# BASIC
# ECONOMICS

## Second Canadian Edition

*Roy Vogt wishes to dedicate*
*this Second Canadian Edition to*
*Ruth,*
*for a friendship more basic than economics.*

# BASIC ECONOMICS

### EDWIN G. DOLAN
GEORGE MASON UNIVERSITY

### ROY VOGT
UNIVERSITY OF MANITOBA

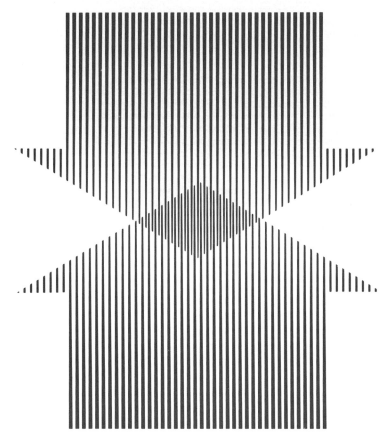

## Second Canadian Edition

HOLT, RINEHART AND WINSTON OF CANADA, LIMITED·TORONTO

**Photo Credits**

Photo of Gerald Bouey, page 208, courtesy of CP Picture Service. Photo of James Coyne,
page 208, courtesy of CP Picture Service. Photo of Milton Friedman, page 258, by C. G. Bloom,
courtesy of the University of Chicago Office of Public Information. Photo of John Kenneth
Galbraith, page 496, courtesy of Professor Galbraith. Photo of Samuel Gompers, page 603,
courtesy of the AFL-CIO. Photo of Harold Adams Innis, page 9, courtesy of the Robert
Lansdale Photography Ltd. Photo of William Stanley Jevons, page 393, courtesy of Historical
Pictures Services, Inc., Chicago. Photo of Harry G. Johnson, page 259, courtesy of Times
Newspapers Limited. Photo of John Maynard Keynes, page 148, courtesy of the Bettmann
Archive. Photo of Oskar Lange, page 667, courtesy of United Press International. Photo of
William Arthur Lewis, page 653, courtesy of Princeton University. Print of Thomas Robert
Malthus, page 643, courtesy of the Bettmann Archive. Photo of Alfred Marshall, page 44,
courtesy of Historical Pictures Services, Inc., Chicago. Photo of Karl Marx, page 663, courtesy
of Miller Pictures Limited. Print of John Stuart Mill, page 138, reproduced from the collection of
the Library of Congress. Photo of Louis Razminsky, page 208, courtesy of CP Picture Service.
Photo of David Ricardo, page 35, courtesy of the Bettmann Archive. Photo of Joan V.
Robinson, page 478, courtesy of Ramsey & Muspratt Studios, Cambridge, England. Photo of
Paul Anthony Samuelson, page 179, courtesy of Professor Samuelson. Photo of Theodore W.
Schultz, page 653, courtesy of Theodore W. Schultz. Photo of Joseph Alois Schumpeter, page
503, courtesy of the Bettmann Archive. Print of Adam Smith, page 6, reproduced from the
collection of the Library of Congress. Photo of James Tobin, page 235, courtesy of James
Tobin. Photo of Graham F. Towers, page 207, courtesy of CP Picture Service.

**Canadian Cataloguing in Publication Data**

Dolan, Edwin G.
  Basic Economics

Includes index.
ISBN 0-03-921671-3

1. Economics.  I. Vogt, Roy.  II. Title.

HB171.5.D58 1984          330          C83-098444-5

Acquisitions Editor:         Michael Roche
Developmental Editor:        Vivien Carter
Managing Editor:             Dennis Bockus
Line Editor:                 Barbara Hehner
Cover Design:                Gord Pronk
Typesetting and Assembly: Compeer Typographic Services Limited

Printed in the United States of America

1 2 3 4 5 6 88 87 86 85 84

# PREFACE

Teaching economics in the 1980s is more of a challenge than ever before. Few economists anticipated the upheavals that our economy began to experience in the early 1970s, and neither politicians nor economists have been very successful in combatting the swings in unemployment and inflation that have characterized those upheavals. The average citizen may question whether economists know what they are doing.

Despite this sense of uncertainty, most economists realize that economic knowledge has advanced significantly in the last decade. In macroeconomics, great strides have been made in understanding the dynamics of inflation and unemployment, the role of monetary policy in the economy, the operation of the labor market, and the importance of expectations as a determinant of economic behavior. In microeconomics, such established fields of study as industrial organization and regulation have taken on a new life. Government involvement in business, the impact of foreign investment on business behavior, and the special role of energy are topics that are justifiably receiving greater attention than in the past.

All this means that teaching economics in the 1980s requires a new kind of textbook—one that brings the new learning into the classroom and confronts student skepticism head on. Students have an uncanny ability, from the first day of classes, to pose exactly those questions that are being debated in the latest journals. They deserve the best answers that can be given; and, in cases where there is no universally accepted answer, they deserve honest explanations of why disagreements persist. They must also have some understanding of the historical roots of Canada's problems. That is why Canadian economic history receives more than usual attention in this text.

Here, in brief, is the strategy used in *Basic Economics, Second Canadian Edition*, to meet the challenge.

## MACROECONOMICS

The effects of monetary and fiscal policy have always been central themes in teaching macroeconomics at the principles level, and this emphasis is continued in *Basic Economics*. However, this book reflects a major shift in economists' perceptions of how fiscal and monetary policies operate. As the late Arthur Okun put it: "The evidence of recent years suggests that through its fiscal and monetary policies the federal government can control—within a reasonable margin—the total growth of GNP measured in dollars. But it cannot control the division of that growth between increases in output and increases in the price level."[1]

The first four chapters of the book provide a sound introduction to economics. Chapter 1 is essentially a preview of the content of the course, discussing the concepts of scarcity and choice and the economic policies related to these two factors. Chapter 2 gives an overview of the concepts of opportunity cost and the market economy. Chapter 3 both introduces supply and demand and provides a detailed discussion of shifts in supply and demand curves. Chapter 4 combines an analysis of the nature of the firm with the role of government in the Canadian economy.

In accordance with the view of how the economy works presented in the early chapters, the crucial distinction between *nominal* quantities, measured in current dollars, and *real* quantities, adjusted for changes in the price level is introduced early (in Chapters 6 and 7). The text then describes the multiplier effects of fiscal policy and the effects of monetary policy as having their primary impact on nominal GNP; it also offers the continual reminder that changes in nominal GNP may represent either changes in real output, or changes in the price level, or changes in both (Chapters 8 to 14). Because of the important role played by the foreign market in Canada's economy, imports and exports are built into the multiplier from the very beginning. A "simple" multiplier without a foreign sector is not an option for the Canadian economy, and there is no reason why students should be given the impression that it is. Chapters 8 to 14 build the foreign sector into the multiplier, and separate chapters (Chapters 15 and 16) are used to describe Canada's international trade and its balance of payments, and to illustrate general equilibrium conditions in both domestic and foreign sectors of the economy. We believe that we have accomplished this without an overly complex technical apparatus. To answer the crucial questions of how changes in nominal GNP are split up between inflation and changes in real output, the book turns to the supply side of the economy. Chapter 17 introduces aggregate demand and supply analysis as well as the Phillips curve, in order to draw initial distinctions between demand-pull and cost-push inflation. Chapter 18 deals with the labor market and the determination of the unemployment rate in terms of job search theory. This chapter also discusses the short-run dynamics of inflation, with special emphasis on the role of inflationary expectations and the phenomenon of inflationary recession. Finally, a new chapter (Chapter 19) explains the major policy alternatives to traditional fiscal and monetary fine-tuning, including innovative approaches to the setting of wages and prices being used in countries such as West Germany and Japan.

---

[1]Arthur Okun, "An Efficient Strategy to Combat Inflation," *Brookings Bulletin* 15 (Spring 1979), p. 4.

## MICROECONOMICS

Microeconomics, like macroeconomics, has a traditional core, represented by Chapters 20 to 23. These chapters give a careful exposition of the theories of consumer behavior, production, costs, and perfect competition. Topics of current concern are discussed in Chapters 24 to 29. Chapter 24 discusses pure monopoly, a traditional topic, and then applies the theory to the case of cartels, a type of market organization receiving greatly increased attention in these days of OPEC. Chapters 25 and 26 explain a wide variety of market forms, organized around the question of when perfect competition is required for satisfactory market performance and when rivalry among a relatively small number of competing firms is enough.

### Policy Questions

This second Canadian edition contains a number of chapters that put students' newly acquired theoretical tools to work on problems of contemporary policy. A reorganized and partially new chapter (Chapter 27) deals with anticombines policy and other attempts by government to limit the growth of private monopoly power and to deal with other forms of market failure. Chapter 28, also new, discusses the special problems of the energy industry, one of the most important sectors in the Canadian economy. Chapter 29 examines the extent to which the performance of the Canadian economy may have been affected by foreign ownership and control of business enterprises and resources.

After a discussion of how various types of income are determined in theory (Chapter 30), two chapters (31 and 32) deal with such issues as collective bargaining, income inequality, and poverty. Finally, in Chapters 33 and 34, the special problems of less developed countries, the so-called *Third World*, and alternatives to our own economic system are described and examined in some detail. There is no better way to confront the student with the interdependence of the world economy and with the potential and the problems of a capitalist economy than to compare that economy with other economies, actual alternatives such as the economy of the Soviet Union. These last chapters should therefore not be considered optional.

## LEARNING AND TEACHING AIDS

The substantive content of a textbook in only part of what makes it usable in the classroom; for the book to be effective, its content must be taught by instructors and learned by students. Therefore, this book pays particular attention to learning and teaching aids.

### Learning Aids

**The Cases** According to a time-honored principle, each generalization should receive a specific illustration, and each illustration should lead to a generalization. Following this principle, numerous short case studies are included in the book. Some of them illustrate general statements about economic policy with specific episodes—for example, Canada's experiment with wage and price controls. Other cases introduce empirical material supporting the discussion in the text—for example, inflation-unemployment trends or data on economies of scale. All cases are placed directly in the text, where they will do the most good, not at the ends of the chapters. Thus they serve as an integral part of the learning process, not just as entertainment or digression.

**Readability**    In *Basic Economics*, readability means two things. First, it means a lively writing style that draws students into the subject matter. Second, it means complete control of the level of difficulty, as measured by standard readability formulas; the book corresponds to the actual reading abilities of today's undergraduate students.

**Vocabulary**    For many students, vocabulary is one of the stumbling blocks to learning economics. This book uses a three-level reinforcement technique to handle the problem. First, each new term is printed in boldface at the point where it is first used and defined. Next, the term and its definition are repeated in the margin of the same page. Finally, the term appears in a complete alphabetical glossary at the end of the book.

**Graphs**    For the benefit of students who may not be used to working with graphs, an appendix on the subject has been added to Chapter 1. This appendix does more than explain techniques. It also addresses the most common problems students face when working with graphs. One of these problems is the tendency to memorize graphs as meaningless patterns of lines. Another is the inability to draw original graphs when they are needed in note-taking or on examinations. The Chapter 1 appendix warns of these pitfalls and carefully explains how they can be avoided. As an added bonus throughout the book, the large page size and single-column format make it especially easy to put graphs exactly where they are needed in relation to the written text.

**Chapter Support Materials**    Each chapter is preceded by a brief statement of learning objectives and a list of terms for review. Each chapter is followed by a concise summary and a set of review questions, and many have an annotated list of suggestions for further reading.

**Study Guide**    A comprehensive Study Guide, published separately, completes the package of learning aids. This guide was developed and written by Beverly Cameron, a very successful teacher of first year economics at the University of Manitoba. Each chapter in the Study Guide contains a list of learning objectives (somewhat more detailed than those given in the chapter openings in the text), a narrative synopsis of the chapter, a programmed review requiring active student involvement and problem solving for immediate reinforcement, and a self-test. The self-test items are carefully coordinated with the test bank in terms of format, coverage, and level of difficulty. Answers to self-test items, with explanations where necessary, are at the back of the study guide.

In addition, the Study Guide contains some unique features. One is a twenty-page guide to careers in economics, written by Keith Evans of California State University at Northridge. Another is a set of case studies, one per chapter, applying concepts learned in the text. The case studies were contributed by Beverly Cameron. Two new components are the "Hands On" and "Don't Make This Common Mistake" sections. The "Hands On" item is featured in almost every chapter and provides a valuable analytical and problem-solving component to the Study Guide. The "Don't Make This Common Mistake" component illustrates for students common misunderstandings in introductory economics.

## Teaching Aids

The text is also accompanied by a complete package of teaching aids.

**Instructor's Manual**  The text is accompanied by an Instructor's Manual, which contains answers to the text's end-of-chapter questions. It also contains a special section entitled "What's Different Here, and Why." This section highlights the unique terminology and underlying models of *Basic Economics*, to help instructors who have used other books in the past convert their courses and lecture notes. For the benefit of users of the First Canadian Edition of *Basic Economics*, this section of the Instructor's Manual also summarizes changes that appear in the Second Edition and explains why they were made. The manual contains additional discussion questions and suggested answers to the application question in the student's Study Guide. Most useful, perhaps, for many instructors, it contains a test bank. The test bank contains several hundred multiple-choice questions, many of which employ graphs or tables. The test items are distributed as evenly as possible among three levels of difficulty: *recognition and understanding, simple application*, and *complex application*. Individual items are coded for level of difficulty and the topic covered. The test items were developed by the authors of the text and Elizabeth Craig of the University of Delaware. As a further teaching aid, transparency masters of some of the most frequently used diagrams from the text are provided.

**Computerized Test Bank**  The printed test bank portion of the instructor's manual will be entered onto 5¼ inch disks for use with a microcomputer. These seven disks will be available to adopters of the text.

## A Word or Two of Thanks

We have been extremely fortunate in getting help of many kinds from many quarters while writing this book. It is a pleasure to acknowledge that help here.

The greatest debt is owed to David E. Lindsey, who provided the theoretical inspiration and many of the technical details for the underlying macroeconomics model of this book—an approach he developed over many years of teaching at Ohio State University and Macalester College.

Next we must thank the reviewers who commented on various drafts of the manuscript and suggested countless improvements. For the Canadian edition of *Basic Economics* these include:

| | |
|---|---|
| Gordon Boreham | University of Ottawa |
| R. Cannon | Fanshawe College |
| G.E. Clarke | Carleton University |
| Peter Durkee | B.C.I.T. |
| Geoffery Hainsworth | University of British Columbia |
| Natalie Hussain | Dawson College |

| | |
|---|---|
| Sadat Kazi | Vanier College |
| Barry Lesser | Dalhousie University |
| A. Paus-Jenssen | University of Saskatchewan |
| B.S. Sahni | Concordia University |
| M.S. Shedd | University of Calgary |
| Bill Wells | Humber College |
| James White | Seneca College |
| Bruce Wilkinson | University of Alberta |

Last but not least, Roy Vogt would like to thank the staff of Holt, Rinehart and Winston of Canada, particularly Michael Roche, Vivien Carter, Barbara Hehner, and Dennis Bockus, for providing excellent assistance in the preparation of the Second Edition. Thanks are again extended to Beverly Cameron for her work on the Study Guide.

# CONTENTS

THE
THEORY
OF
PRICES AND
MARKETS

PART THREE

FACTOR
MARKETS
AND INCOME
DISTRIBUTION

PART FOUR

# AN
# OVERVIEW
# OF THE
# MARKET
# ECONOMY

# PART ONE

# WHAT ECONOMICS IS ALL ABOUT: THE CANADIAN SETTING

---

**WHAT YOU WILL LEARN IN THIS CHAPTER**

*As economists struggle to understand the dramatic economic events of recent years, they are placing increased emphasis on the basics: how individual markets work and how individuals react to changing economic conditions and policies. This chapter will begin explaining these basics with a discussion of the concepts of economic scarcity and choice. Every society has a fundamental economic problem, because in every society virtually unlimited wants must be satisfied by limited resources. The chapter will also distinguish between economics as a science and as policy. The two broadest divisions of economics—macroeconomics and microeconomics—will be defined. Interpretations of Canadian history that have been offered by some of our economists will also be examined. The Appendix to Chapter 1 will introduce the use of graphs in economics.*

---

The 1970s and the early 1980s were years of dramatic change for the Canadian economy. Unemployment and inflation struck in combinations that not so long ago would have been thought flatly impossible. Energy and environmental quality, long ignored or taken for granted, became subjects of national debate and targets of sweeping programs of governmental regulation. The international monetary system was revolutionized, and Canadians watched their dollar lose much of its value on world money markets.

Not surprisingly, all this change and turmoil pushed public interest in economics to new heights. Enrollments in economics have never been higher. Newspapers and television have greatly increased their coverage of economic affairs. The specialized business press has prospered. People want to understand the economic events they are witnessing, and they expect economists to explain them.

Economists are trying hard to do so, and this book is part of the effort. Together with the course of which it is a part, it will help readers become more perceptive of economic news and more constructive participants in discussions of economic issues.

Economics has been undergoing a revolution, part of which has been an increase in modesty among economists. Economists are beginning to understand why the theories and forecasting methods of which they were once so proud came to grief in the 1970s, but they are not fully agreed on what to replace them with. They are beginning to understand why economic policies of the past have not always had the intended effects, but they are not fully agreed on how to design policies that will do better.

There is, however, one thing that economists today seem to agree on: more emphasis on the basics is needed. That means paying more attention to how individual markets operate and how individuals react to changing economic conditions and policies. This emphasis will be very much in evidence throughout the book. The discussion will begin with two of the most basic economic concepts of all: scarcity and choice.

## SCARCITY AND CHOICE IN ECONOMICS

Learning economics means learning to look in a special way at what people do, singling out some features for close attention and placing others in the background. In this respect, economics is much like other social sciences, each of which has its particular way of looking at the world. Psychology emphasizes how people's motivations and personalities shape their behavior toward one another. Political science takes special note of how people's actions are shaped by power relationships within formal and informal political institutions. Economics emphasizes how human actions are influenced by the fact of scarcity and the necessity of choice.

### Scarcity

In economics, *scarcity* means that people do not have as much of everything as they want. Economic scarcity is a subjective concept; it is not measurable by any objective, physical standard. A geologist might say that tin ore is scarce but that iron ore is abundant, meaning that the earth's crust contains much more iron than tin. But an economist would say that both are scarce because people do not have as much of either as they want. An environmentalist might say that sperm whales have become scarce, meaning that there are now barely enough of them to maintain a breeding population. But an economist would say that sperm whales are less scarce than they once were. A century and a half ago, before the discovery of kerosene, whale oil was much in demand as a lamp fuel; today, there are relatively abundant substitutes.

Scarcity as an imbalance between what people have and what they want is sometimes said to be artificial. If people could only learn to limit their wants, then they would solve the problem once and for all. But scarcity is inescapable. Suppose, for example, that you limited your material desires to a single bowl of rice a day and went out into the wilderness to meditate. As soon as you began looking for twigs to build a fire to cook your rice, you would discover that twigs are scarce. You would have to take time off from meditation to look for them. You would build your fire carefully, in such a way as to boil the water without wasting fuel. And in so doing, you would be drawn to meditate that your behavior in the wilderness was shaped by scarcity, much as it was in the world you had left.

### Choice

Economics accepts scarcity as a fact of life, but what makes life interesting, economically speaking, is not scarcity itself so much as the necessity of choosing among ways of coping with it. Earthworms must live with a scarcity of good soil in which to dig their burrows, but they have no choice but to dig. As a result, economists find earthworms nowhere nearly as interesting as people, who can earn their sustenance by burrowing in the soil, by fishing in the sea, or by lecturing on economics to the burrowers and fishers.

As soon as the element of choice is added to that of scarcity, a whole world of economics opens up. How does a person decide how much time to spend fishing and how much to spend farming? Why does one person specialize in farming and another in lecturing on economics? Why is one service more highly rewarded than another? All these questions relate to the way people's lives are shaped by the choices they make among alternatives for coping with scarcity.

## Factors of Production

The limits to our range of economic choice are set by the **factors of production**. Factors of production are the basic components used in the production of all goods and services. They include (1) **natural resources** — land with its original fertility and mineral deposits; (2) **capital** or **capital investment** — manufactured productive resources, such as tools, industrial equipment, structures, and artificial improvements to land; and (3) **labor** — the productive contribution made by people working with their minds and their muscles. Sometimes a special form of human activity, **entrepreneurship**, is identified as a fourth factor of production. An entrepreneur is someone who recognizes new business opportunities and organizes technology and labor to take advantage of them.

Improvements in the quality of factors of production permit the expansion of production possibilities. The quality of labor done by a given population improves as people become healthier and better educated. The quality of capital increases dramatically as technological change improves equipment and brings new methods of production. Most natural resources do not undergo qualitative improvements; in fact, many actually decline in quality as they are depleted by use. So far, in Canada, the increases in quantity and quality of other factors have more than made up for the depletion of natural resources.

## Specialization and the Division of Labor

Individual units of labor, capital, natural resources, and entrepreneurship are different from one another. Units of labor — individual human beings — are the most diverse of all. Because people are not interchangeable parts, we must pay careful attention to the **division of labor** — who gets which job — if we are to do well in our struggle against scarcity.

Suppose that for some reason or other we chose to devote half the nation's labor power to producing education and half to producing other goods, but that we used the wrong half in each place. Skilled production workers would awkwardly mumble their way through lecture notes on Greek history while professors got their thumbs jammed in delicate factory machinery. We would not produce as much as possible of either education or manufactured commodities. Simply by arranging to have the production workers and the professors change places — by using the proper division of

**Factors of production** The basic elements of natural resources, labor, and capital used in the production of all goods.

**Natural resources** As a factor of production, land and mineral deposits.

**Capital** As a factor of production, all manufactured productive resources such as tools, industrial equipment, structures, and artificial improvements to land.

**Labor** As a factor of production, the contributions to production made by people working with their minds and their muscles.

**Entrepreneurship** A unique form of business activity that consists of inventing new ways of doing things, being alert to new opportunities, taking risks, overcoming constraints, and developing new products and organizations.

**Division of labor** The division of the production process for a commodity into numerous specialized functions.

labor—we could increase the output of both manufactured goods and education. That is, production could be increased by *specialization*.

More than two hundred years ago, Adam Smith began the most famous economics book of all time with an example emphasizing the importance of the division of labor. Smith had visited a pin factory and had seen that when one worker specialized in putting heads on the pins, another in sharpening the points, another in placing them on cards, and so on, they all could produce a hundred times more than could the same number of people working separately. Smith went on to show how free markets and private enterprise solve the problem of the division of labor simply by attracting people into the occupations where their potential earnings are greatest. Beginning with Chapter 2, this book will spend many chapters doing the same thing and will have time left over for a look at how governments sometimes try to improve on the market by substituting their own judgments concerning the division of labor.

---

**Adam Smith (1723–1790)**

Adam Smith was born in Kirkaldy, on the east coast of Scotland. He studied first at Glasgow University and then at Oxford. In those days, the universities of Scotland were greater centers of learning than those of England, so Smith returned to the north after finishing his studies at Oxford and obtained a chair at Glasgow. It was not, of course, a chair in economics. Economics had not yet been invented as a distinct discipline, and besides, it was not yet Smith's major interest. His specialty was moral philosophy.

During his long career, Smith wrote just two books. It was his good fortune, however, to have both bring him immediate fame. His first book was *The Theory of Moral Sentiments*, published in 1759. His second, *The Wealth of Nations*, appeared seventeen years later, in 1776. David Hume, a friend of Smith's, commented that "the reading of it necessarily requires so much attention, and the public is disposed to give so little, that I shall still doubt for some time of its being at first very popular." Hume, however, was wrong. The book sold well from the start.

The task Smith set himself first of all was to explain the workings of the economic system—that is, the sources of the "wealth of nations." The greatest source, he discovered, was the division of labor. Chapter 1 opened with the observation that "the greatest improvement in the productive powers of labor, and the greater part of the skill, dexterity, and judgment with which it is anywhere directed, or applied, seem to have been the effects of the division of labor." He then went on to give his famous pin factory example.

It was not enough for Smith just to describe the division of labor, however. He wanted to explain how it came about. His explanation was highly characteristic:

This division of labor, from which so many advantages are derived, is not originally the effect of any human wisdom, which foresees and intends that general opulence to which it gives occasion. It is the necessary, though very slow and gradual consequence of a certain propensity in human nature which has in view no such extensive utility; the propensity to truck, barter, and exchange one thing for another.

Here, for the first time in the book, Smith emphasized the importance of the unintended consequences of human action: each person acting in the marketplace has only narrow ends in mind, but the joint result of the actions of everyone is a general benefit that none intended.

As *The Wealth of Nations* progressed, Smith added another theme, that of the benefits of economic liberty. The free, spontaneous interaction of people in the marketplace is not just one way to bring about the general benefit of mankind; it is the best way. Government attempts to guide or regulate the market end up doing more harm than good. Smith especially attacked the privileges of legally protected monopolies, the

Poor Laws (which he saw as inhibiting the mobility of labor), and the apprenticeship system (which worked against free entry into occupations). All such restraints on the market tended to force trade into "unnatural" and less beneficial channels.

Smith's book has meant various things to various people. To some it has been a handbook of laissez-faire liberalism. To others, it has been the fountainhead of economic science. Still others have found it, not without reason, to be unoriginal and crammed with errors. Whatever its faults, it is a book that continues to be read and debated. In 1976, its bicentennial brought leading economists from all over the world to Glasgow to pay tribute to the professor of moral philosophy who had lectured there so long before.

## AN OVERVIEW OF EARLY CANADIAN ECONOMIC HISTORY

Much of this book is devoted to providing tools and ideas that help to explain the operation of modern economies in general. Throughout this text, however, we will also examine economic institutions and phenomena that distinguish the Canadian economy from others. Canada's early economic history and the way it has been interpreted by leading Canadian economic historians will be outlined in the following pages; more recent developments will be discussed in later chapters.

Canadian economic historians stress the role played by geography in Canada's economic development. It should be noted first that North America faces Europe. Its Atlantic coastline is generally more accessible to landing and settlement than its Pacific coastline. Its climate more closely resembles that of northern Europe than that of the Asiatic countries. While the earliest inhabitants (the native people) came from Asia, for better or for worse the economy of North America was given its basic direction by aggressive European merchants, and their technology and markets gave the impetus to economic expansion in the New World.

Geography also dictated the types of settlements that took root in Canada and their relative success. The early settlements on the Atlantic coast depended on the fisheries, supplemented later by trade in timber and furs, for their existence. They had to compete with European fishing interests and with rivals along the New England coast. A vast, densely wooded hinterland cut them off from the more vigorous settlements developing along the St. Lawrence River.

Commercial ventures setting out from the St. Lawrence penetrated deeply into what later became the United States, because travel from the Great Lakes south via the Mississippi River was much easier than the journey westward over precambrian rock. Initially, the Appalachian Mountains separated the interior from the New England colonies along the eastern seaboard; however, the colonists were soon motivated to overcome this barrier and to expand their own commercial ventures into the Ohio valley and across the trade routes of the Montreal merchants. In 1783, after the successful revolutionary war against England, the American states laid claim to the land west to the Mississippi, and traders from the St. Lawrence were forced to pursue their trade in furs north of the Great Lakes, to the Red River settlement in what is now Manitoba, and beyond.

Economic historians differ as to whether this movement occurred in defiance of or as a natural outgrowth of North American geography. W.A. Mackintosh, for many years a highly regarded scholar at Queen's University, took the former view. He noted that throughout most of North America, rivers and mountains encourage movement north and south. He stressed the difficulty of moving goods and people overland north of the Great Lakes. That the commercial empire of the St. Lawrence was eventually linked up with the western prairies, and that from this linkage there developed a viable nation, occurred, in his opinion, in spite of nature. On the other hand, H.A. Innis, a notable economic historian, was impressed by the penetration of both the St. Lawrence and Hudson Bay into the interior, and by the technology used by the early traders to move quickly and deeply along these watersheds into the Canadian hinterland. Consequently, he concluded that Canada emerged as a nation because of its geography.

Despite differences of opinion about the role of geography, virtually all Canadian economic historians have stressed the importance of staple products in Canada's economic development. A **staple product** is a commodity on which an economy concentrates much of its labor and capital. In Canada's history a succession of staple products—fish, timber, fur, pulp and paper, minerals, wheat, and oil—have provided the impetus for its economic growth. This degree of specialization has had serious implications for the stability, organization, and independence of the Canadian economy.

**Staple product** A commodity on which the economy of a settlement or region concentrates much of its labor and capital.

Given the abundance of land and the relative scarcity of labor and capital, early Canadian settlements answered a European demand for their goods by concentrating on the export of natural resources, or staple products. This set a pattern for Canadian economic strategy for centuries to come. In good times, foreign markets have made exports the leading sector of the Canadian economy, generating new investment in the home production of raw materials and in the further processing of finished goods. However, dependence on foreign markets has also made our country extremely vulnerable to recessions and changes in policies in the countries to which we export. Some regions in Canada have also fallen into what is known as a "staple trap," meaning that they concentrate so much on the export of a few products that they fail to develop other industries. The neglect of a more diversified economic base makes it all the more difficult for the economy of a Canadian region to counteract the negative effects of recessions originating outside the region or country.

The very nature of the staples affected Canada's development. When furs were in great demand, the ease with which fur-bearing animals were caught led to rapid depletion of local supplies and thus to rapid penetration of the Canadian hinterland by traders seeking more pelts. A vast, but frail, economic system evolved, linking eastern headquarters to their sources of supply. Increased amounts of capital were required to overcome the transportation problems created by the great distances over which goods had to travel. This requirement favored strong organizations like the Hudson's Bay Company and led to the growth of monopoly in what had been an extremely competitive industry.

Later, in the nineteenth century, when a nation-state was created on the foundations of this far-flung economic base, massive government subsidies were required to build the canals and railways that were necessary to link the various regions of the country. In the decade after Confederation, when the Canadian population was less than 4 million, the federal government committed more than $60 million to the construction of two railways, linking Central Canada to the Atlantic and the Pacific.

It was the nature of our staple production, therefore, that created conditions of foreign dependence, government assistance, and regional instability, all important features of the Canadian economy to this day.

In recent years the "staple approach" to Canadian economic history has been criticized by some economic historians, but scholars like Melville Watkins of the University of Toronto have argued that on the basis of both new theoretical work and empirical research the staple approach remains one of the most original and useful keys to understanding Canada's economic development.

Many Canadian scholars regard Harold Adams Innis as the most original and influential economist this country has produced. He brought to the study of Canadian economic history a restless and original mind, and the theories he expounded were supported by thorough empirical research. He influenced a wide range of social scientists through his prolific writings and his teaching and leadership at the University of Toronto.

Innis was born near Otterville, Ontario in 1894. He studied at McMaster University, which was then in Toronto, and later did graduate work in economics at the University of Chicago. There he studied with such well-known economists as Frank H. Knight and J.M. Clark, but he was most influenced by the economic historian C.W. Wright. Under Wright's direction he chose to write his doctoral thesis on a history of the Canadian Pacific Railway.

After his graduation in 1920, Innis turned down several offers to teach in the United States, preferring to return to Canada to teach economics at the University of Toronto. Here he plunged into the study of Canadian economic history. He traveled throughout the country, even making a hazardous journey down the Mackenzie River, learning about Canada firsthand and gathering original source materials in private and public archives.

His three major works were published at ten-year intervals: *The Fur Trade in Canada: An Introduction to Canadian Economic History* in 1930, *The Cod Fisheries: The History of an International Economy* in 1940, and *Empire and Communications* in 1950. He wrote dozens of other books and articles, but these three works illustrate most clearly the richness and the development of his approach to economic history.

Harold Adams Innis (1894 – 1952)

In his book on the fur trade, Innis examined the factors that shaped the growth of one of Canada's earliest industries and, in turn, how the development of this industry influenced the creation of a unique Canadian nation. He emphasized the role of geography and technology in the rapid westward expansion of the fur trade, the importance of foreign markets, the high overhead costs involved in creating an effective transportation system, and the way in which the physical characteristics of the furs traded affected the organization and stability of the economy.

This interpretation of economic and social change was carried further by Innis in his other major works. In his study of another staple industry, the cod fisheries, he again focused on the dependence of the industry on foreign markets; the impact of new technology, in this case such things as iron, steam, and refrigeration; and the search for protection after periods of vigorous competition.

Following his work on the fisheries, Innis planned to make a similar study of another major industry, pulp and paper. However, the more he examined this industry the more he became impressed with the profound impact that communications media such as newspapers have on society, and the less he felt able to deal with the industry in a purely economic way. During the 1940s he plunged into an intensive, far-ranging study of how communications media have influenced the growth and decline of civilizations. For example, in media such as stone and parchment he detected what he called a "time bias." Societies using such media tended to restrict the enlargement of their boundaries and fostered traditions and political organizations that favored stability over time. Eventually such societies might be successfully invaded from outside by societies that favored media with a "spatial bias," such as papyrus, paper, and printing. The use of such media encouraged civilizations like the Roman Empire and our own to move quickly over space, conquering territories devoted to stability and "time." However, these more aggressive societies made themselves vulnerable to new forces emerging at the boundaries of their far-flung empires. Internally, their neglect of time and tradition forced them to adopt measures favoring greater social cohesion, political centralization, and monopoly.

Innis documented these ideas in his last major work, *Empire and Communications*. After his death in 1952, these ideas continued to influence scholars in numerous disciplines. In particular they formed the basis for the famous work of Marshall McLuhan. McLuhan's well-known statement, "The medium is the message," is closely linked to Innis's observation that the physical nature of a staple product or communications medium profoundly affects the economic, social, and political life of society.

## ECONOMIC SCIENCE AND ECONOMIC POLICY

A great part of what one reads about economics in the newspapers or hears about it on television is focused on specific problems of economic policy. Should the federal government spend more money and run a larger budget deficit? Should price controls on oil be lifted in the hope of increasing production and decreasing consumption? Should the government encourage or discourage exports of Canadian natural gas? If we are to learn the economic way of thinking, we must learn how economists think about policy issues as well as how they think about pure theory.

The mention of economic policies such as price controls or budget deficits tends to set little lights labeled "hurrah" or "ugh" flashing in our minds. Sometimes our mental circuits work so fast that we do not notice that, between the mention of the policy and the flashing of the lights, a chain of thinking somewhat like the following must occur:

1. If Policy X is followed, Outcome Y will result.
2. Outcome Y is a good (or bad) thing.
3. Therefore, hurrah (or ugh) for Policy X.

In order to understand the contents of this book and how to put them to work, it is important to understand the logic of the three-step chain of thinking. To that end, we will go through it one step at a time.

### Positive Economics

Economic science cannot foretell the future, but it can offer predictions of the "if, then" form: "If A occurs, then B will occur, other things being equal." An economist might, then, make the assertion: "If government spending were increased, then unemployment would decline, as long as no other changes in economic conditions occurred in the meantime." Such a statement is sometimes called a **scientific prediction**. It is a statement of cause and effect but one that is valid only under specified conditions. In making scientific predictions of this form, economists rarely attempt to foretell

**Scientific prediction** A conditional prediction having the form "if A, then B, other things being equal."

whether A will actually occur or whether other things will actually remain constant.

When economists limit their attention to statements that are pure scientific predictions, they are said to be practicing **positive economics**. All sound analysis of economic policy must begin with positive economics as step 1.

**Positive economics** The part of economics limited to making scientific predictions and purely descriptive statements.

**Resolving Disagreements** Of course, economists sometimes disagree about whether a certain scientific prediction is valid. In fact, a great deal of the day-to-day work in which economists engage is directed toward resolving disagreements on matters of positive economics. Some scientific disagreements concern matters of pure theory and are much like the disagreements among mathematicians concerning whether some unproved theorem is true or false. These disputes can, in time, be resolved by a process in which each party tries to state the reasoning as carefully as possible or to detect logical errors.

Frequently, economists try to resolve disputes over matters of positive economics by using **empirical** methods. That means looking at evidence — statistical or otherwise — based on observation of past experience. Much of this work is done by specialists in the statistical analysis of economic data who are called **econometricians**. Suppose that the scientific prediction in dispute said: "If government spending were to increase, then unemployment would decline, other things being equal." An econometrician might enter the debate with the announcement that, according to a study of postwar data on the Canadian economy, an increase in government expenditure has, in fact, been consistently associated with a decline in unemployment, taking into account the probable influence of other factors. Or the econometrician might assert that the data reveal no systematic association at all between government spending and unemployment when advanced statistical techniques are used to eliminate the influence of other changes in economic conditions. Questions of this sort are not usually resolved by a single empirical study, but repeated studies and the gradual accumulation of evidence serve to narrow areas of disagreement and contribute to scientific progress in economics.

**Empirical** A term referring to data or methods based on observation of actual past experience or on controlled experiments.

**Econometrician** A specialist in the statistical analysis of economic data.

This chapter has already described the work of some Canadian economic historians. **Economic historians** explain facts after the event (*ex post*). They direct their attention to how things actually happened and are not so concerned about alternative paths that might have been taken but were not. Therefore, all they require is one *plausible* explanation for a past event. Economists who are, instead, concerned more with the present and the future attempt to build explanatory models that will predict beforehand (*ex ante*) how an economy might develop. They must consider numerous alternative possibilities and do not have the benefit of hindsight (though they use past experience in constructing their models) to confirm their hypotheses. Economic historians are able to provide useful information for such model building and also help us to understand how we got to where we are.

**Economic historian** An economist who explains events after the fact (*ex post*), and is content to find the most plausible reason for an event.

## Normative Economics

A positive economic statement of the type "if Policy X, then Outcome Y" cannot by itself resolve the issue of whether Policy X is desirable. To come to a conclusion on the desirability of the policy, one must decide whether Outcome Y is good or bad. When economists make statements of the type "Outcome Y is good," they are engaging in **normative economics**.

**Normative economics** The part of economics devoted to making value judgments about what economic policies or conditions are good or bad.

Most economists do not consider themselves experts in ethical theory, and few would be prepared to defend their normative statements with the same rigor and clarity they would use to defend their positive economic analysis. Nonetheless, economists who wish to speak persuasively on the subject of economic policy should be able at least to point to some general ethical principles on which their normative conclusions might plausibly be based. Economists who base their like or dislike of a particular policy on personal predilections are less likely to be listened to than are those who speak in terms of consistent and well-thought-out values. With this in mind, we will look at a few basic ideas that frequently arise in discussions of normative economics.

**Efficiency** The property of producing or acting with a minimum of expense, waste, and effort.

**The Efficiency Standard**  The standard of **efficiency** occupies a prominent place among those standards by which economists judge the performance of the systems they observe. In its most general sense, the word *efficiency* means the property of producing or acting with a minimum of expense, waste, and effort.

**Efficiency and Fairness**  Most economists think that efficiency itself is a good thing. This does not mean, however, that any policy promoting efficiency is automatically a good policy. Other norms and values must be introduced into policy analysis to supplement the efficiency standard. Among the most important of the supplementary standards is that of equity, or fairness.

The concept of fairness has two roles to play in relation to the standard of efficiency. First, it may be used to supplement the efficiency standard in cases where the choice is between policies that are equally efficient. Efficiency alone defines not a single, unique pattern of economic life but only a range of possible patterns. Different but equally efficient patterns often involve different distributions of welfare among specific individuals. In one efficient state of the world, Jones may be rich and Smith poor; in another, Smith may be rich and Jones poor; in a third, Jones and Smith may be equally well-off. When such alternatives confront us, we may be led to reason like this:

1. Policies X and Y produce equally efficient outcomes but imply different distributions of individual welfare.
2. The distributional outcome of Policy X is fairer.
3. Therefore, let us undertake Policy X.

A second possible use for the criterion of fairness is to override the criterion of efficiency. For many people, efficiency is a goal that should not be pursued at the expense of fairness but that should, if needed, be sacrificed to the pursuit of fairness. In such cases, the logic might run as follows:

1. Policy X would be bad for efficiency but would help achieve greater fairness.
2. The loss of efficiency is unfortunate, but the gain in fairness outweighs it.

3. Therefore, in the absence of a policy that will serve both goals at once, go ahead with Policy X.

**A Difficulty**　Whichever way it is used, the concept of fairness plays an important role in policy analysis. Using it, however, involves a difficulty that did not occur in the case of efficiency. The difficulty is that fairness has no universally agreed-upon meaning. It means different things to different people, depending on the values they hold and the ideologies they profess. Few things are more harmful to intelligent debate on questions of economic policy than for the parties to a discussion to use words such as *fairness* or *equity* to mean different things.

In the interest of avoiding such misunderstandings, we might wish to establish beyond doubt that a particular meaning of *fairness* is the right one. But to attempt it would take us deep into details of philosophy and far from the main subject of this book. Instead we will simply look at two of the most common conceptions of fairness.

**The Egalitarian Concept of Fairness**　One widely held view associates fairness with an equitable distribution of income. The phrase "from each according to ability, to each according to needs" gives a rough characterization of this point of view. The egalitarian concept of fairness is based on the view that all people—solely by virtue of their birth and their common humanity—merit some share of the total stream of goods and services turned out by the economic system.

There are, of course, degrees and variations of the egalitarian concept of fairness. Some people, for example, believe that all economic goods should be distributed equally among all members of society. Others think that a person's innate claims on economic output are limited to some minimum basket of basic needs and that any surplus above this minimum ought to be distributed according to market principles. Still others see each person's innate claims on output as limited to certain specific types of goods and services. Each person might, for example, have an innate claim to a share of food, shelter, medical care, and education but no such claim to even a minimum share of rum, recreational equipment, or air travel.

**The Libertarian Concept of Fairness**　A second widely held view associates fairness with the right of each individual to act in accordance with private choice, free from force, threat, or coercion by others. This concept of fairness stems from a long tradition in Western political thought, especially the concept of liberty as developed by such thinkers as John Locke and Thomas Jefferson.

The libertarian concept of fairness puts economic rights, such as the right to own property and the right to engage in voluntary exchange with others, on a par with the fundamental civil liberties of freedom of speech, press, and religion. From the libertarian point of view, efforts to promote equality should emphasize equality of opportunity. Attempts to redistribute income by expropriating the income or property of the economically successful or by allowing people unequal access to the marketplace are seen as inherently unfair whether or not they lead to equality of outcome.

## Economic Ideology

**Economic ideology** A set of judgments and beliefs concerning efficiency and fairness as goals of economic policy, together with a set of beliefs concerning matters of positive economics.

Each person carries out the job of policy analysis, whether in a systematic or a casual way, within a personal framework of thought that can be called an **economic ideology.** An economic ideology includes a person's judgments concerning the relative priority (and exact interpretation) of fairness and efficiency and attitudes toward the relative importance of fairness and efficiency as goals of economic policy. Often, it also includes a set of more or less rationally founded beliefs concerning matters of positive economics. Liberalism, Marxism, libertarianism, conservatism—these and many other "isms" are the labels we use to refer to economic ideologies.

To deal with every policy issue from all possible ideological points of view would be too much to attempt in this book. Instead, we will content ourselves for the most part with pointing out the implications of various policies in terms of the standards of efficiency and fairness just discussed. People will have to reach their own conclusions on the ideological level.

## Why Distinguish between Positive and Normative Economics?

When policy analysis is broken down into a three-step process in which positive and normative elements are clearly separated, orderly debate on important economic issues is made easier. The breakdown of policy analysis into positive and normative components makes it clear that disagreements on policy questions can arise from two different sources. If you and I disagree as to whether Policy X is good or bad, it may be either because we disagree on the positive issue of whether Policy X will, in fact, result in Outcome Y, or because we disagree on the normative issue of whether Outcome Y is good or bad. Our analysis also indicates that a particular sort of spurious agreement could arise between us: You might think that Policy X will cause Outcome Y and that Y is good, whereas I might think Y is bad but that X will not cause it! This sort of thing occurs surprisingly often. In any event, it is clear that intelligent policy analysis requires careful thinking.

## Microeconomics and Macroeconomics

**Microeconomics** The study of the economic behavior of individual households and firms and the determination of the market prices of individual goods and services.

**Macroeconomics** The study of large-scale economic phenomena, especially inflation, unemployment, and economic growth.

Having viewed economics in the abstract, it is time to take a closer look at its actual subject matter. Economics is a discipline with many subdivisions and specialties. The broadest distinction within it traditionally has been between the so-called micro and macro branches. **Microeconomics** is the study of the economic behavior of individual households and firms and the determination of the market prices of individual goods and services. The term derives from the Greek word *micro*, which means "small" and which in this case indicates an emphasis on the behavior of small economic units. **Macroeconomics** is the study of large-scale economic phenomena, especially inflation, unemployment, and economic growth. The term comes from the Greek word *macro*, which means "large."

The distinction between micro- and macroeconomics is not a rigorous one. A number of specialties within economics, such as international trade, economic development, and comparative economic systems, cannot neatly be classified as micro or macro. Nonetheless, the micro-macro distinction has proved so useful a device for organizing the teaching of economics that we will follow it through most of the text.

## CONCLUSIONS

In a once-over fashion, this chapter has tried to give some idea of the kinds of things to which economists are sensitive when they look at the world around them. It has shown that economists think in terms of scarcity and choice. It has described the impact of some early features of Canada's economic history—particularly the concentration on staple production—on current economic problems and institutional behavior. It has explained how to distinguish between positive and normative economics and between microeconomics and macroeconomics. What can be said now to sum it all up?

If there is one single feature of overriding importance about the economic way of thinking, it is this: *economics is about people making choices under conditions of scarcity.* Individuals are the units of analysis in all economic theory. Every economic principle developed in this book must be a statement about the way individuals make choices, struggle with the problem of scarcity, and respond to changes in their environment. And all economic policies must be judged in terms of their effect on the welfare of individuals.

Because economics deals with complex entities—people—and not with atoms or other physical particles, economic decision making can never be described adequately in terms of precise mathematical formulas. It has, however, proved very useful in the study of modern economics to summarize and express the past behavior of selected aspects of the economy by algebraic equations and to feed these into computers to predict future behavior. Economic forecasts of this type can be of great usefulness to many business firms, who would like to know what is likely to happen to output, prices, consumer spending, and other such economic variables in the near future. Unfortunately, the way human beings have behaved in the past is not always a reliable guide to how they will act in the future. In order to anticipate new forms of behavior, it is necessary to know something about recent changes in expectations, values, and life styles, and to understand the transformations that important institutions are undergoing. It is also helpful to compare the Canadian experience with that of other countries, who may be slightly further along a path that is similar to ours.

Though the unpredictable behavior of human beings makes accurate economic forecasting quite difficult, it also means that economics can never become stale; it is a vital, dynamic discipline, continually faced with new challenges to our understanding. It is both a science and an art, and it requires both empirical research and an imagination responsive to a broad range of human experiences.

## SUMMARY

1. Learning economics means learning to look at human actions and interactions in a special way, singling out some features for close exami-

nation and placing others in the background. The economic way of thinking places particular emphasis on how people's actions are influenced by the fact of scarcity and the necessity of choice.

2. All economic decisions can be described in terms of scarcity and choice. Limits on our choices are imposed by the availability of factors of production and our ability to take advantage of their most efficient combination.

3. The choices made by Canadians have been shaped by their economic history. Emphasis on staple production has resulted in regional instabilities, dependence on foreign investment and consumer markets, and considerable economic involvement by governments.

4. Positive economics cannot foretell the future, but it can offer scientific predictions in the form "if A occurs, then B will occur, other things being equal." Disputes in positive economics can, in principle, be resolved by reasoned discussion or by the examination of statistical data.

5. Normative economics is concerned with statements about what ought to be. Most economists think that efficiency is, in itself, a worthy goal of economic policy. The efficiency standard must, however, be supplemented by considerations of fairness when policy decisions are to be made. Unfortunately, there is no universal agreement on what fairness means.

6. Economics is often divided into two broad areas: microeconomics, the study of the behavior of small economic units; and macroeconomics, the study of large-scale economic phenomena. It must be remembered, however, that some economic specialties do not fall neatly into one or the other classification.

7. Economics is about people. All economic principles must be framed in terms of the way individuals make choices and respond to changes in their environment, and all economic policies must be judged in terms of their impact on the welfare of individuals.

## DISCUSSION QUESTIONS

1. Suppose you want your grades to be as high as possible this term; yet your time and abilities are limited. Would it be possible to look at the way you spend your time as an economic problem? What constraints and alternative activities do you face?

2. Suppose you won a lottery prize of $20 million. Would this solve all your personal economic problems of scarcity? Explain.

3. Does Canada still rely heavily on the production of a few staple goods? If you think so, what products would you list as staples?

4. Minimum wage laws have been passed in many provinces to provide higher incomes for workers. On the level of positive economics, some people think that a high minimum wage increases the incomes of low-skilled workers, while others think that it reduces the number of jobs available to such workers. On a normative level, people disagree about what distribution of incomes is appropriate. Using the three-step chain of reasoning discussed in this chapter, outline in paragraph form several analyses of the minimum wage issue.

5. Assume that in Country A incomes range from $1,000 to $3,000 a year, and that the median income (half the households below and half above) is $1,600. In Country B, incomes range from $800 to $6,000, and the median income is $3,000. Which of these economies do you think is "fairer" to its citizens? Examine carefully the grounds for your opinion.

6. Do you think that, in your region of the country, trade would flow north and south more naturally than east and west? How could you verify your answer?

# APPENDIX TO CHAPTER 1
# WORKING WITH GRAPHS

## HOW ECONOMISTS USE GRAPHS

At one of our country's well-known colleges, the students have their own names for all the courses. They call the astronomy course "stars," the geology course "rocks," and the biology course "frogs." Their name for the economics course is "graphs and laughs." This choice of names indicates two things. First, it shows that the students think the professor has a sense of humor. Second, it shows that in the minds of students, economics is a matter of learning about graphs in the same sense that astronomy is a matter of learning about stars or geology a matter of learning about rocks.

To begin, then, we can say that economics is not about graphs; it is about people. It is about the way people make choices, use resources, and cooperate with one another in an effort to overcome the universal problem of scarcity. Economics is a social science, not an offshoot of analytic geometry.

The skeptical reader may reply, "If economics is not about graphs, why are there so many of them in this book?" The answer is that economists use graphs to illustrate the theories they develop about people's economic behavior in order to make them vivid, eye-catching, and easy to remember. Everything that can be said in the form of a graph can also be said in words or equations, but saying something two different ways is a proven aid to learning. The purpose of this appendix is to show how to make maximum use of an important learning aid by explaining how to work with graphs.

## PAIRS OF NUMBERS AND POINTS

The first thing to learn is how to use points on a graph to represent pairs of numbers. Consider Exhibit 1A.1. The small table in that exhibit presents six pairs of numbers. The two columns are labeled $x$ and $y$. The first number in each pair is called the $x$ *value*, and the second is called the $y$ *value*. Each pair of numbers is labeled with a capital letter A through E. Pair A has an $x$ value of 2 and a $y$ value of 3; Pair B has an $x$ value of 4 and a $y$ value of 4, and so on.

Next to the table is a diagram. The lines placed at right angles to one another along the bottom and the left-hand side of the diagram are called *coordinate axes*. The horizontal axis is marked off into units and is used for measuring the $x$ value, while the vertical axis is marked off into units for measuring the $y$ value. In the space between these axes, each lettered pair of numbers from the table can be represented as a lettered point. For example, to put Point A in place, go two units to the right along the horizontal axis to represent the $x$ value of 2 and then three units straight up, parallel to the vertical axis, to represent the $y$ value of 3. The other points are placed the same way.

Usually, the visual effect of a graph is improved by connecting the points with a smooth line or curve. When this is done (as shown in the diagram), it can be seen at a glance that as the $x$ value increases, the $y$ value also tends to increase. This line, in turn, can be expressed in the form of an equation. In this example, involving a straight line, the equation is of the form $y = a + bx$, in which $a$ represents the point where the line, when extended leftwards, would cross the vertical axis and $b$ is a number by which $x$ is multiplied to produce the changes in $y$ associated with changes in x. For example, the equation for the line shown in Exhibit 1A.1 would be: $y = 2 + \frac{1}{2}x$. The line starts at 2 (indicating that y is 2 when x is zero), and then rises by ½ unit for every 1-unit movement along the horizontal axis (indicating that y increases by ½ unit for every 1-unit increase in x).

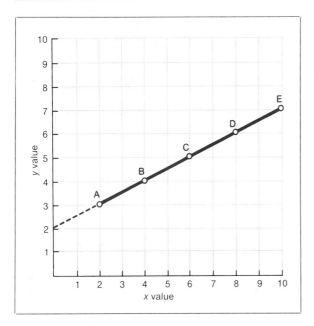

**Exhibit 1A.1**

**Pairs of numbers and points**

Each lettered pair of numbers in the table corresponds to a lettered point on the graph. The x value of each point corresponds to the horizontal distance of the point from the vertical axis, and the y value corresponds to the vertical distance from the horizontal axis.

|   | x | y |
|---|---|---|
| A | 2 | 3 |
| B | 4 | 4 |
| C | 6 | 5 |
| D | 8 | 6 |
| E | 10 | 7 |

## COMMON ECONOMIC GRAPHS

Economics is interested not in abstract relationships between x's and y's but in relationships concerning people and the things they do under various conditions. This means that graphs in economics are labeled in terms of the ideas used in putting together economic theories. Exhibit 1A.2 shows three common ways of labeling coordinate axes. Each of these will be encountered many times in this book.

Exhibit 1A.2a represents the relationship between the price of subway tokens in some city and the number of people who choose to ride the subway each day at any given price. The table shows that as the price of tokens goes up, fewer people choose to ride the subway. The graph shows the same thing. As a matter of tradition in economics, whenever a graph involves both money values and quantity units, the vertical axis is used to measure the money value (in this case, the price of subway tokens) and the horizontal axis to measure the quantity units (in this case, the number of riders per day). The graph clearly demonstrates how subway use declines at higher prices.

Exhibit 1A.2b uses quantity units on both axes. Here, the problem is to represent the various combinations of milkshakes and hamburgers that can be bought at the local carry-out when milkshakes cost $.50 each, hamburgers cost $.50 each, and the buyer has exactly $2.50 to spend on lunch. The table shows that the possibilities are five burgers and no shakes, four burgers and one shake, three burgers and two shakes, and so on.

The graph offers a picture of the "menu" to choose from, given limited money to spend. The points from the table are drawn in and labeled, and any can be chosen. A diagonal line has been sketched in to connect these points, and if the purchase of parts of hamburgers and milkshakes is allowed, the buyer can choose from among all the points along this line (for example, 2.5 burgers and 2.5 shakes). The buyer

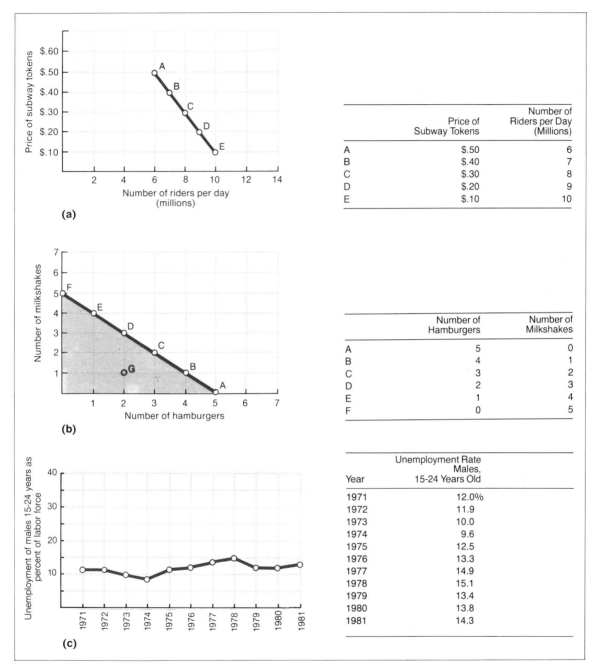

|   | Price of Subway Tokens | Number of Riders per Day (Millions) |
|---|---|---|
| A | $.50 | 6 |
| B | $.40 | 7 |
| C | $.30 | 8 |
| D | $.20 | 9 |
| E | $.10 | 10 |

(a)

|   | Number of Hamburgers | Number of Milkshakes |
|---|---|---|
| A | 5 | 0 |
| B | 4 | 1 |
| C | 3 | 2 |
| D | 2 | 3 |
| E | 1 | 4 |
| F | 0 | 5 |

(b)

| Year | Unemployment Rate Males, 15-24 Years Old |
|---|---|
| 1971 | 12.0% |
| 1972 | 11.9 |
| 1973 | 10.0 |
| 1974 | 9.6 |
| 1975 | 12.5 |
| 1976 | 13.3 |
| 1977 | 14.9 |
| 1978 | 15.1 |
| 1979 | 13.4 |
| 1980 | 13.8 |
| 1981 | 14.3 |

(c)

**Exhibit 1A.2**
**Three typical economic graphs**
This exhibit shows three graphs typical of those used in economics. Part a shows the relationship between the price of tokens and the number of riders per day on a certain city subway system. When a graph shows the relationship between a price and a quantity, it is conventional to put the price on the vertical axis. Part b shows the possible choices open to a person who has $2.50 to spend on lunch and can buy hamburgers at $.50 each or milkshakes at $.50 each. Part c shows how a graph can be used to represent change over time.

Source: Part c is from Department of Finance, *Economic Review,* April 1982, p. 154.

who wanted to have some money left over could purchase a lunch represented by a point within the shaded area, such as Point G (which stands for two burgers and one shake and costs just $1.50). But unless the buyer gets more money, points outside the shaded area cannot be chosen.

Exhibit 1A.2c illustrates still another kind of graph frequently used in economics—one showing how some magnitude varies over time. This graph indicates what happened to the unemployment rate of young males over the years 1971–81. The horizontal axis is used to represent the passage of time and the vertical axis to measure the percentage of young males officially classified as unemployed. Graphs like this are good for getting a quick idea of trends over time. Although young male unemployment has had its ups and downs, with the exception of a break in 1979, the trend has been clearly upward since 1974.

## SLOPES

When talking about graphs, it is frequently convenient to describe lines or curves in terms of their *slopes*. The slope of a straight line drawn between two points is defined as the ratio of the change in the $y$ value to the change in the $x$ value between two points. In Exhibit 1A.3, for example, the slope of the line drawn between Points A and B is 2. The $y$ value changes by six units between these two points, while the $x$ value changes by only three units. The slope is the ratio 6/3 = 2.

When a line slants downward like the line between Points C and D in Exhibit 1A.3, the $x$ value and the $y$ value change in opposite directions. Going from Point C to Point D, the $y$ value changes by −2 (that is, it decreases by two units), while the $x$ value changes by +4 (that is, it increases by four units). The slope of this line is the ratio −2/4 = −1/2. A downward-sloping line such as this is said to have a negative slope.

The slope of a curved line, unlike that of a straight line, varies from point to point. The slope of a curve at any given point is defined as the slope of a straight line drawn tangent to the curve at that point. (A tangent line is one just touching the curve without crossing it). Consider the curve in Exhibit 1A.4. Applying the definition, the slope of this line at Point A is 1, and the slope at Point B is −2. When a straight line is described in equation form, such as $y = a + bx$, the slope of the line is given by $b$, because $b$ indicates the rate at which $y$ changes in relation to changes in $x$. Thus, in Exhibit 1A.1, the equation for the line was $y = 2 + \frac{1}{2}x$, where $b = \frac{1}{2}$, meaning that the slope of the line was ½.

## ABSTRACT GRAPHS

In all the examples so far, we have had specific numbers to work with for the $x$ and $y$ values. Sometimes, though, we know only the general nature of the relationship between two economic magnitudes rather than specific numbers. For example, we might know that when people's incomes rise, they tend to increase their consumption of meat rapidly at first. But then, as they reach very high incomes, their meat consumption levels off. If we want to represent a relationship like this without caring about the numbers involved, we draw a graph like that shown in Exhibit 1A.5. The vertical axis is labeled "quantity of meat consumed per month," without any specific units. The horizontal axis is labeled "income," again without specific units. The curve, which rises rapidly at first and then levels off, tells us the general nature of the relationship between income and meat consumption: when income goes up, meat consumption rises, but not in proportion to the change in income. We will use abstract graphs like this one very frequently in this book. Abstract graphs express general principles, whereas graphs with numbers on the axes summarize specific known information.

## STUDY HINTS FOR GRAPHS

When you come to a chapter in the book that is full of graphs, how should you study it? The first and most important rule is to understand the graphs. I have

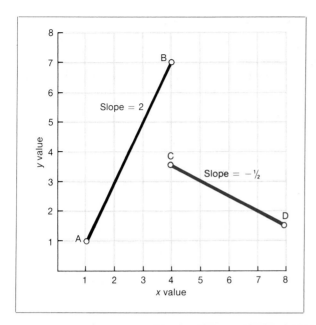

**Exhibit 1A.3**
**Slopes of lines**
The slope of a straight line drawn between two points is defined as the ratio of the change in the *y* value to the change in the *x* value between the two points. For example, the line drawn between Points A and B in this exhibit has a slope of +2, whereas the line drawn between Points C and D has a slope of −1/2.

never taught economics without having at least one student come to me after failing an exam and say: "But I learned every one of those graphs! What happened?" I always tell the students that they should have learned the economics contained in the graphs, instead of merely memorizing graph lines.

Here are some specific study hints for working with graphs: after reading carefully through a chapter that uses graphs frequently, go back through the graphs one at a time. Place your hand over the explanatory note that appears beside each graph and try putting what the graph says into words. If you cannot say at least as much about the graph as the explanatory note does, read the text over again.

If you do all right going from graphs to words, half the battle is won. Next, try

**Exhibit 1A.4**
**Slopes of curves**

The slope of a curve at any given point is defined as the slope of a straight line drawn tangent to the curve at that point. A tangent line is one that just touches the curve without crossing it. In this exhibit, the slope of the curve at Point A is 1, and the slope of the curve at Point B is −2.

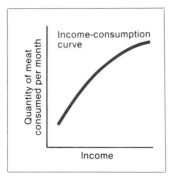

**Exhibit 1A.5**
An abstract graph

When we know the general form of an economic relationship but do not know the exact numbers involved, we can draw an abstract graph. Here, we know that as people's incomes rise, their consumption of meat increases rapidly at first, then levels off. Because we do not know the exact numbers for meat consumption or income, we have not marked any units on the axes.

covering up the graph, and using the explanatory note as a guide, sketch the graph on a piece of scratch paper. If you understand what the words mean and can comfortably go back and forth between the words and the graphs, you will find out that the two together are much easier to remember and apply than either would be separately. If you "learn the graphs" as meaningless patterns of lines, you are lost.

## CONSTRUCTING YOUR OWN GRAPHS

For some students, the hardest kind of question to answer on an exam is the kind that requires construction of an original graph as part of an essay answer. Here are some hints for constructing your own graphs:

1. Put down the answer to the question in words. Try to underline the most important quantities in what you have written. The result might be something like: "The larger the *number of students* who attend a university, the lower the *cost per student* of providing them with an education." Only *after* you have put your ideas clearly into words should you begin to plan your graph.

2. Decide how you are going to label the coordinate axes of your graph. In our example, because it is conventional to put money values on the vertical axis, we label the vertical axis "cost per student" and the horizontal axis "number of students."

3. Do you have exact numbers to work with? If you do, your next step should be to make a table showing what you know and then to use that to sketch your graph. If you do not have numbers, you will be drawing an abstract graph. In this case, all you know is that the cost per student goes down when the number of students goes up. Sketch in any convenient downward-sloping line (as in Exhibit 1A.6), and you will have done as well as can be done.

4. If your graph involves more than one relationship between pairs of economic quantities, repeat steps 1 to 3 for each relationship that you want to represent by a line or curve. When sketching graphs with more than one curve, pay particular

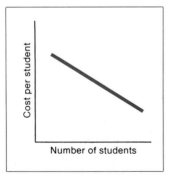

**Exhibit 1A.6**
Constructing a graph

To construct a graph, first put down in words what you want to say: "The larger the *number of students* at a university, the lower the *cost per student* of providing them with an education." Next, label the coordinate axes. Then, if you have exact numbers to work with, construct a table. Here we have no exact numbers, so we draw an abstract graph that slopes downward to show the cost goes down as numbers go up. For graphs with more than one curve, repeat these steps.

attention to points where you think two curves ought to intersect (which will happen whenever both the $x$ and $y$ values of the two relationships are equal) and where you think they ought to be tangent (which will happen whenever the slopes of two curves are equal).

5. After your graph is completed, try translating it back into words. Does it really say what you wanted to say?

## A REMINDER

As you work through this book and are introduced to various specific kinds of graphs, turn back to this appendix now and then. Do not commit the fatal error of memorizing graphs as meaningless pictures. Remember that if you can go back and forth between graphs and words, the underlying theory that both are trying to express will stay with you more vividly than if you rely on either graphs or words alone. Remember that economics is about *people*, not graphs.

## SUGGESTIONS FOR FURTHER READING

Easterbrook, W.T., and Aitken, Hugh G.J. *Canadian Economic History.* Toronto: Macmillan, 1956.
*Though published almost three decades ago, still a very useful chronological treatment of Canadian economic history.*

Easterbrook, W.T., and Watkins, Melville (eds.). *Approaches to Canadian Economic History.* Toronto: McClelland and Stewart, 1967.
*Contains interesting essays by a number of economic historians, including Harold Innis, on the interpretation of Canadian economic history. Part One includes several useful descriptions of the staples approach to our economic history.*

Heilbroner, Robert L. *The Wordly Philosophers.* New York: Simon and Schuster, 1980.
*A popular, well-written, and reliable guide to the thought of leading economists, past and present.*

Mars, William L., and Paterson, Donald B. *Canada: An Economic History.* Toronto: Macmillan, 1980.
*A thematic treatment of Canadian economic history, focusing on the forces and consequences of economic change.*

Robbins, Lionel C. *An Essay on the Nature and Significance of Economic Science.* 2d rev. ed. London: Macmillan, 1935.
*The classic treatment of the topic.*

# THE BASIS OF TRADE, THE PRICE SYSTEM, AND THE MARKET ECONOMY

---

## WHAT YOU WILL LEARN IN THIS CHAPTER

*This chapter will explain the basis for specialization and trade within and between modern economies. It will introduce the role played by markets in determining what is produced, how it is produced, and for whom it is produced. The chapter will explain each of three functions of markets: transmitting knowledge, providing incentives, and distributing income. It will show how the price system broadcasts information on opportunity costs and relative scarcities to buyers, how prices at the same time provide incentives to resource owners and entrepreneurs to put resources to best use, and how the incentive system operates to determine individuals' incomes. It will also introduce the questions of whether the market distributes income fairly and why it does not always operate perfectly. These questions will recur frequently as the discussion of economics progresses.*

## FOR REVIEW

*Here are some important terms and concepts that will be put to use in this chapter. If you do not understand them, review them before proceeding.*
- *Scarcity and choice (Chapter 1)*
- *Factors of production (Chapter 1)*
- *Specialization and the division of labor (Chapter 1)*
- *Efficiency and fairness (Chapter 1)*

---

## OPPORTUNITY COST AND THE PRODUCTION POSSIBILITY FRONTIER

When economists speak of the **allocation of resources**, they mean the determination of *what* will be produced, *how* it will be produced, *who* will produce it, and *for whom* it will be produced. In Canada people can choose from a wide range of occupations and produce a variety of goods and services. Because of scarcity of time and resources, the decision to pursue a particular vocation or produce a particular good involves the sacrifice of other possible activities and goods. Economists call this **opportunity cost**. The opportunity cost of doing something is the loss of the opportunity to do the next best thing instead, with the same time or resources.

How much, for example, does it cost to go to university? The direct, out-of-pocket expense for tuition, books, and room and board might come

**Allocation of resources** Determination of what will be produced, how it will be produced, who will produce it, and for whom it will be produced.

**Opportunity cost** The cost of doing something as measured by the loss of the opportunity to do something else, with the same amount of time or resources.

| (a) Budget of Out-of-Pocket Costs | |
| --- | --- |
| Tuition and fees | $1,400 |
| Books and supplies | 400 |
| Transportation to and from home | 200 |
| Room and board | 2,400 |
| Personal expenses | 600 |
| Total out-of-pocket costs | $5,000 |

| (b) Budget of Opportunity Costs | |
| --- | --- |
| Tuition and fees | $1,400 |
| Books and supplies | 400 |
| Transportation to and from home | 200 |
| Foregone income | 7,000 |
| Total opportunity costs | $9,000 |

**Exhibit 2.1**
Hypothetical student budget, illustrating the difference between out-of-pocket costs and opportunity costs.

to about $5,000. You might draw up a budget like the one shown in Exhibit 2.1a. This budget is called a *budget of out-of-pocket costs*, because it includes all the items, and only those items, for which you or your parents actually have to pay during the year.

Your own out-of-pocket costs may be considerably higher or lower than these average figures, but chances are that the items in this budget are the ones that come to mind when you think about the matter. As you begin to learn the economic way of thinking, however, you may find it informative to recast your university budget in terms of opportunity costs. Which of the items in Exhibit 2.1a represent opportunities foregone in order to go to university? Are there any foregone opportunities that are missing from the original budget? To answer these questions, compare the out-of-pocket budget with the opportunity cost budget shown in Exhibit 2.1b.

The first three items in the out-of-pocket budget appear again in the opportunity cost budget. In order to spend $1,400 on tuition and fees and $400 on books and supplies, you have to give up the opportunity to buy other goods and services, perhaps a car or a stereo set. In order to spend $200 getting to and from university, you have to pass up the opportunity to travel somewhere else or to spend the money on something other than travel. But the last two items in the out-of-pocket budget are not opportunity costs. By spending $3,000 on room, board, and personal expenses during the year, you are not really giving up an opportunity to do something you could have done if you had not gone to university. Whether you went to university or not, you would still have to eat, live somewhere, and buy clothing. Thus these are not opportunity costs of going to university.

Thinking about what you would have done if you had not gone to university suggests a major item that must be added to your opportunity cost budget—one that does not show up at all in the out-of-pocket budget. If you had not gone to university, you probably would have taken a job and started to earn money soon after leaving high school. The average weekly earnings of university-aged young people appear to be about $220. Multiplying this by thirty-two weeks (assuming that you work during summer months even if you go to university) brings the total to about $7,000 per year of university. These potential earnings are something you have to forego to go to university, so the item must appear in your opportunity cost budget.

Which budget you will find useful, of course, depends on the kind of decision you are making. If you are already committed to university and are simply doing your financial planning for the year, then you will use the out-of-pocket budget to make sure that you have enough in savings, scholarships, loans, and parents' contributions to make ends meet. But suppose you are making the more basic decision of whether to go to university or to pursue some alternative career path that does not require university. Then it is the opportunity cost of university that you should take into account, weighing this cost against the benefit of greater future earnings or greater personal satisfaction that you expect to gain from a university education.

It is clear that, in any decision we make, we trade off one opportunity or commodity for another. This is as true for a business or a national government as it is for an individual.

### The Production Possibility Frontier

The production possibility frontier, to be described in the following pages, provides a graphical illustration of opportunity costs. Each movement along the frontier requires the sacrifice of the opportunity to produce one thing in order to produce more of something else.

To see this more clearly, assume that a particular region of Canada, the Maritimes, can produce only two goods, grain and fish. Given existing factors of production, the Maritimes can produce various combinations of these goods.

Even if all the people in the Maritimes devoted all their time and resources to fish, there would be a limit to the quantity of fish that could be produced each year. For the sake of illustration, suppose that this limit is 20 million kilograms. The extreme possibility of producing 20 million kilograms of fish in one year and nothing else is shown by Point A, in Exhibit 2.2. Assume that the maximum rate of output of grain if no resources at all are put into fish is 1,000 million cubic decimetres, shown by Point B. Between these two extremes is a range of possibilities for producing fish and grain in combination. These intermediate possibilities are represented by points such as C and D, which fall along the curve in diagram. This curve is the **production possibility frontier**.

It is a frontier because it is a boundary between the combinations of fish and grain that can be produced and the combinations that cannot possibly be produced. Points A, B, C, and D, which lie right on the curve, represent combinations of fish and grain that can be produced. A combination such as that represented by Point E, in the shaded area within the production possibility frontier, can be produced even if some factors of production remain unemployed or are used wastefully. For example, labor is used inefficiently if people are used for jobs to which they are not suited, or if their use is temporarily halted by strikes or limited by monopolies which restrict entry to a particular labor market.

**Production possibility frontier** A curve showing the possible combinations of goods that can be produced by an economy, given the quantity and quality of factors of production available.

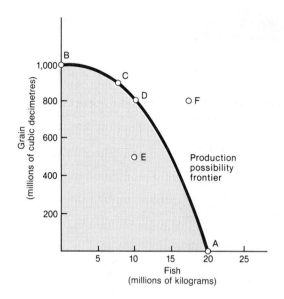

**Exhibit 2.2**
**A production possibility frontier for fish and grain**
This diagram shows a production possibility frontier for fish and grain. Point A represents the maximum production of fish if no grain is produced, and Point B represents the maximum production of grain if no fish are taken. A, B, C, D, and all other points along the frontier, as well as points such as E in the shaded area under it, are possible. Points such as F, outside the frontier, are not possible given the quantity and quality of resources available.

In contrast, a combination of fish and grain such as that represented by Point F cannot possibly be produced in one year without increasing the population, developing new resources, or improving the technology of the region. Therefore, at a given point in time all combinations outside the shaded area are impossible.

At any point along the production frontier, there is a trade-off between fish and grain. More of one cannot be produced without giving up some of the other. For example, suppose we began at Point C, where 8 million kilograms of fish are produced each year and 900 million cubic decimetres of grain are produced. If we wanted to increase the output of fish to 10 million kilograms per year, we would have to give up some grain and use those resources to build extra ships, nets, and processing plants. That would move us to Point D, which represents 10 million kilograms of fish and only 800 million cubic decimetres of wheat.

Now we can see how the production possibility curve allows us to visualize the concept of opportunity costs. In moving from C to D on the production possibility frontier, 2 million extra kilograms of fish can be obtained at the opportunity cost of 100 million cubic decimetres of grain. Putting this on a per-kilogram-of-fish basis, the opportunity cost of fish production in the range between C and D is approximately 50 dm$^3$ of grain per additional kilogram. Geometrically, the opportunity cost of fish in terms of grain is given by the slope of the production possibility frontier.

### Why is the Production Possibility Frontier Curved?
Why is the production possibility frontier a curve rather than a straight line? If it were a straight line, this would mean that the opportunity cost of producing an additional kilogram of fish, measured as a loss of grain production, would be the same no matter how people chose to divide their efforts and resources between fish and grain. When opportunity costs are

constant, each additional unit of output of one good requires a specific and unchanging amount of sacrifice of other goods, as resources are shifted from one use to another. For the analysis of some problems, it is useful to assume constant opportunity cost, but it is highly unlikely that this situation would occur in actual practice. Why?

The answer is that factors of production are not **homogeneous**. That is, individual units of any factor are not all alike. Some are suited to specializing in the production of one thing, others are suited to something else.

**Homogeneous** Having the property that every unit is just like every other unit.

To see why this puts a curve in the production possibility frontier, imagine that starting today the Maritimes wanted to increase the output of fish. The first thing it would need would be more fishermen. The opportunity cost of getting the first few fishermen would be low. Farmers on marginal land, not very interested in farming, could be recruited. Later, however, people and resources more suited to farming would be transferred to fishing. The opportunity cost of fishing would rise, and the production possibility curve would begin to bend as we moved along it.

Soon we would have to start calling in people who were not at all qualified to be fishermen, even though they might be doing a good job at farming. A man who had spent his life tending fields and who had never been in a boat or worked in a fish processing plant might be expected to be much more productive on a farm than in the fishing industry. As more and more unqualified people were moved to fishing, the production possibility frontier would bend still more sharply. In short, differences of ability and specialization among people as well as differences among units of other factors of production can be counted on to give the production possibility frontier its typical concave shape.

The swelling out of the production possibility frontier from the origin illustrates what economists call the **law of increasing costs**.

**Law of increasing costs** As resources are shifted from one use to another, an additional unit of output of one good requires an increasing rate of sacrifice of other goods as greater and greater shifts occur.

## Economic Growth and the Production Possibility Frontier

It is important to note that the limits on our range of choice illustrated by a given production possibility frontier apply only as long as available quantities and qualities of factors of production do not change. If such factors improve with time, the frontier will expand and shift to the right, as shown in Exhibit 2.3. The curve farthest to the left, Curve A, is the *initial* frontier, describing a position of full employment. It is assumed that current resources are fully utilized, so that the curve cannot be shifted simply by using current resources more efficiently. However, the quality of labor and entrepreneurship characteristic of a given population improves as people become healthier and better educated. The quality of capital increases dramatically as technological change improves equipment and brings in new methods of production. Only natural resources do not undergo major qualitative improvements; in fact, many actually decline in quality as they are depleted by use. So far, the increases in quantity and quality of other factors have more than made up for the depletion of natural resources in advanced industrial countries.

In less developed countries it is sometimes extremely difficult to shift the production possibility frontier to the right. Given the scarcity of resources, increases in capital investment require some sacrifice in con-

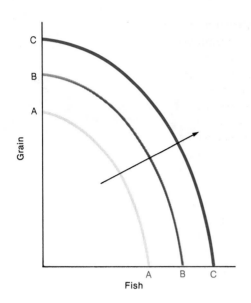

**Exhibit 2.3**
**Expanding production possibility frontier**
The position of the production possibility frontier at any point in time depends on the quantity and quality of the factors of production available. As time goes by, population grows, new capital is accumulated, and technological change takes place, permitting the production possibility frontier to shift outward, as indicated by the arrow in this diagram.

sumption. But in nations where consumption is already very low, no further sacrifices are possible. Economic growth remains for such nations a frustrating dream.

## SPECIALIZATION AND TRADE

We saw in Chapter 1 that economies can increase their output through division of labor, or specialization. Such specialization can occur within a single country, when people are motivated to pursue those occupations that most suit their talents. It can also take place between countries, with one country specializing in the production of certain goods and services to which it is most suited, while another country specializes in other goods and services more appropriate to it. Through both domestic and international specialization, countries can, in effect, push their production possibility frontiers outward.

It must be noted, however, that specialization makes sense only when those who specialize can trade with others. If Farmer Jones decides to concentrate on wheat production, instead of trying to grow all the foods that he would like to consume, he will be forced to exchange some of his wheat for the other goods and services that he needs. Similarly, nations that specialize in the production of some goods will need to obtain others through trade.

Trade can be understood as an alternative way of producing something. If I want a loaf of bread I can either bake it myself or use my earnings from a job to purchase it. If it would take me an hour to bake a loaf of bread and if bread from a bakery costs $1, then if I earn more than $1 an hour at my job I would be foolish—from a strictly financial point of view—to bake my own bread. My opportunity cost of baking a loaf is greater than the baker's cost of producing it.

It can be shown quite easily that individuals and nations will benefit by specializing in, and trading, those goods and services which they produce most efficiently. If you are a better doctor than your neighbor could ever be, but she is a better plumber than you could be, you should stick to your doctoring and get her to do your plumbing, and vice versa. However, economic theory can also show that even if you are *both* a better doctor and plumber than your neighbor, it might still pay you to specialize in medicine and let her do your plumbing. Since this is less obvious, and since it is extremely important for individuals as well as for whole communities and nations, providing the basis of much of our economic activity, it is an idea worth exploring more fully.

To illustrate this, let us create a simplified model of Canada, made up of two regions: the Maritimes and the Prairies. Both regions are assumed to have farms and fishing resources, but the more moderate climate of the Maritimes and their proximity to Atlantic spawning grounds happen to make both their farms and their fishing beds more productive than those on the Prairies. The number of labor hours required to produce a tonne of each product in the two regions is shown in Exhibit 2.4. For simplicity, we shall consider only labor cost in this example. We shall think of other costs as proportional to labor costs. Further we shall assume per-unit labor costs to be constant for all levels of output.

---

**Exhibit 2.4**
**Labor hours per tonne of output in the Maritimes and the Prairies**
The figures in this table show the number of labor hours required to produce each tonne of fish and grain in the Maritimes and the Prairies. The Maritimes have an absolute advantage in the production of both goods.

|       | Maritimes | Prairies |
|-------|-----------|----------|
| Fish  | 2         | 5        |
| Grain | 4         | 5        |

---

## Absolute Advantage and Comparative Advantage

Exhibit 2.4 reveals two kinds of differences in the cost structure of the two regions. First, *both* fish and grain require fewer labor hours to produce in the Maritimes. The Maritimes are said to have an **absolute advantage** in the production of both goods. Second, there are differences in the opportunity costs between the two regions. In the Prairies, producing a tonne of fish means foregoing the opportunity to use 5 labor hours in the fields. A tonne of fish thus has an opportunity cost of 1 t of grain there. In the Maritimes, producing 1 t of fish means giving up the opportunity to produce 0.5 t of grain. In terms of opportunity costs, then, fish are cheaper in the Maritimes than in the Prairies. On the other hand, in terms of opportunity cost, grain is cheaper in the Prairies—where 1 t of grain requires giving up 1 t of fish—than in the Maritimes—where 1 t of grain costs 2 t of fish. The region in which the opportunity cost of a good is lower is said to have a **comparative advantage** in producing that good.

**Absolute advantage** In trade theory, the ability of a region or country to produce a good at absolutely lower cost, measured in terms of factor inputs, than its trading partners.

**Comparative advantage** In trade theory, the ability of a region or country to produce a good at lower opportunity cost, measured in terms of other foregone goods, than its trading partners.

### Pretrade Equilibrium

If no trade takes place between the Prairies and the Maritimes, equilibrium in the fish and grain markets in each region will be established independently. We have simplified things by ignoring all costs but labor costs. Further, to keep the example clear, we have assumed that these costs are constant, even though, as we have seen (p. 29), this is an unrealistic assumption in real-world situations. In pretrade equilibrium, the ratio of the price of fish to the price of grain in each region will thus be equal to the ratio of labor inputs needed to produce the goods. In the Prairies, where a tonne of grain and a tonne of fish both take the same labor to produce, the price of fish will be equal to the price of grain. In the Maritimes, where a tonne of fish takes half as much labor to produce as a tonne of grain, the equilibrium price of fish will be half the price of grain.

Suppose that each region has 1,000 labor hours available for production of fish and grain. This information allows us to construct a production possibility frontier for each region, as illustrated in Exhibit 2.5. The straight-line frontiers reflect the special assumption of this example that costs of the goods in terms of each other remain constant as labor resources are shifted from one good to another in each region.

Since it takes 2 hours of labor in the Maritimes to produce a tonne of fish, and 4 hours of labor to produce a tonne of grain, the Maritimes can produce a maximum of 500 t of fish or 250 t of grain, or a combination of the two goods as indicated by the production possibility frontier. Because the Prairies require 5 hours of labor for each tonne of grain or fish, producers there can produce, at a maximum, only 200 t of fish or 200 t of grain, or a combination of the two goods as indicated by their frontier. The slopes of the production possibility frontiers reflect the trade-off (opportunity cost) between the goods in each region. One tonne of grain can be traded off for two tonnes of fish in the Maritimes, while a tonne of grain can be traded off for a tonne of fish in the Prairies.

---

**Exhibit 2.5**
**Production possibility frontier for the Maritimes and the Prairies, assuming 1,000 labor hours for each region**
With 1,000 labor hours the Maritimes can, in the extreme, produce 500 t of fish or 250 t of grain. The Prairies with the same amount of labor can produce 200 t of fish or 200 t of grain.

The amount of each good produced in each region, before specialization and trade, will depend on demand and consumer tastes. Suppose that demand conditions are such that in the Prairies 80 t of grain and 120 t of fish are produced (Point A in Exhibit 2.5), while in the Maritimes 300 t of fish and 100 t of grain are produced (Point B in Exhibit 2.5). The quantities produced and consumed in pretrade equilibrium are noted in Exhibit 2.6.

**Exhibit 2.6**
**Pretrade equilibrium production of fish and grain in the Maritimes and the Prairies**
If the Maritimes and the Prairies do not engage in trade, each region will have to meet all its needs from its own resources. The quantities of goods produced in each region depend on the strength of regional demand. The relative prices of the two goods in each region will be determined by their labor costs, as shown in Exhibit 2.4.

|  | Maritimes | Prairies | Total for Country |
|---|---|---|---|
| Fish (tonnes) | 300 | 120 | 420 |
| Grain (tonnes) | 100 | 80 | 180 |

## The Possibility of Trade

The stage is now set to consider the possibilities for trade between the Maritimes and the Prairies, considered as two separate economies. A superficial look at labor costs might make us think there were no possibilities for trade. Prairie consumers might like the opportunity to buy some of those cheap Maritime goods, but why should Maritimers be interested? After all, can they not produce everything in their own region more cheaply than it can be produced in the Prairies? If so, how could they gain from trade? A closer look will show us.

Imagine that an enterprising merchant in the Prairies decides to send a carload of grain to the Maritimes. The Maritimers have been used to giving 2 t of fish for 1 t of grain. Prairie farmers have been accustomed to getting only 1 t of fish for 1 t of grain. Any exchange ratio between 1 and 2 t of fish per tonne of grain will seem attractive to both parties. For instance, a trade of 1.5 t of fish for 1 t of grain will make both the Prairie merchant and the Maritime fish producer better off than they would have been had they traded only with others from their own region. Absolute advantage turns out to be unimportant in determining patterns of trade. Only comparative advantage matters.

## Gains From Specialization and Trade

The opening of trade between the Prairies and the Maritimes will soon begin to have an effect on patterns of production in the two regions. In the Prairies, fishermen will discover that instead of working 5 hours to catch 1 t of fish, they can work 5 hours on a farm and exchange the 1 t of grain they get for 1.5 t of fish from the Maritimes. In the Maritimes, people will find that it is no longer worth their while to spend 4 hours on the farm to produce 1 t of grain. Instead, they can fish for 3 hours to catch 1.5 t of fish to exchange for 1 t of grain from the Prairies. In short, Prairie people will find it advantageous to specialize in grain and Maritimers will find it advantageous to specialize in fish.

**Exhibit 2.7**
**Posttrade production and consumption of fish and grain in the Prairies and the Maritimes, in tonnes**
It is assumed that they traded 1.5 t of fish for 1 t of grain. Both are completely specialized. In comparison with pretrade output, shown here in brackets, production in the country has increased, and each region's consumption has increased.

|  |  | Maritimes | Prairies | Total for Country Posttrade | Pretrade |
|---|---|---|---|---|---|
| Fish | Production | 500 | 0 | 500 | (420) |
|  | Consumption | 335 | 165 | 500 |  |
| Grain | Production | 0 | 200 | 200 | (180) |
|  | Consumption | 110 | 90 | 200 |  |

Suppose now that trade continues at the ratio of 1.5 t of fish per tonne of grain, until both regions have become completely specialized. The Maritimes no longer produce any grain and the Prairies no longer produce any fish. The Prairies grow 200 t of grain, 110 t of which are shipped to the Maritimes. Maritimers in turn catch 500 t of fish, 165 t of which are traded to the Prairies. Exhibit 2.7 summarizes their posttrade situations. (It is assumed that each region wishes to consume at least as much of each good as before.)

A comparison of Exhibit 2.7 with Exhibit 2.6 reveals three noteworthy things. First, it shows that Prairie people are better off after trade than before. They have 45 more tonnes of fish to eat, and 10 more tonnes of grain. Second, it shows that Maritimers, too, are better off. They have 10 more tonnes of grain to consume, and 35 more tonnes of fish. Finally, the last columns of the tables reveal that total national output of both grain and fish has risen as a result of specialization and trade. In short, everyone is better off.

### Generalized Mutual Advantage

The principle of mutual advantage from specialization and trade applies to different countries as well as to regions within a country. It is the rational economic basis for international as well as domestic trade. Wherever one country has a comparative advantage over another in producing some good, specialization can increase consumption in each country, and both national and international output can be increased.

It will be observed in several places in this book that Canada's international trade plays a vital role in its economy. Our nation undoubtedly derives great benefit from it and is also subject to some special pressures and problems because of it. There is, however, no need for a special *theory* of international trade. In our previous illustrations, the names of entire countries, such as Portugal and Canada, could have been substituted for the "Maritimes" and the "Prairies," and the same results would have been obtained. That is because the same principles apply. It makes no difference whether buyers and sellers live on the same or opposite sides of political boundaries, as far as the application of the theory of comparative advantage is concerned.

The theory of comparative advantage was first clearly set forth by David Ricardo early in the nineteenth century. Ricardo wanted to show why it would be to England's advantage to maintain active trade with other countries. To do so, he used an example much like the one we have just examined.

---

David Ricardo, the greatest of the classical economists, was born in 1772. His father, a Jewish immigrant, was a member of the London stock exchange. Ricardo's education was rather haphazard, and he entered his father's business at the age of fourteen. In 1793 he married, abandoned strict Jewish orthodoxy, and went into business on his own. These were years of war and financial disturbance. The young Ricardo developed a reputation for remarkable astuteness and quickly made a large fortune.

In 1799 Ricardo read *The Wealth of Nations* and developed an interest in questions of political economy. In 1809 his first writings on economics appeared. They were a series of newspaper articles on "The High Price of Bullion," which appeared the next year as an influential pamphlet. Several other short works added to his reputation in this area. In 1814 he retired from business to devote all his time to political economy.

Ricardo's major work is *Principles of Political Economy and Taxation*, first published in 1817. This work contains, among other things, a pioneering statement of the principle of comparative advantage as applied to international trade. With a lucid numerical example, Ricardo shows why it is to the mutual advantage of both countries for England to export wool to Portugal and to import wine in return, even though both products can be produced at absolutely lower costs in Portugal.

But international trade is only a sidelight of Ricardo's *Principles.* The book covers the whole of economics as then known, beginning with value theory and progressing to a theory of economic growth and evolution. Ricardo, like his friend Malthus and his later follower John Stuart Mill, held that the economy was growing toward a future "steady state." In this state, economic growth would come to a halt, and the wage rate would be depressed to the subsistence level.

Ricardo's book was extraordinarily influential. For more than half a century thereafter, much of economics as written in England was an elaboration of or commentary on Ricardo's work. The most famous of all economists to fall under the influence of Ricardo's theory and method was Karl Marx. Although Marx eventually reached revolutionary conclusions that differed radically from any views Ricardo held, his starting point was Ricardo's labor theory of value and method of analyzing economic growth.

**David Ricardo (1772–1823)**

---

## Trade and Markets

One major precondition for trade of any kind has not yet been examined. If people are to be able to specialize and trade with each other, there must be a coordinating mechanism that brings buyers and sellers together. In the Canadian economy, markets play a central role in providing the necessary coordination. **Markets** are the various arrangements people have for trading with one another. They may be elaborately organized, like the Toronto Stock Exchange or the Winnipeg Commodity Exchange, which match up the sellers and buyers of, respectively, corporation securities and basic agricultural and mining commodities; or informal, like the word-of-mouth network that puts teenage babysitters in touch with people who need their services. But however markets are organized, they perform certain com-

**Markets** All the various arrangements people have for trading with one another.

mon functions: transmitting information, providing incentives, and distributing income. In the following section, case studies will clarify the way widely varied markets carry out these functions.

## THE FUNCTIONS OF MARKETS

### Information and Its Value

Information is the most precious good in any economy. Economic prosperity depends on putting resources to their best uses, and, to do this, the people who make decisions on how resources are to be used must know which uses are best. Like water, economic information is taken for granted when it is cheap and abundant. Its importance becomes apparent only when it is scarce, as the following case study illustrates.

### Case 2.1
### The Role of Information in the Bazaar Economy

At the foot of the Atlas Mountains in Morocco sits the ancient walled town of Sefrou. Once an important stop on the caravan route from Fez to the Sahara, it has been, for about a century now, an important *bazaar*, or market center, for some 15,000 to 30,000 people. Since the mid 1960s, anthropologist Clifford Geertz of the Institute for Advanced Study has been observing the bazaar at Sefrou. What he has discovered is instructive.

According to Geertz, information in the bazaar is poor, scarce, maldistributed, inefficiently communicated, and intensely valued. The level of ignorance about everything from product quality and going prices to market possibilities and production costs is very high. The name of the game in the bazaar is the search for information a person lacks and the protection of information a person has. As in any other economy, capital, skill, luck, privilege, and hard work contribute to individual success; but in the bazaar they do it not so much by increasing the efficiency of production as by enabling a person to secure a strategic location in the market's communications network. The primary problem facing participants in the bazaar is not to balance options but to find out what they are.

Geertz interprets the central features that distinguish the bazaar from a modern, industrialized market economy as responses to the scarcity of information. One of these features is bargaining. In a system where virtually nothing is packaged, standardized, or regulated, every transaction must be preceded by elaborate bargaining over price, quantity, quality, and credit terms. During the bargaining, buyers and sellers naturally try to conceal their minimum acceptable terms from one another, but at the same time they must manage to reveal enough information to form a basis for a mutually advantageous trade.

At this point, the efficiency of the bazaar is apparently improved by a second characteristic feature, which Geertz calls "clientalization." By this he means a tendency of buyers to return repeatedly to the same seller to engage in intensive bargaining rather than to search quickly but extensively among many sellers for the best price. Evidently, repeated bargaining within a stable client-seller relationship improves information exchange by enough to offset any loss of information resulting from frequent examination of alternative sources of supply.

In Geertz's view, the whole structure of the bazaar can be viewed as a set of communications channels designed to serve the needs of people whose interests are opposed in the act of bargaining but joined by the need to coordinate their economic activities. The same is true of any economic system; but since information is relatively scarce in the bazaar, its value is more prominently displayed.

Source: Based on Clifford Geertz, "The Bazaar Economy: Information and Search in Peasant Marketing." *American Economic Review* 68 (May 1978) pp. 28–32. Used by permission.

## The Price System

In the Canadian economy of today, bargaining and client-seller relationships are by no means unknown. Their importance as channels for the transmission of information, however, is completely overshadowed by another mechanism that exists only in rudimentary form in the bazaar economy. This mechanism is the *price system*. In the modern economy, prices typically are not subject to bargaining on a one-to-one basis between buyer and seller every time a transaction is made. Instead, they are widely advertised and published as an invitation to any buyer to enter the market on equal terms with other buyers. The price system is essentially a system for broadcasting information on opportunity costs and on the relative scarcity of various goods and services. A rise in the price of any good relative to the price of other goods signals increasing scarcity of that good. A fall in the price of any good (or, in times of inflation, a failure of its price to rise as fast as the prices of other goods) signals increasing abundance. Buyers can adjust their behavior accordingly.

The following case, supplied by Nobel prize-winning economist F. A. Hayek, brings out the contrast between the price system and the bazaar system. In Hayek's example, prices are the cheap and easily available source of information used by buyers to adjust to complex events occurring far away.

### Case 2.2
### Information and the Price System

Assume that somewhere in the world a new opportunity for the use of some raw material, say tin, has arisen, or that one of the sources of supply of tin has been eliminated. It does not matter for our purpose—and it is very significant that it does not matter—which of these two causes has made tin more scarce. All that the users of tin need to know is that some of the tin they used to consume is now more profitably employed elsewhere, and that in consequence they must economize tin. There is no need for the great majority of them even to know where the more urgent need has arisen, or in favor of what other needs they ought to husband the supply. If only some of them know directly of the new demand, and switch resources over to it, and if the people who are aware of the new gap thus created in turn fill it from still other sources, the effect will rapidly spread throughout the whole economic system and influence not only the uses of tin, but also those of its substitutes and the substitutes of these substitutes, the supply of the things made of tin, and their substitutes, and so on, and all this without the great majority of those instrumental in bringing about these substitutions knowing anything at all about the original cause of these changes. The whole acts as one market, not because any of its members survey the whole field, but because their limited individual fields of vision sufficiently overlap so that through many intermediaries the relevant information is communicated to all.

Source: Reprinted by permission from F. A. Hayek, "The Use of Knowledge in Society," *American Economic Review* 35 (September 1945) pp. 519–530.

By informing people of the value and scarcity of tin, wheat, forklift trucks, and hundreds of thousands of other commodities, the price system reduces countless decisions to the level of pure economizing. Producers and consumers can observe market prices, combine them with their own knowledge of local circumstances, and arrive at valid judgments about the advantages and disadvantages of various production and consumption activities. To be sure, there is more to economic decision making than pure economizing, and the price system does not supply the answers to all economic questions. But entrepreneurial talents and energies, which in a bazaar economy are used up merely in finding out how much things cost, are now liberated to deal with the problem of finding new and better ways of doing things.

### Incentives in the Market Economy

Knowledge of the best use of resources is a necessary condition for efficient coordination of economic activity, but it is not by itself sufficient. In addition to knowing the uses to which resources should be put, the people controlling them must have incentives to devote them to the known best use. Providing those incentives is the second major function of markets. As Adam Smith wrote more than two hundred years ago:

> It is not from the benevolence of the butcher, the brewer, or the baker that we expect our dinner, but from their regard to their own interest.... Every individual is continually exerting himself to find out the most advantageous employment for whatever capital he can command.... By directing that industry in such a manner as its produce may be of the greater value, he intends only his own gain, and he is in this, as in many other cases, led by an invisible hand to promote an end which was no part of his intention.

The market offers different kinds of incentives to different people. Consumers who keep themselves well informed and spend their money judiciously are rewarded by the satisfaction of more needs with their limited budgets. Workers earn higher incomes if they stay alert to job market opportunities and work where their productivity is highest. Real estate brokers earn higher commissions the more efficiently they match suitable buyers and sellers. In every case, people who acquire economic information have an incentive to act on that information and not just file it away.

No doubt the most famous of incentives in the market economy is the profit motive. Profits make up a relatively small part of all income received by individuals. As officially measured by government statisticians, wages and salaries outweigh corporate profits by more than four to one. But profits have an importance entirely out of proportion to their magnitude because they are the reward earned by entrepreneurs for properly coordinating the contributions of workers and other resource owners. A business firm earns a profit by buying inputs at their market prices and using them to produce a product that can be sold for more than the cost of all the inputs. And just as the market rewards firms that use resources productively, it penalizes those who use them wastefully. If the value of the inputs a firm buys exceeds the value of the product it makes out of those inputs, that firm will suffer a loss and will eventually disappear from the market.

### Distributing Income

As a by-product of providing incentives, markets distribute income and wealth. People who possess skills and talents or who own resources that are scarce and highly valued get richly rewarded for putting them to their best use. People whose talents or resources are less scarce or of poor quality get less well rewarded even if they use what they have as wisely as possible. Entrepreneurs who take risks and guess right make large profits; entrepreneurs who take risks that looked just as prudent at the outset but who have guessed wrong suffer losses. In short, the market tends to distribute income in proportion to the contribution each person makes to the process of production.

The distributional function of the market is a source of great controversy, much of it over the normative question of whether the distribution of income in a market economy is *fair*. Not surprisingly, the answer depends largely on what is meant by *fairness*. To those for whom fairness means equal opportunity, the distribution of income in a market economy does appear equitable. People receive what they earn from their own labor and from the voluntary exchange of property with others. All that is required for fairness, in this view, is that the contracts and exchanges be voluntary so they will work out to the mutual benefit of buyers and sellers.

To those who view fairness in terms of equality of income, the market system seems almost by definition to be unfair. Because skills, talents, and resource ownership are not distributed equally among people, the market does not distribute income equally either. Without some form of political intervention, it is unable to solve existing inequalities of this kind.

## IMPERFECTIONS IN THE MARKET SYSTEM

Are markets perfect? Economists from Adam Smith to Milton Friedman sometimes get so enthusiastic about the principles according to which markets operate that they forget to point out that in the real world these principles operate only as tendencies. Imperfections in the market economy stem from a number of sources, which we will consider later. By far the most important is the fact that although the price system *cheapens* the process of transmitting information to a large degree, it does not make information *free*.

Even after the price system has done its best, there is a level of ignorance that cannot be reduced. Producers and consumers remain at least partly ignorant of what is happening in other places and substantially ignorant of what is likely to happen in the future. They may conceal their preferences for strategic reasons when dealing with others and at the same time remain ignorant of the preferences of others. A modern industrial market economy is far ahead of the bazaar at Sefrou in terms of the quality of information available; but as long as information is less than perfect, mistakes will be made.

It must be stressed here that our markets are indeed far from perfect. In produce markets, many firms use their **monopoly power**—their power to raise prices without losing customers—to charge higher prices than consumers would otherwise have to pay. In those industries in which only a few firms control most of the production, prices may be "fixed" by agreement among the firms. New competitors may be kept out of the market by market agreements that favor the existing firms, or by substantial but temporary price reductions that make it difficult for a new firm to gain a foothold in the industry. In the labor market, professionals may restrict the entry of new competitors by setting high admission standards, and unions

**Monopoly power** A seller's power to raise the price of a product without losing all, or nearly all, customers.

may succeed in negotiating contracts that make it difficult for management to replace incompetent workers with new ones. In the financial markets, relatively few banks dominate the industry, with the result that lending rates appear to be the same from one bank to another. In agriculture, marketing boards have virtually destroyed competition in the selling of a wide range of agricultural products.

Such imperfections are both the result of, and the cause of, government intervention in the marketplace. Where the market seems to be destructive of peoples' livelihood, as in agriculture, the government intervenes to alter the market in favor of the producer. In other markets the government may enter in order to increase competition so that the consumer will be favored.

## CONCLUSIONS

This chapter has developed the notions of opportunity cost, the production possibility frontier, and comparative advantage to demonstrate that societies can benefit from specialization and trade.

Trade also requires markets. This chapter has given just a few examples of how markets perform their functions of transmitting information, providing incentives, and distributing income. In later chapters we will examine more closely why markets do not always perform well, and what can be done to improve their performance.

## SUMMARY

1. The production possibility frontier illustrates the fact that every economy operates under conditions of scarcity, and that increased production of one good, in the absence of increases or improvements in the factors of production, can only be obtained at the expense of other goods. Such a trade-off between goods reflects the opportunity cost of producing them.
2. If one trading area is able to produce a good at lower cost, in terms of its factor inputs, than another trading area, it is said to have an absolute advantage. If a trading area is able to produce a good at lower opportunity cost, in terms of foregone goods, than another trading area, it is said to have a comparative advantage.
3. A trading area can utilize its resources more efficiently if it engages in specialization, based on the principle of comparative advantage. Such specialization can take place both within countries, between different regions, and on the international level, between different nations. The benefits of the division of labor are not restricted by political boundaries.
4. Markets play a crucial role in coordinating the division of labor in the market economy. This role includes performance of three basic functions: transmitting information, providing incentives, and distributing income.
5. In an advanced industrial market economy, the price system functions as a mechanism for broadcasting information about opportunity costs and the relative scarcity of resources. Rising relative prices signal increasing scarcity; falling relative prices signal increasing abundance.

6. Knowledge of the best use of resources is a necessary but not sufficient condition for efficient coordination of economic activity. In addition to knowing the uses to which resources should be put, the people controlling those resources must have incentives to devote them to their known best use. Consumers, resource owners, and entrepreneurs all have incentives to heed the information that comes to them through the price system, because doing so increases their satisfaction, income, and profit.

7. As a by-product of their function in providing incentives, markets perform the further function of distributing income and wealth. People who possess skills and talents or who own resources that are scarce and highly valued get richly rewarded for putting the resources to their best use. People whose talents or resources are less scarce or of poor quality get less well rewarded even if they use what they have wisely.

8. Despite their acknowledged effectiveness in coordinating the division of labor, markets are neither necessarily fair nor always perfectly efficient. There is considerable monopoly power in most markets today, posing major problems for consumers and governments.

## DISCUSSION QUESTIONS

1. Suppose you learned that Vladimir Horowitz, the great pianist, was also an amazingly proficient typist. Knowing this, would it surprise you to learn also that he hired a secretary to type his correspondence, even though he could do the job better and faster himself? What does this situation have to do with comparative advantage?

2. Turn to Exhibit 2.4. Suppose that new, high-yield grains were introduced in the Maritimes, so that the number of labor hours needed to grow a ton of grain there were cut from 4 hours to 2 hours. What would happen to trade between the Maritimes and the Prairies? Would it still pay for Maritimers to buy their grain from the Prairies? If the labor hours per ton of grain in the Maritimes fell all the way to 1, what would happen to the pattern of trade?

3. In your opinion, do the wages or salaries of various occupations have much influence on people's decisions about whether to go to university and what to major in? Justify your answer by explaining what it has to do with the functions of markets in transmitting information, providing incentives, and distributing income.

4. If you were the manager of a division of a major automobile manufacturer and you noticed that the price of steel had been going up relative to the prices of other materials used in the manufacturing of automobiles, how would you react? What would you do and have others do to make adjustments? How would you expect your competitors to react? Explain.

5. Even in an advanced industrial economy such as Canada's, not all transactions take place in accordance with uniform, published prices. What sorts of transactions do you know of that are still subject to bargaining between buyer and seller? Why do you think they are carried out by means of bargaining rather than by fixed prices?

# CHAPTER

# SUPPLY AND DEMAND — THE BASICS

# THREE

---

**WHAT YOU WILL LEARN IN THIS CHAPTER**
*Everyday experience teaches that, other things being equal, the quantity of a good that buyers are willing to purchase tends to increase as the price of the good decreases. Similarly, it teaches that the quantity of a good suppliers are willing to sell tends to increase as the price increases. This chapter will show how these commonsense ideas form the basis for supply and demand analysis — one of the most useful analytical tools in all of economics. It will show how terms such as* shortage *and* surplus *can be given a precise meaning and will introduce the concept of market equilibrium. These new concepts will then be applied to practical economic problems.*

**FOR REVIEW**
*Here are some important terms and concepts that will be put to use in this chapter. If you do not understand them, review them before proceeding.*
*• Working with graphs (Appendix to Chapter 1)*
*• Opportunity cost (Chapter 2)*

---

We have seen that market prices are important as a means of transmitting information about the relative scarcities of goods and services. In this chapter we will see how market prices are determined and how they change to reflect changing wants and availabilities. The tools of supply and demand analysis that we will use to explain the determination of market prices are among the most powerful in economics.

The concepts of supply and demand have been familiar to practical merchants and traders of all ages. For as long as there have been markets, sellers have realized that one way to encourage people to buy more of their product is to offer it at a lower price. Similarly, buyers have known that one way to get more of the goods they want is to offer to pay more for them. Only in the last hundred years, though, have economists made the systematic use of the principles of supply and demand the central basis of their science. In the English-speaking world, Alfred Marshall deserves much of the credit for showing how useful the ideas of supply and demand can be. This chapter (and the corresponding chapters in all modern textbooks) builds directly on what he taught his own students a hundred years ago.

## DEMAND

### The Law of Demand

**Law of demand** The law that the quantity of a good demanded by buyers in any market tends to increase as the price of the good decreases and to decrease as the price increases, other things being equal.

Our starting point is the **law of demand**, according to which the quantity of a good demanded by buyers in any market tends to increase as the price of the good decreases and to decrease as the price increases, other things being equal.

The law of demand corresponds closely to common sense and everyday experience. There are two major reasons why we expect people to buy more of a good when its price goes down. First, if the price of one good falls while the price of other goods remains unchanged, people are likely to substitute some of the cheaper good for others they would have bought instead. Thus when the price of fish goes down, with the price of meat remaining the same, people are likely to substitute fish for meat in their menus now and then. Second, when the price of one good falls while prices of other goods and nominal incomes remain the same, people will feel a little richer, much as if a little had been added to their incomes. Feeling richer, they are likely to buy a little more, including more of the good whose price has dropped.

But even though the law of demand is intuitively reasonable, it must be understood clearly if it is to be used properly as a tool of analysis. We will proceed, then, to examine it word for word.

**Alfred Marshall (1842–1924)**

Alfred Marshall was born in London in 1842, the son of a Bank of England cashier. His father hoped that he would enter the ministry, but young Marshall had other ideas. He turned down a theological scholarship at Oxford to study mathematics instead. He received an M.A. in mathematics from Cambridge in 1865.

While at Cambridge, he joined a philosophical discussion group. There, he became interested in promoting the wide development of the human mind. He was soon told, however, that harsh economic reality would prevent his ideas from being carried out. Britain's productive resources, it was said, could never allow the mass of the people sufficient leisure for education. This disillusioning episode appears to have first turned Marshall's attention to economics.

At the time, British economics was dominated by the so-called classical school. Marshall had great respect for the classical writers. Initially, he saw his own work as simply using his mathematical training to strengthen and systematize the classical system. It was not long, however, before he was breaking new ground and developing a system of his own. By 1890, when he brought out his famous *Principles of Economics*, he had laid the foundation of what is now called the neoclassical school.

Attempting to explain the essence of his approach, Marshall included this passage in the second edition of his *Principles*:

In spite of a great variety in detail, nearly all the chief problems of economics agree in that they have a kernel of the same kind. This kernel is an inquiry as to the balancing of two opposed classes of motives, the one consisting of desires to acquire certain new goods, and thus satisfy wants; while the other consists of desires to avoid certain efforts or retain certain immediate enjoyment.... In other words, it is an inquiry into the balancing of the forces of demand and supply.

Marshall's influence on economics, at least in the English-speaking world, was enormous. His *Principles* was the leading text for decades, and the modern student can still learn from reading it. As a professor at Cambridge, he taught a great many of the next generation of leading economists. Today the neoclassical school he founded continues to dominate the profession. It has received many challenges but so far has weathered them all.

## Quantity Demanded

First, what is meant by *quantity demanded?* It is important to understand that "quantity demanded" means the quantity buyers are *willing* and *able* to buy at a given price over a given period, such as a month or year. Quantity demanded is thus a narrower concept than the broad notions of want or need. I might *want* a new Porsche 928, but the last one I saw had a sticker price of $43,000. At that price, my quantity demanded is zero. I might *need* corrective dental surgery to avoid premature loss of my teeth, but I might be very poor. If I were unable to pay and if no other person or agency were willing to pay in my place, my need would not be counted as part of the quantity of dental services demanded at the going price.

## Other Things Being Equal

Second, why is the phrase *other things being equal* attached to the law of demand? The reason is that a change in the price of a product is not the only thing that affects the quantity of that product demanded. If people's incomes go up, they are likely to increase the quantities they demand of a great many goods, even if prices do not change. If people's basic tastes and preferences change, the quantities of things they buy will change. If their expectations about future prices or their own future incomes change, they may change their spending patterns even before those price and income changes actually take place.

Above all, in the law of demand, the "other things being equal" condition indicates that the prices of other goods remain unchanged. What really counts in determining the quantity demanded of some good is its price *relative* to the prices of other goods. If the price of gasoline goes up and consumers' incomes and the prices of all other goods go up by the same proportion, the law of demand does not suggest any change in the quantity of gasoline demanded. But if the price of gasoline goes up 10 percent while the price of everything else goes up 20 percent, an increase can be expected in the quantity of gasoline demanded, because its relative price has fallen.

## Inflation and the Law of Demand

It is especially important to distinguish between changes in relative prices and changes in nominal prices in a world of pervasive inflation. By **nominal prices** we mean the prices at which goods and services are actually sold, without adjustment for inflation. If the nominal price of a good goes up 10 percent while people's incomes and the prices of other goods also go up 10 percent, we would not expect the quantity demanded to decrease in accordance with the law of demand. If the nominal price of a good goes up by 20 percent while incomes and the prices of other goods go up by just 10 percent, the relative price of that good has increased, and we would expect the quantity demanded to decrease. If the price of a good goes up just 5 percent while incomes and the prices of other goods go up 10 percent, the relative price of the good has fallen, and the law of demand would lead us to expect an increase in the quantity of the good demanded.

**Nominal price** The price at which goods and services are actually sold, without adjustment for inflation.

### Exceptions to the Law

Are there exceptions to the law of demand? Are there cases in which an increase in the price of a good causes people to use more of it? Theoretically, such exceptions are possible, although in practice they are quite rare. One kind of exception can occur if the change in the price of a good has such a strong impact on effective purchasing power that it causes a radical change in people's whole pattern of consumption. Imagine a family that lives in Manitoba and habitually spends January each year vacationing in Florida. One year, the price of home heating fuel jumps dramatically. The family reacts by turning down the thermostat a little, but the fuel bills for September through December still go up so much that the family cannot afford to take its Florida vacation in January. Yet, staying at home, even though it is cheaper than going to Florida, requires the family to burn more fuel than during the previous winters, when it left the house unheated for that month. The total effect of the rise in fuel prices is therefore an *increase* in the consumption of the product.

Perhaps other rare kinds of exceptions to the law of demand are also possible.[1] The point is, though, that we have to think so hard to come up with examples that we end up being more convinced than ever of the validity of the law.

[1]A famous example involves what the late American economist Thorstein Veblen called "conspicuous consumption," meaning that some people will buy more of some goods, such as jewelry and furs, at higher prices because a high price is a status symbol.

---

**Exhibit 3.1**

A demand schedule and a demand curve for wheat
Both the demand schedule and the demand curve show the quanitity of wheat demanded at various possible prices. Both show, for example, that when the price is $2/dm³, the quantity is 2 billion cubic decimetres per year.

**(a) Demand schedule**

| Price of Wheat (dollars per cubic decimetre) | Quantity of Wheat Demanded (billions of cubic decimetres per year) |
|---|---|
| $3.20 | 1.4 |
| 3.00 | 1.5 |
| 2.80 | 1.6 |
| 2.60 | 1.7 |
| 2.40 | 1.8 |
| 2.20 | 1.9 |
| **2.00** | **2.0** |
| 1.80 | 2.1 |
| 1.60 | 2.2 |
| 1.40 | 2.3 |
| 1.20 | 2.4 |
| 1.00 | 2.5 |
| .80 | 2.6 |

**(b) Demand curve**

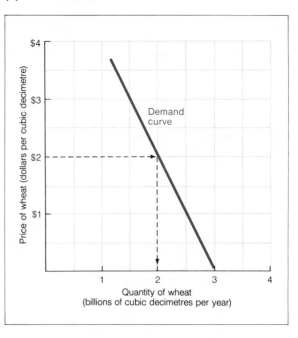

## The Demand Curve

The law of demand associates a quantity of a good or service demanded per unit of time with each possible price for that good or service. This systematic association between prices and quantities demanded for any particular good can be summarized in a table, such as that in Exhibit 3.1a.

From the first line of the table, we learn that when the price of wheat is $3.20, the quantity demanded per year will be 1.4 billion cubic decimetres. Reading further, we see that as the price decreases, the quantity demanded increases. At $3/dm³, buyers are willing and able to purchase 1.5 billion cubic decimetres per year; at $2.80, the quantity demanded is 1.6 billion cubic decimetres. The complete table is called the **demand schedule** for wheat.

The information given by the demand schedule can be expressed just as easily in graphical form. This is done in Exhibit 3.1b. The diagonal line of the graph is called the **demand curve** for wheat. Suppose that we want to use the demand curve to determine what quantity will be demanded when the price is $2/dm³. Beginning at $2 on the vertical axis, we follow across as shown by the arrow until we reach the demand curve. We then go down from that point to the horizontal axis, where we read off the answer— 2 billion cubic decimetres per year. This, of course, is the same answer given in the tabular demand schedule. The demand curve can also be expressed in equation form. The **demand equation** reads: $Qd = f(P)$, or $Qd = a - bP$, meaning that the Quantity demanded (Qd) will be a certain amount ($a$) when the price is zero, and decline as price rises. (In equations of this type, $f$ stands for "a function of" or "related to.") In Exhibit 3.1, $Qd = 3 - \frac{1}{2}P$.

**Demand schedule** A table showing the quantity of a good demanded at various prices.

**Demand curve** A graphical representation of the relationship between the price of a good and the quantity of it demanded.

**Demand equation** This equation can be written as $Qd = a - bP$, where $Qd$ = quantity demanded, $a$ = quantity demanded when the price is zero, and $bP$ expresses the rate at which Qd declines when the price rises.

---

**Exhibit 3.2**

**A shift in the demand curve for wheat**

The effect of a change in the price of wheat, other things being equal, is represented by a movement along the demand curve for wheat, as from Point A to Point B along Demand Curve $D_1$. The effect of a change in something other than a change in the price of wheat (say a change in household income) must be represented by a shift in the entire demand curve, as from the position $D_1$ to the position $D_2$, and a movement from Point A on the old demand curve to Point C on the new one.

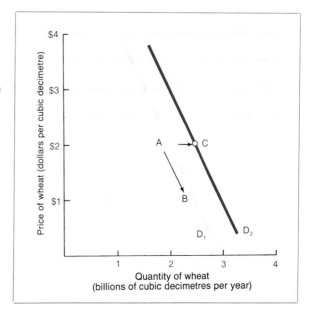

### Movements along the Demand Curve

To repeat what has been said before, the demand curve shows how the quantity demanded changes in response to a change in price, *other things being equal*. When a change in the quantity of wheat demanded occurs as a result of a change in the price of wheat, acting alone, that change is represented graphically as a movement along the demand curve for wheat. If something other than the price of wheat changes, a different graphical representation is required.

Consider Exhibit 3.2. The demand curve labeled $D_1$ is the same as that shown in Exhibit 3.1. It is based on certain assumptions about household income, the prices of other goods, and buyers' expectations about future changes in price. Given those assumptions, the quantity demanded at a price of $2/dm^3$ will be 2 billion cubic decimetres per year, as at Point A, on Demand Curve $D_1$. A fall in the price from $2/dm^3$ to $1/dm^3$, other things being equal, will cause the quantity demanded to increase to 2.5 billion cubic decimetres per year. This change in price is represented by a movement along Demand Curve $D_1$ from Point A to Point B.

**Shifts in the Demand Curve** Return now to Point A. Suppose that the price of wheat does not change but that something else changes—say, household income rises. A sufficiently large increase in household income could cause consumers to demand an additional half billion cubic decimetres per year, even without a change in the price of wheat. This change is represented by a movement from Point A to Point C in the diagram—a movement *off* Demand Curve $D_1$ rather than along it. With household income established at its new, higher level, changes in *price* would now cause movements up or down along the new demand curve, $D_2$, which passes through Point C and lies everywhere to the right of the old demand curve, $D_1$. The new demand curve indicates that, whatever the price of wheat, the quantity demanded, given the new, higher level of household income or higher prices of other goods, will be larger than it would have been at the same price, given the old level of income and prices.

The general point to be established is this: when the demand for some good changes for a reason *other* than a change in the price of the product itself, the change is represented graphically by a *shift* in the entire demand curve to a new position.

It is a rather widely established convention among economists to refer to a shift in a demand curve as a *change in demand*. The phrase *change in quantity demanded* refers to a movement along a given demand curve.

**Normal and Inferior Goods** Economists use some special terms in discussing the sources of shifts in demand curves. Changes in income are one source of such shifts. When a rise in buyers' incomes causes the demand curve for a good to shift to the right (as happened in Exhibit 3.2), the good is called a **normal good**. People tend to reduce their consumption of some goods when their incomes go up. Such goods, called **inferior goods**, are those goods for which there are more desirable but also more costly substitutes. Hamburger and intercity bus travel are examples. An increase in buyers' incomes causes the demand curve for an inferior good to shift to the left.

**Normal good** A good for which an increase in the income of buyers cause a rightward shift in the demand curve.

**Inferior good** A good for which an increase in the income of buyers causes a leftward shift in the demand curve.

**Substitutes and Complements** The position of the demand curve for a good may also be affected by changes in the prices of other, closely related goods. For example, salads can be made from lettuce or from spinach. An increase in the price of lettuce is likely to cause not only a decrease in the quantity of lettuce demanded (represented graphically by a movement up and to the left along the lettuce demand curve) but also an increase in the demand for spinach (represented graphically by a shift to the right of the entire spinach demand curve). When an increase in the price of one good causes an increase in the demand for another good, those two goods are said to be **substitutes** for each other.

Photographic film and flashbulbs tend to be used together. If the price of film were to rise, we would expect not only a  decrease in the quantity of film sold but a decrease in the demand for flashbulbs also. The effect of the change in the price of film is represented graphically as a movement along the film demand curve and as a leftward shift of the flashbulb demand curve. When an increase in the price of one good causes a decrease in the demand for another good, the two goods are said to be **complements.**

**Substitutes** A pair of goods for which an increase in the price of one causes an increase in the demand for the other, other things being equal.

## SUPPLY

The next step in the analysis of markets will be to examine the relationship between the price of a good and the quantity of it that suppliers are willing and able to provide for sale. Everyday experience suggests that, in order to induce sellers to increase the quantity of a good supplied, it is necessary, other things being equal, to offer them a higher price. When this is true, the supply curve for the good in question slopes upward. Exhibit 3.3 shows a **supply schedule** and a corresponding upward sloping **supply curve** for wheat.[2] The supply curve can be expressed in equation form. The **supply equation** reads: $Qs = f(P)$, or $Qs = a + bP$. In Exhibit 3.3, $Qs = 1 + \frac{1}{2}P$.

Why exactly is the supply curve for wheat expected to slope upward? There are a number of possible reasons, any or all of which may operate in a particular case. For one thing, a higher price gives farmers a greater incentive to devote more of their time and energy to wheat production. In addition, it may induce them to substitute wheat for other crops they had been producing. Finally, the higher price may make it possible to attract resources into wheat farming from other lines of production, perhaps even leading to the establishment of new farms. The assumptions that underlie the upward sloping supply curve are covered in more detail in microeconomics courses. For now, these commonsense observations will suffice.

**Complements** A pair of goods for which an increase in the price of one causes a decrease in the demand for the other, other things being equal.

**Supply schedule** A table showing the quantity of a good supplied at various prices.

**Supply curve** A graphical representation of the relationship between the price of a good and the quantity of it supplied.

**Supply equation** This equation expresses the idea that quantity supplied (Qs) is a function of price, or $Qs = a + bP$.

### Shifts in Supply Curves

As in the case of demand, changes in the quantity supplied of a good, represented by movements along a given supply curve, are distinguished from changes in the supply of a good, represented by shifts in the supply curve. A change in the quantity supplied comes about as the result of a

---

[2]Exceptions to the rule that supply curves slope upward are not so rare as exceptions to the rule that demand curves slope downward. A few examples of negatively sloped supply curves will occur later in this book. For the present, however, we will stick to upward sloping curves.

**Exhibit 3.3**

A supply schedule and supply curve for wheat

Both the supply curve and supply schedule for wheat show the quantity of wheat supplied at various prices. An increase in the price of wheat induces farmers to supply a greater quantity of it. This is partly because they have an incentive to devote more time and energy to the crop, partly because they substitute wheat for other crops grown previously, and partly because new resources (and even new farmers) may be drawn into wheat production.

**(b) Supply curve**

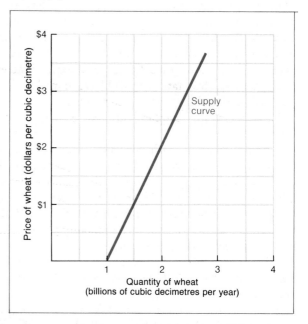

**(a) Supply schedule**

| Price of Wheat (dollars per cubic decimetre) | Quality of Wheat Supplied (billions of cubic decimetres per year) |
|---|---|
| $3.20 | 2.6 |
| 3.00 | 2.5 |
| 2.80 | 2.4 |
| 2.60 | 2.3 |
| 2.40 | 2.2 |
| 2.20 | 2.1 |
| 2.00 | 2.0 |
| 1.80 | 1.9 |
| 1.60 | 1.8 |
| 1.40 | 1.7 |
| 1.20 | 1.6 |
| 1.00 | 1.5 |
| .80 | 1.4 |

change in the price of the good, other things being equal. A shift in the supply curve requires a change in some other factor affecting supply.

One thing that can produce a change in the supply of a good is a change in production technology. If new technology permits more output to be produced from the same quantity of inputs, the supply curve will shift to the right. A second factor that can cause a change in supply is a change in the price of inputs used to produce a good. If input prices go up, for example, suppliers will probably want a higher price than before in order to offer the same quantity of output for sale. This effect is represented by a leftward shift in the supply curve. Finally, the supply curve for one good can be shifted as the result of a change in the price of another good, other things being equal. For example, a rise in the price of soybeans might well cause the supply curve for wheat to shift to the left, as farmers pull land out of wheat production and plant it in the newly profitable soybeans. Some examples of shifting supply curves will be given later in this chapter.

## THE INTERACTION OF SUPPLY AND DEMAND

### Market Equilibrium

Chapter 2 showed how the market transmits information in the form of prices to the people who are potential buyers and sellers of any good. Taking the price of the good into account, together with the other knowledge they possess, these buyers and sellers form plans. Each one decides to enter the market and buy or sell a certain number of units of the good.

Commonly, large numbers of buyers and sellers formulate their market plans independently of one another. When buyers and sellers of some particular good actually meet and engage in the process of exchange, some of them may find it impossible to carry out their plans. Perhaps the total quantity of planned purchases will exceed the total quantity of planned sales at the expected price. In this case, some of the would-be buyers will find their plans frustrated and will have to modify them. Perhaps, instead, planned sales will exceed planned purchases. Then, some would-be sellers will be unable to sell all they had expected to and will have to change their plans.

Sometimes no one will be disappointed. Given the information that market prices have conveyed, the total quantity of the good that buyers plan to purchase may exactly equal the quantity that suppliers plan to sell. The separately formulated plans of all market participants may turn out to mesh exactly when tested in the marketplace, and no one will have frustrated expectations or be forced to modify plans. When this happens, the market is said to be in **equilibrium**.

If we have supply and demand schedules for a market, we can describe more exactly the conditions under which that market will be in equilibrium. Take the market for wheat as an example. In Exhibit 3.4, Columns 1 to 3 give the supply and demand schedules. Reading down Column 2, we see how much wheat producers will plan to sell at each price. Reading down Column 3, we see how much wheat buyers will plan to purchase at

**Market equilibrium** A condition in which the separately formulated plans of buyers and sellers of some good exactly mesh when tested in the marketplace, so that the quantity supplied is exactly equal to the quantity demanded at the prevailing price.

**Exhibit 3.4**

Supply and demand in the market for wheat

When the quantity of a product demanded exceeds the quantity supplied, there is an excess quantity demanded, or shortage, of the product. A shortage puts upward pressure on the price of the product. When the quantity supplied exceeds the quantity demanded, there is an excess quantity supplied, or surplus, of the product. A surplus puts downward pressure on the price. Only when the price of wheat here is $2/dm^3$ is there no shortage or surplus and no upward or downward pressure on price. At $2 the market is in equilibrium.

| Price per cubic decimetre (1) | Quantity Supplied (billions of cubic decimetres) (2) | Quantity Demanded (billions of cubic decimetres) (3) | Shortage (billions of cubic decimetres) 4) | Surplus (billions of decimetres) (5) | Direction of Pressure on Price (6) |
|---|---|---|---|---|---|
| $3.20 | 2.6 | 1.4 | — | 1.2 | Downward |
| 3.00 | 2.5 | 1.5 | — | 1.0 | Downward |
| 2.80 | 2.4 | 1.6 | — | 0.8 | Downward |
| 2.60 | 2.3 | 1.7 | — | 0.6 | Downward |
| 2.40 | 2.2 | 1.8 | — | 0.4 | Downward |
| 2.20 | 2.1 | 1.9 | — | 0.2 | Downward |
| 2.00 | 2.0 | 2.0 | — | — | Equilibrium |
| 1.80 | 1.9 | 2.1 | 0.2 | — | Upward |
| 1.60 | 1.8 | 2.2 | 0.4 | — | Upward |
| 1.40 | 1.7 | 2.3 | 0.6 | — | Upward |
| 1.20 | 1.6 | 2.4 | 0.8 | — | Upward |
| 1.00 | 1.5 | 2.5 | 1.0 | — | Upward |
| .80 | 1.4 | 2.6 | 1.2 | — | Upward |

each price. Comparing the two, it does not take long to discover that only when the price is $2 do the separately formulated plans of buyers and sellers exactly mesh. Thus $2/dm³ is the price at which this market is in something different from $2? Suppose, for example, that a price of $1/dm³ tation that the price will be $2, none of them will be disappointed, and none will have to change plans.

## Shortages

What if, for some reason, buyers and sellers expect the market price to be something different from $2? Suppose, for example, that a price of $1/dm³ somehow becomes established in the market. Column 2 of Exhibit 3.4 tells us that, at this price, producers will plan to supply wheat to the market at the rate of 1.5 billion cubic decimetres per year. Column 3 tells us that buyers will plan to purchase at a rate of 2.5 billion cubic decimetres per year. When the quantity demanded exceeds the quantity supplied, the difference between the two is called an **excess quantity demanded** or, more simply, a **shortage.**[3] In the case of wheat, the shortage (shown in Column 4 of the exhibit) is 1 billion cubic decimetres per year when the price is $1/dm³.

In most markets, the first sign of a shortage is the depletion of inventories of the product available for sale. If inventories run out entirely, or if the market is for a good or service that cannot be stored in inventory at all, a queue of potential buyers may form. Under such circumstances, either sellers take the initiative to raise prices or buyers take the initiative to offer higher prices in the hope of getting part of the available quantity. In either event, the shortage puts upward pressure on price.

As the price of the product rises, producers begin to plan to sell more and buyers begin to plan to purchase less. The higher the price, the smaller the shortage. When the price of wheat in Exhibit 3.4 reaches $2 per cubic decimetre, the shortage is entirely eliminated. With its elimination, there is no further upward pressure on prices. The market is in equilibrium.

## Surpluses

Suppose that, for some reason, the price of wheat becomes established at a level higher than the equilibrium price, say at $3/dm³. At this price, according to Exhibit 3.4, producers will plan to sell 2.5 billion cubic decimetres per year, but buyers will plan to purchase only 1.5 billion cubic decimetres. When the quantity supplied exceeds the quantity demanded, there is an **excess quantity supplied** or a **surplus**. As Column 5 of the exhibit shows, the surplus of wheat is 1 billion cubic decimetres per year when the price is $3/dm³.

When there is a surplus of the product, some producers will be disappointed, since they will not be able to make all their planned sales at the expected price. Inventories of unsold goods will begin to accumulate. Al-

**Excess quantity demanded** The amount by which the quantity of a good demanded exceeds the quantity supplied when the price of the good is below the equilibrium level.

**Shortage** As used in economics, an excess quantity demanded.

**Excess quantity supplied** The amount by which the quantity of a good supplied exceeds the quantity demanded when the price of the good is above the equilibrium level.

**Surplus** As used in economics, an excess quantity supplied.

---

[3]We introduce two equivalent terms—*shortage* and *excess quantity demanded*—in order to make it clear that economists use the term *shortage* in a somewhat narrower sense than it is used in everyday speech. In this book, the word *shortage* will be used most of the time when it is clear that the economic meaning is intended. But sometimes, to avoid possible ambiguity, the more precise term *excess quantity demanded* will be used instead. The same considerations apply to the terms *surplus* and *excess quantity supplied*.

though the details may vary from market to market, the generalization can be made that a surplus puts downward pressure on the product price. Exhibit 3.4 shows that as the price falls, the quantity supplied decreases and the quantity demanded increases. Gradually, the surplus is eliminated until, when the price reaches $2/dm³, the market returns to equilibrium.

## Graphical Presentation

A graphical presentation of the material just covered will help reinforce the points made. Exhibit 3.5 shows both the demand curve (taken from Exhibit 3.1) and the supply curve (taken from Exhibit 3.3) for wheat. With both curves on the same diagram, the quantity demanded and the quantity supplied at any price can be directly compared. The distance from the vertical axis to the demand curve measures the quantity demanded, and the distance from the vertical axis to the supply curve measures the quantity supplied. It follows that the horizontal gap between the two curves measures the surplus or shortage at any price.

As we saw when working through the numerical example for this market, a surplus tends to put downward pressure on the price, and a shortage tends to put upward pressure on it. These pressures result from the actions of frustrated buyers and sellers, who must change their plans when they find they cannot buy or sell the quantities they had intended at the price they had expected. The pressures are indicated by the arrows pointing along the supply and demand curves toward equilibrium.

There is only one price where neither upward nor downward pressure is in force—the price of $2/dm³, the point where the supply and demand curves intersect. There is neither shortage nor surplus at that point. The

**Exhibit 3.5**

**Supply and demand in the market for wheat**

In this diagram, a surplus or shortage is indicated by the horizontal distance between the supply and demand curves. A surplus puts downward pressure on price, and a shortage puts upward pressure on it, as indicated by the arrows following the supply and demand curves. The market is in equilibrium at the point where the supply and demand curves intersect. Compare this diagram with the table in Exhibit 3.4.

quantity that buyers plan to purchase exactly equals the quantity that suppliers plan to sell. Both can carry out their plans exactly as intended, and the market is in equilibrium.

### Changing Economic Conditions and Shifts in Supply and Demand

When underlying economic conditions change, supply and demand curves can shift to new positions. These shifts upset the plans of buyers and sellers, who may have adjusted to some previous market equilibrium, and they bring about changes in prices and quantities. The following case study describes an episode that is typical of the way markets work every day. Particular attention should be paid to the distinction between the kinds of changes that cause shifts in supply or demand curves and the kinds that cause movements along curves.

### Case 3.1
### Supply and Demand in the British Columbia Lumber Industry

This reprinted newspaper article illustrates how the forces of supply and demand changed the price of B.C. lumber in a short period of time in the summer of 1977:

A U.S. home building boom has increased lumber prices in the B.C. market from 15 to 20 percent in the past two-and-a-half months, and local builders fear prices will continue to climb.

Since U.S. builders are the Canadian lumber industry's biggest customers, accounting for half of its sales, they tend to set prices for the Canadian market as well. U.S. housing starts are expected to peak in the last quarter of 1977 at an annual rate of 1.93 million units.

The exchange rate, giving U.S. buyers a better deal for their dollar, hasn't helped any as far as Canadian buyers are concerned.

"The mills are booked two months solid," said Paul Pannozzo, a lumber purchaser for the Lumberland retail chain. He said what happens then is that buyers are forced to bid higher prices in order to snatch enough material for their needs, before it's sold down south.

Pannozzo predicted that "unless California slows down on home-building," B.C. prices could go up another $20 per thousand board feet by 1978. He said there could be a drop in November when cold weather sets in, but prices are likely to jump again in January.

As an example of the recent price jumps, Bob Swannell, general marketing manager for lumber at MacMillan Bloedel Ltd., noted that Western white spruce 2x4s, considered something of a price indicator in the trade, were selling at $190 per thousand board feet on July 29 but had jumped to $209 as of Friday.

He agreed that it's the U.S housing boom causing the rapid price hikes here and noted that unlike Canada, the U.S. is building a large number of single-family houses which consume a high percentage of framing lumber, pushing up lumber consumption.

This year, said Swannel, the U.S. is likely to exceed its record year of 1972 for single-family dwelling starts.

What has happened, he said, is that the U.S. boom came at the same time the B.C. forest industry had let production drop somewhat. With inventory down and demand increasing, prices inevitably started rising.

In addition, he said, the demand came at a time of production drop-offs due to summer holidays and fire closures, especially in Washington and Oregon.

Source: Pat Johnson, "Price of Lumber Zooms," *Vancouver Province*, August 13, 1977. Reprinted in *Dateline Canada*, ed. Peter Kennedy and Gary Dorosh (Scarborough, Ont.: Prentice-Hall, 1978), p.3.

As the article indicates, the price of one particular type of lumber, white spruce 2x4s, rose from $190 per thousand board feet to $209 in a two-week period in 1977. This was the result of changes in demand and supply conditions.

On the demand side, a major factor in the price rise was the home-building boom in the United States. The increased U.S. demand for Canadian lumber was also due to the declining value of the Canadian dollar. This is a good illustration of how our exports increase when the value of our dollar decreases, and it also shows why our prices may rise at the same time.

Exhibit 3.6a gives a graphic representation of growing U.S. demands on Canadian lumber. The immediate result is shown as a rightward shift in the demand curve, from its initial position $D_1$ to a new position $D_2$. Before this shift occurred, the market equilibrium price was $190 ($P_1$). After the shift there was a shortage of white spruce 2x4s as long as the price remained at its previous level. The shortage caused the market price to be bid up. As the price rose, suppliers moved up and to the right along the supply curve $S_1$. When the price had risen to $P_2$, the shortage was eliminated, and if no further changes in economic conditions had occurred, $P_2$ would have been the new equilibrium price.

Other economic conditions did not remain unchanged, however. At the same time the demand shift occurred, conditions were also changing on the supply side of the market. The B.C. forest industry had let production drop,

---

**Exhibit 3.6**
**The effects of changing economic conditions on the price of white spruce (B.C. lumber) between July 29 and August 13, 1977**

Part a shows the effects of a demand shift resulting from increased demand by U.S. home builders. The demand curve is shifted to the right from $D_1$ to $D_2$. The resulting shortage of lumber drives the price up from $P_1$ to $P_2$. Part b shows the effect of a reduction in lumber supply because of production drops in the B.C. lumber industry. Now the supply curve shifts too, from $S_1$ to $S_2$. Together the shift of both curves caused the price of white spruce lumber (2x4s) to rise from $190 per thousand board feet ($P_1$) to $209 ($P_3$) in the two-week period. (Note that $P_2$ is a hypothetical price; it would have been the new price if demand alone had increased. Since supply also changed there is no way of knowing what $P_2$ would actually have been.)

**(a) Quantity of white spruce
(thousand board feet)**

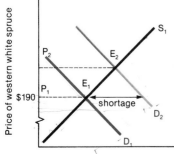

**(b) Quantity of white spruce
(thousand board feet)**

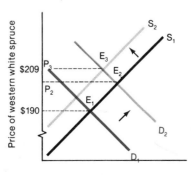

partly due to summer layoffs and fire closures. We can represent the effect of these supply-side changes as an upward shift of the supply curve, from its original position $S_1$ to a new position $S_2$, as shown in Exhibit 3.6b. With the supply curve shifting at the same time as the demand curve shifted, a rise in price from $P_1$ to $P_2$ was no longer sufficient to eliminate the entire shortage of lumber. Instead, the price rose all the way to $P_3$ ($209). In comparison to the equilibrium shown in Part a of the exhibit, we can see that the shift in the supply curve requires a movement of consumers along their new demand curve $D_2$, until equilibrium is finally reached at the point where $S_2$ and $D_2$ intersect. The simultaneous shifts in the supply and demand curves reinforced one another and caused the rise in the price of lumber to be much sharper than it would have been had only one of the changes occurred.

## Markets in Disequilibrium

We have seen that when a market is not in equilibrium, an excess quantity demanded or excess quantity supplied will put upward or downward pressure on the price. If the price is free to respond to this pressure, a new equilibrium will be established at a higher or lower price. Sometimes, though, market prices are not free to fluctuate. Then shortages or surpluses can continue indefinitely, as the following case study shows.

### Case 3.2
### Provincial Rent Controls

In the last decade, most provinces in Canada have chosen to interfere with the market price for apartments and other rental units by establishing some form of rent control. The purpose of such controls is to keep the price for an average apartment or other rental dwelling below what it would be in the absence of government inter-

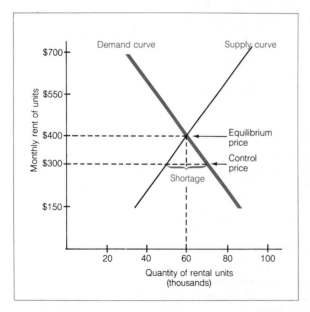

**Exhibit 3.7**
**Effects of rent controls**
This diagram shows hypothetical supply and demand curves for rental units. As the curves are drawn, the equilibrium cost or rent of a unit is about $400. Many provincial governments have established controls to keep the monthly rent below the market equilibrium rent. In this diagram it is assumed that under rent controls the average monthly rent is $300, instead of $400. At this lower price there will likely be a shortage of rental units. Vacancy rates will be at zero and many people may not be able to obtain an apartment or dwelling to rent.

vention. The beneficiaries, of course, are renters. However, some people who would like to rent an apartment or other dwelling may not benefit from such a program. At the control price, too few rental units may be supplied by builders. Vacancy rates may fall to zero, and some of those who would like to rent accommodation may not be able to. Some cities, including Vancouver and Toronto, have experienced vacancy rates very close to zero under rent control programs.

As long as the control price is rigidly maintained below the market equilibrium price, shortages will persist. A new equilibrium will not be established. In order to avoid such persistent shortages, the control programs have generally permitted slight increases in rent, subject to review, and have permitted new rental dwellings to be exempt from the controls for a few years. In addition, builders of rental units have received special tax concessions, known as "tax shelters," to encourage them to build more units than they otherwise would under rent controls. (See discussion question 6, of this chapter.) Reduced taxes mean reduced costs. The supply curve is shifted down to the right, creating an equilibrium with lower price and greater quantity. Exhibit 3.7 shows hypothetical supply and demand curves for rental units and illustrates how rent controls prevent an equilibrium from being established.

## CONCLUSIONS

This completes the presentation of the basics of supply and demand analysis. The chapter will conclude with a few remarks that relate supply and demand to the role of markets as a mechanism for utilizing knowledge and that concern the scope of applicability of supply and demand analysis.

### Information and Equilibrium

There is a simple connection between the idea of equilibrium and the idea of the market as a mechanism for distributing information. The connection is found in the fact that the market can be in equilibrium when, and only when, it has entirely completed its job of distributing information among buyers and sellers.

It is easy to see why this it true. First, if buyers and sellers have incomplete knowledge of prices and of other economic conditions, it is unlikely that their separately formulated market plans will exactly mesh. It may be that both buyers and sellers expect the price tomorrow to be higher (or lower) than it actually will be. It may be that buyers have one idea about what the price will be and sellers another. Whatever the case, someone is bound to be disappointed, and disappointed plans are the stuff of which disequilibrium is made.

On the other hand, if both buyers and sellers have complete and accurate knowledge of both present and future prices and market conditions, how can their plans fail to mesh? No one will plan to sell knowing that there will be no one to buy. With perfect information, people will formulate only such market plans as they know can be carried out on the expected terms, and that is what *equilibrium* means.

Saying that markets are in equilibrium only when all buyers and sellers have perfect information leads to a conclusion that may seem strange. The conclusion is that, in the real world, we can hardly ever expect to find a market in equilibrium! To paraphrase a famous saying, all people know something some of the time, and some people know a great deal all of the time, but everybody does not know everything all of the time. In real markets, prices are always being pushed this way or that by changes in underlying economic conditions. Some people learn of these changes right away, and the buying and selling they do telegraphs that information, via the price system, to others. But the market telegraph does not work with the speed of light. Before everyone who is directly or indirectly interested in what goes on in a particular market learns of some change, other changes have occurred. The whirling stream of human knowledge never quite catches up with an even more fluid reality.

### Applicability

The fact that markets are never fully in equilibrium is, in a sense, a limitation on the applicability of supply and demand analysis, but the emphasis is on showing which way quantities and prices will tend to move. There are other limitations too. Microeconomic theory shows that supply and demand analysis must be applied somewhat differently to different types of markets—depending, for example, on the degree of competition or monopoly in a particular market. Yet, in a general sense, thinking in terms of supply and demand can give extremely useful insights into the way almost all markets work. The usefulness of these tools will be proved in application as we work through this book. Fine points can be left for more advanced courses.

### SUMMARY

1. The law of demand says that the quantity of a good demanded by buyers tends to change in a direction opposite to any change in price, other things being equal. *Quantity demanded* means the quantity buyers are willing and able to buy at a given price, as distinguished from wants or needs not backed up by willingness and ability to buy. By *other things being equal*, economists have in mind such things as buyers' incomes, the price of other goods, and buyers' expectations about future price changes.

2. A change in the quantity of a good demanded that results solely from a change in the price of that good is represented graphically as a movement along a demand curve. When something other than its price changes (for example, buyers' incomes, the prices of substitutes or complements, or buyers' expectations), the result is a change in demand, represented graphically as a shift of the entire demand curve.

3. A supply curve shows the relationship between the price of a good and the quantity of it supplied, other things being equal. Unless there is some particular reason to do otherwise, economists usually draw supply curves with upward slopes. A change in the price of a good produces a change in the quantity supplied, shown by a movement along a supply curve. A change in some other factor—technology, input prices, prices of other goods—produces a change in supply, shown by a shift of the supply curve.

4. Market equilibrium is a condition in which the separately formulated plans of buyers and sellers exactly mesh, so that the quantity supplied is

equal to the quantity demanded. If the price of a product is too high for equilibrium, there will be a surplus of the good, which, in turn, will tend to push the price down. If the price is below the equilibrium, there will be a shortage, which will tend to drive the price up. Equilibrium is possible only when the market has completely carried out its job of distributing information among buyers and sellers.

## DISCUSSION QUESTIONS

1. The *law of demand* states that there is an inverse relationship between the price of a good and the quantity that people will be willing and able to pay for. How is this "law" like the law of gravity? How is it different? Explain.
2. Illustrate the supply of McDonald's hamburgers to an individual consumer. What is the slope of the supply curve?
3. Suppose there were a drought on the Prairies, where the nation's wheat is grown. What would be the impact of the drought on the demand and supply of wheat? What would happen to the price of wheat? Why? How would this be likely to affect the individual consumers of products containing wheat?
4. If you drop a marble into a bowl, it will eventually come to rest at the bottom. You can then say that the marble is at equilibrium at the bottom of the bowl. What is meant by *equilibrium*? In what ways is equilibrium in a market similar to the equilibrium of the marble? In what ways is it different?
5. If you were a wholesaler and you could see sooner than your competitors when the demand curve for the product you deal in was about to shift to the right, how could you use this advance knowledge to make money? Would you be benefiting anyone besides yourself in getting rid of the disequilibrium? Explain.
6. Suppose that rent controls have been placed on rental units such as apartments, and that tax authorities reduce the cost of building apartments by granting tax reductions to those who put their investment funds into new apartments. Illustrate, with reference to Exhibit 3.7, how this would affect the supply curve for apartment units and possibly bring about a new equilibrium at the control price.

## SUGGESTIONS FOR FURTHER READING

Breit, William, and Ransom, Roger L. *The Academic Scribblers*. New York: Holt, Rinehart and Winston, 1971, Chapter 3.
*An essay on Alfred Marshall. The preceding two chapters provide useful background.*

Marshall, Alfred. *Principles of Economics*. Various editions.
*First published in 1891, this book served as the definitive treatise on economics in the English-speaking world for generations. It remains remarkably accessible to browsing, even by the beginning student. For a start, look up Marshall's treatment of the determinants of demand or his discussion (and dismissal) of cases of apparently upward sloping demand curves.*

# THE ROLE OF BUSINESS
# AND GOVERNMENT IN
# THE CANADIAN ECONOMY

**WHAT YOU WILL LEARN IN THIS CHAPTER**

*The business firm is considered to be the basic unit of production in the market economy, and it is important to have some understanding of its organization and function. However, in most market economies, including Canada, the government has come to assume a significant economic role. It is therefore necessary to understand how various levels of government participate directly in the economy and also how they interact with private business firms. This chapter examines some of the more significant features of this "mixed economy," in which business and government share in economic decision making.*

**FOR REVIEW**

*Here are some important terms and concepts that will be put to use in this chapter. If you do not understand them, review them before proceeding.*
- *Entrepreneurship (Chapter 1)*
- *Early Canadian economic history (Chapter 1)*
- *Markets and their function (Chapter 2)*
- *Supply and demand analysis (Chapter 3)*

---

The forces of supply and demand, acting through markets, affect every major economic decision in the Canadian economy. Nonetheless, Canada is not a pure market economy. There are several reasons for this. First of all, many business firms have become large and powerful enough to manipulate market forces at least partially in their favor. Second, there are government agencies that operate to some extent outside of the market but nevertheless affect how resources are used. This chapter first examines the function and behavior of business firms and then shows how governments have developed into a potent economic force.

## COORDINATING ECONOMIC ACTIVITY

Despite their different purposes and different legal forms of organization, all firms—whether mom-and-pop corner stores, or giant steel corporations, or powerful law partnerships—have many things in common. The most basic task all firms must perform is coordinating economic activity.

## Market versus Managerial Coordination

Production in any modern economy, as emphasized in Chapters 1 and 2, is based on a vast division of labor. Many people make individual contributions to the whole effort that must somehow be coordinated. It must be determined what goods are to be produced, who is to produce them, and how they are to be produced. There are fundamentally two kinds of coordination for this vast division of labor: market coordination and managerial coordination.

**Market coordination**
Coordination of economic activity using the price system to transmit information and provide incentives.

**Market coordination** relies on the price system as a source of incentives and a communications network. As relative prices vary in response to the forces of supply and demand, users are induced to substitute low-priced goods and services for scarcer and more expensive alternatives. At the same time, changing relative prices continually create new profit opportunities for entrepreneurs who can devise ways of expanding the output of whatever is particularly scarce and thus particularly valuable to users. All of this is accomplished in a decentralized fashion, with no central authority making decisions or issuing demands.

There are substantial areas of economic activity, however, that do not rely directly on market coordination. Consider, for example, the internal organization of work within a furniture factory. Individual employees do not decide each morning, in response to changing relative prices, that they will spend the day making end tables rather than TV cabinets. Instead, they make end tables because that is what their immediate boss tells them to do. This is the realm of **managerial coordination,** which operates on the principle of direct instruction from manager to subordinate. What makes the instruction effective is the fact that subordinates have pledged obedience to the manager (at least within certain agreed limits) as a condition of employment.

**Managerial coordination**
Coordination of economic activity through directives from managers to subordinates.

## Coordination in the Firm

In a famous essay on the nature of the firm, Ronald Coase posed a question about these two ways of coordinating the division of labor: if the market principle works as well as economists say it does, why is the managerial principle ever used at all?[1] Why do the workers in a furniture factory have to be employees taking orders from a boss? If the market principle were applied everywhere, TV cabinets and end tables would all be built by independent artisans. Changes in the relative prices of various items of furniture would keep the right number of workers at each job.

Coase found an answer to his question. He said that the market is not used for every situation where coordination is required because there are transactions costs to using it. There are costs of finding out what prices are. There are also costs of negotiating contracts, writing bills and receipts, and straightening things out when market contracts are not carried through. If, say, a potential car buyer had to negotiate separately with each person who worked on the car, the cost of coordination would make the car too expen-

---

[1] Ronald H. Coase, "The Nature of the Firm," *Economica*, new series, 4 (November 1937), pp. 386–405.

sive. If the buyer saved negotiating costs by having one or two local mechanics build the car from scratch, the advantages of mass production and the division of labor would be lost, and the vehicle would still cost too much. But when Ford Motor Company acts as an intermediary between the buyer and the workers, thousands of market transactions are eliminated. Cars are sold on the market, but everything in between is coordinated by the managerial principle of simply giving orders and expecting them to be obeyed.

Coase realized, though, that in answering one question, he had just raised another. If managerial coordination works so well, why use the market at all? Why not run the entire economy as one big firm, with all people as employees and a single, central manager running the whole show? Then it would be a matter of not only giving furniture workers or auto workers orders about what to do that day but also giving high school graduates orders about whether to be auto workers or cabinet makers. Not only would the matter of how many end tables and how many TV cabinets be handled by the managerial principle, but so would matters such as how many firms should be in the industry and where they should be located. In the process these would, of course, be a total loss of personal freedom.

Apart from the loss of freedom, such a form of organization would have its own set of problems. Managerial coordination has transactions costs of its own, as well as savings of transactions costs. Under the managerial system, the person actually doing a job does not need to know all the reasons behind the decision to do it, and that is a saving. Offsetting this is the fact that *managers* have to know a great deal about all the different jobs they coordinate, and that is a cost. Sometimes the costs of supplying information to a manager or other central decision maker are greater than the costs of supplying information to people close to the job. When this is the case, managerial coordination loses its advantage over market coordination.

## The Limits of the Firm

Coase saw that the two coordination principles give the key to understanding the nature of the firm and its role in the economy. A firm, he said, is an organization that uses the managerial principle of coordination internally and uses the market to coordinate its activities with those of other firms and individuals. Each firm tends to grow until the transactions cost of organizing one extra task within the firm becomes equal to the cost of organizing the same task outside the firm through the market. In some industries, this rule dictates that firms grow to enormous size. In others, the limit to the growth of the firm occurs at a very small size. By allowing each firm to grow to its optimal size and by leaving coordination among firms to the market, the total costs of organizing economic activity can, in principle, be minimized.

Coase's insights into the nature of the firm have survived the test of time well. They should be kept in mind as the chapter turns from abstract principles to some of the practical details of the organization of business firms.

## ALTERNATIVE FORMS OF BUSINESS ORGANIZATION

Textbook discussions of economic theory inevitably tend to portray business firms as well-defined, homogeneous units of analysis. In the real world, however, they take on a very wide variety of forms. Some firms are tiny, consisting of a single individual doing all production and managerial jobs. At the other extreme are corporate giants like General Motors or ITT. These firms employ more people and dispose of more assets than the governments of all but the world's largest countries. Firms differ not only in size but in their legal form of organization as well. The following three sections will discuss the advantages of the three main types of firms — sole proprietorships, partnerships, and corporations.[2]

### Sole Proprietorships

**Sole proprietorship** A firm owned and usually managed by a single person, who receives all profits of the firm and who personally bears all of the firm's liabilities.

A **sole proprietorship** is a firm that is owned and usually managed by one person. In most cases this person is also an operative employee. Responsibility for the success or failure of the firm rests solely on the proprietor's shoulders. From a legal point of view, he or she owns all the assets and owes all the debts of the organization.

**Advantages** One of the most important advantages for the owner of a sole proprietorship is the complete ownership of all the assets and the right to all the profits of the business. The sole proprietor is legally entitled to 100 percent of any rewards. This right to all the profits is a powerful incentive to the owner to invest money and to work hard to get the revenue from customers from whom profits are derived.

Another of the reasons the sole proprietorship is so widely used is because it is relatively easy to organize. There are very few legal requirements to meet. Consequently, little or no costs of organization are involved. Practically anyone can develop an idea into a sole proprietorship form of organization.

Finally, ease of dissolution may be an important advantage of the sole proprietorship. Just as there are few legal complications about going into business, there are very few in going out of business. Dissolution may simply mean selling the inventory, paying the debts, and locking the door. Ease of dissolution allows the owner to retire or enter another type of business quickly and easily.

**Disadvantages** The sole proprietorship form of organization also has some disadvantages, however. First and foremost among them is unlimited financial liability. This means that in the event of bankruptcy, the sole proprietor's personal property may have to be sold to pay business debts.

Also, because the expansion of a sole proprietorship is limited by what the owner can contribute or borrow, he or she may find it difficult to expand. This difficulty is magnified by the sole proprietor's inability to get into other lines of business because of a lack of capital or of managerial ability.

---

[2] Much of the material in this section is adapted from Robert D. Hay, *Introduction to Business* (New York: Holt, Rinehart and Winston, 1968), pp. 140-148. Reprinted by permission of the author.

Finally, the death, injury, imprisonment, or bankruptcy of the owner may terminate the legal life of the firm. This lack of continuity stems from the legal fact that the individual and the business are one and the same in a sole proprietorship.

## Partnerships

A **partnership** is an association of two or more persons who will carry on a business as co-owners by voluntary legal agreement. Instead of one person being the owner, there are at least two who own all the assets, owe all the liabilities, and have an equity in the business.

**Partnership** A firm formed by two or more persons to carry on a business as co-owners. Each partner bears full legal liability for the debts of the firm.

**Advantages** Like the sole proprietorship, the partnership as a form of legal organization enjoys simplicity and ease in getting started and, in some cases, savings in income taxes. The partnership is able to obtain more equity capital than the sole proprietorship, because the amount available is determined by the personal fortunes of the partners. Many sole proprietorships evolve into partnerships in order to raise more equity capital. For example, a person with a new idea may find another person who is willing to contribute a major share of the needed capital to turn the idea into a profitable business operation for both of them. Thus the necessary amount of capital is acquired through the formation of a partnership.

An advantage closely related to raising equity capital is the enlarged credit standing, or ability to borrow capital, of the partnership. Because the personal wealth of all the partners is available to pay debts of the business organization, a partnership may enjoy a higher credit rating than a sole proprietorship.

Many partnerships are formed to take advantage of greater managerial ability. Because numerous functions are involved in the operation of a business, partners proficient in different functions may complement each other. This combined effort leads to the greater managerial ability.

**Disadvantages** A partnership form of organization does not offer all the answers, because it too has certain disadvantages. As in the sole proprietorship, the chief disadvantage is the unlimited financial liability. In the case of a partnership, the responsibility for the debts of the business is shared individually as well as jointly. Consequently, the unlimited financial liability could result in one partner being forced to pay not only his or her own share but all the debts of the firm.

A further disadvantage of a partnership is that one partner cannot easily withdraw without the cooperation of the others. The partner who wants to withdraw must either find a new partner willing to buy his or her share in the partnership or get the other partners to agree to buy the share. Meanwhile, although the partner wishing to withdraw continues to own a share of the partnership's equity, that equity is "frozen"—it cannot be turned into cash or invested in another undertaking.

In forming a partnership, each partner must accept the others for better or for worse, just as in a marriage. Although better decisions usually result from the combined judgments of the partners, the division of decision making can cause personal difficulties. More partnerships have been dissolved because of such difficulties than for any other reason.

Any change in the combination of partners automatically causes a dissolution of the firm; thus the partnership has limited life. Like the sole proprietorship, the death, incapacity, or withdrawal of any of the partners terminates the original partnership agreement. The admission of a new partner or the sale of a partner's interest also ends the old partnership. Simply because there are more people involved, the limited life poses a larger problem in the partnership than in the sole proprietorship.

## Corporations

**Corporation** A firm in which the ownership is divided into equal parts called shares, with each shareholder's liability limited to the amount of his or her investment in the firm.

Corporations are the third major form of business organization. A **corporation** is a firm organized as an independent legal entity, with ownership divided into equal-value shares. The corporation is the predominant form of organization in the manufacturing sector. About three-quarters of all manufacturing firms in Canada are organized as corporations, and they employ more than 95% percent of all workers in the manufacturing field. Exhibit 4.1, which lists the twenty-five largest industrial corporations in Canada, contains many familiar names. A major feature of the corporation is that it can be dealt with legally just as if it were an individual. This means that the corporation serves as a buffer between the firm's owners and the government and community.

Persons who own the shares of a corporation are called shareholders or stockholders. They elect officers to manage the business. Of course, if they own the majority of voting stock, they can, and often do, elect themselves as managers. Shares can be either common stock or preferred stock. **Common stock** gives the owner the right to vote in the selection of management and the right to share in any dividend payments. **Preferred shares** also confer voting rights, and also the right to a fixed return from profits, payable before payment of dividends is made to common stockholders.

**Common stock or share** A certificate of part ownership in a corporation that gives the owner a vote in the selection of management and the right to share in dividend payments, if any.

**Preferred share** A certificate of part ownership in a corporation that gives the owner voting rights and a fixed return paid out from profits before payments of dividends to common stock holders.

**Advantages**  The main advantage of having the firm as a separate entity is that the owners carry only limited financial liability. This means that creditors can look only to the assets of the corporation for settlement of their claims. They cannot hold the owners liable for the debts of the corporation. If the corporation fails, the shareholders lose only the amount of their investment; their personal assets cannot be attached to pay the corporate debts. This is not the case for a sole proprietorship or a partnership, where the owners are held liable for all the debts and are forced, when necessary, to pay them out of their personal assets.

A corporation can grow to a larger size than a sole proprietorship or partnership because it can attract capital from thousands of individuals. It can expand or increase its size because the advantage of limited financial liability makes investors more willing to purchase additional shares of stock. It is easier for a corporation to raise $1 million by having a thousand people invest $1,000 each than it is for a sole proprietorship to have one person invest $1 million.

The transfer of ownership in a corporation is easily accomplished, especially for those corporations whose capital stock is listed and traded on the major stock exchanges and in the over-the-counter market. Thousands of shares of capital stock change hands daily. As a general rule, corporations allow shareholders to transfer their ownership to anyone at any time (assuming that the price is agreeable to both buyer and seller) without the approval of the other shareholders.

The transferability of ownership of a corporation contributes to the continuity of the firm. Shareholders may withdraw by selling their shares

---

**Exhibit 4.1**

**The twenty-five largest Canadian industrial corporations, 1982**

Each year, *The Financial Post* publishes a list of the five hundred largest industrial corporations in Canada, ranked by sales. This exhibit gives the top twenty-five, based on sales for 1982. The list contains many familiar names. Note that some businesses (for example, Hydro-Québec), use much more capital in relation to sales than others, so that their ranking in terms of assets is quite different.

| Rank by sales 1982 | 1981 | Sales or operating revenue $'000 | Company (head office) | Rank by assets | Assets $'000 |
|---|---|---|---|---|---|
| 1 | 1 | 12,289,487 | Canadian Pacific Ltd. (Montreal) | 3 | 17,273,034 |
| 2 | 2 | 9,570,482 | General Motors of Canada Ltd. (Oshawa) | 29 | 2,751,801 |
| 3 | 3 | 8,618,000 | Imperial Oil Ltd. (Toronto) | 10 | 7,486,000 |
| 4 | 5 | 8,411,300 | Bell Canada Enterprises Inc. (Montreal)[1] | 4 | 13,421,800 |
| 5 | 4 | 7,830,462 | George Weston Ltd. (Toronto) | 41 | 2,072,188 |
| 6 | 6 | 7,335,600 | Ford Motor Co. of Canada (Oakville, Ont.) | 40 | 2,115,700 |
| 7 | 7 | 5,729,303[2] | Alcan Aluminium Ltd. (Montreal) | 6 | 8,212,981 |
| 8 | 8 | 5,149,000 | Shell Canada Ltd. (Toronto) | 18 | 4,660,000 |
| 9 | • | 5,075,000 | Canadian Wheat Board (Winnipeg) July/82 | 20 | 4,109,000 |
| 10 | 10 | 4,768,000 | Texaco Canada Inc. (Toronto) | 25 | 2,966,000 |
| 11 | 9 | 4,682,000 | Gulf Canada Ltd. (Toronto) | 16 | 4,915,000 |
| 12 | 11 | 4,165,000 | Canadian National Railway (Montreal) | 12 | 6,335,971 |
| 13 | 12 | 4,138,671 | Hudson's Bay Co. (Winnipeg) Jan./83 | 21 | 3,952,793 |
| 14 | 17 | 4,011,266 | Canada Development Corp. (Vancouver) | 9 | 7,525,890 |
| 15 | 14 | 3,682,954 | Provigo Inc. (Montreal) Jan./83 | 113 | 621,182 |
| 16 | 31 | 3,657,400 | Chrysler Canada Ltd. (Windsor) | 110 | 680,400 |
| 17 | 27 | 3,501,798 | Nova Corp. (Calgary) | 13 | 6,321,937 |
| 18 | 13 | 3,466,915 | TransCanada PipeLines Ltd. (Calgary) | 17 | 4,716,909 |
| 19 | 231 | 3,445,000[3] | Brascan Ltd. (Toronto) | 23 | 3,365,000 |
| 20 | 21 | 3,411,295 | Hiram Walker Resources Ltd. (Toronto) Sept./82 | 15 | 4,963,552 |
| 21 | 16 | 3,387,630 | Ontario Hydro (Toronto) | 2 | 20,720,832 |
| 22 | 28 | 3,329,255 | PetroCanada (Calgary) | 8 | 7,552,115 |
| 23 | 25 | 3,310,000 | Hydro-Québec (Montreal) | 1 | 23,169,000 |
| 24 | 26 | 3,303,756 | Steinberg Inc. (Montreal) July/82 | 84 | 998,196 |
| 25 | 20 | 3,300,252 | Canada Safeway Ltd. (Winnipeg) Jan./83 | 83 | 1,009,927 |

Source: *The Financial Post 500*, June 1983, p. 68.

or may die, leaving their shares to their heirs without disturbing the legal existence of the corporation.

A further advantage may be the lower income tax paid by a corporation. Canadian-controlled private business corporations pay only about 25 percent tax on the first $150,000 of income, while an individual earning that much could be paying twice as much.

**Disadvantages** The first disadvantage of the corporate form of business organization is the cost of chartering a corporation. The chartering can be done on either the provincial or the federal level and can cost from about five hundred dollars to several thousand dollars in legal fees.

A corporation is subject to special government regulations, and therefore is involved in more red tape and less privacy than other business firms. For example, little is known about the sales and profits of Eaton's in Canada because it is a private company. Corporations, on the other hand, must report such information to their shareholders.

A further disadvantage is the "double taxation" of corporate income. Corporate profits are taxed first before they are paid out as dividends, and dividend income is subsequently taxed when it reaches the shareholders. However, dividend income is subject to "dividend tax credits" that reduce the effective tax rate considerably.

The following case study presents a typical example of the growing pains experienced by a small Canadian firm as it expanded and changed its form.

### Case 4.1
### Rich Hill Candles

A fire strikes a candle factory like a bull hitting a china shop, as Bob and Barb Francis learned. When they had to pick up the pieces of their burned-out company, Rich Hill Candles Inc., in January, 1980, they found themselves inadequately insured and under-funded.

Rich Hill's 70-year-old building in Bracebridge, Ont., about 200 km north of Toronto, was insured for $32,000, the size of the loan with which the Francis's had purchased the combined retail outlet and manufacturing facility in 1976. "But it cost over $50,000 to rebuild," recalls Bob Francis, 35. "We tried to get a small business loan, but the red tape was too much. We had to get moving and come up with the money immediately."

The disaster forced the couple to take out a $40,000 first mortgage and a $20,000 second mortgage, to separate Rich Hill's manufacturing facilities from the firm's retail store, and to re-evaluate their priorities, as well. Says Barb Francis, 29, who runs the retail operation: "It was the first time we'd been forced to sit down and acknowledge we weren't just doing this for fun. We had to say, 'If we don't make a go of this in 3 years, then we should pack it in.' "

More than 3 years later, the Francises have not only rebuilt the company, but boosted production to 3,000 hand-made candles a day, with gross revenues of $300,000 in 1982.

Rich Hill grew out of Bob's amateur candle-making endeavours in the late 1960s at Queen's University in Kingston, Ont. "It was a trendy thing," he says, "and I did it as a hobby. I was strictly giving them away."

In 1970, he and 2 partners decided to set up shop on a dairy farm, called Rich Hill, near Orangeville, Ont., about an hour's drive northwest of Toronto. "We just wanted to live and work in the same place," he says. Contributing $2,000 apiece, they leased the farm and turned out about 100 candles a day. "In the first 2 or 3 years, things went so slowly that we wondered if we'd ever get off the ground," he recalls. In fact, by 1973, Francis had bought out both his partners.

"Things started to grow then," Bob Francis recalls. The company increased the scope of its taper and pillar candle lines, adding dyes and fragrances to the oil-based wax, purchased in Toronto.

This year, the Francises incorporated the company, dividing the shares evenly between themselves. It cost $700, "and now we'll have to fill out more government forms," Bob laments. "But because of the size of the business, we wanted to protect ourselves."

---

Source: Excerpted from *This Magazine Is All About Small Business* (March–April, 1983), pp. 8 and 10.

The success story of Bob and Barb Francis illustrates the pattern followed by many small firms in their early years. Starting as a partnership with a bright idea, they had a difficult time getting adequate financing. Eventually the partnership proved to be too constricting and it was dissolved. Then, in order to protect themselves with limited liability, the Francises chose to become a corporation.

## Co-operatives

The co-operative form of organization is quite important in the Canadian economy, much more so than in the United States. A co-operative is an organization that pools the resources of its members, just as a corporation does, but grants only one vote to each member regardless of the member's investment. Further, earnings not retained are paid out according to the amount of business conducted by the member. Co-operatives may incorporate in order to obtain the benefits of limited liability and continuous existence. Co-operatives are of several types: consumer co-operatives, which engage in retail trade; marketing co-operatives, which sell members' agricultural products; financial co-operatives (for example, credit unions and—in French Canada—*caisses populaires*); insurance co-operatives and service co-operatives (for example, funeral co-operatives).

The chief advantages of the co-operative are the one-member, one-vote form of democracy, the possibility of buying goods and services more cheaply, and the special tax privileges enjoyed under Canadian law. Patronage dividends are not taxable because they are considered to be either volume rebates for goods purchased by members or additional payments for members' goods received by the co-operative.

The chief disadvantages of the co-operative are the difficulty it may have in raising funds, because increased investment by members does not lead to increased control, and the possibility that radical democratic control may lead to inefficient management.

As Exhibit 4.2 illustrates, some co-operatives rank high in the list of industrial corporations in Canada. The top-ranking co-operative, the Saskatchewan Wheat Pool, is fortieth among all industrial corporations in Canada in terms of sales.

**Exhibit 4.2**
**Ten large Canadian co-operatives, 1981**
This list shows the ten largest co-operatives in Canada in
terms of sales. The big Western grain co-ops
predominate. Not included are the large financial
co-operatives.

| Rank | Sales $'000 | Name |
|---|---|---|
| 1 | 1,941,433[1] | Saskatchewan Wheat Pool |
| 2 | 1,390,978[1] | Alberta Wheat Pool |
| 3 | 1,374,576[1] | United Grain Growers |
| 4 | 1,327,037 | Federated Co-operatives |
| 5 | 1,075,873 | Co-opérative Fédérée du Québec |
| 6 | 604,047 | United Co-operatives |
| 7 | 526,935 | Agropur, Co-opérative Agro Alimentaire[2] |
| 8 | 454,304[1] | Manitoba Pool Elevators |
| 9 | 254,025 | Fraser Valley Milk Producers' Association |
| 10 | 196,193 | Co-op Atlantic |

[1]Sales include grain purchased for the account and delivered to the Canadian Wheat Board
[2]Name has been changed from Co-opérative Agricole de Granby.

Source: *The Financial Post 500*, June 1982, p. 100.

## OWNERSHIP AND CONTROL OF CORPORATIONS

Sole proprietorships are owned and controlled by their proprietors and
partnerships by their partners. Corporations are legally owned by their
shareholders, but the matter of control is much less clear-cut than for other
types of firms. Because corporations account for such a large part of Canadian business, no discussion of the nature of the firm would be complete
without some mention of the controversy over control of the corporation.
Many "Canadian" corporations are actually subsidiaries of foreign corporations. Such foreign ownership and control poses unique problems. Regardless of the origin of ownership, the question of who actually makes the
basic decisions within a corporation—shareholders or managers—is a
significant one.

### Shareholder Rights

One of the advantages of the corporate form of business organization is
that capital can be raised from many thousands of separate individuals,
who need not invest a large share of their own portfolios in any one firm.
Legally, those shareholders have the power to control the corporation.
The principal channel for control is the shareholders' power to elect the
corporations's board of directors, who decide company policy. These directors are periodically re-elected and their annual reports must be approved
at shareholder meetings.

However, most shareholders do not actively exercise their ownership
rights. Small shareholders are not really in a position to know what goes on
inside their corporation and why decisions are made as they are. They tend
to accept the policies set by managers as being for the best. If they dis-
approve of management policies, it is easier for them to sell their stock and

buy shares in a better managed company than to try to throw their weight around at annual shareholder meetings. The result is a degree of separation of ownership from control unknown in sole proprietorships and partnerships.

## Shareholders versus Managers

Why is the separation of ownership and control an important issue? The answer given by many economists is that the interests of shareholders and managers may differ. Most shareholders have only one interest in the corporation whose stock they own — that the corporation earn a maximum profit for them. Managers do not always think of their relationship to the corporation in such simple terms.

For one thing, managers are naturally concerned about the security of their own jobs. They know that they must earn at least a respectable minimum of profits or the shareholders may rebel and throw them out. But when it comes to delicate decisions involving marginal trade-offs between risk and profitability, their interests and those of the shareholders may diverge. Shareholders do not normally put all their eggs in one basket. They hold diversified portfolios. If by taking prudent risks they can earn higher average returns, an occasional failure is no disaster. Because a manager's career is more closely tied up with the fate of a single corporation, or even a single project of a corporation, managers may tend to be excessively cautious from the shareholders' point of view.

Corporate growth is another possible area of conflict of interest. Shareholders are interested in growth to the extent that growth means more profit per share, but managers may sometimes favor growth purely for its own sake. The power and prestige of managers, the number of employees they have working under them, and even their salaries are enhanced by growth, regardless of whether that growth increases profit per share.

Finally, it is claimed that managers who identify personally with their firms may be more willing than shareholders to spend money to improve their corporations's image. Lavish headquarters, charitable contributions, community relations projects, and the like may in some cases attract customers and swell profits; but because they also swell managerial pride, there can be a temptation to carry such expenditures too far.

In short, the picture offered by some observers of the corporate scene is one of contrast between the traditional firm singlemindedly pursuing the goal of profit maximization and the modern management controlled corporation for which profits are only one goal among many — and not always the highest ranking one.

## Constraints on Managers

How much truth is there in this picture? The picture offered so far cannot be regarded as complete. There are strong reasons to believe that managers cannot really act as independently of the profit maximizing interests of owners as the preceding arguments might suggest.

For one thing, many corporations have plans that permit management to share directly in company profits. One of the most important types of profit sharing plans is the stock option. Stock options give managers the right to buy a certain number of shares of stock in the corporation at a guaranteed price at some time in the future. For example, say that in July 1984, a manager is given the option to buy a thousand shares of the company's stock in July 1985 at the 1984 price of, say, $25. If the manager, together with other managers, does a good job running the firm in the meantime, the price of the stock stands a good chance of rising. If the market price rises to $35 by July 1985, the option to buy a thousand shares at $25 will be worth $10,000, and the manager will reap a rich reward. But if the company is poorly managed and the share price falls, the option is worthless.

A second important constraint on the power of managers to slacken their pursuit of profits is the threat of a takeover. It is true that when ordinary shareholders do not like a corporation's policy, they may simply sell out and buy other stocks rather than attempt to exercise their influence directly. But what if a great many shareholders sell out? If they do, the price of the stock falls below the value it would have if the corporation were managed by profit maximizers. When this happens, an alert stock market entrepreneur can engineer a takeover bid. The takeover may be made by an individual, a group, or, often, another corporation. The idea is to buy a controlling percentage of the corporation's shares and use the power thus gained to replace current managers with more profit-minded ones. If the gambit succeeds, the listed value of the stock's price will rise as the new management policies attract other buyers. Then the original takeover group will reap very handsome gains.

In periods when stock prices are low by historical standards (for example, during the late 1970s), corporate takeovers become common. Large conglomerate firms that make a specialty of them go on the prowl, and weakly managed companies whose stock is selling at prices not reflecting their long-run profit potential are particularly likely to be bought up. Often, the managers of companies threatened with unfriendly takeovers cast around for a "white knight"—an alternative buyer who will take over the company and let the managers keep their jobs, provided they can convince the white knight of their competence.

The effectiveness of the corporate takeover as a device for keeping management on the profit maximizing track should not be measured solely in terms of the number of takeovers that actually occur. The threat of takeover is a powerful disciplinary device that can work without being used every day.

## Worker Control in the Modern Corporation

Karl Marx, the father of modern scientific socialism, predicted that our system of private enterprise would be destroyed by revolutions, instigated by workers who were not able to share in the ownership and control of business corporations. A century has passed since he made those predictions and during that time revolutions led by communist parties have occurred in countries like Russia and China where, ironically, industrial workers did not make up a significant part of the total labor force. In most of the more advanced industrial nations workers have challenged the rights of corporate owners, not through revolution, but through the establishment of labor unions and the use of the ballot. Such actions have given workers considerably more control over their working conditions.

However, the basic alienation that Marx perceived in western industrial societies persists. Workers, by and large, do not have ownership rights in the corporations for which they work. They are not represented on boards of directors and they have virtually no say in such important decisions as plant relocation and closure. They are "employees," a class set apart from, and below, their employers.

This condition is likely to change in the next decade. Workers have always had the right to buy shares of corporations, like everyone else, but their relatively low earnings and inexperience in the stock market has prevented this from becoming an avenue to worker control. In recent years, however, massive savings have accumulated in worker pension plans and if unions should decide to do so, they could utilize these funds to gain substantial control over their own enterprises. Many companies, seeking to improve productivity by having the worker identify more closely with the interests of the company, have deliberately made stocks available to their workers, in what are known as "profit sharing" programs. There are more than 18,000 such registered plans in Canada at the present time. A parliamentary committee in Ottawa has been considering a bill that would make it compulsory for all companies with more than 100 employees to make voting shares available to their employees. It is debating an even more far-reaching proposal, which would require such corporations to place workers on their boards of directors. In many West European countries, including Sweden and West Germany, workers have been placed on boards of directors for a number of years. These practices are part of a general movement known as "industrial democracy." The Manitoba government appointed two workers to the board of one of its Crown corporations in 1981 and is contemplating appointments to other boards. A few companies in Quebec and Ontario have recently been "bought out" by workers after they got into financial trouble. Worker control in the modern corporation is still in its infancy, but there are reasons to believe that it will assume increasing importance in the future.

## GOVERNMENT AND THE CANADIAN ECONOMY
### How Government Became Involved in the Canadian Economy
In order to understand the important role that governments play in the Canadian economy, it is necessary to recognize the special powers of government and the unique pressures that resulted in the creation of the Canadian nation.

Governments are distinguished from other actors on the economic stage in that they can legitimately use force in economic affairs. When the government taxes incomes, regulates prices, conscripts soldiers, or expropriates land, it does not require the consent of the individuals affected. In addition, governments do not have to prove that their operations are profitable in order to justify them. Such powers were of considerable importance at a time when political and economic pressures made the creation of a Canadian nation seem both highly desirable and very difficult.

It was noted in Chapter 1 that the rapid penetration of the Canadian hinterland, accompanied by the exploitation of staple products, produced a far-flung economic network that was oriented toward foreign trade, was exposed to an aggressive economic and political system in the south, and was heavily dependent on a well-developed transportation and communication network. By the mid-nineteenth century there were strong regional economies in the Maritimes and in Central Canada, but it was far from clear whether, and how, these economies would affiliate with each other and how they should relate to the countries with which they did most of their trading.

Until the 1840s, Central Canada and the Maritimes benefited immensely from their connections with Great Britain, because the latter applied preferential tariffs on most of their exports. However, in the 1840s, a free trade movement in Great Britain resulted in the repeal of the Corn Laws and the Navigation Acts, forcing Central Canada and the Maritimes to compete with other countries in the British market. They found that they could not compete effectively in products like timber and, feeling abandoned by Great Britain, turned increasingly to the American market. For twelve years, beginning in 1854, virtually free trade took place with the U.S. under the terms of the Reciprocity Treaty. However, in 1866, after the conclusion of the American Civil War, the northern states decided to impose protective tariffs against Canadian goods. These events provided a powerful stimulus to the creation of a new east-west economic and political union. Another stimulus was the political deadlock that had developed between the French and English factions in the Central Canadian legislative assembly, and a third was the threat posed by American interests who wished to encroach on the Canadian prairies. Political tensions between Canada's two principal language groups, and the threat of domination by a powerful southern neighbor, gave the impetus to Confederation in 1867, and they remain the major reasons why some Canadians wish to maintain that Confederation and why others question its viability.

The Confederation looked westward, and Manitoba and British Columbia were added to it in 1871 and 1873, respectively, with the promise of a national railway system. The federal government thereby committed itself to a huge public investment project. The governments of Central and Eastern Canada had subsidized railway construction in the 1850s and 1860s by guarantees of bonded debt. Such guarantees had proved to be crippling financial burdens, so when the transcontinental railway system was first proposed in the early 1870s the federal government decided to assist by means of cash and land grants. The Liberal government was prepared to build a government railway in stages, keeping pace with the advance of settlement, but the Conservative government of John A. Macdonald opted for a full-scale transcontinental system utilizing private enterprise and government grants.

In 1880, a group of private investors took up the government offer, and with $25 million in government cash grants and 25 million acres of free land, they proceeded to build the Canadian Pacific Railway—a feat that has become one of the few legends in Canadian history.

Government-supported railway construction was part of a Conservative government development program that has been called the National

Policy.[3] In addition to railway subsidies, it included the establishment of protective tariffs in 1878, a cheap land policy in the west, and the vigorous promotion of immigration. Tariff protection encouraged new industries in Central Canada, and immigration to Western Canada provided greater markets for those industries and a good supply of foodstuffs. The movements of goods and immigrants helped to ensure the profitability of at least some of the railways that were built.

Government and business cooperated so closely in this development policy that the question can be raised whether private business interests used government to promote their own ends or whether government used business to achieve its purposes. Consequently, the distinction between the state and private enterprise in Canada often seems artificial. H.V. Nelles, a historian, has shown, for example, that manufacturing interests in southwestern Ontario were instrumental in getting the Ontario government to take public control of the hydro-electric industry in that province.[4]

Over the years governments at all levels have continued to play an extremely important role in the Canadian economy. According to Vernon Fowke, the programs initiated by the National Policy in 1878 had more or less run out by the early twentieth century, but beginning in the Depression of the 1930s and continuing through World War II to the present, a new "National Policy" can be said to have been set in motion, consisting of a program of public welfare, agricultural assistance, and fiscal and monetary management. In the process, public corporations like the CNR, CBC, and PetroCanada were created to provide a government presence in industries that are privately owned in the United States.

A large part of the remainder of this book will be devoted to exploring the interactions between government and the private market economy. This chapter provides some background material about what governments do and how their activities are paid for. First, however, we will look at the constitutional framework within which the various levels of government are required to operate in Canada.

## The Distribution of Government Powers in Canada

One of the main purposes of a national constitution is to reconcile the conflicting demands of various regional interests with each other and with the interests of the nation as a whole, by creating different levels of government and by assigning specific jurisdictions to each. Canada's constitution, the British North America Act, also sought to do this. However, no completely satisfactory way was found to assign specific functions to the different levels of government, and government action in the economic

---

[3]This policy was examined most thoroughly by Professor Vernon C. Fowke of the University of Saskatchewan in his book, *The National Policy and the Wheat Economy* (Toronto: University of Toronto Press, 1957). Scholars have recently pointed out that the various strategies attributed to the National Policy by Fowke were actually developed quite independently of each other, and if they complemented each other it was quite fortuitous.

[4]See H.V. Nelles, *The Politics of Development: Forests, Mines and Hydro-Electric Power in Ontario, 1849–1941* (Toronto: Macmillan, 1974). Michael Bliss reinforces this viewpoint in "Rich by Nature, Poor by Policy: The State and Economic Life in Canada," in R. Kenneth Carty and W. Peter Ward, eds., *Entering the Eighties: Canada in Crisis* (Toronto: Oxford University Press, 1980, pp. 78–90).

sphere has been made more difficult by disputes over divisions of power. The B.N.A. Act gave the most far-reaching powers to the federal Parliament. The aim, as we have seen, was to produce a strong nation which would withstand its southern rival and avoid the type of civil war that had just occurred there.

Section 91 listed twenty-nine specific matters that belonged in the federal sphere, including the regulation of trade and commerce, taxation, the postal service, defense, banking and currency, and transportation and communication systems that serve two or more provinces. Later amendments gave to the federal government jurisdiction over unemployment insurance and the old age pension (the latter concurrently with the provinces). Most important, the federal government was assigned residual powers (powers not explicitly granted to the other levels of governments) and the general power to engage in any work deemed to be for the advantage of Canada.

In Section 92, the provincial legislatures were given general powers over local concerns and were assigned sixteen specific matters, including the power of direct taxation,[5] jurisdiction over municipal institutions, and most important, all property and civil rights in the province. Section 93 placed education under their jurisdiction.

Agriculture and immigration were assigned to both the federal and provincial governments in Section 95, with the federal government taking precedence in case of a conflict.

The federal government was intentionally placed in a much stronger financial position than the provincial governments. It could levy all kinds of taxes, while the provincial governments were restricted to direct taxes (for example, income and property taxes), which were quite unimportant at the time of Confederation.

During the Great Depression of the 1930s, provincial and municipal governments found it impossible to cope with the social and economic problems that came under their jurisdiction. The Report of the Royal Commission on Dominion-Provincial Relations (the Rowell-Sirois Report) in 1940 called for the redistribution of some tax revenues from the federal to the provincial governments. The latter in turn were urged to transfer more of their revenue to the municipalities.

## The Growth of Government Expenditures

**Government purchases of goods and services (government purchases)**
Expenditures made by federal, provincial, and municipal governments to purchase goods from private firms and to hire the services of government employees.

Exhibit 4.3 gives an indication of how government has grown over time. The chart shows what has happened to federal, provincial, and municipal **government purchases of goods and services** since 1947. Government purchases of goods and services (or **government purchases**, for short) include all the finished products purchased by government (everything from submarines to typewriter ribbons) plus the cost of hiring the services of all government employees (everyone from the prime minister to the courthouse janitor). These purchases are shown as a percentage of gross national product (GNP), a measure of the economy's total output of goods and services. By this measure, government has clearly grown over time. Before

---

[5] A direct tax is a tax applied to the person who is intended to pay it. An indirect tax may be shifted from the person to whom it is applied to another person. For example, the excise tax on cigarettes is an indirect tax because it is applied to the manufacturer but is actually added to the price of cigarettes and eventually paid for by the consumer.

**Exhibit 4.3**

**Government current expenditures on goods and services as a percentage of GNP, 1947 – 1982**

The percentage of total government purchases in GNP has grown substantially over time. Before the Depression of the 1930s, government purchases averaged less than 10 percent of GNP. Now, however, government expenditures have grown to a peacetime average of about 20 percent of GNP.

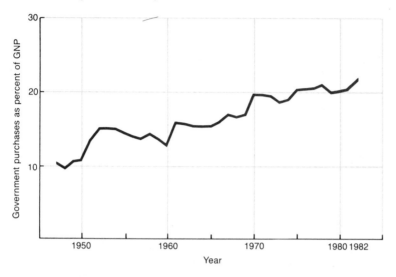

Sources: Department of Finance, *Economic Review*, April 1980, p. 160, and Statistics Canada, *Canadian Statistical Review*, March 1983, p. 18

World War I, government purchases averaged less than 10 percent of GNP. They followed a steady trend upward from about 1947 until 1970. During the 1970s and into the 1980s, total government purchases appear to have leveled off at about 20 percent of GNP. Government purchases have followed almost precisely the same trend, and reached the same levels, in the United States.

Exhibit 4.4 provides a different kind of comparison. This graph gives data for several countries on total government expenditures, including transfer payments as well as government purchases. **Transfer payments** are all payments made by government to individuals that are not in return for goods or services currently supplied. They include such things as family allowance benefits, welfare payments, and unemployment compensation. Using total expenditures rather than government purchases as a measure makes the public sector look somewhat larger. Government purchases plus transfer payments now equal about 40 to 45 percent of GNP in Canada. In comparison with the advanced industrial countries of Western Europe, however, the public sector in Canada is not a particularly large percentage of GNP. As Exhibit 4.5 shows, the general impression held by Canadians that they are burdened with an unusually large civil service is also wrong.

**Transfer payments** All payments made by government to individuals that are not made in return for goods or services currently supplied. Social security benefits, welfare payments, and unemployment compensation are major forms of transfer payments.

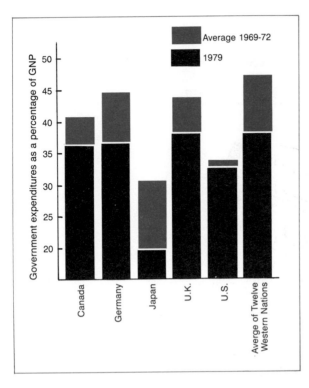

**Exhibit 4.4**
**Total government expenditures as a percentage of GNP for selected countries**
The data in this graph refer to total expenditures of central and local government units, including both government purchases of goods and services and transfer payments. By this measure, the size of government relative to the rest of the economy is larger than when only government purchases are taken into account. Note that although government expenditures in Canada are growing, they are still considerably lower in relation to the size of the economy than for most western nations.

Source: Department of Finance, *Economic Review*, April 1982, p. 175. Twelve western nations (not including Japan) were used for the 1969–72 average, and nine for 1979 (data for three were not available).

It should be noted, however, that the measurements of government activity in Canada shown in Figures 4.3 and 4.4 do not include the expenditures of a wide variety of government-owned enterprises, such as provincial hydro utilities, or crown corporations (such as Air Canada, Canadian National Railway, and Polysar Corporation). If their activities were included, the figures for Canada would be higher.

### The Functions of Government

Governments use the third to two-thirds of GNP that passes through their hands to perform a wide variety of functions. These functions can be classified under five general headings: provision of public goods, transfer of income, economic stabilization, regulation of private businesses, and administration of justice.

**Public goods** Goods or services having the properties that (1) they cannot be provided to one citizen without being supplied also to that person's neighbors, and (2) once they are provided for one citizen, the cost of providing them to others is zero.

**Provision of Public Goods** The first function of government is to provide what economists call **public goods**—goods or services having the properties that (1) they cannot be provided to one citizen without being supplied also to that citizen's neighbors, and (2) once provided for one citizen, the cost of providing them to others is zero. Perhaps the best example of a public good is national defense. One citizen cannot very well be protected against foreign invasion or nuclear holocaust without having the protection "spill over" on neighbors. Also, it costs no more to protect a single resident of a given area than to protect an entire city.

**Exhibit 4.5**
**"Yes we have civil servants, but others have more"**
This exhibit illustrates the percentage of total population comprising public servants in various countries in the period 1980–82. Canada's ratio is relatively low.

% of total population comprised of public servants* 1980/82

*Figure includes all levels of government, military, government agencies and Crown corporations

| West Germany | US | Japan | Canada | UK |
|---|---|---|---|---|
| 7.30 | 7.55 | 3.73 | 2.42 | 1.23 |

Source: Bob Hambly, *Canadian Business*, January 1983, p. 53, based on data supplied by the Public Service Commission, Ottawa; German Information Centre, New York; British Consulate, Toronto; Japan Information Center, Toronto; U.S. National Bureau of Statistics, Washington.

Public goods are traditionally provided by government because their special properties make it hard for private business to market them profitably. Imagine what would happen if someone tried to set up a commercially operated ballistic missile defense system. If you subscribed, I would have no reason to subscribe too and would instead play the "free rider," relying on the spillover effect for my protection. But you would not subscribe, hoping that I would, so that you could be the free rider. The missile defense company would soon go bankrupt.

In Canada, governments also provide a range of public utility services for which the user must pay either the full cost or a substantial part of it. These include provincial hydro utilities, provincial telephone systems, liquor outlets, and others. The government is heavily involved in national transportation. There are three government-owned railways in Canada (in addition to CNR, there are provincially owned railways in Ontario and B.C.), and six government-owned airlines. Government participation in such industries, in addition to government medical care and hospitalization programs, distinguishes our mixed-enterprise system from that in the United States.

Provincially owned utilities such as Hydro-Québec and Ontario Hydro are huge industrial complexes, ranking first and second in assets, respectively, among all industrial corporations in Canada. Exhibit 4.6 shows the ten largest Crown corporations, ranked by their assets.

Federally controlled businesses operate in various forms. The Post Office, for example, was run as a regular government department, until it was changed recently into a Crown corporation. Crown corporations are uniquely Canadian government businesses. They have the legal status of

**Exhibit 4.6**
Ten large Crown corporations, 1981
Here are the ten largest Crown corporations, ranked by
assets. Topping the list is Hydro-Québec, Canada's
largest company in terms of assets but only number 25 in
terms of sales.

| Rank | Assets $'000 | Name |
|------|-----------|------|
| 1 | 20,730,000 | Hydro-Québec |
| 2 | 17,829,621 | Ontario Hydro |
| 3 | 6,911,727 | British Columbia Hydro & Power Authority |
| 4 | 6,612,533 | PetroCanada |
| 5 | 6,140,167 | Canadian National Railway |
| 6 | 5,064,141 | Crown Investments Corp. of Saskatchewan |
| 7 | 2,649,841 | Manitoba Hydro-Electric Board |
| 8 | 2,377,648 | New Brunswick Power Commission |
| 9 | 2,072,162 | Alberta Government Telephones |
| 10 | 1,869,929 | Air Canada |

Source: *The Financial Post 500*, June 1982, p. 100.

independent entities, but have all or most of their assets owned by the government and are ultimately accountable to the federal Parliament or to provincial legislatures through a minister. In 1981, there were 306 federal Crown corporations, ranging from the Canadian Wheat Board to Air Canada.

Some Crown corporations, like the Canadian National Railway and Air Canada (which ranked twelfth and forty-third in assets, respectively, among all industrial corporations in 1982), have special provisions that allow them to finance their operations independently of the government. Others, like Atomic Energy of Canada Limited, are tied more closely to government and are called *agency* Crown corporations.

**Transfer of Income** The second function of government consists of making transfers of income and wealth from one citizen to another. Income or wealth is usually taken from citizens by means of taxation. Benefits are distributed either in the form of direct cash payments or in the form of the free or below-cost provision of goods and services. Among the more familiar types of cash transfers are family allowance payments, welfare benefits, and unemployment compensation. Goods and services used for transfers include public education, public broadcasting (the CBC), public housing, fire protection, and medical care. They are provided at low or zero cost on the basis of political decisions rather than at market prices on the basis of ability to pay.

**Economic Stabilization** Stabilization is a third economic function of government. Particularly since World War II, in an effort to ensure that a severe depression like that of the "dirty Thirties" would not recur, governments have tried to control the rates of economic growth, inflation, unemployment, and the balance of payments. The particular fiscal and monetary policies by which they have tried to do this are referred to as **stabilization policies**.

**Regulation of Private Businesses** A fourth major function of government is the regulation of private businesses. Regulatory control is exercised through a network of specialized agencies and takes a variety of specific forms. Some agencies, such as provincial milk marketing boards, set maximum prices at which certain products can be sold, whereas others set minimum prices. The Food and Drug Directorates of the Department of Health and Welfare exercise considerable control over what can be produced by the firms they regulate. The Canadian Transport Commission sets basic operating conditions for airlines and railways. Regulatory boards have come to influence a wide range of economic behavior and regulation is a subject of widespread research and controversy.

The prices of goods comprising 23 percent of average consumer purchases are now regulated by governments, including alcohol, cablevision, dairy products, eggs, poultry, gasoline, home heating (oil, gas and electricity), transit, bus, rail and air fares, postage, telephone charges, water, and tobacco.

**Administration of Justice** The fifth major function of government is the administration of justice. Usually, the police and courts are not thought of as part of the economic area of government; but their activities do, in fact, have important economic consequences.

Consider what happens, for example, when a judge makes a decision in a case involving an unsafe product, a breach of contract, or an automobile accident. The decision has an immediate effect on resource allocation in the particular case, because one party must pay damages to the other or make some other form of compensation. More importantly, other people will observe the outcome of the decision and, as a result, may change the way they do things. If the courts say that buyers can collect damages from the makers of unsafe products, firms are likely to design their products differently. If certain standards are set for liability in automobile accidents, carmakers, road builders, and insurance companies will take notice.

## How Governments Spend Our Money

In 1982, all levels of government in Canada spent about $160 billion, or slightly more than 40 percent of the gross national product. This compares to expenditures of 25 percent of GNP thirty years ago. What do governments do with this money? As Exhibit 4.7 indicates, almost half is spent on goods and services, meaning primarily the wages and salaries of civil servants, teachers, and medical personnel. One-quarter is allocated to transfer payments. The federal government is responsible for old age security, unemployment insurance, and family and youth allowances, while provincial and municipal governments take care of welfare and relief programs. The federal government also transfers tax revenues to the provinces for the support of health care and postsecondary education, areas that are basically the responsibility of the provinces.

**Stabilization policy** An effort by government to control the level of national income and the related conditions of inflation, unemployment, and the balance of payments.

**Exhibit 4.7**
**Patterns of government expenditures and revenues, 1981**
This exhibit shows the pattern of both expenditures and revenues for all levels of government in 1981. About one-third of total expenditures went to wages and salaries.

| Spending Patterns of All Governments | Revenue Sources of All Governments |
|---|---|
| 1. Expenditures on goods and services<br>47%<br><br>(Of this amount, 70% was made up of wages, including wages of civil servants, teachers, and medical personnel.) | 1. Personal income taxes<br>38% |
| 2. Transfers to persons<br>25%<br><br>(The biggest items were $8.2 billion for old age security, $4.9 billion for unemployment insurance, and $2 billion for family and youth allowances, all from Ottawa. On the provincial level, biggest items were $3.4 billion for postsecondary education and $5.4 billion for charities and relief.) | 2. Indirect taxes<br>33%<br><br><br>3. Investment income<br>14% |
| 3. Interest on the public debt<br>14% | 4. Corporate income taxes<br>8% |
| 4. Capital spending<br>7% | 5. Capital cost allowances<br>4% |
| 5. Subsidies<br>7%<br><br>(The biggest item was $3.8 billion for imports of crude petroleum.) | 6. Other transfers from persons<br>3% |

Source: Department of Finance, *Economic Review*, April 1982; and Catherine Harris, ''What governments do with your money,'' *The Financial Post*, July 31, 1982, p. 8.

Interest on the public debt has risen from 10 percent of GNP in the mid-1970s to 14 percent, but is not much above the 12 percent figure of 1951. Capital spending refers to expenditures on buildings, including hospitals and schools. Its share has declined over the years. Subsidies have increased their share from 2 percent in 1951 to 6 percent in 1981. In the 1950s, most of the subsidies went to agriculture. Now a major portion of subsidies goes to support oil imports and railway transportation.

Federal expenditures as a share of total government expenditures have declined from about 60 percent in the early 1950s to 40 percent in the 1980s, with the provincial and municipal share increasing correspondingly from 40 percent to 60 percent during that same period. This reflects the growing importance of health, education, and welfare expenditures, which are primarily the responsibility of the provinces and municipalities.

## How Large Are Government Debts?

Great concern is expressed in Canada today about the rapid growth of government debt. Tax revenues have not been keeping pace with government expenditures. The federal government incurred a deficit of $26 billion in the 1982–1983 fiscal year alone. These debts seem alarming, and if they continue to accumulate at the current pace, they will pose serious problems for the Canadian economy. It must be noted, however, that we owe most of the government debt to ourselves. (That is, most of the debt is held by Canadians in the form of government bonds, on which they earn interest.)

Further, if we measure the debt in terms of our total output—that is, as a percentage of GNP the picture is somewhat different. Total debt as a percentage of GNP fell from 219 percent in 1945 to 155 percent in 1955 but has risen since then to approximately the 1945 figure. In other words, the weight of the debt has in the past been just as great as it is now, or greater, without jeopardizing the economy. In addition, Canada's annual government deficit as a percentage of GNP compares very favorably with most other industrialized countries, as indicated in Exhibit 4.8. It is considerably less than that of Germany and Japan, two of the most rapidly growing economies in the world. Although this should not make us complacent about our government debt, it shows that the debt need not cause panic either.

**Exhibit 4.8**
**International comparison of annual total government[1] budget balances as percentages of gross domestic product or gross national product**
Canada's annual government deficit was less in recent years than that of most of the countries depicted here.

| | Average 1967–74 | 1975 | 1976 | 1977 | 1978 | 1979 | 1980 | 1981[2] |
|---|---|---|---|---|---|---|---|---|
| Canada | 0.9 | −2.5 | −1.7 | −2.4 | −3.0 | −1.8 | −2.1 | −0.7 |
| France | 0.5 | −2.2 | −0.5 | −0.8 | −1.0 | −0.6 | 0.4 | −2.4 |
| Germany | −0.2 | −5.8 | −3.6 | −2.4 | −2.7 | −2.9 | −3.8 | −4.4 |
| Italy | −6.3 | −11.7 | −9.0 | −8.0 | −9.7 | −9.4 | −7.8 | −9.4 |
| Japan | 0.9 | −2.8 | −3.8 | −3.7 | −5.5 | −4.7 | −4.1 | −3.6 |
| United Kingdom | −0.9 | −4.9 | −5.0 | −3.4 | −4.3 | −3.2 | −3.5 | −2.3 |
| United States | −0.5 | −4.1 | −2.1 | −1.0 | 0.0 | 0.5 | −1.2 | 0.9 |

[1]Includes central and local governments and the social security system, but excludes public corporations.

[2]OECD estimates except for Canada and the United States which are actual.
Source: OECD, *national Accounts of OECD Countries*, 1979, Volume II; OECD, *Economic Outlook*, December 1981; Statistics Canada, *National Income and Expenditure Accounts*, quarterly, cat. 13-001; Executive Office of the President, Council of Economic Advisers, *Economic Report of the President*, updated in some cases with more recent information.

Source: Department of Finance, *Economic Review*, April 1982, Table 9.5, p. 111.

## WHO PAYS FOR GOVERNMENT?

In recent years, people have become increasingly conscious of the costs as well as the benefits of a large, economically active public sector. In one sense, this is nothing new; people have grumbled about taxes ever since taxes were first invented. Nonetheless, in the late 1970s, citizens began to do more than grumble. In the United States, voters forced governments in several states to impose legal limits on state spending or taxes. In Canada, the revolt was not so dramatic, but several changes in government policy may have been due to growing citizen concern over taxes.

## What Kinds of Taxes?

We can begin by looking at the kinds of taxes that federal, provincial and municipal governments use to raise revenue. Exhibit 4.7 gives the breakdowns. Personal income taxes, which include social insurance contributions, are the largest revenue-raising item. Sales and excise taxes form the second largest source of revenue, followed by revenues from government operations and by taxes on corporate profits.

Provincial governments rely heavily on personal income taxes (collected by the federal government but belonging to the provincial government), sales taxes, and transfers from the federal government. Municipalities depend almost entirely on property taxes and transfers from provincial governments (some of which come, in turn, from the federal government). Total taxes, like total government expenditures, amount to about 40 percent of GNP.

## The Problem of Tax Incidence

**Tax Incidence** Measures the extent to which producers and consumers bear the burden of a tax.

Exhibit 4.7 shows the kinds of taxes paid to support various levels of government but not who really pays them. Economists refer to the question of who actually bears the burden of taxation as the problem of **tax incidence**. This problem is not at all an easy one to solve. It is not enough just to look up the tax records of federal, provincial, and municipal governments. That would reveal only who had handed over the tax money to the authorities, not who actually bore the economic burden of the taxes. What makes tax incidence a difficult problem is the fact that the party who is obligated by law to pay the tax can often shift the burden of it to someone else.

**An Illustration of Tax Incidence**  For a simple example, suppose a law is passed that requires all retailers to make a tax payment of $.50 to the government for each pack of cigarettes they sell. Who will bear the economic burden of this tax? A simple supply and demand analysis will provide the answer.

Look at the supply and demand curves shown in Exhibit 4.9. Without the tax, the equilibrium price of cigarettes would be $1 per pack, and 200 million packs per day would be sold. The tax upsets this equilibrium. In effect, the requirement of paying a $.50 per pack tax adds $.50 per pack to the sellers' cost of doing business, which shifts the supply curve upward by $.50. Buyers respond to this "artificial" shift in the supply curve in the same way they would to a genuine increase in the cost of producing cigarettes. They move up and to the left along their demand curve, cutting consumption. A new equilibrium is reached at $1.25 per pack — the intersection of the demand curve with the new supply curve.

Comparing the pretax with the posttax equilibrium, we see that although sellers must hand over $.50 to the government for each pack they sell, they receive only $.25 per pack less than they did before the tax. Thus half the burden of the tax has been shifted to the buyers in the form of a price increase of $.25 per pack. In the new equilibrium, the price paid by buyers is $.50 per pack more than what sellers receive after the tax.

In this example, the economic burden of the tax is divided equally between buyers and sellers, but the division need not always work out that way. If the demand curve had happened to be a little steeper and the supply curve a little flatter, the major share of the burden would have fallen on buyers. If the supply curve had been steeper than the demand curve, sellers would have borne the bigger share of the incidence of the tax. A large part of solving the puzzle of tax incidence, then, is determining just what the shapes of the supply and demand curves really are for the goods and services that are taxed.

---

**Exhibit 4.9**

**The effects of a $.50 per pack sales tax on cigarettes**

Before the sales tax is imposed, the equilibrium price for cigarettes is $1 per pack. The $.50 per pack sales tax can be treated as the sellers' added cost of doing business. It pushes the supply curve up by $.50, as shown. After the shift in the supply curve, the price paid by buyers rises to $1.25 per pack, and the price received by sellers falls to $.75. Thus, when the slopes of the supply and demand curves are equal, as shown in this exhibit, half the burden of the tax falls on sellers, and half is shifted to buyers.

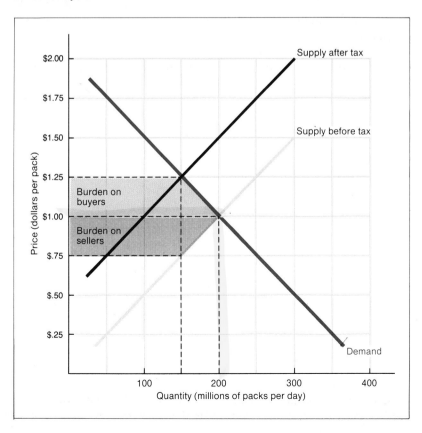

**Progressive tax** A tax that takes a larger percentage of income from people whose income is high.

**Regressive tax** A tax that takes a larger percentage of income from people whose income is low.

**Proportional tax** A tax that takes a constant percentage of income from people of all income levels.

**Fraser Institute** An independent economic and social research organization with headquarters in Vancouver. It is firmly committed to the study and preservation of a competitive market system.

**Net incidence of taxation** The difference between the amount paid to government in taxes and the amount received from government, calculated as a percentage of income.

**Overall Tax Incidence** Taxes can be classified in terms of their incidence as progressive or regressive. A **progressive tax** takes a larger percentage of income from people whose incomes are high, and a **regressive tax** takes a larger percentage of income from people whose incomes are low. A **proportional tax** takes a constant percentage of income from all people. One of the most interesting questions about the economics of taxation is whether the overall effect of federal, provincial, and municipal taxes is progressive, regressive, or somewhere in between.

A study of the real tax burden of Canadian families was published by the **Fraser Institute** of Vancouver in 1979. Exhibit 4.10 is based on data from that study, showing how different types of taxes affect families at different levels of income. Three examples of annual income for 1978—$10,000, $20,000, and $30,000 were chosen to represent low, middle, and high-income families respectively (average family income in Canada was about $20,000). Exhibit 4.10 shows that between the lowest and highest classes all types of taxes were progressive. The overall tax burden increased from 36.9 percent for low-income families to 59.8 percent for high-income families. However, between the lower and middle-income families the picture is quite different. Income taxes were clearly progressive, but property taxes were regressive and the other taxes were almost proportional. This mixture of progressive, regressive, and proportional taxes results in a total tax burden that is only slightly progressive in this range of income.

However, this picture is somewhat misleading. To appreciate what the real tax burden is, something has to be known about the benefits that different income levels receive from government transfer payments. The **net incidence of taxation** can be defined as the difference between the amount paid to governments and the amount received from them, calculated as a percentage of income.

According to Fraser Institute estimates, families in the lowest third of the income scale paid net taxes of $-475 million in 1978, or -1.9 percent of total taxes paid. In other words, they received more from government than they paid. Families in the average income third paid net taxes of $7,021 million or 27.9 percent of total taxes, while families in the highest income third paid net taxes of $18,638 million, or 74.0 percent of total taxes.

It should be noted that these figures are based only on measurable benefits and payments. The argument is sometimes advanced that wealthy

**Exhibit 4.10**
Incidence of selected taxes,
(selected taxes as percentage of cash income)

| Cash Income | Income Tax as Percent of Income | Sales Tax as Percent of Income | Liquor, Tobacco, Other Excise Taxes as Percent of Income | Social Security, Pension, Medical and Hospital Taxes as Percent of Income | Property Taxes as Percent of Income | Total Taxes as Percent of Income |
|---|---|---|---|---|---|---|
| $10,000 | 8.0% | 5.3 | 1.8 | 4.3 | 4.8 | 36.9 |
| $20,000 | 15.7 | 5.5 | 1.9 | 6.0 | 1.5 | 37.3 |
| $30,000 | 20.2 | 7.5 | 2.6 | 5.5 | 6.5 | 59.8 |

Source: Michael Walker and Sally Pipes, eds., *Tax Facts* (Vancouver, B.C.: The Fraser Institute, 1979), pp. 39–41.

people receive sizeable benefits from government in the form of business grants, government-financed training programs, highways, and numerous other types of benefits that cannot be measured. This should be kept in mind in evaluating the above figures.

## CONCLUSIONS

This chapter has offered just a glimpse of some of the complexities lying behind the operation of business firms and governments in our economy. In many branches of economic theory, firms are treated as simple, homogeneous building blocks. In reality, they are neither simple nor homogeneous. Except for the smallest one-person operations, each firm is an organization of separate individuals united for a common purpose—the purpose of carrying out the division of labor effectively. Depending on circumstances, this purpose may best be served by the legal form of a sole proprietorship, a partnership, a corporation, or a co-operative.

This chapter has also examined the services government performs and has looked briefly at who bears the costs of providing these services. But one major question not asked was *how well* the vast machinery of government does its job. This important question involves both normative and positive economics. The normative element comes in deciding what goals the government ought to pursue and the positive element in measuring how closely it meets those goals. This question of *how well* is one to which we shall return repeatedly throughout the book.

## SUMMARY

1. There are two major forms of coordination for the division of labor—market coordination and managerial coordination. Market coordination uses the price system for communication and the profit motive as a source of incentives. Managerial coordination proceeds through directives from superiors to subordinates. It organizes the division of labor within a firm, while market coordination organizes the division of labor among firms. Firms tend to grow until the cost of organizing one more task by managerial means exceeds the costs of organizing that task through the market.

2. Firms may be organized as sole proprietorships, partnerships, corporations or co-operatives. Proprietorships are very common among small firms. They are easy to set up and have the advantage of giving the proprietor rights to all of the firm's profits. They have the disadvantage of unlimited liability. Partnerships also suffer from unlimited liability, but they can allow a firm to grow by bringing in new partners with new skills and new capital. Corporations protect their shareholders with limited liability and permit huge sums of capital to be raised. They suffer the disadvantages of higher taxes and closer regulations than other kinds of businesses, however. Co-operatives have one-member, one-vote democracy, are able to buy goods and services more cheaply than individuals can, and enjoy tax privileges. However, they may have difficulty in raising funds, and their democratic management may be inefficient.

3. It is sometimes argued that managers, rather than shareholders, exercise effective control over corporations. This is an important issue, because the interests of managers and shareholders sometimes conflict. Managers may be less willing than owners to take risks and may sometimes pursue growth at the expense of profits. There are limits to the ability of managers to pursue policies opposed to shareholder interests, though. The most important single constraint is the threat of takeover if profits are too much neglected.

4. Workers in many countries are trying to achieve more ownership rights by assuming positions on boards of directors and by purchasing company shares. This movement is also gaining momentum in Canada.

5. Canadian economic development has been shaped and supported by deliberate government policies, called the "National Policy" by economists like Vernon C. Fowke. This has included subsidies to business, protective tariffs, a cheap land policy, and the promotion of immigration. In recent decades, such policies have been supplemented by programs of public welfare and fiscal and monetary management.

6. Governments in Canada have had their jurisdictions defined by the British North America Act. The different levels of government have been forced to resolve their respective revenue and expenditure difficulties by frequent negotiations and various types of cost-sharing arrangements.

7. Five major economic functions of government are the provision of public goods, the transfer of income, the stabilization of the economy, the regulation of private businesses, and the administration of justice.

8. All levels of government combined now spend about 40 percent of GNP, mostly on the provision of services like health and education. While government debt has risen substantially in the last few years, it does not appear so alarming when measured as a percentage of GNP, or in relation to our ability to pay for it.

9. The determination of the incidence of various kinds of taxes is a difficult problem of applied economics. The burden of many taxes can be shifted from those who bear the legal obligation of paying them to other parties. When all kinds of shifting are taken into account, it appears that the combined federal provincial, and municipal tax systems are neither progressive nor regressive overall.

## DISCUSSION QUESTIONS

1. Your college or university uses a type of managerial coordination to determine which courses should be offered and which professors should teach them. In principle, market coordination could be used instead. The college or university could limit itself to providing classrooms, dormitories, library facilities, and so on. Professors would then be independent businesspeople, advertising certain courses for so much per credit hour and collecting fees directly from the students. Compare the advantages and disadvantages of each system. Why do you think the managerial system predominates? As far as you know, is the market system ever used in education? Explain.

2. On graduation, a classmate whom you barely know suggests that you go into business together selling sports equipment to the students in your university town. He wants to make the business a partnership. "You supply the brains; I'll put up the money," he says. Do you think you might be better off if he set the business up as a sole proprietorship, with you as his employee? As a corpor-

ation, with the two of you holding some of the stock? What would be the advantages and disadvantages to you of each alternative?

3. Suppose that there is only one supermarket in your town and that you think its prices are too high. You decide to organize a food co-operative to compete with it. What transactions costs might you encounter in your efforts to organize the co-op? How would you persuade members to join? Would you limit shopping privileges to members only? If not, how would you keep nonmember "free riders" from reaping all the benefits of your hard work?

4. If workers used their pension funds to buy a majority of shares in the corporation in which they work, would this give them effective control over those corporations? Do you think that this would be a good strategy for workers to use to improve their working conditions?

5. Governments are under growing pressure to balance their budgets. Using total government expenditures in relation to GNP as your criterion, explain whether Canada has made any progress in this direction. What seems to be the main problem? Use recent government statistical reports, such as the monthly *Canadian Statistical Review* to update the data given in Exhibit 4.8.

6. Would you prefer living in a place where income taxes are progressive or regressive? Why?

7. When a tax is imposed on cigarettes, the price paid by consumers goes up and the price received by sellers goes down. The government benefits by the amount of the difference on each pack sold. There is also a second effect of the tax: fewer packs are sold. Who benefits and who is hurt by the second effect? Does the fact that cigarettes are harmful to people influence your answer? What if they were good for people?

8. Describe briefly the major recommendations of the Rowell–Sirois Report. What kinds of problems were these recommendations designed to correct?

9. Does it appear that governments have come to play a significant role in the Canadian economy against the wishes of the private business sector or at the request of business? Discuss, using specific examples from Canadian history.

## SUGGESTIONS FOR FURTHER READING

Coase, Ronald H. "The Nature of the Firm," *Economica*, new series, 4 (November 1937), pp. 386–405.
*The seminal article on the nature of the firm, it explains why there are such things as firms at all.*

Galbraith, John Kenneth. *The New Industrial State*. Boston: Houghton Mifflin, 1967.
*In this provocative and decidedly unorthodox book, Galbraith develops the thesis that the market plays little or no role in coordinating economic activity in the U.S.*

Fowke, Vernon C. *The National Policy and the Wheat Economy*. Toronto: University of Toronto Press, 1957.
*Describes the continuation into the twentieth century, through a series of new government policies, of the national policy begun in the nineteenth century.*

Aitkin, Hugh G.J., ed. *The State and Economic Growth*, pp. 79–114. New York: Social Science Research Council, 1959. Reprinted in *Approaches to Canadian Economic History*, edited by W.T. Easterbrook and M.H. Watkins, pp. 183–221. Toronto: Macmillan, 1978.
*Describes the important role played by government in Canadian economic development, particularly in containment of U.S. expansion.*

# NATIONAL INCOME, INFLATION, AND UNEMPLOYMENT

## PART TWO

# THE CIRCULAR FLOW
# OF INCOME
# AND PRODUCT

CHAPTER

FIVE

---

## WHAT YOU WILL LEARN IN THIS CHAPTER

*This chapter will describe how the circular flow of income and product sends goods from firms to households and factor services from households to firms. At the same time, it will show how payments for these goods and services flow in the opposite direction through the economy. The idea of the circular flow will be used in two ways. First, it will give a framework for a set of important definitions and equalities. Second, it will show how the concepts of supply, demand, and equilibrium can be applied in a macroeconomic context.*

## FOR REVIEW

*Here are some important terms and concepts that will be put to use in this chapter. If you do not understand them, review them before proceeding.*

- *Definition of macroeconomics (Chapter 1)*
- *Factors of production (Chapter 1)*
- *Equilibrium (Chapter 3)*
- *Government purchases and transfer payments (Chapter 4)*

---

This chapter begins putting together a theory that will explain unemployment, inflation, and economic growth and that will offer a framework for thinking about economic stabilization policy. These subjects make up the branch of economics known as macroeconomics.

Because it will take several chapters to complete the study of macroeconomics, it is necessary to have a clear idea of the lay of the land before beginning. The best way to get an overview of the relationships among the major economic aggregates is to represent them in terms of a **circular flow of income and product**. The rest of this chapter, then, will be devoted to the circular flow.

**Circular flow of income and product** The flow of goods from firms to households and factor services from households to firms, counterbalanced by the flow of expenditures from households to firms and factor payments from firms to households.

## THE STRUCTURE OF THE CIRCULAR FLOW

### A Simple Economy

To see the circular flow in its most basic form, begin by imagining an economy made up only of households and business firms—a two-sector economy without a public sector. To make things simpler still, assume that households live entirely from hand to mouth, spending all of their income on consumer goods as soon as that income is received. Similarly, assume that firms sell their entire output to consumers as soon as it is produced.

The circular flow of income and product for this ultra-simple economy is shown in Exhibit 5.1. The diagram is drawn with physical goods and services flowing clockwise and the corresponding money payments flowing counterclockwise.

Two sets of markets link households to firms in this economy. Product markets, which appear at the top of the diagram, are markets where households purchase goods and services—bread, television sets, houses, dry

**Exhibit 5.1**

**The circular flow in a simple economy**
In this simple two-sector economy, households spend all their income on consumer goods as soon as they receive it, and firms sell all their output to households as soon as they produce it. Physical goods and factor services flow clockwise, while corresponding money payments flow counterclockwise.

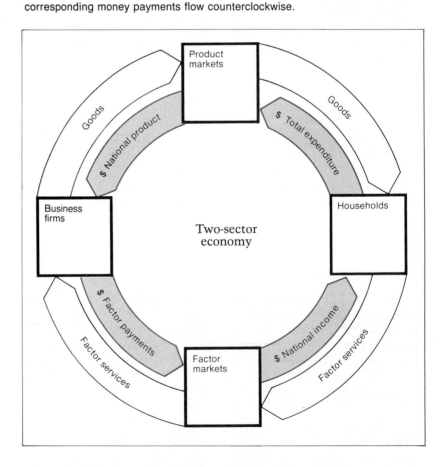

cleaning services, entertainment — for their own direct consumption. Factor markets, which appear at the bottom of the diagram, are the markets in which households sell to firms the **factors of production** they use in making the things sold in product markets.

In return for the natural resources, labor, and capital that they buy from households, firms make **factor payments** in the form of rents, wages, salaries, and interest payments. As a matter of accounting convention, when firms use land, labor, or capital that they themselves own, they are counted as "purchasing" those factors from the households that own the firms, even though no money changes hands and no explicit factor payment is made. For purposes of macroeconomic analysis, profits are thus considered an implicit factor payment from firms to the households that own them.[1]

**Factors of production** The basic elements of natural resources, labor, and capital used in the production of all goods.

**Factor payments** The payments with which firms purchase factors of production (natural resources, labor, and capital).

## Stocks and Flows

Having said this much, let's pause for a moment to concentrate on a word used several times already. Economists call all of the things shown in Exhibit 5.1 **flows** because they are processes that occur continuously through time. Flows are measured in units per time period — for example, in dollars per year, litres per minute, or tonnes per month. Measurements of flows are measurements of rates at which things are happening.

The technical language of economics distinguishes carefully between flows and stocks. A **stock** is an accumulated quantity of something existing at a particular time. (The word *stock* in this general sense has nothing to do with the stock market kind of stocks that are bought and sold on Wall Street.)

For an illustration of the difference between stocks and flows, we can think of a bathtub filling. When we talk about how fast the water is running, we are talking about a *flow*, measured in litres per minute. When we talk about how much water is in the tub at a given moment, we are talking about a *stock*, measured only in litres. Similarly, in the world of economics, we might talk about the rate of housing construction in Toronto, Ontario, in terms of new units per month (the flow) as distinct from the actual number of houses in Toronto as of January 1, 1985 (the stock).

**Flows** Processes occurring continuously through time, measured in units per time period.

**Stocks** Accumulated quantities existing at a particular time, measured in terms of simple units.

*example*

## National Income and Product

Two of the flows in Exhibit 5.1 deserve special attention and have special names. The first is **national income** — the total of all wages, rents, interest payments, and profits received by households. National income is shown in the diagram as an arrow aimed at the box representing households. The second important flow is **national product** — a measure of the total value of the goods and services produced. In the diagram, national product is shown as an arrow passing from the box representing product markets to the box representing firms.

**National income** The total of all incomes, including wages, rents, interest payments, and profits received by households.

**National product** The total value of all goods and services supplied in the economy.

---

[1] For certain purposes of microeconomics, profits are not considered factor payments.

In this economy, national income and national product are equal, simply because of the way they are defined.[2] This equality can be verified in either of two ways. First, consider household expenditures as a link between national income and national product. Households are assumed to spend all of their income on consumer goods as soon as they receive it, and firms are assumed to sell all of their output to consumers as soon as it is produced. The payments made by buyers must equal the payments received by sellers, so national product must equal national income.

Alternatively, consider factor payments as a link between national income and national product. When firms receive money for goods they sell, they use part of it to pay the workers, natural resource owners, and others who contributed factors of production to make the goods. Anything left over is profit. Factor payments, including profits, account for all the money received by firms, so total factor payments must be equal to national product. Factor payments also account for all of the income received by households, so total factor payments must be equal to national income. It again follows that national income and national product must be equal.

## Saving and Investment

The circular flow shown in Exhibit 5.1 is so simple that not very much of interest can be said about it. To build a theory that will be useful for understanding the real-world economy, a few complications must be introduced.

The first change will be to drop the requirement that households immediately spend all of their income to purchase consumer goods and to permit them instead to save part of what they earn. The rate of **saving** by households, under this assumption, is simply the difference between national income and household consumption expenditures.

The second change will be to drop the requirement that firms immediately sell all of their output to consumers. Instead, they will be permitted to sell some products to other firms and to let some accumulate in inventory before selling them to anyone. When firms buy newly produced capital goods (for example, production machinery, newly built structures, or office equipment) from other firms, they are said to engage in **fixed investment**. When firms increase the stock of finished products or raw materials that they keep on hand, they are said to engage in **inventory investment**. The rate of inventory investment can be less than zero in periods when firms are decreasing their stocks of goods or raw materials on hand. The sum of fixed investment and inventory investment will be called simply **investment**.

**Circular Flow with Saving and Investment** Exhibit 5.2 shows how the circular flow of income and expenditure looks when saving and investment are added. (The clockwise arrows showing the flows of goods and services

**Saving** The part of household income not used to purchase goods and services or to pay taxes.

**Fixed investment** Purchases by firms of newly produced capital goods, such as production machinery, newly built structures, and office equipment.

**Inventory investment** Changes in the stocks of finished products and raw materials that firms keep on hand. If stocks are increasing, inventory investment is positive; if they are decreasing, it is negative.

**Investment** The sum of fixed investment and inventory investment.

---

[2] Chapter 6 will show that the equality between national income and product does not hold precisely as these concepts are actually measured by the official statisticians of the Canadian government. It would be pointless, though, to let this statistical detail complicate all theoretical discussions. Everywhere in this chapter, and everywhere from Chapter 7 onward, the necessary simplifying assumptions are made so that national income and product *are* equal.

have been omitted to simplify the diagram.) Hypothetical numbers are used to illustrate how payments to factors of production become the income of households, and how this income, in turn, becomes expenditure on goods and services. Of the $100,000 income received by households, it is assumed that $80,000 is spent directly on consumption, while the other $20,000 is saved. This saving supplies a source of fund for firms to use in making investment expenditure.

On the way from households to firms, the flow of saving passes through a set of financial markets. These markets include a great variety of financial institutions — chartered banks, trust and loan companies, credit unions and caisses populaires, the stock and bond markets, insurance companies, and other institutions that act as intermediaries between households that save and firms that make investment expenditures. Households supply funds to these financial markets. Firms can then borrow from financial markets to obtain the funds they need to make investment expenditures. (Chapter 11 will discuss the operation of financial markets in detail.)

---

**Exhibit 5.2**

**The circular flow with saving and investment**

When saving and investment are added to the circular flow, there are two pathways by which expenditures can travel on their way from households to product markets. Some income is spent directly on consumer goods. The rest is saved and passes to firms via financial markets. The firms then may or may not choose to use the investment expenditures in the product markets.

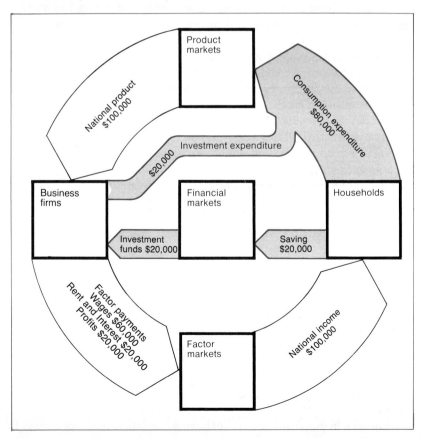

**Equilibrium and Disequilibrium in the Circular Flow**    Adding saving and investment to the circular flow raises an entirely new issue: can total expenditure still be counted on to provide an equalizing link between national income and national product? There are now two entirely different sets of people making expenditure decisions. Households decide how much to spend on consumption, and firms decide how much to spend on investment. How can we be sure that when these two kinds of expenditures are added together, the total will just equal the total value of all goods produced? A new way of applying supply and demand analysis will help find the answers.

## Aggregate Supply and Demand

**Aggregate supply** The total value of all goods and services supplied in the economy; identical to *national product.*

**Aggregate demand** The total value of all planned expenditures of all buyers in the economy.

The term **aggregate supply** refers to the grand total of all goods supplied by all firms in the entire economy. There is already another term for the same thing: national product. *Aggregate supply* and *national product* are two names for the total value of goods and services supplied by all firms. Following the same terminology, **aggregate demand** can be used to mean the grand total of all goods demanded for the whole economy. In defining *aggregate demand* this way, though, care must be taken in the way "demand" is used. The precise way of defining *aggregate demand* is to say that it means the total *planned* expenditures of all buyers in the economy.

Aggregate supply and aggregate demand can be compared to see whether, for the economy as a whole, the plans of buyers mesh with the production activities of sellers, much as supply and demand in a single market can be compared to see if the plans of buyers and sellers mesh.

**A Numerical Example** A numerical example will show how aggregate supply can be compared with aggregate demand. Assume that the various firms in our hypothetical economy, as shown in Exhibit 5.3, have plans to produce consumer goods, such as apples and radios, at a rate of $80,000 a year. They also produce capital goods, such as machinery, at a rate of $20,000 per year. As all firms carry out their plans, output flows at a rate of $100,000 per year. This flow, which can be called either national product or aggregate supply, is detailed in Lines 1 to 3 of Exhibits 5.3a and 5.3b.

While producers are busy carrying out their plans, buyers make plans too. Consumers plan to buy consumer goods at a rate of $80,000 per year, and at the same time the various firms plan to buy machinery at a rate of $20,000 a year. No firm plans either to increase or to decrease the stocks of finished products held in inventory, so planned inventory investment is zero. All these buying plans are expressed in Lines 4 to 8 of Exhibit 5.3a. The total dollar value of all planned expenditures (consumption plus capital investment on machinery plus planned inventory investment) is listed in Line 8 as aggregate demand.

Comparing Line 1 with Line 8 in Exhibit 5.3a, we see that the plans of buyers and sellers exactly mesh. Aggregate supply and aggregate demand are equal. When the plans of buyers and sellers mesh like this, we say that the circular flow as a whole is in equilibrium, just as we say that an individual market is in equilibrium when the plans of its buyers and sellers mesh.

However, in practice, the plans of buyers and sellers need not always fit together as neatly as they do in Exhibit 5.3a. It would be surprising if they did. After all, buyers and sellers do not often consult one another before production takes place. Often, production plans are set before buyers' plans are even formed.

As an example of what happens when buyers' and sellers' plans do not mesh, consider Exhibit 5.3b. The situation there is the same as in Exhibit 5.3a, except that now consumers plan to buy only $75,000 worth of consumer goods, and firms plan to buy only $15,000 worth of capital goods (machinery). Thus aggregate demand (total of Lines 4 and 5 in Exhibit 5.3b) is only $90,000 even though aggregate supply (Line 1) is $100,000.

There are, therefore, some disappointments in store for producers: $5,000 worth of consumer goods and $5,000 worth of capital goods will be left over. What will happen to these unsold goods? Once produced, they cannot vanish into thin air. Instead, they will accumulate as inventories in

---

**Exhibit 5.3**
**A numerical example of a simple economy in equilibrium and disequilibrium**
This exhibit shows a simple economy under conditions where (a) aggregate supply is exactly equal to aggregate demand, and (b) where supply is not equal to demand. In the first case the plans of buyers and sellers exactly mesh and no unplanned inventory changes take place. In the second case the plans don't mesh and unplanned inventory changes do occur.

**(a) The Case of Equilibrium**

| Output resulting from Producers' Plans | | |
|---|---|---|
| 1 Total national product (aggregate supply) | | $ 100,000 |
| 2 Consumer goods (apples, radios) | $ 80,000 | |
| 3 Capital goods (machinery) | 20,000 | |

| Expenditures Resulting from Buyers' Plans | | | |
|---|---|---|---|
| 4 Total consumption expenditure | | $ 80,000 | |
| 5 Planned investment expenditure on machinery | $20,000 | | |
| 6 Planned inventory investment | 0 | | |
| 7 Total planned investment expenditure | | 20,000 | |
| 8 Total planned expenditure (aggregate demand) | | | $ 100,000 |

**(b) The Case of Disequilibrium**

| Output Resulting from Producers' Plans | | |
|---|---|---|
| 1 Total national product (aggregate supply) | | $ 100,000 |
| 2 Consumer goods | $ 80,000 | |
| 3 Capital goods | 20,000 | |

| Expenditures Resulting from Buyers' Plans | | | |
|---|---|---|---|
| 4 Total consumption expenditure | | $ 75,000 | |
| 5 Planned investment expenditure on machinery | $ 15,000 | | |
| 6 Planned inventory investment | 0 | | |
| 7 Unplanned inventory investment (unsold consumer goods of $5,000 + unsold capital goods of $5,000) | 10,000 | | |
| 8 Total planned and unplanned investment | | 25,000 | |
| 9 Total planned and unplanned expenditure (aggregate demand) | | | $ 100,000 |

| Summary of Disequilibrium Case | | |
|---|---|---|
| 9 Total national product | | $ 100,000 |
| 10 Total national expenditure | | 100,000 |
| 11 Planned | $ 90,000 | |
| 12 Unplanned | 10,000 | |

the warehouses of the business firms. Those firms did not *plan* to make any inventory investments, but they find themselves making such investments despite their plans. The $5,000 of unsold consumer goods and the $5,000 of unsold capital goods are thus listed in Line 7 of Exhibit 5.3b as *unplanned* inventory investments.

**An Important Equality** When aggregate buying plans do not mesh with aggregate productions plans, the circular flow is said to be in *disequilibrium*. Aggregate supply and aggregate demand are not equal; national product and total planned expenditure are not equal. One crucial equality does hold, though. National product is still equal to total expenditure *when both planned and unplanned expenditures are taken into account*. The reason is that goods that are produced and not sold *must* be added to inventories, whether firms planned to put them there or not. As long as unplanned inventory investment is counted as part of total expenditure — and it is—total expenditure is by definition equal to national product. Thus, in Exhibit 5.3b, consumption expenditures of $75,000 (Line 4) plus planned investment expenditure of $15,000 (Line 5) *plus unplanned* inventory investment of $10,000 (Line 7) equal $100,000, making total expenditure equal to national product. In equation form, this is written:

$$\begin{matrix}\text{National} \\ \text{product}\end{matrix} = \begin{matrix}\text{Total} \\ \text{planned} \\ \text{expenditure}\end{matrix} + \begin{matrix}\text{Unplanned} \\ \text{inventory} \\ \text{investment}\end{matrix} = \begin{matrix}\text{Total} \\ \text{expenditure}\end{matrix}$$

Another way to write exactly the same thing is:

$$\begin{matrix}\text{Aggregate} \\ \text{supply}\end{matrix} = \begin{matrix}\text{Aggregate} \\ \text{demand}\end{matrix} + \begin{matrix}\text{Unplanned} \\ \text{inventory} \\ \text{investment}\end{matrix}$$

**Reactions to Disequilibrium** In the numerical example outlined in Exhibit 5.3b aggregate demand fell short of aggregate supply. Because buyers' and sellers' plans failed to mesh, there was an unplanned accumulation of inventories. Firms would not want this unplanned rise in inventories to go on and on. In order to stop it, they would reduce their rate of output, or lower prices in order to stimulate sales, or both. These reactions would amount to a reduction in aggregate supply. The size of the circular flow would begin to shrink as the number of dollars received by firms for their products and the number of dollars paid out to workers fell.

At another time, aggregate demand might exceed aggregate supply. With total planned expenditures greater than national product, unplanned inventory depletion would take place. Firms would react in a way opposite to their reaction to an excess of aggregate supply over aggregate demand. Either they would increase output to rebuild inventories, or they would take advantage of the high level of demand to raise prices, or both. Whichever they did, the size of the circular flow would grow as incomes and expenditures rose.

Finally, it is entirely possible that when the plans of buyers and sellers were tested in the market, they would turn out to mesh. In that case, with production and planned expenditure equal, no unplanned inventory investment would occur, and no corrections would be necessary. The circular flow would be in equilibrium.

## Income and Product

Having shown that national product is equal to total expenditure in this economy, we also need to remind ourselves that national product is equal to national income. Go back for a moment to the situation in Exhibit 5.2. Firms are shown to be producing $100,000 worth of goods a year. To produce those goods they make factor payments (including profits) of $100,000 to households, which means that national income is also $100,000. The value placed on goods and services by producers (which equals national product) is, in fact, determined by the payment made to all factors of production. Thus the national product is equal to national income.

## The Place of Government in the Circular Flow

When government enters the circular flow of income, expenditure, and product, things become slightly more complicated. Exhibit 5.4 shows how the circular flow looks when government is added. Two new pathways along which expenditures can flow from households to the product markets are opened up.

First, governments take in revenue from taxes they levy on households. Some of that revenue is immediately returned to households in the form of pension payments, family allowances, and other forms of government assistance called, as a group, *transfer payments*. The difference between what governments take in as tax revenue and what they pay out as transfer payments is called **net taxes.** Funds thus flow from households to government as net taxes and then from government to product markets as government purchases.

Second, if government purchases of goods and services exceed net taxes, the government may need to borrow from the public through financial markets. In this case, the government budget is said to be in **deficit.** When the government runs a deficit, funds flow from households to financial markets as saving, then from financial markets to the government as government borrowing, and finally from government to the product markets as government purchases.

Sometimes, the government budget is in **surplus** rather than deficit. In that case, government's borrowing from the public is less than its repayment of past debts. The net flow of funds between government and financial markets is the reverse of what is shown in Exhibit 5.4. In this exhibit we show the government with a balanced budget. It receives $20,000 in net taxes and spends $20,000 on goods and services. The exhibit also shows the economy in equilibrium: national product of $100,000 is exactly matched by expenditure of $100,000. Consumers spend $70,000 (after reducing their savings from $20,000 to $10,000 in order to pay net taxes of $20,000 out of their $100,000 household income), governments spend $20,000, and businesses have planned investment expenditures of $10,000. What might happen if, for example, governments ran a surplus by spending less than $20,000?

**Net taxes** Total tax revenues collected by government at all levels minus total transfer payments disbursed.

**Deficit** In referring to government budgets, an excess of government purchases over net taxes.

**Surplus** In referring to government budgets, an excess of net taxes over government purchases.

**Exhibit 5.4**
**The circular flow with government included (three-sector economy)**

With government added to the circular flow of income and product, there are two new channels along which funds can flow from households to product markets. Some income is diverted to government in the form of net taxes and then used to finance government purchases. Alternatively, if the government runs a budget deficit, it may borrow from the public via financial markets and use the borrowed funds to finance its expenditures. If the government runs a budget surplus, the flow of funds along this pathway may be reversed, in which case the arrow from government to financial markets will point in the opposite direction from that shown.

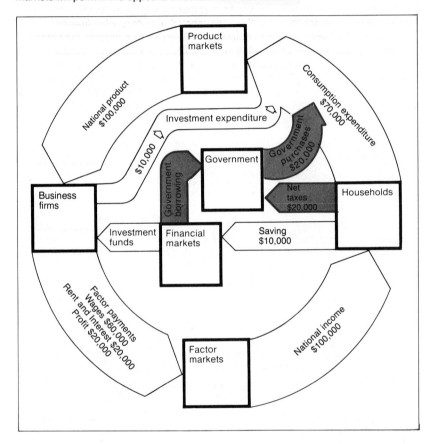

### Adding the Foreign Sector

The final step in constructing the circular flow of income and product is to add the foreign sector, as in Exhibit 5.5. This exhibit shows that some of the expenditures made by consumers, firms, and governments do not flow to domestic product markets, but instead flow to foreign economies to pay for imports of goods and services. It is assumed that $5,000 of government expenditures and $5,000 of business investment expenditures are in the form of imports. In addition, $10,000 of goods bought by consumers are imports, contributing to total imports of $20,000. These expenditures are shown by the arrow labeled *imports* in the exhibit. At the same time, some expenditures on domestically produced goods and services are made by foreigners. These are shown in the exhibit by the arrow labeled *exports,* which passes from the foreign economy sector to domestic product markets.

### Exhibit 5.5

**The circular flow with government and foreign sector (four-sector economy)**
This exhibit adds a foreign sector to the circular flow with government that was shown in Exhibit 5.4. Some consumption, investment, and government purchases are for goods produced abroad; this is shown as the triple arrow pointing toward the imports must be paid for by borrowing from abroad; this is shown by the arrow by foreigners; these are shown as the arrow labeled *exports* running from the foreign sector to domestic product markets. If imports exceed exports, the excess imports must be paid for by borrowing from broad; this is shown by the arrow labeled *loans from foreigners to finance trade deficit*. If exports instead exceed imports, there is a foreign trade surplus, and the direction of that arrow is reversed. Note that all the arrows in this exhibit represent flows of funds, not of physical goods and services. That is why the exports arrow points into the domestic economy and the imports arrow points away from it.

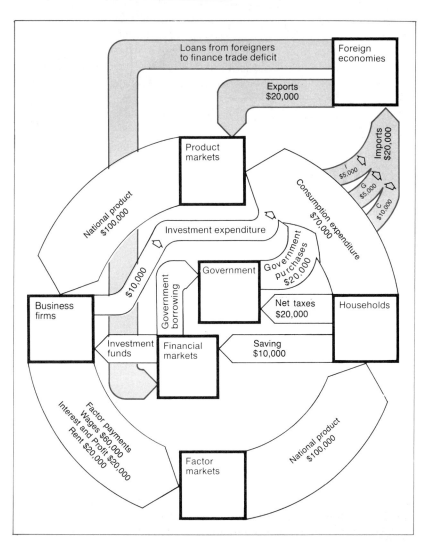

Remember that the arrows in Exhibit 5.5 all represent flows of funds, not flows of physical goods and services. The import arrow thus shows the flow of funds out of the Canadian economy to pay for imported goods and services, and the export arrow shows the flow of funds into the Canadian economy in payment for exports of goods and services. If imports exceed exports, the Canadian economy is said to run a foreign deficit. This deficit must be paid for by borrowing from foreigners; hence the arrow labeled *loans from foreigners to finance trade deficit,* which points from foreign economies to the domestic financial markets. If, instead, Canadian exports exceed imports, Canada is said to run a foreign trade surplus. In this case (not shown), foreign buyers of Canadian goods have to pay for them by borrowing funds in Canadian financial markets, and the direction of the arrow is reversed. In Exhibit 5.5, exports are assumed to equal imports, and the whole economy is pictured as being in equilibrium.

**Leakages and Injections** The first section of this chapter described a highly simplified economy in which households spent all their income on consumption goods, so that all expenditures flowed directly from households to domestic product markets. As financial markets, government, and foreign economies were added, however, it was shown that in the real world, three kinds of purchases of goods and services do not originate directly in domestic households: investment (purchases of capital goods and goods for inventory by domestic business firms), government purchases, and exports (purchases of domestic goods and services by foreigners). From now on, these three kinds of purchases will be referred to collectively as **injections** into the circular flow of goods and services.

Offsetting these injections are imports (expenditures of households, business firms, and units of government on goods produced abroad), plus saving and taxes (the use of household income for purposes other than the direct purchase of goods and services). From now on, saving, net taxes, and imports will be referred to collectively as **leakages** from the circular flow.

**Injections** The part of total expenditures that does not originate from domestic households — that is, investment, government purchases, and exports.

**Leakages** The part of national income not devoted to consumption (saving plus net taxes) plus domestic expenditures on foreign-made goods (imports).

**The Equality of National Income and National Product** Another numerical example will show that adding the government and foreign sectors, with their associated injections and leakages, to the economy does not disturb the fundamental equality between national income and national product on which the circular flow is based. Exhibit 5.6 shows an economy in which consumption is $70,000, investment is $12,000, government purchases are $20,000, and exports are $8,000. Of the consumption, investment, and government purchases shown, $10,000 is spent on imported goods, which cannot be counted as part of the national product of the country represented in the exhibit. National product is thus shown as the total of consumption, investment, and government purchases, plus expenditures on domestic goods by foreigners (exports), minus that part of consumption, investment, and government purchases not spent on domestic goods and services (imports). As Exhibit 5.6 is constructed, the total comes to $100,000.

The production of $100,000 of national product generates $100,000 in factor payments for domestic households. As the bottom part of the table in Exhibit 5.6 shows, this amount is divided among consumption ($70,000), saving ($15,000), and net taxes ($15,000). Introducing the term **net exports** to represent exports minus imports, the relationships shown in Exhibit 5.6 can be written in equation form as:

**Net exports** Total exports minus total imports.

$$\text{National product} = \text{Consumption} + \text{Investment} + \text{Government purchases} + \text{Net exports}$$

or $\quad Y = \quad C \quad + \quad I \quad + \quad G \quad + \quad Xn$

$\quad\quad = \text{Consumption} + \text{Saving} + \text{Net Taxes}$

or $\quad\quad = \quad C \quad + \quad S \quad + \quad Tn$

$\quad\quad = \text{National Income}$

Note, as Exhibit 5.6 shows, that Consumption, Saving, and Net Taxes comprise the way that total income is used by the recipients. On the other hand, Consumption, Investment, Government Purchases, and Net Exports are the expenditures that provide the source of income for the recipients.

**The Equality of Leakages and Injections** It follows from the relationship between national income and national product that total injections must equal total leakages. Beginning with the equation shown above, consumption can be subtracted from both sides, and imports can be added to both sides. The result is:

$$\text{Investment} + \text{Government purchases} + \text{Exports} = \text{Saving} + \text{Net taxes} + \text{Imports}$$

or $\quad I \quad + \quad G \quad + \quad X = S \quad + \quad Tn \quad + \quad M$

Total injections $\quad\quad\quad\quad\quad = \text{Total leakages}$

---

**Exhibit 5.6**

**The equality of national income and product**

This numerical example shows that the equality of national income and product is maintained when the government and foreign sectors, with their associated injections and leakages, are added to the economy. National product is a measure of the goods and services produced in the domestic economy. To arrive at its total, we add consumption, investment, and government purchases of all kinds, plus foreign purchases of domestically produced goods (exports), and we subtract the portion of consumption, investment, and government purchases devoted to foreign-made goods (imports). Using the term *net exports* to stand for exports minus imports, we could say that national product equals consumption plus investment plus government purchases plus net exports. This is equal to national income, which is divided among consumption, saving, and net taxes — as shown in the second part of the table.

| | |
|---|---|
| Consumption | $ 70,000 |
| Plus investment | 12,000 |
| Plus government purchases | 20,000 |
| Plus exports | 8,000 |
| Less imports | –10,000 |
| Equals national product | $100,000 |
| | |
| Consumption | $ 70,000 |
| Plus saving | 15,000 |
| Plus net taxes | 15,000 |
| Equals national income | $100,000 |

*what foreigners buyer*
*what we buy from abroad*

In terms of the circular flow diagrams, which were built up sector by sector, the leakages and injections appear as follows:

| Economy | Injections | Leakages |
|---|---|---|
| Two-Sector | I [*Investment*] | S [*saving*] |
| Three-Sector | I + G [*gov't purch*] | S + Tn [*net taxes*] |
| Four-Sector | I + G + X [*exports*] | S + Tn + M [*imports*] |

Note that this relationship holds even though, in the numerical example of Exhibit 5.6, no individual pair of items on the leakages and injections list exactly matches up. In that example, saving exceeds investment by $3,000, imports exceed exports by $2,000, and net taxes fall short of government purchases by $5,000. The reason total injections must always equal total leakages is that injections include unplanned inventory investment as a balancing item. Suppose, for example, that beginning from the position shown in Exhibit 5.6, government purchases suddenly rise by $5,000, while planned expenditures by households, firms, and foreigners remain constant. The additional purchases made by government cannot come out of thin air; unless or until production of goods and services increases, they must come out of inventory. Total investment, including unplanned inventory disinvestment, thus falls by $5,000 to compensate for the rise in government purchases.

Or suppose, again beginning from the situation shown in Exhibit 5.6, that foreigners suddenly decide to buy $2,000 less of Canadian goods. Exports will fall, but the $2,000 worth of goods that otherwise would have been exported will accumulate as unplanned inventories of Canadian firms, once again maintaining the required equality.

## CONCLUSIONS

This chapter has served two basic purposes. One purpose has been to establish certain key equalities among items in the circular flow of income and product. The two most important of these equalities are the equality of national income and national product and the equality of injections and leakages. The equalities hold by definition, because they are based on the concept of total investment—which includes both planned and unplanned investment.

The other purpose the chapter has served has been to introduce the concepts of equilibrium and disequilibrium in the circular flow. These concepts depend crucially on the distinction between planned and unplanned investments, which are lumped together in defining the basic equalities. To be specific, the circular flow is said to be in equilibrium when, and only when, the plans of buyers and sellers exactly mesh, so that no unplanned inventory accumulation or depletion takes place. If buyers do not demand as much as firms supply, the excess products go into inventory, whether or not firms had planned to put them there. To correct any unplanned inventory accumulation, firms must cut output or reduce prices to boost sales. Either action causes the circular flow to shrink—when this flow is measured in terms of dollars spent on products or earned in incomes. If buyers demand more than firms currently produce, goods come out of inventory, even if firms had not planned to run their inventories down. This unplanned inventory depletion causes firms to raise prices or increase output, either of which causes the volume of the circular flow to grow.

## SUMMARY

1. Two of the most important elements of the circular flow are national income and national product. These two elements are linked on one side by factor payments and on the other by total expenditures. National income and national product are equal.
2. Saving and investment can be added to the circular flow without disturbing the equality between national product and total expenditure. If total *planned* expenditure is not exactly equal to national product, unplanned inventory investment (positive or negative) will make up the difference between the two.
3. *Aggregate supply* is another term for national product and *aggregate demand* another term for total planned expenditure. When aggregate supply is equal to aggregate demand, unplanned inventory investment is zero, and the circular flow is said to be in equilibrium. When aggregate supply and demand are not equal, unplanned inventory investment (positive or negative) must take place. The circular flow is then said to be in disequilibrium.
4. Adding government and a foreign sector to the circular flow of income and product does not disturb the basic equalities of the circular flow. Total injections (investment plus government purchases plus exports) must equal total leakages (saving plus net taxes plus imports). National product (consumption plus investment plus government purchases plus net exports) must equal national income (consumption plus saving plus net taxes).

## DISCUSSION QUESTIONS

1. Contrast the flow of money you put into your bank account each payday with the stock of money indicated by the balance in your passbook. How are the flow and stock related? Why is one referred to as a *flow* and the other as a *stock*?
2. Not all inventory investment is unplanned. Why would a firm plan to increase or decrease its inventories? How would you plan your inventories over the year if you were a seller of children's toys? Of air conditioners? How would you plan your inventories of auto parts if you were a dealer in a town with a steadily growing (or shrinking) population?
3. Rework Exhibit 5.3b for the case of excess aggregate demand. What role do inventory adjustments play in establishing the equality of national income and product? How would producers tend to adjust to these inventory changes?
4. Beginning from a state of equilibrium, as in Exhibit 5.6, trace the effects of each of the following through the circular flow. What happens to inventories? What reactions do firms tend to have? What happens to the size of the circular flow, measured in nominal terms?
   a. Business managers, suddenly becoming more optimistic about the future, decide to increase investment in order to expand productive capacity.
   b. The federal government cuts income taxes.
   c. Good crops throughout the world reduce foreign demand for Canadian farm products.

5. Rework Exhibit 5.6 for the following cases:
   a. Planned investment exceeds saving by $5,000, and the government runs a $10,000 budget deficit.
   b. Imports exceed exports by $6,000, and the government budget is exactly balanced.
   c. Saving exceeds investment, and net taxes exceed government purchases.

   Bonus question: Can you work out an example where saving exceeds investment, the government runs a budget surplus, and imports exceed exports? If not, why not?

# NATIONAL INCOME AND NATIONAL PRODUCT

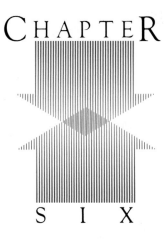
---

## WHAT YOU WILL LEARN IN THIS CHAPTER
*This chapter will explain how the various elements of the circular flow of income and product can be measured. It will describe the methods used by government statisticians to measure both nominal national product and nominal national income and show why these flows, as officially measured, correspond only approximately to the theoretical concepts in the last chapter. The chapter will explain how changes in the price level can be measured by means of price indexes, and it will introduce several specific price indexes in common use.*

## FOR REVIEW
*Here are some important terms and concepts that will be put to use in this chapter. If you do not understand them, review them before proceeding.*
- *Government purchases (Chapter 4)*
- *Transfer payments (Chapter 5)*
- *Basic equalities of the circular flow (Chapter 5)*
- *The circular flow and the foreign sector (Chapter 5)*

---

The last chapter cut the circular flow of income and product into convenient pieces and gave the pieces names like *national income, investment,* and *saving.* These concepts are basic to macroeconomic theory. Because they are so important, it is useful to know how they can be measured, so the theory can be compared to what happens in the real world. This chapter will take a brief tour through some of the basics of national income accounting. The chapter is divided into two parts, corresponding to the important distinction between nominal and real measures of national income and product and their component parts. **Nominal values**, discussed in the first part, are measurements that are made in terms of the actual market prices at which goods are sold. **Real values**, discussed in the second part, are measurements that are adjusted for inflation — for changes in the price level over time.

**Nominal values**
Measurements of economic values made in terms of actual market prices at which goods are sold.

**Real values** Measurements of economic values that include adjustments for changes in prices between one year and another.

## MEASURING NOMINAL NATIONAL INCOME AND PRODUCT

As will be seen below, the value of an economy's total output can be measured either by calculating *expenditures* on output or by calculating the *income* created in the course of production. The expenditure approach will be considered first.

### Gross National Product

**Gross national product (GNP)** The dollar value at current market prices of all final goods and services produced annually by the nation's economy.

**Final goods and services** Goods and services sold directly for household consumption, business investment, or government purchase. Excludes intermediate goods sold for use as inputs in the production of other goods.

Of all economic statistics, perhaps the most widely publicized is the measure of an economy's level of total production called the **gross national product (GNP)**. This statistic represents the dollar value at current market prices (the nominal value) of all final goods and services produced annually by the nation's economy. **Final goods and services** are goods and services sold directly for household consumption, business investment, government purchase, or export. Intermediate goods, such as the flour used to bake bread at commercial bakeries, are not counted in GNP. To count both the value of the flour at its market price (an intermediate good) and the value of the bread at its market price (a final good) would be to count the flour twice, because the value of the flour is included in the price of the bread.

In principle, GNP could be measured directly by constructing a table that shows the quantity of each final good and service produced — massages, apples, submarines, housing units, and all the rest — multiplying these quantities by the prices at which they were sold, and adding the resulting column of figures. But that is not what national income accountants actually do. Instead, they take a shortcut based on the equality of national product and total expenditure. In practice, GNP is measured by summing the nominal expenditures of all economic units on domestically produced final goods and services. This way of measuring aggregate economic activity may be called the expenditure approach to GNP. The result in Canada is officially known as **gross national expenditure** (GNE). Exhibit 6.1 provides an illustration of how it works, using actual 1982 data for the Canadian economy.

**Gross national expenditure** A measurement of aggregate economic activity arrived at by adding together the nominal expenditure of all economic units on newly produced final goods and services.

**Consumption**  Consumption expenditures by households and unattached persons fall into four categories: durable goods, semidurable goods, nondurable goods, and services. In principle, goods that do not wear out entirely in one year — such as automobiles, furniture, and household appliances — are considered durable, and goods that are possibly used up in a shorter period of time, but not instantaneously — such as clothing, books, and magazines — are considered semidurable. Goods used up almost immediately — such as soap, food, and gasoline — are considered nondurable. (In practice, the classifications are often arbitrary.) The remaining item, services, includes things that are not embodied in any physical object when sold, such as haircuts, legal advice, and education. No distinction is made between services that are durable and those that are nondurable in their effects.

Both the goods and the services components of consumption contain items that are produced but that do not actually pass through the market-

*the value of GNP is GNE*

**Exhibit 6.1**

**Nominal gross national expenditure (GNE) 1982 (billions of dollars)**

Gross national product can be measured by the expenditure approach, in which case — in Canada — it is officially called gross national expenditure (GNE). This means adding together the values of expenditures on newly produced goods and services by all economic units to get a measure of aggregate economic activity.

| | | |
|---|---:|---:|
| Personal consumption expenditure | | $206.0 |
| Durable goods | $25.8 | |
| Semidurable goods | 23.1 | |
| Nondurable goods | 66.9 | |
| Services | 90.2 | |
| Plus: gross fixed capital formation (investment) | | 76.4 |
| Machinery and equipment | 26.9 | |
| Residential construction | 12.8 | |
| Nonresidential construction | 36.7 | |
| Plus: changes in inventories (inventory investment) | | −8.7 |
| Plus: government expenditure on goods and services | | 75.7 |
| Plus: net exports of goods and services | | 1.2 |
| Exports | 100.4 | |
| Less imports | −99.2 | |
| Plus: residual error of estimate | | −1.7 |
| Equals gross national expenditure | | $348.9 |

*sum*

Source: Statistics Canada, *Canadian Statistical Review*, March 1983, pp. x and 18.

place on their way to consumers. One such item is an estimate of the food produced and directly consumed on farms. Another is an estimate of the rental value of owner-occupied homes. (Rental payments on tenant-occupied housing are included automatically.)

**Investment** The item in Exhibit 6.1 called *gross fixed capital formation* is the sum of all firms' purchases of newly produced capital goods (fixed investment by both government and private business firms). Fixed investment is broken down into the durable equipment of producers: such as machine tools, trucks, and office equipment; and new construction: including both business structures and residential housing. Separate account is kept of changes in inventory, which we call *inventory investment*. As we saw in Chapter 5, this refers to changes in the stock of finished products and raw materials that firms keep on hand. If such stocks are increasing inventory investment is positive; if they are decreasing (as they did in 1982) it is negative.

When thinking about investment, keep in mind the phrase *newly produced capital goods*. The businessperson who buys a used machine is not engaging in an investment expenditure, according to the national income accountants' definition. The machine was already counted in some previous year. Also, people who speak of making investments in land or corporate bonds are not using the word *investment* in the national income accountants' sense. Real estate and securities are not capital goods. In fact, they are not even part of the more general category, goods and services, with which the measure of GNE is concerned.

**Government Purchases** The contribution that government makes to GNE at the federal, provincial, and municipal levels presents a special problem for national income accountants. Ideally, this contribution should be measured in terms of the value of the services that government produces—

education, national defense, police protection, and all the rest. However, since very few government services are actually sold to consumers and businesses, there are no market prices in terms of which to value them. Instead, national income accountants use government purchases of goods and services to approximate the contribution of government to GNE.

Government purchases of goods and services, as explained in Chapter 4, include the wages and salaries of all civilian and military personnel hired by government plus the purchase of all the buildings, computers, assault rifles, paper clips, and so on used by those employees. Presumably, all the government workers using all that equipment produce an output at least as valuable as the same inputs could have produced in the private sector. In any event, that is the assumption that justifies inclusion of government purchases in GNE. Note that government transfer payments are not included, since they do not represent expenditures made to purchase newly produced goods or current services.

**Net Exports** The final item in GNE is net exports—the difference between the nominal value of goods and services exported abroad and the nominal value of goods and services imported from abroad. Exported goods must be added in because they are products produced in Canada, and thus provide incomes to Canadians, even though they are bought and consumed elsewhere. Imports must be subtracted because some of the expenditures on consumer goods, investment goods, and government purchases that have already been added in were purchases of goods made abroad; and these goods should not be counted as part of national product.

## National Income

The chapter will turn now to a different way of measuring what goes on in the circular flow: the income approach to national income accounting. As the name implies, the **income approach** measures the overall nominal rate of the circular flow by adding up all the different kinds of income earned by households. This is done as shown in Exhibit 6.2. The various incomes add up to what is known as **national income** (or simply national income; see definition in Chapter 5). The categories of income used by national income accountants differ somewhat from the theoretical classification of incomes into wages, rent, interest, and profit; and they deserve some explanation.

The category *wages and other labor income* includes not only wages and salaries but two other items as well. The first is employer contributions for social insurance (Chapter 4 argued that the economic burden of these taxes was borne by employees even though employers actually made the payments.) The second is other labor income, which includes various fringe benefits received by employees, and rental income.

The category *corporate profits* includes all income earned by the owners (that is, the shareholders) of corporations, whether the owners actually receive that income or not. Dividends are the part of that income that the owners actually receive. Another part goes to pay the taxes on corporate profits, and a third part, "undistributed corporate profits," is retained by the

**Income approach** A method of estimating aggregate economic activity by adding together the incomes earned by all households.

**National income** Total income received by a nation's productive factors, including wages and salaries, interest and rent, corporate profits before taxes, and income of unincorporated enterprises. It is also equal to GNP minus capital consumption allowances and indirect business taxes.

*Whether or not the households actually got the income*

**Exhibit 6.2**

**Nominal national income (NI), 1982 (billions of dollars)**

National income is officially estimated by the income approach. This means adding together the values of all income earned by households. Note that some items of income, such as the portion of corporate profits that goes to pay corporate profits taxes, are counted as "earned" by households even though households never actually receive the income.

Source: Statistics Canada, *Canadian Statistical Review*, March 1983, p. x. Figures do not add exactly because of rounding.

| | | |
|---|---:|---:|
| Wages and other labor income | | $201.7 |
| Corporation profits | $21.8 | |
| Less: dividends paid to nonresidents | –3.4 | 18.4 |
| Interest and miscellaneous investment income | | 29.6 |
| Net income of farm and nonfarm unincorporated business, including rent | | 18.7 |
| Inventory valuation adjustment | | –3.8 |
| National income (NI) at factor cost | | 264.8 |

corporations to use for investment purposes. Dividends paid to nonresidents do not form part of income received by Canadians, and are therefore deducted.

The category *interest income* excludes interest paid by government on the public debt, which is considered a transfer payment. Miscellaneous investment income includes profits or losses of government business enterprises.

The category *net income of farm and unincorporated business* is a grab-bag including all income earned by farmers, small unincorporated businesses, and self-employed professionals. No attempt is made to sort out what parts of this income ought theoretically to be classified as wages, interest, or profit. Rental income is the income of persons acting as landlords.

The final item, *inventory valuation adjustment*, refers to the artificial increase in value of inventories resulting from price increases. An appropriate deduction is made for this.

## Reconciling the Income and Expenditure Approaches

In the simplified circular flows of Chapter 5, national income and national product were always equal. In the official national income accounts the two sums do not fit together quite so neatly. Some adjustments must be made in order to reconcile GNP, measured by the expenditure approach (i.e. GNE), with GNP measured by the income approach. Exhibit 6.3 shows these adjustments.

Approached from the left side, expenditures on final goods and services are totalled to arrive at a measure of national output (GNE). As noted in exhibit 6.1, this amounted to $348.9 billion in 1982. Approached from the right side, the incomes generated by current output are totalled to derive national income. This amounted to $264.8 billion in 1982. Why is national income less than GNE? Because some costs which determine the price of final goods, and are "captured" in expenditures on those goods, are not included in the calculation of national income. The indirect taxes which business firms pay are added to other costs in determining price, as are depreciation allowances (for the wearing down of capital), but these costs are not included in national income. They must therefore be added to national income to obtain a GNP figure which will equal GNE. In principle, adding indirect taxes and depreciation to national income should result in a GNP figure which is exactly equal to GNE. However, there is a further difficulty. GNP (via national income) and GNE

**Exhibit 6.3**

**Relation of gross national expenditure (GNE) to gross national product (GNP) and national income (NI), 1982 (billions of dollars)**

Gross national expenditure (GNE) is equal to Canada's gross national product (GNP). In the simple world of elementary economic theory, national product (GNP) and national income (NI) are equal by definition. In the real world, certain adjustments must be made to get GNP and NI to "fit." First indirect taxes and then depreciation are added to NI to obtain GNP. (The figures must also be adjusted for errors in estimates, equal to 0.4% of GNP in 1982).

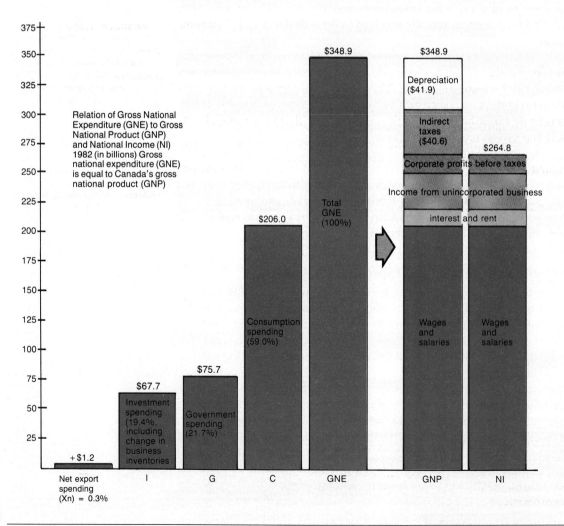

are based on different sets of data. Inevitably, no matter how carefully the work is done, there are some errors and omissions, so that the two sets of figures do not quite fit.

The difference between GNE and GNP measured by the income approach is called the **residual error of estimate**. The discrepancy has no statistical significance; it is simply a "fudge factor" that makes the figures balance (see Exhibit 6.1). In 1982 the "error" was $3.4 billion. This figure was halved; one-half was added to the lower total (in this case the GNP) and one-half was subtracted from the higher figure (GNE) to make the two figures come out even.

**Residual Error of Estimate**
The difference between the initial measurements of GNE and GNP.

**Personal Income** National income, as mentioned several times, is a measure of income earned by households, whether or not those households ever actually get their hands on the income. For some purposes, it is more important to measure what households actually receive than what they earn. The total income actually received by households is called **personal income**.

Exhibit 6.4 shows the steps required to transform national income into personal income. First, two items that are earned by households but not received by them are subtracted. These items are corporate profits taxes and undistributed corporate profits. Next, transfer payments—payments received by households although not earned by them—are added. The result is personal income.

**Personal income** The total of all income, including transfer payments, actually received by households before payment of personal income taxes and other transfer payments to government.

One further income measure is shown at the bottom of Exhibit 6.4: **personal disposable income** (or **disposable income** for short). This income is what households have left of their personal income after they pay personal taxes of various kinds to federal, provincial, and municipal governments, including transfer payments to government, such as pension and unemployment insurance contributions.

**Personal disposable income (disposable income)**
Personal income minus personal taxes.

This completes the discussion of the nominal side of national income accounting. The next section turns to the problem of making adjustments for changing prices.

---

**Exhibit 6.4**

**National income and personal income, 1982 (in billions)**
National income is a measure of all income earned by households, while personal income is a measure of the income they actually receive. To go from national income to personal income, subtract corporate profits taxes and undistributed corporate profits; then add transfer payments. If personal taxes and transfer payments to government are subtracted from this figure, the result is personal disposable income.

| | |
|---|---:|
| National Income | $264.8 |
| Less corporate profits taxes | –9.4 |
| Less undistributed corporate profits | –5.7 |
| Plus transfer payments[a] | 58.1 |
| Equals personal income | $307.8 |
| Less personal taxes and transfer payments to government | –60.7 |
| Equals personal disposable income | $247.1 |

[a] Includes government and consumer interest payments and business transfer payments

Source: Statistics Canada, *Canadian Statistical Review*, March 1983, pp. 18 and 19.

## MEASURING REAL INCOME AND PRICES

### Measuring Real GNP (or GNE)

The investigation of real income and prices will begin with a look at an economy much simpler than that of Canada. This will permit the presentation of the essentials in the clearest possible way before getting into practical details.

Exhibit 6.5 shows nominal GNP accounts in two different years for a simple economy in which only three goods are produced: movies, apples, and shirts. It indicates that nominal GNP grew from $400 in 1972 to $1,000 in 1984. But how are these figures to be interpreted? Do they mean that people really had more of the things they wanted in 1984 than in 1972? More exactly, do they mean that people had 2.5 times as much? These questions require careful answers.

A line-by-line comparison of the two years in Exhibit 6.5 shows that the figures on nominal income do not tell the whole story. The problem is that prices went up sharply betwen 1972 and 1984. Movies cost twice as much as they used to, apples three times as much, and shirts half again as much. So how much more was really produced in the second year than in the first?

We can try looking directly at the quantities of individual goods and services produced. But if we do so, we get conflicting indications: twice as many movies and shirts were produced in 1984 as in 1972 but only half as many apples. Instead, we can approach the matter in another way, by asking how much the total value of output would have changed from 1972 to 1984 *if prices had not changed.*

This approach to the problem gives the results shown in Exhibit 6.6. There, we see that the 1984 output of 100 movies, 500 apples, and 20 shirts, which had a value of $1,000 in terms of the prices at which the goods and services were actually sold, would have had a value of only $500 in terms of the prices that prevailed in 1972. The $500 figure is a measure of *real* GNP for 1984, and it is this measure that we should compare with the 1972 GNP of $400 if we want to know what really happened to physical production in the economy between the two years. Much of the apparent growth of the economy is seen to have been due to higher prices. Thus, instead of having 150 percent more in 1984 than in 1972 (an increase from

---

**Exhibit 6.5**

**Nominal GNP in selected years for a simple economy** In this simple economy, in which only three goods are produced, nominal national income grew from $400 in 1972 to $1,000 in 1984. Prices also went up in that time, though, so people did not really have 2.5 times as much of these things in 1984.

| 1972 | Quantity | Price | Value |
|---|---|---|---|
| Movies | 50 | $ 2.00 | $ 100 |
| Apples | 1,000 | .20 | 200 |
| Shirts | 10 | 10.00 | 100 |
| 1972 nominal GNP | | | $ 400 |

| 1984 | | | |
|---|---|---|---|
| Movies | 100 | $ 4.00 | $ 400 |
| Apples | 500 | .60 | 300 |
| Shirts | 20 | 15.00 | 300 |
| 1984 nominal GNP | | | $1,000 |

$400 to $1,000), the people in this simple economy had only about 25 percent more (an increase from $400 to $500). In nominal terms, the value of goods and services in 1984 is calculated as follows, where P stands for prices and Q stands for quantity:

$P_{84} \times Q_{84} = \$1,000$    *Nominal in 1984*

In real terms, the value of goods and services in 1984 is calculated as:

$P_{72} \times Q_{84} = \$500$    *Real in 1984*

The value of goods and services in 1972 (considered *real* value because 1972 is here used as the base year) is calculated as:

$P_{72} \times Q_{72} = \$400$    *Real in 1972*

---

**Exhibit 6.6**

**Nominal and real GNP in 1984 for a simple economy**

This exhibit shows how the numbers from Exhibit 6.5 can be adjusted to take changing prices into account. The 1984 quantities are multiplied by 1972 prices to get the value of 1984 GNP as it would have been had prices not changed. The total of 1984 quantities valued at 1972 prices is called the real GNP for 1984.

| | 1984 Quantity | 1984 Price | Value at 1984 Price | 1972 Price | Value of 1984 Output at 1972 Price |
|---|---|---|---|---|---|
| Movies | 100 | $ 4.00 | $ 400 | $ 2.00 | $200 |
| Apples | 500 | .60 | 300 | .20 | 100 |
| Shirts | 20 | 15.00 | 300 | 10.00 | 200 |
| Totals | | 1984 nominal GNP = $1,000 | | 1984 real GNP = $500 | |

---

## Price Indexes

In the example covered in Exhibits 6.5 and 6.6, while 1984 nominal GNP rose to a level of $1,000 from a $400 base in 1972, real GNP in 1984 rose only to $500.

The ratio of 1984 nominal GNP to 1984 real GNP provides one possible measure of the rate of price increase between the two years: the reason for the discrepancy between 1984 nominal and real GNP is that the price level doubled between the two years. This measure of the rate of price increase is actually used for some purpose by Canadian national income accountants. The ratio of current year nominal GNP to current year real GNP is the **GNE implicit price deflator** (so called because GNP is measured by the expenditure approach) — known by most economists simply as the **GNE deflator**. It is, in effect, a **weighted average** reflecting changes in the prices of all of the various goods and services of which GNP is composed:

$$\text{GNE deflator} = \frac{\text{Current year output valued at current year prices}}{\text{Current year output valued at base year prices}} \times 100.$$

The GNE deflator is too broad a measure of price change for some purposes, however. To supplement it, Statistics Canada publishes another price index each month, which is a weighted average of the prices of more narrowly defined selections of goods and services.

**GNE implicit price deflator (GNE deflator)** A measure of the price level equal to the ratio of current nominal GNP to current real GNP times 100.

**Weighted average** An average that gives appropriate weights to products in proportion to their relative importance in the total basket of goods purchased.

**Consumer price index (CPI)**
A price index based on a "representative market basket" of about 400 goods and services purchased by urban wage earners. This index is calculated using base year quantities.

*The Consumer Price Index* The index published by Statistics Canada each month is known as the **consumer price index (CPI)**. It differs from the GNE deflator both in the products that are included and in the way the index is constructed. The consumer price index measures the prices of about 400 goods and services purchased by private households in Canadian urban centres with a population of 30,000 or more. The current index is based on a "basket" of goods selected in 1978 and used for the first time in the calculation of the index in 1982. This basket was linked to a previous basket that provided a 1971 basis for the index. Since a fairly constant basket of goods and services is maintained, a continuous price index is possible. Until January 1983, the basis of the index was the prices of 1971. After that date the prices of 1981 formed the basis.

The basket of goods and services typically purchased by consumers is determined through regular family expenditure surveys. Once the basket has been selected, the price of each item in the basket is monitored monthly. Each item is given a "weight," depending on its importance in consumer purchases. The price change of each item multiplied by its weight determines the change in the consumer price index for a given month. The weights are now changed every four years, reflecting changing consumer tastes and buying patterns. Exhibit 6.7 provides a breakdown of the major items contained in the CPI and the weights derived for those items in the year 1967 (which formed the basis for the 1971 index) and the year 1978 (on which the current index is based).

The consumer price index is constructed by using base year quantities rather than current year quantities. The index number is the formula:

$$\text{Price index} = \frac{\text{Value of base year quantities at current year prices}}{\text{Value of base year quantities at base year prices}} \times 100$$

Using base year quantities rather than current year quantities provides an important practical advantage. It means that in order to recalculate the index it is necessary to collect new data only on prices, which are easily available, and not on quantities, which are not quite so readily measured.

| | 1967 | 1978 |
|---|---|---|
| Food | 24.8 | 21.1 |
| At home | 21.0 | 15.5 |
| Away from home | 3.8 | 5.6 |
| Housing | 31.4 | 35.4 |
| Shelter | 17.9 | 20.7 |
| Household operation | 8.5 | 8.7 |
| Furnishing & equipment | 5.0 | 5.9 |
| Clothing | 11.3 | 9.6 |
| Transportation | 15.2 | 16.2 |
| Private transportation | 13.0 | 14.4 |
| Public transportation | 2.2 | 1.9 |
| Health and personal care | 4.5 | 3.7 |
| Recreation, reading & education | 6.9 | 8.6 |
| Tobacco and alcohol | 6.0 | 5.4 |

May not add to totals due to rounding.
Source: Statistics Canada.

**Exhibit 6.7**
**"Weights" of Major Items in the Consumer Price Index**
The consumer price index is calculated by measuring price changes of a wide range of goods and services. The items in a typical consumer basket are given "weights," based on the relative amount spent on each item. Since consumer spending patterns change over time, these weights must be changed periodically. Below are the weights for 1967 and 1978, reflecting the percent of consumer expenditures on major goods and services.

Consequently, Statistics Canada is able to issue up-to-date computations of the consumer price index every month, before data on the GNE implicit price deflator are issued.

**Comparing the CPI and the GNE Deflator** Exhibit 6.8 shows how the consumer price index can be calculated using the data for the simplified economy first displayed in Exhibit 6.5. Notice that the value of the CPI, 237.5, differs from the value of the GNE deflator, 200, calculated from exactly the same underlying data. Which, if either, of the two price indexes is the true measure of change in the price level between the two years?

The reply is that neither the CPI nor the GNE deflator is **the** correct measure of change in the price level. Instead, each is the answer to a different question. The GNE deflator is the answer to the question: how much more did the 1984 output cost at the prices at which it was actually sold than it would have cost if it had been sold at 1972 prices instead? The CPI, in contrast, is the answer to the question: how much more would the 1972 output have cost if it had been sold at 1984 prices instead of at its actual 1972 prices?

Careful inspection of Exhibit 6.5 shows why the answers to the two questions are not the same. In 1972, lots of apples and not very many shirts were produced in comparison to the outputs of 1984. Yet, between the two years, the price of apples increased 300 percent while the price of shirts increased only 150 percent. Because the CPI uses base year quantities, it gives heavy weight to apples, which experienced the greatest price increase, and not much weight to shirts, which experienced only a modest price increase. In contrast, the GNE deflator uses current year quantities, thereby downplaying the importance of apples and emphasizing that of shirts.

---

**Exhibit 6.8**

**Calculation of consumer price index for a simplified economy**

The consumer price index is the base year market basket of goods valued at current year prices, divided by the base year market basket of goods valued at base year prices, multiplied by 100. This exhibit shows how a CPI can be calculated using the data for the simplified economy first given in Exhibit 6.5. The 1972 output cost $400 at the prices at which it was actually sold. If it had been sold at 1984 prices, it would have cost $950. The CPI for 1984 is thus 237.5.

| Good | 1972 Quantity | 1972 Price | Value of 1972 Quantity at 1972 Price | 1984 Price | Value of 1972 Quantity at 1984 Price |
|------|------|------|------|------|------|
| Movies | 50 | $ 2.00 | $100 | $ 4.00 | $200 |
| Apples | 1,000 | .20 | 200 | .60 | 600 |
| Shirts | 10 | 10.00 | 100 | 15.00 | 150 |
| Totals | | | $400 | | $950 |

$$CPI = \frac{\$950}{\$400} \times 100 = 237.5$$

## The Importance of the Consumer Price Index

The consumer price index (CPI) is the most widely used price series produced by Statistics Canada. Its importance derives from its use in measuring the purchasing power of the consumer dollar. All income earners would like to increase their dollar income each year, but what they are most interested in knowing is whether such dollar increases are sufficient to maintain or increase their purchasing power. This cannot be known without a measuring stick such as the CPI. In fact, the purchasing power of the dollar is related inversely to movements in the CPI. According to the CPI, the price of a typical basket of goods in Canada rose from $100 in 1971 to $249.70 in January 1982. This means that prices rose by 149.7 percent during that period, and anyone whose income did not rise by at least 149.7 percent during that same period actually lost purchasing power. Another way of expressing this is to say that the purchasing power of a dollar in January 1982 compared to the 1971 dollar was $0.40

$$(100 \text{ cents} \times \frac{100.00}{249.7} = 40 \text{ cents}).$$

Because of its usefulness in measuring the real purchasing power of the dollar the CPI serves as the bottom line in many salary and wage negotiations; workers insist on getting increases at least equal to the CPI. Many collective agreements contain clauses which guarantee that wages will increase in line with increases in the CPI. Similar cost-of-living-adjustments (COLAs) are often incorporated into pension schemes. Federal social insurance payments, such as Old Age Security, the Canada Pension Plan, and Family Allowances, are indexed to the CPI. The federal government also adjusts income tax exemption levels on the basis of the CPI.

It should be noted that the CPI measures price increases experienced by a sample population in selected areas of the country, so that it may not match the experience of other groups in other places. It also assumes, by maintaining a "fixed" basket of goods, that there is no quality change in goods and that consumers do not switch to cheaper substitutes for goods and services in the basket. Because substitutes *are* made, the CPI may overstate the price inflation experienced by many consumers. Studies indicate, however, that this factor is not very significant.

What the CPI and the GNE deflator do best is to destroy any illusions that we may have about the apparently rapid growth of output and income in a country like ours. Much of the "growth" is caused by price increases. Exhibit 6.9 indicates that per capita GNP (the Gross National Product divided by the population) increased from $4,379 in 1971 to $13,581 in 1981. In other words, it more than tripled in that eleven-year period. This would appear to be a tremendous achievement, giving the average Canadian more than three times as much purchasing power. However, almost all of the increase was due to price inflation. When the GNP figures are translated into real terms, by "deflating" them with the GNE deflator, the performance of the Canadian economy is much less remarkable. In that eleven-year period, real GNP per capita increased from $4,379 to only $5,543, or by about 27 percent. In two years, 1975 and 1980, it actually declined. In terms of purchasing power, therefore, the average Canadian is

**Exhibit 6.9**

**Per capita GNP before and after adjustment by the GNE deflator, 1971–1981**

Largely because of price inflation the per capita GNP (GNP divided by the population) more than tripled between 1971 and 1981. In real terms, however, – after nominal GNP per capita has been deflated by the price index, – per capita GNP in 1981 was only 1.3 times that of 1971.

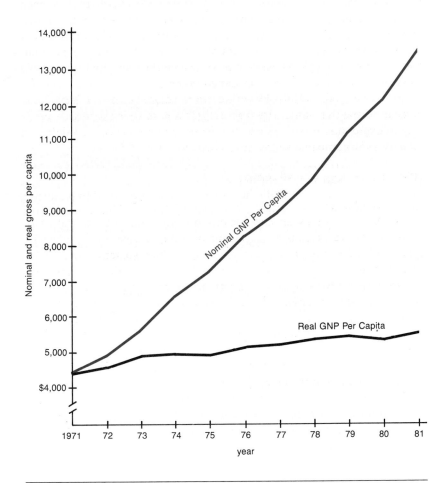

Source: Department of Finance, *Economic Review*, April 1982, pp. 116, 119, and 121.

not much better off in 1981 than in 1971. Without price indices like the CPI and the GNE deflator, we might easily be fooled into thinking that our economy had gone through a decade of enormous growth.

## CONCLUSIONS

We have now looked in some detail at the ways nominal and real GNP are measured. We have also learned how the consumer price index and the GNE deflator are used to change nominal values to real values. In conclusion, it will be well to give some idea of the limitations of GNP measurements. Several points need to be made in this connection.

First, much economic activity is not included in GNP at all. There are whole industries—gambling, bootlegging, narcotics, prostitution—whose multi-billion-dollar sales go unreported because they are illegal. Some legal economic activity also goes unreported for purposes of tax evasion. Other market activity—such as babysitting and casual yard work—goes unreported because it is too scattered to keep track of, even though the total sums involved may be quite large. The size of the underground market economy is surely large—perhaps as much as 10 percent of reported GNP. Even this does not count the enormous amount of nonmarket economic activity that takes place, including such highly valuable services as unpaid housekeeping and child care.

Second, even if real GNP did accurately measure the level of market and nonmarket economic activity, it would still not be a very good measure of welfare or human satisfaction. For example, the way income is distributed may affect the level of satisfaction. The level of real GNP per capita does not directly reflect the number of families in poverty or the relative income status of upper- and lower-income groups.

Third, fewer and fewer labor hours per worker are devoted to producing real GNP as the years go by. It is plausible to think that more leisure will cause satisfaction to rise. Leisure is evidently a scarce economic good valued by workers. However, the substantial increase in the leisure of the Canadian worker in this century is not explicitly reflected in GNP calculations.

Fourth, real GNP is a measure only of currently produced goods and services. Satisfaction also comes from durable consumer goods produced in the past that are still providing services. Surely, the larger the present stock of consumer durables, the higher is satisfaction.

Fifth, the market prices at which goods are sold do not accurately reflect costs or benefits affecting third parties not directly involved in the exchange. For example, environmental pollution caused by productive activities detracts from welfare. Pollution adversely affects people who are neither buyers nor sellers of the goods whose production created it. Like several of the nonmarket goods discussed above that affect satisfaction, pollution is not entered into GNP calculations. Unlike those goods, however, pollution is a "bad"—an output with a negative value. Annual additions to the amount of pollution should, in principle, be subtracted from GNP; but practical problems make this adjustment impossible.[1]

Sixth, an increase in output does not necessarily imply an increase in welfare, even if none of the problems yet mentioned is there. An unseasonably cold winter, for example, or an epidemic of infectious disease could cause the purchases of heating fuel or medical services to rise dramatically. Yet the resulting increases in real GNP would hardly represent an increase in satisfaction! Wartime defense expenditures provide another example of the lack of direct correspondence between output and welfare. We could argue that in principle these kinds of expenditures are for the maintenance of the stock of human beings and should be treated just like

---

[1]The best one can probably do is to subtract from GNP the total expenditures made solely to abate or prevent pollution. Even after such cleanup expenditures, however, enough pollution remains to adversely affect welfare.

investment expenditures that offset depreciation of the capital stock; that is, they should be subtracted from real GNP to get real new output. Putting this idea into practice, however, would be difficult.

Finally, many aspects of human welfare are not related at all to the flow of economic goods and services or to the economic satisfaction obtained from them. Everyone would agree that people do not live by bread alone, but obtaining agreement about exactly what else is important would not be easy. How important are unspoiled natural areas, unalienating work, loving human contact, social justice, income equality, economic growth, and freedom? These are normative questions that each person must answer individually. The economist could never hope to lump these social and economic conditions into an objective measure of social welfare.

For all these reasons, then, real GNP should never be interpreted as a measure of social welfare. Still, it is not completely worthless. It provides a roughly accurate picture of the economy's annual production of final goods and services, which, of course, is all that it was ever intended to do. As will be seen, it is valuable for several purposes even given its limitations.

## SUMMARY

1. Official measurements of national product are made using the expenditure approach. Gross national expenditure (GNE) is obtained by adding together the values of all expenditures on newly produced goods and services.
2. National income is officially estimated by the income approach, which means adding together the values of all income earned by households. In the real world, certain adjustments must be made to get GNE and national income to fit, even though for elementary theoretical purposes, the two are considered equal. The difference between GNE and national income is equal to depreciation plus indirect business taxes plus the residual error of estimate.
3. National income measures all income earned by households, while personal income measures all the income they actually receive. To go from national income to personal income means subtracting corporate profits taxes, and undistributed corporate profits, then adding transfer payments. If personal taxes are subtracted from personal income, the result is personal disposable income.
4. Measurements of aggregate economic activity can be made in real terms in order to adjust for changes in prices. Real GNP or GNE means the total value of current year quantities of output evaluated in terms of the prices of some base year. The GNE deflator is the ratio of current year nominal GNE to current year real GNE.
5. Real GNE does not attempt to be a measure of welfare or satisfaction; it is only a measure of the output of goods and services. It does not do even that job perfectly because of sampling error, omitted items, and biases in price indexes. It is important to remember that a great many things contribute to overall human welfare that are not in any way measured by GNE.

6. The Consumer Price Index (CPI) and the GNE deflator measure changes in prices over a period of time. They are especially useful in determining how much of the growth in output (measured by market prices) is "real" and how much is merely due to changes in prices.

## DISCUSSION QUESTIONS

1. In 1971, the base year for the consumer price index, average earnings of construction workers were $188.27 per week. By 1981, earnings in construction had reached $521.64 per week, but the CPI stood at 236.9. What were real earnings in 1981, stated in 1971 dollars?

2. If all parents in Canada traded off child care services with their neighbors, received a wage for doing their neighbors' work, and hence did none of their own child care, what would happen to GNP as measured by national income accountants? Who, if anyone, would be better off with a situation where everyone got paid? Explain.

3. Do you think transfer payments should be included in the measure of GNP? Explain.

4. In 1933, net fixed business investment was equal to about −$300 million. How could this have been possible?

5. A firm gets rid of its inventory of $10,000 worth of shoes by having a sale to the public. What happens to GNP in this case? What happens to each of its components?

6. If the government increased the unemployment insurance deduction, what would happen to GNP, net national income, and personal disposable income?

7. Determine whether each of the following expenditures of an individual's own earnings is consumption, saving, investment, or something else:
   a. Purchase of a new home.
   b. Purchase of a new automobile for cash.
   c. Payment of a monthly installment on a loan.
   d. Purchase of an item of clothing for $4 plus $.20 sales tax.
   e. Purchase of common stock.
   f. Giving the individual's children a weekly allowance.
   g. Payment of tuition for additional education.
   h. A tip at a restaurant.

8. The following table shows output and prices for a simple economy in 1975 and 1985. Use the data to calculate both the CPI and the GNP deflator for 1985, using 1975 as the base year.

|  | 1975 Quantity | 1975 Price | 1985 Quantity | 1985 Price |
|---|---|---|---|---|
| Cars | 1,000 | $ 2,500 | 2,000 | $ 4,000 |
| Houses | 100 | 20,000 | 150 | 40,000 |
| Hospital services (total days of care) | 500 | 100 | 550 | 250 |

# THE GOALS OF STABILIZATION POLICY AND THE PERFORMANCE OF THE CANADIAN ECONOMY

## WHAT YOU WILL LEARN IN THIS CHAPTER

*The four major goals of stabilization policy are full employment, price stability, growth of real output, and balanced regional development. This chapter reviews the past performance of the economy in terms of each of these goals, and concludes with a discussion of important interrelationships among them. What might be termed a fifth stabilization goal—balance of payments equilibrium—is treated separately in a later chapter.*

## FOR REVIEW

*Here are some important terms and concepts that will be put to use in this chapter. If you do not understand them, review them before proceeding.*
- *Production possibility frontier (Chapter 2)*
- *Marginal tax rate (Chapter 4)*
- *Stocks and flows (Chapter 5)*
- *National income and product (Chapters 5 and 6)*
- *Price indexes including the GNE deflator (Chapter 6)*

---

Economic stabilization policy, one of the major functions of government listed in Chapter 4, can be broken down into the pursuit of four more specific policy goals: full employment, price stability, growth of real output, and balanced regional development.

## FULL EMPLOYMENT

### Definition and Performance

The goal of maintaining full employment has a simple meaning for most Canadians: ensuring the availability of jobs for people who seek them. This simple idea is what the federal government appears to have had in mind when it declared in the **White Paper on Employment and Income of 1945** that it had unequivocally adopted a high and stable level of employment and income as a major aim of government policy. This policy was

**White Paper of 1945**
Committed the federal government to the maintenance of stable, full-employment economic growth.

developed largely in response to the tragically high unemployment rates of the Great Depression in the 1930s. World War II had brought the depression to an end, but there were grave fears that, with the return of peace, the economy might slide into another depression. For this reason, Parliament agreed in principle to pursue policies promoting economic growth and full employment.

Over the years, however, pursuing the goal of full employment has become less a matter of this general principle, and more a numbers game. The particular number that is now the focus of employment policy is the unemployment rate, as measured by Statistics Canada and published in a monthly bulletin, *The Labour Force*. To calculate this rate, each month Statistics Canada first surveys about 55,000 Canadian households to determine how many Canadians are members of the **labor force**. The labor force is made up of those persons 15 years and over who at the time of the survey were either *employed* (which means, among other things, that they were working at least one hour per week as paid employees) or *unemployed* (actively but unsuccessfully looking for work). The **unemployment rate** is the percentage of people in the labor force who are actively looking for employment but who are not currently employed. Persons under 15, adults not actively seeking employment, military personnel, and certain institutionalized persons are counted as outside the labor force, and thus as neither employed nor unemployed.

Clearly, the goal of "jobs for people who want jobs" implies that the officially measured unemployment rate should be kept low. But how low is low? Because of the way the unemployment rate is defined, a zero unemployment rate is impossible. The reason is that even when the economy is performing as smoothly and efficiently as possible, there are a certain number of people who have voluntarily quit their jobs to look for better

**Labor force** All members of the noninstitutionalized civilian population over the age of 15 who are either officially employed or looking for employment.

**Unemployment rate** Percentage of the labor force who are actively looking for employment but who are not employed.

---

**Exhibit 7.1**

**Unemployment in Canada since 1950**

The Economic Council of Canada originally set a 3.5 percent unemployment rate target for the Canadian eocnomy. In the 1970s this target was increased to 4.5 percent and then to 6 percent. In fact, however, unemployment rates below 4.5 percent have been achieved in only nine of the past thirty two years, and rates below 6 percent in only 19 years.

Source: M.C. Urquhart and K.A.H. Buckley, *Historical Statistics of Canada* (Toronto: Macmillan, 1965), and Department of Finance, *Economic Review,* April 1982 ones, or who have entered the labor force for the first time and have not yet found a job. The process of job search, through which workers are matched to the jobs best suited for them, takes time. During the search process, such workers are counted as unemployed, even though their unemployment is voluntary and not always a source of great hardship. Some economists feel that current social welfare programs make it rational behavior for some people to declare themselves unemployed even when jobs are available and that the generous provisions of the Unemployment Insurance Act of 1971 may have increased this type of "voluntary" unemployment.

The White Paper of 1945 did not specify a particular employment target, and subsequent governments have been equally loathe to be precise. However, the White Paper stated that "in setting as its aim a high and stable level of employent and income, the Government is not selecting a lower target than 'full employment'"![1] The Economic Council of Canada has tried to define the percentage of unemployment that is consistent with such **full employment.** It originally chose an "acceptable" unemployment rate of 3.5 percent; by 1972 the target rate had been increased to 4.5 percent and in 1979 to 6 percent. At the First Ministers' Conferences in February and November 1978, the federal government set a goal of 5.5 percent unemployment rate for the early 1980s. Exhibit 7.1 shows the target rates set by the Economic Council of Canada and the actual unemployment rates, from 1950 to 1982.

> **Full employment** The greatest possible utilization of the labor force consistent with price stability and allowing for unavoidable unemployment of workers between jobs.

After averaging about 7.5 percent in the three years 1979 to 1981, Canada's unemployment rose sharply in 1982. About 500,000 jobs were lost that year, and by December the unemployment rate had climbed to 12.8 percent, the highest since the Great Depression of the 1930s. About 90 percent of the jobs were lost in goods-producing industries, in which male workers predominate. This caused the male unemployment rate to increase much more sharply than the female rate, a reversal of the usual pattern. Economic forecasters in the early 1980s saw no significant drop in the unemployment rate for several years.

### Distribution of the Burden of Unemployment

The burdens of unemployment, and hence the potential benefits of a full employment policy, are unevenly distributed over the population. In December 1982, for example, the unemployment rate for Canada was 12.8 percent. However, the rate for young people, aged 15–24, was 24 percent for males and 17.3 percent for females, while for those 25 years and over it was only 10.2 percent for both men and women. For married males the rate is usually lower than for married females. However, at the end of 1982, for males in general the rate was 13.3 percent, while for females it was 12.1 percent, a reversal of the normal pattern.

Although higher education is no longer considered an absolute guarantee against unemployment, persons with a university degree have an

---

[1]Canadian Trade Committee, *Canadian Economic Policy since the War,* 1966, p. 136.

unemployment rate of less than one third of those with only a high school certificate.

The unemployment rate also varied considerably from one region of the country to another. It ranged from a high of 18.1 percent in Newfoundland to a low of 7.3 percent in Saskatchewan. The provinces of Alberta, Saskatchewan, Manitoba, and Ontario had unemployment rates below the national average, while for all the other provinces the rate was above the national average.

The person least likely to be unemployed in Canada, therefore, may be a married male with a university degree living in Saskatchewan. The person most likely to be unemployed is a young, unmarried individual with little formal schooling living in Newfoundland.

Because of such extreme variations by region, sex, age, education, and marital status (not to mention race and other factors that are normally not included in the surveys), it is extremely difficult to deal with unemployment through national economic policies. This point should be kept in mind when appropriate economic policies are discussed in Chapters 17 to 19.

## PRICE STABILITY
### Definition and Performance

In addition to setting unemployment targets, the Economic Council of Canada has suggested goals for price increases in the economy. In its First Annual Review of 1964, the council defined reasonable price stability as a maximum increase of 2 percent per year in the gross national expenditure price deflator. This seemed to be a reasonable objective in the light of the experience of the 1950s, but it turned out to be quite unrealistic for the 1960s and 1970s. In the 1960s, the average rate of price increase was 3.2 percent per year. The council, therefore, in its Ninth Annual Review of 1972, increased the maximum price target to 3.0 percent for the period 1973 to 1975. This goal also proved to be elusive: the GNE deflator rose by 8.4 percent in 1973, by 13.8 percent in 1974, and by 9.7 percent in 1975. Exhibit 7.2, which measures Canada's experience with inflation by means of the Consumer Price Index, rather than by the GNE deflator (the two generally move in very similar ways), shows clearly how poor our performance has been when measured against these unofficial targets. This was especially the case in the 1970s.

After consumer prices rose by 10.9 percent in 1974 and were rising by about 11 percent in 1975, the federal government decided, in October of 1975, to control prices by setting up an Anti-Inflation Board. This board was given the power to limit wages and profits, and its stated objective was to use these indirect measures to hold price increases down to 10 percent in 1975, 8 percent in 1976, 6 percent in 1977, and 4 percent in 1978.

Even such drastic action failed to achieve the government's objectives. As Exhibit 7.2 indicates, consumer prices increased by 10.8 percent in 1975. The annual increase was limited to 7.5 percent in 1976, but instead of falling to 6 percent in 1977, the inflation rate rose to 8 percent, and in 1978 consumer prices increased by 9.0 percent instead of by 4 percent. In 1981 they rose by 12.9 percent. In view of this performance, the federal govern-

**Exhibit 7.2**

**Inflation in Canada since 1950**

The Economic Council of Canada set an inflation-rate target for Canada in 1964 of 2 percent. In 1972 the target was raised to 3 percent, and by the late 1970s it was acknowledged that rates of less than 6 percent were highly unlikely in the near future. The Exhibit shows how the actual inflation rate has exceeded the successive targets.

Source: M.C. Urquhart and K.A.H. Buckley, *Historical Statistics of Canada* (Toronto: Macmillan, 1965), and Department of Finance, *Economic Review*, April 1980.

ment target of a 3.5 percent inflation rate for the 1980s, as announced in November 1978, was very ambitious indeed. The Economic Council of Canada admitted as much, by noting in 1982 that it was highly unlikely that the inflation rate would fall below 8 percent before 1984.

A careful comparison of Exhibits 7.1 and 7.2 reveals an even more distressing feature of our recent macroeconomic record. Until 1968, inflation and unemployment tended to alternate. Only in one year, 1957, was there both unemployment of more than 4.5 percent and inflation of more than 3 percent. Since 1968, however, both goals have been exceeded in every year, with the exception of 1971.

## Who Gains and Who Loses from Inflation?

As in the case of unemployment, the burdens of inflation and the potential benefits of a policy of price stability are not distributed equally among different groups in the population. Various income groups fare very differently in times of inflation. Determining exactly who gains and who loses from inflation, however, is by no means an easy problem. One way to examine the distributional effects of inflation is to look separately at its effects on wage and salary income, transfer payments, interest income, and wealth.

**Wage and Salary Income**  Because wages and salaries rise roughly in step with prices, real income from these sources is among the areas least affected by inflation. For example, between 1971 and the end of 1981, while

**Indexing** The practice of automatically adjusting wages, salaries, or other payments to compensate for changes in the price level.

the consumer price index rose from its base of 100 to a level of 236.9, average earnings in manufacturing rose from $137.64 per week to $355.77 per week, more than keeping pace. In a number of industries, wages are **indexed** — adjusted automatically for changes in the cost of living through escalator clauses. Not all wage and salary earners are equally well protected from inflation. As the inflation rate rose in 1973–74, for example, workers organized in labor unions in larger enterprises were able to increase their wages slightly more than the average. However, some unions were tied into long-run contracts that made it difficult for them to adjust their wages to rising prices. Workers in the forestry, mining, transport, and financial sectors were able to get wage increases larger than the price increases, while those in manufacturing, commercial, and service sectors experienced a reduction in real wages.[2] It should also be noted that food prices have risen much more rapidly in the past decade than other prices, so that poor families who spend a larger proportion of their income on food than other families have suffered more from inflation. Between 1971 and 1981 the food component of the consumer price index went from 100 to 290.4, considerably more than the average.

**Transfer Payments** Over the last decade, total transfer payments have increased much more rapidly than the rate of inflation. Much of the increase, however, can be attributed to changes in social policy not directly related to inflation one way or the other. The relevant question is not whether transfer payments to individuals have increased in real terms but whether they have increased as much as they would have if price stability had been maintained.

There is no way of answering this question with certainty. In many cases, however, recipients of transfer payments appear at least as well protected against inflation as wage and salary earners. One major reason is the indexing of social welfare benefits, which now automatically keep pace with rising prices.

For example, between 1965 and 1975, while prices increased by 47 percent, and the average working family increased its income by slightly more than 70 percent, retired persons dependent completely on public old-age security pensions enjoyed an 85 percent increase in benefits. Persons receiving benefits from private pension plans generally did not receive increases. As a result, the real value of their pensions fell to less than half between 1969 and 1979. In addition to substantial increases in government transfer payments, an increasing proportion of all transfers is now being paid in kind (that is, in the form of free or subsidized housing, medical care, and so forth) rather than in cash. Although the spread of in-kind transfers may not consciously have been intended to protect the poor from inflation, it has had that effect.

**Interest Income — Debtors versus Creditors** What does inflation do to the real income of creditors, who receive interest income from bonds, mortgages, and the like, and to the real income of debtors, who pay this

---

[2]Economic Council of Canada, *Thirteenth Annual Review: The Inflation Dilemma*, 1976, pp. 25, 27.

interest? Although the effects are somewhat more complex than for wage income or transfer payments, they are worth looking at in some detail.

*The Traditional View*   The traditional view of the matter is that inflation injures creditors and aids debtors. Suppose, for example, that I borrow $100 from you today, promising to repay $105 next year. If there is no inflation during the year, I get use of the funds for the year, and you get a $5 increase in your purchasing power. But suppose that during the year the price level goes up 10 percent. In that case, I get the use of the funds for the year, and what is more, I get to pay you back in depreciated dollars. The $105 I give you next year will buy you only as much then as $95 will today. Your real income is negative. I, the debtor, am benefited by inflation; you, the creditor, are hurt.

*Expected and Unexpected Inflation*   It is now recognized, however, that this traditional view of the effects of inflation on debtors and creditors is seriously incomplete, in that it does not distinguish between *unexpected* and *expected* inflation. The example just given implicitly assumes that neither I, the debtor, nor you, the creditor expected any inflation at the time the loan was made. Suppose instead that we both had expected a 10 percent increase in the price level between the time the loan was made and the time it was repaid. You would not then have loaned me the $100 in return for a promise to repay just $105 at the end of the year. Instead, you would have insisted on a repayment of something like $115: $10 to compensate you for the decline in the purchasing power of the $100 principal plus the $5 you originally wanted as real return for relinquishing use of the funds for a year. I, in turn, would have agreed to those terms, expecting that $115 in the next year's depreciated dollars would be no more than the equivalent, in terms of real purchasing power, of the $105 I would have been willing to repay in a noninflationary world. In real terms, then, correctly anticipated inflation is neutral between debtor and creditor.

*Nominal versus Real Interest Rates*   The example just given shows why it is necessary in an inflationary world to distinguish three separate interest rate concepts. The first, the **nominal rate of interest**, means the rate of interest measured in the ordinary way in current dollars. The second, the **expected real rate of interest**, means the nominal rate of interest minus the expected rate of inflation. And the third, the **realized real rate of interest**, means the nominal rate of interest minus the actual rate of inflation.

If no inflation is expected and none actually occurs, all three rates of interest are equal. If inflation does occur and is accurately anticipated, the expected and realized real rates of interest are equal, and both are less than the nominal rate. In the example given above, for instance, an accurately anticipated rate of inflation of 10 percent transformed a 15 percent nominal rate of interest into a 5 percent expected and realized real rate of interest.

If inflation does occur and is not accurately expected, the expected and realized real rates of interest will differ from one another. To extend the example, suppose that you had loaned me the $100 in question at a 15 percent nominal rate in the expectation of a 10 percent rate of inflation but

**Nominal rate of interest** The rate of interest measured in the ordinary way, without adjustment for inflation.

**Expected rate of interest** The nominal rate of interest minus the expected rate of inflation.

**Realized real rate of interest** The nominal rate of interest minus the actual rate of inflation.

that the actual rate of inflation turned out to be 12 percent. Instead of earning your expected real rate of interest of 5 percent (the 15 percent nominal rate minus 10 percent expected inflation), you would actually have earned a realized rate of interest of only 3 percent (the 15 percent nominal rate minus 12 percent actual inflation).

The distinction between nominal and real rates of interest can be used to express precisely the distributional effects of inflation as between debtors and creditors. Accurately expected inflation is neutral between creditors and debtors, because the parties will fully adjust the nominal rate of interest they agree on to take the expected inflation into account. If the actual rate of inflation exceeds the expected rate, debtors will gain at the expense of creditors, because the realized real rate of interest will fall below the expected real rate. If the actual rate of inflation falls short of the expected rate, creditors will gain at the expense of debtors, because the realized real rate will exceed the expected real rate. Note that the traditional view of inflation fits into these generalizations as a special case that applies when the expected rate of inflation is zero.

**Inflation and Wealth** A complete picture of the distributional effects of inflation must consider not only its effects on flows of income to individuals but also its effects on the same individuals' stocks of wealth. The effects of inflation on wealth very much depend on the form in which that wealth is held.

The one group of the population that most clearly benefited from the inflation of the 1970s consisted of those people who had most of their personal wealth tied up in their own homes. In fact, most such people actually benefited in two ways. First, the market value of their houses, at least in most areas of the country, not only kept pace with inflation but outstripped it. Second, many homeowners had long-term, low-interest mortgages negotiated during the 1950s and 1960s. The unexpected increase in inflation during the 1970s benefited them as debtors, allowing them to pay off their mortgages in depreciated dollars. By the early 1980s, house prices have levelled off, and in 1981 to 1982 they fell sharply in some cities. At the same time, renegotiated mortgage rates climbed sharply, to more than 20 percent in 1981, so that for a time homeowners were victims rather than beneficiaries of inflation.

People who held their wealth in common stocks fared very poorly during the inflationary 1970s. This came as a major surprise. For generations, investment advisers had regarded it as dogma that corporate stocks were a sound hedge against inflation. Their reasoning was simple and persuasive. A share of common stock represents a share of ownership of the firm that issues it. If prices double, the firm's costs of doing business will double, but so should its revenues, the prices of the things it sells, the value of its plant and equipment, its profits, its dividends, and so on. The market price of the stocks should thus also be expected to double, leaving the stockholder no worse off as a result of the inflation.

Somewhere toward the end of the 1960s, however, something went wrong. Inflation accelerated, but the stock market failed to respond. The reasons are complex and not yet fully understood, but the facts are clear. By the end of the 1970s, stock prices were fluctuating around an average level no higher in nominal terms than the level they had reached in the mid-1960s. People who had kept their money in the stock market, on the average, lost more than half their real wealth. By the early 1980s, the stock market was recovering; by 1983, prices began to exceed previous high levels.

### Effects of Inflation on Business and Government

What can happen to corporation profits during a period of sudden inflation is illustrated in Exhibit 7.3. During the rapid inflation of 1972–74, Canadian corporations were able to increase both their before- and after-tax profits by much more than the rate of inflation, and at a considerably faster pace than workers were able to increase their wages and salaries. Apparently business firms were able to react more swiftly than workers to the opportunities presented by increased demand in the economy. Since profit levels had been low for a few years before 1972, the 1972 increase might be seen as an overdue return to normal profit rates, but the sharp increases in 1973 and 1974 indicate that many business firms were put into an unusually favorable profit position by rising inflation. By 1975, the picture had changed somewhat. High profit levels were maintained, but profits before taxes increased by only 1.8 percent, while profits after taxes declined by 4.6 percent. At the same time, wages and salaries were finally adjusting to high inflation rates, increasing by 14.2 percent in 1975. It was at this juncture of stable or declining profits and rapidly increasing worker income, that the government, in October 1975, imposed income controls. It has seemed to labor union leaders, and some economists, that the government timed its actions at the most convenient time for business—when prospects for further profit increases were dim—and at a bad time for labor —when renegotiated contracts were just beginning to catch up to the high inflation of the previous few years.

The various levels of government are also affected by inflation. Our federal and provincial governments benefit directly from inflation, because the progressive personal and corporate income taxes which they levy rise steadily with inflation-induced income and profit increases.

---

**Exhibit 7.3**

Percentage change in corporation profits
(and average weekly wages and salaries)

|  | 1972 | 1973 | 1974 | 1975 |
|---|---|---|---|---|
| Corporate profits percentage change before taxes | 24.4 | 42.8 | 28.5 | 1.8 |
| Corporate profits percentage change after taxes | 28.9 | 50.2 | 24.5 | −4.6 |
| Percentage change in average weekly wages and salaries | 8.4 | 7.5 | 11.0 | 14.2 |

Source: Canadian Imperial Bank of Commerce, *Commercial Letter*, No. 4, 1977, p. 5.

Since 1974, however, personal income taxes have been indexed against inflationary effects so that most—though not all—of the bias has been removed from that particular tax, although at the time of writing, the federal government is proposing a partial removal of this concession. Even with indexing, government revenues increase more rapidly than normal in times of inflation. Like all debtors, governments also gain during inflation from a decline in real interest rates. It has been estimated that the federal government gained more than $3 billion dollars in the years 1973–75 through declines, caused by inflation, in the real burden of their debt.[3] In the early 1980s, however, debtors, including governments, generally fared badly, as nominal interest rates went to 20 percent and beyond, and real interest rates were 7 percent and more. Governments must also, of course, pay more in wages and salaries and other costs during inflationary periods.

It will be important to keep the distributional effects of inflation in mind in succeeding chapters as various theories of inflation and proposed anti-inflationary policies are discussed. For the moment, though, attention can be turned to the third major goal of macroeconomic policy —economic growth.

## ECONOMIC GROWTH
### Growth of Potential GNP

Economic growth means the growth of opportunities to satisfy economic wants. At any one time, economic opportunities are limited. Labor, natural resources, and capital are scarce. Their scarcity, together with the state of technological knowledge, limits production possibilities. Not all the goods and services desired can be produced at once.

As time passes, though, the range of possibilities expands. Capital accumulates, and new resources are found. New methods of production make it possible to get more output from each unit of input. People still will not be able to have everything at once, but they can have more things at once than before.

**Growth and the Production Possibility Frontier**  The production possibility frontier, first introduced in Chapter 2, provides a convenient graphical method of representing economic growth. Exhibit 7.4 shows production possibility frontiers for an economy producing only two goods, which will be called "guns" and "butter." "Guns" in this case represent items that do not necessarily improve the living standard of the consumer, while "butter" represents those items that do improve the living standard of the average Canadian.

In any single year, total output is constrained by the production possibility frontier. Over time, however, as new resources become available and as technology improves, the frontier expands outward. Exhibit 7.4 shows four successive production possibility frontiers, each permitting a greater potential real output.

---

[3]Economic Council of Canada, *Thirteenth Annual Review: The Inflation Dilemma*, 1976, p. 71.

**Exhibit 7.4**
**The process of economic growth**
Economic growth can be represented as an outward expansion of the production possibility frontier. In any one year, getting more "guns" means giving up some "butter," as in a movement from B to A. Over time, however, growth could give more of both guns and butter, as in a movement from A to C, D, and E.

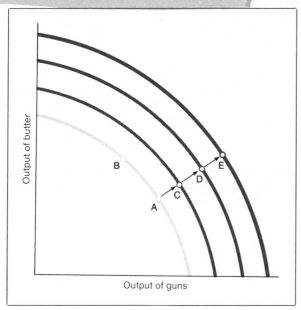

**Actual versus Potential Real Output** In practice, real output may not actually expand exactly in step with the outward shift in the production possibility frontier. Remember that, in any given year, the economy may operate inside the production possibility frontier if resources are not fully employed. Economists use the term **potential real GNP** (or **potential real output**) to indicate the level of real output that the economy could achieve if resources were fully employed. If factors of production are not fully employed, actual output is said to lag behind potential output. Given normal improvements in technology and the growth of the labor force, output in Canada could have grown at least 4 percent annually between 1974 and 1981, whereas it actually increased at an average annual rate of only 2.8 percent.

**Potential real GNP (potential real output)** The level of real GNP that the economy could, in principle, produce if resources were fully employed

## The Growth Record

Economic growth is measured in terms of real gross national product. Although real GNP is not a perfect measure of our ability to satisfy wants, or even of output, it is the best measure we have. In Chapter 6, Exhibit 6.9 shows the growth of per capita real GNP in Canada from 1971 to 1981. This growth rate was quite impressive in earlier years, but has fallen off badly more recently. However, Exhibit 7.5 shows that Canadian economic growth in the 1970s has been relatively good by comparison with that of many other countries. The only country listed that had a better growth rate than Canada over the whole period 1974–1981 was Japan.

**Exhibit 7.5**

**Rates of real GNP growth in seven major countries, 1974–1981**

GDP is used as an alternative to GNP by some countries to measure their output. It stands for Gross Domestic Product, or the value of final goods and services produced within a country (''domestically'') as opposed to Gross National Product, which is based on production by Canadian nationals, regardless of whether it takes place domestically or elsewhere.

| | Average 1974–81 | 1974 | 1975 | 1976 | 1977 | 1979 | 1979 | 1980 | 1981 |
|---|---|---|---|---|---|---|---|---|---|
| | | | | | (per cent) | | | | |
| Growth of real GNP/GDP | | | | | | | | | |
| United States | 2.4 | −0.6 | −1.1 | 5.4 | 5.5 | 4.8 | 3.2 | −0.2 | 2.0 |
| Japan | 3.8 | −1.0 | 2.3 | 5.3 | 5.3 | 5.0 | 5.5 | 4.2 | 3.8 |
| Germany | 1.9 | 0.5 | −1.8 | 5.2 | 3.0 | 3.2 | 4.4 | 1.8 | −1.0 |
| France | 2.6 | 3.2 | 0.2 | 5.2 | 3.1 | 3.7 | 3.5 | 1.2 | 0.5 |
| United Kingdom | 0.5 | −1.0 | −0.6 | 3.6 | 1.3 | 3.3 | 1.4 | −1.8 | −2.0 |
| Italy | 2.5 | 4.1 | −3.6 | 5.9 | 1.9 | 2.7 | 4.9 | 4.0 | 0.0 |
| Canada | 2.8 | 3.6 | 1.2 | 5.5 | 2.1 | 3.7 | 3.0 | 0.0 | 3.0 |
| Seven major countries | 2.4 | 0.3 | −0.5 | 5.2 | 4.1 | 4.0 | 3.5 | 1.0 | 1.2 |
| Total OECD | 2.4 | 0.9 | −0.4 | 4.9 | 3.7 | 3.8 | 3.4 | 1.2 | 1.3 |

Source: Department of Finance, Economic Review, April 1982, p. 106.

## Is Economic Growth Really Desirable?

For many years, everyone thought economic growth was a good thing. The only debates about growth took place between people who thought that the present pace was good enough and those who wanted government action to increase the growth rate. Now things are different.

Today, the people who are satisfied with the record of growth and those who would like to step up the pace have been forced into a defensive alliance. On the other side are two groups. One is made up of people who think that further economic growth is impossible or will soon be so. The other is made up of those who think that further growth may be possible but who do not want it. The matter is important enough to make it worth giving at least an outline of the main issues here.

**Questioning the Desirability of Growth** Look first at the argument that further economic growth is not desirable whether or not it is possible. The heart of this argument is the perfectly valid proposition that GNP is not a measure of human welfare. The trouble, it is said, is that growth of GNP can be offset by a decline in the quality of life. These fears can be expressed in the form of a parable.

Imagine a peaceful little country with a per capita GNP of $100. All the GNP is produced by the women, who work the fields in the morning and relax in the afternoon. The men do nothing but sit around and play cards and drink tea all day. Suppose now that an enterprising foreign company sets up a soap factory and puts all of the men to work. Each man can make $40 worth of soap per year. Previously there was no market for soap in this pastoral nation, but now the soap factory's boilers belch black coal smoke that soils everyone's curtains. The entire output of the soap factory is sold to local housewives, who now spend all their afternoons at the laundromat.

What has happened to the GNP of this country? As any economist will explain, it has gone up by 20 percent to $120 per capita. Farm output has not fallen, and industrial production of $20 per capita has been added. But what has happened to the level of well-being of the people of this country? They have no more to eat than before, their curtains wear out faster than before, and they are working four times as hard as before. They are, say, about one-quarter as well off as before.

Many people believe that this parable applies to the Canadian economy. They are worried not only about pollution but about values that they think will be lost as growth continues. Rapid economic growth makes skills, and hence people, obsolete before their working lives are over. Economic growth crowds out green places and covers them with asphalt. It replaces the community life of the town with the anonymity of the city. Growth is thus said to make life less worth living in ways for which more cars and microwave ovens do not fully compensate.

**Separating the Issues** How valid is this "quality of life" argument? Are people really becoming worse off year by year, or is that claim just romanticism? It cannot be denied that economic growth is a *potential* threat to the quality of life. As it stands, though, the argument is misleading because it confuses two issues. One issue has to do with the size of gross national product and the other with its composition.

In Exhibit 7.6, the production possibility frontier is used to help separate the two issues. The diagram shows an economy in which the two goods produced are called "clean air" and "cars" rather than "guns" and "butter." In any single year, there is a trade-off between the two goods. More cars make the air dirtier; making fewer cars (or spending more money on each car to make them run cleaner) means having better air.

**Exhibit 7.6**
**Pollution and economic growth**
In any single year, there is a trade-off between cars and clean air. More cars make the air dirtier, whereas having fewer cars makes cleaner air possible. As the production possibility frontier moves outward, the choice can be made between two kinds of growth. Many new dirty cars can be made (moving from A to B), if that is what people want. Alternatively, fewer cars can be produced than at B, and more can be spent on each car to make it run cleaner (moving from A to C instead).

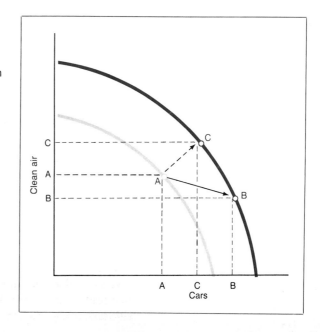

As technology improves and more capital is accumulated, the production possibility frontier shifts outward. If the actual growth path of the economy is from Point A to Point B, people will complain that the quality of life has deteriorated. It is not really economic growth that is to blame, though. The problem is the composition of output that has been chosen. Instead of moving from A to B by producing a great many new dirty cars, the economy could have grown along the path from A to C. That would have meant fewer cars than at B, each more carefully built to cause less pollution. Growth could bring more cars *and* more clean air if people chose to go that way.

**John Stuart Mill (1806–1873)**

John Stuart Mill was in every respect one of the most brilliant and remarkable figures of the nineteenth century. Eldest son of the prominent economist and philosopher, James Mill, John Stuart lived an extraordinary childhood. He began his study of classical Greek at the age of three. By eight, he was reading Plato's dialogues in the original and teaching Latin to the younger members of the Mill family. His education in economics began at thirteen, under his father's tutorship, with a study of Adam Smith's work and the other classics.

This unusual upbringing was bound to produce a strong reaction sooner or later. In his early twenties, Mill went through a spiritual crisis that led him to reject many of his father's ideas. About that time, he met Harriet Taylor and began a long association with her. (Years later, after her husband's death, they were married.) Her ideas on feminism and socialism powerfully influenced Mill's thinking.

Mill published his *Principles of Political Economy* in 1848. This work is seen today as the high-water mark of the classical school, founded by Adam Smith three generations before. As a textbook and authority on economic questions, Mill's *Principles* stood unchallenged until Alfred Marshall transformed "political economy" into "economics" at the end of the century.

Mill's *Principles* is by no means limited to the narrowly technical side of economics. Mill always faced squarely the broad social implications of economic theory wherever they arose. For example, like other economists of the classical school, he believed there were not-too-distant limits to the process of economic growth. "At the end of the progressive state," he wrote, "lies the stationary state. All progress in wealth is but a postponement of this and all advance is an approach to it." Mill was not content, however, simply to describe the mechanics of growth and the technical properties of the stationary state. He wondered what a world without progress would be like. His conclusions so clearly address the concerns of our own age that they are worth quoting at length:

I cannot...regard the stationary state of capital and wealth with the unaffected aversion so generally manifested towards it by political economists of the old school. I am inclined to believe that it would be, on the whole, a very considerable improvement on our present condition. I confess I am not charmed with the ideal of life held out by those who think that the normal state of human beings is that of struggling to get on; that the trampling, crushing, elbowing, and treading on each other's heels, which form the existing type of social life, are the most desirable lot of human kind, or anything but the disagreeable symptoms of one of the phases of our industrial progress....

If the earth must lose that great portion of its pleasantries which it owes to things that the unlimited increase of wealth and population would extirpate from it, for the mere purpose of enabling it to support a larger, but not a better or happier population, I sincerely hope, for the sake of posterity, that they will be content to be stationary long before necessity compels them to.

It should be noted that the choice made may affect the size of output. For example, to force a move from point B to point C may cause a shift in the curve.

Pollution is a serious problem. It cannot be brushed aside. Still, it is wrong to blame pollution primarily on economic growth. To stop growth entirely in order to stop pollution would be to throw the baby out with the bath water. Controlling pollution may require reductions in output of certain types of products, but rather than halting growth in general the economy requires policies to encourage the correct composition of national product.

**Questioning the Possibility of Growth** There is little point in arguing about the direction of growth if resources are being depleted so rapidly that no future growth will be possible. So is growth still possible? A look at the sources of past economic growth may help answer this question.

Refer to Exhibit 7.7, which presents Economic Council of Canada figures on the sources of Canadian economic growth over the period 1950–73. The major source of growth in the past is not of a nature likely to be adversely affected by possible depletion of natural resources in the future. Changes in the quality of the factors of production and the efficiency of their use (factor productivity), which together account for some 35 percent of all growth, use up relatively few natural resources. The category "Labor" takes into account the effects of population growth, which is unlikely to be as rapid in the future as in the past. But although this will slow the growth of total real income, it will not affect the rate of growth of real income per capita.

Although depletion of natural resources may impede the accumulation of capital in some forms, not all capital accumulation takes the form of such resource-intensive items as steel mills and nuclear power plants. Many recent technological developments, in fact, are resource saving. Industry, for example, is learning how to build factories that are somewhat more expensive to construct initially but that require less energy to operate once they are in place. And the trend in the important field of electronics

---

**Exhibit 7.7**

**Sources of Canadian economic growth**

This table shows the relative importance of various sources of economic growth in Canada in the period 1950–73, and as projected by the Economic Council of Canada for the period 1980–85. The role of factors of production (labor and capital) in the growth of national output is calculated by weighting the increase in employment and capital stock by their respective shares in national income. Whatever is not accounted for in actual factor growth by this method is attributed to change in the quality of production or changes in factor productivity due to advances in knowledge, technology, and education.

| Relative contribution of factors of production (in percent) to GNP | | | |
|---|---|---|---|
| | 1950–62 | 1964–69 | 1966–73 | Projected 1980–85 |
| Labor | 32 | 48 | 50 | 44 |
| Capital | 27 | 20 | 20 | 29 |
| Factor productivity | 41 | 34 | 30 | 27 |
| Net national income | 100 | 100 | 100 | 100 |

Source: Economic Council of Canada, *Twelfth Annual Review*, pp. 44–45.

has been to put increasingly more powerful capital devices into smaller and smaller physical packages.

It would appear, then, that most arguments about the impossibility of future economic growth rest on the fallacy of thinking of growth in purely physical terms. To be sure, if economic growth meant nothing other than endlessly piling up duplicates of the gas-guzzling cars and smoke-belching factories of the past, people might someday come up against a blank wall. But exactly because certain important natural resources are gradually being depleted, that is not the direction in which growth need proceed. Instead it could proceed in the direction of developing new generations of capital goods and consumer goods that do their job better with fewer physical inputs and more inputs of technology and human ingenuity.

### The Distributional Effects of Economic Growth

A brief explanation of distributional effects will complete the discussion of economic growth. In the long run, the distributional effects of growth in Canada appear to have been largely neutral except, as shall be noted, when regional differences are taken into account. Workers, resource owners, and recipients of interest and profits appear each to be getting about the same sized slice of the national income pie as a century ago. As the economy has grown, the benefits have been shared by rich and poor alike.

In the context of stabilization policy, however, it is important also to consider the relatively short-term effects of economic growth. In the short run, changes in the year-to-year rate of real economic growth are closely linked to changes in employment. The faster the economy grows, other things being equal, the more jobs are created and the more rapidly the unemployment rate is reduced. In the short run, then, economic growth appears to provide the greatest benefits for those most disadvantaged by high rates of unemployment, unless growth is based largely on improvements in technology.

Besides lowering the overall unemployment rate, economic growth has the additional benefit of making it easier for people to upgrade their jobs and improve their economic circumstances. As one prominent civil rights leader in the U.S. has put it: "A limited-growth policy tends to freeze people to whatever rung of the ladder they happen to be on. That's OK if you're a highly educated 28-year-old making $50,000 per year as a presidential adviser. It's utter disaster if you're unskilled, out of work, and living in a ghetto."[4]

### BALANCED REGIONAL DEVELOPMENT

The Economic Council of Canada pointed out in its first *Annual Review* of 1964 that "Ever since Confederation the notion of 'balanced regional development' has been an implicit, if not explicit, objective of national policy." The Council was itself directed by Parliament "to study how

---

[4]Margaret Bush Wilson, chairman of the National Association for the Advancement of Colored People, quoted in "Review and Outlook: The NAACP Turns a Corner," *Wall Street Journal*, January 12, 1978, p. 12.

national economic policies can best foster the balanced development of all areas of Canada."[5]

As Exhibit 7.8 indicates, there are wide income disparities in Canada, reflecting the unequal distribution of natural resources, markets, transportation systems, and other important economic conditions. Ontario and British Columbia have had income levels considerably above average, while Quebec and the Atlantic region have fared worse than average. The Prairie region has had extremely erratic income behavior, but per capita income on the whole has been close to average.

Exhibit 7.8 also shows that the disparities among provinces have been declining. This is at least partly due to government programs.

**Exhibit 7.8**
**Personal income per capita, Canada and by province, 1951–1980**

| Years | Nfld. | P.E.I. | N.S. | N.B. | Que. | Ont. | Man. | Sask. | Alta. | B.C. | Y.T. & N.W.T. | Canada |
|-------|-------|--------|------|------|------|------|------|-------|-------|------|---------------|--------|
| | (Personal income per capita, by province, as a percentage of personal income per capita at the national level) | | | | | | | | | | | |
| 1951 | 48.3 | 54.5 | 69.2 | 67.1 | 84.0 | 118.3 | 100.8 | 107.2 | 110.6 | 119.2 | 86.8 | 100.0 |
| 1961 | 58.2 | 58.9 | 77.8 | 68.0 | 90.2 | 118.4 | 94.4 | 71.0 | 100.0 | 115.0 | 96.6 | 100.0 |
| 1971 | 63.7 | 63.7 | 77.5 | 72.2 | 88.7 | 117.0 | 94.0 | 80.3 | 99.0 | 109.0 | 86.8 | 100.0 |
| 1980 | 64.0 | 71.1 | 79.1 | 71.5 | 94.5 | 107.1 | 89.5 | 91.1 | 111.6 | 111.2 | 103.2 | 100.0 |

Note: Personal income per capital is obtained by dividing Personal Income by Population as of June. Per cent changes are calculated from unrounded data.
Source: Statistics Canada, *Estimates of Population for Canada and Provinces at June 1; National Income and Expenditure Accounts.*

When Canada was formed in 1867, the federal government made a commitment to the new provinces to pay them subsidies for the tax powers that they lost under the British North America Act. This established a tradition of intergovernmental financial transfers, which has evolved in recent decades into a program of balanced regional development.[6]

In the 1930s, the poorer regions of the country found that their poverty was compounded by their inability to raise enough tax revenues to provide basic social services. A Royal Commission on Dominion–Provincial Relations (The Rowell–Sirois Commission) was established in 1940 to see what could be done to diminish the marked regional disparities that the Depression had exposed. The Commission recommended that the federal government assume the debts of the provinces and take responsibility for the payment of unemployment insurance. The federal government was also asked to collect taxes on behalf of the provinces and to distribute the tax revenues in such a way as to redistribute some of the income from the richer to the poorer provinces.

Beginning in World War II, the federal government was permitted by the provincial governments to levy personal and corporate taxes on their behalf and to return them in the form of cash transfers, known as "tax

[5] Economic Council of Canada *Living Together: A Study of Regional Disparities* (Ottawa: Minister of Supply and Services, 1977), p. 3.

[6] The following section relies heavily on *Financing Confederation*, a 1982 study by the Economic Council of Canada.

rentals." It wasn't until the adoption of an Equalization Program in 1957, however, that such tax sharing was officially used to redress some of the imbalance among the provinces.

Since 1975, the federal government and the provincial governments have concluded a series of agreements regulating financial arrangements between them. At the time of writing, the last agreement in effect was the Federal–Provincial Fiscal Arrangements and Established Programs Financing Act of 1977.

The provisions of this act are extremely significant. Under it, in 1980–81, about $13 billion was transferred to the provinces by the federal government, supporting about 20 percent of total provincial expenditures. In the Atlantic provinces, these transfers represent about 50 percent of total government revenues.

About $10 billion of the $13 billion transfer was intended for equalization of income—involving a transfer of $3.4 billion to seven of the ten provinces—and for the support of health and postsecondary education programs. The intent of this program is to ensure that each province will be able to provide basic levels of social services to its citizens.

On the basis of their greater wealth and taxable resources, three provinces—Ontario, Alberta, and British Columbia—did not receive equalization grants, though they are given the health and education grants. The problem is that the formula on which relative need and wealth is calculated is based on conditions that are rapidly changing. Ontario, in particular, has lost much of its relative position. In its budget of 1980, the Ontario government observed:

The rapid rise of oil and gas prices since 1973 has added a new dimension to the problem of inter-regional sharing. The massive transfer of purchasing power from the oil and gas consuming provinces to the producing provinces is limiting economic growth in the consuming regions. The flow of royalties has expanded the capacity of governments in the Westernmost provinces to improve services and reduce taxes. On the other hand, the federal government finds itself without a sufficient share of oil and gas revenue sources to promote regionally balanced growth and development in Canada, and ensure reasonable harmony in provincial taxation levels. The economic and fiscal imbalances now emerging among the regions and governments of Canada will reach serious proportions in the 1980s unless further oil and gas price increases are accompanied by significantly revised arrangements for sharing and deploying the resource rents that are generated by higher prices.[7]

The problems mentioned in this budget speech make the negotiation of new fiscal arrangements between the federal and provincial governments extremely difficult. Nevertheless, all levels of government remain committed to the basic idea of balanced regional development, and this in turn continues to be one of the major stabilization programs of this country.

## CONCLUSIONS

We have described four goals of economic stabilization policy, reviewed the past performance of the Canadian economy in terms of each goal, and discussed the likely effects of achieving or failing to achieve each goal.

---

[7]Government of Ontario, 1980 Budget Report.

These goals will be used in following chapters to develop a theory of macroeconomics that will explain past performance and, it is hoped, provide some guidance as to the policies that might improve future performance.

Even when stripped of unnecessary complexities, the theory to be introduced is too large to be bitten off and digested in a single piece. It will be necessary to take things one at a time. It would be convenient to break the whole into four separate bodies of theory, one explaining changes in unemployment, a second explaining changes in the price level, a third explaining changes in real output, and a fourth explaining the relative development of the different regions in the country. Unfortunately, that is impossible; the four goals are too closely interrelated. Any policy affecting the performance of a single goal can normally be expected to have effects on the others as well. Instead of organizing the discussion in terms of the four policy goals, it will be organized in terms of the now-familiar distinction between *nominal* and *real* values.

There will first be a discussion of what determines the size and composition of nominal national income and product and an evaluation of various policies that can control nominal aggregate demand. This discussion, in turn, will be divided into two sections. Chapters 8 to 10 will be devoted to matters relating to government spending and taxation policy and their impact on nominal national product. Chapters 11 to 14 will be devoted to the banking system and monetary policy.

Second, when it is understood what determines nominal national income and product, attention will be turned to what determines how changes in nominal national income and product are resolved into changes in employment and real output on the one hand, and changes in the price level on the other. In doing this, we will rely on a simple and important relationship between nominal and real values: *the rate of growth of nominal national income and product is always equal to the rate of change of real national income and product plus the rate of inflation.* Suppose, for example, that in one year nominal GNP increases by 10 percent from $200 billion to $220 billion. This can mean that prices have not changed at all and that 10 percent more real goods and services have been produced, that real output has not changed but that there has been 10 percent inflation, that there has been 5 percent real growth and 5 percent inflation, or that there has been any other combination of a rate of growth of real output and a rate of inflation adding up to the 10 percent growth in nominal GNP. Chapters 17 and 18 will be devoted to explaining why any given change in nominal national income and product is split up in one way rather than another and to a discussion of policies through which the split can be manipulated in the hope of achieving simultaneous full employment, price stability, and balanced growth. Chapter 19 will examine alternative policies used in other countries to produce, hopefully, a more favorable economic performance.

## SUMMARY

1. The general policy of economic stabilization, which means simply the avoidance of harmful fluctuations in economic activity, can be broken

down into the pursuit of four more specific policy goals: maintaining full employment, maintaining price stability, maintaining steady growth of real national income, and maintaining balanced regional development.

2. The White Paper of 1945 committed the Canadian government to pursuing a policy of full employment, by which it meant a job for everyone who wanted a job. Subsequent government statements and Economic Council of Canada reports have proposed numerical targets for unemployment, of from 3.5 to 6.0 percent of the civilian labor force. Other studies suggest an even higher target rate would be realistic. Such low levels of unemployent have rarely been achieved in Canada in the last 30 years.

3. The Economic Council of Canada has also proposed numerical goals for inflation of 2 to 3 percent per year changes in the consumer price index. This goal was achieved through most of the 1950s and early 1960s, but from the late 1960s to the early 1980s, inflation exceeded this goal in every year except one (1971). Recent studies of the distributional impact of inflation suggest that the burden of inflation rests more heavily on older people and on households with relatively high incomes than on younger people and households with low and moderate incomes. Both business and government benefit from inflation, although both may eventually be affected negatively by a combination of persistent high inflation and unemployment.

4. The Canadian economy has recently experienced low rates of growth which, however, compare favorably with those of many other developed countries. In recent years, a controversy has developed over whether rapid economic growth will be possible, or even desirable, in the future. The controversy raises both environmental and distributional concerns.

5. Regional disparities in Canada have prompted a program of intergovernmental equalization grants, which may have helped to reduce previous inequalities.

## DISCUSSION QUESTIONS

1. It is sometimes suggested that the proper goal for employment policy would be a zero level of *involuntary* employment. How might one distinguish between voluntary and involuntary unemployment? What measurement problems might arise in distinguishing the two? Give this matter some general thought now; we will return to it in more detail in Chapter 14.

2. Go to your library and locate recent issues of *The Labour Force* and the *Canadian Statistical Review*, published monthly by Statistics Canada (Catalogue Nos. 71-001 and CSI-003). In each you will find a statistical section that will give you data with which you can update Exhibits 7.1 and 7.2. What progress, if any, is being made toward achievement of the goals of the full employment and price stability? Do you think it will be possible to reach our goals by the mid-1980s?

3. Locate a copy of a good financial newspaper, such as the *Financial Post* or the *Financial Times*, and find out the current interest rates on medium- to long-term Government of Canada bonds. Compare these to the current rate of inflation as measured in terms of the Consumer Price Index. What is the real rate of interest? What does this exercise suggest to you about the current state of inflationary expectations?

4. Make a list of some of the costs and some of the benefits that past economic growth has brought to your particular area or community. Has there been too much or too little economic growth there, in your opinion? Do you think future economic growth in your area or community will bring benefits that outweigh costs? Why or why not?

5. How do you suppose that provinces like Alberta react to the problems mentioned by Ontario on page 142? (Check the Economic Council Study mentioned on page 141.)

## SUGGESTIONS FOR FURTHER READING

Beckerman, Wilfred, *In Defense of Economic Growth*. London: Jonathan Cape, 1974.
*A reply to the Meadows et al. doomsday book listed below.*

Meadows, Dennis L., et al. *The Limits to Growth*. Washington, D.C.: Potomac Associates, 1972.
*A report on a highly controversial and widely debated computer simulation study purporting to show sharp limits to economic growth in the relatively near future.*

Mill, John Stuart. *Principles of Political Economy*. 1871 ed.
*Excerpts available in Pelican Books edition of 1970 and many other editions. Book VI, "Of the Stationary State," contains Mill's views on the limits to growth.*

# THE DETERMINANTS OF PLANNED EXPENDITURE

---

**WHAT YOU WILL LEARN IN THIS CHAPTER**

*British economist John Maynard Keynes made aggregate demand a key element of his economic theory. This chapter will follow his approach by looking at the determinants of each of the major components of aggregate demand. The first component, consumption expenditure, depends to a substantial extent on the level of national income. The second, planned investment expenditure, depends on the expected real rate of interest and on business expectations concerning the profitability of investment projects. Government purchases and exports are determined by forces outside the scope of elementary economic theory and will be treated as "givens" for the sake of further analysis. Imports are a part of consumption expenditures, investment expenditures, and government purchases. Since they play an important role in our consumption expenditures, it is assumed that they depend at least partly on the level of national income.*

**FOR REVIEW**

*Here are some important terms and concepts that will be put to use in this chapter. If you do not understand them, review them before proceeding.*
- *Aggregate demand (Chapter 5)*
- *Planned and unplanned investment (Chapter 5)*
- *Relationships among gross national product, national income, personal income, and disposable income (Chapter 6)*
- *Real and nominal interest rates (Chapter 7)*

---

Chapter 5 introduced the circular flow and the ideas of aggregate supply and demand. Chapter 6 showed how national income accountants go about measuring the elements of the circular flow, including consumption, investment, government purchases, and net exports. Chapter 7 set forth a number of goals and reviewed recent macroeconomic experience in terms of those goals. Now it is time to put all these preliminary concepts and definitions to work and to begin developing a theory—one that will explain why national income and product are at one level rather than another in any particular year, and why they have their ups and downs over time.

### Some Simplifications

In economics, theory building always begins by making some simplifications in order to concentrate on essentials. One simplification that will be used throughout this discussion of macroeconomic theory is the elimination of indirect taxes, depreciation, and the residual error of estimate. Getting rid of these elements of the national income accounts makes things much easier. Gross national product and national income once again become equal by definition, as they were in the simplified circular flow diagrams of Chapter 5.

A second simplification that will be used throughout the following chapters is the omission of undistributed corporate profits. With neither indirect business taxes nor undistributed corporate profits, personal income will be equal to national income minus net taxes. (The term *net taxes*, as in Chapter 5, means all taxes—personal income tax, transfers to government, and corporate profits tax—minus all transfer payments by government.)

A third simplification will be the concentration for the time being on *nominal* values of national income, consumption, and so on—primarily a matter of taking one thing at a time. Chapters 8 to 16 will be explaining why nominal income is, say, $200 billion rather than some other value in a certain year. Then, Chapters 17 and 18 will turn to the question of why changes in nominal income sometimes take the form of changes in prices rather than in real output.

In these early chapters, where the discussion is entirely in terms of nominal values, the term *nominal* will not be repeated every time consumption, investment, income, or whatever is mentioned. Keep in mind, though, that nominal values are meant in every case, unless real values are explicitly specified.

---

**John Maynard Keynes
(1883–1946)**

John Maynard Keynes was born into economics. His father, John Neville Keynes, was a lecturer in economics and logic at Cambridge University. John Maynard began his own studies at Cambridge with an emphasis on mathematics and philosophy. His abilities soon so impressed Alfred Marshall, however, that the distinguished teacher urged him to concentrate on economics. In 1908, after Keynes had finished his studies and done a brief stint in the civil service, Marshall offered him a lectureship in economics at Cambridge, which he accepted.

Keynes is remembered above all for his *General Theory of Employment, Interest, and Money*, published in 1936, although that was by no means his first important work. Keynes's reputation as the outstanding economist of his generation lay in the departure from classical and neoclassical theory he made there. It is hardly necessary to say much about the substance of the *General Theory* in these paragraphs, because they are extensively discussed in every modern textbook on economics. It will be enough to note that its major features are a theory boldly drawn in terms of broad macroeconomic aggregates and a policy position tending toward activism and interventionism.

Keynes was no "narrow" economist. He was an honored member not only of the British academic upper class but also of Britain's highest financial, political, diplomatic, administrative, and even artistic circles. He was intimately involved with the colorful "Bloomsbury set" of London's literary-Bohemian world. He was a friend of Virginia Woolf, E. M. Forster, and Lytton Strachey; and in 1925, he married ballerina Lydia Lopokovia. He was a dazzling success at whatever he turned his hand to, from mountain climbing to financial speculation. As a speculator, he made an enormous ·

fortune for himself, and as bursar of Kings College, he turned an endowment of £30,000 into one of £380,000.

In even the briefest discussion of Keynes, it would be unforgivable not to give his most famous quotation. Writing in the *General Theory*, he pronounced that

the ideas of economists and political philosophers, both when they are right and when they are wrong, are more powerful than is commonly understood. Indeed the world is ruled by little else. Practical men, who believe themselves to be quite exempt from any intellectual influences, are usually the slaves of some defunct economist. Madmen in authority, who hear voices in the air, are distilling their frenzy from some academic scribbler of a few years back.... There are not many who are influenced by new theories after they are twenty-five or thirty years of age, so that the ideas which civil servants and politicians and even agitators apply to current events are not likely to be the newest.

Was Keynes issuing a warning here? Whether or not he had any such thing in mind, his words, forty years later, have become one of the great ironies in the history of economic ideas.

Keynes had a profound and direct impact on economic policymaking in Canada. A number of Canadian economists worked with or studied under him, before and during World War II. One of them, W. A. Mackintosh, who during the war was Director General of Economic Research in the Department of Reconstruction and Supply in the Canadian government, and later became Principal of Queen's University, wrote a government White Paper on Employment and Income in 1945 that was based on Keynesian ideas. Mackintosh said of that document: "Though the battle over Keynesianism had been pretty well conceded, I had some interest in seeing how far some of the elements of Keynesianism could be presented as the most ordinary of common sense." As was noted in Chapter 7, the White Paper was one of the first commitments by any government to a high employment policy.

## Keynes

One further note is in order at the beginning of the discussion of macroeconomic theory—the introduction of the British economist, John Maynard Keynes, whose writings have strongly influenced macroeconomic thought since the 1930s. Although many of Keynes's particular conclusions have been challenged by contemporary economists, the fact that these challenges occur within his basic theoretical framework attests to his lasting influence. Keynes's ideas underlie all of modern macroeconomic theory as well as the contents of this book, even in places where they are not specifically acknowledged.

Keynes made the concept of **aggregate demand** a key element of his theory. He taught that macroeconomic analysis should begin by asking what determines each of the separate types of planned expenditure that make up aggregate demand: consumption, planned investment expenditure, government purchases, and net exports. This chapter will follow his plan by discussing each of these areas in turn.

**Aggregate demand** Total planned expenditure for an economy, consisting of consumption, planned investment, government purchases, and net exports.

## CONSUMPTION

### The Consumption Schedule

Keynes began his theory of consumption expenditure from the observation that each year, consumers spend most, but not all, their disposable personal income on personal consumption. This tendency is as clearly observable

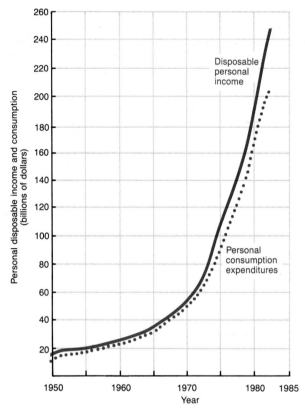

Sources: Statistics Canada, *National Income and Expenditure Accounts*, Vol. 1, Annual Estimates, 1926–1974, No. 13-531, and Vol. 2, Quarterly Estimates, 1947–1974, No. 13–533; Department of Finance, *Economic Review*, April 1982, and Statistics Canada, *Canadian Statistical Review*, March 1983, pp. 18 and 19.

**Exhibit 8.1**
**Disposable personal income and personal consumption expenditures in the Canadian economy, 1950–1982**

As this exhibit shows, Canadian consumers each year spend most, but not all, of their disposable personal income on personal consumption. The percentage of disposable personal income devoted to consumption has remained roughly constant over the period shown.

for the postwar Canadian economy as it was in Keynes's day. As Exhibit 8.1 shows, nominal disposable income in Canada grew from $13.3 billion in 1950 to $247.1 billion in 1982. Each year, consumers spent somewhat over 85 percent of their disposable income on personal consumption.

Reasoning on the basis of this observation, Keynes hypothesized a theoretical relationship between disposable personal income and personal consumption somewhat like the one displayed in Exhibit 8.2. This exhibit shows how consumption changes in response to changes in disposable income — not for the actual Canadian economy but rather for a simplified economy in which consumers each year devote exactly $.75 out of each $1 of added disposable income to consumption. The relationship shown in Exhibit 8.2 is known as a **consumption schedule**.

**Consumption schedule**
A graphical or numerical representation of how nominal consumption expenditure varies as nominal income varies, other things being equal.

**Autonomous consumption**
The level of consumption shown by a consumption schedule for a zero disposable income level.

**Autonomous Consumption** Note that the consumption schedule in Exhibit 8.2 includes a constant term. Even when aggregate disposable income is zero, aggregate consumption expenditure is equal to $100. This, of course, could only be true in the short run. The constant term in the consumption schedule is often referred to as **autonomous consumption**.

Taken literally, the $100 level of autonomous consumption would indicate that aggregate consumption expenditures would be $100 even if aggregate disposable income were zero. In reality, of course, aggregate

**Exhibit 8.2**

**The consumption schedule**

The table and graph both show a simple numerical example of the relationship between disposable income and consumption. The level of autonomous consumption is shown on the graph by the height of the intersection of the consumption schedule with the vertical axis. The slope of the consumption schedule is equal to the marginal propensity to consume.

**(a)**

| Nominal Disposable Income (1) | Nominal Consumption Expenditure (2) | Change in Income (3) | Change in Consumption (4) | Marginal Propensity to Consume (5) |
|---|---|---|---|---|
| $ 0 | $ 100 | | | |
| 100 | 175 | $100 | $75 | 0.75 |
| 200 | 250 | 100 | 75 | 0.75 |
| 300 | 325 | 100 | 75 | 0.75 |
| 400 | 400 | 100 | 75 | 0.75 |
| 500 | 475 | 100 | 75 | 0.75 |
| 600 | 550 | 100 | 75 | 0.75 |
| 700 | 625 | 100 | 75 | 0.75 |
| 800 | 700 | 100 | 75 | 0.75 |
| 900 | 775 | 100 | 75 | 0.75 |
| 1,000 | 850 | 100 | 75 | 0.75 |
| 1,100 | 925 | 100 | 75 | 0.75 |
| 1,200 | 1,000 | 100 | 75 | 0.75 |

**(b)**

The consumption function can be written as $C = a + b(Y - T)$ where C is total consumption, a is autonomous consumption, and b is the marginal propensity to consume. $Y - T$ is nominal income minus net taxes, or nominal disposable income. In the example at right, $a = \$100$ and $b = 0.75$.

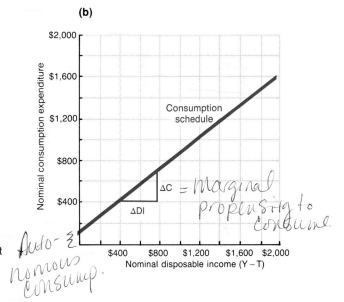

disposable income never falls to zero. Individual households, however, may temporarily experience zero disposable income; and when they do, they do not cut consumption expenditures to zero. Instead, they borrow or draw on past savings to maintain some minimal level of consumption. To that extent, the concept of autonomous consumption is rooted in actual consumer behavior.

**Marginal Propensity to Consume** Look now at Columns 1 to 4 of Exhibit 8.2a. The numbers in these columns show that whenever household income increases, some of the additional income is devoted to consumption above and beyond autonomous consumption. The fraction of each added dollar of disposable income that goes to added consumption is called the **marginal propensity to consume**.

**Marginal propensity to consume** The proportion of each added dollar of disposable income that goes to added consumption. Algebraically it can be written:

$$\text{MPC} = b = \frac{\Delta C}{\Delta DI}$$

where MPC is the marginal propensity to consume, C is consumption, and DI is personal disposable income.

For example, a $100 increase in disposable income, from $500 to $600, raises consumption by $75 from $475 to $550. Similarly, a $100 decrease in disposable income from $500 to $400 would cause consumption to fall by $75, from $475 to $400. The value of the marginal propensity to consume for this numerical example is thus 0.75 (75 divided by 100).

In geometric terms, the marginal propensity to consume is equal to the slope of the consumption schedule. In Exhibit 8.2b, a horizontal movement of $100 in disposable income corresponds to a vertical movement of $75 in planned consumption. The slope of the consumption schedule is thus 75 divided by 100 equals 0.75, the same as the marginal propensity to consume.

## Saving Schedule

**Saving schedule** A graphical or numerical representation of how nominal saving varies as nominal disposable income varies, other things being equal.

Once we know the level of consumption corresponding to each level of disposable income, we can easily calculate the level of saving that corresponds to each level of disposable income. The relationship between saving and income, called the **saving schedule**, is given in numerical form in Exhibit 8.3a. The numbers in this table are calculated simply by subtracting consumption from disposable income.

The saving schedule is shown in geometric form in Exhibit 8.3b. This figure can be constructed simply by plotting the numbers from Column 3 of the table. The saving schedule can also be derived directly from the consumption schedule, which is Exhibit 8.3c. The level of saving corresponding to each level of disposable income is equal to the vertical distance between the consumption schedule and the 45 degree reference line.

**Dissaving** Negative saving—the difference between disposable income and consumption expenditure when consumption exceeds disposable income.

In the numerical example, a **dissaving**—negative saving—of $100 occurs when disposable income is zero. Saving at a zero disposable income is the negative of autonomous consumption. At the $400 level of disposable income there is a breakeven point at which neither saving nor dissaving occurs. Below that point, consumption exceeds disposable income; and above it, consumption falls short of disposable income.

**Marginal propensity to save** The proportion of each added dollar of disposable income that is not consumed. Algebraically, it can be written:

$$MPS = \frac{\Delta S}{\Delta DI},$$

where MPS is the marginal propensity to save, S is saving, and DI is personal disposable income.

The **marginal propensity to save** is the fraction of each additional dollar of disposable income that is not consumed. Because all disposable income is, by definition, either saved or consumed, it follows that the marginal propensity to save (MPS) is equal to 1 minus the marginal propensity to consume (MPC):

$$MPS = 1 - MPC$$

In geometric terms, the marginal propensity to save is equal to the slope of the saving schedule, which is 0.25 in Exhibit 8.3.

## Short Run versus Long Run

In practice, the marginal propensities to consume and save depend on, among other things, the time horizon under discussion. Over long historical periods, aggregate consumption expenditures have risen by about $.90 for each $1 increase in aggregate disposable income. In the short run, however, people tend to change their consumption by somewhat less than

**Exhibit 8.3**

**The saving schedule**

The saving schedule shows the relationship between saving and income. In the table (Part a), saving is found by subtracting consumption from disposable income. In Part b of the exhibit, the saving schedule is given in graphical form. It could be constructed directly from the numbers in Column 3 of the table or from the consumption schedule shown in Part c.

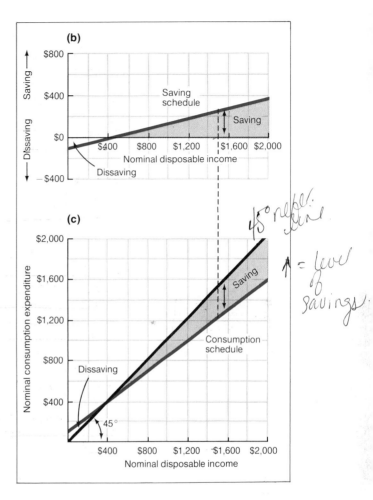

**(a)**

| Nominal Disposable Income (1) | Nominal Consumption (2) | Nominal Saving (3) |
|---|---|---|
| $     0 | $  100 | −$100 |
| 100 | 175 | −75 |
| 200 | 250 | −50 |
| 300 | 325 | −25 |
| 400 | 400 | 0 |
| 500 | 475 | 25 |
| 600 | 550 | 50 |
| 700 | 625 | 75 |
| 800 | 700 | 100 |
| 900 | 775 | 125 |
| 1,000 | 850 | 150 |
| 1,100 | 925 | 175 |
| 1,200 | 1,000 | 200 |
| 1,300 | 1,075 | 225 |
| 1,400 | 1,150 | 250 |
| 1,500 | 1,225 | 275 |
| 1,600 | 1,300 | 300 |
| 1,700 | 1,375 | 325 |
| 1,800 | 1,450 | 350 |
| 1,900 | 1,525 | 375 |
| 2,000 | 1,600 | 400 |

$.90 out of each $1 change in income that they perceive as being only temporary. A household accustomed to a yearly disposable income of $15,000 would tend to economize somewhat on its consumption if its income dropped, in one exceptional year, to $12,000. But as long as it expected better times to return, it would tend to spend more in that year than if it expected the decline in income to be permanent.

Because this book focuses primarily on short-run problems of economic stabilization policy, the numerical examples in this and the following chapters employ a marginal propensity to consume of 0.75, which is lower than the long-run marginal propensity to consume of about 0.9. No claim is made that 0.75 is exactly the value of the marginal propensity to consume for the Canadian economy, but for the short run it is probably close enough.

## Shifts in the Consumption Schedule

In working with the consumption schedule (as in many areas of economics) it is important to distinguish between movements along the schedule and shifts in the whole schedule. The consumption schedule represents the relationship between nominal consumption expenditures and nominal disposable income, other things being equal. A change in consumption brought about by a change in nominal disposable income, then, is represented by a movement *along* the schedule. A change in consumption brought about by a change in something other than nominal disposable income is represented by a *shift* in the schedule. Among the possible causes of shifts, the following are particularly important: changes in wealth, changes in expectations, changes in the price level, and changes in the rate of inflation.

**Changes in Wealth**  The consumption decisions that a household makes may be influenced not only by its current flow of income but also by its accumulated stock of wealth. Other things being equal, a household with a monthly income of $1,000 and $100,000 in the bank can be expected to spend more freely than a household living on the same monthly income and having few, if any, financial reserves. What is true for individual households is also true for the economy as a whole. Any increase in the aggregate wealth of all households, then, can be expected to produce an upward shift in the consumption schedule—that is, more consumption spending at each given level of disposable income. For example, many people hold a substantial part of their wealth in the form of corporate stocks. A rise in the average value of those stocks would increase the aggregate wealth of stockholders and would tend to produce an upward shift in the consumption schedule. A decline in aggregate wealth, other things being equal, would tend to reduce consumption and shift the consumption schedule downward.

**Changes in Expectations**  People's consumption decisions depend not only on their current income but also on their expectations regarding their future income. Other things being equal, an increase in the expected future nominal income tends to increase present consumption expenditure, even before the increase in income is actually realized. This effect is represented by an upward shift in the consumption schedule. Similarly, a decrease in expected future income tends to depress current consumption spending. For example, if consumers feared a coming recession, in which many of them would lose their jobs and hence their sources of income, they might cut back on their consumption expenditures even before the expected decline in income actually occurred. This would be represented by a downward shift in the consumption schedule.

**Changes in the Price Level**  All changes in nominal disposable income are represented as movements along the consumption schedule, whether they refer to changes in real disposable income with the price level constant, changes in the price level with real income constant, or some mix of the two. It is worth enquiring, however, whether a change in the price level might cause a shift in the consumption schedule as well. Two possibilities are worth considering.

First, it seems reasonable to assume that a single, permanent change in the price level, once consumers fully adjust to it, will produce a proportional change in autonomous consumption—the point at which the consumption schedule intercepts the vertical axis. Think of real autonomous consumption as the level of consumption that consumers would maintain in the hypothetical event that real aggregate disposable income fell to zero. If the price level doubles, the nominal value of autonomous consumption will also have to double in order to keep the real value of autonomous consumption constant. This implies that an increase in the price level will tend to shift the nominal consumption schedule upward.

A second effect of changes in the price level, however, tends to offset the first effect. The second effect results from the fact that many of the forms in which people hold their wealth—bank deposits, private and government bonds, life insurance, private pension rights, and so on—have values that are fixed in nominal terms. An increase in the price level thus decreases the real value of household wealth. If the price level doubles, a savings account or life insurance annuity or other savings instrument ends up with only half the purchasing power it had before. By itself, therefore, the effect of an increase in the price level on real wealth tends to cause the consumption schedule to shift downward.

In practice, it is not known which of these two effects acts more strongly on short-run consumption decisions. To simplify the discussion, this and the following chapters will assume that the two effects exactly offset one another. They will thus treat the nominal consumption schedule as not shifting either up or down in response to a single, permanent change in the price level.

**Changes in the Rate of Inflation**  The preceding section discussed the effects of a single, permanent price level change to which consumers are fully able to adjust. Equally, if not more, important as a determinant of consumer spending are changes in the rate of inflation—that is, variations in the rate of change of the price level. Once again, two different consumer reactions to changes in the rate of inflation must be distinguished.

First, consumers tend to view increases in the rate of inflation as a sign of hard times to come. They may not expect their nominal wages and salaries to keep up with inflation, or they may expect government to fight the inflation with policies that increase unemployment and that may therefore cost them their jobs. To the extent that consumers treat inflation as a sign of hard times to come, an increase in the rate of inflation tends to depress consumer spending, thereby shifting the consumption schedule downward.

However, an increase in the rate of inflation can also have the opposite effect. When consumers see the rate edging up, they may decide to buy before prices go up still more. This anticipatory buying tends to increase consumer spending, which shifts the consumption schedule upward.

There is no way to be certain which of the two effects of inflation on consumer spending will predominate. There are indications, however, that in the late 1970s the anticipatory buying effect was strong, and evidence of accelerating inflation stimulated consumer spending. However, by the early 1980s, the "hard times" effect began to predominate and depress consumer spending.

## Adjusting for Taxes

Up to this point, consumption has been discussed only in relation to disposable income. But the consumption schedule can also be adjusted for taxes and expressed in terms of national income rather than disposable income. (These chapters assume that there are no indirect taxes or undistributed corporate profits, which means that national income is considered equal to disposable personal income plus net taxes.)

In adjustment of the consumption schedule for taxes, two separate cases will be considered. In the first case, illustrated by Exhibit 8.4, all taxes and transfers are of the **lump sum** form — that is, they do not change as income changes. Columns 3 and 4 of the table give the familiar consumption schedule in terms of disposable income, while Columns 1 and 4 show the relationship between national income and consumption expenditure.

In the second case, illustrated by Exhibit 8.5, the government employs a personal income tax. Here, the amount of tax collected does change as the level of national income changes. In construction of the table, the assumption has been that everyone pays a straight 20 percent income tax, regardless of the amount of earnings. (The actual income tax is much more complicated, of course.) Again, Columns 3 and 4 give the consumption schedule in terms of disposable income, and Columns 1 and 4 give the schedule in terms of national income.

Compare the two cases. With lump sum taxes, an additional $1 of national income results in an additional $.75 of consumption expenditure and an additional $.25 in saving. With an income tax, the additional $1 of national income results in an additional $.60 of consumption, an additional $.20 of saving, and an additional $.20 of net taxes. One might say

**Lump sum taxes** Taxes that do not vary as income varies.

---

**Exhibit 8.4**

**National income and consumption with lump sum taxes**

Lump sum taxes are taxes that do not change when the level of income changes. This table shows how the consumption schedule can be expressed in terms of either disposable income (Columns 3 and 4) or national income (Columns 1 and 4) for an economy where all taxes are of the lump sum variety. In the simple economy on which the table is based, there are no undistributed corporate profits or indirect business taxes, so national income is equal to disposable income plus net taxes.

| Nominal National Income (1) | Nominal Lump Sum Taxes (2) | Nominal Disposable Income (3) | Nominal Consumption Expenditure (4) | Nominal Saving (5) |
|---|---|---|---|---|
| $ 100 | $100 | $ 0 | $100 | −$100 |
| 200 | 100 | 100 | 175 | −75 |
| 300 | 100 | 200 | 250 | −50 |
| 400 | 100 | 300 | 325 | −25 |
| 500 | 100 | 400 | 400 | 0 |
| 600 | 100 | 500 | 475 | 25 |
| 700 | 100 | 600 | 550 | 50 |
| 800 | 100 | 700 | 625 | 75 |
| 900 | 100 | 800 | 700 | 100 |
| 1,000 | 100 | 900 | 775 | 125 |
| 1,100 | 100 | 1,000 | 850 | 150 |
| 1,200 | 100 | 1,100 | 925 | 175 |

**Exhibit 8.5**

National income and consumption with a 20 percent proportional income tax

With an income tax, net taxes rise as income increases. Each additional $1 of national income results in an additional $.60 of consumption, an additional $.20 of saving, and an additional $.20 of net taxes. Three-quarters of each added $1 of *disposable* income goes to consumption, but only 60 percent of each added $1 of *national* income goes to consumption.

| Nominal National Income (1) | Nominal Net Taxes (2) | Nominal Disposable Income (3) | Nominal Consumption Expenditure (4) | Nominal Saving (5) |
|---|---|---|---|---|
| $   100 | $   20 | $   80 | $160 | −$80 |
| 200 | 40 | 160 | 220 | −60 |
| 300 | 60 | 240 | 280 | −40 |
| 400 | 80 | 320 | 340 | −20 |
| 500 | 100 | 400 | 400 | 0 |
| 600 | 120 | 480 | 460 | 20 |
| 700 | 140 | 560 | 520 | 40 |
| 800 | 160 | 640 | 580 | 60 |
| 900 | 180 | 720 | 640 | 80 |
| 1,000 | 200 | 800 | 700 | 100 |
| 1,100 | 220 | 880 | 760 | 120 |
| 1,200 | 240 | 960 | 820 | 140 |

that, in the second case, there are two different marginal propensities to consume. The propensity to consume out of national income (0.6) is lower than the propensity to consume out of disposable income (0.75).

The Canadian government does make heavy use of the personal income tax, so the second of the two cases considered here is the more realistic. On the other hand, lump sum taxes simplify the job of theory building. In the chapters that follow, the simplifying assumption of lump sum taxes will be used whenever possible. When it is important for questions of policy, though, the effects of an income tax will also be discussed.

## The Stability of the Consumption Schedule

So many things can produce shifts in the consumption schedule that its usefulness can be questioned. What good does it do to draw a relationship between consumption expenditure and disposable income, other things being equal, if the "other things" change so frequently?

There is some validity to this criticism. Short-run predictions of changes in consumer spending have not always proved accurate, even when forecasters have taken precautions to correct for changes in wealth, expectations, and inflation. The concern in this book, however, is not with practical forecasting techniques but rather with establishing a general theoretical understanding of important macroeconomic relationships. For present purposes, then, the consumption schedule will be treated as a reasonably stable relationship between nominal consumption expenditures and nominal disposable income. Shifts in the schedule will be introduced only when strictly necessary.

## PLANNED INVESTMENT EXPENDITURE

Another major component of aggregate demand is planned investment expenditure. Planned investment, as discussed earlier, includes both fixed investment and planned inventory investment. Total investment, as measured in the national income accounts, includes planned investment plus unplanned inventory investment. Our immediate interest is in what determines aggregate demand, so unplanned inventory investment will be ignored for the moment.

### A Simple Theory of Investment

Business firms must constantly invest. They must acquire new plant and equipment to replace what wears out each year. They must invest in additional plant and equipment to grow and to adapt to changing conditions, such as international competition and higher energy costs. They must invest in inventory to smooth out the imperfect synchronization of input purchases, production, and sales of final products. To do all this, they must somehow acquire the funds to purchase the investment goods they need. Many firms are fortunate enough to have steady flows of profits, some of which can be used for investment before the remainder is paid out to the firms' owners. Other firms obtain funds by borrowing directly from the public or through financial intermediaries. Still others bring in new partners or stockholders as a means of raising investment funds.

**The Opportunity Cost of Capital**  Whatever the source of a firm's investment funds, acquiring new fixed capital or inventories always involves an opportunity cost. The opportunity cost of capital is the interest rate that must be paid for funds obtained from outside the firm or that could be earned by investing the firm's own funds elsewhere. There is no free capital. A firm that spends its own retained profits on new office equipment could instead have earned interest on the funds by depositing them in a bank, buying government securities, or loaning them to another firm. A firm that borrows to buy its capital goods must pay the interest rate lenders are currently charging. And a firm that obtains investment funds by drawing in new partners or stockholders must offer those new owners a rate of return on the capital they bring with them that is at least equal to what they could have obtained by putting their funds to work elsewhere.

In the real world, of course, the opportunity cost of capital to a particular firm may vary according to the source of funds. The job of the finance department of such a firm is to choose carefully among and balance the sources of funds so as to minimize the firm's overall cost of capital. Because this is not a course on managerial finance, however, we will ignore such details; as far as we are concerned, the firm will face a unique opportunity cost, equal to the interest rate regardless of the particular source of funds.

**How Much to Invest**  At any given time, dozens or hundreds of investment opportunities may present themselves to a firm. A regional sales office may be built in a distant city. Production equipment may be modernized. Greater supplies of raw materials may be kept on hand to guard against supply

**Exhibit 8.6**

**Evaluation of returns from GFMI insulation project**

This exhibit shows the returns that a hypothetical firm, GFMI, might receive as a result of investing in various quantities of insulation for the roof of its warehouse. As the table shows, each 15 cm of added insulation costs $10,000. Each time the quantity of insulation is increased, the rate of heat loss falls. Thus, as Column 5 shows, the annual savings in heat loss as a percentage of the added investment decreases as the quantity of insulation increases.

| Centimetres of Insulation Added (1) | Heat Loss in Dollars per year (2) | Change in Heat Loss in Dollars per Year (3) | Cost of Added Insulation (4) | Savings as Percent of Investment (5) |
|---|---|---|---|---|
| 0 | $12,000 | — | — | — |
| 15 | 6,000 | $6,000 | $10,000 | 60 |
| 30 | 4,000 | 2,000 | 10,000 | 20 |
| 45 | 3,000 | 1,000 | 10,000 | 10 |

disruptions. Somehow, the firm's management must decide which projects to undertake and how far to carry each project. In doing so, it must balance the potential benefits, in terms of enhanced future profits, against the opportunity cost of obtaining the investment funds.

A simple example will illustrate the main elements of investment decision making. Consider the case of the hypothetical small firm, Great Falls Manufacturing, Inc. (GFMI). GFMI is disturbed about high energy costs. It hires a consultant to see what can be done. The consultant reports that the firm is losing $12,000 a year through the roof of its warehouse. The problem can be substantially reduced by installing insulation. But how much should be installed?

To help GFMI's management reach a decision, the consultant presents the table shown in Exhibit 8.6. This table gives the costs and heat losses associated with various quantities of insulation. If the firm does nothing, it will continue to waste $12,000 in energy each year. For $10,000, the firm can put in 15 cm of fiberglass insulation. This will cut the heat loss in half, to $6,000 per year. For another $10,000 the firm can increase the insulation to 30 cm. The consultant's engineering calculations show that this will reduce the heat loss by another $2,000 per year, to $4,000. For still another $10,000 the insulation can be brought up to 45 cm, cutting the heat loss to $3,000 per year, for a further $1,000 annual saving. Once the insulation is installed, it will never have to be replaced, so that the savings will continue indefinitely.

To determine how much insulation to install, GFMI must compare the potential cost savings with the opportunity cost of capital. To make the comparison easier, both quantities can be expressed in percentage terms. Column 5 of Exhibit 8.6 gives the cost savings as a percentage rate of return. The first 15 cm of insulation saves $6,000 per year, an annual return equal to 60 percent of the initial $10,000 investment. The second 15 cm yields a saving of $2,000 annually on the additional $10,000 investment, for a rate of return of 20 percent. The third 15 cm costs another $10,000 but saves only an additional $1,000 per year, a rate of return of just 10 percent. Each added 15 cm of insulation thus brings a smaller and smaller saving.

A local bank is willing to supply the funds for the project, secured by a mortgage on the warehouse, at an interest rate of 18 percent per year. We take this to be the firm's opportunity cost of capital. The 60 percent rate of return on the first 15 cm of insulation far exceeds the 18 percent cost of capital. (Annual interest payments on the first $10,000 borrowed would be $1,800, compared with the $6,000 annual saving.) The second 15 cm is also profitable, since its 20 percent rate of return still is greater than the opportunity cost of capital. The third 15 cm, however, would not pay for itself. The rate of return of 10 percent obtained by going from 30 to 45 cm of insulation falls far short of the 18 percent cost of funds. It would be worth borrowing $10,000 to install the final 15 cm of insulation only if the interest rate were 10 percent or less.

**The Planned Investment Schedule** Simple though it is, this example illustrates two important principles that underlie all theories of investment. First, as a firm's annual investment outlays increase, the expected rate of return obtained on the last dollar invested tends to fall. In the language of economics, the **marginal efficiency of investment** is said to decrease as the annual flow of investment increases. Second, it is profitable for a firm to expand its annual investment outlays up to, but not beyond, the point where the marginal efficiency of investment drops below the opportunity cost of capital, as represented by the market rate of interest.

Putting these two principles together makes it possible to draw a **planned investment schedule** for a firm and, by extension, for the economy as a whole. Such a schedule shows the quantity of planned investment associated with each interest rate; the height of the schedule at each point is equal to the marginal efficiency of investment. Exhibit 8.7a shows the insulation investment schedule for GFMI that is implicit in the consultant's report of Exhibit 8.6. At an interest rate of 60 percent or more, it would not be worthwhile to do any insulating. As soon as the interest rate drops below 60 percent, the first $10,000 of insulation is worth installing. The second increment of insulation begins to pay for itself when the interest rate falls below 20 percent, and the third when the interest rate drops below 10 percent. Given the 18 percent rate shown in the diagram, investment expenditure is cut off at $20,000 per year.

Exhibit 8.7b shows a generalized investment schedule for the economy as a whole. With tens of thousands of firms and millions of potential investment projects, the stair steps of the single-firm, single-project investment schedule are smoothed out. As the schedule is drawn, an 18 percent interest rate is associated with $180 billion of planned investment spending for the economy as a whole.

Any change in the interest rate, other things being equal, will produce a movement along the planned investment schedule. As the schedule in Exhibit 8.7b is drawn, for example, a decrease in the interest rate to 12 percent will increase planned investment to $210 billion. Similarly, an increase in the interest rate to 24 percent will reduce total planned investment to $150 billion.

**Marginal efficiency of investment** The rate of return expected to be obtained on an additional dollar of planned investment.

**Planned investment schedule** A downward-sloping schedule showing the relationship between planned investment and the interest rate, other things being equal.

**Exhibit 8.7**
**Planned investment schedules for a firm and for the economy as a whole**
Part a of this exhibit shows, in graphical form, the planned investment schedule for GFMI, based on the data in Exhibit 8.6. Part b shows a hypothetical planned investment schedule for the economy as a whole. In both cases the quantity of planned investment increases as the interest rate decreases, other things being equal.

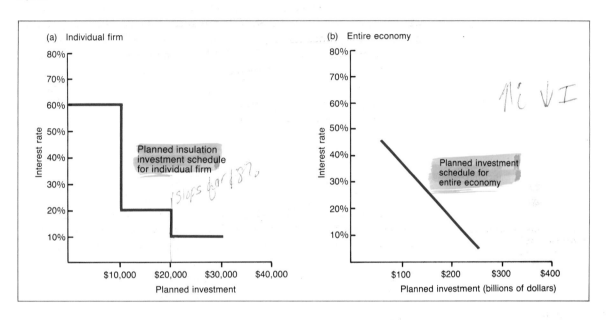

**Shifts in the Planned Investment Schedule** Any change in one of the conditions covered by the "other things being equal" assumption will shift the planned investment schedule. A complete analysis would have to consider two kinds of changes: changes in the price level and changes in the expected return on investment. In this section, however, we are dealing with an economy in which there is no inflation, so that the price level never changes.[1]

As a general rule, anything that increases the expected rate of return on investment will shift the planned investment curve to the right, and anything that decreases the expected return will shift it to the left. Consider GFMI's warehouse insulation project. An increase in the cost of heating fuel, other things being equal, will increase the expected rate of return from any given quantity of insulation. For example, if the cost of fuel doubles, the saving from each added layer of insulation will be twice as great as was shown in Exhibit 8.6. Increasing the thickness of insulation from 30 to 45 cm will then yield a saving of $2,000 rather than just $1,000.

---

[1] If the planned investment schedule is drawn with the nominal interest rate on the vertical axis and nominal planned investment on the horizontal axis, a change in the expected rate of inflation, other things being equal, will shift the planned investment schedule upward by a distance equal to the expected change in the inflation rate. A once-and-for-all increase in the price level with no change in the subsequently expected rate of inflation will shift the planned investment schedule proportionately to the right.

At any interest rate up to 20 percent, it will be worth installing a full 45 cm of insulation if the cost of fuel is expected to double.

Many investments are made to increase productive capacity rather than to reduce costs per unit of output. Sometimes technological developments can spur investment in a major sector of the economy, as was the case with railroads in the nineteenth century, automobiles earlier in this century, and electronics today. More broadly, expectations regarding long-term growth trends and population trends influence the level of planned

**Exhibit 8.8**
**Investment expenditures in the Canadian economy, 1929–1982**
Investment expenditure in the Canadian economy has often changed sharply from year to year. The changes shown here were caused partly by changes in interest rates and partly by changes in expected rates of return. The inventory component of total investment expenditure is particularly unstable. The data on inventory investment shown here lump together planned and unplanned inventory expenditure.

**(a) Gross fixed investment**

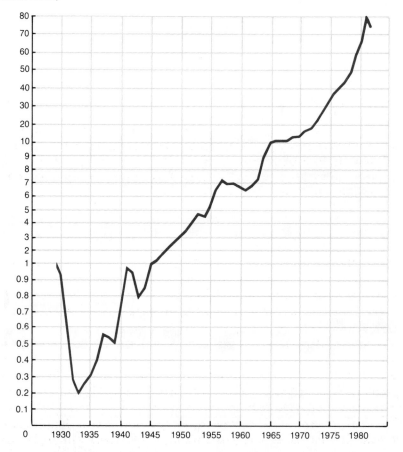

**(b) Change in business inventories**

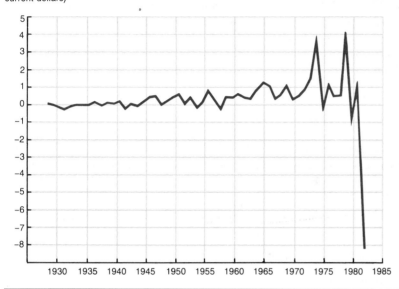

Absolute scale
(billions of
current dollars)

Source: Statistics Canada, *National Income and Expenditure Accounts* (Annual), Catalogue No. 13-201, 1983.

investment. In the short-run, forecasts of business conditions in coming years and quarters can strongly influence the timing of fixed investments and can even more strongly influence the level of planned inventory investment or disinvestment. Whatever the source, an increase in business confidence regarding the long-run or short-run economic future will tend to shift the planned investment schedule to the right. A decrease in business confidence, based on forecasts of poor profit opportunities, will tend to shift the planned investment schedule to the left.

## The Stability of Planned Investment

Because the rate of planned investment depends so heavily on expectations, and because expectations can sometimes change quickly, planned investment expenditure can vary considerably from year to year. As Exhibit 8.8a shows, there have been times in Canadian economic history when investment has undergone wide swings over short periods.

Inventory investment is a particularly unstable component of total investment expenditure, as Exhibit 8.8b shows. Unfortunately, it is impossible to distinguish statistically between year-to-year changes in *planned* inventory investment and year-to-year changes in *unplanned* inventory investment. As the theory developed in the following chapters will make clear, changes in planned inventory investment can be considered a *cause* of instability for the economy as a whole, while changes in unplanned inventory investment can be considered a *consequence* of disequilibrium originating elsewhere in the economy. Exhibit 8.8b lumps together planned and unplanned inventory investment.

## OTHER TYPES OF EXPENDITURE

### Government Purchases

A third major component of aggregate demand, after consumption and planned investment, is government purchases of goods and services. As noted in Chapter 4, such purchases by the various levels of government in Canada have been growing more rapidly than national output, to the point where they now account for slightly more than 20 percent of the gross national product. In several of the years since 1969, they have exceeded the amount spent by business enterprises on investment.

Despite the importance of government purchases, their level is traditionally considered, in macroeconomic analysis, to be determined by political decision processes that are "outside" the economic system. In adhering to that tradition here, we do not mean to pretend that the legislators and executives who make spending decisions at various levels of government are uninfluenced by economic considerations such as the level of national income or the rate of unemployment. Our later analysis of fiscal policy will show that they are guided very much by such considerations. However, the relationships, whatever they are, between government spending and unemployment and national income, are too indirect and complex to be put into a simple theory.

### Net Exports

Net exports are the fourth and final component of aggregate demand. Net exports represent the difference between the value of goods and services exported to foreigners and the value of goods and services imported from foreign countries. As will be shown more fully in Chapter 15, foreign trade is extremely important to the Canadian economy, accounting for about 30 percent of Canada's GNP annually. It is important, therefore, to understand some of the factors that determine the levels of our imports and exports.

Before we examine these factors, however, it should be noted that it is the *difference* between exports and imports (*net* exports) that determines the impact that the foreign market will have on the Canadian economy. Net exports are normally only 1 or 2 percent of Canadian GNP, but that small size may understate their importance as a source of disturbances in aggregate demand, because net exports can be very volatile. For example, from 1970 to 1975, net exports fell from +$.953 billion to −$5.137 billion, a total swing equivalent to about 3.5 percent of GNP (see Exhibit 8.9).

A comprehensive picture of the balance of payments accounts will be presented in Chapter 15. Here we content ourselves with a brief examination of how export and import expenditures are determined so that their role in aggregate demand can be understood.

**Exhibit 8.9**

Canadian net exports and gross national product (billions of current dollars)

| Year (1) | Gross National Product (2) | Exports (3) | Imports (4) | Net Exports (5) |
|---|---|---|---|---|
| 1958 | $ 34.777 | $ 6.329 | $ 7.321 | −$ .992 |
| 1959 | 36.846 | 6.674 | 8.028 | −1.354 |
| 1960 | 38.359 | 7.004 | 8.092 | −1.088 |
| 1961 | 39.646 | 7.624 | 8.480 | −.856 |
| 1962 | 42.927 | 8.234 | 9.045 | −.811 |
| 1963 | 45.978 | 9.068 | 9.561 | −.493 |
| 1964 | 50.280 | 10.503 | 10.913 | −.410 |
| 1965 | 55.364 | 11.182 | 12.341 | −1.159 |
| 1966 | 61.828 | 13.045 | 14.259 | −1.214 |
| 1967 | 66.409 | 14.663 | 15.234 | −.571 |
| 1968 | 72.586 | 16.719 | 17.010 | −.291 |
| 1969 | 79.815 | 18.761 | 19.821 | −1.060 |
| 1970 | 85.685 | 21.167 | 20.214 | .953 |
| 1971 | 93.462 | 22.187 | 22.019 | .168 |
| 1972 | 103.952 | 24.502 | 25.251 | −.749 |
| 1973 | 120.438 | 30.684 | 31.003 | −.319 |
| 1974 | 140.880 | 38.488 | 40.675 | −2.187 |
| 1975 | 165.428 | 40.452 | 45.589 | −5.137 |
| 1976 | 191.492 | 45.685 | 49.997 | −4.312 |
| 1977 | 210.132 | 52.716 | 57.232 | −4.516 |
| 1978 | 231.835 | 61.913 | 67.174 | −5.261 |
| 1979 | 260.533 | 76.412 | 82.051 | −5.639 |
| 1980 | 289.859 | 90.258 | 93.443 | −3.185 |
| 1981 | 328.501 | 98.999 | 107.177 | −8.178 |
| 1982 | 348.925 | 100.395 | 99.150 | 1.245 |

Source: Department of Finance, *Economic Review*, April 1983 and previous years.

## The Determinants of Net Exports

Imports are a part of total consumption, investment, and government expenditures. As such, they are the result of the same forces that underlie those expenditures: income, prices, interest rates, and a multitude of other factors. The major determinants are generally assumed to be national income and the prices of foreign goods relative to the prices of domestic goods. As incomes rise, we tend to import more cameras from Japan and more stylish clothes from Paris. The cost of foreign goods is affected by the foreign exchange rate. Suppose, for example, that a certain golf ball costs $2.20 in Canada in Canadian currency and only $2.00 in the United States in U.S. currency. If the two currencies exchange at a ratio of 1:1, Canadians will be inclined to import that golf ball from the United States, because they can do so for only $2.00 in Canadian currency. However, if the value of the U.S. dollar rises relative to the Canadian dollar so that it costs $1.10 in Canadian dollars to purchase $1.00 U.S., Canadians will be forced to spend $2.20 in Canadian currency to purchase the two U.S. dollars required to pay for the golf ball in the United States. This will make it just as expensive to purchase the ball in the United States as in Canada, even though the price of the ball in the U.S. is still only $2.00 in U.S. currency.

**Import schedule** A graphical or numerical representation of how nominal import purchases vary as nominal income varies, other things being equal. It is assumed here that: Imports (M) = Ma + $m$ DI, where Ma is autonomous imports, $m$ is the marginal propensity to import, and DI is disposable income.

**Autonomous Imports** (Ma) is the amount of imports when disposable income is zero.

**Marginal propensity to import** The proportion of each added dollar of disposable income (DI) that goes to added imports.

$$MPM = m = \frac{\Delta M}{\Delta DI}$$

In our model of the economy, where the only difference between disposable income and national income is a lump-sum tax, the marginal propensity to import out of disposable income will be the same as the marginal propensity to import out of national income. For purposes of analysis we will often express MPM in terms of national income, i.e.

$$MPM = \frac{\Delta M}{\Delta Y}, \text{ where}$$

Y = national income.

Therefore, changes in prices and in the exchange rate can affect imports. Usually these are assumed to be constant in order to relate imports to another important variable: disposable income (DI). In constructing an **import schedule**, we will assume in this text that imports, like consumption, consist of **autonomous imports** (Ma) *and* an element that is related to disposable income through what we shall call the **marginal propensity to import** (MPM). This indicates the proportion of each added dollar of disposable income that goes to added imports. In the short run this MPM has been found to be as high as 0.49.[2]

In our model, where the only difference between disposable income and national income is a lump-sum tax (T), the marginal propensity to import out of disposable income will be the same as the marginal propensity to import out of national income. Assume, for example, that imports (M) = Ma + $m$(DI), where $m$ denotes the marginal propensity to import (MPM). If Ma = $65 and $m$ = 0.15, then:

(1) $\quad M = \$65 + 0.15 \, DI$

Now, in our model, disposable income = national income minus net taxes, or DI = Y – T. Equation (1) can then be rewritten as follows:

$$M = Ma + m \, (Y - T)$$

If we add a net tax of $100 to the other money values, M = $65 + 0.15 (Y – $100), or M = $65 + 0.15 Y – $15. This simplifies to:

(2) $\quad M = \$50 + 0.15 \, Y$

The two equations show that the marginal propensity to import ($m$) is the same for both DI and Y. What changes is the value of Ma. When disposable income is used as a basis, Ma = $65. When national income is used, Ma is reduced to $50. This occurs because disposable income is less than national income at every level of national income. A given level of imports will then be a larger proportion of disposable income than of national income, even though imports will *change* at the same rate in relation to *changes* in national income and disposable income. For example, if imports = $80, national income = $200, and disposable income = $100, it is consistent with the data to say either that M = $65 + 0.15 DI or M = $50 + 0.15Y. For purposes of equilibrium analysis, in which values are expressed in terms of national income, it is useful to relate changes in imports to changes in national income. This is what will be done in the next few chapters. However, in Chapter 10, where brief consideration will be given to the impact of changes in taxes on national income, it will prove helpful to express the import function in terms of disposable income, since tax changes affect expenditures in the economy through changes in disposable income.

Having clarified some of the terms to be used, something more specific must be said about the export and import functions that will be used in the following analysis. Exports are related primarily to the income of other

---

[2]T.R. Robinson, "Canadian Imports and Economic Stability" *Canadian Journal of Economics* 1, May 1968, p. 421. In another study Robinson indicates that a longer run MPM is about half as large. "Foreign Trade and Economic Stability," *Studies of the Royal Commission on Taxation*, No. 5, Ottawa, 1967, p. 175.

**Exhibit 8.10**
Hypothetical export, import, and net export schedules

**(a) Imports and exports**

Exports

M

X

Imports

Nominal national income          500

**(b) Net exports**

Net exports

Xn

*export* ↑ *+ve*

Xn = 0

Nominal national income          500

*imports* ↑ *-ve*

countries and to relative prices. They are therefore treated similarly to government purchases: as a very important demand component that is connected to forces "outside" the system. A "constant" value is therefore assigned to exports. It is assumed in Exhibit 8.10a that exports (X) equal $125 at each level of nominal national income, while imports (M) are $50 plus 0.15 of national income (that is, the MPM is 0.15). If exports and imports behave in this way, then at a level of national income of $500 exports would equal imports (both would equal $125). Note carefully that at levels of income below $500 exports would be larger than imports; that is, net exports would be positive. At levels of income higher than $500 imports would be greater than exports, and net exports would be negative. Recall that *net exports* equal exports minus imports, or X − M. Since, in this hypothetical example, exports = $125 and imports = $50 + 0.15 national income, net exports (X − M) = $125 − ($50 + 0.15 national income) or $75 − 0.15 national income. If income were zero, exports would be $125 and imports would be $50; therefore, net exports would be $75. This situation is illustrated in Exhibit 8.10b. As national income increases, exports remain the same but imports increase, so that net exports fall with rising income. At an income level of $500, net exports become zero (at the point where exports = imports in Exhibit 8.10a), and, at income levels higher than $500, net exports will be negative, meaning that imports will be greater than exports.

This hypothetical example corresponds to the type of export and import behavior that a country like Canada can expect. As the level of income in Canada rises, imports may be stimulated more than exports, resulting in a growing deficit in the export-import balance.

## CONCLUSIONS

The objective in this chapter has been to look at the determinants of each kind of planned expenditure in order to understand how aggregate demand as a whole is determined. The chapter has shown that consumption depends on disposable income, that planned investment depends on the expected real interest rate (among other things), that government spending depends on the political process, and that net exports depend on income, in addition to many other things. Now these relationships can be pulled together and applied — in a new chapter.

## SUMMARY

1. Following the tradition of Keynesian economics, the theory building begins by looking at what determines each separate component of aggregate demand — consumption, planned investment, government purchases, and net exports.
2. The consumption schedule shows that as nominal disposable income increases, nominal consumption expenditure also increases — but not by as much as the increase in income. The fraction of each added dollar of income that is devoted to consumption is called the marginal propensity to consume. The part of disposable income that is not consumed is saved. The marginal propensity to save is equal to 1 minus the marginal propensity to consume.
3. Planned investment expenditure depends on the rate of interest and the expected rate of return on investment projects. The planned investment schedule represents the way planned investment varies as the expected rate of interest varies, other things being equal. Other kinds of changes that affect the expected rate or return on investment are represented graphically as shifts in the planned investment schedule.
4. For purposes of elementary theory, we consider government purchases to be determined by forces not directly related to national income. It is assumed that the export component of net exports is determined by forces that exist outside the Canadian economy, but that the import

component is related to our national income. Imports rise with income so that net exports (which equal exports minus imports) decline with income. They may become negative at high levels of income.

## DISCUSSION QUESTIONS

1. Autonomous consumption is the level of consumption that would occur if national income were zero. Since national income will never be zero, why do we talk about autonomous consumption? In other words, what does it really mean? And how does it affect the consumption schedule? What word or expression might you use in place of *autonomous* when talking about autonomous consumption?

2. Since saving and consumption are related, is there an autonomous saving that can be related to autonomous consumption? How would you find this "autonomous saving"?

3. Suppose you unexpectedly won $1,000 in a lottery. How much of the winnings would you devote to current consumption, and how much would you save? Do you think you would spend as large a fraction of the one-time lottery prize as you would of a $1,000 increase in your annual income that you expected to be permanent? Would it surprise you to learn that some economic studies have indicated that, on the average, the fraction of windfalls spent on current consumption is less than the overall marginal propensity to consume? Explain.

4. Have you ever consciously engaged in anticipatory buying, fearing that if you did not buy some item now, its price would only be higher later? Did your fears prove justified? Would you have been better off in preparing for the coming inflation by increasing your rate of saving, thereby building a pool of funds to help you through the hard times that inflation might bring? Explain.

5. Explain carefully why it is assumed that net exports will decline as national income increases.

# THE MULTIPLIER THEORY OF NATIONAL INCOME DETERMINATION

## WHAT YOU WILL LEARN IN THIS CHAPTER

*Chapter 8 discussed the determinants of each of the major components of aggregate demand—consumption, planned investment, government purchases, and net exports. This chapter takes the next step in theory building by showing how knowledge of these determinants makes it possible to discover the level of nominal national income for which the circular flow is in equilibrium. Any shifts in the components of aggregate demand will be shown to result in changes in the equilibrium level of nominal national income.*

## FOR REVIEW

*Here are some important terms and concepts that will be put to use in this chapter. If you do not understand them, review them before proceeding.*
- *Aggregate supply and demand (Chapter 5)*
- *Equilibrium and disequilibrium in the circular flow (Chapter 5)*
- *Injections and leakages (Chapter 5)*
- *Consumption, saving, investment, and import and export schedules (Chapter 8)*

Chapter 5 showed that the circular flow could be in equilibrium only when aggregate demand was equal to aggregate supply—that is, only when total planned expenditures were equal to total national product. If planned expenditures exceeded national product, buyers' attempts to purchase more than was currently being produced would lead to unplanned decreases in business inventories. Business firms would react to these decreases by increasing output or by raising prices, thereby causing the level of the circular flow—as measured in nominal terms—to increase. If planned expenditures fell short of national product, business inventories would accumulate at a rate faster than planned, and firms would react by cutting production or lowering prices so the nominal level of the circular flow would drop.

These are the ideas on which the Keynesian theory of national income determination is based. All that need be done now is to add a bit more precision by making use of the detailed analysis of planned expenditure developed in the last chapter.

## THE AGGREGATE DEMAND AND SUPPLY SCHEDULES

### Aggregate Demand Schedule

The first step in constructing a theory of nominal income determination is to prepare an **aggregate nominal demand schedule** — a schedule that shows what the nominal level of total planned expenditure will be for each possible level of nominal national income. Exhibit 9.1 indicates how such a schedule can be built up from the separate consumption, investment, government purchase, and net export components discussed in the previous chapter.

Look first at the tabular form of the aggregate nominal demand schedule

> **Aggregate nominal demand schedule** A graph showing the relationship between aggregate nominal demand (the nominal value of total planned expenditure) and nominal national income.

**(a)**

| Nominal National Income Y (1) | Nominal Consumption Expenditure C (2) | Nominal Planned Investment I (3) | Nominal Government Purchases G (4) | Nominal Exports X (5) | Nominal Imports M (6) | Nominal Net Exports Xn (7) | Nominal Total Planned Expenditure (Aggregate Demand) (8) |
|---|---|---|---|---|---|---|---|
| $ 100 | $ 100 | $110 | $150 | $125 | $ 65 | +$60 | $ 420 |
| 200 | 175 | 110 | 150 | 125 | 80 | + 45 | 480 |
| 300 | 250 | 110 | 150 | 125 | 95 | + 30 | 540 |
| 400 | 325 | 110 | 150 | 125 | 110 | + 15 | 600 |
| 500 | 400 | 110 | 150 | 125 | 125 | 0 | 660 |
| 600 | 475 | 110 | 150 | 125 | 140 | − 15 | 720 |
| 700 | 550 | 110 | 150 | 125 | 155 | − 30 | 780 |
| 800 | 625 | 110 | 150 | 125 | 170 | − 45 | 840 |
| 900 | 700 | 110 | 150 | 125 | 185 | − 60 | 900 |
| 1,000 | 775 | 110 | 150 | 125 | 200 | − 75 | 960 |
| 1,100 | 850 | 110 | 150 | 125 | 215 | − 90 | 1,020 |
| 1,200 | 925 | 110 | 150 | 125 | 230 | −105 | 1,080 |
| 1,300 | 1,000 | 110 | 150 | 125 | 245 | −120 | 1,140 |
| 1,400 | 1,075 | 110 | 150 | 125 | 260 | −135 | 1,200 |
| 1,500 | 1,150 | 110 | 150 | 125 | 275 | −150 | 1,260 |
| 1,600 | 1,225 | 110 | 150 | 125 | 290 | −165 | 1,320 |

**(b)**

**Exhibit 9.1**
**Construction of the aggregate nominal demand curve**
Aggregate nominal demand is the nominal value of all planned expenditures. This exhibit shows how an aggregate nominal demand schedule can be built up from the separate components of consumption, planned investment, government purchases, and net exports. In the simplified economy represented in this exhibit, consumption and imports are the only elements of expenditure that vary as nominal national income varies (net exports vary because of imports). The slope of the aggregate demand schedule is thus equal to the marginal propensity to consume (0.75) minus the marginal propensity to import (0.15), that is, 0.6.

in Exhibit 9.1a. The consumption schedule in Column 2 is based on an assumed marginal propensity to consume of 0.75, an autonomous consumption of $100, and lump sum net taxes of $100. Interest rates and business conditions are assumed to remain constant and yield the $110 of planned investment expenditure shown in Column 3. This component of expenditure is assumed not to vary as nominal income varies. Nominal government purchases (Column 4) are also assumed not to vary.

Exports, imports, and net exports (Columns 5-7) are assumed to vary as described in Exhibit 8.10. Aggregate nominal demand (Column 8) is equal to the sum of consumption, planned investment, government purchases, and net exports.

The procedure for constructing the graphical form of the aggregate nominal demand schedule, shown in Exhibit 9.1b, is as follows: first, a set of axes is drawn with nominal national income on the horizontal and nominal planned expenditure on the vertical. Next, the consumption schedule is drawn in—adjusted for taxes so that it is stated in terms of national income (as given in Column 2 of the table). This schedule is labeled C in Exhibit 9.1b.

Then, planned investment expenditure is added. Given the shape and position of the planned investment schedule and the rate of interest (which is assumed to be constant), planned investment is fixed and does not change as national income changes. A line, labeled C + I, is thus drawn parallel to the consumption schedule, separated from it by a distance equal to the level of planned investment.

The next component of aggregate demand to be added is government purchases, which are assumed to be constant at $150. Adding this component gives a new line, labeled C + I + G.

Net exports are assumed in this exhibit to have a value of $75 − 0.15 national income, because net exports equal X − M and X = $125 and M = $50 + 0.15 national income. When national income is zero, Xn (net exports) adds $75 to aggregate expenditure. Thereafter the gap between C + I + G + Xn and C + I + G declines as Xn declines. When national income is $500, Xn is zero and C + I + G + Xn = C + I + G. At higher levels of income, where Xn is negative, C + I + G + Xn actually lies below C + I + G. (The declining Xn function is illustrated in Exhibit 8.10b.)

## Aggregate Supply Schedule

Chapter 5 introduced the term *aggregate nominal supply* to refer to the total nominal value of goods and services produced by the economy. The term, it was pointed out, is a synonym for *nominal national product*. Making use of this relationship of aggregate nominal supply and nominal national product allows an **aggregate nominal supply schedule** to be introduced to show the level of nominal national product associated with each level of nominal national income.

In this simplified economy, there are no indirect business taxes, capital consumption allowances, or statistical discrepancies. As a result national product is, by definition, equal to national income. This means that the aggregate supply schedule is extremely easy to draw. Because the level of nominal national product associated with any given level of nominal

**Aggregate nominal supply schedule** A graph showing the relationship between aggregate nominal supply (nominal national product) and nominal national income. The schedule has the form of a 45 degree line passing through the origin.

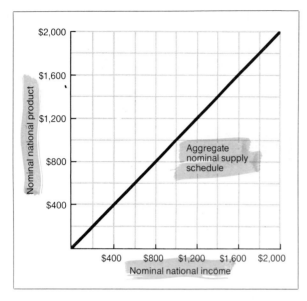

**Exhibit 9.2**
**The aggregate nominal supply curve**
*Aggregate nominal supply* is another term for *nominal national product*. Given the simplifying assumptions used in these chapters (no indirect business taxes, capital consumption allowances, or statistical discrepancies) nominal national product and nominal national income are, by definition, equal. The aggregate nominal supply curve, which shows the relationship between aggregate nominal supply and nominal national income, is thus a 45 degree line passing through the origin, as shown here.

national income is equal to that level of nominal national income, the aggregate supply schedule is simply a straight 45 degree line (see Exhibit 9.2). It can easily be checked that each point on the schedule is equally far from the horizontal axis (national income) and the vertical axis (national product).

## FINDING THE EQUILIBRIUM LEVEL OF NOMINAL NATIONAL INCOME

### The Keynesian Cross

Taken together, the aggregate nominal supply and demand schedules make it possible to determine the equilibrium level of nominal national income. Drawing the aggregate nominal supply and demand schedules together on the same diagram, as in Exhibit 9.3, gives a figure that economists call the **Keynesian cross**. A diagram much like this was used by early followers of Keynes to show how the equilibrium level of national income is determined.

**Keynesian cross** A figure formed by the intersection of the aggregate nominal demand and aggregate nominal supply schedules.

From Chapter 5, we know that the circular flow will be in equilibrium only when total planned expenditure (aggregate demand) is equal to national product (aggregate supply). The point of intersection of the two schedules that comprise the Keynesian cross shows exactly which level of national income permits aggregate supply and demand to be equal. That point, which corresponds to a nominal national income of $900 in Exhibit 9.3, is the equilibrium point (E).

It is easy to see that no other level of nominal national income can represent equilibrium in the circular flow. If national income were lower than the equilibrium level, say $600, planned expenditure (aggregate demand) would exceed national product (aggregate supply). There would be unplanned depletion of business inventories equal to the vertical distance

**Exhibit 9.3**

**Using the Keynesian cross to determine equilibrium national income**

The aggregate nominal supply and demand schedules drawn on one diagram form a figure called the Keynesian cross. This figure provides a simple way to determine the equilibrium level of nominal national income, given the assumptions concerning planned expenditure on which the aggregate demand curve is based. Any national income higher than the equilibrium level would result in excess aggregate supply, unplanned inventory accumulation, and downward pressure on nominal national income. Any national income below the equilibrium level would result in excess aggregate demand, unplanned inventory depletion, and upward pressure on nominal national income.

between the aggregate demand schedule and the aggregate supply schedule, as shown in Exhibit 9.3. Firms would try to restore inventories to their planned levels by increasing production and/or prices. That increase would in turn cause nominal national income to rise until equilibrium was reached.

If, on the other hand, nominal national income were to be higher than the equilibrium level, say $1,200, then planned expenditures would fall short of national product. The unsold goods would go to unplanned inventory investment equal to the gap between the aggregate demand schedule and the aggregate supply schedule. Business firms would react to the unplanned buildup in inventories by cutting production and/or prices. The cutback would cause nominal national income to fall until equilibrium was restored.

## A Numerical Example

The same story is told in Exhibit 9.4, which gives numerical values for nominal national income, planned expenditure, and other variables that correspond to the Keynesian cross diagram of Exhibit 9.3. The table confirms that $900 is the only level of national income that allows equilibrium in the circular flow. Column 5 shows that national income tends to move toward equilibrium whenever it is at any level other than $900.

## Leakage-Injection Approach

The leakage-injection approach to determining the equilibrium level of nominal national income is an alternative method for arriving at the same conclusion reached with the aid of the Keynesian cross. It uses the saving schedule rather than the consumption schedule as its starting point.

**Exhibit 9.4**
**Finding equilibrium nominal national income: a numerical example**
This exhibit gives a numerical example of the determination of equilibrium nominal national income, based on the same assumptions that underlie Exhibit 9.3. At every level of nominal national income except the equilibrium level, aggregate supply either falls short of aggregate demand, causing unplanned inventory depletion, or exceeds aggregate demand, causing unplanned inventory accumulation. Unplanned inventory depletion stimulates firms to raise output or prices or both, causing nominal national income to increase; unplanned inventory accumulation causes firms to cut output or prices or both, causing nominal national income to decrease.

| Nominal National Income | Nominal Planned Expenditure (Aggregate Demand) | Nominal National Product (Aggregate Supply) | Unplanned Inventory Change | Tendency of Change in National Income |
|---|---|---|---|---|
| $ 100 | $ 420 | $ 100 | −$320 | Increase |
| 200 | 480 | 200 | −280 | Increase |
| 300 | 540 | 300 | −240 | Increase |
| 400 | 600 | 400 | −200 | Increase |
| 500 | 660 | 500 | −160 | Increase |
| 600 | 720 | 600 | −120 | Increase |
| 700 | 780 | 700 | − 80 | Increase |
| 800 | 840 | 800 | − 40 | Increase |
| 900 | 900 | 900 | 0 | No change |
| 1,000 | 960 | 1,000 | + 40 | Decrease |
| 1,100 | 1,020 | 1,100 | + 80 | Decrease |
| 1,200 | 1,080 | 1,200 | +120 | Decrease |
| 1,300 | 1,140 | 1,300 | +160 | Decrease |
| 1,400 | 1,200 | 1,400 | +200 | Decrease |
| 1,500 | 1,260 | 1,500 | +240 | Decrease |
| 1,600 | 1,320 | 1,600 | +280 | Decrease |

Exhibit 9.5 illustrates the use of this approach. Columns 2 to 5 of Part a show how national income is divided into consumption, saving, net taxes, and imports. Saving, net taxes, and imports are all leakages from the circular flow. In Part b, a diagonal line is drawn to show how total leakages vary as national income varies. The slope of the line representing total leakages is equal to the marginal propensity to save (0.25) plus the marginal propensity to import (0.15).

Columns 7 to 9 of Part a show planned injections: planned investment, government purchases, and exports. Under the simplifying assumptions adopted earlier, none of these is assumed to vary as nominal national income varies. The planned injections line in Part b is thus perfectly horizontal. These injections represent planned expenditures on final goods and services that do not originate in domestic households.

The point in Part b where the injections and leakages schedules cross denotes the equilibrium level of nominal national income. At that point, planned injections are equal to total leakages. Under the saving approach, then, nominal national income is in equilibrium when, and only when, saving plus net taxes plus imports are equal to planned investment plus government purchases plus exports.

A careful comparison of Exhibits 9.5 and 9.3 reveals that the gap between the leakage and injection schedules at any level of nominal national income is exactly equal to the gap between the aggregate nominal demand and supply schedules at the same level of nominal national income.

_leakages_    _injections (constant)_

**(a)**

| Nominal National Income (1) | Consumption (2) | Saving (3) | Net Taxes (4) | Imports (5) | Total Leakages (6) | Planned Investment (7) | Government Purchases (8) | Exports (9) | Total Planned Injections (10) |
|---|---|---|---|---|---|---|---|---|---|
| $ 100 | $ 100 | −$100 | $100 | $ 65 | $ 65 | $110 | $150 | $125 | $385 |
| 200 | 175 | −75 | 100 | 80 | 105 | 110 | 150 | 125 | 385 |
| 300 | 250 | −50 | 100 | 95 | 145 | 110 | 150 | 125 | 385 |
| 400 | 325 | −25 | 100 | 110 | 185 | 110 | 150 | 125 | 385 |
| 500 | 400 | 0 | 100 | 125 | 225 | 110 | 150 | 125 | 385 |
| 600 | 475 | 25 | 100 | 140 | 265 | 110 | 150 | 125 | 385 |
| 700 | 550 | 50 | 100 | 155 | 305 | 110 | 150 | 125 | 385 |
| 800 | 625 | 75 | 100 | 170 | 345 | 110 | 150 | 125 | 385 |
| 900 | 700 | 100 | 100 | 185 | 385 | 110 | 150 | 125 | 385 |
| 1,000 | 775 | 125 | 100 | 200 | 425 | 110 | 150 | 125 | 385 |
| 1,100 | 850 | 150 | 100 | 215 | 465 | 110 | 150 | 125 | 385 |
| 1,200 | 925 | 175 | 100 | 230 | 505 | 110 | 150 | 125 | 385 |
| 1,300 | 1,000 | 200 | 100 | 245 | 545 | 110 | 150 | 125 | 385 |
| 1,400 | 1,075 | 225 | 100 | 260 | 585 | 110 | 150 | 125 | 385 |
| 1,500 | 1,150 | 250 | 100 | 275 | 625 | 110 | 150 | 125 | 385 |

**Exhibit 9.5**
**The leakage-injection approach to national income determination**
This exhibit shows how the equilibrium level of nominal national income can be determined by finding the point where planned injections to the circular flow (planned investment plus government purchases plus exports) are equal to total leakages from the circular flow (saving plus net taxes plus imports).

**(b)**

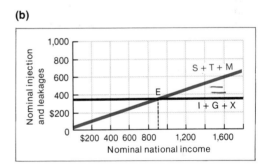

## CHANGES IN NOMINAL NATIONAL INCOME AND THE MULTIPLIER EFFECT

### Expenditure Changes

A great many economic factors can affect the level of planned expenditure. The aggregate demand schedule singles out the effects of changes in national income on planned expenditure. The effects of these changes are represented by movements along a given aggregate demand schedule.

Other factors also influence planned expenditure. Changes in consumer expectations, in wealth, or in the rate of inflation cause the level of autonomous consumption to vary. Changes in the expected real rate of interest or the expected real return on investment projects cause the level of planned investment to vary. Changes in policy cause the government purchases component of planned expenditure to vary, and changes in the world economy affect the volume of net exports. All the changes in planned expenditure that arise from reasons other than changes in national income must be represented by shifts in the aggregate demand schedule.

Consider Exhibit 9.6, which shows the effects of a $100 increase in planned expenditure at all levels of income. For the moment, it does not

**Exhibit 9.6**
**The multiplier effect of a shift in the aggregate demand schedule**
A shift in the aggregate nominal demand schedule produces a more than equal change in equilibrium nominal national income. This is known as the multiplier effect. Here, a $100 upward shift in the aggregate nominal demand schedule produces a $250 increase in equilibrium nominal national income from $900 to $1,150. The ratio of the change in equilibrium income to the original shift in demand, known as the multiplier, thus has a value of 2.5 in this example.

matter whether this increase originates in the consumption, investment, government purchases, or net export component of aggregate demand. The effect in any case is to shift the aggregate nominal demand schedule upward by $100, from the position $AND_1$ to the position $AND_2$.

### The Multiplier Effect

What happens to the equilibrium level of national income when the planned expenditure schedule shifts upward by $100? The immediate effect is that planned expenditure exceeds national product, so that inventories start to be depleted. Firms react to this unplanned inventory depletion by increasing output and/or prices. Nominal national income rises to its new equilibrium level of $1,150.

Notice what has happened: a $100 upward shift in the aggregate demand schedule has induced a $250 increase in equilibrium nominal income. This ability of a given shift in aggregate demand to create a larger increase in equilibrium national income is the famous **multiplier effect**, a central pillar of Keynesian macroeconomics.

**Multiplier effect** The ability of a $1 shift in the aggregate nominal demand schedule to induce a change of more than $1 in the equilibrium level of nominal national income.

**Round by Round**  One way to view the multiplier effect is to imagine the effects of the initial upward shift in aggregate demand percolating down through the economy "round by round." Suppose that the original shift is caused by a $100 per year increase in the rate of autonomous consumption expenditure on domestic goods and services. When autonomous consumption expenditures increase, it is likely that part of the increase will be spent on foreign goods and services. The result will be both increased imports and increased expenditures on domestic goods and services. We have chosen here to focus only on the net increase in consumption expenditure devoted to domestic goods and services. This means, in terms of Exhibit 9.1b, that the consumption function will shift upwards by

In 1970, the Swedish Academy of Sciences awarded its Nobel Memorial Prize in Economics to MIT Professor Paul Samuelson. In doing so, the academy announced that "Professor Samuelson's extensive production, covering nearly all areas of economic theory, is characterized by an outstanding ability to derive important new theorems and to find new applications for existing ones. By his contributions, Samuelson has done more than any other contemporary economist to raise the level of scientific analysis in economic theory." The multiplier theory of national income determination is just one of dozens that has been refined, restated, and sharpened by Samuelson's penetrating mind.

Samuelson began his task of raising the level of scientific analysis in economic theory early in his career. His doctoral dissertation at Harvard, written when he was just twenty-six, was boldly entitled *Foundations of Economic Analysis*. (Contrast this with the narrow, ultraspecialized topics of most dissertations!) Published in 1947, the *Foundations* immediately became—and to a great extent remains—the definitive statement in modern mathematical dress of much of neoclassical economics.

In the nineteenth century, leading economists had seen their major theoretical statements go on to become textbooks to future generations. Alas, Samuelson's *Foundations* could not serve that purpose. One must already be well educated in economics and mathematics even to read it. Something had to be done to bring the advances in economic theory made during the 1930s and 1940s into the college classroom. Samuelson solved the problem with his famous *Economics*. That book was based on the simple assumption that beginning students did not need to be taught a different *kind* of economics than the kind economists wrote in their own professional journals. What they needed was a lucid, step-by-step presentation. The formula was so successful that Samuelson's *Economics* sold millions of copies as it went through a total of twelve editions.

On policy issues Samuelson ranks as a liberal and an activist. He derides the laissez-faire market economy as a "system of coercion by dollar votes." Unlike many like-minded colleagues, however, Samuelson did not move to Washington during the Kennedy-Johnson years. He was called on frequently for his opinions and advice, but he resisted service on the Council of Economic Advisers. Although much sought as a lecturer and writer of popular articles, Samuelson remains fundamentally an economist's economist. "In the long run," he has said, "the economic scholar works for the only coin worth having—our own applause."

**Paul Anthony Samuelson (1915–     )**

this net amount and there will be no downward shift in the net export function (because nothing explicit has been said about the change in imports). Therefore, the aggregate demand function shifts upward by $100. In response to the $100 increase in demand, business firms raise their prices and/or output enough to cause a $100 increase in nominal national product. The increase in national product results in $100 of additional nominal income for some people in the form of higher profits, wages, rents, or interest payments. All of what has happened so far can be called the first-round effect of the shift in aggregate demand for domestic goods. The second round consists of tracing the effects of the $100 in new income generated by the first round. Given an assumed marginal propensity to consume of 0.75 and a marginal propensity to import of 0.15, the people who receive this income will spend $75 of it on consumer goods and services, of which $15 will be spent on imports. The net effect is to increase the aggregate demand for domestic goods and services by $60. This spending will cause firms to step up output by $60 more and generate $60 in new factor payments and income.

**Exhibit 9.7**

**The multiplier effect, round by round**

This exhibit shows the round-by-round multiplier effects of an initial $100 upward shift in the aggregate nominal demand schedule for domestic goods and services. Each increase in aggregate nominal demand for domestic output produces an equal increase in nominal national income. Each $1 increase in nominal national income in turn produces $.75 of new consumer demand, in which is included a $.15 increase in expenditures on imports. This means that each $1 increase in national income produces $.60 of new demand on domestic goods and services. In total, the infinite series of rounds produces a $250 increase in aggregate nominal demand for domestic output and nominal national income. In comparing this exhibit with Exhibit 9.6, note that the original $100 increase in aggregate demand corresponds to the upward shift in the aggregate demand schedule, whereas the subsequent increases in aggregate demand for domestic goods and services correspond to movements along the new schedule.

| Round | Increase in Total Aggregate Demand | Increase in Imports | Increase in Aggregate Demand for Domestic Goods and Services | Increase in National Income |
|---|---|---|---|---|
| 1 | $100.00 | $ 0 | $100.00 | $100.00 |
| 2 | 75.00 | 15.00 | 60.00 | 60.00 |
| 3 | 45.00 | 9.00 | 36.00 | 36.00 |
| 4 | 27.00 | 5.40 | 21.60 | 21.60 |
| 5 | 16.20 | 3.24 | 12.96 | 12.96 |
| 6 | 9.72 | 1.94 | 7.78 | 7.78 |
| 7 | 5.84 | 1.17 | 4.67 | 4.67 |
| 8 | 3.50 | .70 | 2.80 | 2.80 |
| All later rounds | 5.24 | 1.05 | 4.19 | 4.19 |
| Totals | $287.50 | $37.50 | $250.00 | $250.00 |

Another way of handling this would be to focus on the *gross* change in autonomous consumption and to specify the proportion of such a change spent on imports. For example, assume that gross autonomous consumption increases by $125, of which $25 is spent on imports. In terms of Exhibit 9.1b, the consumption function (C) would shift upwards by $125, the net export function would decline by $25 (because autonomous imports have increased by $25) and the net result would again be a $100 upward shift in the aggregate demand function (C + I + G + Xn).

Because, for reasons of simplicity, we have chosen not to specify the proportion of autonomous expenditures allocated to imports, the changes in autonomous expenditures considered here with the multiplier analysis are always net of imports. That is, the initial change in autonomous expenditures always refers to a change in expenditures on domestic goods and services only.

In the third round, three-quarters of the $60, or $45, is spent, of which $9 is spent on imports. This means that the aggregate demand for domestic goods and services increases by $36. Nominal income will go up by the same amount. In the fourth round, total aggregate demand will increase by $27 (= 0.75 × $36), $5.40 of which will go to imports (= 0.15 × $36). Therefore, the aggregate demand for domestic goods and services will rise by $21.60. This will continue until the increments become too small to worry about. When all the increments to income induced by the original $100 upward shift in the aggregate nominal demand function for domestic goods and services are added together, the total is:

$100 + $60 + $36 + $21.60 + $12.96... = $250

just as expected. This round-by-round version of the multiplier effect is summarized in Exhibit 9.7.

**The Multiplier** Exhibit 9.7 shows quite clearly that as income increases in response to the original upward shift in the aggregate demand schedule, national income "catches up" with planned expenditure. For each $1 increase in nominal national income there is an equivalent increase in output, but expenditure on domestic output increases by only a fraction of a dollar. The fraction is equal to the marginal propensity to consume minus the marginal propensity to import. At the new equilibrium, the difference between planned expenditure on domestic goods and services and national income is eliminated.

The ratio of the induced increase in national income to the original increase in planned expenditure on domestic output is called the **multiplier**.[1] The value of the multiplier depends on the fraction of each added dollar of income that goes to added planned expenditure on domestically produced goods and service. More precisely, the multiplier is given by the formula:

$$\text{Multiplier} = \frac{1}{1-(\text{MPC}_D)} \text{ where MPC}_D = \text{MPC} - \text{MPM}\text{[2]}$$

MPC stands for the marginal propensity to consume, MPM for the marginal propensity to import, and $\text{MPC}_D$ for the marginal propensity to consume domestic output. Applying the figures used previously:

$$\text{Multiplier} = \frac{1}{1-(.75-.15)} = \frac{1}{.4} = 2.5$$

As the formula for the multiplier indicates, the value of the multiplier is related to that portion of any change in income that is spent on domestic goods and service. This equals MPC minus MPM.

Alternatively, the multiplier can be related to that portion of any change

**Multiplier** The ratio of an induced change in the equilibrium level of national income to an initial change in planned expenditure. For an economy in which imports play an important role, the value of the multiplier is given by the formula

$$\text{Multiplier} = \frac{1}{1 - (\text{MPC} - \text{MPM})}$$

or $\dfrac{1}{1 - \text{MPC}_D}$

$\text{MPC}_D$ is the marginal propensity to consume domestic output.

$$\text{MPC}_D = \frac{\Delta C}{\Delta DI} - \frac{\Delta M}{\Delta DI}$$

Note that
$\text{MPC}_D + \text{MPM} + \text{MPS} = Y$
where $Y$ = national income.

---

[1] An algebraic derivation of the multiplier formula is given in the Appendix to Chapter 10.

[2] If the foreign market were not so important to Canada, one could ignore the effect of income on imports and derive a simpler multiplier using only the MPC. This simpler multiplier, used in many American texts, $= \frac{1}{1 - \text{MPC}}$. If MPC is 0.75 and MPM is 0.15 note that our multiplier will equal 2.5, while the simpler multiplier will equal 4. In other words, introducing import leakages reduces the multiplier. The "Buy Canadian" campaigns that are occasionally promoted on billboards are prompted by the desire to lessen the leakage of spending from the Canadian economy.

in income that is not spent on domestic output. This is equal to the marginal propensity to save (MPS) *plus* the marginal propensity to import (MPM).

Therefore, an alternative formula for the multiplier is:

$$\text{Multiplier} = \frac{1}{\text{MPS} + \text{MPM}}$$

Using previous figures

$$\text{Multiplier} = \frac{1}{.25 + .15} = 2.5$$

Whichever way we write the formula, the multiplier is larger, the larger the propensity to consume and the smaller the marginal propensity to import; and it is smaller, the larger the marginal propensity to save and the larger the marginal propensity to import.

## CONCLUSIONS

The multiplier effect plays a central role in Keynesian economic theory and economic policy analysis. The central implication of the multiplier is that even small changes in planned expenditure will have magnified effects on the national economy. Early Keynesian economists saw the instability of planned expenditure, magnified by the multiplier effect, as an explanation for the cycle of boom and bust that had plagued capitalist economies since the nineteenth century. They also saw in the multiplier effect the key to a new policy for economic stabilization. This part of their analysis is important enough that a separate chapter is devoted to it.

## SUMMARY

1. For a given aggregate demand schedule, the circular flow can be in equilibrium at only one level of nominal national income. The equilibrium condition is achieved when planned expenditure on domestic output and national product are equal. If planned expenditure exceeds national product, there will be unplanned depletion of inventories and upward pressure on income. If national product exceeds planned expenditure, there will be unplanned accumulation of inventories and downward pressure on national income.

2. The injection-leakage approach to the determination of the equilibrium level of nominal national income shows that equilibrium can occur only when planned injections (planned investment plus government purchases plus exports) are equal to total leakages (saving plus net taxes plus imports). In equation form:

   $$S + T + M = I + G + X$$

3. A shift in the aggregate demand schedule changes the equilibrium level of nominal national income. According to the multiplier effect, the induced change in equilibrium nominal national income will be larger than the initial shift in planned expenditure. The ratio of the change in income to the shift in planned expenditure is known as the multiplier.

## DISCUSSION QUESTIONS

1. It is possible to analyze the determinants of national income and product with either the circular flow or the Keynesian cross. Which do you prefer? Why? Does each contribute some insights of its own? Explain.
2. Explain the "round-by-round" effect of the multiplier by using the circular flow model.
3. If you expected a depression in the near future, would it be to your advantage to save in order to prepare for it? What would happen if we all tried to save a larger fraction of our income than usual to prepare for an expected depression?
4. If planned saving exceeds planned investment, will gross national product increase or decrease? Suppose you know the government's budget is exactly in balance. Now can you answer the question? What else, if anything, do you need to know?
5. What would be the size of the multiplier if the marginal propensity to consume were 0.5, 0.75, and 0.8 and the marginal propensity to import in each case were 0.25?
6. In what ways are the Keynesian cross and the supply and demand diagram of previous chapters similar, and in what ways are they different?
7. What changes in the economy would force a movement along the aggregate demand curve? What changes would result in a shift of the curve?
8. Suppose that consumers suddenly increase their marginal propensity to consume from 0.70 to 0.80 while the marginal propensity to import is and remains 0.1. What effect will the increase have on the aggregate demand curve? Trace the impact of this change using the Keynesian cross diagram.

# FISCAL POLICY AND THE MULTIPLIER THEORY

## TEN

## WHAT YOU WILL LEARN IN THIS CHAPTER

*This chapter applies the multiplier theory of national income determination to some important practical problems of economic stabilization policy. It shows how taxes and government purchases can be adjusted in an attempt to achieve a level of nominal national income judged compatible with the goal of full employment. Later chapters deal at greater length with the problems of price stability, real economic growth, and balance of payments stability. In addition to discussing the use of discretionary changes in taxes and government purchases for stabilization purposes, the chapter also looks briefly at certain built-in automatic stabilizers contained in the economy. The chapter ends with a review of the long-standing controversy about the economic burden of the national debt.*

## FOR REVIEW

*Here are some important terms and concepts that will be put to use in this chapter. If you do not understand them, review them before proceeding.*

- *Government debts and deficits (Chapter 4)*
- *Nominal values for gross national product and net national income (Chapter 6)*
- *Goals of stabilization policy (Chapter 7)*
- *Multiplier theory (Chapter 9)*

The multiplier theory, introduced in the previous chapter, shows how shifts in aggregate demand cause changes in the equilibrium level of national income. This chapter applies the theory to shifts in aggregate demand produced by changes in the levels of net taxes or government purchases. The control of aggregate demand through these changes is known as **fiscal policy**.

In this chapter, as in the last two, the discussion continues in nominal terms. This is quite natural, in that government budgets are ordinarily cast in nominal terms. However, it should be kept in mind that manipulating the level of nominal national income is only an intermediate policy goal. The ultimate policy goals of full employment, price stability, the growth of real output, balanced regional development, and stability in the foreign

**Fiscal policy** The collective term for the policies that determine the levels of government purchases and net taxes.

trade sector are affected only indirectly by changes in the nominal level of national income.

These changes can take the form of changes in either real output (with accompanying changes in employment) or the price level — or some combination of the two. When fiscal policy is used to stimulate aggregate demand and drive up the level of nominal national income, policy makers naturally hope that all or most of the expansion will take the form of job-creating increases in real output. Part of the expansion of nominal income, however, may also take the form of unwanted inflation and unwanted increases in imports. Similarly, when fiscal policy is used to moderate aggregate demand and slow the growth of nominal income, it is hoped that most of the slowdown will take the form of a reduction in the rate of inflation. However, some of it may also take the form of a slowdown in real economic growth, possibly accompanied by a rise in unemployment.

It will be several chapters yet before we have assembled all the pieces of macroeconomic theory needed to determine exactly what part of a change in nominal income will take the form of changes in real output and what part will take the form of changes in the price level. For the time being, we should keep in mind that the manipulation of nominal aggregate demand is a powerful but imperfect means of achieving full employment, price stability, real economic growth, regional economic balance, and balance of payments stability.

## FISCAL POLICY IN ACTION

### The Target Level of Nominal National Income

We turn now to the matter of applying fiscal policy, once it has been decided what level of nominal national income is most likely to promote the goals of full employment, price stability, economic growth and a healthy

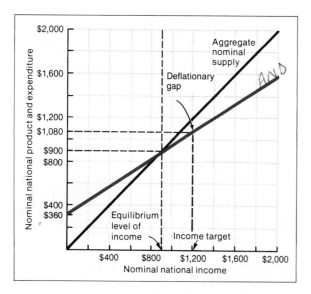

**Exhibit 10.1**

**A deflationary gap**

A deflationary gap is said to occur whenever planned expenditure (aggregate demand) is less than national product (aggregate supply) at the target level of national income. Under this condition, the equilibrium level of nominal national income is below the target level. If national income were at the target level, unplanned inventory accumulation would put downward pressure on the level of income and cause it to contract.

foreign-trade sector. That level of income, whatever it is, can be referred to as the **target level of nominal national income** (or the **income target** for short).

If, at any time, the equilibrium level of nominal national income is equal to the target level, no active fiscal policy is called for. To see fiscal policy in action, we need to look at the more interesting cases in which equilibrium nominal income either falls short of or exceeds the income target.

**A Deflationary Gap** Consider the case shown in Exhibit 10.1. As the aggregate supply and demand curves are drawn, they determine an equilibrium level of nominal national income of $900. Suppose policy makers consider $900 too low and set their target instead at $1,200. With the planned expenditure schedule shown, $1,200 cannot be the equilibrium level of income, because planned expenditures will fall short of national product by $120 if income is at the target level. At the income level of $1,200 planned expenditure will be only $1,080.

Whenever planned expenditure is less than national product at the target level of income, there is a **deflationary gap**. The size of the gap represents the rate of unplanned inventory accumulation that will take place at the target level of income with the given aggregate demand schedule. Geometrically, the gap is measured by the vertical distance between the aggregate demand and supply schedules at the target level of national income. The word *deflationary* refers to the fact that unplanned inventory accumulation tends to cause the level of nominal national income to fall if income is at the target level. Both prices and output may fall.

**An Inflationary Gap** Alternatively, the equilibrium level of nominal national income may be higher than the target level. Such a case is shown in Exhibit 10.2, where the aggregate demand schedule is $280 higher than the

**Target level of nominal national income (income target)** The level of nominal national income judged by policy makers to be most nearly compatible with the goals of full employment, price stability, real economic growth, regional economic balance, and balance of payments stability.

**Deflationary gap** The difference between planned expenditures and national product at the target level of national income when aggregate supply exceeds aggregate demand at that level.

---

**Exhibit 10.2**
**An inflationary gap**
An inflationary gap is said to occur whenever planned expenditure (aggregate demand) is greater than national product (aggregate supply) at the target level of national income. Under this condition, the equilibrium level of nominal national income is above the target level. If national income were at the target level, unplanned inventory accumulation would put upward pressure on the level of income and cause the circular flow to expand.

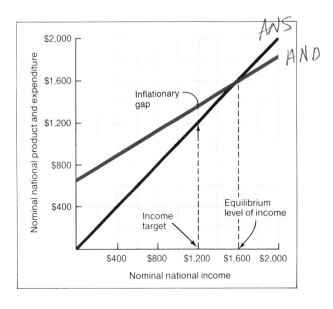

one shown in Exhibit 10.1. Now planned expenditures will exceed national income at the target level of national income. Instead of unplanned inventory accumulation and a deflationary gap at the target income, there is unplanned inventory depletion and an **inflationary gap**.

**Inflationary gap** The difference between planned expenditures and national product at the target level of national income when aggregate demand exceeds aggregate supply at that level.

When such a gap exists, nominal national income is again not in equilibrium at the target level. If national income were to be at the target level, unplanned inventory depletion would cause the circular flow, measured in nominal terms, to expand. This will likely cause price inflation.

### Filling a Deflationary or Inflationary Gap

When there is an inflationary or deflationary gap in the economy, fiscal policy can be used to fill it. In the case of a deflationary gap, consumption, planned investment, government purchases, and net exports combined are not great enough to equal national income at the target level. Policy makers can try to fill the gap directly by increasing government purchases or indirectly by stimulating consumption through reduced taxes. In the case of an inflationary gap, consumption, planned investment, government purchases, and net exports are together so great that they exceed national income at the target level. Policy makers then try to eliminate the gap by cutting government purchases or discouraging consumption with a tax increase.

**Leakage-Injection Approach** Chapter 9 introduced the leakage-injection approach as an alternative way of determining the equilibrium level of national income. This approach sheds additional light on the process of eliminating inflationary and deflationary gaps. According to the approach, in equilibrium, saving plus net taxes plus imports must equal planned investment plus government purchases plus exports.

When there is a deflationary gap, leakages exceed planned injections at the target level of nominal income. Unless fiscal policy intervenes, the difference is taken up by unplanned inventory investment, which holds nominal national income below the target level. Fiscal policy can close the gap by adding to injections with government purchases or by reducing leakages through a cut in net taxes.

When there is an inflationary gap, saving plus net taxes plus imports fall short of planned investment plus government purchases plus exports at the target level of nominal national income. Fiscal policy can bring the two into balance either by increasing leakages in the form of taxes or by reducing injections in the form of government purchases.

In outline, this is how fiscal policy works. Now we turn to an examination of the details of multiplier theory.

### Government Purchases Policy

We begin with a simple case in which the government fills a deflationary gap by increasing government purchases. In Exhibit 10.3a, initial conditions are represented by the aggregate nominal demand curve $AND_1$. The consumption schedule on which this curve is based assumes a marginal propensity to consume of 0.75, autonomous consumption of $100, and lump sum taxes of $100. Interest rates and business conditions generate

$110 of planned investment expenditure, and government purchases are $150. Net exports are $75 – 0.15 of national income. The result is an initial equilibrium nominal national income of $900. There is a deflationary gap of $120, measured vertically at the target level of national income of $1,200.

Policy makers want to fill the deflationary gap, and one way to do so is by increasing government purchases. To illustrate: suppose policy makers authorize spending an extra $120 to accelerate the completion of a stretch of interprovincial highway. If the policy is to work, this added spending must be paid for, not by increased taxes, but instead by borrowing from the public. The consequences of the increased spending can be considered from three viewpoints: round by round, aggregate supply and demand, and leakage-injection.

**Round by Round**  First, we can take a round-by-round approach. Spending $120 on the highway project creates $120 in new income for the construction workers, which raises total national income in the first round from $900 to $1,020. Given a marginal propensity to consume of 0.75, the workers save one-quarter of their new income and spend the rest ($90) on, say, clothing. Because 15 percent of the increased income ($18) is spent on clothing produced outside the country, the increased expenditure generates $72 of new income for domestic clothing workers and retailers, which raises total income to $1,092 in the second round. In the third round, clothing workers spend three-quarters of their new income on something else, including 15 percent on imports, which adds $43.20 more to the stream of income and expenditure. As further rounds progress, the target level of $1,200 national income is approached more and more closely.

**Aggregate Supply and Demand Approach**  Instead of taking the round-by-round approach, we can refer to Exhibit 10.3a, which shows the effects of the increased government purchases in terms of the Keynesian cross. The decision to spend $120 on the highway project shifts the aggregate demand schedule upward by $120 to the position labeled $AND_2$. At the initial level of national income, $900, planned expenditures exceed national income and hence national product by $120. This added demand initially causes inventories to decline unexpectedly. In response, firms either step up output or raise prices or both, which sends nominal national income and product upward. The unplanned depletion of inventories is not eliminated entirely until the new equilibrium level of nominal national income is reached — at the point where the new aggregate demand schedule intersects the aggregate supply schedule. This new equilibrium occurs at the target income of $1,200.

**Leakage-Injection Approach**  Finally, we can consider the effects of increased government purchases in terms of the leakage-injection approach. In Exhibit 10.3b, increased government purchases shift the injection schedule upward by $120, from $(I + G + X)_1$ to $(I + G + X)_2$. At the $900 income level, planned investment, government purchases, and exports add up to more than total leakages, so that inventories are unexpectedly depleted and incomes begin to rise. With a marginal propensity to save of

**Exhibit 10.3**

**Use of fiscal policy to fill a deflationary gap**

This exhibit illustrates the use of fiscal policy to fill a deflationary gap and move equilibrium nominal national income to the target level. Part a illustrates this process with the Keynesian cross and Part b with the injection-leakage approach. In both cases, a $120 increase in government purchases results in a $300 increase in equilibrium nominal national income.

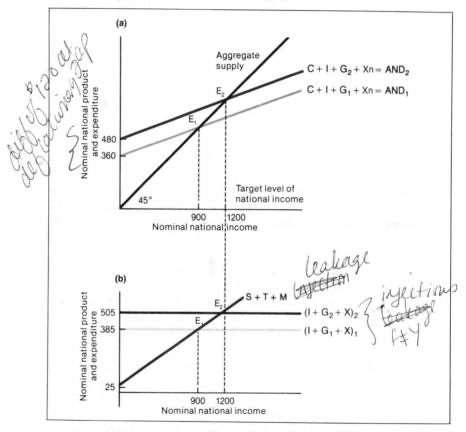

0.25, $.25 in new saving results from each $1 of added income. By the time national income reaches $1,200, saving has increased by $75 and imports by $45 (so that leakages have increased by $120) and equilibrium is restored.

**The Multiplier** Whichever approach we use, we come to the same conclusion: when government purchases are increased while taxes, planned investment, the net exports schedule, and the consumption schedule remain unchanged, equilibrium nominal national income changes by an amount equal to the change in government purchases times the multiplier. In this case, where the change in government purchases is $120 and the multiplier is 2.5, the change in equilibrium income is 2.5 × $120 = $300.

$$\text{Multiplier} = \frac{1}{1-\text{MPC}_D} = \frac{1}{1-(0.75-0.15)} = \frac{1}{0.4} = 2.5$$

This can also be written as follows:

$$\text{Change in national income} = \frac{1}{1-\text{MPC}_D} \times \text{Change in government purchases}$$

$$\$300 = 2.5 \times \$120$$

## Net Tax Policy

Instead of stimulating aggregate demand by increasing government purchases or moderating it by cutting purchases, fiscal policy authorities can instead manipulate demand by raising or lowering net taxes. Net tax policy is potentially as capable of filling a deflationary or inflationary gap as government purchase policy, but the chain of effects through which it operates is sufficiently different to warrant a separate discussion.

**Net Taxes and Consumption Expenditure** The major difference between the two types of fiscal policy is that changes in government purchases are themselves changes in aggregate demand, whereas changes in net taxes operate on aggregate demand only indirectly—through changes in consumption expenditures. The immediate effect of a $1 tax cut is a $1 increase in the part of national income left to households as disposable income. The effect of this change on aggregate demand—on domestic goods and services—depends on the marginal propensity to consume and the marginal propensity to import. If the marginal propensity to consume is 0.75, and the marginal propensity to import is 0.15, as assumed in the recent examples, a $1 tax cut produces a $.75 increase in consumption expenditure, other things being equal, and a $.15 increase in imports or a $.60 increase in expenditure on domestic goods and services.

Geometrically, this initial effect of a tax cut appears as an upward shift in the aggregate nominal demand schedule. With a marginal propensity to consume of 0.75 and a marginal propensity to import of 0.15, each $1 cut in taxes shifts the demand schedule up by $.60. (A $1 increase in net taxes would cut $1 from disposable income, which in turn would shift the aggregate demand schedule downward by $.60.) Once the aggregate demand schedule has shifted, the multiplier process takes over. The $.60 in new first-round expenditure on domestic goods and services stimulated by each $1 cut in net taxes becomes someone's second-round income. Sixty percent of this second-round income is spent on further domestic output, which generates third-round income, and so on. Equilibrium is reestablished only when the economy has moved along the new, higher aggregate nominal demand curve to the point where it intersects the aggregate nominal supply curve.

**The Net Tax Multiplier** The change in equilibrium nominal national income produced by a change in taxes is equal to the multiplier times the amount of the shift in the aggregate demand curve produced by the tax change. This shift is opposite in direction to the tax change (up for a tax cut, down for a tax increase) and equal in magnitude to the amount of the tax change times the marginal propensity to consume minus the marginal propensity to import. With a marginal propensity to consume of 0.75 and a marginal propensity to import of 0.15, the multiplier has a value of 2.5. A $1 tax cut shifts the aggregate demand curve up by $.60. Multiplying this by 2.5 gives an increase in equilibrium nominal national income of $1.50. Similarly, a $1 tax increase shifts the aggregate demand curve down by $.60, which produces a $1.50 fall in equilibrium nominal national income.

**Net tax multiplier** A multiplier showing how much equilibrium nominal national income will change in response to a change in net taxes. The formula for the net tax multiplier is
$$-\frac{(MPC - MPM)}{MPS + MPM} \text{ or } \frac{-MPC_D}{1 - MPC_D}$$

This analysis of the effects of a change in taxes can be used to define the **net tax multiplier**—the change in equilibrium nominal national income resulting from a $1 change in net taxes. The net tax multiplier is negative because a change in net taxes causes an opposite shift in the aggregate demand curve. It is also smaller than the previous multiplier, because the size of the shift in the aggregate demand curve produced by each $1 change in disposable income is equal only to $1 times the marginal propensity to consume minus the marginal propensity to import. Using MPC to represent the marginal propensity to consume, MPS to represent the marginal propensity to save, MPM to represent the marginal propensity to import, and $MPC_D$ to represent the marginal propensity to consume domestic output (MPC−MPM), the formula is:

$$\frac{\text{Net tax}}{\text{multiplier}} = -\frac{(MPC-MPM)}{MPS+MPM}, \text{ or } -\frac{(MPC-MPM)}{1-(MPC-MPM)}, \text{ or } -\frac{MPC_D}{1-MPC_D}$$

If MPC = 0.75, MPM = 0.15, the $MPC_D$ = 0.6 and the net tax multiplier is:

$$-\frac{0.6}{1-0.6} = -\frac{0.6}{0.4} = -1.5$$

The complete algebraic derivation of the net tax multiplier is given in the Appendix to Chapter 10.

**Taxes and Transfers**  A final comment on net tax policy: the term *net taxes*, as explained earlier, means taxes collected by government minus transfer payments. The net tax multiplier thus applies to changes in transfer payments as well as to changes in taxes paid. A $1 increase in transfer payments is a $1 decrease in net taxes, and a $1 decrease in transfer payments is a $1 increase in net taxes. With a marginal propensity to consume of 0.75 and a marginal propensity to import of 0.15, a $1 increase in transfer payments can be expected to produce a $1.50 increase in equilibrium nominal national income. This is the result of applying the net tax multiplier of 1.5 to the change in net taxes of −$1.

### The Multipliers Compared

Two multipliers have now been introduced. With a marginal propensity to consume of 0.75 and a marginal propensity to import of 0.15, and hence a marginal propensity to consume domestic output of 0.6, there is a multiplier related to changes in expenditures of 2.5 and a net tax multiplier of 1.5. If the marginal propensity to consume were 0.9 and the marginal propensity to import remained at 0.15, the expenditure multiplier would be 4 and the net tax multiplier would be 3.

However, these multipliers should be interpreted with caution. A change in government spending is the most powerful tool of fiscal policy, in the sense that it takes advantage of the full value of the multiplier. That power does not mean, though, that a change in government spending is necessarily the best way to eliminate an inflationary or deflationary gap. Any of the two policies can be as effective as the other, so long as a big enough change in taxes or transfer payments is used.

### The Balanced Budget Multiplier

The fact that the multiplier for an increase in government expenditures is greater than the net tax multiplier opens up the interesting possibility that a balanced increase in both government spending and net taxes will have a net, stimulative effect on the economy. A government need not go into debt in order to move the economy toward a full employment equilibrium when a deflationary gap exists.

To understand this possibility, imagine an initial situation in which national income is at its equilibrium level and the federal budget is exactly in balance. Beginning from this position, suppose that government purchases are raised by $100 and that, at the same time, taxes are increased by a lump sum $100. This combination of policy moves will leave the budget exactly in balance at the initial level of national income.

However, using the same multipliers as previously, the $100 increase in government spending will increase the income level by $250, while the tax increase of $100 will reduce income by only $150 (the net tax multiplier of – 1.5 multiplied by the change in tax). The net result should be a $100 increase in the equilibrium level of income.

The ability of an increase in government purchases, matched dollar for dollar by an increase in taxes, to raise the equilibrium level of nominal national income is known as the **balanced budget multiplier effect**. If a tax increase (or cut) initially reduces (or increases) consumption by the full amount of the marginal propensity to consume, a dollar change in government purchases matched by a dollar change in net taxes will produce a dollar change in equilibrium nominal national income. In this case, the value of the balanced budget multiplier is 1.

In a decade when balanced federal budgets are only a fading memory, the balanced budget multiplier effect might seem to be little more than a theoretical curiosity. Not so. The balanced budget multiplier operates whenever net taxes and government purchases are changed by equal amounts, whether or not the budget is initially in equilibrium.

> **Balanced budget multiplier effect** The ability of an increase in government purchases, matched dollar for dollar by an increase in taxes, to raise the equilibrium level of nominal national income.

## DISCRETIONARY FISCAL POLICY AND AUTOMATIC STABILIZERS

### Discretionary Policy

Up to this point, it has been assumed that policy makers are free to adjust taxes and government purchases as they please, for no other purpose than

**Discretionary fiscal policy**
Changes in the levels of taxes, transfers, or government purchases made for the specific purpose of economic stabilization.

to manipulate aggregate nominal demand. Policy actions of this type are known as **discretionary fiscal policy**. The following case study illustrates this type of fiscal policy. It concerns a proposal to use discretionary fiscal policy to deal with a deflationary gap.

### Case 10.1
### The Turner Tax Concessions

In May 1972, Canada's Minister of Finance, John Turner, announced tax concessions for manufacturing and processing firms. Beginning in 1973, such firms would receive tax reductions based on the portion of their income devoted to investment. Though the economy was not in a slump, the unemployment rate was rising and it was felt by the government that more investment was needed in the 1970s to assure a high rate of growth for the Canadian economy.

In 1975, after the tax concessions had been in effect for almost three years, the government undertook a study to assess the impact of the tax reductions on industrial investment. The report claimed that the reductions were responsible for $2.5 billion of new investment, some 73,000 new jobs, and $4.8 billion in increased sales. A multiplier effect was also claimed, with about $1.2 billion new investment in the second round. It was conceded that the government lost over $1 billion in tax revenue as a result of the tax reductions, but much of this was regained through increased tax revenues resulting from the alleged growth in output. Businessmen surveyed, however, were not so sure that the government's fiscal strategy was primarily responsible for the growth in investment, output, and employment. Only 32 percent indicated that they had been favorably influenced by the tax reductions. It is finally impossible, of course, to know what would have been done in the absence of special government tax measures. The minister pointed out that in the year before the measures came into effect, real investment had declined by 2.1 percent. In contrast to this, in 1973 and 1974, investment increased annually at an average rate of 20 percent. It seems reasonable to assume that at least part of that increase was due to fiscal policy, but there is no way of knowing how much.

## Automatic Stabilizers

Although discretionary fiscal policy is what makes the headlines, not all fiscal policy is of a discretionary nature. Some policy changes occur automatically, without any positive action taken by Parliament or the federal cabinet. Although ignored in the simplified examples up to this point, where lump sum taxes were assumed, these automatic changes are quite important in practice. For example, many kinds of taxes — including corporate and personal income taxes, payroll taxes, and sales taxes — automatically increase as the level of nominal national income increases. Also, many kinds of transfer payments tend to decrease as nominal national income increases. Unemployment benefits are a case in point.

Because these nondiscretionary changes in taxes and transfer payments tend to have a contractionary influence when the economy is expanding and an expansionary influence when it is contracting, they are called **automatic stabilizers**. In effect, these stabilizers reduce the value of the simple multiplier for the economy. Because of them, the economy is less sensitive than it otherwise would be to unexpected changes in planned investment, government purchases, autonomous consumption expenditure, and net exports.

**Automatic stabilizers**
Changes in taxes, transfers, and government purchases that occur automatically as nominal GNP rises or falls.

Automatic stabilizers are not by themselves enough to guarantee full employment and price stability. They do, however, provide a useful supplement to discretionary fiscal policies.

## FISCAL POLICY AND THE NATIONAL DEBT

This chapter so far has drawn a very symmetrical picture of fiscal policy. If the economy is in a slump, the government cuts taxes or increases expenditures; the resulting deficit acts as an injection of new demand into the circular flow, and national income and product are boosted toward their target level. If the economy is overheated, with inflation and tight job markets, spending is cut or taxes are raised; enough of this results in a surplus, which withdraws demand from the circular flow and cools off the economy.

In the 32 years from 1950 to 1981 inclusive, the federal government of Canada has varied surpluses and deficits in a fairly even way: it has had surpluses in 14 years and deficits in 18. All levels of government together have had surpluses in 16 years and deficits in 16. There are critics of government policy, however, who have been disturbed by the size of government deficits in recent years and are worried about the increase in government debt. (See Chapter 4 for a review of the figures.)

After running a surplus of more than $1 billion in 1974, the federal government incurred a deficit of more than $3 billion in each of the years 1975 and 1976. In 1977 the deficit soared to $7.4 billion. In 1978 it increased to $11.4 billion and in 1982–83 it jumped sharply to $26 billion. It is small wonder that there is growing concern about these deficits.

In the late 1970s, political support began to grow in both the United States and Canada for stricter limits on discretionary fiscal policy. Constitutional amendments were proposed in the United States to force governments to restrain spending and keep their budgets in balance. Little attention has been given in Canada to such legal or constitutional restraints, but both provincial and federal governments sense a growing public desire for what is sometimes called "fiscal responsibility." Do these political developments represent the last gasp of an economic conservatism that dates back to pre-Keynesian times, or do they instead represent a justified disenchantment with the results of several decades of deficit spending? The debate is likely to continue for years to come, so it is worthwhile to look at the economic arguments advanced by each side.

### In Defense of Deficit Spending

In the opinion of fiscal activists, the important thing is to provide the right amount of stimulus or restraint each year, in order to move toward the goals of full employment, price stability, economic growth, and balance of payments stability. If this requires running budget deficits more often than surpluses, then so be it. There is no reason to make controlling the size of the national debt a separate, fifth goal of policy. No one is hurt if the national debt grows, so nothing should be sacrificed in order to keep it small. Four arguments underlie this position:

**Trend of the National Debt**  The first argument given for not being concerned with the size of the national debt is that the trend of the debt, in relation to gross national product, has been steadily down, not up. If ever the national debt was a burden, it was at the end of World War II. In 1946, the government of Canada debt stood at an all-time high of 135 percent of GNP. By the mid-1970s, it had been reduced to less than 25 percent of the GNP.[1]

**The Power of Taxation**  A second argument for not being concerned with the size of the national debt is that the federal government never need worry about bankruptcy, no matter how large its debt becomes. The federal debt is backed by the federal power of taxation, which is enormous. As long as the power of taxation exists, people will continue to lend the government money to refinance the debt as it becomes due, confident that they will be repaid on time, in full, and with interest.

**We Owe It to Ourselves**  The third argument is that the size of the national debt is not a matter of serious concern because it is a debt that the Canadian people owe largely to themselves. It is a mere bookkeeping entry that can be cleared by shuffling funds from one account to another with no net drain on the real resources of the country. From the point of view of the circular flow, interest payments on the national debt are only transfer payments.

**Can't Build Today's Houses with Tomorrow's Bricks**  Finally, it is said that there is no reason to be concerned that the national debt will put an unfair burden on future generations. Even if those in authority want to do so, the argument goes, today's houses cannot be built with tomorrow's bricks. Real goods and services, that is to say, cannot be transferred from the future to the present. No matter how government spending is financed today, annual real income consists in the real goods and services we produce—no more and no less. The same has been true at every time in the past and will be true at every time in the future.

**Beware False Comparisons**  Taken together, these arguments add up to a warning not to make false comparisons between the national debt and the debts of individual families or private firms. Individuals and private firms can go bankrupt if their debts get larger than their ability to repay. Repayments of private debts (unless they are debts to people within the same family or firm) are not mere bookkeeping entries but instead are real flows of purchasing power from those within to outsiders. Thus private debts do represent a real burden on the future consumption or investment capacity of the unit that incurs them. But none of these things, it is said, hold true for the national debt.

---

[1]In 1816, during the course of England's industrial revolution, the national debt was more than twice the size of the gross national product. Source: Arthur Redford, *The Economic History of England, 1760–1860* (London: Longmans, 1960), p. 103.

## Reservations about Deficit Spending

Although acknowledging that the four arguments for deficit spending are valid as far as they go, modern fiscal conservatives nonetheless have grave reservations about the wisdom of unlimited deficit spending and limitless growth of the national debt. They raise four points of their own.

**Reversal of the Trend**  First, although recognizing the downward postwar trend of the national debt in relation to GNP, they are alarmed by the apparent break with the trend that occurred in the late 1970s and early 1980s. Although the debt remained fairly low in relation to GNP, the size of the annual deficits—which measure the rate at which new debt is accumulated—reached a postwar high. Furthermore, although the debt ratio was still quite low, interest rates had risen to historic highs, so that the proportion of GNP needed to service the debt was as high as at the end of World War II.

**Limits to Taxation**  Second, those people who are concerned about the size of the national debt are skeptical of assurances that taxes can be raised without limit to repay debts. There are the examples of cities like New York and Cleveland, which have already found their taxing power insufficient to repay past debts on schedule. Cities in Canada have not reached the same crisis stage, but they too are severely pinched by a narrow tax base and growing demands for services. The federal government does have one power that makes it more able to meet debt payments than provincial and municipal governments, but it is not the power of unlimited taxation. Instead, it is the power to create money. This power, discussed in coming chapters, does indeed guarantee that the federal government need never default on its debts; but in the long run, use of this power can impart an inflationary bias to stabilization policy.

**Rising Foreign Share of the Debt**  Third, fiscal conservatives reject the notion that national debt payments have no economic impact because they are mere costless transfers from one group of people to another. For one thing, because of administrative costs and the disincentive effect of taxes, no transfer is truly costless. Each dollar in debt repayment imposes an opportunity cost of more than a dollar on someone.

On a more practical level, it is no longer as true as it once was that the national debt is something citizens owe to themselves. Between 1966 and the late 1970s, the share of the federal government debt held by other countries increased from about 4 percent to 6 percent. In 1978 alone, the federal government increased the outstanding amount of government securities held by Canadians by $8.2 billion, while it increased the amount held by foreigners by $2.3 billion.

**Possible Burdens on Future Generations**  Fourth, critics of excessive deficit spending are not convinced that borrowing to finance government spending imposes no burden on future generations. True, it is literally impossible to build today's houses with tomorrow's bricks. But future generations can be burdened with the necessity of exporting some of those future bricks to pay off borrowing from abroad. In addition, heavy government borrowing today may indirectly cause real national product to be lower in the future than it otherwise would have been. The reason is that the government and private firms must compete in financial markets for the same pool of funds created by savers. At some point, government borrowing may begin to crowd out the private investment on which future economic growth depends. (More on this subject will appear in later chapters.)

To summarize, modern fiscal conservatives are willing to accept the arguments used in defense of deficit spending by fiscal policy activits, but only up to a point. The national debt—at least that part of it held by people within Canada—is indeed not strictly comparable to private debts. The federal government is admittedly not in danger of literal bankruptcy. Nonetheless, there is a danger that excessive short-run reliance on deficit spending as a means of promoting full employment may in the long run threaten the ability of the economy to achieve price stability and real economic growth.

## CONCLUSIONS

The discussion of stabilization policy has now been carried about as far as it can be on the basis of the multiplier theory alone. Already, the discussion of the controversy over the national debt has had occasion to mention money and the federal government's power to control its supply. Monetary policy is, in fact, the second side of stabilization policy, and it is as important as fiscal policy. The next three chapters will discuss the banking system and monetary policy. Then, Chapter 14 will take a fresh look at what this chapter has explained and will discuss the interactions between monetary policy and fiscal policy.

## SUMMARY

1. If the equilibrium level of nominal national income is different from the target level, there is a gap between total planned expenditure and national product measured at the target level of income. If the equilibrium level of income is lower than policy makers want it to be, a deflationary gap is said to exist. If the equilibrium level of nominal income is too high, the gap is said to be inflationary.
2. One way to fill a deflationary gap is by increasing government purchases without increasing net taxes. When such purchases are increased while net taxes, planned investment, the consumption schedule and the net export schedule remain unchanged, equilibrium nominal national income changes by an amount equal to the change in government purchases times the multiplier.
3. A deflationary gap can also be filled by cutting net taxes without changing government purchases. When net taxes are changed while government purchases, planned investment, autonomous consumption, autonomous net exports, the marginal propensity to consume, and the

marginal propensity to import remain unchanged, equilibrium nominal national income changes in the direction opposite to the change in taxes by an amount equal to the change in net taxes times the net tax multiplier.

4. Changes in taxes, transfers, or the level of government purchases made for the specific purpose of achieving the goal of economic stabilization are called discretionary fiscal policy. In addition to discretionary fiscal policy, other changes in taxes, transfers, and even government purchases occur automatically as the level of national product varies. Examples are changes in income taxes and unemployment benefits. These are called automatic stabilizers.

5. At least since the 1930s, there has been a running controversy between fiscal conservatives, who would like to see the federal government balance its budget at least most of the time, and fiscal activists, who think that persistent deficit spending is no real cause for worry. The issue centers largely on whether the national debt (and the repayment of it) imposes a real burden, present or future, on the economy. The fiscal activists have succeeded in establishing that naive fears of national bankruptcy are based on misleading analogies between private debt and the national debt. But fiscal conservatives counter that in the long run, excessive government borrowing and indebtedness can pose a threat to economic growth and price stability.

## DISCUSSION QUESTIONS

1. Is the target level of national income always the level of national income at which there will be equilibrium?
2. Should the major tool of fiscal policy be changes in government spending or changes in taxation? Justify your position.
3. Use the circular flow to trace the effect of government spending in closing a deflationary gap.
4. What importance does the size of the marginal propensity to consume and the marginal propensity to import have for the effectiveness of fiscal policy in closing both inflationary and deflationary gaps?
5. Explain why a given change in government spending has a greater impact on the economy than does the same change in taxation.
6. If there were a deflationary gap, would there be some advantage in simply paying workers to dig ditches and then fill them in? Under what circumstances would this policy be beneficial?
7. Who pays the cost and who receives the benefits of (a) increased government spending and (b) increased taxes? Does your answer to this question differ now from what it would have been just after you read Chapter 4?
8. Do you think that there is an inflationary gap in the economy right now (as you are taking this course)? A deflationary gap? How can you tell? What is the government doing about the gap if there is one?
9. Evaluate the following possible rule for the conduct of fiscal policy: set the level of government purchases by looking at the actual economic merit of spending projects without considering macroeconomic effects. Then, if the resulting budget does not provide the right amount of macroeconomic stimulus, aim for the target level of national income by adjusting net taxes upward or downward as required. Is this rule compatible with active use of discretionary fiscal policy?

# APPENDIX TO CHAPTER 10
# AN ALGEBRAIC APPROACH TO INCOME DETERMINATION AND THE MULTIPLIER

All the theoretical propositions illustrated with graphs and numerical examples in the last three chapters can also be expressed in terms of elementary algebra. Begin with the consumption schedule. Using $a$ for the constant term in the schedule (autonomous consumption), $b$ for the marginal propensity to consume, C for nominal consumption expenditure, T for net taxes, Y for nominal national income, and M for imports, M$a$ for autonomous imports, and $m$ for the marginal propensity to import, the consumption schedule and the import schedule can be written:

$$C = a + b(Y - T)$$
$$M = Ma + m(Y - T)$$

**10A.1**

Note that the expression $(Y - T)$ that appears in the right-hand side of this expression represents nominal disposable income.

With the consumption schedule as a basis, the aggregate nominal demand (AND) schedule is put together by adding planned investment (I), government purchases (G), and exports (X) and subtracting imports (M). This gives:

$$AND = C + I + G + X - M$$

**10A.2**

Substituting in Equation 10A.1:

$$AND = a + b(Y - T) + I + G + X - Ma - m(Y - T)$$

**10A.3**

It is convenient to rewrite this equation by grouping the constant terms, so that it becomes:

$$AND = (a - bT + mT + I + G + X - Ma) + bY - mY$$

**10A.4**

The term in parentheses in Equation 10A.4 represents the constant term, or vertical intercept, of the aggregate nominal demand schedule; and $b$, the marginal propensity to consume, minus $m$, represents its slope.

This equation can now be used to determine the equilibrium level of nominal national income. The theory set forth in Chapter 9 showed that for the economy to be in equilibrium, national income must be equal to planned expenditure, so that there is no unplanned inventory accumulation or depletion. This equilibrium condition can be written:

$$Y = AND$$

**10A.5**

Substituting Equation 10A.4 into Equation 10A.5, the equilibrium condition becomes:

$$Y = [a - bT + I + G + X - (Ma - mT)] + bY - mY$$

**10A.6**

Solving Equation 10A.6 for Y then gives this formula for the equilibrium value of nominal national income:

$$Y^* = \frac{1}{1 - b_d}[a - bT + I + G + X - (Ma - mT)]$$

where $b_d$ is the marginal propensity to consume domestic output which equals $b - m$.

**10A.7**

The asterisk after the Y in this formula is a reminder that the equation holds only for the equilibrium value of nominal national income.

Equation 10A.7 can now be applied to solve a number of problems.

**Problem 1** Use Equation 10A.7 to derive the formulas for the multiplier and the net tax multiplier.

*Solution* The multiplier was defined in Chapter 9 as the ratio of an induced change in the equilibrium level of nominal national income to an initial shift in the aggregate nominal demand schedule for domestic output. In algebraic terms, a shift in the aggregate nominal demand schedule means an increase or decrease in the intercept term $[a - bT + I + G + X - (Ma - mT)]$. For ease in notation, let A represent this intercept term:

$$A = [a - bT + I + G + X - (Ma - mT)] \qquad \textbf{10A.8}$$

Equation 10A.7 then becomes:

$$Y^* = \frac{1}{1 - b_d} A \qquad \textbf{10A.9}$$

Suppose now that this constant term changes from an initial value of $A_0$ to a new value, $A_1$, thereby producing a shift in the aggregate nominal demand schedule of $A_1 - A_0$. This increases the equilibrium value of nominal national income from

$$Y_0^* = \frac{1}{1 - b_d} A_0$$

to a new value of

$$Y_1^* = \frac{1}{1 - b_d} A_1$$

The multiplier, as the ratio of the change in equilibrium income to the shift in the aggregate nominal demand schedule, can now be calculated as follows:

$$\text{Multiplier} = \frac{Y_1^* - Y_0^*}{A_1 - A_0}$$

$$= \frac{(A_1 - A_0)/(1 - b_d)}{A_1 - A_0} = \frac{1}{1 - b_d}$$

This is exactly the result given in Chapter 9, except that $b_d$ is used in place of $MPC_D$ to represent the marginal propensity to consume domestic output.

Once this multiplier is established, finding the net tax multiplier is easy. Suppose that net taxes change by an amount $\Delta T$. From Equation 10A.8, it is apparent that the resulting shift in the aggregate nominal demand schedule will be $\Delta A = -b\Delta T - m\Delta T$. The change in equilibrium income can be found by applying the multiplier to the shift in the aggregate demand curve, which gives:

$$\Delta Y^* = \frac{1}{1 - b_d} \Delta A = -b + m \frac{1}{1 - b_d} \Delta T \text{ or } -b + m \frac{1}{1 - b_d} \Delta T$$

Simplifying the last expression on the right:

$$\Delta Y^* = \frac{-b + m}{1 - b_d} \Delta T, \text{ or } \Delta Y = -\frac{b_d}{1 - b_d} \Delta T$$

The net tax multiplier is thus equal to $-\dfrac{b_d}{1 - b_d}$ or $-\dfrac{MPC_D}{1 - MPC_D}$

as given in the text.

**Problem 2** Suppose that $a = 100$, $b = 0.75$, $T = 100$, $I = 110$, $G = 150$, $X = 125$, and $M = 65 + 0.15(Y - T)$. What is the equilibrium value of aggregate nominal demand?

*Note:* $b - m = 0.75 - 0.15 = 0.6$.

*Solution* Simply substitute the various values into Equation 10A.7. This gives:

$$Y^* = \frac{1}{(1 - 0.6)} [100 - 0.75(100) + 110 + 125 + 125 - (-65 - 15)]$$

$$= 2.5(360)$$

$$= \$900$$

Compare this result with Exhibits 9.3 and 9.4, which provide graphical and numerical solutions to the same problem.

**Problem 3** Suppose that, initially, all variables and constants have the values given in Problem 2 but that the government adopts a target value for nominal national income of $1,200. Assuming no change in taxes, how much will government purchases have to be in order to reach the income target?

*Solution* Substitute the known values for $a$, $b$, T, I, **X**, and M into Equation 10A.7, leaving G as the unknown. Use the target income of $1,200 in place of Y*. This gives:

$1,200 = 2.5[100 - 0.75(100) + 110 + 150 - 75 + G]$

Solve for G as follows:

$1,200 = 525 + 2.5G$

$2.5\,G = 675$

$G = 270$

# CHARTERED BANKS AND OTHER FINANCIAL INTERMEDIARIES

---

## WHAT YOU WILL LEARN IN THIS CHAPTER
*This chapter provides an introduction to the financial sector of the economy. It explains how banks, thrift institutions, insurance companies, pension funds, and securities markets operate as financial intermediaries to channel funds from savers to investors. Because banks will play a particularly important role in the subsequent analysis, the balance sheets of Canadian chartered banks are discussed here in some detail. The chapter also introduces the Bank of Canada, which plays an important role in regulating the Canadian banking system and in conducting monetary policy.*

## FOR REVIEW
*Here are some important terms and concepts that will be put to use in this chapter. If you do not understand them, review them before proceeding.*
- *Circular flow of income and product (Chapter 5)*
- *Nominal and real interest rates (Chapter 7)*

---

This chapter is the first of four devoted to the financial sector of the Canadian economy. This sector consists of a set of markets that provide the monetary and financial arrangements necessary to facilitate the production and distribution of real goods and personal services.

**Financial Intermediaries** The chapter focuses on the important institutions in the financial sector that are know as **financial intermediaries** because of their role in channeling funds from savers to investors. Financial intermediaries include chartered banks, credit unions and caisses populaires, insurance companies, securities markets, and a number of other institutions. They are a necessary part of the economy because the needs of individual lenders and individual borrowers do not necessarily match in terms of quantity of funds, time horizons, or attitudes toward risk.

The job of financial intermediaries is to reconcile the diverse interests of lenders and borrowers. For example, intermediaries can pool the funds of

**Financial intermediary** Any financial institution that performs the function of channeling funds from savers to investors.

many small savers and use the proceeds to make large loans. They can tap the steady stream of funds flowing through the chequing accounts of households and firms (funds that remain in these accounts for only a few days or weeks at a time) and use them as a basis for extending long-term loans. And, as will be shown, they can reconcile the needs of people who want to borrow in order to undertake somewhat risky investments with the needs of people who want to find relatively risk-free uses for their savings. A list of selected financial intermediaries in Canada in 1982 indicated that they had assets of $429.35 billion, equal to 125 percent of GNP.[1]

---

[1]Gordon F. Boreham, "The Changing Nature of Canadian Banking," *Canadian Banker and ICB Review,* February 1983, p. 9.

**Exhibit 11.1**

**The circular flow with financial intermediaries**

This diagram of the circular flow of income and product features the role of the financial intermediaries that operate in the economy's financial markets. Their role is to channel funds from savers to investors. Households are net savers, as shown by the large arrow; but they also do some borrowing. Businesses are net borrowers, but they also do some saving. Units of government run deficits (borrow) in larger amounts than they run surpluses (save).

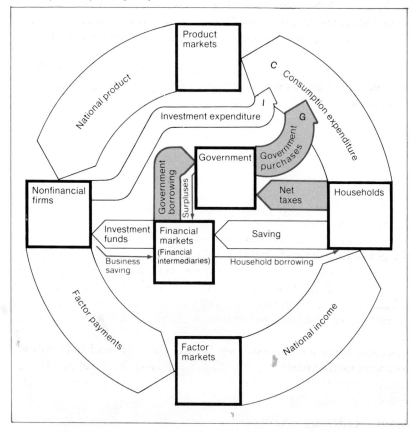

**Financial Intermediaries in the Circular Flow**  Exhibit 11.1 shows the place of financial intermediaries in the circular flow of income and product. This exhibit is similar to Exhibit 5.4, except that it has additional arrows to show flows both into and out of the markets in which financial intermediaries operate. The large arrow from households to financial markets indicates that households are net lenders; but, as the small arrow from financial markets to households indicates, they do some borrowing. Non-financial business firms, on the other hand, are net borrowers, although they do provide loanable funds to financial markets in lesser amounts than their borrowings, as shown by the smaller arrow. Similarly, the government sector is on the average a net borrower, because government budget deficits tend to be larger than surpluses. However, the units of government that do run budget surpluses are a source of funds to financial markets.

Now that the general introduction to the function of financial intermediaries has been given, the chapter will consider the various major classes of intermediaries one by one. It will begin with chartered banks.

## CHARTERED BANKS

Chartered banks are financial intermediaries that accept a wide variety of deposits from firms and households and in turn make loans to the public in a wide variety of forms. They are, in many respects, the most important and least specialized of financial intermediaries. In Canada the name "bank" can be used only by institutions that obtain a special charter from Parliament and operate under the Bank Act, which was revised most recently in 1980. This makes them subject to control by Canada's central bank (discussed later in this chapter). It also gives them the right to accept deposits for chequing purposes and to transfer such cheques from one bank to another through clearing houses maintained by the Canadian Payments Association.

The best way to get an idea of how chartered banks operate is to look at their total balance sheet. This will make it clear just where the funds handled by banks come from and where they go.

### A Balance Sheet for Chartered Banks

Exhibit 11.2 shows the consolidated balance sheet of Canada's chartered banks as of November 30, 1982. Like all balance sheets, this one is divided into two columns. The left-hand column lists all the banks' *assets* — all the things to which the banks hold legal claim. The right-hand column shows the banks' *liabilities* — all the claims held against the banks by outsiders — and their *net worth* — the difference between assets and liabilities. Net worth represents claims against the banks' assets by the owners of the banks. It includes shareholders' equity and reserves for losses.

Because of the way the terms are defined, the right-hand and left-hand columns exactly balance — hence the *balance sheet*. For all balance sheets, whether of banks or of any other financial unit or aggregate, it must always be true that

Assets = Liabilities + Net worth

**Exhibit 11.2**

**Consolidated balance sheet of chartered banks, November 30, 1982 (in billions of dollars)**

This table shows the consolidated balance sheet for all the Canadian chartered banks. Listed as assets are all the things that the banks own. Liabilities are all claims against the banks' assets held by individual firms or institutions other than the banks' owners. The banks' net worth is obtained by subtracting liabilities from assets.

| Assets | | Liabilities and Net Worth | |
|---|---|---|---|
| Bank of Canada reserve deposits and notes | 6.1 | Canadian demand deposits | 17.6 |
| Treasury bills | 9.4 | Canadian savings and notice deposits | 148.7 |
| Mortgages | 31.6 | Deposits held by foreigner (foreign currency liabilities) | 160.7 |
| General loans | 121.9 | | |
| Canadian securities | 10.1 | Other liabilities | 28.7 |
| Foreign securities and deposits with foreign banks | 156.9 | Total liabilities | 355.7 |
| Other assets | 33.1 | Net worth | 13.4 |
| Total assets | 369.1 | Total liabilities plus net worth | 369.1 |

Source: *Bank of Canada Review*, January 1982, p. 534-536.

The balance sheet shows that most of the assets held by banks are financial claims against others. These claims are mostly loans granted to individuals and businesses, and securities issued by business and federal, provincial, and municipal governments. On the liability side of the balance sheet, the biggest items are demand and notice deposits, which are claims against the bank owned by depositors. The net worth figure represents what would be left to the owners of the bank if they were to sell all their assets and pay off all their liabilities at "book" values.

## Reserves

**Reserves** (of chartered banks) Money held by chartered banks as cash or non-interest-bearing deposits with the Bank of Canada.

The **reserves** item on the asset side of the balance sheet deserves some further explanation. Historically, the reason that banks hold some of their assets in the form of reserves is that at any moment depositors may want to withdraw their money from the bank, either by writing a cheque to someone who will deposit it in another bank, or by walking up to the teller's window and asking for currency. In the Canadian banking system today, the quantity of reserves that banks hold is not left up to the judgment of individual bankers. Instead, the Bank Act sets certain reserve requirements for chartered banks. These take the form of fixed percentages of deposits that banks must hold as reserves. These percentages are called **required reserve ratios**. They vary according to the type and size of deposits, and are set down in the Bank Act, which is reviewed every ten years. The rates at the time of the last review, in 1980, were 12 percent for demand deposits and 4 percent for notice deposits. They were set to decline gradually to 10 and 3 percent, respectively by 1984. In addition to these "primary" reserves, chartered banks are required to maintain *secondary* reserves, consisting of short-term, highly liquid assets such as three-month government bonds.

**Required reserve ratios** Legally required minimum quantities of reserves, expressed as ratios of reserves to various types of deposits.

## THE BANK OF CANADA

Canada's central bank is a child of the Depression. In 1933 the federal government responded to growing demands for better monetary leadership in typical Canadian fashion, by appointing a Royal Commission to investigate the situation and make recommendations to the government. The commission made its report that same year and recommended the establishment of a central bank for Canada. Early in 1934, in remarkably quick fashion, Parliament acted on these recommendations and passed the Bank of Canada Act, thereby establishing a central bank for Canada.

Initially all shares of the Bank of Canada were sold to the public, making it a private bank. The first governor, Graham Towers, and the directors of the Bank were appointed by the government, but provision was made for future election of the directors by the private shareholders. However, political pressure developed to make the Bank more subject to government control. Therefore, in 1936, the federal government acquired 51 percent of the Bank's shares, and in 1938 it bought the rest. The Bank of Canada thereby became a true government bank.

### Structure of the Bank of Canada

The structure of the Bank of Canada is quite simple. The Bank is managed at the top by a Board of Directors, consisting of the governor, the senior deputy governor, and twelve directors. The deputy minister of finance is also on the board as a non-voting member. The directors are appointed for three-year terms by the minister of finance, with the approval of the federal cabinet. Unlike the Federal Reserve System in the United States, the Bank of Canada does not have formal regional divisions, but the directors on the board are always chosen on a regional basis, and periodical meetings are held across the country. In addition, the bank has branch offices in most major Canadian cities.

The governor and senior deputy governor are appointed by the board of directors, with cabinet approval, to seven-year terms. An executive committee, consisting of the governor, senior deputy minister, and two directors selected by the board, plus the nonvoting deputy minister of finance, is the real power within the Bank and meets weekly to implement board policy. The full board is called together at least eight times a year to review and ratify policy.

From its establishment in 1934 to the present day, the Bank of Canada has had only four governors. The first governor was Graham F. Towers, a native of Montreal and an economist and accountant by training. He served longer than any other governor, from 1934 to 1954, and developed for the Bank of Canada a worldwide reputation for monetary responsibility and imaginative direction. International recognition of his work led to his appointment as alternate governor of the International Monetary Fund from 1946 to 1954. In the post-World War II period, Towers followed an expansionary policy and maintained low interest rates in order to stimulate investment. He was criticized in the early 1950s for not fighting growing signs of inflation with a more restrictive policy, but he remained primarily concerned with the possibility of recession.

His successor, James Coyne, a lawyer and a native of Winnipeg, was criticized in the late 1950s for following a much more restrictive course at a time when the government and many economists felt that the economy needed some stimulation. The Minister of Finance, Donald Fleming, asked Coyne to change course, and when Coyne refused the minister asked for his resignation. Coyne refused to resign, whereupon the government initiated action in Parliament to declare his office vacant. After an appearance before the Senate and before being evicted by the government, Coyne did resign, on July 13, 1961.

**Graham F. Towers (1897–1975)**

**James Coyne (1910– )**

James Coyne was succeeded by the third governor, Louis Rasminsky, an economist from Montreal. Upon taking the office, he publicly declared that, while the Bank of Canada has the responsibility for monetary policy, if the government disapproves of this policy and asks the Bank to change it, the governor of the Bank is faced with only one choice: he must either change his mind and follow the government's advice, or resign.

When the Bank Act was revised in 1967, it provided for closer and more continuous consultation between the minister of finance and the governor of the Bank of Canada and clarified the steps to be taken in case of a disagreement.

The fourth and current governor, Gerald K. Bouey, an economist from Saskatchewan, took over from Louis Rasminsky in 1973. About the time that Governor Bouey assumed his duties, Canada came to be plagued by unusually high rates of inflation *and* unemployment. The years since 1973 have been marked by a vigorous debate among economists and government advisers about which of these problems poses the greater danger to the Canadian economy. The Economic Council of Canada has often given more weight to the unemployment problem and has urged the government to take steps to stimulate the economy. The governor of the Bank of Canada, obviously in harmony with the various ministers of finance, has placed greater stress on the inflation problem and has attempted to follow a fairly restrictive monetary policy.

**Louis Rasminsky (1908– )**

**Gerald K. Bouey (1920– )**

### Functions of the Bank of Canada

The Bank of Canada is expected to formulate and execute monetary policy for Canada, and it is designed to be reasonably free from political interference. When it attempts, for example, to control inflation by cutting down on the amount of money that people have to spend, it may run into considerable opposition from members of the public. The government may then be pressured into changing the Bank's policy. It obviously wouldn't do for the Bank to give in to such pressure whenever it develops. The governors of the Bank of Canada have tried to maintain a certain tradition of independence, especially the second governor, James Coyne, who refused to follow government policy and was eventually forced to resign (see the profile of the governors).

The government, of course, as the sole shareholder of the Bank, and as the body that is responsible for overall economic policy, has ultimate control over the Bank. There is regular, close consultation between the minister of finance and the governor, and in case of serious disagreement, it is clearly the minister who holds the upper hand. Some argue that the Bank should be a mere arm of government, a division of the Ministry of Finance, since the elected representatives of the government are answerable to the people and should formulate all economic policy for the country. Despite this view, it has been considered advisable to give the Bank as much independence as possible.

The work of the Bank is carried out through several departments, including Securities (to handle open-market operations), Research, and International Transactions. Through its nationwide network of offices and its role as the ultimate clearing agency, the Bank not only manages to regulate monetary operations in the country, but it is one of the few government agencies that regularly produces a surplus on its operations. Probably the most visible function of the Bank is its currency processing. While the Royal Canadian Mint is responsible for coins, the Bank of Canada is the sole issuer of paper currency. Each year it produces more than 600 million new bills, of which more than 90 percent are used to replace worn-out bills.

The chartered banks are required to submit regular reports on their operations to the minister of finance and the Bank of Canada. Their most closely watched duty is to keep reserve deposits with the Bank of Canada. The importance of reserve deposits will be discussed in more detail in Chapter 12.

## THE BANKING SYSTEM

The Canadian banking system consists (in early 1983) of thirteen chartered banks. It resembles the British system and is very different from the banking system of the United States, which has 15,000 separate banks. Amalgamation of banks, and the creation of a branch system such as ours, has been discouraged in the United States. The power of large branch banks is feared, and the objective has been to make the banks serve the needs of industry in local communities. In Canada we have only a few banks with about 7,500 branches. The emphasis has been on consolidation and safety. Managers are moved around frequently to prevent a local branch from losing its objectivity in advancing loans to local business. Credit unions and other financial institutions have often taken advantage of this situation by providing the kind of local service that small banks in the U.S. provide.

The chartered banks of Canada play an extremely important role in the economy, and they have done so with admirable success. There has not been a bank failure since 1923. The kind of bank crisis described in Arthur Hailey's novel *The Money Changers*, in which an individual bank is brought close to bankruptcy when depositors panic and withdraw their money, could hardly occur in this country. No branch bank would be left on its own to weather a run on its deposits.

Exhibit 11.3 illustrates the large assets built up by some of the banks, and their relative positions. The biggest bank, the Royal Bank of Canada, ranks twenty-eighth in size (in terms of deposits) among all world banks. The top five banks hold about 86 percent of the assets and play a major role in determining economic activity in the country. The combined assets of all the banks in November 1982 were $369.1 billion, or about 107 percent of Canada's gross national product.

Bank assets constitute around 80 percent of assets of all financial intermediaries in Canada. Because of the powerful role they play, frequent concern is expressed about the degree of competition in the industry. Though the number of chartered banks is small, some comfort may be derived from the fact that between 1967 and 1982 the share of total bank assets

**Exhibit 11.3**
Assets of the chartered banks, 1981

| Bank | Millions of Dollars | Percentage of Total |
|---|---|---|
| Royal Bank of Canada | $87,516 | 25.0% |
| Canadian Imperial Bank of Commerce | 66,845 | 19.1 |
| Bank of Montreal | 63,780 | 18.2 |
| Bank of Nova Scotia | 50,138 | 14.3 |
| Toronto Dominion Bank | 44,862 | 12.8 |
| National Bank of Canada | 19,157 | 5.5 |
| Mercantile Bank of Canada | 4,102 | 1.1 |
| Bank of British Columbia | 2,996 | 0.9 |
| Others | 10,000 [a] | 2.9 |

[a] Figure approximate.

Source: *The Financial Post 500*, July 1982.

held by the five largest banks declined from 94 percent to 87 percent. Competitiveness has also been increased through the introduction of more than 50 foreign bank operations to Canada in 1982 alone.[2] Bank profits, in fact, are about average for Canadian industry as a whole.

## NONBANK FINANCIAL INTERMEDIARIES

Banks are by no means the only financial institutions active in the economy. Many other institutions—including trust and mortgage-loan companies, credit unions and caisses populaires, and consumer loan companies—perform some, although not all, of the same functions as banks. In particular, these institutions function as go-betweens for savers with funds to lend and investors with the need to borrow. For this reason they are considered financial intermediaries, as are banks.

Exhibit 11.4 illustrates the important role played by some of these intermediaries, as well as the chartered banks, in providing loans and mortgages to private persons. (The chartered banks extend many other forms of credit in addition to those listed here, including more than $73 billion dollars in business loans in 1981. Life insurance companies also provide funds to business and to other institutions through the purchase of securities.)

The various financial intermediaries can be classified into several groups: near-banks, contractual savings institutions, and securities markets.

### Near-Banks

The most familiar financial intermediaries, after the chartered banks, are the so-called **near-banks**. They include trust and mortgage-loan companies, credit unions, caisses populaires, and the Quebec savings banks. These institutions accept deposits on which cheques can be written, but they are currently not subject to reserve requirements with the Bank of Canada. With some exceptions, they are subject to provincial regulations. In recent

**Near-banks** Institutions that accept deposits on which cheques can be written but that are not chartered banks and not subject to direct Bank of Canada control.

[2]Gordon F. Boreham, "The Changing Nature of Canadian Banking," *Canadian Banker and ICB Review*, February 1983, p. 8.

**Exhibit 11.4**

**Selected loans of major financial institutions, 1981 (end of period)**

| Types of Institutions | Millions of Dollars | |
| --- | --- | --- |
|  | Consumer Loans | Mortgage Loans |
| Chartered banks | $32,312 | $30,887 |
| Credit unions and caisses populaires | 6,083 | 16,038 |
| Trust and mortgage companies | 1,872 | 45,574 |
| Life insurance companies | 2,375 | 915 |

Source: *Bank of Canada Review*, January 1982, pp. S34, S36, S92–94, and S110. Data for 16 life insurance companies only.

years, credit unions alone have accounted for personal or consumer loans to Canadians equal to about 20 percent of the loans issued by chartered banks.

## Contractual Savings Institutions

**Contractual savings institutions** are financial intermediaries such as insurance companies and pension funds, to which individuals and groups commit savings on a long-term, contractual basis. More savings are committed to such institutions annually than to the near banks. Since the important role played by these institutions is not always clearly understood, a further description of some of their functions is in order.

**Contractual savings institutions** Financial intermediaries such as insurance companies and pension funds, to which individuals and groups commit savings on a long-term, contractual basis.

**The Insurance Industry** The insurance industry is really two industries. One part of the business of an insurance company is selling protection against risk. The other is operating as a financial intermediary.

*Risk Protection* Insurance companies sell protection against risk on the principle that although exposure to risk is inherently unpredictable for any single individual, it is highly predictable for large numbers of individuals. No family, for example, can be certain that its house will not burn down during the coming year. An insurance company, however, can predict quite accurately, on the basis of past experience, that (say) one in every thousand houses in a given type of neighborhood will burn down each year. Knowing this, it can sell insurance. Each family pays a premium each year equal to a thousandth of the value of its house, and the pool of funds thus collected is used to compensate the unlucky one family in a thousand whose house burns down.

Today, one can buy insurance against risks of almost any kind. Fire insurance, automobile accident insurance, and health insurance are the most common types. All of them protect the buyer against losses that might never occur but that would be very costly if they did.

Life insurance is a very important kind of insurance. Superficially, it differs somewhat from the other kinds of insurance mentioned in that the risk it appears to insure against—death—is something certain to befall everyone. On closer examination, however, it turns out that what life insurance really does is protect the buyer against the risk of *premature* death. Although everyone can be certain of dying sometime, death during any single year is a risk, not a certainty—much like the risk of having a house burn down.

Pensions and annuities are closely related to life insurance. They are arrangements under which a person pays in a premium each year up to a given age, say sixty-five years, and then receives a fixed sum each year until death. In a sense, pensions and annuities insure people against the risk that they will live too long. Pension premiums and benefits are based on participants' average life expectancy at retirement. Those who die sooner than expected will, in a sense, not get their money's worth out of the program. But those who live longer than expected will receive payments totaling more than the value of the premiums they paid in.

*Insurance Companies as Financial Intermediaries* This picture of what insurance companies do is, of course, an extremely simplified one. If the companies actually paid out benefits as rapidly as they took in premiums, they would not be able to cover administrative expenses, let alone make a profit. In part, insurance companies allow for administrative expenses and profit by charging premiums that are somewhat higher than the level dictated by the exact probability of risk. (In the earlier example, this would mean collecting from each purchaser of a fire insurance policy somewhat more than a thousandth of the value of the insured home.) But insurance companies and pension funds have another important source of income as well—namely their operations as financial intermediaries.

Insurance companies are able to operate as financial intermediaries because all insurance involves an element of saving. This results because

**Exhibit 11.5**
**The Fifteen Largest Insurance Companies in Canada and the Growth of Pension Funds**

Exhibit 11.5a lists the 15 largest insurance companies, with assets of about $55 billion, or about 14 per cent of chartered bank assets.

**(a)**

| Rank [a]81 | 80 | Name | Total Assets $000 | Total Insurance $000 |
|---|---|---|---|---|
| 1 | 1 | Sun Life Assurance Co. of Canada | 8,797,314 | 72,351,176 |
| 2 | 2 | Manufacturers Life Insurance | 6,931,192 | 32,117,891 |
| 3 | 3 | Great-West Life Assurance | 5,816,616 | 68,039,473 |
| 4 | 4 | London Life Insurance | 4,200,248 | 36,179,000 |
| 5 | 5 | Canada Life Assurance | 4,148,349 | 46,412,151 |
| 6 | 6 | Mutual Life Assurance Co. of Canada | 3,886,184 | 26,470,230 |
| 7 | 7 | Confederation Life Insurance | 3,471,055 | 46,955,343 |
| 8 | 10 | Crown Life Insurance | 2,834,402 | 41,065,709 |
| 9 | — | Laurentian Group[b] | 2,800,000 | 24,800,000 |
| 10 | 8 | Standard Life Assurance[c] | 2,792,578 | 3,025,751 |
| 11 | 9 | Metropolitan Life[c] | 2,755,781 | 24,648,667 |
| 12 | 11 | Prudential Insurance Co. of America[c] | 2,095,422 | 23,296,509 |
| 13 | 12 | North American Life Assurance | 1,891,602 | 17,638,306 |
| 14 | 14 | Prudential Assurance Group[c] | 1,332,594 | 8,171,099 |
| 15 | 15 | Dominion Life Assurance | 1,082,103 | 7,038,983 |

[a]Fiscal year ended Dec. 31, 1981 for all companies except Standard Life, which has Nov. 15, 1981 yearend.
[b]Consolidates results of all insurance operations including those of Imperial Life which ranked 13 last year.
[c]Figures are for Canadian operations.

premiums are collected before benefits are paid out, which generates in the meantime a pool of funds controlled by the insurance company. In the case of life insurance and pension funds, the lag between receipt of premiums and payment of benefits is often particularly long, which gives these companies billions of dollars to put to work in financial markets. The assets of life insurance companies alone are nearly as large as the assets of thrift institutions.

Exhibit 11.5a lists the fifteen largest insurance companies in Canada, ranked by value of assets. Their combined assets totalled $55 billion in 1981, or about 14 percent of chartered bank assets. Exhibit 11.5b indicates the tremendous growth taking place in the accumulation of pension funds. The $85.2 billion figure projected for 1983 placed the value of such pension savings at about one-fifth of the GNP.

These vast quantities of funds are put to work principally through the purchase of securities such as corporate stocks and bonds. Insurance companies and pension funds also often buy commercial mortgages and some-

**Assets of trusteed pension funds,
1960, 1965, 1970–1980,
projected: 1981–1983**

Exhibit 11.5b illustrates the tremendous growth of pension funds in Canada. By 1983 these funds totalled about 20 percent of GNP.

**(b)**

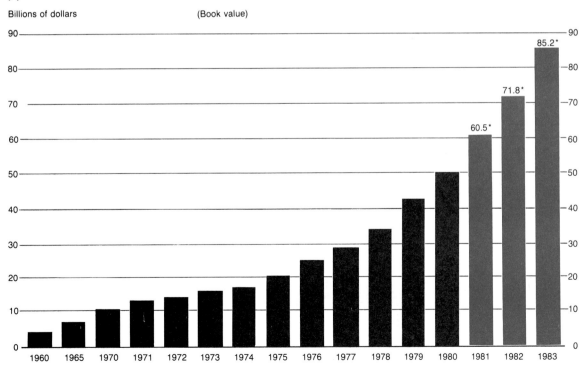

Billions of dollars · (Book value)

*Not to scale, estimates only
Source: (Part a) *Canadian Business*, July 1982, p. 97 (Part b) *The Financial Post 500*, June 1981, p. 137.

times invest directly in real estate. Certain types of life insurance policies also permit policyholders to take out personal loans from these companies at advantageous interest rates.

### Securities Markets as Financial Intermediaries

The chapter has mentioned government and corporate securities—bills, bonds, stocks, mortgage notes, and the like—without mentioning a further important class of financial intermediaries—the markets in which such securities are bought and sold. These institutions too play an important role in channeling savings from households to business and government borrowers. Conceptually, the securities markets can be divided into two classes—primary and secondary.

*Primary Markets*  Primary securities markets are those in which new borrowing takes place. Suppose, for example, General Motors wants to build a new assembly plant or testing facility. It might finance the project with a bank loan, but it has an alternative that is often more attractive: it can sell newly issued bonds or stocks to the public. Bonds are a promise to repay a fixed nominal amount at a later date, with periodic interest payments to be made in the meantime. Stocks represent a share in the ownership of the firm, including the right to receive part of future profits in the form of dividends.

A corporation seeking to raise money through the sale of stocks or bonds does not normally approach individual households directly. Instead, it uses the services of brokers and underwriters—specialists in putting individuals and firms with funds to loan in touch with companies wishing to sell newly issued bonds and stocks. Brokers and underwriters thus act as financial intermediaries. Since the purchaser of the new securities may itself be a bank, savings institution, or insurance company, the funds involved may pass through a chain of two or more financial intermediaries on their way from the original saver to the ultimate borrower.

*Secondary Markets*  When most people think of securities markets, however, it is not these primary markets that they have in mind. Instead, they think of highly publicized institutions such as the New York Stock Exchange or Toronto Stock Exchange. These exchanges are *secondary* markets; they stand in relation to the primary markets discussed above exactly as used car dealers stand in relation to new car dealers. The sellers in secondary security markets are typically not themselves issuers but instead are savers or financial institutions who own and now wish to sell stocks or bonds issued by firms or government units at some time in the past.

Strictly speaking, then, secondary security markets are not financial intermediaries. Rather than channeling money from savers to investors, they permit savers to exchange "used" securities for money or money for securities. Indirectly, however, these markets are very important to the operation of the economy's system of financial intermediaries. They give households, banks, thrift institutions, insurance companies, pension funds, and all the rest a much-needed flexibility in their financial operations.

A corporation makes a long-term financial commitment when it uses a new bond or share of stock, but the buyer need not make an equally long-term commitment. Because the secondary market with its network of brokers is always there, the buyer can resell the security tomorrow, obtaining cash to spend on goods, services, or some different kind of asset.

## CONCLUSIONS

This chapter has wandered rather far from macroeconomic policy — but for a reason. Chartered banks and other financial intermediaries play a crucial role in regulating the circular flow of income and product, which is what macroeconomic policy seeks to stabilize. The focus here has been on their functions in channeling funds from savers to investors. The next chapter will look at the function of banks as creators of money and at the Bank of Canada as the regulator of the money supply.

## SUMMARY

1. Financial intermediaries are institutions that channel funds from savers to investors. They are a necessary part of the circular flow of income and product because the needs of individual lenders and borrowers do not necessarily match in terms of quantity of funds, length of commitment, and degree of risk.
2. Chartered banks are the least specialized and most important class of financial intermediary. They accept demand deposits, savings deposits, and time deposits from households and firms and earn income by making loans and purchasing securities. Banking practices are regulated by the Bank Act and by federal and provincial regulatory bodies. One of the most important Bank Act regulations is that chartered banks must maintain reserves with the Bank of Canada.
3. A number of nonbank financial intermediaries also operate in the Canadian economy. They include savings institutions, insurance companies, and organized securities markets. Each plays an important role in channeling funds from savers to investors.

## DISCUSSION QUESTIONS

1. Do you have a chequing or savings account in a local chartered bank? If so, go to that bank (and if not, go to any convenient chartered bank) and ask for a copy of its most recent balance sheet. Compare the balance sheet for your bank with the consolidated chartered bank balance sheet shown in Exhibit 11.2.
2. Go to your library and look at a recent issue of the *Bank of Canada Review*. Use the data in the section of tables at the back of the issue to update the chartered bank balance sheet shown in Exhibit 11.2. Also examine the detailed breakdowns of loans, securities, and so on into particular subcategories.
3. Do you maintain an account at a local trust company or credit union? If so, see if you can obtain a copy of that institution's balance sheet. (If not, obtain the balance sheet of any convenient savings institution.) Compare it to the balance sheet for the chartered bank that you obtained for Question 1.
4. What kinds of insurance do you carry: health insurance? auto insurance? life insurance? If it is convenient, call your insurance agent and ask for a copy of your insurance company's balance sheet. What kinds of assets and liabilities does it hold? Compare this balance sheet to that of a chartered bank.

5. Go to your library and find a recent copy of the business section of the *Globe and Mail*. Look carefully through the ads and the columns and tables relating to stock and bond markets. Which items refer to secondary markets? (Hint: the Dow-Jones Industrial Average is one such item. It is an average of industrial stock prices on the New York Stock Exchange, which is a secondary market.) Which items refer to primary markets? (Hint: look for individual advertisements mentioning the sale of new stocks or bonds, or look for daily or weekly columns discussing new issues in the stock and bond markets.)

## SUGGESTIONS FOR FURTHER READING

Boreham, Gordon F., et al. *Money and Banking: Analysis and Policy in a Canadian Context*. 2nd ed. Toronto: Holt, Rinehart and Winston, 1979.
*A comprehensive description of Canada's banking system and banking policy.*

Boreham, Gordon F. "The Changing Nature of Canadian Banking," *The Canadian Banker and ICB Review*, Part I, January–February 1983; Part II, March–April 1983; Part III, May–June 1983.
*These articles provide a recent overview of new developments in the Canadian banking system.*

# THE SUPPLY OF MONEY

---

**WHAT YOU WILL LEARN IN THIS CHAPTER**
*This chapter is about money — what it is, how it is created by the banking system, and how the Bank of Canada controls the quantity of it in circulation. The first section examines the thorny problem of how to define and measure the stock of money in the economy. The next, through a series of examples based on a simplified banking system, shows how chartered banks create money on the basis of reserves supplied by the Bank of Canada. The final section discusses the policies used by the Bank of Canada to control the money supply and shows why these policies are not always completely reliable.*

**FOR REVIEW**
*Here are some important terms and concepts that will be put to use in this chapter. If you do not understand them, review them before proceeding.*
*• Assets, liabilities, and balance sheets (Chapter 11)*
*• Chartered banks and other financial intermediaries (Chapter 11)*
*• The Bank of Canada (Chapter 11)*

---

Chapter 11 emphasized the role of banks and savings institutions as financial intermediaries. In that capacity, they play a crucial role in channeling investment funds from savers to investors, thereby lowering transaction costs and facilitating the circular flow of income and product. The chapter also introduced the Bank of Canada, concentrating on its regulation of banks in their role as financial intermediaries. But there is much more to be said about the role of banks and the Bank of Canada in the economy. In fact, the most important function of these institutions is one that has not been mentioned yet.

To be specific, nothing has yet been said about the role of banks and the Bank of Canada in the creation of money. In fact, no formal definition of *money* has been given. This chapter will fill the gap by explaining what money is, where it comes from, and how its supply is controlled by the Bank of Canada. The next two chapters will then return to the theory of national income determination, showing how monetary policy is used side by side with fiscal policy in pursuit of the goals of economic stabilization.

## MONEY AND ITS FUNCTIONS

**Money** Anything that serves as a unit of account, a medium of exchange, and a store of purchasing power.

Money can best be defined in terms of what it does. It serves as a means of payment, a store of purchasing power, and a unit of account. Its physical form is of secondary importance; gold, beaver skins, paper currency, and electronic bookkeeping records have all been found serviceable as money at various times and places because each has served these three central functions.

**Means of Payment** As a means of payment, money facilitates the many exchanges we make and enables us to avoid the inconvenience of barter. Because it performs this function, we do not have to find out what the dentist wants for dinner before we get our teeth fixed. Instead of taking a dozen eggs or a side of bacon with us, we take money; and the dentist stops off at the supermarket on the way home to pick up whatever looks good.

**Store of Purchasing Power** As a store of purchasing power, money makes it possible to arrange economic activities conveniently through time. Income and expenditures thus need not be synchronized exactly. Instead, a stock of money can be kept on hand to dip into if expenditures run ahead of income or to add to if income runs ahead of expenditures.

**Unit of Account** Finally, as a unit of account, money makes it possible to measure and record economic stocks and flows in consistent terms. Movies, apples, and shirts cannot be added together to get gross national product; but dollars' worth of movies, dollars' worth of apples, and dollars' worth of shirts can be added up to get GNP measured in dollars.

### Money as a Liquid Asset

Economists refer to all the things of value that people own as assets. A typical household's assets might include a house, a car, other personal possessions, maybe a few stocks or bonds, and, of course, some money. All assets serve to one degree or another as stores of purchasing power, because they can be sold and the proceeds can be used to buy something else.

Money, however, has two important properties that no other asset has to the same degree. First, money itself can be used as a means of payment without first having to be exchanged for something else. Second, it never experiences a gain or loss in nominal value. The nominal value of a house or a bond or a share of corporate stock can go up or down for any number of reasons, but the nominal value of a dollar is always a dollar. The constancy of the nominal value of money is a consequence of the fact that money is itself the unit of account in terms of which nominal values are defined.

**Liquid** Description of an asset that can be used as a means of payment or easily converted to a means of payment without risk of gain or loss in nominal value.

Because it can be used directly as a means of payment, and because its nominal value never changes, money is said to be **liquid**. No other asset is as liquid as money, although some assets can be exchanged for money quickly and easily, with little danger of a change in their nominal value, and are thus fairly liquid.

## MEASURING THE QUANTITY OF MONEY

For the purpose of economic policy, it is important to know not only what money is but also how much money there is in the economy at any time. In all modern economies, the quantity of money in circulation is controlled by government.

### Types of Money

In modern economies, there are two things that perform all three of the basic functions of money: currency and demand deposits. By **currency** we mean coins and paper money. **Demand deposits** are the accounts in chartered banks that we commonly call chequing accounts. By conventional definition, money is held only by households and firms other than banks. No currency or demand deposits that belong to the Bank of Canada, chartered banks, or the federal government are included in the definition of money. When we speak of the economy's stock of money in this book, this is what we mean: the total currency outside banks plus the public's holdings of demand deposits in chartered banks. This total is generally called $M_1$.

Some other assets closely resemble money. Of these, the most important are **notice deposits** in chartered banks. By notice deposits we mean term and savings deposits. Some economists think that when we total up the economy's money stock we should add these in too. When this is done, the total is called $M_2$. Exhibit 12.1 shows us the total amount of each component of the money stock for Canada, according to recent data.[1]

**Currency** Coins and paper money.

**Demand deposits** Deposits at chartered banks that permit the depositor to make payments to others by writing a cheque against the deposit. Demand deposits are what we commonly call chequing accounts.

**$M_1$** The money supply defined as currency plus demand deposits in chartered banks.

**Notice deposits** Interest-paying accounts at chartered banks against which it is not ordinarily possible to write cheques.

**$M_2$** The money supply defined as $M_1$ plus notice (savings and term) deposits at chartered banks.

---

**Exhibit 12.1**
**Components of money and near-money, December 1982 (billions of current dollars)**
Money takes several forms in the Canadian economy. Currency held by the public, and private demand deposits, fully perform all three of the major functions of money. Together they are called $M_1$. Savings, term, and notice deposits act as stores of value but generally not as means of payment. Such "near-money" plus $M_1$ is called $M_2$.

| Type | Amount in circulation |
|---|---|
| Currency outside banks | $10.9 |
| Demand deposits | 15.8 |
| Money supply $M_1$ | 26.7 |
| Chequable notice and personal term deposits | 104.9 |
| Money supply $M_2$ | 131.6 |

Source: *Bank of Canada Review*, January 1983, p. S54.

---

### Currency outside Banks

Since 1945, the Bank of Canada has been solely responsible for issuing the nation's currency. Prior to 1945, this privilege was shared with the chartered banks. Before the establishment of the Bank of Canada in 1934, the federal government and the chartered banks were in charge of currency issues.

Paper money and coins are no longer backed by any intrinsically valuable commodity. The Bank of Canada will not give anything in exchange for a

---

[1]Other definitions of money are also used. For example, the Bank of Canada regularly keeps records of MIB, which is similar to $M_2$, except that it does not include personal notice and term deposits that are not chequable. There is also $M_3$, which includes *total* private bank deposits (i.e. business as well as personal deposits), plus foreign currency deposits held by Canadian residents.

$10 bill other than $10 in paper money and/or coins—another promise to pay. Until the beginning of World War II, the Bank of Canada supported the currency with gold. It was required to hold the equivalent of 25 percent of its note and deposit liabilities in gold. This provision was suspended during the war, because the money supply had to be increased substantially to support the war effort. The requirement was abolished in 1967. We now have a currency whose value is based entirely on the public's faith in its ability to exchange it for all kinds of goods and services.

### Demand Deposits

Demand deposits are bookkeeping entries of chartered banks. They represent obligations of these banks to their depositiors. As shown in Exhibit 12.1, demand deposits account for about 60 percent of the money supply $(M_1)$, but this figure actually understates their importance. Demand deposits turn out to be used to conduct some 90 percent of the dollar volume of all transactions in the economy. Although demand deposits are issued by chartered banks, there are limits on the volume of such deposits that banks can create. We shall discuss these limits shortly.

### Near-Money

**Near-money** Assets that are less than perfectly liquid but still liquid enough to be reasonably good substitutes for money.

Currency, demand deposits, and savings deposits are only three of a great many kinds of assets held by households and firms. Some of the other assets are sufficiently liquid that they are known as **near-money**. It should be noted that demand and savings deposits at nonbank financial institutions, such as credit unions and trust companies, hardly differ from similar deposits in chartered banks. Securities such as government bonds, commercial paper, and treasury bills are also very liquid.

### Credit and Credit Cards

In their efforts to make transactions ever more convenient for their customers, bankers have succeeded in blurring not only the distinction between money and near-money but also the distinction between money and credit. A case in point is the "plastic money" that almost everyone carries around in purses and billfolds these days—Master Charge cards, Visa cards, and all the rest. But money and credit cards are different things, and it is important to understand why.

What distinguishes a credit card both from money and from near-money is that it is not a store of purchasing power. Instead, it is just a document that makes it easy for its holder to obtain a loan. When you go into a store, present your credit card, and walk out with a can of tennis balls, you have not yet paid for your purchase. What you have done, instead, is borrow money from the bank that issued the credit card. Simultaneously, you have instructed the bank to turn over the proceeds of the loan to the merchant. Later, the bank will send money to the merchant, thus paying for the tennis balls; and later still, you will send money to the bank to pay off the balance on your credit card account. A credit card is a means of deferred payment.

Although credit cards are not a form of money, a discussion of them is not entirely out of place here. The reason is that credit cards allow households to *economize* on the use of money. If people use credit cards, they do not have to keep as much cash in their billfolds or as large a balance in their chequing accounts as they otherwise would. In this strictly limited sense, it is not altogether wrong to think of credit cards as "plastic money."

## THE CREATION OF MONEY BY THE BANKING SYSTEM

The chapter has so far discussed in some detail the problem of how the quantity of money is to be measured. It turns now to the important matter of how the quantity of money is controlled by the Bank of Canada.

Although currency is issued directly by the Bank of Canada, demand deposits—the most important component of the money supply, however measured—are mainly created by chartered banks. The Bank of Canada's control over the money supply is thus inherently indirect, and it is exercised primarily through its powers to establish reserve requirements and to determine or influence the outstanding amount of chartered bank reserves. To understand how this control works, we must first understand how money, in the form of demand deposits, is created by the chartered banking system.

### A Simplified Banking System

To keep things simple, we will ignore certain complexities of real-world financial markets in this section. Once the major principles governing the supply of money are made clear, we will introduce some of the complexities in a discussion of monetary policy.

Our simplified banking system is comprised of just ten banks, all of which are identical in every respect. The liabilities of these banks consist entirely of demand deposits, which are also the only form of money in the system. There is no currency, and the banks have zero net worth. On the other side of the banks' balance sheets, only three kinds of assets are found. The first is reserves, which consist entirely of non-interest-bearing deposits with the Bank of Canada. In addition to reserves, the banks hold two kinds of interest-bearing assets—loans and government securities.

**Regulation and Required Reserves** The banks in our simple system are subject to regulation by an equally simplified version of the Bank of Canada. The only assets of this simplified Bank of Canada are Canadian government securities, and the only liabilities are bank reserve deposits. All bank demand deposits are subject to a uniform **required reserve ratio** of 10 percent. This means that they are required to hold ten cents in reserves for each dollar of demand deposits.

**Required reserve ratio** The fraction of each type of deposit that the Bank of Canada requires chartered banks to hold in the form of non-interest-bearing assets.

**Balance Sheet Equilibrium** Like any other firms, our simplified banks want to earn the maximum possible profit for their shareholders. The source of their income is interest earned on securities and loans. To maximize profits, then, they want to expand their loans and security holdings to the greatest extent possible. Given the choice between holding assets in the form of non-interest-bearing reserves or interest-bearing loans and securities, they choose loans and securities. They thus tend to expand

**Excess reserves** Reserves held by chartered banks in excess of required reserves.

their loans and securities to the greatest extent they can without violating their required reserve ratio. In doing so, they try to avoid holding any **excess reserves**—reserves in excess of the required amount. A bank that has expanded loans and security holdings to the maximum extent possible is said to have its balance sheet in equilibrium.

**Balance Sheets** To further set the stage for our discussion of the banking system's creation of money, we can fill in some numbers in the balance sheets of our simplified chartered banks and of the simplified Bank of Canada. Each of the 13 chartered banks will start from the following equilibrium balance sheet position:

**Representative Chartered Bank Balance Sheet**

| Assets | | | Liabilities | |
|---|---|---|---|---|
| Reserves: | | $10,000 | Demand deposits | $100,000 |
| Required | $10,000 | | | |
| Excess | 0 | | | |
| Loans | | 45,000 | | |
| Securities | | 45,000 | | |
| Total assets | | $100,000 | Total liabilities | $100,000 |

The simplified Bank of Canada will begin with a balance sheet that looks like this:

**Simplified Bank of Canada Balance Sheet**

| Assets | | Liabilities | |
|---|---|---|---|
| Canadian government securities | $100,000 | Chartered bank reserve deposits | $100,000 |

**The Process of Deposit Creation** The stage is now set in such a way as to give the Bank of Canada control of the quantity of reserves at chartered banks. This in turn makes it possible for the Bank of Canada to control the quantity of money supplied by the banking system in the form of demand deposits. Suppose, for example, that the Bank of Canada decides to increase the quantity of money available to the economy. Here is how it might typically proceed.

*An Open Market Purchase Injecting New Reserves* The easiest way for the Bank of Canada to set in motion an expansion of demand deposits is through an **open market operation**—an open market purchase in this case. (In terms of monetary policy this would be called an "easy money" policy.) To be specific, suppose the Bank of Canada's securities department decides to buy $10,000 in securities from a member of the public.

**Open market operation** A purchase of securities from the public or a sale of securities to the public made by the Bank of Canada for the purpose of altering the quantity of reserves available to chartered banks.

The Bank of Canada pays for these securities with a cheque—a special cheque drawn on itself, not on one of the chartered banks. The seller of the securities deposits this special Bank of Canada cheque in his or her local chartered bank account. To keep track of things, we will call this bank the Alberta Bank. That bank in turn deposits the cheque in its account with the Bank of Canada, at which point the objective of injecting $10,000 of reserves into the system has been accomplished. After all this has taken place, the balance sheets of the Bank of Canada and the Alberta Bank now look like this:

**The Bank of Canada**

| Assets | | Liabilities | |
|---|---|---|---|
| Canadian government securities | $110,000 (+10,000)a | Chartered bank reserve deposits | $110,000 (+10,000) |

aHere and in subsequent balance sheets, changes are shown in brackets.

**Alberta Bank**

| Assets | | | Liabilities | |
|---|---|---|---|---|
| Reserves at Bank of Canada | | $20,000 (+10,000) | Demand deposits | $110,000 (+10,000) |
| Required | $11,000 (+1,000) | | | |
| Excess | 9,000 (+9,000) | | | |
| Loans | | 45,000 | | |
| Securities | | 45,000 | | |
| Total assets | | $110,000 (+10,000) | Total liabilities | $110,000 (+10,000) |

Notice how the $10,000 in new reserves at the Alberta Bank is distributed between required reserves and excess reserves. Deposits have gone up by $10,000, which means that the bank must hold $1,000 more in required reserves. The other $9,000 is not required to be held as reserves, so it is listed as excess reserves. The bank is no longer in equilibrium; it can increase its income by putting those reserves to work. What happens when it does is the subject of the next section.

*Making a New Loan* Suppose that the Alberta Bank decides to put its $9,000 to work by making a new loan of $9,000. It does this simply by crediting $9,000 to the chequing account of the borrower, James Anderson. At the moment the loan is completed, the balance sheet of the bank will look like this:

**Alberta Bank**

| Assets | | | Liabilities | |
|---|---|---|---|---|
| Reserves | | $20,000 | Demand deposits | $119,000 (+9,000) |
| Required | $11,900 (+900) | | | |
| Excess | 8,100 (−900) | | | |
| Loans | | 54,000 (+9,000) | | |
| Securities | | 45,000 | | |
| Total assets | | $119,000 (+9,000) | Total liabilities | $119,000 (+9,000) |

The bank now has $9,000 in new assets (loans) matched by $9,000 in new liabilities (the increase in the borrower's demand deposits). Required reserves have increased sufficiently to maintain a level of 10 percent of deposits. The bank still has excess reserves of $8,100, but it does not make further new loans, because it knows that the situation is only temporary. Anderson did not borrow $9,000 just to leave it sitting idle in his chequing account; he borrowed it to buy a car.

*Chequing Away the Proceeds of the Loan*    Anderson pays for the car by writing a cheque on his account in the Alberta Bank. The dealer from whom he buys the car—Joyce Barnard—has her account at the Brandon Bank.

When Barnard deposits Anderson's Alberta Bank cheque in her Brandon account, the Brandon Bank sends it to the Bank of Canada for collection. The Bank of Canada credits $9,000 to Brandon's reserve account and debits (subtracts) $9,000 from Alberta's reserve account. Then it puts the cheque itself (the actual piece of paper) in the mail so that the Alberta Bank can eventually forward it to Anderson for his personal records. When all these transactions have taken place, the balance sheets of the two banks look like this:

**Alberta Bank**

| Assets | | | Liabilities | |
|---|---|---|---|---|
| Reserves | | $11,000 | Demand deposits | $110,000 |
| | | (−9,000) | | (−9,000) |
|   Required | $11,000 | | | |
| | (−900) | | | |
|   Excess | 0 | | | |
| | (−8,100) | | | |
| Loans | | 54,000 | | |
| Securities | | 45,000 | | |
|   Total assets | | $110,000 | Total liabilities | $110,000 |
| | | (−9,000) | | (−9,000) |

**Brandon Bank**

| Assets | | | Liabilities | |
|---|---|---|---|---|
| Reserves | | $19,000 | Demand deposits | $109,000 |
| | | (+9,000) | | (+9,000) |
|   Required | $10,900 | | | |
| | (+900) | | | |
|   Excess | 8,100 | | | |
| | (+8,100) | | | |
| Loans | | 45,000 | | |
| Securities | | 45,000 | | |
|   Total assets | | $109,000 | Total liabilities | $109,000 |
| | | (+9,000) | | (+9,000) |

No further changes take place in the Bank of Canada's balance sheet totals. Now we can see why the Alberta Bank could not loan out more than its initial $9,000 of excess reserves. It knew that the new $9,000 deposit it created by the loan was not likely to stay there for long. As soon as the cheque cleared, Alberta lost $9,000 in total reserves. Its required reserves went down by only $900 (10 percent of the amount of the loss in deposits), so the $8,100 of the excess reserves that Alberta had immediately after making the loan was needed to make up the difference.

*Buying Securities*    When all transactions were completed, the Alberta Bank ended up with $10,000 more in deposits and $10,000 more in assets.

But that is not the end of the story. The $8,100 in excess reserves that the bank lost did not disappear from the banking system. The Brandon Bank's excess reserves rose by exactly the same amount that Alberta's fell. Brandon gained $9,000 in deposits and $9,000 in reserves, of which only $900 were required reserves. The remaining $8,100 became excess reserves for Brandon.

Although the Alberta Bank has now returned to a state of balance sheet equilibrium, the Brandon Bank is out of equilibrium. To increase its earning assets to the maximum, it must put its excess reserves to work. It could, like Alberta, make a new loan, but it decides instead to buy $8,100 in securities. It purchases these securities from a private dealer and pays for them by writing a cheque on its own account. The seller then deposits the cheque in the Cornwall Bank. This time we omit Brandon's intermediate balance sheet showing the situation after the securities are bought but before the cheque is cleared. After the cheque has been cleared through the Bank of Canada, here is what Brandon's and Cornwall's balance sheets look like:

**Brandon Bank**

| Assets | | | Liabilities | |
|---|---|---|---|---|
| Reserves | | $10,900 | Demand deposits | $109,000 |
| | | (−8,100) | | |
| Required | $10,900 | | | |
| | (no change) | | | |
| Excess | 0 | | | |
| | (−8,100) | | | |
| Loans | | 45,000 | | |
| Securities | | 53,100 | | |
| | | (+8,100) | | |
| Total assets | | $109,000 | Total liabilities | $109,000 |

**Cornwall Bank**

| Assets | | | Liabilities | |
|---|---|---|---|---|
| Reserves | | $18,100 | Demand deposits | $108,100 |
| | | (+8,100) | | (+8,100) |
| Required | $10,810 | | | |
| | (+810) | | | |
| Excess | 7,290 | | | |
| | (+7,290) | | | |
| Loans | | 45,000 | | |
| Securities | | 45,000 | | |
| Total assets | | $108,100 | Total liabilities | $108,100 |
| | | (+8,100) | | (+8,100) |

*[handwritten: 10% of 8,100]*

**The Multiple Expansion of Deposits**  We really do not have to trace much farther the effects of the Bank of Canada's initial injection of $10,000 of new reserves into the chartered banking system. A clear pattern is beginning to emerge. Bank A received a deposit of $10,000, of which it set aside 10 percent as required reserves and used the remainder to finance a loan of $9,000. Bank B received a deposit of $9,000, of which it set aside 10 percent as required reserves and used the remainder to finance securities purchases of $8,100. Bank C received a deposit of $8,100, of which it put aside $810 as required reserves. It used the remaining $7,290 to finance either loans or securities purchases. (The examples above show that it makes no difference which.) Each bank makes new loans and/or securities purchases equal to 90 percent of the deposit it receives, thereby generating new deposits for the next bank in line. Total new deposits generated by the initial injection of $10,000 of new reserves is thus equal to the sum of the infinite series $10,000 + $9,000 + $8,100 + $7,290 + $6,561 + $5,905 + ... = $100,000. The whole process is referred to as the multiple expansion of deposits by the chartered banking system.

**A Shortcut** Just to check what we have learned, we can go back to the beginning and look at the effects of the injection of new reserves, using a shortcut method based on the consolidated balance sheet for all 13 member banks. The initial purchase by the Bank of Canada of $10,000 in securities from a member of the public puts $10,000 in new reserves into the banking system. The first bank to get those reserves does not hold on to all of them; it holds only the required portion (10 percent) and passes the remainder on to some other bank. Another 10 percent of these reserves come to rest as required reserves in the second bank, another 10 percent of the remainder in the third, and so on.

The multiple expansion of deposits continues in this way until all reserves have eventually come to rest as required reserves in one bank or another. But no matter how often the reserves are passed from hand to hand, the total increase in the quantity of reserves in the banking system remains $10,000. Total deposits have to rise by enough to convert all of the initial $10,000 of excess reserves into required reserves. With a 10 percent required reserve ratio, this takes $100,000 in new deposits. In the eventual equilibrium position, the consolidated balance sheet for the ten identical member banks looks like this:

**Consolidated Balance Sheet of All Chartered Banks
(Final Position)**

| Assets | | | Liabilities | |
|---|---|---|---|---|
| Reserves | | $110,000 (+10,000) | Demand deposits | $1,100,000 (+100,000) |
| Required | $110,000 (+10,000) | | | |
| Excess | 0 | | | |
| Loans and securities | | 990,000 (+90,000) | | |
| Total assets | | $1,100,000 (+100,000) | Total liabilities | $1,100,000 (+100,000) |

## Contraction of the Money Supply

If the Bank of Canada withdraws reserves from the simplified banking system, the whole process works in reverse. Suppose, for example, that the Bank of Canada begins by selling $1,000 in securities to a member of the public. The seller pays for the securities with a cheque drawn on the Dalhousie Bank. Dalhousie loses $1,000 in deposits and $1,000 in reserves. That leaves it $900 short of required reserves, as the following balance sheet shows (assuming the same initial balance sheet for the Dalhousie Bank as for all the banks in the previous examples):

**Dalhousie Bank**

| Assets | | | Liabilities | | |
|---|---|---|---|---|---|
| Reserves | | $9,000 (−1,000) | Demand deposits | | $99,000 (−1,000) |
| Required | $9,900 (−100) | | | | |
| Excess | −900 | | | | |
| Securities | | 45,000 | | | |
| Loans | | 45,000 | | | |
| Total assets | | $99,000 (−1,000) | Total liabilities | | $99,000 (−1,000) |

In order to meet its legal reserve requirements, the Dalhousie Bank must somehow obtain $900 in new reserves. One obvious way to do this is to sell $900 in securities. When someone writes a cheque to pay for these securities, another bank, say the Edmonton Bank, loses $900 in deposits and $900 in reserves, leaving it with an $810 shortfall from required reserves. Edmonton in turn sells securities to meet its requirements, and the operation of the multiple contraction process continues until it causes a total loss of $10,000 in deposits.

## The Money Multiplier

We will conclude our analysis of the simplified banking system by drawing an important generalization from both the expansionary and contractionary examples just given: in every case, the ultimate change in total demand deposits (and hence in the total money supply) in the simplified chartered banking system must be equal to the initial change in reserves divided by the required reserve ratio. The ratio of the change in the money supply to the initial change in reserves can be called the **money multiplier** for the banking system. (More precisely, it can be called the demand-deposits-to-total-reserves multiplier.)

In the simplified banking system, the formula for the money multiplier is:

$$\text{Money multiplier} = \frac{1}{\text{Required reserve ratio}}$$

With the required reserve ratio of 0.10 used in the examples, the money multiplier is 10. Hence the $10,000 injection of new reserves results in a $100,000 expansion of the money supply, and a $1,000 withdrawal of reserves results in a $10,000 contraction. Hence,

Change in the money supply = money multiplier × change in reserves
$100,000 = 10 × $10,000

**Money multiplier** The ratio of the quantity of money to the total reserves in a banking system. Various money multipliers can be defined, depending on the definition of money used. In the simplified banking system, the formula for the money multiplier is: Money multiplier =
$$\frac{1}{\text{Required reserve ratio}}$$

## THE INSTRUMENTS OF MONETARY POLICY

We turn now from the simplified banking system to the real world. On the surface, everything looks similar. Demand deposits still make up the most important part of the money supply, although not all of it. The Bank of Canada still has the power to control bank reserves and to impose reserve requirements. And changes in the total reserves of the banking system still result in multiple expansions or contractions of the money supply.

On closer examination, however, the actual banking system of Canada differs from that of the simplified economy in a number of details, which, taken together, crucially affect both the methods and the success of the Bank of Canada in controlling the nation's money supply.

The Bank of Canada uses five major instruments to orchestrate its monetary policy. These are *open market operations* (sales and purchases of government securities in the open market), *moral suasion* (attempts by the Bank of Canada to persuade the chartered banks to follow a certain policy), *draw downs* and *redeposits* (transfers of government deposits between the Bank of Canada and the chartered banks), changes in the *Bank rate* (the interest rate paid by chartered banks to borrow reserve funds from the Bank of Canada), and changes in the *required reserve ratios* for chartered banks.

Open market operations have already been illustrated for the simplified banking system. By the purchase and sale of securities, the Bank of Canada can inject new reserves directly into the banking system or withdraw reserves from it. Something more must be said about the other methods used by the Bank of Canada.

### Moral Suasion

Because the number of chartered banks in Canada is so small, the Bank of Canada can easily contact their presidents to obtain their support in implementing a certain policy. This may be done through general discussion or special directives. The Bank of Canada might request that the chartered banks, for example, tighten up on their loans or raise their interest rates. Because of its legal supervisory powers, the Bank of Canada has considerable clout when it engages in such **moral suasion**.

**Moral suasion** Direct attempts by the Bank of Canada to influence the practices of the chartered banks.

### Draw Downs and Redeposits

The federal government has substantial deposits with the Bank of Canada and the chartered banks. With the permission of the minister of finance, the Bank of Canada can transfer government deposits from itself to the chartered banks, thereby increasing the reserves of the banks, or it can reduce those reserves in support of a tight money policy by transferring government deposits from the chartered banks to the Bank of Canada. These **draw downs** and **redeposits** have become one of the most important short-term techniques used by the Bank of Canada in implementing monetary policy.

**Draw downs and redeposits** Transfer of government deposits between the Bank of Canada and the chartered banks.

### The Bank Rate

**Bank rate** The interest rate paid by chartered banks to borrow reserve funds from the Bank of Canada. Acts as a signal as to desired changes in interest rates charged by chartered banks.

Another policy instrument that the Bank of Canada can use is the **Bank rate**, or discount rate as it is called in the United States. A rise in the Bank rate, other things being equal, has the effect of discouraging chartered banks from borrowing to augment their reserves. A decline in the Bank rate has the opposite effect.

Actually, the chartered banks in Canada rarely borrow from the Bank of Canada to augment their reserves. They can call in loans or sell assets in the market to satisfy the reserve requirements. Changes in the Bank rate act more as a signal to the chartered banks, telling them whether the Bank of Canada would like them to raise or lower their own interest rates. Most market interest rates, including the "prime rate" that chartered banks charge their best customers, tend to follow the Bank rate. In the late 1950s and again in the 1980s the Bank of Canada allowed this rate to "float" in relation to the interest rate on short-term government bonds known as Treasury bills. Since the rate on such bonds is itself affected by the Banks' open market operations, interest rates are still subject to Bank of Canada influence. (The Bank has adopted a practice of "auctioning" government bonds every Thursday to financial institutions. The bidding on these bonds in effect determines the rate of interest to be charged. The Bank may use a reserve bid to keep interest rates within certain limits.)

## Changes in Required Reserve Ratios

The fifth instrument of monetary policy, changing required reserve ratios, is more powerful in the United States than in Canada. In Canada the rates for so-called cash or primary reserves are set when the Bank Act is reviewed. As noted previously (Chapter 11), the reserve rate for demand deposits is set to go down to 10 percent by 1984, and the rate on notice deposits to 4 percent. These rates were established in the Bank Act of 1980.

The Bank of Canada actually lost its right to vary primary reserve ratios when the Bank Act was amended in 1967. Instead, it was given the right to establish secondary reserve requirements for the chartered banks, and to vary these requirements. Chartered banks can now be required to hold up to 12 percent of their total Canadian deposits in the form of such liquid, interest-bearing assets as short-term Treasury bills and day-to-day loans. These are the secondary reserves. The Bank of Canada has, since 1967, varied the secondary reserve ratio from 5 to 9 percent.

## PRACTICAL PROBLEMS OF MONETARY POLICY

The Bank of Canada has relied on the major tools of monetary policy described in the preceding section to control the growth of the money supply for many years, but it began to publicize its monetary growth targets in advance, only in the last half of the 1970s.

During the rapid inflation of 1975, the Governor of the Bank of Canada, Gerald Bouey, followed the example of other central bankers and announced annual growth targets for $M_1$, the most immediately spendable money. High growth rates in the money supply were linked in the minds of many economists with the rapidly increasing inflation. The target growth rate in the money supply for the first few years was set at 10 percent to 15 percent annually. By February of 1982 this target had been reduced to a 4 percent to 8 percent annual growth rate. Later that year, the Bank decided to de-emphasize such a specific target and focus on a broader set of objectives, such as interest rates, exchange rates, and other concerns of monetary policy. It had evidently been found that control of $M_1$ did not ensure that there would be adequate corrective to high inflation and unemployment because of financial innovations.

Despite the variety of policy instruments available, and despite the announced targets, monetary policy in practice is a far more imprecise affair than in the simplified economy described earlier in this chapter. The real world is full of many problems and pitfalls not yet mentioned. As a result, the Bank of Canada, even with the best of intentions, has had only mixed success in meeting the monetary policy objectives it has set for itself.

### Variations in Money Multipliers

The key to control over the money supply in the simplified banking system was a fixed money multiplier, equal to the reciprocal of the required reserve ratio on demand deposits. In the real world, the closest equivalent to this multiplier is the so-called $M_1$-to-total reserves multiplier (the $M_1$ multiplier, for short). As the name implies, this multiplier is the ratio of $M_1$ to total reserves of the chartered banking system. It is more complicated and subject to more variation than the money multiplier of our simple banking system.

**Structure of Reserve Requirements** One major reason for the greater complexity of this real-world money multiplier is that required reserve ratios vary from one kind of deposit to another. Some reserves must be used to support savings deposits that are not counted as part of $M_1$. Other things being equal, the greater the ratio of savings and time deposits to demand deposits at banks, the lower the $M_1$ multiplier.

In the last decade and more, new business and banking practices, including electronic banking and cash controls, and new forms of savings deposits with more attractive interest rates, have led the public to put a greater portion of their income into savings deposits and less into demand deposits. Between 1974 and 1981 $M_1$ grew annually by 8.1 percent, while $M_2$ grew at an annual rate of 14.3 percent. This has led to a substantial reduction of $M_1$ in relation to GNP.

**Near-Banks** A second major reason for variations in the $M_1$ multiplier is the existence of near-banks such as trust companies and credit unions. They offer savings and term deposits that compete with those offered by chartered banks, but their deposits are not considered part of the money supply. Hence shifts in deposits among banks and near-banks are also a source of variability in the money multiplier.

**Excess Reserves** Yet a third reason for variability in the $M_1$ multiplier is the fact that real-world banks, unlike those in the simplified banking system, cannot always keep their excess reserves exactly at zero, nor do they always want to. Banks sometimes find it hard to keep up with unexpected deposit flows resulting in excess reserves. Such excess reserves, while only a small amount on average, do show some variation over time.

**Currency** The Bank of Canada allows chartered banks to count currency on hand (so-called vault cash) as reserves, which means that when individuals or firms withdraw money from their banks in the form of currency, they drain total reserves from the banking system. When this happens, a multiple contraction of the money supply takes place unless the Bank of Canada offsets the shift with an injection of new reserves.

In addition, currency is a form of money that is not a liability of the banking system and thus is not itself subject to reserve requirements. Even if the Bank of Canada maintains the level of reserves, the larger the fraction of their money balances people choose to hold as currency, the larger the $M_1$ multiplier.

## CONCLUSIONS

This chapter has examined in some detail a few questions concerning the supply of money: how the money supply can be measured, how money is created by the banking system, and how the Bank of Canada attempts to exercise control over the money supply. Now it is time to return to a theme sounded briefly at the beginning of the chapter — the relationship between monetary policy and the goals of full employment, price stability, economic growth, and balance of payment stability. It is the importance of money to these goals of stabilization policy, after all, that justifies the attention to technicalities in this chapter.

The next chapter will turn from the supply side of the money market to the demand side. Chapter 14 will examine the effect of variations in money demand and supply on nominal national income and product.

## SUMMARY

1. Money is defined in terms of what it does. As a unit of account, it allows us to keep accounts and measure aggregate economic magnitudes. As a means of payment, it allows us to escape the inconvenience of barter. And as a store of purchasing power, it helps us arrange our economic activities in an orderly way through time.

2. One traditional definition of money, $M_1$, includes currency plus demand deposits at chartered banks. Another definition, $M_2$, adds notice (term and savings) deposits at banks to this total. In addition to the money included in $M_1$ and $M_2$, there are other highly liquid assets, such as deposits at savings and loan associations, short-term government securities, credit union shares, money market mutual fund shares, and repurchase agreements. Recent innovations in banking practices have made it necessary to rethink the traditional definitions of money.

3. In a simplified banking system, an injection of new reserves sets off a multiple expansion of deposits and the money supply. Each bank receiving new reserves makes loans or buys securities equal to its excess reserves. In that way, it passes along part of the reserves to the next bank in line. The process continues until deposits have risen enough to convert all the new reserves into required reserves. The ratio of money to reserves is known as the money multiplier.

4. In the actual Canadian banking system, the Bank of Canada has available five main instruments of monetary policy: open market operations (buying and selling securities on the open market), changes in required reserve ratios, changes in the bank rate (the rate charged to chartered

banks for loans of reserves), moral suasion (efforts by the Bank of Canada to get the chartered banks to follow a proposed policy), and draw downs and redeposits (transfers of government deposits between the Bank of Canada and the chartered banks).

5. The Bank of Canada's instruments of monetary policy do not give it precise control of the money supply. A major reason is that the money multiplier can change for reasons not under direct control of the Bank of Canada. Shifts of funds from one type of bank to another, from banks to near-banks, from one type of deposit to another within banks, and from deposits to currency can all affect the money multiplier. So can changes in banks' excess reserves. In addition, shifts of funds from chartered bank deposits to currency can alter the total reserves available to the banking system.

## DISCUSSION QUESTIONS

1. List the functions that money performs in the economy, and illustrate them with examples of how you yourself have used money for each purpose. Have you ever used something other than money for any of the three purposes?

2. Do you have an account at any bank or other financial institution? If so, is your account part of $M_1$? Of $M_2$?

3. Is it possible that with increased use of credit cards we will eventually do away with currency and demand deposits? Explain. Would we be doing away with money if this did occur?

4. Go to your library and look in any back issue of the *Bank of Canada Review*. Where the recent banking data are reported, find the current values for currency, demand deposits, and time deposits at chartered banks. Use these values to update Exhibit 12.1. Next, examine the data given for $M_1$ and $M_2$ and the definitions of these quantities. Is the Bank of Canada still using traditional definitions, or has it modified them?

5. Using the same starting position given in the text for the simplified banking system, work through the multiple expansion (or contraction) process for the following policy actions:
   a. An injection of $5,000 in new reserves via an open market purchase.
   b. A withdrawal of $500 in new reserves via an open market sale.
   c. A selective reduction in the required reserve ratio for the Alberta Bank only — from 10 percent to 8 percent. (Assume that once the expansion process gets underway, no one ever deposits new reserves in the Alberta bank but uses only the other nine banks.)
   d. A general reduction in the required reserve ratio for all banks from 10 percent to 8 percent.

6. Go to your library and obtain copies of the *Globe and Mail* business section or the *Financial Post*. Usually, these papers contain short news items or columns reporting weekly changes in the money supply, which the Bank of Canada has announced. What is happening to the money supply? What comments do the papers make regarding Bank of Canada policy? Are any comparisons of actual and target money growth given?

# THE DEMAND
# FOR MONEY AND THE
# MONEY MARKET

## WHAT YOU WILL LEARN IN THIS CHAPTER

*This chapter discusses the determinants of the quantity of money that people wish to hold at any given time — that is, people's demand for money. People value money for its liquidity, but because money normally earns no interest, the nominal rate of interest represents an opportunity cost of holding it. The relationship between the demand for money and the rate of interest can be used to draw a demand schedule for money. This schedule can be combined with the supply of money to show how equilibrium is established in the money market.*

## FOR REVIEW

*Here are some important terms and concepts that will be put to use in this chapter. If you do not understand them, review them before proceeding.*
* *Nominal and real interest rates (Chapter 7)*
* *Liquidity (Chapter 12)*
* *Control of the money supply by the Bank of Canada (Chapter 12)*

Chapter 12 defined money, discussed the various things that serve as money and near-monies in the Canadian economy, and explained how the supply of money is determined. This chapter turns first to the determination of the demand for money and then to the interaction of the supply and demand for money in the money market. It will lay the groundwork for the discussion of the interaction of monetary and fiscal policy in Chapter 14.

## THE DEMAND FOR MONEY

Having viewed the determinants of the supply of money in some detail, we turn now to the demand for money. In examining the demand for money, as in dealing with other subjects in economics, it is important to distinguish between stocks and flows. The demand for money is the demand for a stock. The question is not one of how much money people would like to spend per day or per month; that would be a flow of money. Instead, the demand for money is a matter of how large a share of their total wealth people would at any point in time like to hold in the form of money, as opposed to assets such as securities, real estate, or consumer durables.

### Early Views of the Demand for Money

**The Equation of Exchange** One early view of the demand for money developed from the so-called **equation of exchange**. This equation can be written in the form

$$MV = \underset{\longrightarrow\ \text{nominal income}}{PQ}$$

**Equation of exchange** An equation showing the relationship between the money stock (M), the velocity of money (V), the price level (P), and the level of real income (Q), written MV = PQ.

where M stands for the quantity of money, V for the **velocity** of money (that is, for the average number of times each dollar of the money stock is spent each year for income-producing purposes), P for the price level, and Q for the real quantity of output, or real national income. This equation must always hold, given the way the term *velocity* is defined. Suppose, for example, that real output is 1,000 units of goods and services and that the price level is $2. Nominal national income will thus be $2 × 1,000 or $2,000 per year. If each dollar is spent for income-producing purposes an average of five times per year, a money stock of $400 will be required to sustain the $2,000 per year nominal national income. To sustain that income with a smaller money stock will require each dollar to be used more than five times per year. If the money supply is larger, the same level of nominal national income can be sustained with a velocity less than five. In short, the stock of money times the velocity of money must always, because of the way *velocity* is defined, equal nominal income (real income times the price level).

**Velocity** The ratio of nominal national income to the money stock; a measure of the average number of times each dollar of the money stock is used each year for income-generating purposes.

The equation of exchange itself is not a theory of anything; it simply presents a definitional relationship of money, velocity, real income, and the price level. An early step toward a theory of the demand for money, however, was to assume velocity to be a constant. This constant number of times each dollar could be spent each year was supposedly determined by custom and institutional factors, such as how often workers were paid and how fast banks could clear cheques. With velocity constant, the quantity of money required to sustain any given level of nominal national income could be found by dividing nominal national income by velocity. In equation form, using MD to stand for money demand, PQ to stand for nominal income, and V to stand for velocity, this theory of money demand could be written as:

$$MD = \frac{PQ}{V}$$

**Keynes on the Demand for Money** When John Maynard Keynes began work on his *General Theory of Employment, Interest, and Money,* he was not content with the simple view that because velocity was constant, the demand for money would be proportional to nominal income. Instead, he developed a more complex theory, based on three motives for holding money.

Keynes called the need to hold money as a means of payment the *transactions motive* for holding money. In addition to holding money to make normal day-to-day purchases, people may also hold some extra money to deal with unexpected circumstances. Keynes called this the *precautionary motive* for holding money. He believed that both the transactions and the precautionary motives were roughly proportional to nominal income, as in the equation of exchange.

In addition, however, Keynes distinguished a third motive for holding money, somewhat different from the other two. People may sometimes want to hold part of their wealth in the form of money, Keynes said, if they believe other forms of wealth are temporarily too risky. Suppose, for example, that interest rates are at an unusually low level, which often implies high prices for bonds. Under these circumstances, people may be reluctant to hold bonds, for fear the prices will fall and they will suffer capital losses. Thus when bond prices are unusually high, Keynes suggested, people may prefer to hold much of their wealth in the form of money, hoping to exchange the money for bonds after interest rates rise and the price of bonds falls. Keynes called this the *speculative motive* for holding money.

In sum, then, Keynes thought that the demand for money depends both on the level of nominal income and on nominal interest rates. As nominal income rises, other things being equal, the demand for money will increase because of the transactions and precautionary motives. But given the level of nominal national income, the speculative motive will tend to make the demand for money increase as nominal interest rates decrease and to make it decrease as nominal interest rates increase.

---

Although many economists have contributed to the modern theory of money demand, the central concept of "portfolio" theory always brings the name James Tobin to mind. In a series of papers written in the 1950s, Tobin showed how Keynesian macroeconomic theory could be strengthened by discarding the somewhat artificial categories of transactions, precautionary, and speculative motives for holding money. In their place he offered a portfolio theory that firmly integrated micro- and macro-level analysis while making room for a wide spectrum of assets with varying rates of return, liquidities, and degrees of risk. Tobin's refinements of the Keynesian system were a major factor in the development of a "post-Keynesian synthesis" that bridged many gaps between early followers of Keynes and non-Keynesian economists.

Educated at Harvard, Tobin has spent most of his professional career at Yale. He has received many awards and honorary degrees. In 1971 he served as president of the American Economics Association. In 1981 he received the Nobel Memorial Prize in economics for his early work on portfolio theory.

Although he won his reputation mainly in the pages of scholarly journals, Tobin has never ducked issues of policy. In 1961 he went to Washington as a member of John Kennedy's Council of Economic Advisers. There he played a major role in promoting expansionary tax and expenditure policies. Although he remained on the council only briefly, he has continued to serve as a consultant and adviser to Democratic administrations and liberal causes ever since.

During the 1970s and early 1980s the liberal activist policies with which Tobin had been identified came increasingly under attack. As this happened, Tobin assumed the role of leading critic of the new conservative trend. Several of his more noteworthy scholarly papers of recent years have taken the form of critiques of the economic theories on which the shift to a more conservative national economic policy has in part been based.

**James Tobin (1918– )**

### The Modern View of the Demand for Money: The Importance of Liquidity to a Balanced Portfolio

Today most economists accept the notion that the demand for money is sensitive to changes in both nominal national income and interest rates. Keynes's original three-way classification of motives for holding money is now widely regarded as too rigid, however, and his view of the link between interest and money demand as too narrow. Today following the work of James Tobin and others, the tendency is to explain the demand for money in terms of the importance of liquidity to a balanced portfolio. (Economists use the term **portfolio**—which originally just meant a case for carrying papers—as a shorthand term for a person's collection of assets, including money, stocks, bonds, and real estate.)

**Portfolio** A shorthand term for a person's collection of assets.

An asset is said to be liquid, we should recall, if it can be used directly as a means of exchange and if it has a fixed nominal value. There are thus two potential advantages to holding a liquid asset such as money instead of relatively illiquid assets such as stocks or bonds. The first advantage is that liquidity reduces transactions costs. One doesn't want to have to make a trip to a bank or a broker to exchange stocks or bonds for money to buy each week's groceries. The second advantage of holding liquid assets is avoidance of the risk of loss of nominal value associated with less liquid assets.

**The Opportunity Cost of Liquidity** Offsetting the advantage of liquidity is a major disadvantage: more liquid assets generally tend to pay less interest. Currency and chartered bank demand deposits generally pay little or no interest. Some of the assets included in $M_2$ will pay higher interest rates, but even these assets tend to pay a smaller return than alternatives such as stocks or long-term bonds when yields are averaged over an extended period.

The loss of the higher interest rates available on alternative assets is thus an opportunity cost of holding money, to be weighed against money's liquidity value. More precisely, we should say that it is the higher *nominal* rates of interest that measure the opportunity cost of holding non-interest-bearing forms of money. Recall that the nominal interest rate is equal to the real interest rate plus the inflation rate. Suppose, for example, that the nominal interest rate is 10 percent and the inflation rate is zero. Under these circumstances, a person holding money in a non-interest-bearing form such as currency maintains a constant purchasing power but earns zero real return, whereas a person holding a bond or other interest-bearing asset earns a real rate of return equal to the assumed 10 percent nominal rate of interest.

On the other hand, suppose that when the nominal rate of interest is 10 percent, the inflation rate is 6 percent. Under these circumstances the bondholder earns only a 4 percent real rate of return, but the person holding currency loses real purchasing power at the rate of 6 percent per year. The difference between the real return on bonds and the real return on money is 10 percent in either case. Thus, regardless of the rate of inflation, the nominal interest rate properly measures the opportunity cost of holding non-interest-bearing money.

## The Demand for Money in a Two-Asset Economy

In order to bring out more clearly some of the essential features of the demand for money, it will be useful to introduce a simplified economy in which there are only two financial assets available to portfolio holders. These assets are money (in the narrow sense of non-interest-bearing currency and demand deposit balances at the chartered banks) and long-term bonds.

### The Price of Bonds and the Rate of Interest

A short digression on the subject of bonds is needed at this point. **Bonds** are simply IOUs of firms and government units. They have been mentioned several times without explanation of one of their important features—the inverse relationship between the price of a bond and the rate of interest.

In Canada, long-term corporate bonds are often issued in denominations of $1,000. The issuing firm promises to pay the bondholder a certain sum per year for a certain number of years (usually twenty to thirty years) until maturity and, upon maturity, to repay the initial $1,000. The annual sum the bondholder receives until maturity is set according to the nominal rate of interest prevailing at the time the bond is issued. If the interest rate is 8 percent, the annual payment on a $1,000 bond will be $80; if the interest rate is 10 percent, the payment will be $100; and so on.

As Chapter 11 showed, there are active secondary markets in which bonds of this type can be bought and sold. The original purchaser need not hold the bond until maturity. There is no guarantee, however, that the bond can be sold in the secondary market "at par"—that is, at its original purchase price of $1,000. Instead, the price at which the bond can be resold depends on what has happened to the interest rate between the date of issue and the date of resale.

To illustrate: suppose a certain firm issues a twenty-five-year bond at a time when the nominal interest rate on such bonds is 10 percent, agreeing to pay $100 per year for twenty-five years plus $1,000 on maturity. The original purchase price is $1,000. A year later, the original buyer wants to sell the bond; but in the meantime, the nominal interest rate has gone up to 12.5 percent. That means brand new $1,000 bonds are scaled to pay $125 per year to their purchasers, so no one is willing to buy last year's bond with the $100 payment unless its price is cut to approximately $800—since $100 is 12.5 percent of $800. The original buyer of the bond with the $100 annual payment suffers a capital loss of $200 in selling the bond.

If, instead, the interest rate had fallen, say to 5 percent, new bonds would be paying only $50 per year. In that case, the old bond carrying a $100 annual payment could be sold at a premium in the secondary market—for roughly $2,000, in fact.

Actually, there is a little bit more to calculating how much a bond is worth on the secondary market, because we have not taken into account the fact that all bonds are worth the same $1,000 amount at maturity regardless of the annual payment the bondholder receives in the meantime. That is why the prices in the above examples are stated as approximations. However, as long as we stick to long-term bonds for which the date of maturity lies in the rather distant future, the price of the bond is determined almost entirely by the interaction of the size of the annual payment

**Bond** A promise, given in recognition of a loan, to make a fixed annual or semiannual payment over a period of years plus a larger final payment equal to the sum initially borrowed.

and the nomimal interest rate. In any event, the important thing to remember is this: *a rise in the nominal rate of interest depresses the price of bonds in the secondary market, and a fall in the nominal rate of interest raises the price of bonds in the secondary market.*

**Portfolio Balance in the Simple Economy** The quantity of money demanded by the inhabitants of the simplified economy depends on how they decide to balance their portfolios between money and bonds. Two factors can be expected to influence their decision.

First, the higher the nominal income in the simplified economy, the greater the desired quantity of money. The reason is the transactions motive. People's purchases increase when their income increases, so their demand for money also increases.

Second, the higher the nominal rate of interest, the lower the desired quantity of money. There are two reasons for this. One is that a high nominal rate of interest means a high opportunity cost to holding money; holders of money could be earning a high income by holding bonds instead. Second, relative to what has been experienced in the past and what is expected in the future, the higher the rate of interest, the lower the price of bonds. If the price of bonds is perceived as low, people will be inclined to hold more bonds relative to money in the hope that their price will go up and they can be resold for capital gain. Conversely, if the interest rate is low, the price of bonds will be high and people are likely to be reluctant to hold them for fear the price will drop and they will be stuck with a capital loss. In this situation, people will be inclined to hold more of their portfolio in money. The speculative motive for holding money is thus seen to influence people's decisions regarding the balance of their portfolios between bonds and money.

**A Money Demand Schedule** The quantity of money demanded, then, increases as the nominal interest rate falls and as nominal income increases. The relationship among the amount of money demanded, the interest rate, and the level of nominal income that prevails in a given economy in a given period is known as that economy's **money demand schedule**. Exhibit 13.1 shows what the schedule might look like for the simplified economy. The entries in Exhibit 13.1a give the quantity of money demanded when the interest rate is that indicated at the left-hand border of the table and the level of nominal national income is that shown at the top of the table. For example, when the interest rate is 10 percent per year and the level of nominal national income is $600, the quantity of money demanded is $72.

Exhibit 13.1b gives the money demand schedule in graphical form. At any given level of income, the relationship between the quantity of money demanded and the interest rate can be shown by a downward-sloping curve that looks much like an ordinary demand curve. For example, the curve labeled $MD_1$ shows the way money demand varies as the interest rate varies when income is $600. This curve is drawn from the data in the $600 column of the table in Part a. A change in the level of income would produce a shift in the money demand curve. For example, if income were to increase to $1,200, the money demand curve would shift to the position

**Money demand schedule** A schedule showing the quantity of money that people desire to hold in their portfolios given various values for the nominal interest rate and the level of nominal income.

**(a)**

| Nominal Interest Rate (Percent) | Level of Nominal National Income | | | | | |
|---|---|---|---|---|---|---|
| | $200 | $400 | $600 | $800 | $1,000 | $1,200 |
| 2 | $120 | $240 | $360 | $480 | $600 | $720 |
| 4 | 60 | 120 | 180 | 240 | 300 | 360 |
| 6 | 40 | 80 | 120 | 160 | 200 | 240 |
| 8 | 30 | 60 | 90 | 120 | 150 | 180 |
| 10 | 24 | 48 | 72 | 96 | 120 | 144 |
| 12 | 20 | 40 | 60 | 80 | 100 | 120 |
| 14 | 17 | 34 | 51 | 68 | 85 | 102 |
| 16 | 15 | 30 | 45 | 60 | 75 | 90 |

**Exhibit 13.1**

**Money demand schedule for a hypothetical economy**
The table and diagram show how the quantity of money demanded varies as the nominal interest rate and the level of nominal income vary in a simplified economy like the one used in these numerical examples. The entries in the body of the table show the quantity of money demanded at the nominal interest rate corresponding to the row and the nominal income corresponding to the column. Each column of the table can be graphed to get a money demand curve like that shown in Part b of the exhibit. The curve $MD_1$ assumes income to be fixed at $600. A rise in income to $1,200 would shift the money demand curve to the position $MD_2$. Keynes referred to this as "the liquidity preference schedule."

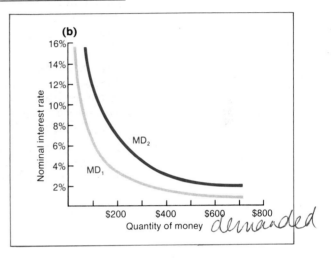

labeled $MD_2$ in the figure. The data given in the last column of the table indicate that when income doubles, the quantity of money demanded at any particular level of the interest rate doubles.

**Money Demand and Velocity** As Exhibit 13.1b is drawn, the ratio of nominal income to money demanded is constant for all levels of income, given a particular interest rate. For example, when the nominal interest rate is 6 percent, each $1 of the money stock must support $5 of nominal national income; when the interest rate rises to 12 percent, each $1 must support $10 of nominal income, and so on.

In the actual Canadian economy, there is a tendency for money demand and velocity to vary with the interest rate, just as in the simple two-asset economy. But for practical purposes of conducting monetary policy, knowledge of such a tendency is not necessarily enough. It is also important to know how stable the demand for money is—how closely it follows a given money demand schedule from year to year—and whether the money demand schedule itself is subject to shifts over time. The following case study presents some data bearing on these questions.

**Case 13.1**
**The Stability of Money Demand in the Canadian Economy,**
**1963–1981**

Exhibit 13.2 provides two viewpoints on money demand for the Canadian economy for the years 1963 through 1981. First, Exhibit 13.2a shows the relationship between the nominal interest rate, on the vertical axis, and the quantity of money demanded per dollar of nominal GNP, on the horizontal axis. This graph looks much like one of the money demand curves in Exhibit 13.1, except that money demand is divided by nominal income in order to make the graph easier to interpret. Changes in nominal national income do not shift the curve in Exhibit 13.2a as they shifted the curves in Exhibit 13.1. Exhibit 13.2b shows the relationship between velocity and nominal interest rates over the same period. Velocity is measured here as the ratio of nominal GNP to $M_1$. Because the horizontal axis in Part a measures $M_1$ divided by nominal GNP, whereas the horizontal axis in Part b measures nominal GNP divided by $M_1$, the two figures are mirror images of one another.

At first glance the relationships shown by the broad shaded bands in the figures are much as would be expected. As nominal interest rates have risen over almost twenty years, the demand for money as a fraction of nominal GNP has fallen, and velocity has risen. A closer inspection of the two figures, however, shows that the relationship has not been completely stable. In Part a, the dots for the years 1963–1970 are clustered closer to the right than those for the years 1973–1981. In Part b, the earlier years are clustered to the left of the later years. It appears, then, that the underlying money demand function shifted substantially during the 1970s. These shifts, unlike the demand-curve shifts shown in Exhibit 13.1, were not caused by changes in nominal income; such income-induced shifts are eliminated by the way the horizontal axes are drawn in these figures.

If rising nominal income did not cause the apparent shifts in the money demand relationship, what did cause them? Economists are divided on the explanation, but the shifts have probably been caused by new forms of savings not included in $M_1$, new corporate cash management practices, and new information-processing systems that allow money holders to keep exact track of their available funds and thereby economize on their $M_1$ cash balances.

## EQUILIBRIUM AND DISEQUILIBRIUM IN THE MONEY MARKET

Now that both the supply and the demand for money have been analyzed, the next step will be to put the two together and investigate the nature of equilibrium and disequilibrium in the money market. Exhibit 13.3 shows the basic diagram that will be used to do this. It contains a downward-sloping demand curve for money (taken from Exhibit 13.1) and a money supply curve; and it uses an assumed national income of $1,200. The money supply curve is simply a vertical line; it reflects an assumption that in the simple economy the money supply is determined solely by Bank of Canada policy and is not directly affected by changes in economic conditions. As Exhibit 13.3 is drawn, the quantity of money supplied is assumed to be $180. Given a certain MS (money supply), MD shows a willingness to hold onto M. At higher rates of interest, people with money will be trying to loan it out. At lower rates of interest they will be happier to hang on to it because, (a) the opportunity cost of liquidity is now low, and (b) they hope that interest rates may rise in the near future.

It is important to remember that both the demand for money and the supply of money are measured in terms of stocks, not flows. The supply

**Exhibit 13.2**
**Velocity and interest rates in the Canadian economy, 1963–1981**
Part a of this exhibit traces the relationship between the demand for money ($\tilde{M}_1$) as a fraction of GNP and the nominal rate of interest on three-month Treasury bills from 1963 to 1981. Part b shows the relationship between the income velocity of money (measured at the ratio of GNP to $M_1$) and the same interest rate. The two graphs are mirror images—alternative ways of looking at the same underlying relationship. Note that there has been an apparent shift in the relationships depicted here, beginning in the early 1970s, and again more recently.

Source: Department of Finance, *Economic Review*, April 1982, pp. 221 and 230, and previous years.

**(a) Money demand plotted against three month Treasury bill rate (annual data 1963–1981)**

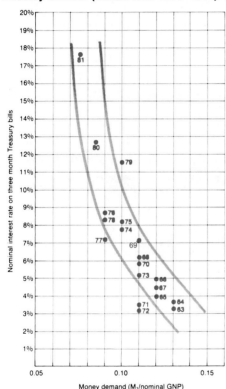

**(b) Velocity plotted against three month Treasury bill rate (annual data 1963–1981)**

represents the stock in existence at a given time, and the demand represents the stock that people desire to hold in their portfolios under given conditions.

## Equilibrium

It is apparent from the diagram that there is only one nominal rate of interest, 8 percent, at which the stock of money that people want to hold is equal to the stock of money supplied by the banking system in accordance with Bank of Canada policy. At any higher rate of interest, there would be an excess quantity of money supplied.

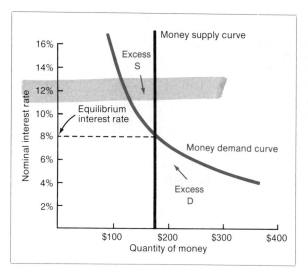

**Exhibit 13.3**
**Equilibrium in the money market**

The money demand curve in this diagram is based on the data given in Exhibit 13.1, and it uses an assumed nominal national income of $1,200. The money supply curve assumes a quantity of money supplied of $180. The equilibrium nominal interest rate is 8 percent. At any higher interest rate, an excess quantity of money supplied would put downward pressure on the interest rate. If the interest rate were below equilibrium, there would be an excess quantity of money demanded and upward pressure. Both money supply and money demand are measured in stock terms.

**Reactions to an Excess Supply of Money**  At an interest rate of 12 percent, for example, the excess quantity supplied would be $60. This quantity reflects the fact that people do not want to hold as much money in their portfolios as the Bank of Canada has caused the banking system to put into circulation.

Individual asset holders react to an excess quantity of money supplied by using their excess money to buy other assets. Given the high interest rate, they are particularly attracted to the idea of replacing some of the money in their portfolios with bonds. However, although some individual asset holders can successfully reduce the quantity of money in their portfolios by buying bonds, not all asset holders can do so at once. Every time someone takes money out of his or her portfolio to buy a bond from someone else, that money ends up in the portfolio of the seller.

No matter how much money is churned around from portfolio to portfolio in pursuit of bonds, every cent of the fixed stock of money supplied by the banking system has to be in someone's portfolio at each moment. What occurs as a result of all this churning is not a fall in the money stock but a rise in the price of bonds. This rise in bond prices means a fall in the nominal rate of interest on bonds. As the interest rate falls, the excess quantity of money supplied is reduced, not because the extra money disappears but because the amount of money that people desire to keep in their portfolios rises until it catches up with the quantity of money supplied. Soon the nominal interest rate reaches its equilibrium level, and the excess demand is entirely eliminated.

**Reactions to an Excess Demand for Money**  If the interest rate were for some reason below the equilibrium level, there would be an excess quantity of money demanded, and a process opposite to that just described would occur. People would want to sell bonds in order to get the greater quantity of money they would prefer to hold at the low interest rate. This would not increase the total supply of money available in the system, but it would depress the price of bonds—which in turn would raise the interest rate until equilibrium were restored.

Equilibrium in the money market thus associates one and only one nominal interest rate with a given quantity of money and a given nominal income. The reactions to excess supply and demand just discussed play a critical role in the adjustment of the money market to two important types of disturbances, as will now be shown.

### Effects of a Change in Money Supply

The first step will be to examine the effects of an increase in the money supply resulting from an open market purchase of securities from the public by the Bank of Canada. Suppose that initially the money supply is $180, as shown by the money curve MS$_1$ in Exhibit 13.4. A nominal national income of $1,200 gives the money demand curve MD. The equilibrium interest rate is 8 percent, and the money multiplier is 9.0.

Imagine that the Bank of Canada makes an open market purchase of $20 worth of government securities, paying for them with one of its own cheques. The immediate effect of this purchase is to increase the money supply by $20 and to raise bond prices slightly and lower the rate of interest slightly.

If this were the end of the story, the money supply curve would be put in the position indicated as MS$_2$, and the market would be put in a new equilibrium at the intersection of that curve with the money demand curve. But this is not the end of the story. As soon as the original Bank of Canada cheque is deposited in the bond seller's bank, the total reserves of the banking system go up by $20 to a new level of $40. This sets off the process of deposit expansion described in Chapter 12, and by the time the reserves-to-money multiplier has worked itself out, the money supply will reach $360. This will shift the money supply curve all the way to the position MS$_3$.

↑ money supply
↑ money demand

**Exhibit 13.4**

**Effects of an increase in the money supply**
Initially, a money supply of $180 puts the money supply curve in the position MS$_1$. An open market purchase of $20 by the Bank of Canada has the immediate effect of moving the money supply curve to MS$_2$. That is not the end of the story, however. With a money multiplier of 9.0, the money supply reaches $360 (MS$_3$) before the deposit expansion process works itself out completely. The new equilibrium nominal interest rate is 4 percent.

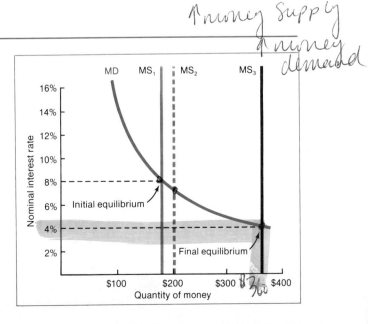

**New Equilibrium** Now there will be a large excess quantity of money supplied. Asset holders will not desire to hold the new money at the old interest rate and will try to reduce their money holdings. It is likely that some excess money balances will be spent on physical assets, including consumer durables, and it is certain that some will be spent on bonds. As before, the actions of portfolio holders will bid up bond prices and lower interest rates. When the interest rate falls low enough (to 4 percent as this example is constructed), the demand for money will rise sufficiently to re-establish equilibrium. In the new equilibrium, total money balances outstanding will be larger than initially, and the nominal interest rate will be lower.

### Effects of an Increase in Income

In looking at the money market effects of an increase in the money supply, we assumed that nominal income remained unchanged throughout. Now we will look at the effects of a change in nominal income, assuming that the money supply will remain fixed. This will complete the groundwork for the next chapter, where the two types of changes will be considered in combination.

**A Shift in the Money Demand Curve** Exhibit 13.5 sets the scene for exploring the effects of a change in nominal income. Suppose that initially the economy is in equilibrium with a money supply (MS) of $180, a nominal income (MD$_1$) of $600, and an interest rate of 4 percent. At this interest rate, the desired quantity of money holdings is $180, just equal to the money supply—as of course it must be in equilibrium.

Now suppose that for some reason nominal income rises to $1,200. The increase in income causes the money demand curve to shift to the new position, MD$_2$. With the money supply still at $180, this means a very substantial excess quantity of money demanded. To meet the increased

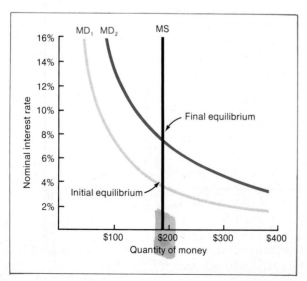

**Exhibit 13.5**

Effects of an increase in national income
Initially, a nominal income of $600 puts the money demand curve at MD$_1$. The equilibrium nominal interest rate is 4 percent with the money supply at $180. If an increase in nominal income to $1,200 shifts the money demand curve to MD$_2$, the interest rate will have to rise to 8 percent to restore equilibrium.

demand for money, portfolio holders will have to sell some of their earning assets, especially bonds. This will depress the price of bonds and raise the nominal interest rate.

As the nominal interest rate rises, the desired ratio of money to income falls, since the higher interest rate raises the implicit cost of holding money balances. When the nominal interest rate rises high enough, the desired quantity of money will fall to $180, entirely eliminating the excess quantity of money demanded. This will happen at an interest rate of 8 percent for the current example. Therefore, the new equilibrium rate of interest is 8 percent.

## CONCLUSIONS

This completes the initial discussion of the supply and demand for money. The important next step — to apply this theory to the problem of national income determination — is the aim of the next chapter. That chapter will show how the inclusion of the money market in the analysis of national income determination leads to some important modifications of the multiplier theory and sets the stage for the discussion of inflation and unemployment.

## SUMMARY

1. The equation of exchange illustrates the relationship between the quantity of money, velocity, real income, and the price level. John Maynard Keynes tried to clarify the relationship between the quantity of money and income by examining the motives of people for holding money. He noted that money is demanded for transactions purposes, for coping with uncertainties, and for speculative purposes. His theory has been amplified and modified in modern "portfolio theory."

2. The collection of various assets a person owns (money, real estate, consumer durables, bonds, stocks, or whatever) is called a portfolio. Portfolio holders try to maintain a balance among the various kinds of assets they own, shifting from one to another as economic conditions change. As nominal income rises, people tend to want more money in their portfolios to satisfy their transactions demand. As the nominal rate of interest rises, people tend to want less money in their portfolios, because the opportunity cost of holding money increases and because their speculative demand for money decreases.

3. A downward-sloping money demand curve can be drawn to indicate, in graphical form, how the quantity of money demanded changes as the interest rate changes, given some level of nominal income. An increase in the level of nominal income shifts this curve to the right, and a decrease shifts it to the left.

4. If the money supply is assumed to be fully controlled by Bank of Canada policy, the money supply curve can be represented by a vertical line. Together, the money supply and money demand curves associate one and only one nominal rate of interest with each quantity of money supplied and each level of nominal income. With nominal income unchanged, an increase in the money supply must be followed by a fall in the nominal

rate of interest, other things being equal. With the money supply unchanged, an increase in nominal income causes the nominal rate of interest to rise, other things being equal.

## DISCUSSION QUESTIONS

1. List the items that you might consider part of your portfolio. Is your portfolio basically similar to the one discussed in the text? In what ways is it similar? In what ways is it different?
2. Which is most important in determining your own demand for money—the transactions motive, the precautionary motive, or the speculative motive? Explain.
3. If the interest rate paid on savings deposits were increased, would you change your portfolio? Would you invest more or less in a savings account? Explain.
4. What is the average balance in your chequebook during a typical month? How much currency do you carry on a typical day? The sum of these two figures will give the quantity of money demanded. In order to get a point on your demand for money schedule, a price is needed. What price should be used?
5. Evaluate the following statement: It is at best a mere metaphor, and at worst seriously misleading, to speak of the money "market." Money cannot be bought and sold; it is just the means of payment we use in buying and selling everything else. Since it cannot be bought and sold, it cannot have a true market.
6. Do you know what the interest rate is on three-month Treasury bills at the time you are reading this chapter? Try to find out.

## SUGGESTIONS FOR FURTHER READING

Boreham, Gordon F., with Shapiro, Eli, Solomon, Ezra, and White, William. *Money and Banking: Analysis and Policy in a Canadian Context*, 2nd ed. Toronto: Holt, Rinehart and Winston, 1979.
*Chapters 10 and 18 parallel the discussion of this chapter but offer additional details.*

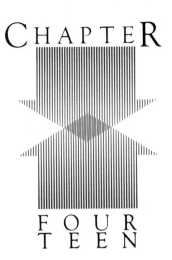
# THE INTERACTION OF MONEY AND THE MULTIPLIER

---

**WHAT YOU WILL LEARN IN THIS CHAPTER**

*This chapter ties together the analysis of fiscal and monetary policy given in previous chapters. First, it shows how the two policies interact to establish simultaneous equilibrium in the money market and the circular flow. Next, it shows how the effects of fiscal policy actions are modified when monetary reactions to fiscal policy are taken into account. Finally, after discussing the basic tools of fiscal and monetary policy analysis, the chapter introduces some important controversies concerning the relative importance and effectiveness of fiscal and monetary policy.*

**FOR REVIEW**

*Here are some important terms and concepts that will be put to use in this chapter. If you do not understand them, review them before proceeding.*

• *Real and nominal interest rates (Chapter 7)*
• *Theory of investment (Chapter 8)*
• *Fiscal policy (Chapter 10)*
• *Supply of money (Chapter 12)*
• *Demand for money (Chapter 13)*

---

This chapter ties together the multiplier analysis of Chapters 8 to 10 with the analysis of the financial sector presented in Chapters 11 to 13. In doing so, it makes a transition from what economists call partial equilibrium analysis to what they call general equilibrium analysis.

The difference between the two lies in the role played by the "other things being equal" assumption. In **partial equilibrium analysis**, it is said that if Event X occurs, the effect on Market Y will be Z, provided that the equilibrium of other markets is not disturbed. In **general equilibrium analysis**, in contrast, it is said that if Event X occurs, the effect on Market Y will be Z, provided that other markets also adjust fully to the event in question.

So far, the multiplier theory and the theory of money have been examined only from the partial equilibrium point of view. Chapter 8 described the determinants of planned expenditure and noted how one type of expenditure, investment, is linked negatively to the rate of interest. However, this linkage was not explored further in the development of the multiplier. Chapter 10 analyzed the effect of a change in fiscal policy on

**Partial equilibrium analysis** An approach to the study of markets along the lines of: if Event X occurs, the effect on Market Y will be Z, provided that the equilibrium of other markets is not disturbed.

**General equilibrium analysis** An approach to the study of markets along the lines of: if Event X occurs, the effect on Market Y will be Z, provided that other markets also adjust fully to the event in question.

the equilibrium level of the circular flow without considering the possible effects that the change might have on the demand for money, on the nominal interest rate, and on the level of planned investment. Similarly, Chapter 13 looked at the effect a change in the money supply would have on the equilibrium nominal interest rate without considering the possible effect of such an act of monetary policy on the level of nominal national income or the position of the money demand curve.

This chapter will also look at fiscal and monetary policy, but now using the general equilibrium approach. After delineating some basic principles, it will turn to important controversies surrounding the relative strength and effectiveness of monetary and fiscal policy.

## THE INTERACTION OF MONEY AND NATIONAL INCOME

### The Conditions for General Equilibrium

The chapter begins by showing what the economy looks like when the circular flow and the money market are simultaneously in equilibrium. Consider Exhibit 14.1, which shows two main channels of interaction (represented by large arrows) between money and the level of nominal national income. Each of these channels requires some comment.

**Nominal Income and Money Demand** The first interaction runs from the level of nominal national income, as determined by aggregate supply and demand, to the position of the money demand curve. As shown in the last chapter, the quantity of money demanded depends both on the nominal rate of interest and on the level of national income. A change in the nominal interest rate produces a movement along a given money demand curve, whereas a change in nominal national income produces a shift in the money demand curve. In order to put the money demand curve in its proper position, then, it is necessary to know the equilibrium level of nominal national income.

**Interest Rates and Investment** The second channel of interaction runs from the money market to the aggregate demand schedule by way of the effect of interest rates on the level of planned investment. Low interest rates encourage investment; and investment, in turn, is an important component of aggregate nominal demand.

**Finding the Equilibrium Values** The money market and the circular flow can be in equilibrium simultaneously only if a certain pair of values for the interest rate and nominal national income prevail. Let the required level of nominal income be Y and the required interest rate be r. Then the value of r must be just right to induce the level of planned investment needed to put equilibrium nominal national income exactly at the level Y, and the value of Y must be just right to put the money demand curve in the position needed to keep the equilibrium interest rate at r.

As Exhibit 14.1 is drawn, an interest rate of 8 percent and a nominal national income of $1,200 are called for. The aggregate demand schedule is drawn on the assumptions that autonomous consumption is $100, the marginal propensity to consume is 0.75, government purchases are $280,

**Exhibit 14.1**

**A general equilibrium view of national income determination**

The money market and the circular flow can both be in equilibrium at once only if a certain pair of values for the interest rate and nominal income prevail. The large arrows in this figure show how the interest rate and nominal national income interact. The equilibrium interest rate helps determine the position of the aggregate demand curve through its effect on planned investment spending. The level of nominal national income helps determine the interest rate through its effect on the position of the money demand curve.

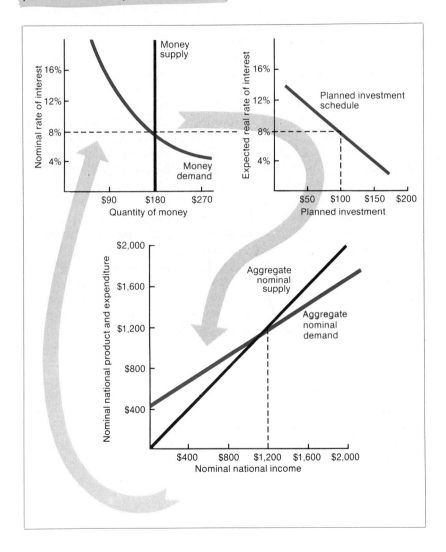

net exports are $75–0.15 national income, and net taxes are $100. If planned investment is $100, equilibrium nominal national income will be $1,200. A check of the planned investment schedule reveals that an interest rate of 8 percent is just what is needed to encourage that amount of planned investment.

Turning to the money market, where a money supply of $180 is assumed, the money demand curve must be in exactly the position indicated in Exhibit 14.1 for the equilibrium rate of interest to be 8 percent. This position, which corresponds to a nominal national income of $1,200, verifies that r = 8 percent and Y = $1,200 are an equilibrium pair for the interest rate and nominal national income.

**The Equilibrium Is Unique**  For any given set of assumptions about autonomous consumption, the marginal propensity to consume, government purchases, net taxes, net exports, the money supply, and the position of the planned investment schedule, there is just one pair of values for the interest rate and nominal national income that permits both the money market and the circular flow to be in equilibrium. Thus, equilibrium values of nominal national income and the interest rate are unique.

To see this, assume momentarily that one of the values is different, and then show that this does not permit both markets to be in equilibrium. Suppose, for example, that the interest rate were only 4 percent, while all underlying economic conditions were the same as before. The planned investment schedule in Exhibit 14.1 shows that a 4 percent interest rate would cause planned investment to rise to $150. With planned expenditure $50 higher than before, equilibrium nominal national income would rise by $125 to $1,325 under the impact of the multiplier effect. Thus an interest rate of 4 percent requires an equilibrium nominal national income of $1,325.

The money market part of Exhibit 14.1 shows that 4 percent cannot be the equilibrium rate of interest when the money demand curve is in the position shown and the money supply is $180. The money demand curve would have to shift to the left to make 4 percent the equilibrium rate of interest. But an increase in nominal national income from $1,200 to $1,325 would shift the curve not to the left but to the right. There is no way that 4 percent can be an equilibrium rate of interest when the level of nominal national income is $1,325, given the assumed money supply. There is also no way that the equilibrium level of nominal national income can be anything but $1,325 when the rate of interest is 4 percent. Given the assumed underlying economic conditions, it is necessary to conclude that when the interest rate is 4 percent, there is no value of nominal national income that permits both the money market and the circular flow to be in equilibrium.

The same reasoning could be repeated for any value of r other than 8 percent and any value of Y other than $1,200. This pair of equilibrium values for nominal national income and interest rate is unique.

## A Revised Look at the Effects of Fiscal Policy

Chapter 10 discussed the effects of two kinds of changes in fiscal policy: changes in government purchases and changes in net taxes. Each of these kinds of fiscal policy must now be reconsidered from the point of view of general equilibrium analysis. For purposes of comparison with what follows, recall the conclusion reached in Chapter 10 about the effects of a change in government purchases: when government purchases are increased while taxes, planned investment, the consumption schedule, and the net export schedule remain unchanged, equilibrium nominal national income will change by an amount equal to the change in government purchases times the multiplier.

**Effects of a Change in Government Purchases** Beginning with government purchases, assume that the economy is initially in equilibrium with interest rate r and nominal national income Y. Then assume that fiscal policy makers decide to increase government purchases of domestic goods and services by $100, with no accompanying change in taxes. Consider the effects of this fiscal policy as they work their way through the economy.

The first effect of the increase in government purchases is to shift the aggregate demand schedule upward by $100. Planned expenditure now exceeds national product at the initial income level. This causes unplanned depletion of inventories, to which business firms respond by increasing output and/or raising prices. The level of nominal national income begins to rise.

**Money Market Effect** As nominal national income rises, the change in fiscal policy begins to affect the money market. The increase in nominal national income causes the money demand curve to shift rightward. In Exhibit 14.2 this is shown as a shift from the initial position of the money demand curve, $MD_1$, toward a new position, $MD_2$. The money demand curve shifts because when incomes rise, people tend to want more money in their portfolios. Because the money supply does not increase, people's attempts to get more money by selling bonds simply drives down the price of bonds and drives up the rate of interest. Altogether, then, the effect on the money market of the increase in government purchases is to push up the rate of interest

**The Crowding Out Effect** Attention can now be shifted from the money market to the planned investment schedule, also shown in Exhibit 14.2. Increased money demand has driven up the rate of interest. Firms find it more costly to undertake fixed investment projects and to increase inventories of raw materials or finished goods. They therefore reduce their planned investment expenditures, shown by a movement upward and to the left along the planned investment schedule. This decrease in planned investment expenditures, as an indirect effect of an increase in government purchases, is called the **crowding out effect.** The amount of investment crowded out is labeled $\Delta I$ in the exhibit.

Exhibit 14.3 shows what happens in terms of aggregate supply and demand. The original position of the aggregate demand curve is shown as $AND_1$. Considered in isolation, the increase in government spending would have pushed the schedule all the way up to the position $AND_2$. When the crowding out effect is taken into account, though, it is apparent that the upward shift in aggregate demand is less than the amount of increase in government purchases. If $\Delta G$ stands for the increase in government purchases and $\Delta I$ for the amount of investment crowded out, the upward shift is reduced to $\Delta G - \Delta I$. This puts the final position of the aggregate demand curve at $AND_3$.

**Crowding out effect** The tendency of expansionary fiscal policy to cause a drop in private planned investment expenditure as a result of a rise in the interest rate.

**Exhibit 14.2**

**The crowding out effect**

An increase in government purchases causes nominal national income to rise via the multiplier effect. The increase in income shifts the money demand curve from its initial position, $MD_1$, to the new position, $MD_2$. The equilibrium interest rate rises from $r_1$ to $r_2$. An amount of private investment equal to $\Delta I$ is "crowded out."

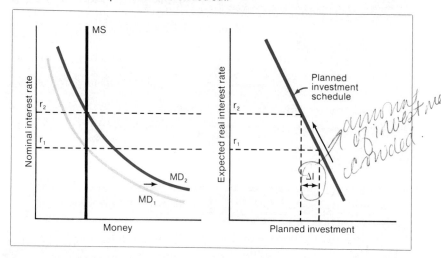

*amount of investment crowded.*

Looking at Exhibits 14.2 and 14.3 together, now, notice that both income and the interest rate have changed. The new equilibrium interest rate, $r_2$, and the new equilibrium nominal national income, $Y_2$, are higher than they were to begin with. Government purchases and private consumption are higher than initially, but private investment is lower.

**Crowding Out and the Multiplier** Because an increase in government purchases crowds out some private investment, nominal national income does not rise by the full amount of the multiplier times the increase in government purchases. This fact does not, however, directly contradict the conclusion reached in Chapter 10 and repeated above. The trouble is that the earlier conclusion, which was based on partial equilibrium analysis, included the assumption that planned investment would not change when nominal national income changed. The general equilibrium approach taken here shows that that assumption is invalid. This makes it necessary to modify the way the multiplier theory is applied to the analysis of fiscal policy. The multiplier must now be applied not just to the change in government purchases but rather to the change in government purchases minus the induced change in private planned investment expenditure.

The new way of applying the multiplier theory to the analysis of fiscal policy can be put in the form of a simple equation. Using the symbol $\Delta Y$ to represent the change in nominal national income resulting from a change

**Exhibit 14.3**

**The crowding out effect in terms of aggregate supply and demand**

Here the crowding out effect is shown from the perspective of aggregate supply and demand. Taken by itself, the increase in government purchases ($\Delta G$) would have pushed the aggregate demand curve from $AND_1$ to $AND_2$. The crowding out effect chops $\Delta I$ off private investment, however, so the actual shift is only from $AND_1$ to $AND_3$, a distance equal to $\Delta G - \Delta I$.

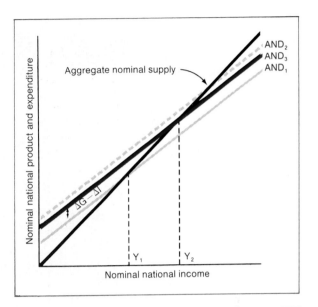

in government purchases, $\Delta G$, and using $(1/1 - MPC_D)$ to stand for the multiplier:

$$\Delta Y = \frac{1}{1 - MPC_D} (\Delta G - \Delta I)$$

*national income resulting from a $\Delta G$.*

**Other Fiscal Policies** The crowding out effect applies to other types of fiscal policy as well as to changes in government purchases. When taxes are lowered, or when the level of government purchases is increased while the budget is kept in balance, nominal national income rises. This pushes interest rates up and crowds out some investment. The result is that the overall effectiveness of these fiscal policies is somewhat less than would be predicted by the simple applications of the tax multiplier.

It must also be remembered that when taxes are raised or government purchases lowered, as might be done to eliminate an inflationary gap from the economy, the crowding out effect works in reverse. The deflationary impact of fiscal policy is somewhat diminished, because as incomes fall, the demand for money and the interest rate fall too. These effects stimulate new planned investment expenditure, somewhat offsetting the downward shift in the aggregate demand schedule that the deflationary policy produces.

## A Revised Look at the Effects of Monetary Policy

Chapter 13 described the effects of a change in the money supply from a partial equilibrium point of view, taking into account only what happens in the money market. This section will reconsider the effects of changes in the money supply in a general equilibrium context, taking into account the interaction of money and the multiplier theory of income determination.

**An Open Market Purchase**  To be specific, suppose that the Bank of Canada initiates an expansion of the money supply through an open market purchase of bonds. It will not be necessary to give separate consideration to the expansion of the money supply by the use of other instruments of monetary policy because the effects are very little different from those of an open market operation.

Chapters 12 and 13 analyzed initial effects of the open market purchase. The open market purchase creates an increase in chartered bank reserves, and banks are induced to begin the process of deposit expansion. When the expansion is complete, the money supply will have increased by an amount equal to the expansion in the reserves times the money multiplier. This is indicated in Exhibit 14.4 by the shift in the money supply curve from the position $MS_1$ to the position $MS_2$.

As the money supply expands, people find that they have more money than they want to hold in their portfolios at the original rate of interest. They attempt to reduce these holdings by buying other assets, including bonds. This tends to push the price of bonds up and the interest rate down. In the diagram, the process is represented by a movement along the original money demand curve, $MD_1$, toward its intersection with the new money supply curve, $MS_2$.

**Income and Expenditure Effect**  As the interest rate begins to fall, business executives are encouraged to increase their level of planned investment,

---

**Exhibit 14.4**

**Money market and investment effects of an increase in the money supply**

An increase in the money supply shifts the money supply curve from $MS_1$ to $MS_2$. The immediate effect of this shift is a movement down along the money demand curve, $MD_1$, toward its intersection with the new money supply curve. The interest rate then falls and planned investment expenditure rises, which stimulates nominal national income through the multiplier effect. The rise in income in turn shifts the money demand schedule to a new position, $MD_2$, which cuts short the fall in the interest rate — and a new equilibrium is established.

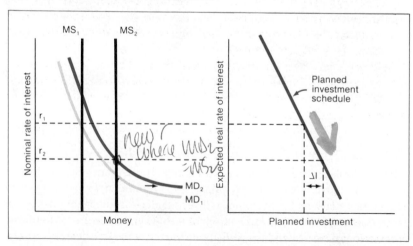

**Exhibit 14.5**
**The effect of an increase in the money supply on aggregate demand and nominal national income**
An increase in planned investment spending, caused by an increase in the money supply, shifts the aggregate demand curve upward. The amount of the shift is equal to the change in investment, $\Delta I$. A new equilibrium is established, with nominal national income increasing from $Y_1$ to $Y_2$.

which is indicated by a movement down and to the right along their planned investment schedule. The increase in investment expenditure shifts the aggregate nominal demand schedule upward, as shown in Exhibit 14.5. Planned expenditure now temporarily exceeds nominal national income; and by the familiar multiplier process, nominal national income begins to increase.

As this income increases, the money market is once again affected. Now the money demand curve begins to shift to the right, moving toward the position marked $MD_2$ in Exhibit 14.4. This shift cuts off the fall in the interest rate, and a new equilibrium interest rate is established where $MD_1$ and $MS_2$ intersect.

Once this interest rate is established, planned investment stops expanding. The aggregate nominal demand schedule comes to rest at a new equilibrium position, $AND_2$, as shown in Exhibit 14.5. That means the new equilibrium level of nominal national income will be higher than it was before the increase in the money supply.

In short, general equilibrium analysis shows that an increase in the money supply will result in new equilibrium values for both the interest rate and nominal national income. With zero inflationary expectations, as assumed, both the nominal interest rate and the expected real interest rate will be lower than before the monetary expansion took place, and the level of nominal national income will be higher.

## Accommodating Monetary Policy

Now that the separate effects of fiscal and monetary policy have been described, it is not difficult to envision how the two policies might be used

**Accommodating monetary policy** A policy under which the Bank of Canada expands the money supply, in an attempt to keep interest rates from rising, and provides the money to allow financial intermediaries to buy the bonds when the government sells bonds to cover a budget deficit.

in combination. Although not every possible combination of policies will be discussed here, one case is important enough to deserve at least a brief mention: the case of accommodating monetary policy.

The Bank of Canada is said to pursue an **accommodating monetary policy** when, in the face of expansionary fiscal policy, it expands the money supply in an attempt to keep interest rates stable. To see why the Bank might want to do this, consider what happens when the government increases its purchases without raising taxes in order to stimulate aggregate demand. It must finance the deficit by selling bonds to the public. This depresses the price of bonds, thereby raising the interest rate. The increase in the interest rate is unwelcome—for two reasons. First, it crowds out some private investment. This partially negates the intended stimulative effect of the increased government purchases. Second, it makes it more expensive for the government to raise the money needed to finance the deficit. By making open market purchases of bonds at the same time the government is selling new bonds to finance the deficit, the Bank of Canada keeps the interest rate from rising, thereby "accommodating" the government.

But, of course, by feeding new reserves to the banking system, the Bank of Canada's actions cause the money supply to expand. In effect, *the combined actions of the Bank of Canada and the government mean that the government is paying for its purchases with newly created money.*

To understand accommodating monetary policy more fully, refer back to Exhibit 14.2, which described the crowding out effect. Increased government purchases increased interest rates from r to $r_2$, by increasing the demand for money from $MD_1$ to $MD_2$. Higher interest rates lowered planned investments. By engaging in accommodating monetary policy, through the purchase of bonds in the open market, the Bank of Canada causes the money supply curve to shift to the right. This lowers interest rates and increases planned investment.

In times gone by, governments did not always bother with such niceties as bonds and open market purchases when they wanted to spend more than they collected in taxes. Instead, they just cranked up their presses and printed new currency. In remembrance of this ancient custom, economic journalists to this day sometimes refer to the combination of deficit spending and accommodating monetary policy as "deficit finance via the printing press."

## CONTROVERSIES OVER MONETARY POLICY

The analysis of the interactions of monetary and fiscal policy just worked through may appear to be perfectly straightforward and perhaps not particularly exciting. Yet some of the major economic controversies of the twentieth century revolve around the ideas presented in the preceding pages. Taking things in historical sequence, the so-called Keynesian-monetarist controversy will be the first one looked at.

### The Keynesian-Monetarist Controversy

Keynes's general theory of employment, interest, and money was intended to be "general" in the sense that it would take into account both monetary and fiscal influences on the economy.[1] However, in the first years after the publication of Keynes's book, it was not the general theory as a whole that dominated the thinking of the economics profession. Instead, some followers of Keynes tended to place one-sided emphasis on planned expenditure and to downplay the role of money in the economy. Early followers of Keynes interpreted the experience of the Great Depression as justifying the view that "money doesn't matter." They attributed the fact that monetary policy had failed to prevent both the 41 percent decline in nominal income and the increase in the unemployment rate to 19 percent of the labor force that occurred in Canada between 1929 and 1933 not to poor conduct of monetary policy but to its ineffectiveness. The fact that the Great Depression did not end until World War II had brought on a massive increase in government spending appeared to support this view.

After the war, many of the early Keynesians forecast a new depression and economic stagnation. They thought that private investment opportunities would dry up with the disappearance of wartime government spending. Experience proved them wrong. Canada, the United States, and the countries of Western Europe experienced rapid postwar recovery. Central banks in most of the major economies pursued "easy" monetary policies during these years, and inflation was a more widespread problem than depression. Those countries that succeeded in controlling inflation did so only by orthodox monetary policies. Economists began to wonder if perhaps money mattered after all and began to look once again at the general theory as a whole.

**The Monetarists** The reaction against the one-sided theories of the early Keynesians received major support during the 1950s and 1960s from a group of economists working under the intellectual leadership of Milton Friedman of the University of Chicago. Friedman's empirical research led him to think that monetary policy had had a much greater influence on the course of economic events than the Keynesians were willing to admit. It appeared to be possible to explain even the Great Depression in this way. Because of the emphasis they gave to monetary phenomena, Friedman and his followers became known as **monetarists**.

The economics profession generally remained skeptical about monetarism. In fact, the 1960s were in some respects the heyday of Keynesian policy, as such prominent Keynesians as Walter Heller, James Tobin, and Gardner Ackley left their academic posts to join the Council of Economic Advisers under American Presidents Kennedy and Johnson. Nonetheless, the ideas of the monetarists proved influential in persuading the Keynesians to return to the idea of a general theory in which monetary and fiscal policy played co-equal roles.

In Canada, economists like David Laidler, Thomas Courchene, and Michael Parkin of the University of Western Ontario, and Jack Carr of the

**Monetarists** Economists who believe that movements in the money supply are the primary causes of ups and downs in business activity.

[1] John Maynard Keynes, *The General Theory of Employment, Interest, and Money* (New York: Harcourt, Brace, & World, 1936).

Milton Friedman (1912–    )

In October 1976, Milton Friedman received the Nobel Memorial Prize in economics, becoming the sixth American to win or share in that prize. Few were surprised. The main surprise was that this most original and influential of economists had had to wait in line so long! The explanation is that Friedman has built his career outside the economics establishment — built it, in fact, by challenging virtually every major establishment doctrine.

Friedman was born in New York in 1912, the son of immigrant garment workers. His hard-working parents sent him across the river to Rutgers University in New Jersey, where Friedman came under the influence of Arthur Burns, then a young assistant professor. From Burns, Friedman learned the importance of empirical work in economics. Statistical testing of all theory and policy prescriptions became a key characteristic of Friedman's later work. From Rutgers, Friedman went to the University of Chicago for an M.A. and then east again to Columbia University, where he got his Ph.D. in 1946. With his degree in hand, he returned to Chicago to teach. There, he became the leading member of the "Chicago School," which provides the main intellectual counterweight to the Eastern Establishment in U.S. economics today.

If one were to single out the theme that underlies all of Friedman's work, it would be his conviction that the market economy works — and works best when left alone. This can be seen in his best-known work, *A Monetary History of the United States*. Written with Anna Schwartz, the work challenges two major tenets of orthodox Keynesian economics: first, the idea that the market economy is inherently unstable without the guiding hand of government, and second, that monetary policy had been tried and found useless as a cure for the Great Depression. Friedman and Schwartz found both beliefs to be the opposite of the truth. "The Great Depression," Friedman later wrote, "far from being a sign of the inherent instability of the private enterprise system, is a testament to how much harm can be done by mistakes on the part of a few men when they wield vast power over the monetary system of the country."

Friedman strongly favors a hands-off policy by governments in almost every area, not just in monetary matters. The trouble, in his view, is not that government is evil by nature but rather that so many policies end up having the opposite of their intended effects. "The social reformers who seek through politics to do nothing but serve the public interest invariably end up serving some private interest that was no part of their intention to serve. They are led by an invisible hand to serve a private interest." Transport regulation, the income tax, public education, agricultural subsidies, and housing programs are among the many policy areas where Friedman believes the government has done more harm than good and where a free competitive market would do better.

Today, Friedman continues to take on new challenges. He promotes his ideas before congressional committees, in professional journals, in his *Newsweek* column, and in face-to-face debate with his colleagues. Economics has never had a more respected heretic.

---

University of Toronto, among others, began to provide a monetarist critique of Canadian economic policy in the 1970s. A number of them are graduates of the University of Chicago.[2] A famous Canadian economist, the late Harry G. Johnson, took an eclectic, Keynesian-Monetarist approach to the analysis of economic change. Many economists similarly elude classification into a single school of thought.

---

[2] Students are sometimes surprised to discover how the ideas of their professors can apparently be traced back to the schools in which they studied. The influence of Friedman and the so-called "Chicago School" can now be traced through two generations in Canada. As mentioned, a number of monetarists at the University of Western Ontario received their training at Chicago. In turn, one of the more vocal young monetarists, Michael Walker, chief economist of the Fraser Institute in Vancouver, studied economics at Western.

One of the world's most famous interpreters of macroeconomics, until his death in May 1977, at the age of 53, was Harry G. Johnson. Johnson was born in Toronto and, after studying economics at the University of Toronto and Cambridge University, he taught economics for several years in Canada. After completing his Ph.D. at Harvard University in 1958 he became Professor of Economics at the University of Chicago. For a number of years, from 1966 to 1973, he was also Professor of Economics at the London School of Economics, jetting back and forth across the Atlantic to teach and advise students at both universities. At the time of his death he was professor at the University of Geneva as well as at Chicago.

Johnson was a prodigious worker and a prolific writer. One colleague observed that "he seemed to be intellectually 'all Muscle.' Physically too he gave an impression of tremendous power under easy self-control. He was broad, thick-chested, inclined towards a solid plumpness."[3] During his brief career, he published hundreds of articles on economics and more than a dozen books, dealing largely with the interpretation and application of Keynesian theory.

Though most of Johnson's career was spent outside of Canada, he retained a lively interest in the Canadian economy, as evidenced by several of his major books (for example, *The Canadian Quandary* and *Canada in a Changing World Economy*) and the numerous lectures that he gave in this country. Just a year before his death he gave the Harold Innis Lecture at the meetings of the Canadian Economics Association, on the topic: "Keynes's General Theory: Revolution or War of Independence?" In keeping with his previous work, he argued in this lecture that Keynes had produced some new and interesting ideas for economists to follow but that they did not amount to a revolution in economic thought. Johnson felt that pre-Keynesian ideas still had considerable validity, as shown by, among others, his colleague at the University of Chicago, Milton Friedman. Johnson felt that Keynes's view had been too short-run. For example, not enough attention was given in Keynes's work on the multiplier process to the shocks and adjustments that affect the process over time. However, Johnson thought that Keynes had revitalized the study of economics and had provided it with helpful new tools of directions.

Harry G. Johnson (1923–1977)

As a result of his cosmopolitan experience and outlook, Johnson was very critical of Canadian nationalism. He firmly believed in the benefits of free trade and competition and decried the defeatist, defensive attitude that he detected among many Canadians. He was frequently invited to lecture in less-developed countries, and there too he was outspoken in his criticism of centralized direction of the economy and the extreme nationalism of some of those countries. He will be remembered by most of his students and readers as one of the clearest interpreters of macroeconomics since Keynes.

---

Monetarist ideas began to make an impact on government and Bank of Canada policy. Courchene, who had earlier criticized the Bank of Canada for contributing to the inflation of the early 1970s, noted with delight in 1976 that "the Bank of Canada has embraced the tenets of the monetarist approach to stabilization policy."[4]

**Monetarism versus Keynesianism: Unresolved Issues**   Today, the theoretical gap between monetarism and Keynesian economics has been narrowed but not altogether eliminated. The analysis presented in the first part of

[3]Edward Shils, "Harry Johnson, Memoir," *Encounter*, November 1977, p. 87.

[4]Thomas J. Courchene, *Monetarism and Controls: The Inflation Fighters* (Montreal: C.D. Howe Research Institute, 1976), p. 1. However, Courchene has subsequently criticized the Bank for its very narrow monetary strategy. See his more recent work, *No Place to Stand? Abandoning Monetary Targets: An Evaluation* (Montreal: C. D. Howe Research Institute, 1983).

this chapter can be used as a framework for discussing some of the important unresolved issues, including the following:

1. What is the relative importance of monetary and fiscal policy in determining nominal national income?
2. How are the effects of monetary policy actions transmitted through the economy?
3. To what extent is monetary policy a determinant of the rate of inflation, in both the long run and the short run?
4. What kind of monetary and fiscal policies are best suited to achieve the goals of economic stabilization?

The first two of these issues will be discussed in the remainder of this chapter. The third and fourth will be left for Chapters 16 to 19.

**How Large a Crowding Out Effect?** The debate over the relative importance of monetary and fiscal policy as determinants of nominal national income is, to a considerable extent, a debate over the importance of the crowding out effect. Exhibit 14.6 shows why. Suppose that the money demand curve has the shape shown by $MD_1$, indicating that the demand for money is not very sensitive to changes in the interest rate. If this is the case, the portfolio adjustments required when the money demand curve shifts relative to the money supply curve (as when nominal income changes) or when the money supply curve shifts relative to the money demand curve (as in the conduct of monetary policy) will bring about large changes in the rate of interest. Suppose that at the same time the planned investment schedule is relatively flat, like the curve $I_1$, so that a change in the rate of interest will induce a large change in planned investment expenditure.

Taken together, the curves $MD_1$ and $I_1$ tend to give the sort of results expected by monetarists. An expansion of government purchases leads to a large increase in the rate of interest, a large drop in private investment spending, and hence a large crowding out effect. Also, an increase in the money supply leads to a large decline in the rate of interest and a large increase in investment spending. Therefore, given curves of these shapes, fiscal policy tends to be relatively ineffective and monetary policy relatively effective.

On the other hand, if the money demand curve has the shape $MD_2$ and the planned investment schedule the shape $I_2$, the situation is reversed. Fiscal policy will have relatively little impact on interest rates; and interest rates, in turn, will have relatively little impact on private investment. Changes in taxes or government purchases will then operate on aggregate nominal demand without much hindrance from the crowding out effect. At the same time, the economy will become much less sensitive to changes in the money supply. The world will behave more like a Keynesian would expect it to.

**The Transmission Mechanism** In addition to disagreeing about the size of the crowding out effect, monetarists and Keynesians continue to disagree about the nature of the mechanism by which the effects of monetary policy are transmitted through the economy.

Keynesians tend to emphasize the chain of causation running from changes in monetary policy to changes in interest rates to changes in

**Exhibit 14.6**

**Alternative views of monetary and fiscal policy effectiveness**

If the money demand curve has a shape like $MD_1$, while the planned investment schedule is shaped like $I_1$, monetary policy will tend to be more effective than fiscal policy. A change in the money supply will have a big impact on planned expenditure, while fiscal policy will be severely hampered by the crowding out effect. On the other hand, a money demand schedule like $MD_2$, with a planned investment schedule like $I_2$, will give the advantage to fiscal policy. Changes in the money supply will have little impact on investment spending, and the crowding out effect will be small.

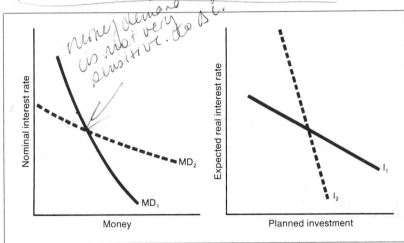

planned investment spending. This is the transmission mechanism emphasized so far in the chapter. Keynesians also suggest that there may be a secondary chain of causation running from a decrease in interest rates to an increase in stock prices and, hence, via an increase in wealth, to an increase in consumer spending.

Monetarists, without disagreeing that interest rates and planned investment play an important role in transmitting the effects of monetary policy, tend to emphasize that changes in the money supply affect the economy in many other ways as well. In particular, they point out that it can be very misleading to think in terms of a world in which money and bonds and perhaps stocks are the only assets that people hold in their portfolios — however convenient such a two- or three-asset economy may be as an expositional device for writers of textbooks.

Instead, when the Bank of Canada injects new money into the economy — more money than people initially want to hold — those who first receive the new money are likely to try to rebalance their portfolios by purchasing a broad variety of assets. These assets might include not only bonds of various types and maturities as well as stocks, but also productive capital equipment, housing, and even consumer durables. Increased demand for all these assets tends to drive their prices up, which in turn stimulates construction firms to build more houses, corporations to issue new stock and purchase new capital equipment, and durable goods makers to increase production to replace depleted inventories. The effects of expansionary monetary policy are thus transmitted through a great variety of channels, including some that are not adequately reflected in market interest rates, to many parts of the economy. The implication is that monetary policy may thus be more effective than the traditional Keynesian transmission mechanism would imply.

**Evidence** Not surprisingly, a number of attempts have been made to bring empirical evidence to bear on the Keynesian-monetarist controversy. These efforts have succeeded in narrowing, although not entirely closing, the gap between the two schools of thought. The following case studies represent two of a number of possible approaches to evaluating the relative importance of fiscal and monetary policy as determinants of nominal national income. One approach, discussed in Case 14.1, is to look at critical policy episodes when monetary and fiscal policy move in opposite directions. Unfortunately, this happens too infrequently to provide conclusive answers. The alternative approach, discussed in Case 14.2, is to sort out monetary from fiscal influences in periods when the two policies have worked in the same direction.

## Case 14.1
### A Recent Episode in Canadian Economic Policy

During the early 1980s, Canadian monetary and fiscal policy moved in opposite directions. The Bank of Canada was worried about possible overheating of the economy and restricted the growth of the money supply. During the same period, the federal budget swung into a deep deficit, because the government was worried about growing unemployment and because of falling tax revenues. The outcome, as described previously in Chapter 7, was the worst recession since the 1930s, which apparently indicated that the restrictive monetary policy outweighed the effect of the rising federal deficit. Neither policy was successful. Years of restrictive monetary policy failed to bring down inflation. Government deficits failed to bring down the unemployment rate. We shall return to this serious dilemma in Chapters 17 and 18, and note in Chapter 19 how some countries have resolved the problems of inflation and unemployment better than we have.

## Case 14.2
### A Monetarist vs. Keynesian Analysis of the 1974 Inflation

In Chapter 7, we noted the double-digit inflation (10.9 percent) that Canada experienced in 1974. The causes of the inflation that ensued will be examined in greater detail in Chapters 16 and 17. However, it can be observed here that the controversy between monetarists and Keynesian fiscal theorists is reflected in their differing interpretations of what caused the inflation of 1974. Those who support the ideas of Keynes argue that prices rose because of increased demand for our goods and services, and because of rising costs such as wages and profits. All these things happened. But monetarists argue that such demand and cost factors could not have caused higher prices if the Bank of Canada had not allowed the money supply to increase. It takes more money to increase prices in general. Therefore it is the monetary authorities who control the process of inflation.

This is the viewpoint, for example, of Thomas Courchene, who maintains that "money is at the root of all inflation.... Inflation is always and everywhere a monetary phenomenon."[5] He notes that in 1974, in one quarter alone, $M_1$, the narrowly defined money supply, increased by 20 percent. Though spending and cost pressures had increased, it was the rapid expansion of the money supply that made the inflation possible.

To some extent the debate on this issue boils down to a question of immediate versus primary cause. When someone shoots another person, the immediate cause is the firing of the pistol. It is possible to argue that the particular murder would not have occurred in that particular way if a gun had not been made available to the murderer. To apply the analogy to the inflation process, the gun is the money supply, and its availability enables a person with inflationary intent to increase purchases, which causes prices to rise. This is the immediate cause that monetarists focus on.

Keynesians tend to look for the primary cause. Given that murderers need weapons, the primary question is: what conditions brought about the murderer's intent to kill? To apply it to inflation, given that spenders need money, what brought about the increased spending pressure? It is from this difference in focus that some of the controversy between monetarists and Keynesians stems.

## Monetary Policy, Inflationary Expectations, and Interest Rates

The fact that inflationary expectations change in response to changing economic conditions and policies makes it necessary to modify the analysis of the effects of monetary policy on interest rates. Under the simplifying assumption of zero inflationary expectations used earlier in the chapter, expansionary monetary policy led to a new equilibrium in which interest rates were lower. In the real world, however, things are not always so simple. The distinction made between real and nominal interest rates in Chapter 7 helps us to understand more realistically what can happen.

**Long-Term Effect**  Imagine for example, that the economy is initially in an equilibrium with zero inflationary expectations and the nominal and real rates of interest both at 4 percent. Suppose that the Bank of Canada then undertakes a sustained, rapid expansion of the money supply, stimulating the growth of nominal GNP. Some of this growth will presumably take the form of growth of real output; but in the present case, suppose that nominal GNP grows too rapidly for real GNP to keep up. The difference between the growth of nominal and real GNP must be made up by inflation.

Initially, no inflation is anticipated; but as inflation continues, it comes to be expected. This drives a wedge between the nominal rate of interest and the expected real rate of interest. If inflation is rapid enough and continues long enough, the wedge will grow large enough to begin pushing up the nominal rate of interest. If, say, everyone comes to expect 6 percent per year inflation as the long-term norm, the initially assumed 4 percent nominal rate of interest surely cannot be maintained. The nominal rate would in principle rise to 10 percent, enough to restore the expected real rate to its original 4 percent. The conclusion, then, is that if the money supply is continuously expanded sufficiently to produce sustained inflation, the long-term effect will be to raise, not lower, nominal interest rates.

---

[5]Thomas Courchene, *Money, Inflation, and the Bank of Canada* (Montreal: C.D. Howe Research Institute, 1976) p. 263.

**Short-Term Effects** As a long-term proposition, this conclusion is now widely accepted. The short-term effects of monetary policy on interest rates are less settled, however, and depend in part on whether one emphasizes adaptive or rational expectations.

With purely adaptive expectations, the short-term effects of monetary expansion might well be exactly as represented earlier in this chapter: both the nominal and real interest rates would be depressed. Only later, after the actual rate of inflation accelerated, would more rapidly rising prices begin to be reflected in expectations and in a higher nominal rate.

Rational expectations, however, introduce new possible short-term effects of policy changes. For example, the Bank of Canada until recently undertook to announce its plans for monetary expansion up to a year in advance. If it were possible to predict exactly the effects on the rate of inflation of the Bank's policy, borrowers and lenders would begin to take that amount of inflation into account from the day the announcement was made. If the announcement implied a higher than previously expected rate of inflation, nominal interest rates would jump upward immediately, even before the announced policy was put into effect. With full adjustment of the nominal rate, the expected real rate of interest might not change at all.

In practice, perfect forecasting of inflation is not possible. "Bank of Canada watchers" try to guess the significance of every speech made by the governor of the Bank, and every week's data on the monetary aggregates. More often than not, however, these watchers cannot even agree among themselves. The short-run effects of monetary policy remain difficult to forecast.

## CONCLUSIONS

In tying together fiscal and monetary policy, this chapter has rounded out the discussion of the determination of nominal national income and product. As the discussion of monetary policy and inflationary expectations made clear, it is time now to turn to the question of how the growth of nominal income is split up between inflation and the growth of real income. Only when we have thoroughly investigated that question will we be able to make a judgment as to what fiscal and monetary policy can and cannot hope to accomplish in promoting full employment, price stability, economic growth, and balance of payments stability.

## SUMMARY

1. Analysis of the interaction between money and the multiplier requires moving from partial equilibrium analysis to general equilibrium analysis. What happens in the money market affects aggregate demand because any change in the interest rate changes planned investment expenditure. What happens to aggregate demand affects the money market, because movements in nominal national income shift the money demand curve.

2. The money market and the circular flow can both be in equilibrium at once only if a certain pair of values for the interest rate and nominal income prevail. With the money supply, autonomous consumption, the

marginal propensity to consume, net taxes, net exports, and the position of the planned investment schedule given, the equilibrium values for nominal national income and the interest rate are unique.

3. An increase in government purchases has a somewhat weaker impact on the equilibrium level of nominal national income than a simple application of the multiplier theory predicts. The reason is that any growth in nominal income shifts the money demand curve to the right and pushes up the interest rate. This in turn crowds out some private investment, partially offsetting the increase in government purchases.

4. If the expected rate of inflation is assumed not to change, an increase in the money supply has the initial effect of depressing the interest rate. This stimulates planned investment, and aggregate demand increases. As nominal national income rises, the money demand schedule shifts to the right, limiting but not completely cancelling out the fall in the interest rate. In the new equilibrium position, the interest rate will be lower and the level of nominal national income higher than before the monetary expansion.

5. Keynesian and monetarist economists have long debated the relative effectiveness of monetary and fiscal policy and the transmission mechanisms through which they influence the economy. The inflationary experiences of the 1970s and early 1980s have added new elements of controversy—for example, over the role played by inflationary expectations in determining the effects of monetary policy.

## DISCUSSION QUESTIONS

1. Suppose that you wanted to study the effect of a variation in rainfall on the prices of three agricultural products: corn, soybeans, and hogs. Do you think a general equilibrium approach or a partial equilibrium approach would give you more insight into the problem? Explain.

2. Use the theory presented in this chapter to trace the effects of a tax increase. What happens to national income, the interest rate, investment, consumption, and net exports?

3. Use the theory presented in this chapter to trace the effects of an increase in required reserve ratios on demand deposits. What happens to national income, the interest rate, investment, consumption, and net exports?

4. Suppose there is a deflationary gap in the economy. For the sake of discussion, assume that the government can with equal ease bring national income up to its target level by using expansionary monetary policy or by increasing government purchases. Suppose that the government also has a long-term goal of promoting rapid economic growth. Can you think of any reason for the government to use one policy rather than the other? Explain.

5. Would you say that the governor of the Bank of Canada is one of the most powerful people in Canada? Would your opinion have been the same before you read this chapter? Before you started this course?

6. Suppose that the Bank of Canada decided on a policy of pegging the interest rate at some level, r, by smoothly expanding or contracting the money supply. (This policy could be represented graphically by drawing a horizontal rather than a vertical money supply curve.) Assume zero inflationary expectations. How would the policy affect the effectiveness of fiscal policy? What would happen to the crowding out effect? (Bonus question: Suppose the Bank attempted to peg the nominal interest rate in the face of rising inflationary expectations. What do you think would happen?)

# APPENDIX TO CHAPTER 14
# THE ELEMENTARY ALGEBRA
# OF MONEY AND
# INCOME DETERMINATION

This appendix is a continuation of the Appendix to Chapter 10, which developed a simple algebraic version of the multiplier theory. It adds no new theory to what has been presented in the body of Chapter 14. Nonetheless, readers who feel comfortable with elementary algebra may find the approach presented here useful in consolidating their understanding of the general theory of nominal income determination. Throughout this appendix, the real rate of inflation is assumed to be zero, as in the first part of the chapter.

## AGGREGATE DEMAND

The basic equation for aggregate nominal demand or planned expenditure is:

$$AND = C + I + G + X - M \tag{14A.1}$$

In the Appendix to Chapter 10, the C in this equation was replaced with a consumption schedule, which was written as:

$$C = a + b(Y - T) \tag{14.A2a}$$

and imports with a schedule written as:

$$M = Ma + m(Y - T) \tag{14A.2b}$$

where $a$ and $b$ were constants representing autonomous consumption and the marginal propensity to consume, $Y - T$ stood for nominal disposable income, $Ma$ was autonomous imports, and $m$ was the marginal propensity to import. Now, I in Equation 14A.1 will also be replaced with a simple planned investment schedule:

$$I = c + dr \tag{14A.3}$$

where I stands for planned investment and r for the interest rate, and where $c$ and $d$ are constants. The constant $d$, which is the reciprocal of the slope of the planned investment schedule, will have a negative value, because planned investment increases as the rate of interest falls.

Putting together Equations 14A.1, 14A.2a and b, and 14A.3, the following general expression for the aggregate demand schedule is arrived at:

$$AND = a + c + b(Y - T) + dr + G + X - Ma - m(Y - T) \tag{14A.4}$$

## MONEY DEMAND

For a general equilibrium analysis of nominal income determination, a money demand schedule is also needed. The one used in Chapters 11 and 12 gave a money demand curve in the shape of a rectangular hyperbola. (Exhibit 12.2, for example, is based on the formula $MD = 1.2Y/r$.) To retain this kind of money demand schedule would involve the use of quadratic equations and would unnecessarily complicate the arithmetic, so it is replaced with a linearized money demand schedule written as:

$$MD = e + fY + gr \tag{14A.5}$$

where MD stands for the quantity of money demanded, r for the interest rate, and Y for income and where $e$, $f$, and $g$ are constants. The constant g is the reciprocal of the slope of the money demand schedule. It is negative because money demand decreases when the interest rate rises.

The reader is cautioned that this linear formulation of the money demand function has certain drawbacks. One is that, except for a certain central range of the variables, algebraic solution of the equilibrium equations (to be presented below) may produce negative values for income or the interest rate. Such negative values have no reasonable economic meaning. Care will be taken to keep within the safe range of values in the examples.

## NUMERICAL VALUES

The constants in these equations can be replaced with representative numerical values to show how the algebraic formulations of planned expenditures and money demand can be put to work. Using $a = 100$, $b = 0.75$, $c = 210$, $d = -500$, $e = 80$, $f = 0.2$, $m = 0.15$, and $g = -400$, Equations 14A.4 and 14A.5 can be rewritten as:

$$AND = 310 + 0.75(Y - T) - 0.15(Y - T) - 500r + G + X - Ma \qquad \textbf{14A.6}$$

and

$$MD = 80 + 0.2Y - 400r \qquad \textbf{14A.7}$$

## EQUILIBRIUM CONDITIONS

As shown in the text of Chapter 12, the economy as a whole can be in equilibrium only when both the money market and the circular flow are in equilibrium. Money market equilibrium requires that money supply equal money demand, and equilibrium in the circular flow requires that national product be equal to planned expenditure. These equilibrium conditions can be written as:

$$MS = MD \qquad \textbf{14A.8}$$

for the money market, where MS stands for the money supply, and

$$Y = AND \qquad \textbf{14A.9}$$

for the circular flow.

Substituting Equations 14A.6 and 14A.7 into Equations 14A.8 and 14A.9:

$$MS = 80 + 0.2Y - 400r \qquad \textbf{14A.10}$$

and

$$Y = 310 + 0.75(Y - T) - 0.15(Y - T) - 500r + G + X - Ma \qquad \textbf{14.A11}$$

which simplifies to:

$$Y = 775 - 1.5T + 2.5(G + X - Ma) - 1250r \qquad \textbf{14A.12}$$

Equilibrium in the economy is possible only for pairs of values for r and Y that simultaneously satisfy Equations 14A.10 and 14A.12.

## POLICY VARIABLES

Besides r and Y, there are five variables in Equations 14A.10 and 14A.12 for which numerical values have not yet been specified. Two of these values are X (exports) and M (imports). The problems that follow assume that exports (X) are autonomous, while imports (M) are partly autonomous (Ma) and partly related to disposable income [$m(Y - T)$]. The remaining three variables are G (government purchases), T (net taxes), and MS (the money supply). These are collectively referred to as policy variables, because they stand for the elements of the economy that are under the direct control of the government. The following problems will show how the manipulation of these variables can be used by policy makers in their attempts to hit their economic targets.

**Problem 1:** Government policy makers set their policy variables at the values G = 125, T = 100, MS = 300, Ma = 50, and X = 245. Apply Equations 14A.10 and 14A.12 to determine the equilibrium values of r and Y.
*Solution:* Equation 14A.10 becomes:

$$300 = 80 + 0.2Y - 400r$$

and Equation 14A.12 becomes:

$$Y = 775 - 150 + 800 - 1250r$$

Simplifying and setting the equations equal to zero:

$$220 - 0.2Y + 400r = 0$$

$$1425 - Y - 1250r = 0$$

The usual methods for solution of simultaneous equations give the pair of values r = 0.10 and Y = 1,300 as the equilibrium levels for interest rate and national income.

**Problem 2:** Using the solution to Problem 1 as a starting point, assume that the authorities want to raise the equilibrium level of national income to a target level of $1,400, using monetary policy alone. How much will the money supply have to be increased to accomplish this objective?
*Solution:* Substitute Y = $1,400, G = 125, T = 100, X = 245, and Ma = 50 into Equation 14A.12 in order to find the required equilibrium value for r.
The substitution gives:

$$1400 = 775 - 150 + 800 - 1250r$$

which simplifies to:

$$25 - 1250r = 0$$

The solution to this last equation is r = 0.02.
Next, substitute the equilibrium values Y = 1,400 and r = 0.02 into Equation 14A.10 in order to determine the money supply necessary to give a 0.02 rate of interest when national income is $1,400. This gives:

$$MS = 80 + 0.2(1400) - 400(0.02) = 352$$

The solution to the problem, then, is that the money supply must be increased by $52 — from $300 to $352 — in order to raise national income to $1,400.

**Problem 3:** Using the solution to Problem 1 as a starting point, show that an increase of $26 in government purchases will be more effective in raising the equilibrium level of national income if the Bank of Canada pursues an accommodating monetary policy than if it leaves the money supply unchanged.
*Solution:* An accommodating monetary policy is one that expands the money supply enough to keep the interest rate unchanged — in this case, equal to 0.10. Substitute the values T = 100, G = 151, Ma = 50, X = 245, and r = 0.10 into Equation 14A.12 to get the new value that equilibrium national income will reach if accommodating monetary policy is pursued. Without going into details, the new equilibrium Y with accommodating monetary policy is $1,365. (Further substitution of Y = $1,365 and r = 0.10 into Equation 14A.10 shows that the money supply would have to be increased to $313 to achieve this result.)
Without accommodating monetary policy, the new values of Y and r are found by going through the same steps outlined in the solution to Problem 1, using G = 151. Again without going into details, the solution turns out to be Y = $1,340 and r = 0.12. Substitution of the new, higher value of the interest rate into the investment schedule (I = 210 − 500r) shows that $10 of the original $160 in private planned investment is crowded out by the $26 increase in government purchases. This accounts for the lower equilibrium value of Y when accommodating monetary policy is not used.

# INTERNATIONAL TRADE AND THE BALANCE OF PAYMENTS

CHAPTER

FIFTEEN

## WHAT YOU WILL LEARN IN THIS CHAPTER

*Up to this point we have not given detailed attention to a very important aspect of Canada's economy—the foreign sector. Exports and imports were built into the aggregate expenditure model developed in Chapter 8. It remains to describe more fully how, and to what extent, Canada is involved in international trade and how international transactions affect the Canadian economy. This chapter re-examines the basis for specialization and trade which, as we saw in Chapter 2, is rooted in the theory of comparative advantage. This theory is now applied to international trade. The arguments for and against free trade are examined, and Canada's experience in international trade is described.*

## FOR REVIEW

*Here are some important terms and concepts that will be put to use in this chapter. If you do not understand them, review them before proceeding.*
* *Comparative advantage (Chapter 2)*
* *Net exports (Chapter 8)*
* *Net exports in the multiplier process (Chapter 9)*

Several important elements associated with Canada's participation in international trade and finance have been discussed in previous chapters. The bases for both domestic and international trade were examined in Chapter 2. The macro model that we began to construct in Chapter 8 included net exports as one of the important components of planned expenditure. The multiplier formula of Chapter 9 incorporated the leakage effect of imports, and it was shown how such leakages change the impact of fiscal and monetary policies. Thus, through much of the preceding analysis, Canada has been treated as an open economy, heavily dependent on trade with other countries.

However, the notion of comparative advantage was not applied specifically to international trade, and arguments for and against its application have not yet been examined. This will now be done. In addition, a closer look at Canada's trade with other countries will help us to appreciate the important role that international trade plays in determining the level of economic activity in Canada. Not only the exchange of goods and services but also the purchase and sale of international bonds and stocks are important to our economy. It is this complex of international transactions that is described in this chapter.

## AN INTERNATIONAL APPLICATION OF COMPARATIVE ADVANTAGE

We saw in Chapter 2 that trade between regions or countries is economically beneficial whenever such regions or countries have a comparative advantage in the production of some goods. They have such an advantage when they can, in comparison with other regions, produce a good at lower *opportunity cost*, measured in terms of other foregone goods. The concept was illustrated graphically in Exhibit 2.4, where on the basis of different opportunity costs for the production of fish and grain in the Maritimes and the Prairies, production possibility frontiers for the two regions were developed, and the advantages of specialization and trade were examined.

The concept of comparative advantage can again be illustrated graphically, using a set of production possibility frontiers for two countries, Spain and Norway, instead of two regions. This is done in Exhibit 15.1, which shows three production possibility frontiers. Part a is the production possibility frontier for Spain. It is assumed that Spain can produce up to 500 t of grain per year if it produces no fish (Point B). If it produces no grain, up to 250 t of fish per year can be caught (Point D). The combinations of grain and fish that Spain can possibly produce are thus represented by the line running from D to B.

Exhibit 15.1b shows the corresponding production possibility frontier for Norway. If Norwegians devote all their time to fishing, they can catch up to 200 t of fish per year (Point B'). If they devote all their time to farming, they can grow up to 200 t of grain (Point D'). The line between B' and D' thus represents the Norwegian production possibility frontier.

### Pretrade Production and Consumption

Let us assume that before trade begins Spain produces and consumes 350 t of grain and 75 t of fish. This is shown as Point A on Spain's production possibility frontier. Correspondingly, Norway is assumed to produce and consume 100 t each of fish and grain. This is shown by Point A' on Norway's frontier.

### The World Production Possibility Frontier

A production possibility frontier for the world as a whole (consisting of just these two countries in our example) can be constructed as in Exhibit 15.1c. The world frontier is constructed as follows. First, assume that both countries devote all their labor to grain. That gives 500 t of grain from Spain plus 200 from Norway, or 700 t of grain in all (Point R in Exhibit 15.1c). Starting from there, assume that world fish output is to be increased. For maximum efficiency Norwegian farmers should be the first to switch to fishing, because the opportunity cost of fish is lower (1 t of grain per tonne of fish) than in Spain (2 t of grain per tonne of fish). As Norwegians switch to fishing, then, world production moves up and to the left along Line Segment RQ.

**Exhibit 15.1**

**A graphical illustration of comparative advantage**

This exhibit shows production possibility frontiers for Spain, Norway, and the two countries combined. Before trade, Spain produces and consumes at Point A and Norway at Point A'. Together, these correspond to World Consumption Point P, which is inside the world production possibility frontier. After trade begins, Spain specializes in producing grain (Point B) and trades part of the grain for fish, moving to Consumption Point C. Norway similarly specializes in producing fish (Point B') and reaches Consumption Point C' through trade. As a result, world efficiency is improved, and Point Q is attained on the world production possibility frontier.

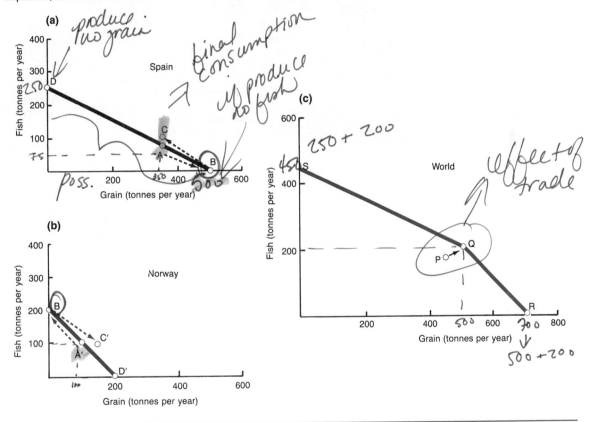

When all Norwegians have abandoned farming for fishing, the world will have arrived at Point Q—500 t of grain (all Spanish) and 200 t of fish (all Norwegian). From that point on, the only way to get more fish is to have Spanish farmers switch to fishing. At the opportunity cost of 2 t of grain per tonne of fish, this moves the economy along Line Segment QS. When all Spanish farmers are fishing, the world arrives at Point S, where 450 t of fish and no grain are produced. The production possibility frontier for the world as a whole is thus the kinked line RQS.

## The Effects of Trade

The pretrade production point for the world as a whole lies inside the world production possibility frontier. Adding the quantities of fish and grain from A and A' together, we arrive at Point P in Exhibit 15.1—450 t of grain and 175 t of fish. This is inefficient; the world economy as a whole could produce more of both goods. To improve efficiency, both countries must specialize.

Suppose that Spain shifts its production from 350 t of grain and 75 t of fish (Point A) to 500 t of grain and no fish (Point B). It then trades the extra 150 t of grain for 100 t of Norwegian fish. Spain's consumption thus ends up at Point C while its production remains at B.

At the same time, Norway shifts its production from A' to B', specializing entirely in fish. The extra 100 t of fish are traded for the 150 t of Spanish grain, moving Norwegian consumption to Point C'.

As the result of specialization plus trade, then, both Spain and Norway have moved to points that lie outside their own national production possibility frontiers. As they do so, the world as a whole moves from Point P inside its production possibility frontier to Point Q on the world frontier. As in the numerical example, specialization improves world efficiency, increases world production of both goods, and leaves both countries better off than they would be in the absence of trade.

## PROTECTIONISM VERSUS FREE TRADE

Our illustration of the theory of comparative advantage has been for a very simple trading world, little different than that discussed by Ricardo (see Ricardo's profile, Chapter 2). In the century and two-thirds since Ricardo's time, the theory has been extended many times to cover more complex and realistic situations. The extensions have covered situations in which there are more than two countries, in which there is more than one factor of production and more than two commodities, and in which production possibility frontiers are not straight lines, to name just a few. The result of all this additional theoretical work has been to show that the theory of comparative advantage is very general. Regardless of the initial assumptions or the complexity of the situations, international trade, following the principles of comparative advantage, offers all countries involved an opportunity for mutual gain compared with the no-trade alternative.

But if international trade is so unequivocally beneficial, why do free-trade policies always and everywhere face opposition? Why does every government feel pressure to create **protectionist** policies, such as **tariffs** and **import quotas**, that will restrict the free importation of goods from abroad? The sources and logic of protectionism form the subject of this section.

**Protectionism** Policies of shielding domestic industry from foreign competition.

**Tariff** A tax levied on imported goods.

**Import quota** A limitation on the quantity of a good that can be imported in a given time period.

### The Terms-of-Trade Argument

One argument in favor of trade restrictions concerns the possibility of manipulating the international terms of trade. In our example of Spain and Norway, we supposed that the terms of trade of grain for fish would be set by competitive bargaining and haggling by private traders from each country. Such a process might not always result in the exact 1.5-to-1 trading ratio of grain to fish assumed in the example, but it would not be surprising to see the gains from trade divided fairly evenly when the terms of trade are competitively set.

In the real world, however, a country may sometimes find reason to interfere with the competitive determination of the terms of trade. Note, for example, that Canada is one of the world's leading producers and exporters of nickel (producing about 35 percent of world output) and a leading importer of textiles. To take advantage of its partial monopoly power in the nickel market, Canada might restrict nickel exports, hoping to drive up the world price. Similarly, to take advantage of its buying power in the textile market, it might restrict textile imports, hoping to drive the world price down. The export and import restrictions would, of course, have the effect of reducing the total volume of trade. Worldwide gains from trade would thus be less than they would be in the absence of protectionist measures. Nonetheless, manipulating the terms of trade might leave Canada with a bigger share of the smaller world total of gains from trade, making Canadians better off, on balance, than under a free-trade policy.

The terms-of-trade argument for protectionism, which has been known for more than a hundred years, has its limitations, however. One major limitation concerns the possibility of retaliation by trading partners. If other countries react to Canadian trade restrictions by imposing trade restrictions of their own, the attempt to manipulate the terms of trade may well fail. The volume of world trade will then shrink even more, and all countries will be left worse off than under free trade.

## The Income Distribution Argument

A more complete understanding of the origins of trade restrictions requires consideration of their effects on the distribution of income within each trading country. Take, as an example, the effects on the Canadian economy of increased imports of Chinese textiles after a period in which such imports were somewhat restricted. The impact of increased textile imports can be divided into three parts. First, all consumers of textiles in Canada will benefit because textiles will be cheaper than before. Second, the Chinese may increase their purchases of Canadian goods, which will benefit workers in Canadian export-oriented industries. Finally, Canadian textile workers and manufacturers will suffer a decreased demand for their products.

Textile workers and manufacturers with relatively mobile skills or assets can escape most of the impact by moving to other industries. Some workers, however, are less mobile because of personal circumstances or the specialization of their skills. They are likely to suffer a loss of income that will more than offset the benefits they receive as consumers of cheaper textiles. In the aggregate, the loss to the group adversely affected is more than offset by the gains to others in the economy. But this fact is not likely to make much impression on unemployed textile workers. They will see free trade as a threat and will campaign for protection. The government will then have a difficult political decision to make. Suppose that the government decides that the textile workers deserve consideration. Does this mean protectionism should be supported? Not necessarily. The policy of protection might be compared with alternative policies that could have the same distributive effects. One such alternative may be to subsidize the retraining and relocation of textile workers who lose their jobs. Another may be simply to offer these workers cash compensation.

How do these alternatives rate? In terms of efficiency they are not perfect, but probably they are better than tariffs or quotas. They seem to offer two advantages. One is that benefits are more precisely concentrated on the people who need them. The other is that the tax burden required to fund the alternative programs is likely to be distributed more equitably than the burden of higher textile prices would be.

## The National Security Argument

Another argument advanced for the restriction of trade involves considerations of nation building and defence. It was pointed out in Chapter 4 that Canada and the U.S. experimented with free trade on certain products for twelve years, between 1854 and 1866. Following the American Civil War, a wave of nationalism led the U.S. to build tariff barriers against other countries, including Canada. Canada retaliated with barriers of its own, also in the name of nationalism. It was felt that tariffs would help industry in central Canada to grow more quickly, and a strong industrial base was considered essential for the building of a Canadian nation. Exponents of such views are not deterred by counter arguments that their policies may lead to inefficiency. In their view it is more important to have a relatively inefficient *Canadian* industry than a more efficient non-Canadian industry. In time of emergency, it is argued, it would be important to have adequate Canadian supplies of strategic goods such as energy and basic metals. One problem is that tariffs may actually result in *more* foreign ownership of Canadian industries, as foreigners try to get behind the Canadian tariff wall.

## The Infant Industry Argument

Canada appears to have a strong comparative advantage in the production of natural resources, which it has in abundance and to which it has attracted considerable capital, and a comparative disadvantage in the production of many manufactured goods, particularly those that are labor intensive. Does this mean that Canada is destined forever to have a weak manufacturing sector? There are those who argue that this need not be the case. Some industries, it is argued, might fare well after a while if they received support only during their developmental or infant phase until they were mature enough to compete with the industries of other countries. The Canadian steel industry, for example, is as efficient in some of its branches as comparable branches of that industry in other countries. It has been permitted, so the argument runs, to develop expertise and capital over the long run to make itself competitive. This argument may well be sound for some industries, but many industries in Canada, for resource or climatic reasons, may never be able to compete. How can one distinguish one request for protection from another, or know which infants will eventually thrive? Once the protection is applied, how easy is it to remove? These are difficult practical problems that must be faced in evaluating this argument for trade restrictions.

Canada's relative strength in international trade is indicated in Exhibit 15.2. In 1981, Canada had a net surplus of $23.4 billion in the importing/

**Exhibit 15.2**

**Canada's trade balance by commodity group, 1981**

This exhibit shows that Canada exports more food, crude, and semiprocessed "fabricated materials" than it imports, but it usually imports considerably more finished or end products, including autos, than it exports.

| Commodity Group | Trade Balance (billions of dollars) |
|---|---|
| Food and related products | $4.3 |
| Crude materials and related products | 3.1 |
| Fabricated materials | 16.0 |
| Auto and related products | −2.9 |
| Other end products | −17.7 |

Source: Ottawa, Dept. of Finance, *Economic Review*, April 1982, p. 73.

exporting of food and related products, crude materials, and semiprocessed "fabricated materials," (top three rows) while it had a net deficit of $20.6 billion in automobile and end products.

## THE EXTENT OF PROTECTION AND ITS COST

Ever since Confederation, Canada has used tariffs or customs duties (which are really a tax on foreign goods), licenses, quotas, and special purchasing arrangements (whereby, for example, governments in Canada may choose to buy certain foreign goods only if they are priced at least 15 percent below equivalent domestic goods) to raise revenues for government, to restrict the flow of foreign goods into the country, and to protect Canadian industry against foreign competition. Case 15.1 illustrates how tariffs and quotas are being applied in Canada to protect its shoe industry.

### Case 15.1   Protection for Canada's Shoe Industry

Trade retaliation or demands for financial compensation loom large now that Canada has restored stringent import quotas on leather footwear. The quotas returned just seven months after they were lifted and several partners say they are upset at another sign of protectionism.

"For us it's a worrying trend and we will respond as a matter of principle," says one French trade official. "It's a risk the government must take," says Trade Minister Ed Lumley.

The quotas, which have applied to canvas footwear imports since November are being extended to buttress Canada's flagging shoe industry in the face of a damaging 19 percent increase in leather-wear import penetration during the first four months of 1982. During the same period, Canadian demand for footwear dropped 4 percent.

Imports now account for 67 percent of the Canadian footwear market, but the quotas will hold foreign-made canvas and leather products to 46.6 million pairs this year. Had the import surge continued, Edward Rowe, president of Aurora-based Sisman's of Canada, estimates 55 million pairs of imported footwear would have entered the country this year.

The global quotas have been invoked under article XIX of the General Agreement on Tariffs and Trade (GATT), which permits temporary protective measures to counter disruption of domestic industry caused by increased imports. Ottawa argues this year's sudden surge contributed to declines in production and industry employment of 13 percent. Altogether 7,000 of the footwear industry's 20,000-strong work-force are said to be out of work.

The quotas will not be directed specifically at exporting countries such as Brazil and Italy, which trade officials say are the chief forces behind the jump in leather footwear imports. Importers will simply be given certain quotas which they are free to fill from any foreign source. Consequently, some trade officials say compensation may be demanded by shoe exporting countries that did not contribute to the problem but which may be hurt by the protectionist measures.

The action was lauded by footwear manufacturers, but decried by importers and retailers who say the quotas will disrupt contracts. In announcing the measures, Trade Minister Lumley vowed to lift the quotas in November, 1984. In the meantime, he urged the industry to continue modernizing and restructuring to become globally competitive.

Source: Giles Gherson, "Shoe quotas put the boot to importers and retailers." *The Financial Post* Toronto, July 17, 1982, p. 3. Reprinted with permission.

## Canada's Trade Relations

Protection such as that described in Case 15.1 is being applied at a time when many other trading nations are resorting to similar measures to protect their industries. It should be noted that Canada has engaged in international trade negotiations with other nations in attempts to reduce tariffs among all major trading countries. Since 1947, it has signed several *General Agreements on Tariffs and Trade* (GATT) designed to promote freer world trade. The result of this, in terms of Canadian trade relations with other countries is summarized in Exhibit 15.3. It shows that on those goods subject to tariffs, the tariff rate had fallen from a high of 31.6 percent

**Exhibit 15.3**
**Average rates of duty on imports from all countries, by principal tariff legislation, 1865–1980**

Tariff rates have fallen considerably since the early 1930s, and the proportion of goods entering free has increased.

|  | | Rate on | | Proportion of Imports Entering Free |
|---|---|---|---|---|
|  | Legislation | Dutiable Imports | Total Imports | |
|  | | (Percent) | | |
| **Canada** | | | | |
| 1869–71 | Dominion tariff | 19.5 | 12.6 | 35.3 |
| 1875–79 | Mackenzie tariff | 21.2 | 14.2 | 33.4 |
| 1880–87 | National policy | 26.2 | 19.8 | 24.2 |
| 1888–90 | 1887 amendment | 31.6 | 21.7 | 31.2 |
| 1891–97 | Conservative tariffs | 30.5 | 19.0 | 37.7 |
| 1898–07 | Fielding's 1st tariff | 27.7 | 16.7 | 39.7 |
| 1908–14 | 2nd tariff | 26.4 | 16.8 | 36.7 |
| 1914–21 | | 24.1 | 15.7 | 35.0 |
| 1922–30 | Liberal Progressive tariffs | | | |
| 1931–35 | R.B. Bennett tariffs | 28.5 | 17.6 | 38.2 |
| 1936–41 | Canada-U.S. trade agreements | 24.2 | 13.2 | 45.7 |
| 1942–51 | | | | |
| 1952–60 | GATT | 17.8 | 10.2 | 42.5 |
| 1961–70 | GATT | 16.7 | 8.2 | 51.2 |
| 1970–1980 | GATT (Tokyo Round) | — | 5–7 | — |

Source: Hugh McA. Pinchin, "The Regional Import of the Canadian Tariff," *Economic Council of Canada*, Ottawa, 1979, p. 6.

in the late nineteenth century to slightly more than 16 percent by the late 1960s. During roughly the same period, the proportion of imports without any duty or tariff rose from about one-quarter to one-half. In the Tokyo Round of GATT meetings held in 1979, Canada agreed to reduce its tariffs by another 40 percent by 1987, as did most of its trading partners.

Despite these movements toward free trade, many industries still receive considerable protection. In 1970, the average protection on agricultural products by nominal tariff rates was about 2 percent, while rates between 10 and 22 percent were applied to such goods as textiles, clothing, furniture, metal fabricating, and electrical products.

The most recent round of GATT agreements (known as the Tokyo Round), came into effect in 1980. Tariffs on industrial products are to decline from 14 to 9 percent, and tariffs on average from the previous level of 8.2 percent to between 5 and 7 percent. In general, protection remains high for finished products and low for raw or semiprocessed goods, a policy designed to encourage domestic production in areas for which Canada's comparative advantage is least obvious.

## Free Trade for Canada?

A question often asked is: would Canada benefit from a policy of completely free trade? Economic theory strongly suggests that it would. Empirical studies are more ambiguous in their results, because they deal with industries that have enjoyed protection for some time and where, at least in the short-run periods of readjustment, there might be severe hardships in terms of unemployment and relocation.

Assume, for example, that Canada eliminated tariff barriers in trade with the U.S. One recent study estimates that real income for Canada as a whole might increase by about 2 percent. The increase would result from a shift in the resources used in the most protected industries, like textiles, to less protected industries like natural resources, in which Canada has a more obvious comparative advantage. However, the increase in general income levels would mask a decline in real wages, because the effect of past tariff policy has been to protect labor-intensive industries. Under free trade, there would be a redistribution of income from labor in these industries to the owners of resources whose production would expand.

Freer trade might also be accompanied by marked regional effects. Income per capita would increase by about 4 percent in the Prairies and in the Atlantic regions, as well as in British Columbia (because of the shift to natural resources), and decline *relatively* in Ontario and absolutely in Quebec.[1] Many Canadian industries would thrive in a freer climate, but the adjustments in others make governments pause in moving Canada to even greater free trade. What this indicates is that despite the very strong theoretical arguments for free trade, based on the idea of comparative advantage, the movement *toward* freer trade in a country where many industries are currently protected by tariffs, and in a world economy in which protectionist pressures are very strong, may not be as easy and as decisively beneficial as the theory suggests. In the long run, however, it

---

[1]Based upon Roma Dauphin, *The Impact of Free Trade*, Economic Council of Canada, 1978.

should be the strategy of every country to reduce protection, because the economic arguments for free trade are indeed compelling. In addition, for a nation like Canada, the removal of tariff barriers could help reduce foreign ownership of Canadian industry.

## BALANCE OF PAYMENTS

Exports and imports are important elements in Canada's gross national expenditure. In the five years 1977–81 Canada exported an average of 29 percent of its GNP annually, while it imported about 31 percent. In other words, we depend upon foreigners to buy about 29 percent of the goods and services we produce, and we depend upon them for about 31 percent of the goods and services that we consume. Such imports are part of our consumption, investment, and government expenditures. Separate accounts, called **balance of payments** accounts, are kept of these international transactions, as well as of other important transactions that we carry on with other countries.

In the balance of payments accounts, Canada's international receipts and payments are broken down into three categories: (1) transactions in goods and services produced in the current year, summarized in what is called the *current account*; (2) transactions in short- and long-term securities and bonds, summarized in the *capital account*; (3) changes in official holdings of reserves, recorded as a *net change in official reserve account*.

> **Balance of payments**
> A record of all economic transactions between Canada and other countries in a given year. The balance is in surplus when receipts in the current and capital account exceed total payments to foreigners. It is in deficit when such receipts are less than total payments.

> **Current account** The account whose transactions include imports and exports of goods and services plus international unilateral transfer payments.

### The Current Account

Exhibit 15.4 illustrates the relationship among these accounts for the year 1981. In that year Canada ran a current account deficit of $6,576 million. In merchandise trade, Canada, as it usually does, exported considerably more than it imported, so that it had a sizable surplus on this part of the current account (line 3). However, as is also quite customary, it had a deficit in its service transactions (line 14) large enough to more than offset the surplus in merchandise trade. The service sector includes travel—in which Canada normally has a deficit—and receipts and payments for interest and dividend transactions. Canada normally pays much more to foreigners in the form of interest and dividends than it receives from them, indicating that foreigners have invested much more in the Canadian economy than Canadians have invested abroad. Net transfers are private and government transfer payments in the form of pension payouts, inheritances, and migrant transfers which produced a net credit of $1,602 million.

It is important to note that imports and exports include trade in both merchandise goods and services, but not transfers. Therefore the overall export-import balance (or net exports, line 15) is equal to exports of goods and services minus imports of goods and services, or about –$8,178 million for 1981. To this amount is added net transfers of $1,602 million to obtain the current account balance.

The deficit on the current account of $6,576 million means that Canadians were required in 1981 to obtain at least that much foreign currency from sources other than trade to pay for their purchases of foreign goods and services. Fortunately, the capital account provides such an alternative source.

## The Capital Account

Current account transactions are not the only ones that take place between residents of different countries. We must also consider international lending and borrowing, and international sales and purchases of assets. A Canadian company might, for example, obtain a short-term loan from a Milwaukee bank to finance the purchase of a shipload of beer for import to Canada. The Ontario government might get a long-term loan from Citibank of New York to help finance construction of a hydroelectric

---

**Exhibit 15.4**

**Canadian balance of international payments, 1981 (millions of dollars)**

This exhibit shows in simplified form the actual Canadian balance of payments for 1981. In merchandise trade, Canada had a surplus of $6,636 million (line 3). However, in service transactions, it had a negative balance of $14,814 million (line 14), caused largely by negative balances in travel and in the payment and receipt of interest and dividends. Net exports (= exports of goods and services) was therefore –$8,178 million (line 15). Adding a balance in transfers of $1,602 million produces a current account deficit of $6,576 million (line 17).

The current account deficit was more than balanced by a capital surplus of $7,792 million (line 27). This was the result of large sales of Canadian stocks and bonds to foreigners, (line 20) and increases in short-term bank deposits abroad (line 27). The result was a current *and* capital account balance of $1,216 million (the difference between lines 17 and 27). After allowing for errors and omissions and the allocation of special drawing rights, Canada's official foreign reserves increased by $1,216 million (line 31).

**(a) Current account**

| | | | |
|---|---|---:|---:|
| 1. | Merchandise exports | $84,140 | |
| 2. | Merchandise imports | 77,504 | |
| 3. | Merchandise balance | | $6,636 |
| 4. | Service receipts | 14,859 | |
| 5. | travel | $3,731 | |
| 6. | interest & dividends | 1,607 | |
| 7. | freight & shipping | 4,193 | |
| 8. | other | 5,328 | |
| 9. | Service payments | 29,673* | |
| 10. | travel | $4,888 | |
| 11. | interest & dividends | 8,589 | |
| 12. | freight & shipping | 3,950 | |
| 13. | other | 12,245 | |
| 14. | Services balance | | – 14,814 |
| 15. | Balance of goods and services (net exports) | | – 8,178 |
| 16. | Net transfers | | + 1,602 |
| 17. | Current account balance | | –$6,576 |

**(b) Capital account**

| | | | |
|---|---|---:|---:|
| | Long-term capital flows | | |
| 18. | Direct investment in Canada (net) | –$5,300 | |
| 19. | Direct investment abroad | – 4,900 | |
| 20. | Net issues of Canadian securities | 10,777 | |
| 21. | Other | 763 | |
| 22. | Total net long-term capital flows | | $1,340 |
| | Short-term capital flows | | |
| 23. | Change in the chartered banks' foreign currency position | $17,890 | |
| 24. | Errors and omissions (net) | – 8,438 | |
| 25. | Other | – 3,000 | |
| 26. | Total net short-term capital flows | | $6,452 |
| 27. | Total net capital flows | | $7,792 |

**(c) Net change in official reserves**

| | | | |
|---|---|---:|---:|
| 28. | Special drawing rights allocations | –$ 210 | |
| 29. | Official international reserves | 382 | |
| 30. | Official international liabilities | 1,044 | |
| 31. | Total of drawing rights and reserves | | $1,216 |

*Total is inexact due to rounding.

Source: Department of Finance, *Economic Review*, April 1982, pp. 78 and 200–208.

project. A Canadian millionaire might open an account in a Swiss bank. Or an oil-rich Middle Easterner might purchase Saskatchewan farmland or shares in a Canadian corporation.

All of these transactions and others like them are called transactions on **capital account**. Purchases of Canadian assets by foreigners and borrowing by Canadians from foreigners create a flow of Canadian dollars into Canada, and are thus called **capital inflows**. Purchases of foreign assets by Canadians or loans by Canadians to foreigners create a flow of Canadian dollars away from Canada, and are thus called **capital outflows**.

Long-term capital flows relate to the buying and selling of bonds that have a maturity of one year or more, and to "direct investment," that involves the acquisition of controlling rights in a business. Short-term capital flows involve obligations with a maturity of less than one year, consisting largely of the foreign currency business of the chartered banks.

As Exhibit 15.4 shows, in 1981 there was a net outflow of $10,200 million (lines 18 and 19) for direct investments, of which $5,300 million (net) was spent by Canadians on the acquisition of foreign-owned corporations in Canada. Much of this was due to the effort made to "Canadianize" the oil industry. Money left the country to pay for these acquisitions. Another $4,900 million (net) was used to acquire businesses abroad.

While $10,200 million (net) left Canada to pay for such acquisitions, Canadian borrowers retrieved $10,777 million (net) by selling long-term bonds and securities abroad. Much of this selling was made possible by establishing interest rates on Canadian bonds that were higher than interest rates prevailing in the countries where the bonds were sold. This policy, and its implications, is discussed more fully in the next chapter. The result of such borrowings was to generate a net *inflow* of long-term foreign capital into Canada of $1,340 million (line 22).

The net inflow of long-term capital was supplemented by an even larger net inflow of short-term capital. Chartered banks financed a large part of the corporate takeover activity mentioned above, and in turn raised funds abroad. This increased their holdings of foreign currency by $17,890 million (Line 23). When offset by "errors and omissions" of $8,438 (Line 24), which refers to transactions that go unrecorded, net short-term capital inflows totalled $6,452 million (Line 26). The combined short- and long-term capital inflow for Canada was therefore $7,792 million (Line 27).

This amount was available to pay for the current account deficit of $6,576 million, and to add $1,216 million to a third account—Canada's reserves of foreign currency (Line 31).

### The Official Reserve Account

One important category of international transactions has yet to be explained: the sales and purchases of foreign currency reserves held by the Bank of Canada and the corresponding central banks of other countries. These sales and purchases are not included in the current account because they are not made to pay for imports or exports or to make unilateral transfers. They are not included in the capital account, because they are not necessarily made for investment purposes. Often, sales and purchases of foreign currency reserves by central banks are made instead to offset an

**Capital account** The account whose transactions include all international borrowing and lending and all international purchases and sales of assets for investment purposes.

**Capital inflow** Purchases of domestic assets by foreigners and borrowing by domestic residents from foreigners.

**Capital outflow** Purchases of foreign assets by domestic residents and borrowing by foreigners from domestic sources.

excess supply or demand of dollars or other currencies. These sales and purchases are referred to as transactions on the **official reserve account**. In 1981, Canada's foreign reserves increased by $1,426 million (Lines 29 and 30), but Canada allocated $210 million to the International Monetary Fund (IMF) in the form of so-called **special drawing rights** (Line 28). These drawing rights (called **SDRs**) refer to accounts that the larger trading nations hold with the IMF to settle their international transactions with each other.

The balance of Canada's international payments can be summed up as follows: Canada traditionally buys more goods and services from others than it sells. This shows up as a deficit on the current account. This deficit is financed by a net inflow of foreign currency on the capital account. In 1981, this surplus on the capital account was large enough to add to Canada's holdings of foreign reserves. Deficits in one or more of the accounts within the balance of payments are matched by surpluses in other accounts, so that the overall account is always in balance.

**Official reserve account**
The account whose transactions include purchases and sales of reserves of foreign currency by central banks.

**Special drawing rights (SDRs)** Accounts that the larger trading nations hold with the International Monetary Fund to settle their international transactions with each other.

**Exhibit 15.5**
**Canada's balance on current account since 1970**
In most years—with 1982 being the most recent exception—a surplus on trade in goods is not sufficient to offset substantial service deficits. This means that the current account balance in total is usually in deficit, which creates unique problems for Canada.

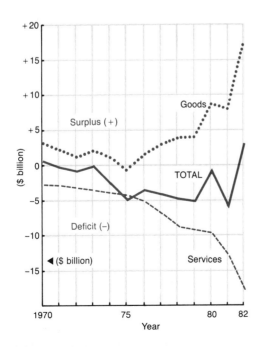

Source: *Financial Post*, January 22, 1983, p. 10.

### The Current Account Reviewed

While the overall balance is always in balance, the perennial deficit in Canada's current account deserves special consideration. Within the current account, Canada generally has a favorable balance on trade in goods, known as the merchandise balance. This balance has been negative in only two years since 1960. However, in the service sector, particularly in the receipts and payments associated with travel and interest and dividend transactions, Canada almost always has a deficit more than large enough to counteract the favorable merchandise balance. As Exhibit 15.5 shows, the total current account balance has been favorable in only two years in over a decade—in 1973 and again in 1982. In fact, since 1950, the current account has had a positive balance in only four years.

This situation poses unique and severe problems for the Canadian economy. It means that Canada is constantly under pressure to borrow enough foreign currency through its capital account to pay for the deficit experienced in the current account. For this purpose, interest rates must be kept at a level high enough to entice foreign lenders, but perhaps too high to generate enough domestic investment to create full employment. It is problems of this kind that are discussed in the next chapter.

## CONCLUSIONS

The post-World War II period as a whole has seen a broad movement toward freer trade. A series of multilateral agreements among the major trading nations, including Canada, have resulted in mutual reductions in tariffs and facilitated an upsurge in world trade. However, recessions in recent years have prompted many nations to seek new forms of protection against foreign competition. Canada also is under pressure from domestic producers to increase restrictions on imports. Because almost one-third of our output is sold abroad, Canada is particularly vulnerable to breakdowns in world trade. Canada would have more to lose than most nations if the freer trade movement of recent decades were to be reversed. In fact, Canada might have more to gain than most from the freest possible trade with other countries.

## SUMMARY

1. A country is said to have a comparative advantage in the production of any good that it can produce at a lower opportunity cost than that of its trading partners. Trading nations can realize mutual benefits if each specializes in products for which it has a comparative advantage. Such specialization can give consumers in each country more of all goods than they would have without international trade.

2. Although the theory of comparative advantage shows that all countries benefit from free international trade, a country with selling or buying power in international markets can sometimes manipulate the terms of trade by using tariffs or quotas. The resulting improvement in terms of trade can theoretically more than offset the loss in efficiency. However, if other countries retaliate with protectionist measures of their own, all

will end up losers. The same can be said of most other protectionist measures.

3. Some of the arguments for protection—the infant-industry argument, for example—are not without merit, but most economists favor the freest possible trade on the basis of the theory of comparative advantage.

4. The post-World War II period has generally been one of increasingly free trade. However, free trade faces challenges in the 1980s from new protectionist movements.

5. The many kinds of international transactions that take place in the world economy can conveniently be classified into three "accounts." The first is the current account, which comprises imports and exports of goods and services and unilateral transfers. The second is the capital account, which includes all international borrowing and lending and all international purchases and sales of assets for investment purposes. The third is the official reserve account, which is made up of central bank purchases and sales of foreign currency reserves. Because all inter-national transactions are included in one account or another, the sum of the surpluses or deficits on these three accounts must always be zero.

6. Canada depends on foreign trade for almost one-third of its total pur-chases and sales. It normally has a positive balance on merchandise trade, but its current account is usually in deficit because of service payments. This deficit requires a surplus in the capital account.

## DISCUSSION QUESTIONS

1. Consider the following statement: "The Common Market, Japan, Russia, all areas of the world are beating us.... It's no longer economical for us to produce anything." On the basis of what you have learned about the principle of comparative advantage, do you think it is really possible to reach a point when it is no longer economical to produce anything—that is, when it is economical to import everything? Explain.

2. Suppose you, a convinced advocate of free trade, became Prime Minister. Would your policy be to cut off all Canadian tariffs and quotas at once, or would you bargain with your trading partners, saying that you would cut Canadian tariffs only if they cut their own tariffs? Why would a mutual reduction be better than a one-sided reduction?

3. Simple trade theory suggests that countries will export goods in which they have a comparative advantage and import goods in which they have a compara-tive disadvantage. In fact, countries often import the same kinds of goods they export. For example, most countries that are big exporters of automobiles are also big importers of automobiles. Why do you think that happens?

4. Is the current account balance the same as net exports? Is net exports the same as the merchandise balance?

5. On the basis of Exhibit 15.5, explain what kind of transactions result in demand by Canadians for foreign currency, and what kind result in a supply of foreign currency to Canadians.

6. Why might it be better to subsidize workers harmed by freer trade than to protect them by imposing tariffs on foreign imports?

7. The federal trade minister, Mr. Lumley, vowed to lift the quotas on certain types of footwear in 1984 (see Case 15.1). Write to the minister to determine if that vow is being kept. On the basis of this chapter, what is your prediction about the likelihood of this happening?

# THE INTERACTION OF THE FOREIGN SECTOR AND THE MULTIPLIER

---

**WHAT YOU WILL LEARN IN THIS CHAPTER**
*This chapter completes the general equilibrium analysis introduced in Chapter 14 by integrating the foreign sector into the multiplier process. First, the determination of exchange rates is examined briefly. An explanation of balance of payments equilibrium follows. Equilibrium in the foreign sector is related to equilibrium in the money market and in the circular flow, and to monetary and fiscal policy. The effects of fixed and floating exchange rates are also examined. The last part of the chapter discusses the functioning of the international monetary sector and concludes with a brief summary of Canada's current problems.*

**FOR REVIEW**
*Here are some important terms and concepts that will be put to use in this chapter. If you do not understand them, review them before proceeding.*
- *Supply and demand (Chapter 3)*
- *Net exports (Chapter 8)*
- *Net exports in the multiplier process (Chapter 9)*
- *Integration of the money market and the circular flow (Chapter 14)*
- *Balance of payments accounts (Chapter 15)*

---

Chapter 15 provided information about Canadian trade patterns and policies and about Canada's international balance of payments, which form a necessary background to our understanding of how the foreign sector forms an integral part of our total economy. Though close attention was given to the role played by imports and exports, it was noted that foreign trade is just one aspect of Canada's international transactions.

Exports and imports form the current account component of Canada's balance of payments, but, as Chapter 15 indicated, the balance of payments also consists of capital flows, recorded in the capital account, and changes in reserves of foreign currency. A deficit or surplus in one account must be offset by surpluses or deficits in the other accounts.

The balancing process is affected by fiscal and monetary policy and in turn determines the effectiveness of such policies. A main concern of this chapter is to extend the general equilibrium approach of Chapter 14, in order to show how fiscal and monetary policy interact with the foreign sector, and how this in turn influences conditions in the money market and in the circular flow.

## THE THEORY OF EXCHANGE RATE DETERMINATION

### How supply and demand determine the short-run value of the Canadian dollar

One of the most popular topics of conversation among Canadians (next to the weather) is the fluctuating value of the Canadian dollar. Why was our dollar worth more than the American dollar for many years prior to 1976, and why has it become much less valuable since then? The supply and demand analysis described in Chapter 3 helps to explain this.

At any given time, there is a demand for our dollars by foreigners who wish to buy from us. Those Canadians from whom foreigners make their purchases want to be paid in Canadian dollars. Foreign purchasers must go to the foreign exchange market to obtain Canadian dollars for their transactions. This results in a demand for Canadian dollars in the foreign exchange market. On the other hand, each time a Canadian purchases goods or services from abroad, he must exchange Canadian dollars in the foreign exchange market for the currency of the country where the purchase is made. This results in a supply of Canadian dollars in the foreign exchange market, and a corresponding demand for other currencies. The value of our dollar is determined through such demand and supply forces.

**Foreign exchange market**
The complex of institutions through which the currency of one country may be exchanged for that of another.

The term **foreign exchange market** refers to the whole complex of institutions, including banks, specialized foreign exchange dealers, and official government agencies through which the currency of one country may be exchanged for that of another.

### The Supply and Demand for Foreign Exchange

All kinds of goods and services are exchanged between countries, as was noted in Chapter 15. Payments on *current account* consist of payments for imports of goods and services, including payment of interest and dividends to foreigners for past loans and investments. For the moment, assume that no other transactions occur between the citizens of the various countries of the world.

Suppose, for example, that an American clothing importer wants to buy a shipment of parkas from Canada. The importer plans to finance the purchase with U.S. dollars held in a New York bank account. However, the parka manufacturer wants to be paid in Canadian dollars, which can be used to meet payrolls and buy materials in Canada. The American bank sells the necessary quantity of U.S. dollars on the foreign exchange market, receiving Canadian dollars in return. These are then forwarded to the Canadian manufacturer to pay for the parkas.

Meanwhile, thousands of other Canadians and Americans are also buying and selling dollars for their own purposes. The overall activity in the foreign exchange market, like that in any other market, can be characterized in terms of supply and demand curves, such as those shown in Exhibit 16.1. This market has been drawn so that it shows the supply and demand for Canadian dollars, with the price (that is, the exchange rate) shown in terms of U.S. dollars per Canadian dollar. But it could equally well have been drawn to show the supply and demand for U.S. dollars with the price in Canadian dollars per U.S. dollar.

Look first at the demand curve for Canadian dollars that appears in this market. The shape and position of the demand curve for Canadian dollars depends on how American demand for Canadian goods varies as the exchange rate varies, other things being equal. It is easy to see that the demand curve will normally be downward sloping. Suppose, for example, that parkas sell in Canada for $50. At an exchange rate of 1 U.S. dollar per Canadian dollar, American consumers would have to pay $50 U.S. They might buy a total of, say, 200,000 parkas per year, thus generating a demand for 10 million Canadian dollars in the foreign exchange market. If the exchange rate were to fall to 0.8 U.S. dollars per Canadian dollar while the parka price remained unchanged, American consumers would be able to buy parkas more cheaply for U.S. dollars. At that lower price, they would presumably buy a greater quantity, say, 510,000 parkas. The demand for Canadian dollars on the foreign exchange market would thus increase to $25.5 million.

The supply curve for dollars in Exhibit 16.1 ($S_1$) is drawn with an upward slope, indicating that more Canadian dollars will be supplied to the foreign exchange market as the price of Canadian dollars, in terms of U.S. dollars, rises. This will be the case whenever Canadian demand for American goods increases so much when the value of the Canadian dollar rises that more Canadian dollars are actually spent and supplied to Americans. Suppose, for example, that a certain model American-built motor home has a price of $20,000 U.S. At an exchange rate of 1 U.S. dollar per Canadian dollar, the motor home would sell for $20,000 in Canada (forgetting about shipping costs and other charges). If, say, 5,000 of the motor homes per year were sold at that price, Canada would have to supply 100 million Canadian dollars to the foreign exchange market in order to get the 100 million U.S. dollars needed to pay the American manufacturer. Suppose next that the exchange rate rose to 1.25 U.S. dollars per Canadian dollar, so that Canadian buyers could get the motor home for just 16,000 Canadian dollars. If the quantity imported rose to 7,500 per year as a result of the increase in the value of the Canadian dollar, Canadians would supply 120 million Canadian dollars to the exchange markets.

Exhibit 16.1 also helps to illustrate how exchange rates can change as a result of shifts in demand and supply. As that Exhibit is drawn, the foreign exchange market is initially in equilibrium at an exchange rate of 1 U.S. dollar per Canadian dollar. Suppose, then, that some change in Canadian spending habits occurs. Canadians might decide to travel more in the

**Exhibit 16.1**

**Equilibrium between demand and supply in the foreign exchange market**

The demand curve for Canadian dollars (D) indicates that Americans will desire a greater quantity of Canadian dollars as the cost per U.S. dollar declines. The quantity supplied ($S_1$) increases at higher exchange rates.

When only current account transactions are taken into account, the process by which equilibrium is maintained in the foreign exchange market is very simple. Suppose that a sudden increased preference of Canadians for travel in the United States shifts the supply curve for Canadian dollars to the right, from $S_1$ to $S_2$. This creates an excess supply of dollars and puts downward pressure on the exchange rate. As the exchange rate falls, Americans are induced to spend more on Canadian goods, and Canadians to spend less on American goods. The exchange rate reaches a new equilibrium at 0.8 U.S. dollars per Canadian dollar.

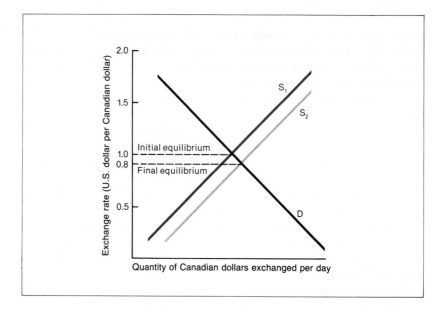

Quantity of Canadian dollars exchanged per day

United States and pay more to Americans in the form of interest and dividends. This could increase the supply of Canadian dollars in the foreign exchange market, at the existing exchange rate. This is shown in Exhibit 15.1 as a shift in the Canadian dollar supply curve from $S_1$ to $S_2$. The shift in the supply curve initially creates an excess supply of Canadian dollars, which tends to depress the exchange rate. As the exchange rate falls, Canadian goods become cheaper for Americans to buy, encouraging an increase in the quantity demanded of Canadian dollars. This is represented by a movement down along the demand curve in Exhibit 16.1. At the same time, American goods become more expensive for Canadian buyers, somewhat decreasing the quantity of Canadian dollars supplied. This appears as a downward movement along the new Canadian dollar supply curve. As the figure is drawn, the supply and demand for Canadian dollars comes into equilibrium again at an exchange rate of 0.8 U.S. dollars per Canadian dollar.

In the terminology of foreign exchange markets, the Canadian dollar is said to **depreciate** when its price falls in terms of foreign currency, as in the example above. Seen from the American point of view, a fall in the price of the Canadian dollar in terms of U.S. dollars is equivalent to a rise in the price of the U.S. dollar in terms of Canadian dollars. The American dollar, then, can be said to have **appreciated** against the Canadian dollar.

> **Depreciation and appreciation of the exchange rate** The Canadian dollar is said to depreciate when its price falls in terms of foreign currency, and to appreciate when its price rises in terms of foreign currency.

## Foreign Exchange Markets with Current and Capital Accounts

When only current account transactions were considered, equilibrium in foreign exchange markets required that every dollar's worth of goods or services imported be paid for by a dollar's worth of goods or services exported. Once capital account transactions are introduced, however, this need no longer be the case. Imports of goods or services can now be paid for either by exports, or by capital inflows; that is, by borrowing from foreigners or selling assets to foreigners. Similarly, a country can export more goods and services than it imports, so long as it provides its trading partners with the means to do so, by making loans to them or buying assets from them.

Consider the hypothetical case shown in Exhibit 16.2. In the year for which these accounts are drawn, Canada is shown as importing more in goods and services than it exports, and running a current account deficit of $5 billion. (In the table, all flows of dollars away from Canada are shown with a minus sign and all flows of dollars toward Canada are shown with a plus sign.) At the same time, however, borrowing from foreigners plus sales of Canadian assets to foreigners (capital inflows) exceed loans to foreigners plus purchases of foreign assets (capital outflows) by $5 billion. Canada thus has a $5 billion capital account surplus that exactly balances the current account deficit.

It is not necessary to draw a new set of foreign exchange supply and demand curves to take both current and capital transactions into account. There is still just one supply curve of Canadian dollars, one demand curve for Canadian dollars, and one exchange rate for the Canadian dollar in

---

**Exhibit 16.2**
**Hypothetical balance of payments accounts, current and capital accounts only (billions of Canadian dollars)**
In a world where the only international transactions are those taking place on current and capital account, any current account deficit must be balanced by a capital account surplus, and vice versa. In this hypothetical example, Canada is shown importing more than it exports, thus running a current account deficit. This is financed by a capital inflow; that is, by borrowing from abroad or by sales of assets to foreigners. Note that all outflows of dollars are listed with a minus sign and all inflows with a plus sign.

| | | |
|---|---|---|
| Exports (including travel by foreigners in Canada and receipt by Canadians of interest and dividends from abroad) | | +$62 |
| Imports (including payments by Canadians for travel abroad and for interest and dividends to foreigners) | | −$67 |
| Transfers | | 0 |
| Current account deficit | | −$5 |
| Sales of Canadian assets to foreigners and borrowing from foreigners | +$7 | |
| Purchases of foreign assets and loans to foreigners | −$2 | |
| Capital account surplus | | +$5 |

terms of any other currency, such as the U.S. dollar. However, there are now additional sources of shifts in the supply and demand curves, such as a rise in Canadian interest rates. One immediate effect of this would be to make Canadian securities more attractive than before to foreign buyers. Their increased demand for Canadian dollars with which to buy these securities would show up as a rightward shift in the demand for Canadian dollars in the foreign exchange market. That would tend to cause the Canadian dollar to appreciate against the U.S. dollar. As will be discussed later in this chapter, the Bank of Canada might deliberately cause interest rates in Canada to be higher than those in the U.S., in order to get the demand curve for the Canadian dollar to shift to the right. The exchange rate would then rise above 0.8 U.S. dollars per Canadian dollar. It is shifts in the type of international transactions just described that explain, through demand and supply analysis, how the value of our dollar changes in the short run.

### Foreign Exchange Markets with Official Reserves Added

We saw in Chapter 15 that transactions in the official reserve account involve purchases and sales of reserves of foreign currency by central banks. Such transactions can prevent or moderate exchange rate fluctuations.

An example of how official reserve transactions might affect exchange rates appears in Exhibit 16.3. This diagram begins with the same scenario as did Exhibit 16.1: initially, the market is in equilibrium at an exchange rate of 1 U.S. dollar per Canadian dollar. This is shown by the intersection of $D_1$ and $S_1$. Next, an increase in Canadian transfer payments causes a rightward shift in the dollar supply curve to $S_2$, which creates an excess supply of Canadian dollars at the original exchange rate. Normally, this would cause the Canadian dollar to depreciate against the U.S. dollar. Instead of permitting the exchange rate to fall, however, the Bank of Canada could decide to use some of the U.S. dollars it holds as part of its foreign currency reserves to purchase the surplus Canadian dollars. Alternatively, the U.S. Federal Reserve might sell U.S. dollars in order to build up its reserves of Canadian dollars, or both central banks might act together, coordinating their efforts. In any event, the transactions would show up on the exchange market diagram as a rightward shift in the demand curve for Canadian dollars. As Exhibit 16.3 is drawn, sufficient official reserve purchases of Canadian dollars are made to shift the demand curve all the way to Position $D_2$. The entire excess supply of Canadian dollars is thus soaked up, and the exchange rate does not change.

So far, only the mechanics of exchange rate determination have been discussed; exchange rates, like other prices, are determined by supply and demand. The next step is to look beyond the supply and demand curves for a theory explaining why, at any particular time, the curves intersect at one exchange rate rather than another. Once that step has been taken, the next section will discuss the conditions for equilibrium in both the domestic and foreign sectors of the economy. This will then be followed by an examination of how and why governments use interest rate policies and reserve transactions to intervene in foreign exchange markets.

**Exhibit 16.3**
**Official intervention in the foreign exchange market**
This exhibit begins with the same scenario shown in
Exhibit 16.1. Starting from an exchange rate of one U.S.
dollar per Canadian dollar at the intersection of $D_1$ and
$S_1$, an increase in transfers from Canada shifts the
Canadian dollar supply curve to the right, to $S_2$. That
shift creates a surplus of Canadian dollars and puts
downward pressure on the exchange rate. To prevent the
exchange rate from falling, the Canadian or U.S.
government begins official reserve purchases of dollars.
These purchases shift the demand curve for dollars to
the right, to $D_2$ until the demand curve intersects the new
supply curve at the old exchange rate.

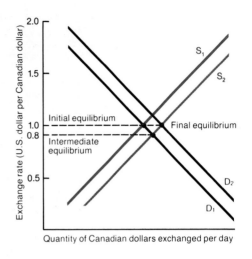

Quantity of Canadian dollars exchanged per day

## THE LONG RUN: PURCHASING POWER PARITY

The leading theory of exchange rate determination in the long run is the
so-called **purchasing power parity theory**. According to this theory, the
price of a unit of Currency A in terms of Currency B (that is, the exchange
rate) will, in the long run, tend to equal the ratio of the price level in
Country B to the price level in Country A.

In a world where all goods and services were traded internationally, with
no transportation costs or other barriers to trade, the purchasing power
parity theory would presumably hold exactly. Suppose, for example, that
the Canadian and German domestic price levels are such that $100 will buy
exactly twice as large a market basket of goods in Canada as can be bought
for 100 marks in Germany. The purchasing power parity theory will then
imply that the exchange rate must be 2 marks per dollar. If a dollar could be
exchanged for more than 2 marks, Canadian consumers would all try to
turn in their dollars and do their shopping in Germany. Their attempt to do
so would immediately drive the price of the dollar back down to 2 marks.
Similarly, if a dollar could be purchased for less than 2 marks, Germans
would try to turn in all their marks for dollars and shop in Canada. This
would quickly push the price of the dollar up to 2 marks. In such a world, in
fact, the expressions "100 dollars" and "200 marks" would simply be different names given in Germany and Canada to equal-sized lumps of abstract
purchasing power.

In practice, exchange rates do not always reflect purchasing power parities exactly. The difference can be explained in part by the fact that
purchasing power parities reflect the prices of all goods and services, while
exchange rates tend to reflect the value of goods and services traded
internationally.

Also, deviations of exchange values from present purchasing power parities may reflect future expectations as much as current realities. For

**Purchasing power parity
theory (of exchange rates)**
The theory holding that the price
of a unit of Currency A in terms
of Currency B will, in the long
run, tend to be equal to the ratio
of the price level in Country B to
the price level in Country A.

*exchange rate*

example, if participants in foreign exchange markets come to expect Canadian inflation in the future consistently to average higher in relation to German inflation than they thought in the past, they may "speculate" against the dollar by shifting out of dollar-denominated assets into mark-denominated assets. These capital account transactions can depress the value of the dollar even before enough actual inflation takes place to justify the new exchange rate in terms of purchasing power parities. Similarly, if participants in foreign exchange markets speculate that future real economic growth will cause the demand for a country's exports to increase more rapidly than its demand for imports, the present exchange rate for its currency may be bid up in anticipation of the expected future improvement in its current account balance.

With the necessary reservations, as noted, the purchasing power parity theory can be thought of as determining exchange rates in the long run.

## THE INTERACTION OF MONEY, NATIONAL INCOME, AND THE BALANCE OF PAYMENTS

### The Conditions for General Equilibrium

It was shown in Chapter 14 that the money market and the circular flow can be in equilibrium only if there is a perfect matching of interest rates and nominal national income. Exhibit 14.1 illustrated a general equilibrium situation for the money market and the circular flow. No consideration, however, was given to equilibrium in the balance of payments.

It was observed in Chapter 15 that, in a purely accounting sense, the balance of payments will always be shown to be in equilibrium, because in principle the sum of the current, capital, and reserve accounts will always be exactly zero. However, economists define a **balance of payments equilibrium** as a situation in which there are no changes in reserves. That is, the balance of payments is considered to be in equilibrium when the capital account exactly balances the current account. This means that any loss of foreign currency required to pay for a deficit on the current account is matched by a net capital inflow of the same amount, while a surplus in the current account will be utilized to finance net capital outflows. If such balancing occurs, there will be no loss or build-up of foreign currency reserves.

As we have seen (Chapter 15), Canada usually runs a deficit on its current account. An equilibrium in Canada's balance of payments can be said to exist only when capital inflows exceed capital outflows by the amount of the current account deficit. (When capital inflows do exceed capital outflows it is defined as a positive *net* capital inflow.) This kind of equilibrium might be considered a minimal objective. Even more desirable would be a balance or near-balance in the current account itself, with exports equaling imports, easing the pressure to increase inflows of foreign capital to help to pay for a current account deficit. However, the minimal objective will be considered here.

To have a balance of payments equilibrium, negative net exports (deficit on current account) must be matched by positive net capital inflows (surplus on capital account), or positive net exports must be matched by negative net capital inflows.

**Balance of payments equilibrium** A situation in which transactions in the capital account exactly match transactions in the current account, so that there is no loss or build-up of foreign currency reserves.

Net exports, as shown in Exhibit 8.10b, have a positive autonomous element. However, because imports increase with nominal national income, and exports are assumed not to increase, net exports decline as nominal national income increases. The current account, therefore, becomes negative at high levels of income.

We can again make use of the net export function illustrated in Exhibit 8.10b and in Exhibit 16.4c. Exports are assumed to be $125 regardless of income, and imports are $50 plus 0.15 of nominal national income. Net exports (exports minus imports) are equal to $75 −0.15 national income. At an income level of $500 net exports would be zero, and at levels of income above $500 they become negative.

To have a minimal equilibrium in the balance of payments, net exports must be matched by capital flows. Capital flows are related primarily to interest rates. The higher our interest rates are compared to those of other countries (for example, the United States), the more inclined Canadians will be to borrow in those countries and the less inclined foreigners will be to borrow in Canada. What is important is not the absolute level of our interest rates but the differential between our rates and those of other countries. However, it will be assumed here that as our rates go up the differential increases. Net capital inflows will then be related positively to the rate of interest.

It follows from these assumptions that at a specific level of nominal national income, which produces a particular level of net exports, it will require one particular rate of interest to create capital flows that exactly match the net exports. Therefore, equilibrium in the foreign market requires a matching of interest rates and nominal national income, just as a matching of interest rates and national income was required to create equilibrium simultaneously in the money market and in the circular flow. In fact, as we shall see, *general equilibrium in an economy requires that the money market, the circular flow, and the balance of payments all be brought into equilibrium simultaneously by a unique combination of interest rates and nominal national income.*

### General Equilibrium Including the Foreign Market

The nature of such a general equilibrium, and its necessity, was illustrated in Exhibit 14.1. An interest rate of 8 percent caused the demand for money to be equal to the supply of money. Simultaneously that interest rate resulted in investment spending of $100, which, together with the other spending flows in the economy, was consistent with a nominal national income of $1,200. Therefore, that interest rate, in combination with that particular level of nominal national income, created equilibrium in both the money market and the circular flow.

However, nothing was said in that illustration about equilibrium in the foreign market—that is, in the balance of payments. For that reason it was not really correct to call it a situation of *general* equilibrium.

Exhibit 14.1 told us what was happening to net exports. At a nominal national income of $1,200 they were −$105. Were they matched by a corresponding inflow of capital? We don't know, because up to that point no capital flow function had been developed. This gap must now be filled.

**Exhibit 16.4**
**A general equilibrium view of the circular flow and the foreign market**
Demand and supply forces in the money market (not shown here) have created an interest rate of 8 percent. This interest rate generates a net capital inflow of $105 (16.4a). This is exactly sufficient to pay for the $105 deficit on the current account shown in 16.4c. The latter resulted from a nominal national income of $1,200, which in turn was caused partly by a level of investment of $100. That level of investment was due to the 8 percent rate of interest, as illustrated in 16.4b. A different rate of interest would have led to a net capital inflow and a nominal national income level such that the current and capital accounts would not have been equal. A unique combination of interest and income is required for equilibrium in the foreign sector.

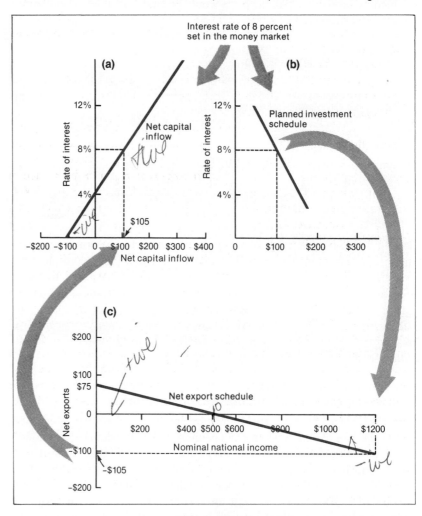

The requirements for simultaneous equilibrium in the circular flow and in the balance of payments are illustrated in Exhibit 16.4. It is assumed that an interest rate of 8 percent has been established in the money market, based on the first diagram in Exhibit 14.1. A hypothetical net capital inflow function is shown in Exhibit 16.4a. At low rates of interest, below 4 percent, it is assumed that net capital inflows would be negative.

More capital would leave the country, in order to take advantage of higher interest rates elsewhere, than would enter the country, resulting in net capital outflows (or a negative net capital inflow). At rates of interest above 4 percent, capital inflows would begin to exceed capital outflows. At 8 percent interest, it is assumed that net capital inflows would equal $105.[1]

At the same time, at a rate of interest of 8 percent, investment would equal $100, as illustrated in Exhibit 16.4b. This, together with the other expenditure flows noted previously, would result in an equilibrium level of nominal national income of $1,200 (Exhibit 16.4c). Exhibit 16.4c also shows that an income of $1,200 produces net exports of − $105. These net exports are exactly matched by the net capital inflows which the 8 percent rate of interest produced.

We thus have the following simultaneous equilibrium conditions:

1. In the money market, supply and demand forces have been brought into equilibrium at a rate of interest of 8 percent. Given those forces, only that rate of interest will produce equilibrium.

2. In the circular flow, the 8 percent rate of interest helps to create expenditure flows (through the investment function), which produce an equilibrium level of nominal national income of $1,200. Given a rate of interest of 8 percent, no income level other than $1,200 will produce an equivalent level of planned expenditures. Therefore, the circular flow is uniquely in equilibrium at a rate of interest of 8 percent and a nominal national income of $1,200.

3. In the foreign market, the 8 percent rate of interest creates a net capital inflow of $105. Simultaneously, the nominal national income of $1,200 results in a current account deficit of $105. Equilibrium in the foreign market, therefore, results from a perfect matching of interest rates and nominal national income.

The important result is this: a unique combination of a particular rate of interest and a particular level of income is required to produce a general equilibrium for the economy. Government policy may be able to establish interest rates and income levels that achieve equilibrium in two markets but not in all three. Failure to achieve equilibrium in one may frustrate policies designed to maintain equilibrium in the others. (As we shall see, this is strictly true only when exchange rates are not permitted to move freely in response to imbalances in the foreign sector. It should also be noted that the general equilibrium sought here is assumed to be the most desirable one, namely one with full employment, low inflation, and a balance of payments achievable on the basis of policies that promote the overall objectives.)

### The Difficulty of Achieving General Equilibrium (with Fixed Exchange Rates)

To understand the difficulty of achieving an equilibrium situation, assume that the government decides to increase nominal national income, because

---

[1]The net capital inflow function utilized here is expressed by the equation $F = -\$105 + 2625(r)$, where F = the net capital inflow, $105 is the autonomous net capital inflow, and the number 2625 expresses the rate at which F will change in relation to interest rates (r). E.g., if $r = .08$, $F = -\$105 + 2625(0.8) = -\$105 + \$210 = +\$105$.

there is too much unemployment when national income is $1,200. Suppose that the Bank of Canada increases the money supply in order to reduce interest rates to 4 percent. This lower rate of interest would increase investment to $150, and—as noted in Chapter 14—the nominal national income would eventually increase by $125, to a new level of $1,325. Before, when only the circular flow and the money market were considered, the economy was judged to be in general equilibrium at the new interest rate and the new level of income. However, note now what happens to equilibrium in the foreign market. At a rate of interest of 4 percent, net capital inflows will fall to zero, while simultaneously, at the income level of $1,325, net exports will decline to −$113.75. (Xn = $75 − 0.15($1,325)) The current account deficit has grown larger as a result of the monetary policy, but at the same time the net capital inflow required to pay for the deficit has diminished. The balance of payments is in serious disequilibrium.

If fiscal policy, without accommodating monetary policy, were used to increase national income, the effects on the balance of payments would not be as clear cut. The rise in income would increase the current account deficit, but higher interest rates would simultaneously increase net capital inflows. It is highly unlikely that the current and capital accounts would change by the same amount (one down, the other up), so that the end result would probably be either a small overall surplus or a small deficit.

What is likely to happen in an economy in which the foreign market is in serious disequilibrium, perhaps because of a monetary policy designed to lower interest rates and increase income? The result will depend largely on whether the exchange rate is fixed or whether it is allowed to change because of the pressures created by changed interest rates and income.

If the exchange rate is fixed, and the interest rate remains at 4 percent, the deficit in the balance of payments will not be self-correcting. However, the Bank of Canada will have to use up its reserves of foreign currency to pay for the imbalance. In the process of selling foreign currency to private dealers who need the foreign currency to pay for the deficit, the Bank will receive cheques in Canadian currency from those dealers, which will reduce deposits of the chartered banks. This will reduce the money supply, thereby increasing interest rates once again and lowering the level of income. Unless the Bank of Canada counterbalances such reductions in the money supply with new infusions of money, the economy will revert to its old equilibrium level. The result is that the monetary policy designed to increase the level of income and reduce the level of unemployment has been completely stymied. Monetary policy, therefore, may be made ineffectual by fixed exchange rates.

### Achieving General Equilibrium with Flexible Exchange Rates

Very different results are possible with flexible exchange rates. When the money supply is increased, and the current account deficit increases while net capital inflows diminish, the value of the Canadian dollar will decline.

This will happen because the *supply* of Canadian currency in the foreign exchange market will *increase* (as Canadians react to lower interest rates and higher incomes by exchanging more Canadian dollars for foreign currency, in order to purchase more bonds and goods and services from foreigners), and the *demand* for Canadian dollars will *decrease* (as foreigners react to our lower interest rates by buying fewer bonds from us). The decline in the value of our dollar should reduce the current account deficit. Foreigners will find our goods and services cheaper than before, while Canadians will find that foreign goods and services have become more expensive.

*exports - imports = two*

In terms of Exhibit 16.4, the net export schedule in Exhibit 16.4c will shift to the right, because at a given level of income more will now be exported and less imported. In fact, it can be assumed that the value of the Canadian dollar will keep dropping until net exports and net capital inflows are equal (meaning that the net export schedule in Exhibit 16.4c shifts so far to the right that net exports equal zero at an income level of $1,325). The foreign market then will have achieved a new equilibrium, at interest rates of 4 percent and the target income level of $1,325. With flexible exchange rates, policy makers have some hope of moving the economy in the desired direction.

Flexible exchange rates may appear to make fiscal policy more potent than our previous examples of the multiplier effect (in Chapter 10) indicated. Partly because of import leakages, the multiplier in our example was only 2.5 for an increase in government expenditures. However, if the government uses an expansionary fiscal policy to increase income, the increased deficit on the current account resulting from higher imports may result in a depreciation of our currency. This will decrease imports and increase exports, thereby increasing the demand forces and the level of income. Yet, higher interest rates will accompany this increased demand, in the absence of increases in the money supply, and the higher rates will attract more foreign capital, driving the exchange rate back up. At the same time, the higher interest rates will discourage domestic investment. Therefore the net result is indeterminate.

### Exchange Rate Policy

In general, flexible exchange rates are favored by most economists because they eliminate imbalances in the foreign sector that might result from monetary and fiscal policy, so that domestic stabilization policies can be pursued without too much worry about repercussions in the balance of payments.

However, the real world is one in which other considerations also play an important role, so that fixed or semifixed exchange rates are more often the rule than the exception. In the 1950s (until 1961) Canada allowed its exchange rate to fluctuate freely; in the 1960s it operated with fixed exchange rates, and in the 1970s and early 1980s rates were semiflexible, being controlled partly by special purchases and sales of foreign currency by the Bank of Canada.

### The Case for and against Fixed Rates

**Real Effects of Currency Disturbances**   The first point made by proponents of fixed rates is that variations in exchange rates have significant real effects on the economy. When a country's currency appreciates, its export industries find it harder to compete in world markets. At the same time, industries that face import competition find it difficult to compete in domestic markets. When a country's currency depreciates, in contrast, export and import-competing industries boom, but industries that rely on imported energy or raw materials suffer. If the appreciation or depreciation in question reflects fundamental long-term changes in patterns of world trade, these adjustments in import and export industries may be necessary and desirable. But it is argued that short-term random, cyclical, or speculative changes in exchange rates should not be allowed to disturb the domestic economy. After all, labor and other factors of production cannot make costless moves from sector to sector at a moment's notice.

**The J-curve Effect**   A second reason frequently advanced for fixing exchange rates is that, in the short run, the depreciation of a country's currency may worsen rather than improve its balance of payments on current account. This is known as the J-curve effect, and is illustrated in Exhibit 16.5. When a country's currency first depreciates, few additional export sales are made immediately, and importers do not or cannot immediately reduce the quantity of goods they purchase. At the lower exchange rates, however, importers do have to offer greater quantities of the domestic currency in order to obtain the foreign currency they need to buy the unchanged physical quantity of imports. The current account balance thus moves toward deficit, putting further downward pressure on the exchange rate. Eventually, the lower exchange rate attracts new export buyers and encourages importers to find domestic substitutes. Supporters of fixed rates emphasize possible negative short-term effects of flexible rates. Supporters of flexible rates can argue that, in the long run, such rates do produce favorable results. Something like this appears to have happened after Canada's dollar fell sharply in value toward the end of 1976. It took some time—as Chapter 17 will discuss—before the foreign market benefited from the exchange rate depreciation.

---

**Exhibit 16.5**

The J-curve effect

The so-called J-curve effect occurs because a devaluation may initially worsen a country's balance of payments on its current account before eventually improving it. Here, the country has been experiencing a moderate current account deficit for some time. At the point shown, it devalues its currency. At first, the current account drops farther into deficit, but eventually it rises into surplus, following the J-shaped path shown.

**Inflationary Effects** A third argument in favor of fixed exchange rates is based on the relationship between exchange rate variations and inflation. Countries experiencing relatively rapid inflation can expect their currencies to depreciate—in accordance with the purchasing power parity theory. However, the causation may also run the other way; a currency depreciation may cause domestic cost-push inflation. This occurs in part directly, because the prices of imported goods and raw materials rise, and in part indirectly, because domestic import-competing industries feel free to raise their prices when the prices of imports rise.

Under the proper conditions, a vicious cycle that runs something like this can be touched off: inflation in, say, Canada causes the dollar to depreciate. Depreciation brings a round of cost-push inflation. International asset holders see the worsening inflation and react by pulling their funds out of Canadian banks and securities, thereby creating a capital account deficit. Especially if the J-curve effect of the depreciation is creating a current account deficit at the same time, the value of the dollar can plunge out of control in the absence of official intervention.

Meanwhile, a less inflationary country, say Switzerland, enters a "virtuous" cycle that is the mirror image of the vicious cycle described for Canada. Currency appreciation lowers import prices, further dampening inflation. International investors rush to put their funds in the ultra-safe Swiss franc, thereby creating a capital account surplus that causes further appreciation. But while the banks of Zurich grow fat, Swiss watchmakers find themselves increasingly priced out of the world market on which their livelihood depends.

The way to prevent such runaway vicious-virtuous cycles, it is said, is to prevent exchange rate fluctuations in the first place. Rather than letting differential rates of inflation disturb exchange markets, countries should use the time gained by exchange rate intervention to undertake domestic policies to control inflation.

*Arguments for Floating Rates* Floating-rate advocates begin by pointing out that fixed rates do not truly protect the domestic economy from the real effects of international disturbances. For example, if inflation occurs under a fixed-rate system, foreign competition may prevent prices from rising in industries facing strong international competition. As costs and prices rise in other sectors of the domestic economy, the industries facing foreign competition will be squeezed and resource allocation will consequently be disturbed. As was indicated previously, the J-curve effect is likely a short-term one. In the long run, it is not really an argument for fixed rates.

Floating-rate advocates are similarly unconvinced by the argument that currency depreciation creates a vicious cycle through cost-push inflation. The impact of exchange rate fluctuations on domestic inflation depends on whether the domestic money stock is held constant or increased. If the money stock is held constant—instead of being increased to accommodate the inflationary impact of currency depreciation—price increases in some markets will tend to be offset by price decreases elsewhere. Floating-rate advocates concede that in a floating-rate world, central banks would not always have the necessary discipline to avoid inflationary monetary policy, but they suggest that the blame should be placed on the banks, not on the monetary system.

It is time now to turn from theory to a brief review of the postwar history of the international monetary system.

## The International Monetary System

After World War II, the major trading nations of the world met under United Nations auspices at Bretton Woods, New Hampshire, to forge a new world monetary system of the fixed rate variety. The Bretton Woods conference also set up the International Monetary Fund (IMF), with headquarters in Washington, D.C., to administer the system. The rules of the international monetary game as it was played under the Bretton Woods system are presented here.

It was not quite an ideal fixed rate system. Instead, it featured what might best be called an "adjustable peg." Par values for each currency were established in terms of the U.S. dollar. Exchange rates were pegged at the par values; thus they were allowed to fluctuate under the influence of supply and demand within a narrow range of 2.25 percent above par to 2.25 percent below par. (The limits were only 1 percent until December 1971.) When the value of a currency rose to the upper limit or fell to the lower one, the government of the country in question was obligated under IMF rules to intervene and prevent further movement. A government faced with an excess demand for its currency at the limit rate had to sell enough of its own currency in exchange for dollars to soak up the excess demand. A government faced with an excess supply of its currency had to buy it in exchange for dollars if necessary to keep its price from slipping below the limit.

Although governments were supposed to intervene in exchange markets to counteract temporary distrubances, they had another option if they felt the disturbances reflected fundamental long-term changes. In the face of such changes, they could adjust the peg—change the par values of their currencies. This could be done in either of two slightly different ways. One way was to declare immediately a new par value above or below the initial value. The other was to float the currency temporarily, letting it find a new equilibrium value under the influence of supply and demand without government intervention. A new par value would later be fixed at the market determined rate when things seemed to have settled down. (A few countries, notably Canada, let their currencies float for years at a time in the postwar period. This, however, was considered to be a violation of at least the spirit, if not the letter, of IMF rules.)

## Problems of the Bretton Woods System

**Resisting Adjustment**  Under the Bretton Woods system, a country whose currency fell to the lower limit of the permissible range either was supposed to buy it until the imbalance was corrected or was supposed to adjust the peg, make a new start at a new par value, and try to keep serious imbalances from arising again in the future. Unfortunately, governments often did neither when faced with downward pressure on their currencies.

Fearing unemployment and high interest rates, they refused to make purchases of their own currency. And, concerned about possible sectoral effects, they resisted downward adjustment of their par value. In desperate attempts to prop up their currencies, they engaged in all sorts of trade restrictions. They imposed tariffs and quotas to try to improve current account balances, and they slapped on foreign exchange controls to prevent free international movements of capital, all in the hope of improving the capital account. But these mechanisms usually did little more than postpone the day of reckoning.

Crises   Because adjustments were seldom fully automatic, the system was crisis-prone. Governments often resisted making small adjustments when the adjustments would have been only slightly painful. Instead, they waited for pressures to build up, and these pressures eventually tore the system apart.

Here is the scenario for the kind of international monetary crisis that repeatedly occurred under the Bretton Woods rules. Some country, say the United Kingdom, runs a persistent balance of payments deficit. A chronic excess supply of British pounds sterling appears on the world's exchange markets. The British government is forced to support the pound. It resists monetary restraint. Gradually, dollar reserves are run dangerously low, and the British government is forced to borrow from the IMF or the U.S. Treasury. It may try imposing exchange controls or other trade restrictions, but its efforts are met with threats of retaliation and domestic political resistence. It becomes harder and harder to keep the pound from breaking through the floor. The final scene in the sterling crisis is set when speculators, observing the decline in the value of the pound, start to pour hundreds of millions of pounds into the foreign exchange markets. The excess supply of sterling becomes overwhelming, and the last straw forcing an actual devaluation is the speculative pressure occurring in anticipation of the devaluation.

## The End of the Bretton Woods System

In early 1973, an especially severe crisis occurred, involving the U.S. dollar, the German mark, and the Japanese yen. In response to this crisis, the major trading nations took the bold step of abandoning the adjustable peg and allowing their currencies to float relative to each other. The relative values of the yen, the dollar, and the mark were allowed to find their own levels under the influence of supply and demand.

The international monetary system that emerged from the crisis of 1973 is still a mixed system. It contains a number of features that do not conform exactly to a pure floating rate system. Although it is much more flexible than the adjustable peg, two important restrictions must be kept in mind.

First, not every currency floats against every other currency. Rather, the system is one in which major blocks of currencies float against one another. A number of Western European countries have attempted to peg their currencies against one another in an arrangement known as the European Monetary Union. Countries with strong trading ties to the United States have pegged their currencies to the dollar. Those with strong ties to Britain have pegged theirs to the pound. Movements between blocks have been substantial, though. Because increased flexibility has been introduced, several currencies have swung by as much as 20 to 30 percent. Occasionally there have been swings of 2 or 3 percent in a single day.

Second, governments have not taken a strictly hands-off attitude toward exchange rates. Instead, they have frequently intervened in foreign exchange markets to damp what they perceive to be temporary or unjustified fluctuations in exchange rates. This intervention is, however, not guided by any specific rules, as under the Bretton Woods agreements. The present mixture of floating rates and sporadic intervention is often referred to as a "dirty float." During much of the postwar period, the Canadian dollar has been allowed to float within limits, so that the value has been set largely through demand and supply forces.

## CANADA'S DILEMMA IN THE FOREIGN MARKET

Most of our international transactions are conducted with the United States, and Canada's basic problems in the foreign market can best be illustrated by referring to our dealings with that country.

Canada's balance of payments position vis-à-vis the U.S. can be summarized briefly. We almost always have a deficit in our current account with the United States. This is largely due to the interest and dividends on investments in Canada that we pay to American investors. These investors want to be paid in U.S. dollars, so companies in Canada paying interest and dividends to them must purchase U.S. dollars in the foreign exchange market. Doing so pushes up the value of the U.S. dollar. Therefore, our heavy dependence on American investment has created a perennial problem for us, by saddling us with heavy debt payments that push down the value of our dollar. In order to stabilize the value of the dollar around **par**, we have tried to lure more investment into Canada by keeping our interest rates above those prevailing in the United States. Because of our higher interest rates, Americans are induced to buy our securities in preference to their own. It is operations of this kind that have counterbalanced the negative impact on the value of our dollar caused by the normal deficits in our current account.

> **Par** The point at which one unit of a currency is traded for exactly one unit of another currency.

In 1976, several factors coincided to bring about a substantial decline in the value of our dollar. First, we allowed our interest rates to approach those of the United States, so that fewer Canadian bond issues were sold in the United States. There was therefore little counterpressure to the normal downward pressure on the dollar. Second, our inflation rate had been allowed to rise above that of the United States, so that we had additional problems in our current account. Third, the victory of the Parti Québecois in the province of Quebec, which threatened the unity of the country, probably led to some speculative action against the dollar by people anticipating a diminution of Canadian resources as a result of Quebec's secession.

By 1981, as Exhibit 16.6a illustrates, the value of the Canadian dollar had stabilized at about $.83 U.S. The Bank of Canada has tried to use interest rate policy and special intervention with reserve funds to prevent the value of the dollar from falling lower than that. Exhibit 16.6b illustrates

**Exhibit 16.6**

**The behavior of Canada's exchange rate and Bank rate**

Part a gives each currency a value of 100 in 1971 and then shows how the value of the Canadian dollar has changed relative to the U.S. dollar since 1973. Part b illustrates the way in which the Bank of Canada has moved its Bank rate up in accordance with changes in the U.S. discount rate, to maintain a differential between interest rates in Canada and the U.S., so as to create a capital account surplus, offsetting our current account deficits.

**(a)**

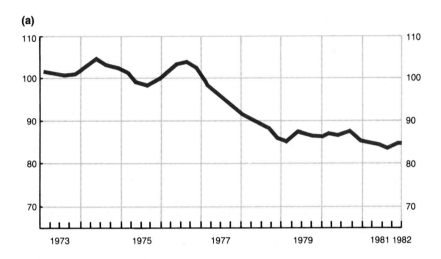

**(b) Canada's bank rate in relation to the U.S. discount rate.**

Source: Minister of Finance, *Economic Review*, April 1982, pp. 81 and 230.

the way in which our interest rates have been maintained at a level at least 1 percent, and sometimes as much as 7 percent, above those of the United States. When the Federal Reserve Bank of the United States pushes U.S. interest rates up, ours follow. In mid-1981 this brought about an increase in the Bank of Canada rate to its highest level ever, more than 21 percent. The move to this high, unpopular rate prompted the Bank to allow the Bank rate to *float*—that is, to move in accordance with the market rate of short-term government bonds.

One of the main concerns of the Bank of Canada, and of the federal government, seems to be to prevent the value of the Canadian dollar from falling too far below the value of the American dollar. High interest rates, and purchases of Canadian dollars in the foreign exchange market by the Bank of Canada, have been used alternately or in combination to achieve this end.

The Bank has been severely criticized for such actions. It is pointed out by critics that a flexible, perhaps temporarily lower, exchange rate would help to overcome the perennial deficit in the current account by stimulating exports and discouraging imports. High interest rates, say the critics, discourage investment and add to unemployment; they also add to the costs of doing business and therefore contribute to inflation. By attracting foreign capital, high interest rates also add to the large interest payments that already create problems in the current account. Our borrowings in the capital account add to the interest payments in the current account.

The Bank counters that high interest rates are necessary to prevent a massive outflow of capital from this country to the United States and other countries into which Canadians channel their money. Unless we want to resort to foreign currency controls, which are judged to be very difficult to manage, the capital outflow would seriously drain this country of funds for investment. Furthermore, the governor of the Bank of Canada argues, if Canada's exchange rate were allowed to drop freely in response to market pressures, our cost of imports would rise, thus adding to Canada's inflation rate.

A recent study examined the relative cost contribution to inflation of high interest rates and the lower exchange rate that would result from a lowering of our interest rates. The study concluded, on the basis of available data, that the strategy of the Bank of Canada, fighting inflation by maintaining an artificially high exchange rate through high interest rates, is almost exactly counterbalanced by the contribution that such high interest rates make to inflation by raising costs of production. Or, to say it in another way, a lowering of our exchange rate, by reducing the interest rate differential between Canada and the United States, would not increase the inflationary pressures upon us any more than now comes about through the maintenance of high interest rates. In addition, the Bank of Canada's interest rate policy must be more of a contributor to a higher unemployment rate than a lower interest rate policy would be. As N.E. Cameron wryly concludes, in the study referred to above: "A strategy of raising interest rates to protect the dollar must be justified by a belief that we need more recession rather than less."[2]

---

[2]N.E. Cameron, "Interest Rates and Inflation," *Western Economic Review* 1 (July 1982), p. 13.

What, then, is the solution? It is not clear that a further devaluation of the Canadian dollar would be disastrous—and it might in fact be quite beneficial. For a few months in the early 1980s the Canadian dollar dipped below $.80 U.S. without creating panic. As our purchasing power parity theory showed, the long-run value of the Canadian dollar in terms of the U.S. dollar should settle at a ratio equal to the ratios of their purchasing power. Therefore, though there might be a decline of our dollar to below 80 cents U.S. in the short run, (in the absence of higher interest rates), in the long run it should move in a range between $.85 and $.90 U.S., reflecting the fact that costs in the U.S., and hence prices, are considered to be about 15 percent lower than in Canada. To solve our problems in the international sector will not be easy, but the pain of short-run currency devaluations may be better than the long-run pain of increasing deficits and high interest rates.

## CONCLUSIONS

As the international economy moves through the 1980s, the world of Bretton Woods fades more and more into history. The academic debates over fixed versus floating rates that characterized the fifties and sixties have been overtaken by events. At present, it is clear that the dirty float is here to stay for quite a while. Critics of free floating exchange rates argue that such rates have been tried and found wanting. Supporters of such rates counter that they haven't been tried enough, especially recently, to know whether they could do the job.

What Canada has currently is a dirty float, in which our dollar is allowed to move up and down as long as it stays somewhere above $.80 U.S. The Bank of Canada intervenes in the foreign exchange markets to prevent the dollar from falling too drastically. We may not know for some time whether truly flexible rates would solve some of our serious economic problems.

## SUMMARY

1. Despite the inevitable zero balance for all the accounts in our balance of payments, an imbalance or disequilibrium in the balance can be said to exist whenever deficits or surpluses in the current account are not matched by equal surpluses or deficits in the capital account. Such an imbalance will require the use of foreign currency reserves, and under a system of floating exchange rates will be reflected in exchange rate fluctuations.

2. A unique combination of interest rates and nominal national income is required to produce equilibrium in the foreign sector. General equilibrium can be said to exist only when the money market, the circular flow, and the foreign market are all in equilibrium. Under fixed exchange rates, monetary policy will create disequilibrium in the foreign sector which will negate the effectiveness of such policies.

3. The mechanics of exchange-rate determination can be explained by means of supply and demand analysis. In the long run, international exchange rates tend to reflect, at least approximately, changes in the purchasing power parity of various national currencies.

policy combine to bring about a nominal GNP growth rate of, say, 10 percent per year, it clearly makes a great deal of difference whether the rate is 8 percent real growth and 2 percent inflation or 2 percent real growth and 8 percent inflation.

## UNEMPLOYMENT, INFLATION, AND THE KEYNESIAN CROSS

### Keynesian Theory

During the first two postwar decades, when periods of high unemployment alternated with periods of inflation, most economics textbooks featured a theory of unemployment and inflation that was based on simple Keynesian multiplier analysis. For want of a better term, this theory can be called the "crude Keynesian theory."

Exhibit 17.1 contains a Keynesian cross diagram of the familiar kind. Notice, though, that one significant change has been made. A point on the horizontal axis has been labeled "full employment national income." That label replaces the indication of a "target" level of national income that some of the earlier diagrams contained.

To get a theory of unemployment and inflation from this diagram, we can reason as follows: first, suppose that consumption, planned investment, government spending and net exports are just sufficient to put the aggregate demand schedule at the level of $AND_1$. In this position, it intersects the aggregate nominal supply schedule exactly at the "full employment" level of nominal national income. By assumption, when equilibrium nominal national income is at this level, just enough goods will be demanded to keep everyone who wants a job busy. (To put it less casually, just enough goods will be demanded to keep all but 5 to 6 percent of the labor force at work, as measured by official statistics.)

**Exhibit 17.1**

**Inflation and the Keynesian cross**

The crude Keynesian theory of inflation is based on this Keynesian cross diagram and some additional assumptions. When the aggregate demand curve is in position $AND_1$, it is assumed that real GNP will be sufficient to keep everyone employed. If the aggregate demand curve shifts to $AND_2$, it is assumed that the resulting fall in nominal GNP will take the form of reduced real output and increased unemployment. If the aggregate demand curve shifts to $AND_3$, it is assumed that all of the subsequent increase in nominal GNP will take the form of a price increase.

**Contraction of Nominal Demand Causes Unemployment** Next, suppose that, because of an error in policy or some unexpected change in private consumption, planned investment, or net exports, the aggregate demand schedule slips to the level marked AND$_2$. This move creates a deflationary gap. Applying the multiplier theory, one can predict that this downward shift in planned expenditure will be followed by a downward movement of nominal national income. Now, one more crucial assumption is added. The assumption is that in the short run, at least, all or most of the downward movement of nominal national income below the full employment level will take the form of a fall in real income and product, and not much, if any, will take the form of a decline in prices. Because the lower level of real output requires fewer workers to produce it, the economy will experience a period of relatively high unemployment and price stability.

**Expansion of Nominal Demand Causes Inflation** Finally, assume that for one reason or another the aggregate nominal demand schedule shifts upward, reaching the position labeled AND$_3$ in Exhibit 17.1. This high level of planned expenditure produces an inflationary gap. In accordance with the multiplier theory, nominal national income rises. Remember, though, that everyone, or almost everyone, who wants a job now has one, although people not previously in the labor force, such as teenagers and housewives, may be drawn into the labor force by an expanding market. It is not physically possible to squeeze more than a little extra real output from the economy above the full employment level. The rise in nominal national income that the multiplier theory requires can take place only in the form of an increase in the price level. As a result, the inflationary gap brings on a period of lower unemployment and inflation of the general price level.

## Does it Work?

Like the crude quantity theory, the crude Keynesian theory has considerable intuitive appeal if applied in the proper time and place. In particular, the theory provides a fairly plausible reading of the record of inflation and unemployment in Canada in the 1950s and 1960s. Nonetheless, it cannot be judged entirely satisfactory for several reasons.

First, proponents of this theory have always had difficulty explaining why downward movements in nominal national income affect real output so much more strongly than they affect prices, at least in the short run. A number of hypotheses have been advanced by various authors, but none of them has ever been universally accepted.

Second, where inflationary gaps are involved, the crude Keynesian theory tells us at most how much prices will rise but not how fast. Because inflation is by nature a matter of speed of change in the price level, the theory is thus seriously incomplete.

Finally, the crude Keynesian theory by itself is unable to explain how high (and even rising) unemployment can occur simultaneously with high (and even rising) rates of inflation. For this reason, the theory has lost some of its intuitive appeal as an explanation of unemployment and inflation in the 1980s, though when supplemented by other analytical tools it is still a useful basis for understanding some of our current problems.

## MODIFYING THE MODEL

In the model used for the multiplier analysis of Chapters 9 and 10, no attempt was made to separate money or nominal effects from real effects, or to identify price and employment changes accompanying changes in aggregate nominal demand. To begin a modification of this model, assume that nominal national income is initially in equilibrium at $1,600, as depicted by the $AND_1$ curve in Exhibit 17.2a. To separate the real from the money components of this nominal income, assume that it consists of 800 physical units of goods and services, selling at an average price of $2. This is illustrated at Point A in Exhibit 17.2b, which matches a real output level of 800, measured along the horizontal scale, with a price level of $2, measured on the vertical scale. Point A is also crossed by an **aggregate real demand curve** ($ARD_1$), which gives the real purchasing power of $1,600 at different price levels. Along $ARD_1$, about 727 units could be purchased at an average price of $2.20 (total purchasing power equals $1,600), or 910 units could be purchased at a price of about $1.76. Because we assume initially that the price level is $2, it follows that, with purchasing power of $1,600, 800 units would be purchased.

> **Aggregate real demand curve** A curve showing the amount of real output purchased at any given price level for a given aggregate nominal demand.

We will assume further that employment is linked to real output—not to nominal income, as was assumed in previous models—and that, at a real output level of 800 units, 80 percent of the available labor force is employed (that is, the unemployment rate is 20 percent). In an effort to reduce this high unemployment rate, government authorities might reason as follows: if real output of 800 units (with a value of $1,600) provides employment for 80 percent of the labor force, an output of 900 units, one-eighth higher than the current output level, should provide jobs for another 10 percent of the labor force and reduce unemployment to 10 percent (employment would rise by one-eighth, from 80 percent to 90 percent). If the price level remained at $2, the nominal income level would have to rise from $1,600 to $1,800 (= 900 units × $2) to accomplish this. If, say, the effective multiplier is 2 (after allowing for crowding out effects), increased government expenditures of $100 would be enough to increase equilibrium income to $1,800 and output to 900 units. The expenditure increase is illustrated by $AND_2$ in Exhibit 17.2a. Autonomous expenditures have increased by $100 and nominal national income rises to $Y_2$, or $1,800. The $AND_2$ curve is translated into an aggregate real demand curve in Exhibit 17.2b, represented by $ARD_2$. Since the price level remains at $2, real output increases from Point A to Point B in Exhibit 17.2b (from 800 to 900 units). It can now be seen that Points A and B represent two points along an **aggregate real supply curve**. This is simply a curve showing the relationship between aggregate real supply and the price level.

> **Aggregate real supply curve** A curve showing how much real output is produced at different price levels.

The government will undoubtedly be very pleased with its fiscal initiative. Real output has increased by the anticipated amount and the unemployment rate has declined to 10 percent. Encouraged by these results, the government might decide to increase government spending by another $100, hoping thereby to drive nominal income up to $2,000 and real output up to 1,000 units, which should be sufficient to provide jobs for the 10 percent of the labor force that is still unemployed. However, as new spending is undertaken, the following might happen: due to the lower

**Exhibit 17.2**

**Moving from the Keynesian cross to aggregate real demand and supply**

The Keynesian mode, which depicted equilibrium income at the point where nominal aggerate demand "crossed" the nominal aggregate supply line is reproduced in part a of this exhibit. It is then transformed into real aggregate demand and supply functions in part b, by separating nominal values into real output along the horizontal axis and prices on the vertical axis. The aggregate real demand curve shows the amount of real output purchased at any given price level for a given aggregate nominal demand. The aggregate real supply curve describes one possible real output scenario, as government fiscal policy is used in an attempt to increase real output and employment to the full employment level at 1,000 units.

**(a)**

Nominal national income (Y)

**(b)**

Real ouput (Q)

level unemployment, both employees and employers decide that now is the time to increase their incomes. Workers demand considerably higher wages, and employers increase their profit margins. Since wage costs and profit margins are both rising, prices will have to be increased. Assume that aggregate spending rises from $1,800 to $2,000, but prices rise on average from $2 to $2.20. In Exhibit 17.2a, the increased nominal spending is represented by $AND_3$ and is translated into real terms in Exhibit 17.2b by $ARD_3$. The b part of the Exhibit shows that at a price level of $2.20 a purchasing power of $2,000 is consistent with a real output level of only 909 units, not 1,000 units as the government had planned. This is indicated at Point C, and it means that output will move from Point B to Point C along the aggregate real supply curve. The increased spending has been divided between a small increase in real output and a substantial increase in prices. If real output rises only to 909 units only about 91 percent of the labor force will be employed, and the unemployment rate will have fallen only to about 9 percent. Because of the behavior of the aggregate real supply curve, government planners have been stymied in their attempts to reduce the unemployment rate significantly; instead, they have been greeted by a substantial dose of inflation!

Should the government increase its spending even more and approach more closely to the real output target of 1,000 units (here assumed to be the full employment output level, and depicted as $Q_f$ in Exhibit 17.2b), it may find that the ARS curve rises more steeply; each spending increase is accompanied by a small decline in unemployment but ever larger increases in prices. Should the full employment output level actually be reached, further increases would simply raise prices, a situation represented by the vertical range of the ARS curve above Point D.

## The Aggregate Real Supply Curve

The analysis of this book has focused almost entirely on aggregate demand, but to understand some of our current problems more attention must be given to aggregate supply, expressed here in real terms. Exhibit 17.2b depicts a real supply curve that is horizontal at low levels of output representing high levels of unemployment, begins to slope upward as output increases and full employment is approached, and becomes vertical at the full employment level.

In the real world, the aggregate real supply curve may slope upwards over most of its length, as illustrated by $ARS_1$ in Exhibit 17.3. To understand why, assume once again that the economy is in equilibrium at a real output level considerably below full employment. If aggregate demand increases, business firms may find that the increased demand enables them to make higher profits by charging higher prices. The profit per unit of a good equals the price of that good minus the cost per unit. As demand increases, costs may remain more or less fixed for awhile. Wages, which account for about 75 percent of costs on average, may have been set through long-term union contracts and if so will not rise very quickly. The business firm may have long-term price contracts on the purchase of raw materials, payments of rent, and so on. By raising its selling price, the firm can quickly increase its profits. The chance to increase profits will also

**Exhibit 17.3**

**A shift of the aggregate real supply curve**
As input prices (e.g. wages) rise, or as productivity of the
inputs falls, unit costs of production rise and the ARS
curve shifts upward from ARS$_1$ to ARS$_2$. The opposite
shift occurs when input prices fall and productivity rises.

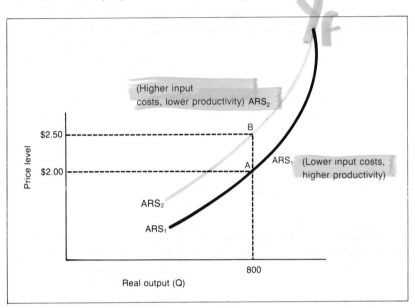

induce it to expand output. Therefore, production and prices rise together
until the economy reaches full employment and the ARS$_1$ curve becomes
vertical.

## Shifts of the Aggregate Real Supply Curve

The slope of the aggregate real supply curve reflects the possibility that
firms will be encouraged to produce more at higher prices through the lure
of higher profits. However, the curve may not stand still. The basic input
costs, which were initially assumed to be more or less fixed, become less
fixed as production increases and prices start to rise. New labor contracts
will be negotiated at higher rates, as will raw material and other contracts.
This increases the unit cost of output and depresses profit margins. At any
given level of real output, higher prices will now be necessary to maintain
previous profit margins. In Exhibit 17.3, the ARS curve shifts upward from
A to B at 800 units. The new ARS curve, ARS$_2$, also becomes vertical at
the full employment level. Note that it is a rise in money wage rates, or in
the price of other inputs, that shifts the ARS curve upward. A fall in input
prices will shift it downwards. Such shifts can also occur through changes
in productivity of factors of production. Decreased productivity increases
costs and shifts the ARS curve upward, while increased productivity reduces
unit costs and shifts the ARS curve downward.

## APPLICATIONS OF AGGREGATE REAL SUPPLY AND DEMAND

The aggregate real supply and demand curves introduced in this chapter make it possible for us to analyze a variety of policy issues. In the examples that follow, we will see the economy in recession and expansion, and we will compare a variety of causes of increases and decreases in the price level. These conditions are brought about by shifts in the aggregate real demand curve, the aggregate real supply curve, or both.

### The Economy in Recession

In the following paragraphs we will look at a classic recession. First, however, a point must be made about the terminology used for this discussion. At several places in this chapter and the next we will mention an "initial," "original," or "equilibrium" level of real output and unemployment. This refers to the belief of some economists that at any given time an economy will have what might be called a minimum level of unemployment. That is, given worker attitudes, the level of social assistance, minimum wage-support, and other social and economic factors, it might prove impossible to lower the unemployment rate below that level *without* creating considerable inflationary pressure. In other words, the equilibrium rate is not considered fixed, but is a minimum rate below which the economy presumably cannot go without encountering rising prices. Given changes in underlying conditions this rate may itself change. The Economic Council of Canada, which periodically "determines" such a rate, claims that it rose from less than 4 percent in the late 1960s to above 8 percent in the late 1970s (see Chapter 7 and more recent E.C.C. reports). Because there is considerable disagreement about the existence, location, and significance of such a rate, it is not highlighted in our analysis. It is generally sufficient to say that, at a point approaching full employment, attempts to increase real output and decrease unemployment will be subject to increasing upward pressure on prices.

*The Onset of Recession* A classic recession is brought about by a drop in aggregate demand. Exhibit 17.4 illustrates the process. The story begins with the economy in equilibrium at "an equilibrum" level of real output, here assumed to be 1,600 units, close to a full employment output of 2,000 units. The price level is initially assumed to stand at a level of $1.50. Aggregate nominal demand is $2,400, putting the economy at Point $E_1$, the intersection of the aggregate real supply curve $ARS_1$ with the aggregate real demand curve $ARD_1$.

Beginning from this situation, suppose that aggregate nominal demand falls to $1,200, half its former level. This could be caused by contractionary monetary or fiscal policy, by a decrease in planned investment and consumption expenditures, or by some combination of the two. In terms of the diagram, the effect of the collapse of aggregate nominal demand is to shift the aggregate real demand curve leftward to the new position, $ARD_2$. This shift sets off a familiar sequence of events. Sales lag behind production, causing unplanned inventory investment. Firms react by cutting output and prices in a combination indicated by the slope of the aggregate real supply curve. As the recession deepens, the economy moves downward toward the new short-run equilibrium, $E_2$. In this equilibrium, both real output and the price level are lower than they initially were, and unemployment is higher.

*Two Paths to Recovery* From $E_2$ there are two pathways that the economy might take to return to the previous level of real output. One path depends on a rebound of aggregate demand to its prerecession level. The recovery of aggregate demand might take place spontaneously if the causes of the initial collapse in planned expenditure were temporary. Alternatively, active monetary or fiscal policy might be required to restore aggregate nominal demand to its former level. In either case the aggregate real demand curve would shift back to its original position, $ARD_1$. The path of recovery would be back up along aggregate real supply curve $ARS_1$.

But even if aggregate nominal demand were to stay permanently at the $1,200 level, the economy might not remain at Point $E_2$. Firms that at first had reacted to slack demand largely by cutting back output would begin to reevaluate their policy as the slump continued. Prices of basic commodities might fall in the recession, reducing the costs of manufacturing firms and giving them leeway to cut prices more. The high rate of unemployment brought on by the recession could hold down labor costs, although, as will be shown in Chapter 18, such adjustments might occur very slowly. As firms realized that prices were falling throughout the economy, they would gradually revise their expectations. The aggregate real supply curve would begin to shift down. As it did so, the economy would slowly work its way down along aggregate real demand curve $ARD_2$ toward a new long-run equilibrium, at $E_3$. There, real output would regain its previous level of 1,600 units, with aggregate nominal demand at $1,200 and the price level at $.75. The aggregate real supply curve would come to rest at $ARS_2$ once expectations had completely adjusted to the new reality.

---

**Exhibit 17.4**

**The economy in recession**
The recession illustrated in this exhibit begins when aggregate nominal demand drops from $2,400 to $1,200, shifting the aggregate real demand curve from $ARD_1$ to $ARD_2$. In the short run, the economy moves along the supply curve SR-$ARS_1$, from $E_1$ to $E_2$, with both real output and the price level falling. What happens next depends on the behaviour of demand. If nominal demand remains at $1,200, firms and households gradually adjust to the lower price level, and the economy moves back toward the higher level of output at $E_3$. A more likely path out of the recession results from a recovery of aggregate nominal demand, in which case the economy moves back to $E_1$.

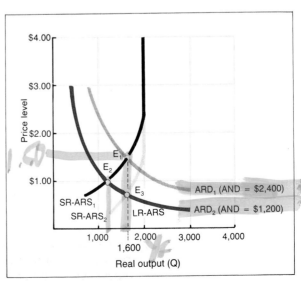

## Demand-Pull Inflation

**Demand-pull inflation**
Inflation caused by an expansion of aggregate nominal demand relative to the productive capacity of the economy.

The opposite of recession is **demand-pull inflation** — an increase in the price level caused by expansion of aggregate nominal demand relative to the productive capacity of the economy. Exhibit 17.5 provides a graphical illustration of demand-pull inflation.

The scenario begins with the economy in equilibrium at Point $E_1$. The price level stands at $1.00, and real output is at a level of 1,600 units. Suppose that a rapid expansion of the money supply lifts the level of aggregate nominal demand from $1,600 to $3,200. This is shown as a shift in the aggregate real demand curve from $ARD_1$ to $ARD_2$.

Manufacturers, getting a flood of new orders and sensing the opportunity to make more profit, will tend to put their work forces on overtime, use standby capacity, and possibly hire more labor. Prices will be raised and real output will rise. The economy will move up and to the right along $ARS_1$. Following this path, the economy will reach a new short-run equilibrium at $E_2$. As Exhibit 17.5 is drawn, the price level will have increased from $1 to $1.60 and real output from 1,600 to 2,000 units.

*Long-Run Adjustment* It is not possible, however, for the economy to remain permanently at $E_2$. In order to raise real output above its previous level, firms have had to run overtime, use standby capacity, and draw extra workers into the labor force. They have done so because each firm saw, or thought it saw, a chance to get some extra profit from the demand surge. As soon as price increases begin to be reflected in costs, firms will begin to revise their expectations. Expected increases in the prices of inputs that firms buy will cause the short-run aggregate real supply curve to shift upward. Workers too will come to expect a higher cost of living and will be unwilling to supply the same quantity of labor services without a matching rise in nominal wages. Assuming no further increase in aggregate nominal demand, the economy will move up and to the left along aggregate real demand curve $ARD_2$ as the aggregate real supply curve shifts upward. By the time the aggregate real supply curve reaches the position $ARS_2$, real output will have returned to its previous level. If everyone now expects the price level to remain at $2, a new long-run equilibrium is possible at $E_3$, where all the original doubling of aggregate nominal demand has finally been converted into a doubling of the price level.

In sum, the demand-pull inflation scenario is divided into two phases. During the first phase, the expected level of prices and costs lags behind the increase in demand, permitting real output to rise above its previous level. During the second phase, expectations catch up with the increase in demand; more and more of the increase in nominal GNP is converted into inflationary price icreases, until real output returns to or near to its original level. In the end, only prices have changed.

## The Inverse Relationship between Inflation and Unemployment

When the price level changes because of a change in demand, the unemployment level will tend to move in a direction opposite to the price change. The price level and real output move together, but as real output

**Exhibit 17.5**
**Demand-pull inflation**
If aggregate demand increases when the economy is already producing at near-full employment, the result is demand-pull inflation. In the short run, prices do not adjust in full proportion to the increase in demand, so that real output temporarily rises above its previous level. Before long, however, expectations begin to adjust to the inflation that is taking place, and the aggregate real supply curve begins to shift upward. If aggregate nominal demand stabilizes at $3,200, in this example, a new long-run equilibrium will be possible at $E_3$. There, real output will have returned to its previous level, and the price level will have doubled.

increases, unemployment will normally decline. When demand declines, as illustrated in Exhibit 17.4, prices and real output both decline as the economy moves from $E_1$ to $E_2$. Unemployment will then increase. When there is demand-pull inflation, as illustrated in Exhibit 17.5, prices and real output both increase, as the economy moves from $E_1$ to $E_2$ in that diagram. This should cause unemployment to decline.

The negative or inverse relationship between price changes and unemployment was explored by A.W.H. Phillips, after whom a famous curve in economics has been named.

## THE PHILLIPS CURVE

### Early Empirical Work

Economists place a strong emphasis on empirical work—work based on real-world data—as well as on abstract theorizing. Sometimes a single empirical study can suggest a whole new direction for a theory to take. A well-known research paper by A.W.H. Phillips, outlined in the following case study, had such an impact.

**Case 17.1**
**A.W.H. Phillips and the Phillips Curve**

In 1958, A.W.H. Phillips published the results of some attempts he had made to test the simple hypothesis that wage rates tend to rise faster when unemployment is low than when it is high. The data he had available covered a very long period in the economic history of Great Britain, stretching from 1861 to 1957. The statistical evidence he assembled seemed to support the idea that the rate of change in money wages can be explained by the level of unemployment.

Phillips presented his results in a series of charts, one of which is reproduced here as Exhibit 17.6. This diagram contains a curve that represents the average relationship between unemployment and the rate of change of wages during the period 1861 to 1913. The points scattered near the curve show wage and unemployment data for the years 1948 to 1957. The fit of the modern years in Phillips's study to the curve calculated on much earlier data is remarkably close.

Source: A.W.H. Phillips, "The Relationship between Unemployent and the Rate of Change of Money Wage Rates in the United Kingdom, 1861–1957," *Economica* New Series 25 (November 1958), pp. 283-299.

> **Phillips curve** A curve showing the relationship between the rate of inflation and the level of unemployment. Inflation, usually placed on the vertical axis of such a figure, can be measured in terms of either the rate of change in wages or the rate of change in a price index.

Since the publication of Phillips's article, curves like the one in Exhibit 17.6 have come to be called **Phillips curves**. In recent years, the term *Phillips curve* has been broadened to include similar curves drawn on diagrams where the vertical axis measures the rate of change of prices (that is, the rate of inflation) instead of the rate of change of wages. Recent data for Canada is presented in Exhibits 17.8 and 17.9.

## Interpreting the Phillips Curve

The intuitively appealing concept of the Phillips curve is open to serious misinterpretation when applied to economic policy. One tempting but misleading interpretation is to regard the curve as a menu of alternatives from which policy makers can choose a preferred compromise between the evils of inflation and unemployment.

**The Phillips Curve as a Menu** Suppose, for example, that the minister of finance was presented with data that suggested the Phillips curve shown in Exhibit 17.7. It can easily be imagined that if the administration were an NDP one, strongly influenced by union labor or sympathetic to the plight of the unemployed, it might pursue expansionary policies and aim for a point high up and to the left, such as the point marked D in the figure. In contrast, a Conservative or Liberal cabinet, dominated by conservative businesspeople and bankers, might aim for a point such as R, near the intersection of the Phillips curve and the horizontal axis.

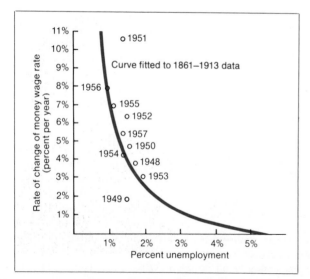

**Exhibit 17.6**

**One of A. W. H. Phillips's original Phillips curves for the British economy**

In 1958, A. W. H. Phillips published an influential paper that looked at the relationship between unemployment and the rate of change in wages over a long period in Great Britain. He found that data from the period 1948 to 1957 fit rather closely a curve based on data from the period 1861 to 1913, as shown here. Curves like this have since come to be called *Phillips curves*.

Source: A. W. H. Phillips, "The Relationship between Unemployment and the Rate of Change of Money Wage Rates in the United Kingdom, 1861–1957." *Economica* New series 25 (November 1958), pp. 283–299. Reprinted by permission.

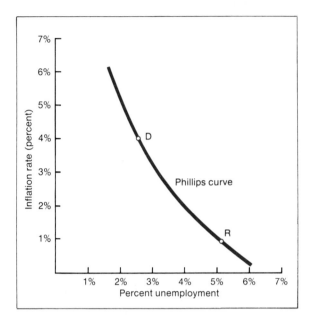

**Exhibit 17.7**
**The Phillips curve as a policy menu**
The Phillips curve is sometimes misleadingly interpreted as a policy menu offering a fixed trade-off between inflation and unemployment. If the curve for the Canadian economy had the shape shown here, it could be imagined that New Democrats would want to choose a point like D, where low unemployment would be "bought" at the price of high inflation, while Liberals or Conservatives might prefer a point like R. Unfortunately for this interpretation, the Phillips curve is not stable. Policies designed to produce movements along it can cause it to shift to a new position.

**Shifts in the Phillips Curve** The trouble with interpreting the Phillips curve as a policy menu is that it may not stand still while the diners enjoy their meal. As the 1960s progressed, economists in Canada began to notice that inflation-unemployment points for recent years did not fit the Phillips curves they had plotted using data from the 1950s. It became common to speak of an upward drift in the Phillips curve. The menu seemed to be getting less appetizing as time went by. If the upward drift had been entirely spontaneous, policy makers could simply have been told to make the best of disappointing circumstances and still choose the point they liked best

A. W. H. Phillips was an economist whose reputation was based largely on a single paper published on the right topic at the right time. In the late 1950s, the relationship between inflation and unemployment ranked as the major unsolved problem of macroeconomic theory. The curves that Phillips drew in his famous article in *Economica* suggested a simple, stable relationship between inflation and unemployment. Phillips's paper offered little by way of a theoretical explanation of the relationship, but his curves became the peg on which all future discussion of the problem was hung. Almost immediately, every article on inflation and unemployment became a discussion of what was the shape of the Phillips curve, what point on the Phillips curve was best as a policy target, how the Phillips curve could be shifted, and so on. Today, the term is so well established that Phillips's name enjoys a sort of immortality even though his own interpretation of the famous curve has fallen into disrepute.

Phillips was born in New Zealand, but he made London his base for most of his academic career. He taught at the London School of Economics during the 1950s and 1960s until moving to the Australian National University in 1967. Phillips was originally trained in electrical engineering, and this training seems to have influenced his approach to economic problems, which has been characterized as "scientistic." In the mid-1950s he was suggesting the use of an "electric analog machine or simulator" as an aid to the study of economic dynamics. This idea perhaps foreshadowed the intensive use of electronic computers in contemporary economic research.

**A. W. H. Phillips (1914–1975)**

from the new, higher Phillips curve. However, to the extent that the shifts in the Phillips curve have been caused by the particular policies chosen to move the economy along a supposedly fixed curve, the idea of the Phillips curve as a policy menu needs to be reevaluated altogether.

Turning from the realm of theory to the real world, one can find some similarities between the hypothetical Phillips curve and recent experience with inflation and unemployment in Canada, but there are also significant differences.

### Case 17.2
### The Phillips Curve in the 1960s

In 1958–61 the Canadian economy was in a very depressed state. There was virtually no growth in real GNP and unemployment averaged 7 percent. Despite this, the government and the Bank of Canada followed restrictive policies. Interest rates were kept high, and the small deficit that the government incurred was due not to expansionary fiscal measures but to lower tax revenues resulting from the recession. In the last few years of the Diefenbaker government, from mid-1961 until the defeat of the government in 1963, the government reversed some of its policies, and the Bank of Canada, under a new governor, Louis Rasminsky, began to follow a more expansionary policy. The expansion that began in 1961 was reinforced during the Pearson era (1963–68) and continued almost unabated until the end of 1969. This has been called the longest period of expansion in Canadian peacetime history. Exhibit 17.8 shows the unemployment-inflation record for the economy up to the end of the Pearson era.

Expansionary policy at first produced substantial gains in employment with little inflation penalty. However, between 1962 and 1966, with the exception of 1964, each successive reduction in unemployent was accompanied by a bigger jump in prices. In 1967, unemployment began to increase, and in 1968 there was a further increase in unemployment, accompanied by a further increase in prices. A new phenomenon, inflationary recession, or *stagflation*, began to occur.

*Limitations of the Phillips curve*  The experience of the last twenty years, represented in the next chapter in Exhibit 18.6, tells us that sometimes inflation and unemployment have been inversely related, in keeping with the Phillips curve, but at other times they clearly have not been. Our theory needs to be modified to accommodate the seemingly ambiguous reality. Demand-pull inflation by itself is not an adequate theory of inflation. A demand curve moving up a stable, positively sloping supply curve will increase real output, prices, and reduce unemployment. But unemployment has not always been reduced during periods of rising prices. Similarly, a demand curve moving down a stable real aggregate supply curve should produce lower prices, lower real output, and higher unemployment. This has often happened, but again there are exceptions, as in the years 1954 to 1955. What is undoubtedly happening is that the supply curve is not necessarily stable. Shifts in the supply curve can produce results not envisioned in the scheme of things represented by the Phillips curve. This takes us to a second type of inflation known as cost-push inflation.

**Exhibit 17.8**
**The Phillips curve in the 1960s**
During the 1960s, the economy expanded rapidly.
Growing demand accompanied by inflation reduced
unemployment and kept it low for several years in a row.
At the end of the 1960s, however, both unemployment
and inflation began to rise—the economy seemed to be
departing from the traditional Phillips curve.

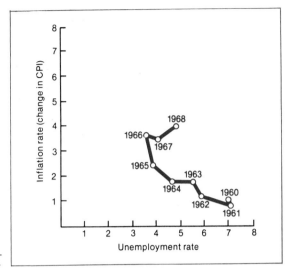

Source: Department of Finance, *Economic Review*, April 1980, pp. 202, 216.

## Cost-Push Inflation

Increases in aggregate nominal demand relative to the productive capacity
of the economy are a sure source of inflation, but they are by no means the
only source. Inflation can also occur when the aggregate real supply curve
shifts while the aggregate real demand curve remains stationary. Because
shifts in the aggregate real supply curve are associated with changes in the
level of costs, this kind of inflation has come to be known as **cost-push
inflation.** As we will see, cost-push inflation comes in two variants,
depending on the nature of the shift in the aggregate real supply curve.

> **Cost-push inflation** Inflation
> produced by an upward or
> leftward shift in the aggregate
> real supply curve relative to the
> aggregate real demand curve.

*Increases in Input Costs as a Cause of Inflation*  The first variant of cost-
push inflation takes place when, for example, labor costs or the costs of
other inputs are increased. This shifts the aggregate real supply curve
upward while the level of aggregate nominal demand is unchanged or
increases less rapidly. This can happen when firms and households have
become accustomed to past inflation and expect inflation to continue in
the future.

Exhibit 17.9 shows how the expectation of inflation can actually cause
inflation. This time the scenario begins at $E_3$, which is the end point of the
episode of demand-pull inflation shown in Exhibit 17.5. Firms and households have just lived through a doubling of prices, from a level of $1 at $E_1$ to
a level of $2 at $E_2$. During the demand-pull episode, inflation caught people
at least partially unaware, but now the price level has reached $2 and peo-
ple expect it to keep going right on up to $3. They will start to demand
higher wages.

Graphically, the increase in input costs is represented by an upward
shift in the aggregate real supply curve, from $ARS_2$ to $ARS_3$. What happens
next depends on the government's management of aggregate nominal
demand. We will consider two alternatives.

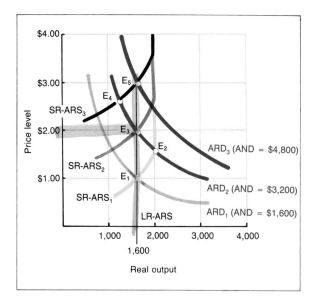

**Exhibit 17.9**
**Cost-push inflation**
Once inflation becomes an established pattern, input costs may rise, pushing the aggregate real supply curve upward, even after aggregate demand, which initially caused the inflation, has stablized. In this exhibit, we assume that demand has temporarily stablized at $ARD_2$ after a jump from $ARD_1$ but that people expect the price level to keep right on rising from $2.00 to $3.00. They begin to demand higher wages. That pushes the aggregate real supply curve up to $ARS_3$. In the short run, real output falls and prices rise as the economy moves up along $ARD_2$ to $E_4$. By raising aggregate nominal demand to $4,800 ($ARD_3$), policy makers could accommodate the inflationary expectations; real output would recover, but at the expense of still more inflation. Alternatively, policy makers could hold the line at $ARD_2$, and eventually price expectations might shift back downward. The path back to the previous level of real output, $E_3$, might be a slow and painful one, however, after considerable unemployment has been created.

First, suppose that aggregate nominal demand is held fixed at $3,200, so that the aggregate real demand curve remains stationary at $ARD_2$. As firms expect the prices of inputs they buy to rise, they will try to protect themselves by passing the cost increases on to their customers, at least in part. Because workers expect the cost of living to rise, firms will find it hard to hire them without raising nominal wage rates. This will put further upward pressure on costs and prices. But with aggregate nominal demand fixed, every increase in prices means that less real output can be sold. As unsold inventories accumulate, production will be cut back. The economy will move up and to the left along $ARD_2$ toward its intersection with $ARS_3$, at $E_4$. There is both growing inflation and growing unemployment.

$E_4$ may be only a temporary equilibrium, however. Slowly, excess plant capacity and high levels of unemployment will put downward pressure on wages and prices, and the economy will move back down along $ARD_2$ toward $E_3$, the previous level of real output.

Clearly, the sequence of events just described is a painful one. The economy initially experienced an **inflationary recession**—(or what is often called an inflationary stagnation or "stagflation") a worst-case episode in which prices and unemployment went up while real output went down. To avoid the recessionary part of the inflationary recession, the government can instead increase aggregate nominal demand to $4,800, shifting the aggregate real demand curve up to the position $ARD_3$. As the aggregate real demand curve moves up, the economy will move up from $E_3$ to $E_5$. The drop in real output will be avoided — but only at the cost of even more inflation.

In short, it appears that cost-push inflation caused by expected increases in the price level puts policy makers in a cruel dilemma. Either they clamp down on aggregate nominal demand, putting the economy through a painful inflationary recession, or they accommodate inflationary expectations

**Inflationary recession (or stagflation)** An episode characterized by simultaneous high (or rising) inflation, low (or falling) real output, and high (or rising) unemployment.

with matching increases in nominal demand, avoiding recession only at the risk of setting off an inflationary spiral. Much of the history of economic policy in the 1970s and 1980s has been a search for an escape from this dilemma. We will return to this issue in some detail in Chapters 18 and 19.

*Supply Shocks as a Source of Inflation*  In Exhibit 17.9, cost-push inflation was set off by an increase in input costs that shifted the aggregate real supply curve upward. The effects of the supply curve shift on real output and the price level in turn depended on whether fiscal and monetary authorities chose to accommodate or resist the inflationary pressure. A variation on this cost-push inflation scenario occurs when a supply shock shifts the aggregate real supply curve upward.

As before, the starting point is $E_1$, with a price level of $1.00, aggregate nominal demand of $1,600, and aggregate real output at 1,600 units. Beginning from this point, some catastrophe occurs; for example, foreign oil prices suddenly rise sharply, as happened with the formation of the OPEC oil cartel in 1973. Manufacturers in eastern Canada, depending on foreign oil for their industry, find their input costs rising dramatically. The ARS curve rises, even without prior inflationary expectations created by demand-pull inflation. A dilemma similar to the previous one ensues. Prices and unemployment once again rise together, in defiance of the Phillips curve discussed earlier. Because this kind of a shift in the ARS curve does not occur in response to inflationary expectations, a reversal of such expectations may not end the inflationary spiral.

## When Does an Inflationary Recession End?

We have just described several situations in which demand-pull and cost-push forces can combine to cause both higher prices and higher unemployment. The tools of aggregate supply and demand enable us to understand the basic nature of our recent stagflation dilemma. But the theory developed so far does not help us to anticipate the route that the economy may continue to take. Will prices and unemployment continue to rise? For how long? We need to have a more dynamic understanding of the inflationary process to deal with such questions. We also require a better understanding of the internal mechanisms that cause prices and input costs to behave in certain ways, and we need a few more tools of analysis to understand the kind of "spiral" depicted in Exhibit 18.6. This is the purpose of Chapter 18.

## CONCLUSIONS

Fitting together the pieces of the unemployment–inflation puzzle is perhaps the most important single job for economists today. The problem of inflationary recession or "stagflation" has been with us in acute form for about a decade—a seemingly long period of time for the typical student but not a very long time for many practicing economists. They look upon it as a very recent "disease" whose symptoms are fairly well understood (like cancer) but whose cure is still elusive.

Aggregate real supply and demand analysis, as developed in this chapter, has proved a powerful tool for exploring problems in stabilization policy. It helps us to understand concepts like demand-pull and cost-push inflation, and to explain the reality that lies behind both the Phillips curve and departures from it.

Other things being equal, an increase in aggregate nominal demand tends to draw real output above its previous level and to pull up the price index. The result is demand-pull inflation. Similarly, other things being equal, a decrease in aggregate nominal demand tends to depress real output and to lower the price level. The result is a recession or depression. For a given level of aggregate nominal demand, an upward or leftward shift in the aggregate real supply curve will cause the price level to rise and real output to fall. The result is an inflationary recession. In the case of an upward supply curve shift caused solely by an increase in the expected price level, the reduction in real output will be temporary. In the case of a leftward shift caused by a supply shock, the reduction in real output may persist indefinitely.

In summary, shifts in aggregate real supply curves can be viewed as constraints on the ability of monetary and fiscal authorities to achieve the goals of full employment, price stability, and economic growth. Their control over aggregate nominal demand allows them, in effect, to select freely from a menu provided by the short- and long-run aggregate real supply curves. But unless they use tools other than those of monetary and fiscal policy, they cannot deviate from this menu.

In developing these conclusions, we have used aggregate real supply and demand analysis to help us take a giant step forward in understanding the macroeconomy. For those who want a more complete perspective, however, there are some important questions that aggregate real supply and demand analysis alone does not adequately address. One set of questions concerns the linkages between changes in the levels of prices and real output and the levels of employment and unemployment. We have not looked closely at the foundations on which employment and unemployment behavior rest. Chapter 18 will go beyond what we have seen so far to explore an entire branch of macroeconomics devoted to employment and unemployment.

A second set of questions concerns the short-run dynamics of inflation, unemployment, and real output. Aggregate supply and demand analysis is based on the comparison of equilibrium levels of prices and real output before and after once-and-for-all policy changes. It is not specifically equipped, however, to analyze the time paths of prices, real output, and employment as the economy moves from one equilibrium to another, especially under conditions where policies are changed and changed again before the economy reaches a new long-run equilibrium. To fill this gap, Chapter 18 supplements the aggregate real supply and demand approach with an additional set of analytical tools that focus more directly on inflationary dynamics.

## SUMMARY

1. The aggregate real demand curve shows the relationship between the real purchasing power represented by a given aggregate nominal de-

mand (horizontal axis) and the price level (vertical axis). By definition, aggregate real demand times the price level equals aggregate nominal demand. As the economy moves along the aggregate nominal demand curve, the government is assumed to take any policy actions necessary to keep aggregate nominal demand at a constant target level. Changes in the level of aggregate nominal demand result in shifts in the aggregate real demand curve.

2. Aggregate real supply is the level of real output that firms choose to produce at a given price level. Aggregate real supply curves relate real output to the price level. At full employment the aggregate real supply curve is vertical.

3. Before full employment is reached, prices adjust to changes in aggregate demand. Part of any increase in nominal GNP takes the form of a change in real output, and part takes the form of a change in the price level. The result is an upward-sloping short-run aggregate real supply curve.

4. The aggregate real supply curve is subject to both vertical and horizontal shifts. A change in input costs, responding to changes in the price level, results in a vertical shift of the short-run aggregate real supply curve. Adverse supply shocks, such as oil price increases or crop failures, shift real supply curves to the left. Economic growth shifts supply curves to the right.

5. In the short run, a decrease in aggregate nominal demand moves the economy down and to the left along its aggregate real supply curve. The result is a recession. Similarly, an increase in aggregate nominal demand moves the economy up and to the right along the supply curve, causing demand-pull inflation. If no further changes take place in the level of aggregate nominal demand following a recession or an episode of demand-pull inflation, expectations may eventually adjust to the new situation, producing a shift in the aggregate real supply curve. The result will be a new equilibrium, in which real output returns to its previous level and the price level changes in proportion to the initial change in aggregate nominal demand.

6. Cost-push inflation occurs when the aggregate real supply curve shifts up or to the left. An upward shift can be caused by the momentum of inflationary expectations following an episode of demand-pull inflation. A leftward shift can be caused by a supply shock. If aggregate nominal demand remains fixed while the supply curve shifts up or to the left, the immediate result is an inflationary recession, in which real output falls, unemployment increases, and the price level rises, all at the same time.

7. The existence of cost-push inflation tends to destroy the inverse relationship between unemployment and inflation that was described by A.W.H. Phillips.

## DISCUSSION QUESTIONS

1. Tax cuts are an established technique for stimulating aggregate nominal demand. Some tax cuts may also stimulate aggregate real supply by providing greater incentives to work and invest. Using aggregate real supply and demand

curves, compare the effects of the following:
   a. A one-time tax rebate with no significant incentive effects.
   b. A permanent cut in income tax rates that provides an immediate incentive to work harder and produce more.
   Assume that the effects of the two on aggregate demand are identical.
2. Using the aggregate real demand and supply curves developed in this chapter indicate what would happen to real output, prices, and unemployment under the following circumstances:
   a. An increase in productivity due to a more skilled labor force.
   b. An increase in net exports.
   c. A decrease in the money supply.
   d. Increased government expenditures accompanied by sharp increases in the general wage level.
3. Some people maintain that unemployment is a painful human tragedy while inflation is just a matter of dollars chasing dollars. What sort of choice would such a person make if faced with a Phillips curve "menu" (assuming, for the sake of discussion, that the menu were a stable one)? Do you think that inflation, like unemployment, also affects people? If inflation is not "about people" but only "about dollars," why is it studied in an economics course?
4. Assume that in a country where everything else is fine, there is suddenly an outbreak of hoof and mouth disease that sharply decreases the supply of beef cattle. Would the resulting rise in the price of beef be true cost-push inflation? Trace this kind of inflation through the marketing chain for beef. At what points would it look different from demand-pull inflation? At what points would it be hard to tell the difference?
5. Assume that aggregate nominal demand has been growing for several years while real output has remained steady at its natural level. The result of these events has been steady inflation. If the government wants to stop inflation by suddenly stopping the growth of aggregate nominal demand, should it:
   a. Go quietly about the necessary fiscal and monetary policy moves with as little fanfare as possible?
   b. Explain and publicize its program as much as possible?
   How would the effects of the two alternatives differ? Why might one be better than the other in terms of the major goals of stabilization policy?

# THE DYNAMICS OF INFLATION AND UNEMPLOYMENT

---

**WHAT YOU WILL LEARN IN THIS CHAPTER**

*This chapter focuses on the determinants of the inflation rate—how fast the price level moves from one level to another in response to changes in aggregate demand or supply. It explains why expansionary demand management policy produces a favorable trade-off between inflation and unemployment in the short run and why the trade-off becomes less favorable over time. The theory developed in this chapter is also used to explain why stopping inflation is so costly once everyone has become accustomed to it. New tools of analysis, involving labor market behavior and the relationship between rates of unemployment and economic growth are developed and utilized.*

**FOR REVIEW**

*Here are some important terms and concepts that will be put to use in this chapter. If you do not understand them, review them before proceeding.*

• *Definition of inflation and unemployment (Chapter 7)*
• *Cost-push and demand-pull inflation (Chapter 17)*
• *Phillips curve (Chapter 17)*

---

Inflation has entered our discussion at many points in this book, but we have not yet tried to examine in any systematic way what determines the inflation rate. We came closest to an explanation in Chapter 17, which used aggregate real supply and demand curves to show the conditions under which the price level would move from one equilibrium level to another. What has not yet been done in any systematic way, however, is to explain what determines the rate of inflation itself. What determines which part of a given growth rate of nominal GNP will take the form of real output growth and which part the form of inflation? Why did the average annual rate of inflation take such a big jump in the 1970s in comparison with all previous peacetime experience? And once the genie of inflation is out of the bottle, why is it so difficult to get it back in?

The suspicion that these questions have been put off because economists just do not know the answers is in a sense correct. Rapid peacetime inflation is only a little over ten years old in this economy, and explaining the phenomenon has required some very serious rethinking of previous economic theory.

What is more, it is not only economists who have needed time to adjust their thinking to chronic inflation. Consumers, business managers, and government decision makers have been adjusting too. People have now come to view inflation as the norm rather than the exception. Expecting inflation, they plan to protect themselves from it. The reactions of the economy to expected inflation are thus very different from its initial reaction to unexpected inflation. This has been a complicating factor in the search for an adequate theory.

Nonetheless, the fact that economists may not yet know all the answers is no reason to avoid giving a progress report. Despite disagreements on details, virtually all modern theories of inflation contain certain elements in common. In an introductory treatment such as this, it will be enough to concentrate on these common elements and leave the details to be worked out as time goes by.

## THE EFFECTS OF ACCELERATING INFLATION

The fundamental insight on which modern theories of inflation are based is that it is not so much the rate of inflation itself as changes in it that affect employment and real output. This insight will be put to work first by an examination of the case of accelerating inflation. The examination will make use of four building blocks for a theory of inflation.

### Building Blocks for a Theory of Inflation

The first building block is the theory of nominal income determination developed in Chapters 8 through 16; this theory explains the effects of monetary and fiscal policy on nominal income, national income, and product.

Second, at all times, the rate of growth of nominal national product must be equal to the growth rate of real output plus the rate of inflation. With this rule and with a given rate of change of nominal national product, the job of a theory of inflation becomes simply that of determining how the given rate of change in nominal national income will be split up between change in real output and change in prices. Will a 10 percent increase in nominal GNP come out as a 3 percent gain in real output and 7 percent inflation? As no inflation and a 10 percent gain in real output? As 12 percent inflation and a 2 percent drop in real output? The outcome must lie somewhere along this spectrum of possibilities.

The third building block is the relationship between the rate of growth of real output and changes in the unemployment rate. According to **Okun's law**, named after its discoverer, the late American economist Arthur Okun, the unemployment rate will remain unchanged in any year in which actual real output grows at the same rate as potential real output. At present, the growth rate of potential real output appears to be approximately 3 percent per year. Deviations from this long-run trend are associated with changes in the unemployment rate. More specifically, for each three percentage points by which real economic growth exceeds (or falls short of) the long-run trend in any year, the unemployment rate will tend to fall (or rise) by 1

**Okun's law** Each 1 percent increase (decrease) in unemployment results in a 3 percent decrease (increase) in real economic growth. Or, conversely, each 3 percent increase (decrease) in real economic growth results in a 1 percent decrease (increase) in unemployment.

percentage point. Conversely, for every 1 percent change in the unemployment rate, the real growth rate of the GNP will change by 3 percent.[1] The growth of Canada's "potential" output has been around 3 percent per year, based on a "normal" unemployment rate of about 5 percent. **Potential output growth** is the average growth that can be expected each year as a result of changes in population, changes in labor force participation (the percentage of those in the employable age who want to be part of the labor force), and changes in labor productivity.

**Potential output growth**
The average growth that can be expected each year as a result of changes in population, in labor force participation, and in labor productivity.

The fourth and final building block is a better understanding of our pricing and wage-setting system. The following section looks at this more closely.

## Price- and Wage-Setting Practices

Many business firms use what is known as a "markup" policy in setting prices. That is, they calculate the costs of producing a unit of output and add a markup of, say, 10 percent, to provide them with profit.

As we have noted previously, various costs enter into the total cost of a typical product, but since labor costs average about 75 percent of net national income, it is not too inaccurate, and useful for purposes of our analysis, to focus on them as the prime determinant of cost. For simplicity, let us assume that labor costs are the only cost in manufacturing a certain product. In that case, the unit cost of the product would be calculated as the wage payment per one unit of output. The unit cost obviously depends upon both the wage rate and the productivity of labor.

**Unit labor cost** The wage payment per one unit of output.

Assume that the hourly wage rate paid by a company is $5, and that the output of each unit of labor is 5 units per hour. The unit cost of the output equals the wage rate/output (W/Q), or $1. As long as wage rates increase at the same rate as output, the unit cost will not rise. (If wages rise to $6 per hour, and output increases to 6 units per hour, the unit cost remains at $1.) Further, as long as the profit markup remains at 10 percent there will be no increase in prices. The price for the product should be set and remain at $1.10.

What would happen if, given the above situation, wages were suddenly negotiated to increase from $5 to $6 per hour, while labor output increased only from 5 to 5.5 units per hour? Obviously, the unit cost would increase, from $1 to almost $1.10 ($6/5.5). If the manufacturer continues to apply a markup of 10 percent, the price will rise from $1.10 to $1.21. An inflationary process is underway. But what might have caused wages to rise faster than productivity in the first place? Maybe economy was experiencing an increased demand for most products, and labor was able to wring from management an unusually large wage increase because, given the favorable demand situation, management assumed that it would be able to pass on the higher unit cost to consumers in the form of higher prices. Or perhaps the whole process started because managers anticipated an opportunity to improve their profits under the new demand conditions and proceeded to increase profit margins beyond the previous 10 percent limit.

---

[1]Results similar to those traced by Okun in the U.S. have been obtained for Canada. See Economic Council of Canada, *Performance and Potential: Mid-1950s to Mid-1970s*, 1970, p. 18.

The higher prices threw labor into a panic. If they didn't get substantially higher wage increases their earning power would be eroded.

Serious attempts have been made by numerous economists in recent years to understand the labor market and its response to unanticipated inflation and unemployment. The theory below, known as "job search" theory, is one such attempt.

## JOB SEARCH: A THEORY OF LABOR MARKET BEHAVIOR

In Chapter 7, the unemployment rate was defined as the ratio of two groups (or "stocks") of workers — those officially counted as unemployed to those officially counted in the civilian labor force. Changes in the unemployment rate thus occur as the result of flows into and out of the underlying stocks.

Additions to the stock of the unemployed occur whenever people enter the labor force and are unable to find work or when they leave a job and begin immediately to look for a new one. (If they don't look for a new one they are not considered part of the labor force and are no longer counted among the unemployed.)

### The Duration of Unemployment

The length of time that people are out of work will affect the unemployment rate. An economy in which each worker was out of work for about three weeks of each year would have an unemployment rate of about 6 percent (6 percent of the working weeks are lost). An economy in which each worker was out of work for about five weeks would have an unemployment rate of about 10 percent.

There is a tendency, therefore, for the unemployment rate to move closely together with the average duration of unemployment. For this reason, much recent work on the theory of unemployment has focused closely on the process of job search as a key to the average duration of unemployment and hence to the measured unemployment rate. A recent Economic Council of Canada study found that in any one month of 1977 there were more than one million jobseekers in Canada, about three-quarters of whom were unemployed and one-quarter employed.[2] The figure undoubtedly increased substantially in the early 1980s. Another Economic Council of Canada study found that the duration of unemployment has a profound effect on the unemployment rate. "The average unemployment spell is short; about 55 percent of those recorded in 1980 ended within one month. But the long spells—those lasting more than six months—accounted for a disproportionate share of total unemployment." Specifically the study found that "unemployment spells exceeding three months accounted for 45 percent of total unemployment."[3] Short-term unemployment is usually referred to as "frictional" unemployment, while long spells are termed "structural" unemployment.

---

[2] Abrar Hasan and Surendra Gera, *Job Search Behaviour, Unemployment, and Wage Gain in Canadian Labour Markets*, Economic Council of Canada, 1982.

[3] Economic Council of Canada, *In Short Supply, Jobs and Skills in the 1980s*, 1982.

There are many variations of the job search theory of unemployment and new ideas are still being put forth and tested. Just a brief outline of some basic assumptions and approaches is given here. Economists realize that when people are looking for work they will not automatically take the first job offered. A search is made for the best wages and working conditions.

## The Reservation Wage

There is a limit, however, to the length of time people will search for a job when jobs are available. That limit can be expressed in terms of a reservation wage. A person's **reservation wage** is the wage (adjusted for nonmonetary advantages of the job, as always) below which he or she will not accept an offer. A person who has a reservation wage of $150 per week, for example, will reject any offer of $149 a week or less and take any job that offers $150 a week or more.

People's reservation wages tend to decline the longer their job search continues. There are at least two reasons for this. First, the people may initially be very optimistic, overestimating their own worth in the eyes of potential employers, and then gradually become more realistic as the hoped-for top-level offers do not materialize. Second, even if unemployment insurance is available, long periods without work tend to cut into people's savings, and financial pressure to get back to work increases. Empirical studies confirm the idea that reservation wages decline as the job search period lengthens.

**Reservation wage** The wage (adjusted for nonmonetary advantages and disadvantages of a job) below which a person will not accept a job offer.

## Determining the Duration of Unemployment

The idea of repeated sampling to find the best job offer plus the idea of a declining reservation wage offers a simple theory of the duration of unemployment. Exhibit 18.1 gives a graphical presentation of the theory. An upward-sloping curve is drawn in the diagram to show that, on the average, a worker can find a better job offer by spending more time in the job search.

**Exhibit 18.1**
**Determinants of the duration of unemployment**
In this exhibit, the duration of unemployment is determined by the intersection of a wage offer curve and a reservation wage curve. The latter records the lowest wage offer a worker is willing to accept at any point during the job search. The first wage offer meeting this minimum is accepted, ending the period of unemployment after an average of ten weeks, according to this exhibit.

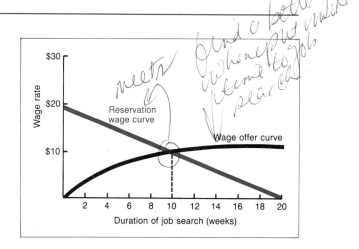

A downward-sloping curve is drawn to show how the worker's reservation wage falls as time goes on. The two curves come together the first time the worker gets a job offer that meets that worker's reservation wage. This takes ten weeks on the average as the figure is drawn. The worker takes the job, and the period of unemployment is at an end.

Two things should be stressed about this figure. First, the curves express averages for workers of similar skills and experience. Individual workers may, simply by good luck, find offers meeting their reservation wage on the first or second try. Others, less lucky, may have to look longer than average before they find something they will accept. Second, the positions of the curves, and hence the average length of the job search, may be very different for workers at different skill levels. In particular, for many types of unskilled workers, wage offers received are likely to be very low. At the same time, hope for something better, even if unrealistic, keeps the reservation wage from falling very rapidly. This can stretch out the period of unemployment to many months.

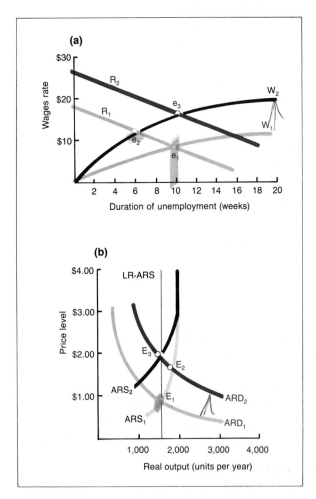

**Exhibit 18.2**

**Unemployment and demand-pull inflation**

This exhibit uses both the job search diagram (Part a) and aggregate real supply and demand curves (Part b) to show how unemployment behaves during an episode of demand-pull inflation. Rising aggregate demand (to $ARD_2$ from $ARD_1$ in Part b) first affects the wage offer curve in Part a, shifting it upward to $W_2$. The average duration of unemployment falls from $e_1$ to $e_2$ as real output rises (to $E_2$ from $E_1$). After workers adjust their reservation wages to the increased price level ($R_2$), the economy returns to a new long-run equilibrium where unemployment is back at its original rate ($e_3$) and real output is back at its original level ($E_3$).

## CAUSES OF CHANGES IN THE UNEMPLOYMENT RATE

### Unemployment and Demand-Pull Inflation

The reservation wage and wage offer curves just introduced can be combined with the aggregate real supply and demand curves of Chapter 17 to show what happens to the unemployment rate as macroeconomic conditions change. Let's first consider the case of demand-pull inflation, represented in Exhibit 18.2.

Initially, we will suppose that the reservation wage curve $R_1$ and the wage offer curve $W_1$ apply, giving an average duration of unemployment of ten weeks (Point $e_1$ in Exhibit 18.2a). The economy is in equilibrium with aggregate real demand curve $ARD_1$ and aggregate real supply curve $ARS_1$ (Point $E_1$ in Exhibit 18.2b).

Now suppose that expansionary policy shifts the aggregate real demand curve to the right, to the position $ARD_2$. Given the tendency of the economy to adjust prices only gradually to changes in demand, firms respond by expanding output. In part, they may do so by putting existing workers on overtime, but they will increase their hiring of new workers too. They may also bid against one another for workers, thereby raising nominal wages as well as the quantity of job openings available. In Exhibit 18.2a, this upturn in the job market is shown as an upward shift in the wage offer curve, from $W_1$ to $W_2$.

How will workers react to this change in the job market? To understand their initial reaction, we have to keep in mind that workers operate in a world of incomplete information. Because the wage offer curve has shifted upward, they will, on the average, find a job at any given wage level after a shorter search period than before. But at least at first, individual job seekers are likely to interpret such job finds as isolated pieces of good luck rather than as a general increase in nominal wages. Given their reservation wages, as represented by $R_1$ in Exhibit 18.2a, they will eagerly pounce on the new jobs after an average of just six weeks of search. In the short run, then, the job market will move from Point $e_1$ to Point $e_2$. The average duration of unemployment will fall, and measured unemployment will drop below its previous "equilibrium" rate. In Part b of the exhibit, the declining unemployment corresponds to rising output, as the economy moves from $E_1$ to $E_2$.

Neither $e_2$ in Part a nor $E_2$ in Part b can be a permanent equilibrium, however. After a time, workers will become aware that the average wage level has risen and will re-evaluate their wage prospects accordingly. At the same time, they will find out that prices have begun to rise, as shown in Exhibit 18.2b. That will cause them to re-estimate the level of nominal wages they need to maintain their accustomed standard of living. The realization that average nominal wages have risen combined with the expectation of a higher price level will push up the reservation wage level of job seekers. They will not snap up the abundant job offers quite so quickly now. The duration of unemployment and the unemployment rate will begin to rise.

In Exhibit 18.2b, these events correspond to an upward shift in the aggregate real supply curve, from $ARS_1$ to $ARS_2$. As indicated in Chapter 17, more and more of the initial increase in aggregate nominal demand is converted to an increase in the price level as this happens. If there were no further demand disturbances, the economy could reach a new equilibrium at Point $E_3$. This would correspond to the intersection of wage offer curve $W_2$ with the new reservation wage curve, $R_2$, in Exhibit 18.2a. Unemployment would return to its equilibrium rate at $e_3$.

To summarize: in the short run, beginning from overall equilibrium, an increase in aggregate demand raises real output, increases the quantity and quality of job offers, and reduces the average duration of unemployment and the unemployment rate. In the long run, assuming no further disturbances, real output returns to its initial rate at a higher price level, reservation wages adjust fully to the new economic conditions, and the average duration of unemployment and the unemployment rate go back to where they started from.

We have now described four building blocks that can be used to describe a dynamic inflationary process. We will call this the **accelerationist theory of inflation**. The first building block is the notion that policy makers, through the use of fiscal and monetary policy, have some control over the volume of national income. The second is the rule that the growth rate of nominal national income must be equal to the growth rate of real output plus the rate of inflation. The third building block is the rule of thumb known as Okun's law by which, for each three percentage points that real output growth exceeds the normal potential growth rate of 3 percent, the unemployment rate falls by about one percentage point. The fourth building block is provided by business pricing policies, and by job search theory, indicating how the beginning of an inflationary process first reduces unemployment and then results in labor market pricing adjustments frustrating further declines in unemployment.

**Accelerationist theory of inflation** A theory according to which changes in the inflation rate, rather than the rate itself, influence real output and employment.

### Some Preliminary Simplifications for the Accelerationist Theory

In putting these building blocks to work, we will make two simplifying assumptions. These assumptions will permit a clear exposition of the basics of the accelerationist theory.

First we will assume that the growth rate of potential real GNP is zero. During the early 1980s that growth rate in Canada did in fact approximate zero. But the zero potential growth assumption is made less in recognition of this recent slowdown than in an effort to simplify the application of Okun's law. That law, it will be recalled, relates changes in unemployment to the difference between the growth of actual and potential real GNP. With potential real GNP growth assumed to be zero, Okun's law can be represented in simplified form by the following formula:

$$\Delta U = -\frac{\dot{y}}{3}$$

in which $\Delta U$ stands for the percentage point change in the unemployment rate over a year's period, and $\dot{y}$ stands for the growth rate of real output.

Second, we will make a simple assumption about the formation of inflationary expectations. We will assume that the expected inflation rate in any year is equal to the actual inflation rate in the previous year. The idea that people form their expectations of inflation entirely on the basis of the actual inflationary experience of the recent past is known as the **adaptive expectations hypothesis**. To assume that expectations are formed solely on the basis of the experience of the most recent year is a very strict version of adaptive expectations, but it is not altogether unrealistic. Although economists who have studied the matter have identified many factors that influence the expected rate of inflation to some degree, all would agree that the inflationary experience of the recent past has a strong impact on inflationary expectations for the near-term future.[4]

> **Adaptive expectations hypothesis** The hypothesis that people form their expectations of the future rate of inflation primarily on the basis of inflationary experience in the immediate past.

With these four building blocks and two simplifying assumptions in hand, we turn now to an analysis of the effects of accelerating inflation. As our simplifying assumptions do not exactly fit the Canadian economy, we will cast our discussion in terms of a hypothetical country. We will assume that this country is a democracy dominated by two political parties, which we will call the Reds and the Whites.

## Expansionary Policy from a Standing Start

Our analysis begins in Year 0 with the economy in a "standing start" position. By this we mean that both the actual and the expected rates of inflation are zero; the growth rate of actual real GNP is equal to the growth rate of potential real GNP, which in this case is also zero; and unemployment is at its "equilibrium" rate, here assumed to be 6 percent. In Year 0 an election is held. The Reds base their campaign on a promise to "get the country moving." They convince the electorate that 6 percent is too high an unemployment rate and that a little economic growth would be a good thing. Upon taking over the machinery of government, they reset the dials of fiscal and monetary policy to raise the growth rate of nominal GNP from zero to, say, 8 percent per year. What will happen next?

Exhibit 18.3 indicates how the economy will react to this dose of expansionary policy. The exhibit shows a negatively sloped short-run Phillips curve labeled $Ph_1$. In Year 0 the economy is at Point A. As the expansionary policy takes hold, a familiar train of events unfolds. Increased aggregate demand causes inventories to fall throughout the economy. Some firms react by increasing output, others by raising prices, and others by doing a little of both. In terms of the diagrams of Chapter 17, the economy is moving up and along its initial aggregate real supply curve at this time.

*Effects on the Labor Market*  Soon the effects of the expansionary policy will be felt on the labor market. The firms that are stepping up their output will be recruiting new workers. Some will offer higher wages, knowing that improved demand conditions will allow them to pass along

[4]There is another theory, known as the *rational expectations hypothesis*, which assumes that people form their inflationary expectations not solely on the basis of inflationary experience of the immediate past, but also on forward-looking judgements of the probable course of economic policy and its effects, in the light of macroeconomic relationships as they understand them.

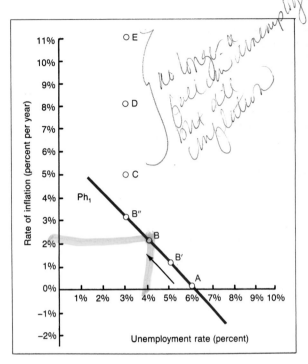

*[handwritten note: no longer a decline in unemployment but still inflation]*

**Exhibit 18.3**
**The effects of expansionary policy from a standing start**

This exhibit shows the effects of an increase in the growth rate of nominal GNP to 8 percent from a standing start. As the economy moves from A to B, the unemployment rate drops by two percentage points. Following Okun's law, this means a 6 percent growth rate of real output. The remaining 2 percent of the 8 percent growth of nominal GNP is accounted for by 2 percent inflation. The 8 percent growth rate of nominal output is more than enough to reach Point B' and less than enough to reach Point B". No inflation-unemployment combination other than B is possible under the circumstances. If increased spending thereafter is accompanied by rapidly rising costs, prices will continue to rise but there will be no further decline in the unemployment rate. A movement to points such as C, D, and E will occur.

the higher labor costs, at least in part, to their customers. In terms of the job search diagrams (Exhibit 18.2), the wage offer curve will be shifting up at this point. Job seekers will find both the quantity and the quality of employment opportunities better than before. Acting with incomplete knowledge of current and future economic trends, however, they will not immediately adjust their reservation wages. Instead, each job seeker at first will be likely to interpret the improved labor market conditions as personal good luck. The newly offered jobs will thus be quickly snapped up. The average duration of unemployment will fall, and the unemployment rate will fall with it.

*Moving up the Phillips Curve* At this point the economy is moving up and to the left along the Phillips curve, with the unemployment rate falling and the inflation rate rising. How far up the Phillips curve will it go? The answer can be found by combining two of the building blocks described at the start of this chapter. First, the economy must move to a point where the inflation rate plus the growth rate of real output equal the 8 percent growth rate of nominal GNP. Second, according to Okun's law, the growth rate of real GNP must be equal to three times the change in the unemployment rate. (This is the simplified form of Okun's law, using zero growth of potential real GNP.) Putting the two together, we conclude that the economy will move to a point on the Phillips curve where the inflation rate plus three times the change in the unemployment rate equal the growth of nominal GNP. This condition is met at Point B in Exhibit 18.3. The inflation rate at B is 2 percent, and the two percentage point drop in the unemployment rate (from 6 to 4 percent) produces a 6 percent increase in real output, for a total of 8 percent. *(unemployment has fallen by 2%*

*∴ 6% ↑ in output*
*(2 × 3)*

No other point on the Phillips curve satisfies the required condition. Consider Point B', for example. There the inflation rate is 1 percent, and the unemployment rate has fallen by 1 percent, giving a 3 percent real growth rate. The 1 percent inflation plus 3 percent real growth add up to only 4 percent, well short of the assumed 8 percent growth rate of nominal GNP. Or consider Point B''. There the inflation rate is 3 percent, and unemployment has fallen by three percentage points, giving a 9 percent rate of real growth. Adding the rate of inflation to the rate of real growth tells us that Point B'' could be reached only if nominal GNP grew at 12 percent rather than at the assumed 8 percent.

In short, once the growth rate of nominal output, the initial unemployment rate, and the expected inflation rate are given, only one combination of inflation and unemployment is possible. (The expected inflation rate determines the position of the Phillips curve.)

In terms of real aggregate demand and supply analysis, and in terms of our theory about price setting and job search, what has happened can be interpreted in the following way. Responding to the increased demand in the economy, both workers and employers have tried to increase their income. Since workers may be tied to long-term wage contracts, they may have responded less successfully than employers. The latter have moved up the real aggregate supply curve, increasing the profit markup, charging higher prices, and at the same time increasing output. In order to increase output they may have improved their wage offers somewhat, so that the wage offer curve shifts upward (see Exhibit 18.2); the duration of unemployment and the unemployment rate have declined.

## The Effects of Repeated Expansionary Policy

The Reds have every reason to be proud of the economic record of their first year in office. From the stagnation of the standing start position, a little dose of expansionary demand management in Year 1 has cut unemployment by a third and jumped the growth rate of real output to 6 percent at the cost of only a 2 percent inflation rate. These results are so encouraging that the Reds repeat exactly the same policy and maintain the 8 percent growth rate of nominal GNP in Year 2. Exhibit 18.3 again shows what will happen.

The economy is now forced off the original Phillips curve to Point C. What has happened is this: anticipating the increased demand in the economy, both workers and employers have once more tried to increase their income. However, both of them were fooled by the first increase in demand. They were operating on the assumption that general prices would not increase (a phenomenon known in economics as "money illusion"). Managers hoped that the increased prices for their own products would not be matched by general price increases, so that their relative prices would go up. Because of the general inflation this has not happened.

Workers hoped that the small increases in wages offered by employers in their attempts to increase output would not be eroded by inflation. But inflation did occur, and both groups failed to increase their real incomes as much as they had planned.

In Year 2, both workers and employers have the inflationary experience of Year 1 behind them. They will now respond to a second 8 percent increase in demand by raising wages and prices not only enough to take advantage of that demand but to resolve the 2 percent inflation loss of Year 1. The original Phillips curve did not anticipate such an inflation catch-up—it was built on zero inflationary expectations. If inflation had not taken place, the economy would have continued to move leftward along the Phillips curve, to point B″ and beyond. However, the trade-off between the unemployment rate and the inflation rate is no longer so favorable, once the wage- and price-setting factors build an inflationary adjustment into their new wages and prices.

In terms of aggregate demand and supply analysis, the movement off the Phillips curve to Point C is represented by an upward shift in the aggregate real supply curve (see Exhibit 17.5). In terms of the job search diagrams, it is represented by an upward adjustment of the reservation wage curve.

Having concluded that the economy in Year 2 will move to some point like C, we next need to determine just why that point is reached. Exactly the same reasoning can be applied as before: in Year 2 the economy must move to a point where the rate of inflation plus the rate of real growth equal the rate of nominal GNP.

As before, the growth rate of real GNP can be calculated using Okun's law, but now the starting point is the 4 percent unemployment rate reached in Year 1 rather than the 6 percent equilibrium rate. Real output will grow in Year 2 only to the extent that the unemployment rate falls further. If it stays at 4 percent, no real growth will occur. A little trial and error quickly shows, then, that the economy must end up in Year 2 at Point C. There, a further one percentage point drop in the unemployment rate, from 4 to 3 percent, will yield a 3 percent growth rate of real output. That, plus a 5 percent inflation rate equal the assumed 8 percent growth rate of nominal GNP.

### The Effects of Continued Acceleration

Clearly, the Reds' record in Year 2 is not quite as good as in Year 1. The growth rate of real output has slowed to 3 percent, and the inflation rate has risen to 5 percent. On the plus side, though, unemployment has dropped to just 3 percent. All in all, the campaign promise to get things moving has been redeemed. So let's suppose that the growth rate of nominal GNP is held at 8 percent for a third year.

As Exhibit 18.3 indicates, in Year 3 the whole of the demand pressure is translated into higher prices. Workers and employers increase their wages and profit margins so that prices are forced to rise by 8 percent. The economy moves straight up from Point C to Point D. There is no room for any further decrease in unemployment or any growth of real output. The entire 8 percent growth rate of nominal GNP is absorbed in an 8 percent inflation rate.

This result leaves the Reds with little to brag about except a continued low unemployment rate. Clinging to this one remaining accomplishment, the Red economic strategists decide that in Year 4 they will maintain the 3 percent unemployment rate at all costs. As we shall see, this may force them to increase demand spending beyond the previous rate of 8 percent, leading to an even greater inflationary spiral.

*A Point-by-Point Description of Inflation* Some economics interpret these events in terms of a constantly upward shifting Phillips curve, but since the economy jumps from one point on such a hypothetical curve to another, without moving along any curve for very long, if at all, a point-by-point description of what can happen is attempted here instead. This approach is illustrated in Exhibit 18.4.

Exhibit 18.4a provides hypothetical numbers for the economy sketched above. It is assumed (Column 2) that the productivity of the input factors remains constant over the five-year period, at 5 units of real output. The cost of each input (primarily labor) is $5 initially (Column 3). We will refer to this as the wage rate. The initial unit input cost is therefore $1. We assume that business firms initially apply a 10 percent markup to these costs, so that the price of each unit of output becomes $1.10 (Column 6). In Year 0, there is no increase in demand, a 6 percent unemployment rate,

---

**Exhibit 18.4**
**Response of prices and unemployment to demand increases with markup pricing and job search**

With a "standing start" in Year 0, it is assumed that initially demand in the economy increases each year by 8 percent (Column 7). Workers and employers respond by increasing input costs and profit markups, resulting in higher unit input costs and prices. Initially, in the first two years, low (even zero) inflationary expectations prompt relatively small increases in such costs, and real output is permitted to expand, and unemployment declines. However, as both workers and employers respond to unanticipated, rising inflation, their wage demand and profit markups increase, prices rise more sharply, output ceases to grow, and unemployment falls no further.

**(a)**

| 1 | 2 | 3 | 4 | 5 | 6 | 7 | 8 | 9 | 10 | 11 |
|---|---|---|---|---|---|---|---|---|---|---|
| Year | Real Output per Unit of Input | Cost of Input (wage rate) | Unit Input Cost | Profit Markup % | Output Price | Increase in Demand % | Unemployment Rate % | Inflation Rate % | Percent Change in Nominal Input Income % | Percent Change in Real Input Income % |
| 0 | 5 | $5.00 | $1.00 | 10 | $1.10 | — | 6 | 0 | 0 | 0 |
| 1 | 5 | 5.05 | 1.01 | 11 | 1.12 | 8 | 4 | 2 | 1 | −1 |
| 2 | 5 | 5.25 | 1.05 | 12 | 1.18 | 8 | 3 | 5 | 4 | −1 |
| 3 | 5 | 5.60 | 1.12 | 13 | 1.27 | 8 | 3 | 8 | 6²/₃ | −1⅓ |
| 4 | 5 | 6.20 | 1.24 | 14 | 1.41 | 11 | 3 | 11 | 11 | 0 |
| 5 | 5 | 6.95 | 1.39 | 15 | 1.60 | 13 | 3 | 13 | 12 | −1 |

**(b)**

| Alternate route if in Years 4 & 5 demand increase had remained at 8% (Col. 7) | | | | | | | | | | |
|---|---|---|---|---|---|---|---|---|---|---|
| 4 | 5 | 6.20 | 1.24 | 14 | 1.41 | 8 | 4 | 11 | 11 | 0 |
| 5 | 5 | 6.95 | 1.39 | 15 | 1.60 | 8 | 5²/₃ | 13 | 12 | −1 |

zero inflation, and no change in nominal or real input income. In Year 1, demand increases by 8 percent (Column 7). Workers cannot respond very quickly but they receive a wage increase of 1 percent (Column 3), resulting in a 1 percent increase in unit input cost (Column 4). Employers are able to respond more successfully and raise their markup from 10 to 11 percent (Column 5). This represents a 10 percent increase in the markup rate. The price of the output rises by about 2 percent, from $1.10 to $1.12 (Column 6). Given that demand has increased by 8 percent and prices by 2 percent, how much can the unemployment rate fall? It can fall by 2 percent, to a lower level of 4 percent. Following Okun's law, the real output increase will be about 6 percent, leaving prices to rise by 2 percent. Note that worker wages rose by 1 percent (Column 10), but since the inflation rate is 2 percent there is a 1 percent decrease in *real* worker income (Column 11). Employers manage to increase their markup by more than the inflation rate, but they too may be disappointed that some of the increase was eroded by inflation.

In Year 2, workers demand a 4 percent wage increase (from $5.05 to $5.25), in order to compensate themselves for the 2 percent inflation of Year 1 which resulted in an erosion of their real wages, and to take advantage of the increased demand in the economy. Employers raise their markup rate to 12 percent, and prices rise to $1.18 (Column 6). This represents a 5 percent inflation rate, which means that since demand increased by only 8 percent, real output can rise by only 3 percent, and unemployment can fall by only one percentage point, to 3 percent (Column 8). Note that workers thought they were gaining on inflation by increasing their nominal wages by 4 percent, but in Year 2 inflation is actually 5 percent, so real worker income again *falls* by 1 percent (Column 11).

In Year 3, workers and employers try even harder to raise incomes, as demand once again grows by 8 percent. Their wage and pricing practices cause prices to rise by 8 percent to $1.27, leaving no room for further increases in real output or further declines in the unemployment rate.

In Year 4, workers and employers, having found that their expectations of a 5 percent inflation rate in Year 3 were actually exceeded by 3 percent, will increase their wages and profit margins even more aggressively, if they can. Assume that workers now try to raise their nominal income by 11 percent, to compensate them for the previous year's inflation of 8 percent and to take advantage of increasing demand. Employers raise their markup rate to 14 percent. This results in a price increase of 11 percent. Such an increase is possible only if it is accommodated by increased demand in the economy of 11 percent. In terms of Exhibit 18.3, the economy will move to Point E, with unemployment remaining at 3 percent and prices rising by 11 percent. Note that this result is possible only because of even more expansionary monetary and fiscal policy than before. The cost of maintaining the low rate of unemployment, then, is accelerating inflation.

### Some Generalizations

Let's leave the world of the Reds and Whites for a moment now and draw some generalizations from our example. The first is that starting from a base of high unemployment and low inflation, expansionary monetary and fiscal policy initially produces an attractive combination of falling unemployment and rapid real growth, with only a moderate inflationary penalty. The second is that as people begin to adjust their expectations to the inflationary effects of such expansionary policy, the trade-off between inflation and unemployment becomes increasingly less favorable. And the third generalization is that the unemployment rate can be kept below the equilibrium rate for a prolonged period only at the expense of a constantly accelerating inflation rate, which keeps the actual inflation rate always above the expected rate.

## INFLATIONARY RECESSION AND THE STOP-GO CYCLE

Given our assumption of purely adaptive expectations, there is no limit to the number of years that unemployment can be held below its equilibrium rate by continuously accelerating inflation. In practice, though, political pressures eventually build up to the point where something has to be done about inflation. Let's suppose that this happens in the land of the Reds and the Whites. In Year 3 another election is held. The Reds are running on a promise to increase spending by 11 percent, but the economy is threatened by 11 percent inflation and there is stagnant real output. They point proudly to the low unemployment rate they have achieved, but the Whites' campaign promises to do something about inflation results in a change of administration. True to their promise, the Whites, once in office, put on the monetary and fiscal brakes.

### The Effects of Deceleration

Specifically, let's assume that nominal spending on GNP will be cut back to 8 percent from the planned 11 percent depicted in Exhibit 18.4a. The previous Year 4 experience is repeated, except that the new monetary and fiscal authorities allow demand to grow by only 8 percent (Column 7, Exhibit 18.4b). In this case, the increased wages and profits set by workers and employers can be realized only if real output declines. If real output declines by 3 percent, a nominal spending increase of 8 percent is consistent with a price increase of 11 percent. (Remember, the rate of growth of nominal national product ($\Delta Y$) equals the rate of growth of real output ($\Delta Q$) plus the rate of inflation ($\Delta P$). In this case,

$$\Delta Y = \Delta Q + \Delta P$$
$$8 = -3 + 11$$

As shown in Exhibit 18.4b, unemployment therefore rises from 3 percent to 4 percent (Column 8). Unfortunately, despite the fact that spending increases have been limited to 8 percent and the unemployment rate has been allowed to rise to 4 percent, the inflationary spiral is not brought under control. Because prices did in fact rise by 11 percent, rather than the anticipated 8 percent (based on Year 3's inflation rate), workers and employers will again pursue much larger wages and profit margins. The inflation rate may rise to 13 percent in Year 5, which, if spending increases are again held to 8 percent, will require a further increase in the unemployment rate to 5⅔ percent.[5]

We already have a name for these events: inflationary recession (or stagflation). Every possible bad thing is happening at once. Real output is falling. Unemployment is rising. And inflation, instead of slowing down, is still being carried upward by the momentum of inflationary expectations generated by recent experience. Economists used to think that such a combination of events just couldn't happen.

To make certain that we clearly understand the mechanics of inflationary recession, we can relate the events of Exhibit 18.4b to the graphical frameworks used in this and the previous chapter. In terms of Chapter 17's diagrams, an inflationary recession is produced when rising inflationary expectations push the short-run aggregate real supply curve up while the aggregate real demand curve remains stationary or (as in this case) rises less rapidly. As the aggregate real supply curve shifts upward, firms become worried about rising costs and insist on higher prices in order to maintain their rates of real output. But with aggregate nominal demand rising only slowly, there is not enough real purchasing power to absorb a constant rate of real output at a higher price level. Inventories accumulate, and firms react by cutting back output. The economy moves up and to the left along its aggregate real demand curve.

The events of the inflationary recession can also be interpreted in terms of the kind of job search diagram used in this chapter. Because workers are expecting ever higher prices, given recent inflationary experience, they raise their reservation wages. But the reversal of demand management policy means that the wage offer curve is no longer being pushed up as fast as reservation wages are rising. Workers find it harder and harder to find the jobs they want. However, operating with incomplete information, they at first attribute their difficulties to individual bad luck. They stubbornly keep looking, stretching out the average duration of unemployment. The unemployment rate thus rises.

### Turning the Corner

Although the events of Years 4 and 5 win no applause for the Whites, let's suppose that they remain determined to "wrestle inflation to the ground." Accordingly, in Year 6 they allow nominal spending to rise by only 6 percent. What is likely to happen? The results are not entirely predictable. Output has been declining, and the profit margins of firms may be forced down whether they like it or not. Unemployment is increasing and workers are moving further down the reservation wage curve as the duration of unemployment increases and the wage offer curves are possibly shifted downward. It may be that for another year labor will choose to insist on wage increases of 14 percent, to compensate for the previous year's inflation of 13 percent, and profit margins may at least be maintained. Prices would then rise by 14 percent, but this could only be accomplished, in the

---

[5]Note: $\Delta Y = \Delta Q + \Delta P$, or $\Delta Q = \Delta Y - \Delta P$. If $\Delta P = 13\%$ and $\Delta Y = 8\%$, the required change in $Q = 8 - 13 = -5\%$. Since for every drop in Q of 3% the unemployment rate increases by 1%, the unemployment rate will now rise another 1⅔%.

face of a 6 percent increase in nominal spending, by reducing output by 8 percent and increasing unemployment by 2⅔ percent to a new level of 8⅓ percent. The inflation rate is still rising, and unemployment is still increasing. However, a similar restrictive policy in the following year might induce labor as well as management to accept lower wage increases and lower profit margins, despite the apparent loss in real earnings. If nominal spending in Year 7 were to increase by 4 percent, and prices rose by only 8 percent, output would still be forced to decline, and unemployment would rise by another 1⅓ percent, but a downturn might soon be accomplished. Because prices are coming down, wage and profit demands might decline even more.

A large "reserve army of the unemployed," to use a term coined by Marx, is now present to challenge those members in the labor force who would still like to insist on high wage increases, and there would now be enough bankruptcies in business, due to falling output, to caution business firms against raising prices sharply. At tremendous expense, in terms of high unemployment rates and lost business, the inflation rate might fall below the increase in nominal spending, permitting an increase in output and a decline in the unemployment rate. By year 7 or 8, let's say, the inflation rate and the unemployment rate may both have declined to more acceptable levels.

But Year 8 is an election year again. What kind of record are the Whites running on? In Year 4 they took over an economy with 11 percent inflation. By Year 8 they have cut that figure considerably, but the reduced inflation rate has been won only at the cost of a major recession. The unemployment rate is still higher than it was four years before, and real output is lower. By this time, voters are likely to remember the Red era more as one of prosperity than as one of unacceptable inflation.

Furthermore, the Whites' austerity program offers the Reds a uniquely tempting opportunity. If the Reds win, for one crucial year following the election, they can pursue an expansionary policy while still taking advantage of the downward momentum of inflationary expectations. This procedure is known as **reflation**.

**Reflation** An episode in which demand management policy becomes more expansionary while the expected rate of inflation is falling.

Because firms will still be expecting their costs to drift downward, they will react to a renewed burst of demand almost entirely by expanding real output and hardly at all by raising prices. Because workers are expecting a moderation of the rate of increase in the cost of living, they will eagerly snap up the newly created employment opportunities without much of an increase in nominal wages. As a result, the economy will move almost horizontally to the left, along a new, lower Phillips curve. Real output will grow, and unemployment will fall, at the cost of very little inflation.

## The Stop-Go Cycle

Compared with the prospect of continued austerity under a re-elected White government, the Reds' promise of reflation and prosperity is likely to swing the election. But the reflation trick works only for one year. After that, for all the now-familiar reasons, the inflationary penalty that must be

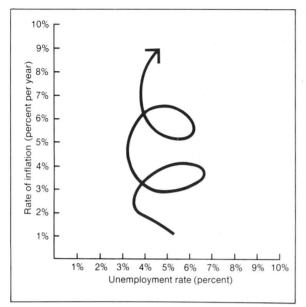

**Exhibit 18.5**
**Stop-go with an inflationary bias**
The so-called stop-go cycle means the alternation of acceleration, inflationary recession, deceleration, and reflation, as political pressure builds up first to do something about inflation and then to do something about unemployment. If the pressures to reduce unemployment are, on the average, stronger than the pressures to control inflation, the stop-go cycle may be given an upward bias. Each time around, the cycle spirals higher, as this sketch indicates.

borne to keep unemployment below the equilibrium rate will grow every year. The economy will enter a new upswing until political pressures again mount to do something about inflation.

Alternating periods of expansionary demand management policy and austerity produce what the British colorfully call a stop-go policy cycle. If

**Exhibit 18.6**
**Recent Canadian experience with inflation and unemployment**
Since 1954, inflation and unemployment have spiraled upward in a series of roughly circular loops. One cycle, that following the 1957 recession, was cut off before the previous peak of inflation had been reached. In 1973-75, inflation reached an especially high peak because internationally generated commodity inflation was added to domestic inflationary pressures. Prices rose persistently from 1976 to 1981, without reducing unemployment. The inflationary cycle finally seemed to break in 1982, accompanied by the highest unemployment rate since the Great Depression of the 1930s.

Source: Department of Finance, *Economic Review*, April 1982, pp. 159, 171.

the political system is, on the average, more sensitive to the evils of unemployment than to the evils of inflation, an inflationary bias is added to the stop-go cycle, with each upswing lasting longer than each downswing. Without pursuing the matter in detail, we can say that the result is an upward spiral of the economy, shown schematically in Exhibit 18.5.

Admittedly, the assumptions that produce the stop-go policy cycle in the world of the Reds and Whites are highly restrictive and stylized. The actual economy of Canada is far more complicated, as is the political system that goes with it. Nonetheless, as the following case study shows, the path followed by the Canadian economy during the post–World War II period bears a disquieting resemblance to the schematic spiral of Exhibit 18.5.

## Case 18.1
### Recent Canadian Experiences with Unemployment and Inflation

Exhibit 18.6 presents actual data on inflation and unemployment in the Canadian economy from 1954 to 1982. One part of this record — the expansion of the 1960s — has already been examined in Exhibit 17.8. Now some other features will be explored.

The overall impression one gets from the figures for the latter half of the 1950s and for the 1960s is that of roughly circular clockwise loops. Although the lengths and strengths of successive accelerations and decelerations are rather irregular, it does not take much imagination to see an upward spiral of sorts. This figure at least roughly resembles that of Exhibit 18.5.

For the period after 1969, the picture is somewhat different, although the movements are generally in line with the theory presented here. The growing inflation in the latter half of the 1960s brought about a more restrictive monetary policy by 1968. The inflationary process was brought under control, but the result was a sharp increase in the unemployment rate between 1969 and 1971. By 1970, monetary policy was again expansionary and prices began to rise sharply in 1972. Canada then began to go through a period of accelerating inflation, accompanied by only small declines in the unemployment rate. The inflation was now fed by sharply increased demand from abroad for our agricultural products and other resources, by increased costs for imported foodstuffs, and by the upsurge of oil prices associated with the OPEC oil cartel. Rising prices may have been induced by demand forces, but they were soon supported and accentuated by cost-push factors, based on new inflationary expectations. The process began to resemble the inflationary recession described in Exhibit 18.3.

The government stepped in with wage and profit controls in October 1975 and this seemed to dampen inflation in 1976. However, in the years 1977 and 1978 prices again rose sharply, led by increases in food and energy costs. Unemployment remained high, increasing to 8.4 percent in 1978. In view of the increased inflation, one might have expected unemployment to decline. In other words, one would have expected the trend line to move upward to the left after 1976, rather than upward to the right.[5] Prices rose persistently from 1976 to 1981, and in defiance of the normal Phillips curve, unemployment did not drop. The inflationary cycle finally seemed to turn in 1982, accompanied by the highest unemployment rates since the 1930s.

---

[5]A recent study by Clarence Barber and John McCallum (see suggestions for further reading) suggests that the unemployment rate would have fallen to 6.9 percent in 1978 if restrictive monetary policy prior to 1977 had not held back our foreign sector by keeping the value of our dollar at an unrealistically high level. By 1979 Canada was benefiting from a depreciated dollar — having overcome the J effect — and the unemployment rate fell to 7.5 percent. Was this the beginning of a new short-run Phillips curve?

## THE POLICY DILEMMA

Macroeconomic theory demonstrates the powerful role that monetary and fiscal policy play in the modern economy. "Demand management" through such policies undoubtedly contributed a great deal to the rapid growth and stability of the Canadian economy in the first few decades after World War II. However, in the past decade, growing instability—as measured by unusually large increases in both inflation and unemployment—and a decline in the growth rate have prompted economists to search for new tools of analysis and prescription. The last two chapters have featured some of the new analysis, which indicates that the results of demand management depend critically on the behavior of pricing and wage-setting policies. But these are "institutional" factors long relegated by economists to the realm of microeconomics, and not considered significant in examining macroeconomic problems. We obviously cannot go on making this assumption. What is needed are new prescriptions, and these will have to take seriously the way in which costs and prices are determined in our economy. Fiscal and monetary policies will continue to play a vital role in determining our level of economic activity, but their results will continue to depend on the institutional framework within which costs and prices are established. Such a framework, with suggested policy changes, is provided in Chapter 19.

## CONCLUSIONS

This chapter almost brings our macroeconomic theory building to a close. Of course, only the basics of each piece of the theory have been presented in this introductory book. Advanced texts will offer a wealth of extensions, details and controversies not even mentioned here. Nonetheless, the ideas built up since Chapter 5 do represent a reasonably accurate outline of contemporary macroeconomic thinking.

Having made it through the heavy part of the macroeconomics course, then, we are ready for dessert. In the next chapter, we will turn from analyzing the effects of economic policy on the economy to analyzing alternative proposals for improving the conduct of economic policy. As we do so, we will find widespread agreement that serious policy mistakes have been made in the past. But we will find much less agreement as to how the course of policy ought to be changed for the future.

## SUMMARY

1. According to modern, dynamic theories of inflation, it is unexpected *changes* in the rate of inflation, rather than simply the rate of inflation, that affect unemployment and real output.

2. The dynamic theory of inflation rests on four building blocks. The first is the notion that the government, through monetary and fiscal policy,

can control aggregate nominal demand with a reasonable degree of accuracy. The second is the rule that the growth rate of real output plus the rate of inflation must equal the growth rate of nominal output. The third is Okun's law, relating changes in real output to changes in unemployment. The fourth is pricing and job search theory, relating unemployment to the actual and expected rates of inflation.

3. Especially critical to the analysis of dynamic inflation is an understanding of how prices and wages are established by firms and workers. Labor costs are by far the most significant cost in the production of most goods. The "unit cost" of a firm's output is, therefore, determined largely by current wage rates and the productivity of labor. Many business firms simply add a markup to these costs in setting their sale prices. Whatever the origin of an initial rise in prices, it is the response of wage costs and markups to such a price rise that will determine whether the price increase will be sustained or will even accelerate, and whether it will be accompanied by falling or rising unemployment.

4. Job search theory has helped to explain the likely response of workers to changes in the economy. On average, increasing the length of the job search period improves the best job offer a worker discovers. This fact is represented by an upward-sloping wage offer curve. At the same time, the lowest offer a worker is willing to accept tends to decline as the period of job search lengthens, producing a downward-sloping reservation wage curve. The intersection of the two determines the duration of unemployment. It also provides some clues as to how workers will react, for example, to changes in demand. An increase in aggregate demand pushes up the wage offer curve. In the short run, before workers begin to adjust their expectations to the long-run inflationary implications of the increase in demand, the reservation curve will be unchanged. Thus, the short-run effect of inflation that is not fully anticipated is to reduce the average duration of unemployment and the measured unemployment rate, without a major increase in inflation. As time goes by, however, and both workers and employers come to expect inflation, the trade-off between inflation and unemployment becomes less favorable. Wages and markups increase substantially, in a "catch up" fashion, and inflation rises faster and faster.

5. If the growth rate of nominal demand is slowed after a period of accelerating inflation, an inflationary recession will result (called *stagflation*). Until inflationary expectations are dampened, the inflation rate and the unemployment rate may both continue to rise while real output falls. However, if unemployment becomes severe enough, wages and prices may begin to decline despite inflationary expectations, leading, in turn, to a drop in the inflation rate. This deceleration may continue, or it may be interrupted by a renewal of expansionary policy— called *reflation.*

6. Alternating expansionary and contractionary demand management policies produce a stop-go policy cycle. On the inflation-unemployment diagram, the economy moves in clockwise loops. If the political system is, on the average, more sensitive to the problem of unemployment than to the problem of inflation, the loops may become an upward spiral. Actual post–World War II macroeconomic experience in Canada closely fits such a pattern.

## DISCUSSION QUESTIONS

1. Many economists believe that unemployment compensation, by lowering the opportunity cost of job search, tends to raise workers' reservation wages. Using the graphical framework introduced in this chapter, show the effect of unemployment compensation on the duration of job search and the unemployment rate.

2. During an episode of cost-push inflation, the expected price level sometimes rises faster than the actual price level. What do you think such an episode would do to the position of the reservation wage curve relative to the position of the wage offer curve? What would it do to the average duration of unemployment and the unemployment rate?

3. In what sense does an abnormally high or low rate of unemployment indicate that the market is not performing very well its function of distributing information?

4. Suppose that some private economic research organization discovered a 100 percent accurate and reliable method of forecasting next year's rate of inflation. Under what circumstances, if any, might the government want to suppress such a forecast?

5. What effect do you think shortening the period between national elections would have on economic policy? What effect would lengthening the period have?

6. Using the most recent issue of the Economic Review, published each April by the Minister of Finance, find inflation and unemployment statistics to update Exhibit 18.6. Do the points fall where you expect them to? Write a paragraph or two interpreting the data.

## SUGGESTIONS FOR FURTHER READING

Hasan, Abrar and Gera, Surendra. *In Short Supply: Jobs and Skills in the 1980s.* Economic Council of Canada, 1982.
*An in-depth look at the Canadian labor market, with forecasts about future trends in jobs and unemployment levels.*

Donner, Arthur W., and Peters, Douglas D. *The Monetarist Counter-Revolution, A Critique of Canadian Monetary Policy, 1975–1979.* Toronto: James Lorimer, 1979.
*A critique of recent economic policy — in particular, Bank of Canada policy.*

Barber, Clarence L., and McCallum, John C.P. *Unemployment and Inflation, The Canadian Experience.* Ottawa: The Canadian Institute for Economic Policy, 1980.
*A critique of recent monetary policy and a defense of traditional Keynesian policies.*

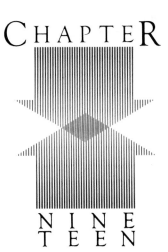

# COMBATTING INFLATION AND UNEMPLOYMENT

## WHAT YOU WILL LEARN IN THIS CHAPTER

*This chapter provides a critique of past policies applied to these problems, and a look at new approaches, both at home and abroad. The primary focus of stabilization policy in the post–World War II period has been the management of aggregate nominal demand. Demand management policy has not been notably successful in recent years, however, when measured in terms of the goals of full employment, price stability, and economic growth. This chapter discusses a variety of suggestions for making demand management work, some of which go beyond traditional monetary and fiscal policy tools. A number of the suggestions have been developed and tested in other countries. It may not be too late for Canada to learn from them.*

## FOR REVIEW

*Here are some terms and concepts that will be put to use in this chapter. If you do not understand them, review them before proceeding.*

- *Inflation, unemployment, and growth (Chapter 7)*
- *Aggregate real supply and demand (Chapter 17)*
- *Demand-pull and cost-push inflation (Chapter 17)*
- *Equilibrium rate of unemployment (Chapter 17)*
- *Job search theory and the labor markets (Chapter 18)*

The Great Depression of the 1930s had many lasting effects on economic policy and economic thought. One of those effects was to give the government increased responsibility for economic stabilization—a responsibility that was formalized in the White Paper on Employment and Income of 1945.

The primary focus of stabilization policy, as it developed over the years, was the management of aggregate nominal demand. Basically, the idea was that if the economy went into a slump and too many people were out of work, aggregate demand could be boosted with expansionary fiscal or monetary policy, and the economy could be gotten moving again. If a boom got too hot and prices rose too fast, putting the damper on aggregate demand was supposed to cool things off. The hope was that, by judicious use of expansionary and contractionary policy, the economy could be fine-tuned for prosperity without inflation.

As we have seen, however, things have not worked out particularly well in recent years for the would-be stabilizers and demand managers. The degree of instability experienced in the 1970s and early 1980s has, in fact, seriously called into doubt the adequacy of traditional demand management policies. Currently, the debate over how stabilization policy ought to be conducted centers on three questions. First, there is the short-term question of how best to reduce the current high rates of inflation and unemployment at minimum cost. Second, there is the longer-term question of how best to conduct demand management policy in order to avoid a repetition of the recent instability. And third, there is the question of whether a stabilization policy for the future should focus less exclusively on the traditional tools of demand management and pay more attention instead to the operation of our wage- and price-setting mechanisms. These questions are discussed in this chapter. To set the stage, we will first recapitulate what we have learned in previous chapters about how the economy works.

## INFLATION, UNEMPLOYMENT, AND AGGREGATE DEMAND: A RECAP

### The Tools of Demand Management

Aggregate nominal demand is the total value of all planned expenditures by all buyers in the economy. The concept of demand management thus encompasses all policies that affect the consumption plans of households, the investment plans of business firms, the plans of government units regarding the purchases of goods and services, and the plans of international traders of goods and services. Demand management policies fall into two groups—fiscal and monetary.

Fiscal policy acts by varying the volume of planned expenditure injected into the circular flow through government purchases or withdrawn from the circular flow through taxation. Fiscal policy actions in turn affect private consumption, investment, and international trading decisions.

Monetary policy injects new infusions of money rather than new flows of expenditures into the economy. As people adjust their portfolios to accommodate the changed money supply, changes occur in the prices of other assets, interest rates, planned investment spending, consumer durables purchases, and so on. Although indirect, the effects of monetary policy on aggregate nominal demand are potentially quite powerful.

Just how powerful monetary policy is relative to fiscal policy is still a matter of controversy between Keynesian and monetarist schools of economics. Despite differences in emphasis, however, economists generally agree that fiscal policy and monetary policy in some appropriate combination can be used to expand or contract aggregate nominal demand, thereby altering the equilibrium level of nominal national income and product.

### The Dynamics of Inflation and Unemployment

Through fiscal and monetary actions, then, policy makers are able to exercise reasonably close control over national income and product measured in nominal terms. The manipulation of nominal national income and product, however, is only an indirect means of pursuing the ultimate policy goals of full employment, price stability, real economic growth and balance of payments stability. To know the effects of demand management policy on these ultimate goals, then, it is crucial to know how any given change in nominal output will be split up between changes in the price level and changes in real output and employment. The aggregate real supply and demand analysis introduced in Chapter 17 provided a minimal set of tools with which to examine the effects of changes in aggregate nominal demand on real output and the price level Chapter 18 supplemented this basic framework with more detailed discussions of the labor market and of inflationary dynamics. But even without the refinements of the last two chapters, certain principles emerge from a basic analysis of inflation and unemployment.

*Demand-Pull Inflation*  One of the surest principles of macroeconomics is that, if aggregate nominal demand grows faster for a sustained period than the economy's real productive capacity, the price level will rise. Such an increase in the price level is called demand-pull inflation. However, an increase in the growth rate of aggregate nominal demand does not immediately produce an exactly proportional increase in the rate of inflation. Instead, in an economy like that of Canada, prices typically adjust only gradually to increases in aggregate nominal demand. In the short run, before the price level adjusts completely, a part of any increase in nominal GNP thus takes the form of an increase in real output.

Because of gradual price adjustment, then, episodes of demand-pull inflation tend to be associated with low or falling unemployment and high or rising real output. Thus, a policy of deliberate inflation can, for a time, pull output above its equilibrium level and unemployment below its equilibrium rate. However, the favorable output effects of demand-pull inflation are short-lived. If any given steady rate of expansion of aggregate nominal demand is maintained, workers and firms will adjust their expectations accordingly. As this happens, the increase in nominal GNP will eventually be fully converted into price effects, and real output will tend to return to its equilibrium level. Only if aggregate demand is allowed to grow at a constantly increasing rate, so that expectations never quite catch up with the actual rate of price increases, can unemployment be kept below its equilibrium rate and real output above its equilibrium level for a sustained period. But the price of such a policy is, of course, constantly accelerating inflation.

*Inflationary Recession*  The same principle of gradual price adjustment that produces favorable real output effects during demand-pull inflation produces adverse real output effects when the economy's monetary and fiscal brakes are applied. If the growth rate of aggregate nominal demand is suddenly stopped or slowed at a time when firms and workers have come to expect ongoing inflation, prices and wages will not immediately stop in their tracks. As the momentum of inflationary expectations continues to push the price level up, the purchasing power of the relatively restricted level of aggregate nominal demand will be inadequate to absorb the high level of real output attained during the previous inflationary period. Rising inventories will cause output and employment cutbacks while prices continue to rise. The result is an inflationary recession—a worst-of-all-possible-worlds situation in which the goals of full employment, price stability, and real growth are all simultaneously out of reach.

*Restoring Price Stability*  Fortunately, the combination of circumstances that produces an inflationary recession cannot persist for long. If fiscal and monetary authorities do not accommodate inflationary expectations by resuming rapid expansion of nominal demand, and if workers and employers react to growing unemployment and business failure by dampening wage and price demands, the price level, although rising, will begin to rise less rapidly. As firms and workers become aware that inflation is slowing, they may eventually stop taking actions to protect themselves from price increases they mistakenly were expecting. When the inflation rate drops to the reduced growth rate of nominal GNP, real output will stop falling.

Inflation is now decelerating, real output has stopped falling but remains below its potential level, and unemployment has stopped rising but remains above its equilibrium rate. At this point, the government will be tempted to bring a quick end to the recession by resuming rapid expansion of aggregate nominal demand. If it does so, it will win a temporary respite in the upward inflationary spiral, but it will not restore actual price stability. To restore long-run price stability by use of demand management tools alone, policy makers must follow the inflationary recession not by a quick recovery but by a sustained gradual slowing of the growth rate of nominal demand. If real output is held below its equilibrium level and unemployment above its equilibrium rate for a sustained period, inflationary expectations will continue to be revised downward until they approach zero. At that point, in theory, at least, the economy can be eased to a better position in which inflation will fall to zero, real output will return to its equilibrium level, and unemployment will return to its equilibrium rate.

*Markets, Expectations, and the Distribution of Information*  The preceding paragraphs provide a rough synopsis of the theory of inflation and unemployment put together in the last two chapters. It is worth noting how this theory builds on the fundamental idea, introduced in Chapter 2, that markets are mechanisms for transmitting information. Business decision makers, workers, and households operate with incomplete information in the best of times, so that their plans do not always mesh. Some people are always incurring losses through miscalculation while others are reaping unexpected windfall gains. But during periods of macroeconomic stability, these numerous microeconomic mistakes tend to cancel one another out.

Unanticipated changes in the inflation rate or in the direction of macroeconomic policy, however, add something new to the picture. Such changes can mean that, temporarily at least, a great many people may suffer from similar misinformation. As a result, everyone may tend to make the same kinds of mistakes at once. When aggregate demand first begins to expand, firms may increase output more and increase prices less than they would if they knew the increase in demand was economy-wide and not just a locally favorable trend in their own market. As inflation first begins to accelerate, workers may be willing to accept nominal wage offers that turn out to be not so good when they find out that the cost of living has gone up more than expected. Conversely, when inflation first begins to slow down, firms may find themselves pricing goods higher and paying higher wages than they would if they had correctly anticipated the slowdown. And workers may damage their short-term employment prospects by trying to protect themselves against expected inflation that turns out not to be so bad after all. These widespread errors of information contribute to the fluctuations in employment and real output that typically accompany changes in the inflation rate.

Does the theory say, then, that people act foolishly? Not at all. People are smart. They learn from experience. All the theory says is that the market does not transmit information at the speed of light, so that learning takes time. Between the time events change their course and the time people adjust their plans and expectations to the new conditions, people may be led to do things they never would have done had they possessed accurate information all along.

## GOING BEYOND DEMAND MANAGEMENT

Given this view of how the economy operates, how can demand management best be conducted to promote the goals of full employment, price stability, and real growth? In particular, what steps, if any, should be taken to reduce the current levels of inflation and unemployment in Canada?

It must be recognized that demand management policy to promote price stability implicitly relies on the creation of a recession and its painful side effects in order to curb inflation. A restrictive demand management policy may ultimately be successful in fighting inflation because, in the course of creating an inflationary recession, business failures increase and unemployment rates increase to the point where they become intolerable to workers and employers. This certainly happened in the 1982 to 1983 period. Business bankruptcies reached post-Depression heights, and unemployment increased to 12.8 percent, also the highest figure since the Depression. Though the government introduced a so-called "6 and 5" wage guideline in 1982, in an effort to encourage wage and price settlements to move down to those levels in 1983 and 1984, it was the severe recession itself that probably brought about reductions in both wages and prices, resulting in a reduction in the inflation rate. In fact, several recent studies indicate that market-set wages and prices fell much more rapidly in the 1982 to 1983 period than prices and wages set by government. It was found that government-determined prices, which constitute nearly 25 percent of all prices in our economy, were growing 50 percent faster than privately set prices. In the three-year period 1979 to 1981, wages in the private sector rose by 24 percent, while wages in the federal government increased by 38 percent.[1]

---

[1]Reference is made here to two studies by the Bank of Canada and Statistics Canada, as reported in Michael Walker, "Government sector keeps inflation rate from falling," *The Financial Post*, October 2, 1982, p. 6.

While labor and business began to adjust their wage and price increases downwards in the early 1980s, producing a declining inflation rate and new hope for economic recovery, the events that produced such adjustments were tragic for millions of Canadians. Many people were asking quite justifiably: is this the best that the market system can do?

It would appear that the Canadian policy makers, at least, with their past policies of demand management, have failed quite miserably to cope with recent increases in prices and unemployment. We have mentioned that once the inflationary process begins, labor and management cannot be accused of acting irrationally when they set wages and prices so as to keep up with the inflation rate. But their combined actions are irrational in another sense, even if they are understandable—they are self-defeating, and they contribute to the very problem that they are trying to solve. It seems foolish for any particular labor group to hold back its wage increases when it cannot count on other groups to do the same thing, and when all are experiencing price increases. Similarly, it seems foolish for a firm to hold down its prices when labor costs and other costs are increasing. Nevertheless, such wage and price increases merely add fuel to the inflationary fires. In the end, almost no one will be better off, and many people will be much worse off.

There has been a tendency in our news media to identify a "villain" in all of this, *either* labor or management. But both of these actors are merely trying to keep pace with forces that they are unable to see are caused by them. Labor feels that it must get wage increases in order to keep wages in line with prices, and management feels that it must raise prices to pay for increased wage and production costs.

Exhibit 19.1 depicts the annual average increase in industrial wages and salaries, both in nominal and in real terms, from 1971 to 1981. Money wages increased at about 8 percent a year before the inflationary upsurge of 1974. Wages then began to rise sharply, the annual increase exceeding 14 percent in 1975, the year that price and wage controls were imposed. Between 1975 and 1978 the annual increases dropped considerably, only to increase once more, in line with inflationary pressures after 1978. What is most significant, however, is the trend for real wage increases, based on average wages and salaries that have been adjusted for price increases. During the inflationary period 1973 to 1975, labor managed to keep ahead of inflation, as evidenced by the positive real increases they obtained. (However, the best real increase, it may be noted, was in 1976, after the first full year of wage controls, when prices started to come down and even nominal wage increases were reduced.) During the most recent inflationary period, in contrast, the greater nominal increases that labor enjoyed did not keep up with the inflation rate. In all four years, 1978 to 1981, real increases were negative. Therefore, though industrial labor did increase its wages quite sharply, it failed to keep pace with inflation.[2]

---

[2]Though labor demands in this sense cannot be said to have been "excessive" or unreasonable, this is not to say that they may not have contributed to the inflationary pressures. Between 1971 and 1980, output per person employed in manufacturing increased by 19.5 percent, while labor compensation per unit of output increased by 108.8 percent. This would certainly promote price increases. (See Department of Finance, *Economic Review*, April 1982, p. 166.)

**Exhibit 19.1**
**Nominal and real annual increases in wages and salaries, 1971–1981,**
**compared with changes in the CPI**
Though labor generally managed to raise its nominal wages during periods of rapid
inflation, during the most recent severe inflation it failed to increase wages as
rapidly as inflation, depicted by the negative rates of change in real wages during
that period.

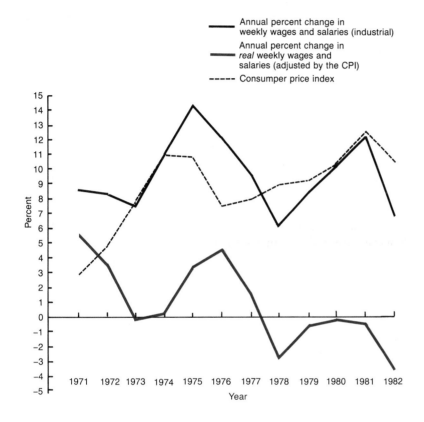

Source: Department of Finance, *Economic Review*, April 1982, pp. 14, 167, and 171.

Case 19.1 indicates that business firms are similar to labor in their behavior. Strong efforts are made to increase the rate of return on capital invested, in line with inflation increases. During recent inflation bouts the after-tax rates of return on equity have increased sharply, but the rates of change have not kept pace with inflation.

**Case 19.1**
**How Business Builds an Inflation Factor into Return Targets**

Exhibit 19.1 indicates rates of return on shareholders' equity over the past few years. The projection by Sharwood & Co. indicates the forecast trend over the next three years. These projections are somewhat higher than most, because corporate presidents, unable to deal with the complexities of inflation accounting, have set target rates of return at the traditional rate of 10–12 percent plus the inflation rate.

Accordingly, it is not uncommon to see "hurdle rates" for corporate investments of 25 percent (the "hurdle rate" is the minimum rate of return a corporation requires for approval of a proposed investment). Payback periods on internal projects are often set at two years, which really represents a 50 percent hurdle rate.

It is quite startling to see how sharply rates of return have climbed over the past few years. Below is a representative sample of some better-managed major corporations that have substantially improved their rate of return over the past few years. As you can see, not all are in the resource sector, so rates of return are improving generally.

|                            | 1975 | 1979 |
|----------------------------|------|------|
| Stelco                     | 11.7 | 20.8 |
| Abitibi                    | 4.1  | 19.6 |
| Consolidated Bathurst      | 7.1  | 19.7 |
| Ivaco                      | 6.6  | 22.1 |
| Westburne International     | 15.6 | 22.7 |
| Cara Operations            | 18.3 | 24.0 |
| Magna International         | 21.0 | 24.0 |

The chart is based on one by the Finance Department, about which they comment that, "while rates of return have been trending upwards on a current basis, when adjusted for inflation they have been trending downwards."

This is true, but returns have taken a sharp rise in the past two years and my view is that they will continue to do so.

After wage and price controls ended and it became apparent in 1977–78 that we were in for a long period of inflation, I think corporate presidents and planners began to build assumptions about continued inflation into their forecasts. It became important to increase prices to give that kind of improvement in rates of return, and I would think that corporate price behavior has fueled inflation over the past few years as corporations have striven to bring their rate of return up to a more appropriate level.

Source: Gordon Sharwood, "Business Building Inflation Factor into Return Targets," *The Financial Post*, May 5, 1981, p. 15. Reprinted by permission.

## What is the Real Problem?

Canada's inflation and unemployment problems are rooted in numerous complex factors, and there are no simple solutions. We have had to cope with increases in our labor force that were extraordinary in comparison with our previous experience and in comparison with those of other Western nations. We have been the victims of sharp increases in commodity prices that gave a profound shock to our whole system in the 1970s. We have been under unusual pressure to keep our interest rates high because of high interest rates in the United States and elsewhere. Our foreign sector has suffered from increasing protectionism and from severe recessions in our major trading partners. Along with much of the rest of the industrial world, we have seen disturbing drops in productivity, which some attribute to the "working down" (decline in impact) of previous technological breakthroughs. There is a growing premonition, too recent to be tested, that the new applications of computer technology will pose even greater threats to our efforts to reach full employment than the forces we have coped with in the recent past.

In view of all these problems, and others that could easily be elaborated upon, it would be quite presumptuous to say that there is *one real* cause

**Exhibit 19.2**
**After-tax rates of return on equity, private**
**non-financial corporate sector, all industries Canada**

In 1977, the list of corporations included in the Statistics Canada sample was revised on the basis of the 1974 corporate population. Overlapping estimates of rates of return can be constructed for the period 1975–1977. Both the unrevised and revised estimates are shown in the chart.

Estimate by
Sharwood & Co.

1979 data are seasonally adjusted data referring to the first three quarters only

After adjustments to remove foreign assets and related income, eliminate double-counting of intercorporate shareholdings, and count deferred tax liabilities as equity

Source: Statistics Canada and *The Financial Post*, May 5, 1981, p. 15.

for the Canadian economic dilemma. Nevertheless, there are undoubtedly a few factors that lie at the core of our recent stagflation experience, and it is worthwhile to identify them and examine them briefly. Our previous analysis indicates that a serious problem facing our market system is the absence of a mechanism to get major economic role-players like labor and management to act in concert so that their actions truly benefit them. When the inflationary spiral begins, there seems to be nothing, short of a major recession, to stop the process.

This is the point made in Case 19.2. Two leading American economists, Robert Heilbroner and Lester Thurow, have argued in a recent book that no country—at least not Canada or the United States—has succeeded in forging a consensus among groups like labor and management that is capable of placing a ceiling on the inflationary spiral before it does considerable damage to the economy. Their argument is perhaps somewhat extreme. As we shall see, Canada has experimented with some new initiatives, and there are other countries that have successfully (or at least much more successfully than Canada) created mechanisms for setting wages and prices that have reduced both inflation and unemployment rates.

### Case 19.2
### Does a "depression-proof Economy" Breed Inflation?

The five economic challenges that face North America are inflation, recession, big government, the falling dollar, and the energy crisis — so say two distinguished American economists, Robert Heilbroner and Lester Thurow.

These two men believe that the manner in which we deal with these crises will determine the quality of our lives in the years ahead. Their book, *Five Economic Challenges,* is a lucid analysis written in a way we can all understand.

Lester Thurow gained recent attention with his book, *The Zero Sum Society.* Professor Heilbroner teaches at the New School for Social Research in New York. His most widely known book is *The Wordly Philosophers.*

At 62, Heilbroner is small, neatly suited, serious and persuasively articulate and frank. He was in Toronto recently, where he spoke with Financial Post contributor Alan Pearson.

**Pearson: Why is it that economists can disagree with each other so fundamentally?**

**Heilbroner:** Well, economics is not a science the way engineering is. There are real disagreements based on insufficient knowledge. Milton Friedman, for instance, is convinced that if you change the money supply you change the rate of inflation. Sounds logical. In fact, what we know about this, in terms of tracing it statistically, is very muddy. There are nations that have increased money supply and haven't had inflation. The linkage is not mechanical, it's a circuitous one. So, there's room for honest disagreement.

The other basis for disagreement is that economists are, consciously or unconsciously, pushing for moral values. Such as more egalitarianism or less, helping the working class, helping the capitalist class, helping the farmer... or what have you. So, they select and sift the evidence without any sense of deliberately distorting the evidence to favor their own policies.

**What is the genesis of inflation?**

It seems to me that inflation derives from the fact that we live in an economy which has been made depression-proof. It has floors under it (one of them is massive government spending). Such an economy, instead of being unstable downwards, is unstable upwards and, ultimately, the cure is to add ceilings on top of the floor. Those ceilings may be wage and price controls, they may be what is called incomes policy, they may be appropriate tax policies.

No Western country has succeeded in forging those ceilings, largely for political reasons. They have not achieved the consensus needed or, if you will, the coercion needed. That's the inflationary challenge in a nutshell: forging the political consensus to put in the appropriate economic ceilings.

The real problem with big government is the extraordinary misconceptions the public has. They think of the public sector as being entirely deadweight; they think of the private sector as being entirely dynamic. If you look at both with an appraising eye, you'll see they both have waste.

Source: *The Financial Post,* May 23, 1981, p. 10. Reprinted by permission.

## SOME NEW ALTERNATIVES

We have seen that, although traditional tools of demand management are not likely to be abandoned soon, economists have become pessimistic about the ability of discretionary fiscal and monetary policies alone to return the economy quickly to the desired path of full employment, price stability and balanced economic growth. Not surprisingly, they have cast about for supplementary policy tools. This section will examine several such tools, beginning with incomes policies.

## Incomes Policies

An **incomes policy** is any policy that directly controls wages, salaries, and earnings for the purpose of fighting inflation. Ordinarily, such a policy also includes direct controls on wholesale and retail prices. Canada has experimented with incomes policies, and they have become a permanent feature of economic life in many Western European countries. It will be worthwhile to look at how these policies work and why they are highly controversial.

**Incomes policy** A policy that attempts to control wages, salaries, earnings, and prices directly in order to fight inflation.

**The Theoretical Case for an Incomes Policy** From a theoretical point of view, the case for an incomes policy is strongest when the policy is intended as a temporary measure to fight inflationary recession. The previous chapter showed that when policy makers put on the brakes after a long period of accelerating inflation, the economy is thrown for a time into the worst of all possible worlds. Workers and employers base their plans on the expectation of more inflation; yet aggregate demand is actually tailing off. Wages, prices, and unemployment all rise at once—until expectations adjust to reality.

Now enters the timely use of an incomes policy. Suppose that just at the moment the fiscal and monetary brakes are put on, the government announces a program of strict price and wage controls, as the White party did, in the example given in Chapter 18. This is done with great fanfare and a show of grim determination to lick inflation once and for all. What is hoped is that workers and businesspeople will believe that these controls are going to stop inflation. If they do, they will revise their inflationary expectations downward much more rapidly than if they have to wait to learn from experience. This revision of expectations will get rid of the cost-push element of the inflationary recession. Workers will know that they do not have to push for high wages to beat inflation, so they will accept the controls. Firms will know that they will not have to pay higher wages, so they will keep their prices in line and concentrate on increasing their sales. The readjustment to price stability and full employment will be more rapid and less painful than it would be without an incomes policy.

**Problems with Controls** So much for theory. Granting that wage and price controls are helpful in squeezing the cost-push element out of an inflationary recession, does that mean that they are a cure-all for the country's economic problems? Not really. The problem is that controls can be of help in correcting past mistakes in demand management policy, but they cannot work as a substitute for sound demand management. Unfortunate things can happen if the government tries to use an incomes policy to fight inflation without also slowing the growth of aggregate demand, or if it leaves controls in force after a recession is over and a new boom gets underway, as we saw in Chapter 18.

If aggregate demand rises in nominal terms, one of three things must logically happen. First, national product (aggregate supply) may rise in real terms to meet the increased nominal demand without a rise in prices. Second, prices may rise to meet the increase in nominal demand without an increase in output. Finally, neither prices nor output may rise, in which case the aggregate quantity of goods demanded will exceed the aggregate quantity of goods supplied, and there will be an overall shortage of goods. A combination of these three alternatives may sometimes occur, but no fourth alternative is logically possible.

Naturally, the first alternative is the most attractive. It will mean real economic growth without inflation. Real economic growth can come from only two sources, however. One is an increase in potential GNP, which can be hoped for at the rate of about 3 percent per year in the long run. The other is a fall in unemployment. This source of growth is temporary, because unemployment will soon reach a level below which it can fall no further. In the long run, then, real growth without inflation or shortages is possible only if demand management limits the growth of nominal GNP to the potential long-term growth rate of real GNP.

An incomes policy cannot buy real growth without inflation or shortages if that rule of demand management is not followed. All it can do is determine which of the second two alternatives will occur. If aggregate demand is allowed to run away without controls, the result is runaway inflation. If controls are applied and demand still runs away, the result is shortages, rationing, and black markets.

## Canadian Experience with Controls

There have been several experiments with wage and price controls in the Canadian economy. One was during World War II. Then, huge wartime government spending made it impractical to control aggregate demand. The effects of controls in those conditions were as predicted. Rationing was introduced, and there were widespread shortages and black markets. All this was tolerated because people felt that rationing was the fairest way to distribute essentials during the emergency. As soon as the war had been won, controls were abandoned with a sigh of relief.

Another experiment, of an entirely voluntary nature, was attempted in the late 1960s when prices started rising after a period of price stability. The government suggested in 1966 that wage increases should not exceed 6 percent annually. However, these guidelines were soon broken by the government itself, when it granted a 15 percent increase to members of the Seafarers' Union after a long strike.

In 1969, the government tried to reestablish a voluntary program of restraint by creating a Prices and Incomes Commission. This commission made some thorough studies of the causes of inflation and sought voluntary support for a restraint program, but labor unions, which felt that wages would be more closely monitored than profits, refused to cooperate. These attempts came to an end with the aboliton of the commission in 1972.

A third, major experiment with controls was initiated by the Trudeau government in October 1975, after prices in the previous year had risen by more than 10 percent. There is some evidence that inflationary pressures were beginning to ease just at the time the controls were set up. However, an Anti-Inflation Board was established with the mandate, and with considerable powers, to reduce annual price increases to 4 percent by 1978. The price and wage controls applied to about 50 percent of the economic activity of the country. Excluded were the prices of foodstuffs, imports and exports, and the prices of public services. About 2.4 million workers had their wages controlled by the board by late 1976. The board restricted its control to the profits and prices of firms employing more than 500 employees. However, direct price controls were eliminated in June 1976, because of the complex problems that arose in enumerating the huge variety of goods and services. Corporations were still required to justify price increases, and large profit margins were seen as evidence of excessive price changes and grounds for ordering price rollbacks.

The Anti-Inflation Board and the control program were discontinued in the spring of 1978, so the experiment was in effect for about two-and-a-half years. In terms of its major objective, the substantial reduction of annual price increases, the program must be considered a failure. As we saw in Exhibit 19.1, the inflation rate did drop considerably in 1976, to 7.5 percent, but by 1978 the annual rate of increase was up to 9 percent, instead of down to the target of 4 percent.

There are several reasons for this. First, many goods, particularly imports and foodstuffs, were not controlled at all. The Canadian consumer is heavily dependent on both. In late 1976, the problem of import prices was compounded by a serious and prolonged decline in the exchange rate of the Canadian dollar. This helped to boost exports and ease some of the demand pressure on imports, but it also meant a substantial increase in the effective price that Canadians paid for their imports.

The failure of governments to control utility prices also contributed to the maintenance of high inflation. In addition, because many income earners were not monitored at all, or not monitored as closely as those subject to union management negotiations in large corporations, unions understandably did not support the program. Therefore, cost-push factors were not eased nearly as much as had been hoped.

Whether the program helped to diminish inflationary expectations is not clear. Inflation continued to run high until 1981, and both wages and rates of return on investment rose sharply as well.

We don't know what inflation would have been like without the program, or if the program had been more systematically enforced. But the results of this radical incomes experiment in Canada, like those of similar programs in other countries, have not been very satisfying.

## The Future of Controls

Not everyone is willing to give up on the idea of controls, though. A very bold British experiment with incomes policy was established in 1976. It had one novel feature. In return for accepting lower wage increases, the government promised to cut taxes for wage earners. The idea was that this would protect workers' real incomes without making labor power so expensive that firms could not afford to hire new workers. In combination, the wage controls and tax incentives were intended to cut both inflation and unemployment at the same time. Incomes policy is likely to be talked about and experimented with as long as inflation remains at its recent unacceptable levels.

**Exhibit 19.3**

Inflation and unemployment experience of countries with and without new forms of ''industrial democracy''

Countries in the bottom left corner, with relatively low rates of unemployment and inflation in the late 1970s and early 1980s, are compared with countries in the upper right corner, which have higher inflation and unemployment. A basic difference between the two sets of countries is that the first has created forms of social consensus between groups like labor and management, while the other has not.

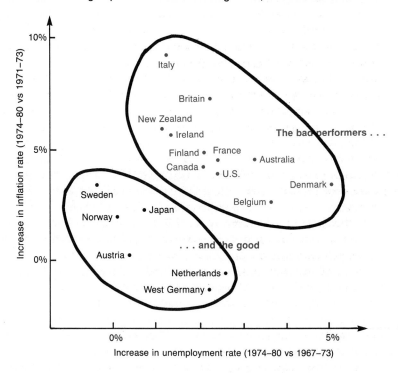

Source: John McCallum, ''We Need a Way as Well as a Will,'' *Financial Post*, November 20, 1982, p. 10.

## Experiments with Industrial Democracy

Incomes policies generally seek to *impose* a solution on workers and employers, trying to coerce them into more "rational" forms of behavior. This type of policy appears at times to be necessary in countries where there is no natural form of cooperation between labor and management, or no mechanism through which they can work at certain problems cooperatively.

Several industrialized countries have tried in the last few decades to create mechanisms permitting labor and management to work at mutual solutions, without destroying their ability to bargain over matters like wages and working conditions. Such efforts have come to be described as experiments in **industrial democracy**. This is a very broad term and refers to a wide range of practices which, however, have the common objective of increasing the participation of workers in economic decision making

**Industrial democracy**
Arrangements whereby workers are able to participate more fully in economic decisionmaking.

within their plant and enterprise, in the process encouraging greater co-operation between workers and employers.

The countries that have advanced quite far in this direction are Sweden, Norway, Japan, Austria, the Netherlands, and West Germany. Before we describe some of the features of their experiments, and examine briefly the motivation behind them, it is instructive to note how the economic performance of these countries has differed from our own.

In a recent study, two Canadian economists have observed that, in the control of inflation and unemployment, there is a substantial difference between countries like those listed above, and countries that have not developed forms of consensus.[3] Nations like Canada, Australia, the United States, and France have suffered far higher rates of both inflation and unemployment than have the set of countries experimenting with industrial democracy. The difference in performance is illustrated quite vividly in Exhibit 19.3. As one of the authors of that study notes, "the six successful countries have not only superior tools [of demand management] but also superior social consensus. These are the countries with the lowest average strike rates over the whole postwar period and with the most effective system of labor-management cooperation at the plant level (works councils)."[4]

No one would pretend that these countries have found a panacea for all of their major economic problems. Indeed, in the case of West Germany and Japan, unemployment worsened considerably in 1982–83. They are clearly not impervious to some of the strong currents affecting us. But the empirical evidence is too ample for us to ignore: some of these countries have developed a system of setting wages and prices and settling other matters involving workers and employers that is quite different from ours, and this system appears to have an impact on their macroeconomic performance.

The systems now in place usually grant workers more rights on at least two different levels:

1. Within the plant where the worker is employed, decisions involving working conditions, including holiday time, pay schedules (though not usually pay rates, which are bargained for collectively), overtime, dismissals, and layoffs are regulated by agreements between management and labor worked out in plant-wide labor bodies, often called workers' councils. Grievances are subject to binding arbitration.

2. At the level of the whole enterprise, which might have many plants or other sub-units within it, workers are allowed to be members of the highest company board, which decides matters such as plant relocations, new investments, and the hiring of management. This practice has been carried furthest in West Germany, where the highest board is called the supervisory board. The following description gives some indication of the ambitious scope of the German attempts at industrial democracy.[5]

---

[3]Clarence Barber and John McCallum, *Controlling Inflation: Learning From Experience in Canada, Europe and Japan* (James Lorimer & Company, Toronto: 1982).

[4]John McCallum, "We Need a Way as Well as a Will," *The Financial Post*, November 20, 1982, p. 10.

[5]Roy Vogt, "Property Rights and Employee Decisionmaking in West Germany," *Journal of Economic Issues* 15 (June, 1981), p. 383.

The Co-Determination Act of 4 May 1976 establishes three different forms of worker participation on supervisory boards. In the first type, in stock companies with up to 2,000 employees (outside coal and steel), one-third of the seats on the supervisory board are allocated to workers' representatives. In the second type, in stock companies with more than 2,000 employees (outside coal and steel), the board consists of an equal number of workers' and shareholders' representatives. On a board with twenty members, six of the ten workers' representatives must be white- and blue-collar personnel elected by the workers, three are union representatives nominated by the union and elected by the workers, and one must be an executive legal "worker" nominated by all senior executives and voted for by all executives. The chairman is to be elected with a two-third majority vote of the board. Failing that, he is elected by the shareholders' representatives. He casts an additional vote in the event of a tie. These boards came into full effect on 1 July 1978. The third type exists in the coal mining and iron and steel producing industries (based on the Stock Act of 1965 and the Mining Co-Determination Act of 21 May 1951). The board consists of an equal number of shareholders' and workers' representatives, plus a "neutral" chairman agreed upon by both sides.

Famous German companies like Volkswagen are organized this way, and operate very successfully. Workers on the company board have access to all financial information about the company. In fact, they are provided with funds by the company to hire their own lawyers and accountants to make sure they understand what is happening. When the company is doing badly no one has to tell them—they know it for themselves. Several times in Volkswagen's history, the workers have held back wage increases or even taken a cut when the company was in jeopardy. On the other hand, they have benefitted from good years, knowing precisely how good they were and what the company could afford. The wages of German workers have risen more than the average for workers in Europe. Further, when Volkswagen wanted to build an assembly plant in the United States in the 1970s, it was required that a detailed "social" plan be worked out in advance with workers, providing satisfactory remuneration for those who would be laid off if such a move were to be made, and the chance to move to the new location for workers who so desired.

Salary negotiations are carried out on the national level, keeping in mind the needs of each industry and overall problems in the economy. Government may get involved in this process, reminding the parties that for the sake of German exports and full employment, wage and price settlements should not go above a certain level.

Countries like West Germany have developed such models of mutual decisionmaking for a number of reasons. First, they think it will improve efficiency, by helping the worker to identify more closely with his company. Second, it is hoped that decisions made will be more "rational," that is, corresponding to both worker and management goals and also to the needs of the economy. Third, it is considered a worker's *right* to be involved in decision making. He commits his time, energy, and talents to the company, and is clearly more involved in it than the average shareholder. Why should he not be able to have a greater say in the institution to which he is most committed?

As Case Study 19.3 indicates, Japan has adopted similar practices for similar reasons.

## Case 19.3
## The Japanese Style of Doing Business

ST-LAURENT, Quebec — The sign on the factory door reads: ''Sorry — no jobs available. No applications accepted.''

In that regard, Y.K.K. Canada Inc. is like most manufacturers, restraining employment to help ride out the economic storm.

In other ways, however, the company differs significantly from most Canadian producers. The zipper-maker is owned in Japan, and has brought with it many Japanese labor practices. For example, no Y.K.K. employee in Canada has ever been furloughed, says personnel manager Robert N. King, even though ''I could easily have laid off twenty-five or thirty people on six or seven occasions.''

The parent company, Yoshida Kogyo K.K., espouses what president Tadao Yoshida calls ''the cycle of goodness.'' The concept is built on the concern's 9,700 employees in Japan, who are required to deposit at least 10 percent of wages and 50 percent of bonuses with the company.

These savings ultimately ''enrich the lives of every citizen,'' Yoshida suggests. The company has the use of the money for its needs, the workers receive interest, and the government collects higher taxes.

Partly because of differences in laws, the program does not function in Canada. Still, the 230 employees, mostly in Montreal, Toronto and Winnipeg, are offered a stock ownership plan, whose interest rates have so far exceeded those available from banks, says Joe Y. Mizumaki, president of Y.K.K. Canada. Of 118 workers who are eligible, 63 are participating.

No profits from the Canadian operation — or from any other non-Japanese subsidiary — are repatriated to the parent. ''If we make a profit we reinvest it in that country,'' Mizumaki says. Operating earnings are divided equally among employees, through bonuses; customers, through reduced prices; and the community, through such projects as scholarships and charities.

Unlike their Japanese peers, the Canadian workers neither chant nor practise gymnastics on the job. ''That wouldn't work here,'' says personnel manager King. There is no formal quality-control circle, either. Instead, Y.K.K. uses a committee system to lubricate communications between employees and management. The 190 or so factory hands are divided into groups of ten to fifteen. Each of the fourteen groups chooses a representative who brings complaints and suggestions to the top and circulates management's proposals among his or her group. Meetings are held at least once a month.

Since Y.K.K. began manufacturing in Canada in 1971, it has twice moved to larger premises. The present plant in the Montreal suburb of St-Laurent covers 19,600 square metres (211,000 square feet). Investment totals $16.5 million, including land and machinery. The business reported after-tax earnings of $1.8 million on revenues of $21.2 million last year, and Mizumaki maintains it holds more than two-thirds of the Canadian zipper market.

There are other ways of measuring the philosophy's success. Union organizers who tried to sign up the staff early in 1979 were sent packing. ''Our employees have in mind that Y.K.K. is good, and they pass that on to newcomers,'' King maintains.

Wages at Y.K.K. average $9.50 to $10 an hour, including fringe benefits. King describes this as ''a fair amount better than the industry we're in (clothing) but nowhere near what a GM worker gets.''

Despite the attempt to blend into the various communities in which the Y.K.K. group operates, four of the seven senior executives in Canada are Japanese. (There are also eight Japanese technicians at the factory.) ''Our managers here don't have that much experience with zippers or management, so I'm waiting,'' Mizumaki says. ''Eventually more of our executives will be Canadian. Even the president.''

The firm's unblemished slate may end if the depression drags on long enough. "I don't say Y.K.K. has a policy that it will never lay off," Mizumaki acknowledges. "Nobody knows what will happen tomorrow."

Such a step, though, would not be taken lightly. "Our workers are my family—my brothers, my sisters," the president continues solemnly. "So I have the responsibility for looking after their lives."

Source: Alan Gray, "The Japanese Way in Canada," *The Financial Times of Canada*, October 18, 1982. Reprinted by permission.

### Which Way for Canada?

There is no reason to think that the changes described in Case 19.3 could not be adopted in Canada, and that they would not prove beneficial. In 1982, the Manitoba government appointed two workers to the board of Manitoba Forestry Resources, one of its Crown corporations. Chrysler made headlines a few years ago when, in the midst of a financial crisis, it appointed the head of the United Automobile Workers to its board, in order to seek worker cooperation. There was a renewed vote of confidence in Douglas Fraser when he was re-elected company director of Chrysler in May, 1983 (see Case 19.4). Parliament authorized a Sub-Committee in 1982 to study the possibility of encouraging more profit-sharing plans for workers and to examine "alternate forms of employee participation on boards of directors and in company decision-making generally."[6]

Unfortunately, both business and labor leaders are often apprehensive about these developments. Management thinks that such changes are an encroachment on their rights, and that workers will use increased power irresponsibly. Union leaders fear that they will be "co-opted" into serving management goals. Cooperation may appear to be an act of surrender to those who are accustomed to thinking almost entirely in adversarial terms.

In a careful study of late nineteenth century workers' response to industrial capitalism, Gregory J. Kealey[7] has shown that workers initially sought to retain co-decision making powers with management. They had had considerable power over the setting of prices, determining the quality of their product, and setting their working hours and wages under the old handicraft system, and they wished to retain an equal footing with management. They did not want to be pushed into a separate class of people called "employees," because it seemed to them an essential human right to have some basic say about working conditions. Workers were, however, pushed into a lower, less powerful class and eventually they joined unions to fight against a new adversary.

Perhaps the time has come to break down the barriers that were created then and to restore some of the rights that were taken away. With a new way of setting our wages and prices, in a more trusting environment in which essential information is available to all participants, and in which both local and national objectives can be considered, we may discover at

---

[6]House of Commons Standing Committee on Finance, Trade, and Economic Affairs, June, *Report of the Sub-Committee to Promote Profit Sharing by Employees in Business,* June 1982.
[7]Gregory S. Kealey, *Toronto Workers Respond to Industrial Capitalism, 1867–1892,* (Toronto, University of Toronto Press, 1980).

least one other method of solving some of our current problems. Our examination of macroeconomics ends where it should: in a concern not only for better economic performance but for the methods that should be used in achieving such performance.

## Case 19.4
## A Union Boss on the Board

When the Chrysler Corp. re-elected soon-to-retire United Auto Workers President Douglas Fraser to a fourth one-year term as a company director, the significance of the move was clouded in uncertainty. For one thing, the election, which took place during the company's annual meeting in Detroit, signalled Chrysler's continued willingness to grant a union chief unprecedented access to the rarefied air of the boardroom. But the renewal of Fraser's tenure also disguised a controversy surrounding the bold Swedish-style experiment in labor-management relations and growing concern that the seat will not be offered to Fraser's successor, who will take power this month. Chrysler broke new ground in 1980 by selecting Fraser to become the only labor representative to sit on the board of a major U.S. corporation. That seat came about as a result of collective bargaining action in 1979 to help the number three U.S. automaker avoid bankruptcy. But industry insiders say that Chrysler may be preparing to reverse its policy.

According to Chrysler spokesman Douglas Nicoll, the stockholders re-elected Fraser—who began his career at Chrysler in 1941 as a metal finisher at a DeSoto plant—because of his uniquely extensive knowledge of the industry. Still, that does not mean his successor will become a board director, says Nicoll. Even Chrysler Vice-Chairman Gerald Greenwald stated flatly earlier this year, "We do not have board seats by heredity."

For his part, Fraser says that he is "confident" that the seat will be handed over to his probable successor, Owen Bieber. But industry analysts are less certain. They point out that Bieber, now the UAW vice-president in charge of the General Motors department, is considered to be an old-style labor leader who is unlikely to embrace Fraser's conciliatory style. According to Arvid Jouppi, a Detroit-based auto analyst, Bieber was endorsed by the union's international executive board to succeed Fraser largely because he is viewed as a leader "unwilling to hold hands with management." By supporting Bieber, Jouppi said, "the union is indicating to the Big Three [automakers] that North American union members are not ready to work with management from the board level all the way down to the shop floor."

Fraser's own position on the board has been criticized by some union members, who charge that he has lost some of his militancy at the bargaining table. But Fraser disagrees, arguing that the benefits have included access to details about Chrysler's financial conditions and valuable advance warnings about company decisions involving employees. "Getting a grip on plant closings and economic dislocation before the event" has helped the workers involved, he said. With that knowledge, the UAW was able to forestall the planned closings of the trim, forge and glass plants in Detroit and the Indianapolis electric plant. The labor leader also says that his board-level intervention during the sale of Chrysler's tank division to General Dynamics Corp. in February, 1982, prevented 119 Chrysler workers from losing their seniority rights at the Warren, Mich., plant.

As for the company, Chairman Lee Iacocca says that Fraser's presence in the boardroom has opened up a better line of communication with the union. "Doug Fraser has been an invaluable member to the board," he said.

Despite such accolades, the future of the arrangement remains in doubt, as does its long-term benefit for the labor movement. One skeptic is Robert White, director of the Canadian United Auto Workers. He says that the boardroom presence is not something that has won widespread acceptance. "One executive on the board cannot change a corporation," he declared. But he conceded that Fraser's post did help the UAW to win the right in 1982 to have its officials present workers' concerns directly to the boards of the Big Three. If Fraser is the last union leader to sit with his employers, even those small gains may not be repeated.

Source: Carol Bruman, "A Union Boss on the Board," *Maclean's*, May 16, 1983, p. 35.

## CONCLUSIONS

Macroeconomics as it is now known was born in the crisis of the Great Depression. Before that time, the distinction between what is now called macroeconomics and microeconomics was not as sharp as it later became. In particular, part of what made Keynes's ideas catch on was their macro quality. To the followers of Keynes, it seemed that the really important features of national economic life could be captured in a few key relationships between broad aggregate quantities. Macroeconomics meant building with big blocks labeled "consumption," "investment," "aggregate supply," "money," and so on. The demand management policies of the 1960s grew out of this macroeconomic approach.

Today, the distinction between macroeconomics and microeconomics is once more becoming blurred. One thing more than any other unites the critics of the theory and policy of the past — a belief in the great importance of understanding the detailed microstructure of economic life. This is as true of economists who are liberals as of those who are conservatives. It is as true of neo-Keynesians as it is of monetarists. And it is true of those who simply look for the truth with no labels attached.

The exciting topics of macroeconomics today are such micro questions as: How can we understand unemployment in terms of the job search decisions of individual workers? How is cost-push inflation generated? How do workers and businesspeople form their expectations and plans for the future? How can they learn to make decisions together that will benefit both groups in the long run?

We are back, it seems, to the theme with which the book began. Economics is about people. It is not about aggregate demand or expansionary gaps or Phillips curves — except when these things are understood as expressions of the way individual people think and act and plan.

## SUMMARY

1. Unexpected increases in the inflation rate pull unemployment below its equilibrium rate. If policy makers allow inflation to run faster and faster every year, they can keep unemployment low for quite a while. When inflation slows after a long period of acceleration, however, the result is temporarily the worst of all worlds — an inflationary recession in which inflation and unemployment both rise. Recession cures inflation, but, at least in recent Canadian experience, the price of the cure in terms of employment and real output is quite high.

2. Wage and price controls, more formally known as incomes policies, are one common suggestion for reducing the cost of eliminating inflation. The theory is that incomes policies, if applied in conjunction with restrictive monetary and fiscal measures, will break the momentum of inflationary expectations and permit a faster return to price stability.

Experience with wage and price controls during the 1970s is not particularly encouraging, however.

3. Less coercive forms of mutually-set wages and prices, as practised in different forms of industrial democracy, could help, in the long run, to improve our economic performance. There is empirical support for such a hope, though it would be foolish to think panaceas are just around the corner.

## DISCUSSION QUESTIONS

1. Now that you have completed your first study of macroeconomics, how have your views on problems like inflation and unemployment changed? Have you become more, or less, pessimistic about the effectiveness of past policies and about our ability to improve our situation in the future?
2. Why doesn't unemployment seem to affect people as badly today as it appears to have done in the Great Depression of the 1930s? Why didn't Canadian workers riot, with unemployment rates above 12 percent, and one-and-a-half million workers unemployed?
3. In 1982 to 1983, the inflation rate began to show significant declines, but unemployment rates remained high. How would you explain this, in view of the theory developed in the last three chapters?
4. At the moment you are reading this, what do you perceive to be the main problem in the country, inflation or unemployment? How would you propose to cope with the problem if you were advising the Minister of Finance? Do you think that more cooperative relationships between labor and management would help? Why or why not?
5. "We have political democracy, but very little economic democracy." What do you think is meant by this assertion? Discuss its validity.

## SUGGESTIONS FOR FURTHER READING

Barber, Clarence L., and McCallum, John C.P. *Controlling Inflation, Learning from Experience in Canada, Europe and Japan.* Toronto: James Lorimer, in association with the Canadian Institute for Public Policy, 1982.
*In addition to describing the inflation problem, this study examines solutions attempted elsewhere. Tax-based incomes policies are also evaluated.*

Anton, Frank R. *Worker Participation, Prescription for Industrial Change.* Calgary: Detselig Enterprises, 1980.
*One of the most recent Canadian studies of industrial democracy, describing practices in West Germany, the Netherlands, the United Kingdom, and in the European Economic Community generally.*

Carnoy, Martin, and Shearer, Derek. *Economic Democracy, The Challenge of the 1980s.* New York: M. E. Sharpe, 1980.
*A vigorous argument by two American economists in favor of extending more rights to workers in order to solve current and coming problems.*

Heilbroner, Robert and Thurow, Lester. *Five Economic Challenges.* Englewood Cliffs, N.J.: Prentice-Hall, 1981.
*An interesting survey of basic problems facing modern capitalism, by two economists who combine good economic analysis with a strong concern for the human implications of economic processes.*

# THE
# THEORY
# OF
# PRICES AND
# MARKETS

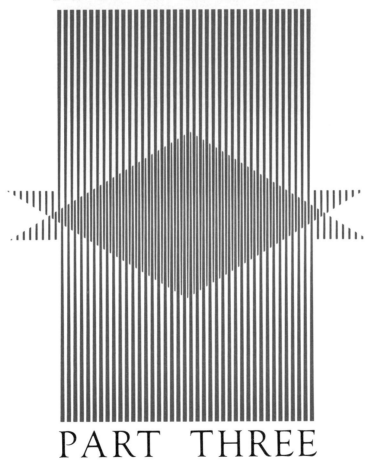

# PART THREE

# SUPPLY AND DEMAND: BUILDING ON THE BASICS

CHAPTER

TWENTY

---

**WHAT YOU WILL LEARN IN THIS CHAPTER**

*This chapter begins with a review of the principles of supply and demand, first covered in Chapter 3, for the benefit of those who have just completed the study of macroeconomics. Next it introduces the concept of elasticity as a way of measuring the responsiveness of the quantity of a good supplied or demanded to a change in the price of that good. It then extends the concept of elasticity to apply to changes in variables affecting the demand for a good other than changes in the price of the good itself.*

**FOR REVIEW**

*Here are some important terms and concepts that will be put to use in this chapter. If you do not understand them, review them before proceeding.*
- *Market equilibrium (Chapter 3)*
- *Shortage and surplus (Chapter 3)*
- *Substitutes and complements (Chapter 3)*
- *Normal and inferior goods (Chapter 3)*

---

The principles of supply and demand are the most widely applied principles in all of economics. Those readers who have just completed the study of macroeconomics will have seen many applications since the principles were first introduced. As you move from the study of macroeconomics to the study of microeconomics, the principles of supply and demand will become more important than ever. This chapter will set the stage for what is to come by briefly reviewing the principles presented in Chapter 3 and then adding some new details.

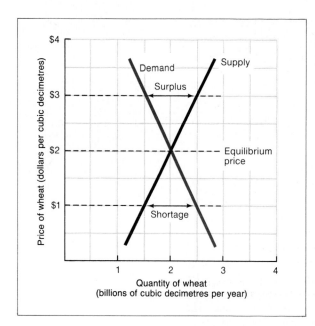

**Exhibit 20.1**
**Equilibrium in the market for wheat**
The equilibrium price is found at the point where the downward-sloping demand curve and the upward-sloping supply curve intersect. That is the only price at which there is neither a shortage nor a surplus, so that no person has an incentive to change the price asked or offered.

## A REVIEW OF THE BASICS

### The Supply and Demand Curves

Exhibit 20.1 uses the market for wheat to set the scene for a review of the basics of supply and demand. The demand curve for wheat is drawn with a negative slope in accordance with the law of demand: as the price of wheat decreases, other things being equal, the quantity demanded increases. The supply curve is drawn with a positive slope, indicating that, other things being equal, farmers are willing to increase the quantity of wheat they will supply if they are offered the incentive of a higher price.

Both the supply and demand curves are drawn on the basis of other things being equal in order to isolate the effects of changes in the price of wheat from the effects of other things that might influence the decisions made by buyers and sellers. To be specific, the demand curve is drawn on the assumption that population, consumer tastes, consumer incomes, the prices of other goods, and consumer expectations about future prices remain unchanged as the price of wheat changes. Similarly, the supply curve for wheat is drawn on the assumption that production technology, the prices of inputs to the production of wheat, and supplier expectations about future prices remain unchanged as the price of wheat changes.

### Equilibrium

The price of $2/dm^3$, where the supply and demand curves intersect, is shown as the *equilibrium price* in the exhibit. It is the equilibrium price because it is the only price at which no person has an incentive to change the price asked or offered for the product.

Consider, by contrast, any price higher than $2. At a price of, say, $3 the quantity supplied would be 2.5 billion cubic decimetres and the quantity demanded only 1.5 billion. There would be a surplus (an excess quantity supplied) of 1 billion cubic decimetres per year. Farmers could not sell all they were willing to offer at that price. Those who were unable to find buyers for their crops would then have an incentive to cut the price at which they offered their wheat for sale. As the price fell, the quantity demanded would increase and the quantity supplied would decrease. The surplus would gradually be eliminated, and equilibrium would be restored.

In much the same way, there would be an incentive for price changes if the price of wheat were below $2. As Exhibit 20.1 is drawn, for example, at a price of $1, buyers would want to purchase 2.5 billion cubic decimetres of wheat per year, but producers would be willing to supply only 1.5 billion cubic decimetres. There would be a shortage (excess quantity demanded) of 1 billion cubic decimetres. Not all buyers would be able to get as much wheat as they wanted. Unsatisfied buyers would have an incentive to offer higher prices in order not to be left out altogether. Farmers would willingly accept these offers, and the price would rise toward equilibrium. Eventually the shortage would disappear.

## Changes in Equilibrium

As economic conditions change, the equilibrium price and quantity for the market change also. In analyzing changes in equilibrium, it is important to distinguish between shifts in supply or demand curves and movements along those curves.

When a change occurs in the price of a good, other things being equal, the effect is seen in a movement along the demand curve for that good. Economists refer to such a movement as a *change in the quantity demanded*. In contrast, when the behavior of buyers is affected by a change in something other than the price of the good for which the demand curve is drawn, the result is shown as a shift in the entire demand curve. Such a shift is, by convention, referred to as a *change in demand* for the good in question. All the items covered by the other-things-being-equal clause in the law of demand are potential sources of shifts in the demand curve. Changes in the demand for a good can thus occur as the result of changes in population, consumer tastes, consumer incomes, the prices of other goods, or consumer expectations regarding future prices.

The same distinction between movements along a curve and shifts in the curve applies to the supply curve. When a change in the price of the good occurs, other things being equal, the effect is shown as a movement along the supply curve. This is called a *change in the quantity supplied*. A change in one of the things covered by the other-things-being-equal clause — production technology, input prices, or supplier expectations — produces a shift in the supply curve. Such a shift is referred to as a *change in supply*.

The points regarding shifts in curves and movements along curves are illustrated in Exhibit 20.2. In Exhibit 20.2a, an increase in consumer incomes shifts the demand curve for wheat to the right, from the position $D_1$ to the position $D_2$. This shift creates a shortage of wheat, which in turn drives up the price. As the price rises, the market moves up along the supply curve, from the original equilibrium position $E_1$ to equilibrium

**Exhibit 20.2**
**Changes in price caused by changes in demand and supply**
Part a of this exhibit shows the effects of a change in the demand for wheat caused by an increase in consumer incomes. The demand curve shifts to the right, from $D_1$ to $D_2$, creating a shortage at the initial price of $2/dm^3$. The market moves up along the supply curve, as shown by the arrow, until a new equilibrium is established at $E_2$, with a price of $3/dm^3$. Part b shows the effects of a change in supply caused by an increase in labor costs. The supply curve shifts upward from $S_1$ to $S_2$, creating a shortage at the original price. The market moves along the demand curve to the new equilibrium $E'_2$.

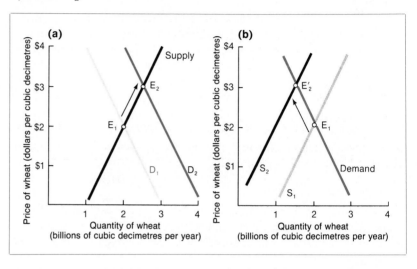

position $E_2$. In Exhibit 20.2b, a price rise is touched off by a decrease in supply. An increase in labor costs shifts the supply curve upward, from $S_1$ to $S_2$. This creates a shortage of wheat at the initial price, which again pushes the price upward. As the price rises, the market moves along the demand curve from the original equilibrium position $E_1$ to the new equilibrium position $E'_2$.

## ELASTICITY

### Elasticity and Changes in Revenue

The review of supply and demand just presented emphasized the effects of changes in price on the quantity of a good demanded. This section shifts focus somewhat to look at the effects of price changes on the total revenue generated by the sale of a good—total revenue being calculated as the quantity of the good sold multiplied by the price at which it is sold.

As Exhibit 20.3 shows, a change in the price of a good can have one of three effects on total revenue, depending on the shape and position of the demand curve. In the case of good A, a decline in price from $5 per unit to $3 per unit increases the quantity demanded from three units to six units. Total revenue thus increases from $15 to $18 as the price falls. In the case of good B, the same decline in price from $5 to $3 is shown as increasing the

**Exhibit 20.3**

**Elastic, inelastic, and unit elastic demand**

This exhibit illustrates the relationship between changes in price and changes in revenue for three different demand curves. As the price of good A decreases from $5 to $3, revenue increases from $15 to $18; the demand for good A is elastic. As the price of good B decreases over the same range, revenue falls from $15 to $12; the demand for good B is inelastic. As the price of good C decreases, revenue remains unchanged; the demand for good C is unit elastic.

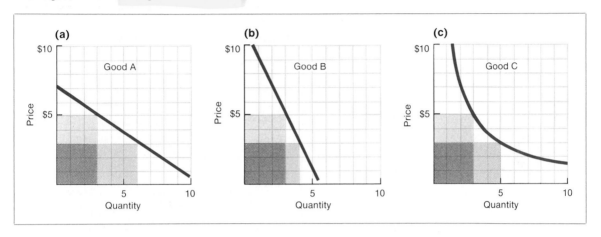

quantity demanded by only one unit, from three units to four units. Total revenue thus decreases from $15 to $12. Finally, in the case of good C, a drop in price from $5 to $3 increases the quantity demanded from three units to five units, leaving total revenue unchanged at $15.

The effects of changes in price on total revenue illustrated in Exhibit 20.3 can be expressed in terms of the relationship between the percentage by which the quantity demanded changes and the percentage by which the price changes. The ratio of the percentage change in the quantity demanded of a good to the percentage change in the price of the good is known as the **price elasticity of demand**, or simply the **elasticity of demand**, for that good. If quantity changes by a larger percentage than price, as in Exhibit 20.3a, so that total revenue increases as the price decreases, demand for the good is said to be **elastic**. If quantity changes by a smaller percentage than price, so that total revenue decreases as the price decreases, as in Exhibit 20.3b, demand is said to be **inelastic**. And if price and quantity change by the same percentage, as in Exhibit 20.3c, so that total revenue remains unchanged, demand is said to be **unit elastic**.

In addition to the cases of elastic, inelastic, and unit elastic demand illustrated in Exhibit 20.3, there are two limiting cases illustrated in Exhibit 20.4. Exhibit 20.4a shows a demand curve that is perfectly vertical. No matter what the price, the quantity demanded is a constant five units—no more, no less. Such a demand curve is referred to as **perfectly inelastic**. Exhibit 20.4b shows a demand curve that is perfectly horizontal. Above the price of $5, none of the good can be sold. But as soon as the price

**Price elasticity of demand (elasticity of demand)** The ratio of the percentage change in the quantity of a good demanded to the percentage change in the price of the good.

**Elastic demand** The situation in which quantity changes by a larger percentage than price along the demand curve, so that total revenue increases as price decreases.

**Inelastic demand** The situation in which quantity changes by a smaller percentage than price along the demand curve, so that total revenue decreases as price decreases.

**Unit elastic demand** The situation in which price and quantity change by the same percentage along the demand curve, so that total revenue remains unchanged as price changes.

**Perfectly inelastic demand** The situation in which the demand curve is a vertical line.

**Exhibit 20.4**
**Perfectly elastic and perfectly inelastic demand**
Part a of this exhibit shows a demand curve that is a vertical line. No matter what the price, the quantity demanded is a constant five units. Such a demand curve is referred to as perfectly inelastic. Part b shows a perfectly elastic demand curve, which is a horizontal line. Above the price of $5, none of the good can be sold. At the price of $5, suppliers can sell as much of the good as they want without further reductions in price.

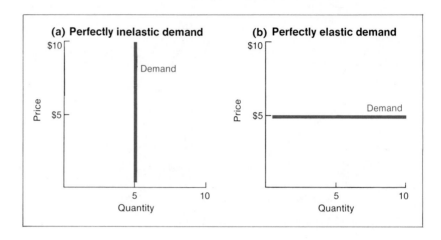

drops to $5, producers can sell as much of the good as they care to produce without cutting the price any more. A horizontal demand curve such as this one is described as **perfectly elastic**.

**Perfectly elastic demand**
The situation in which the demand curve is a horizontal line.

## The Importance of Elasticity

If elasticity were nothing more than another way of describing the shape and position of demand curves, it would not deserve a great deal of attention. But what makes elasticity an important concept is not so much its descriptive usefulness as its analytic usefulness. Decision makers in business and government often would like to know what the elasticity is for particular products. This is illustrated in the following case study.

## Measuring Elasticity of Demand

For some purposes, it is useful to put a numerical value on elasticity of demand, rather than simply to classify demand as elastic or inelastic. The basis for such numerical measurements is the definition of the *elasticity of demand* as the ratio of the percentage change in quantity demanded to the percentage change in price.

### Case 20.1
### Measuring Elasticity of Demand in the Wine Market

The price of beer, liquor, and wine is set by provincial liquor control commissions. In setting prices, the commissions take account of world demand and supply conditions as well as local demand and supply forces. They would like to know something about the elasticity of demand for their various products in order to guess how changes in price will affect the quantity demanded.

The news item below, taken from the *Winnipeg Free Press* of January 19, 1974, illustrates this:

The jump in price of European wines June 1 has shown some pretty predictable results at the local liquor control commission.

(Prices, particularly of French wines, shot up drastically last year as a result of a combination of factors, including increased world demand, increased shipping charges, a few poor vintages and the devaluation of the United States dollar.)

To compensate for the expected decrease in sales of French wines, the Manitoba liquor control commission expanded its range of Italian, German, Spanish, and Portuguese wines last spring.

Statistics made public this week by the commission indicate that, between October 1972, and October 1973, the purchase of French wines had decreased by 13 percent and the sale of Italian wines, by 55 percent. German wines were up 66 percent from October 1972; Spanish and Portuguese wines were up 53 percent.

The statistics on decreased purchases of French wines apply mainly to those which increased drastically in price. For example, until May, Chateauneuf du Pape sold at $3.90 a bottle and, between January and May, the commission sold a total of 5,200 bottles. After June 1, the price of the wine soared to $11.95 and between June and December sales dropped to 400 bottles. It's a wonder even 400 bottles were sold at this terribly inflated price.

The Manitoba liquor control commission was forced to raise the price of French wines because of demand and supply changes noted in the second paragraph of the newspaper article. The commission correctly anticipated that the quantity of French wines demanded by the Manitoba public would decline and that the demand for other wines would increase. However, it could not predict how much the price increase would affect the quantity demanded of French wines. In other words, it couldn't say how elastic or inelastic the demand for a given French wine actually was.

The last paragraph in the news article gives us some useful information about the demand for one particular brand of French wine, Chateauneuf du Pape. In the five-month period before June 1, the value of sales of this wine totaled $20,280 (5,200 × $3.90). In the seven-month period after the June 1 price increase, sales declined to $4,780 (400 × $11.95). Would you say that the demand for this wine is elastic or inelastic? Note that the calculation of elasticity in this example is complicated by the fact that the comparision is drawn out over a full year. Elasticity is meant to measure consumer response to a change in price over such a short period of time that other factors like income and tastes cannot be said to influence consumer behavior. Over a year, of course, such factors do alter, so that it is difficult to say how much of the change in the quantity demanded was caused by the price change.

**Percentage Changes** In order to apply this definition to the measurement of elasticity, we need to be somewhat more precise than before about how to calculate percentage changes. Suppose, for example, we are dealing with a $.25 increase in the price of strawberries, from $.75/L to $1/L. In everyday usage, we would call this a 33 percent increase in price ($.25/$.75 = 0.33). However, if we observed a $.25 decrease in the price of strawberries, from $1/L to $.75, we would call it a 25 percent decrease ($.25/$1 = 0.25).

In measuring elasticity, it would be awkward to have to specify whether we were dealing with a price increase or a price decrease before calculating the percentage change. To get around this difficulty, we will adopt the convention of using the midpoint of the price range as a basis for calculating the percentage. The midpoint in this case is ($.75 + $1)/2 = $.875, so the percentage change, as we define it, becomes $.25/$.875 = 0.285 (approximately). Calculated this way, the percentage is the same for an increase as for a decrease over the specified range of price.

Using $P_1$ to represent the price before the change and $P_2$ the price after the change, this convention for calculating the percentage change in price can be written in terms of a general formula as:

$$\text{Percent change in price} = \frac{P_1 - P_2}{(P_1 + P_2)/2}$$

The same problem arises in defining the percentage change in the quantity demanded that results from a given change in price. Suppose that when the price of strawberries falls from $1 to $.75, the quantity demanded increases from 100L per day to 150L. We can use the average of the higher quantity and the lower quantity to calculate the percentage change in quantity. If $Q_1$ and $Q_2$ are the quantities before and after a change in price, the formula for the percentage change can be written as:

$$\text{Percentage change in quantity} = \frac{Q_1 - Q_2}{(Q_1 + Q_2)/2}$$

Applying this formula to the example just given, we would say that either an increase in quantity from 100 to 150 or a decrease in quantity from 150 to 100 represented a 40 percent change in quantity:

$$\text{Percentage change in quantity} = \frac{150 - 100}{(150 + 100)/2} = 0.40$$

**An Elasticity Formula**  Defining percentage changes in this way allows us to write a practical formula for calculating elasticities. The formula can be applied to the elasticity of either supply or demand. Using $P_1$ and $Q_1$ to represent price and quantity before a change and $P_2$ and $Q_2$ to represent price and quantity after the change, the formula is:[1]

$$\begin{matrix} \text{Price} \\ \text{elasticity} \\ \text{of demand} \end{matrix} = \frac{(Q_1 - Q_2)/(Q_1 + Q_2)}{(P_1 - P_2)/(P_1 + P_2)} = \frac{\begin{matrix}\text{Percentage change}\\\text{in quantity}\end{matrix}}{\begin{matrix}\text{Percentage change}\\\text{in price}\end{matrix}}$$

The following problem illustrates the use of this formula.

**Problem:** A change in the price of strawberries from $1/L to $.75/L causes the quantity demanded to increase from 100L per day to 150L per day.

---

[1] Given the definition of percentage changes, we could write the elasticity formula as:

$$\frac{\dfrac{Q_1 - Q_2}{(Q_1 + Q_2)/2}}{\dfrac{P_1 - P_2}{(P_1 + P_2)/2}}$$

This is unnecessarily complicated, however, because the 2s cancel out. The formula given in the text is the simplified equivalent of this one.

What is the price elasticity of demand for strawberries over the range of price and quantity indicated?

*Solution:*
$P_1$ = Price before change          = $1
$P_2$ = Price after change           = $.75
$Q_1$ = Quantity before change = 100
$Q_2$ = Quantity after change     = 150

$$\text{Elasticity} = \frac{(100 - 150)\,/(100 + 150)}{(\$1.00 - \$.75)\,/(\$1.00 + \$.75)}$$

$$= \frac{-50\,/250}{\$.25/\$1.75}$$

$$= \frac{-0.2}{\$.1428}$$

$$= -1.4$$

Note that when the formula is applied to a good having a negatively sloped demand curve — as most, if not all, goods do — it yields a negative value for elasticity. The reason is that the quantity changes in the opposite direction to the change in price. It will be the practice in this book to drop the minus sign, however, and to speak of price elasticity of demand as a positive number; that is, the elasticity of demand for a good will be given as 2 or 0.5 or whatever rather than as −2 or −0.5. This convention of dropping the minus sign is widely used in economic writing, although it is not followed universally. If this convention is applied to the preceding problem, the elasticity of demand for strawberries will be said to be 1.4 over the range of price and quantity shown.

### Elasticity Values and Changes in Revenue

The chapter earlier introduced the terms *elastic, inelastic, unit elastic, perfectly elastic* and *perfectly inelastic demand*. They were defined in terms of the relationship between change in price and change in total revenue. Each of these elasticity terms corresponds to a certain numerical value or range of numerical values of elasticity as calculated according to the elasticity formula. A perfectly inelastic demand curve has a measured elasticity of 0, because any change in price produces no change in quantity demanded. The term *inelastic* (but not perfectly inelastic) *demand* applies to measured elasticities in the range from 0 up to, but not including, 1. *Unit elasticity*, as the name implies, means a numerical elasticity of exactly 1. *Elastic demand* means any value for elasticity greater than 1. *Perfectly elastic demand*, corresponding to a horizontal supply curve, is not defined numerically; as the demand curve approaches horizontal, the denominator of the elasticity formula approaches 0, so that the measured value of elasticity approaches infinity.

### Varying and Constant Elasticity Demand Curves

The formula just given for calculating the elasticity of demand shows the elasticity of demand over a certain range of price and quantity. Measured

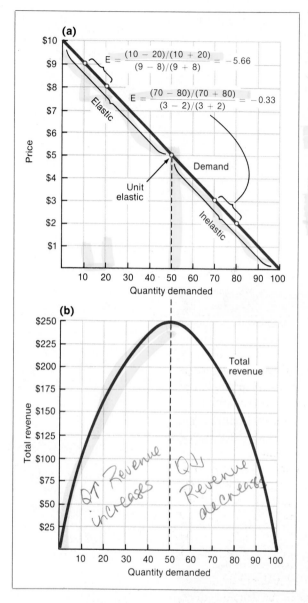

**Exhibit 20.5**
**Variation in elasticity along a straight-line demand curve**

This exhibit shows how elasticity varies along a straight-line demand curve. At low quantities, demand is elastic; for example, in the range from ten to twenty units, the elasticity of the demand curve shown in Part a of the exhibit is 5.66. At fifty units of output (halfway down the curve), a point of unit elasticity is reached. From there to a hundred units of output, demand is inelastic; in the range seventy to eighty units, for example, elasticity is 0.33. Part b of the exhibit shows that total revenue increases as quantity increases over the elastic portion of the demand curve and decreases as quantity increases over the inelastic portion. Total revenue reaches a maximum at the point of unit elasticity.

over some other range of price and quantity, the elasticity of demand for the same good may or may not be different. Whether the elasticity of demand for a good changes along the demand curve turns out to depend on the exact shape of the curve. This is illustrated in Exhibits 20.5 and 20.6.

**A Linear Demand Curve** First consider Exhibit 20.5a, which shows a straight-line demand curve like most of those drawn in this book. The elasticity of demand is not constant for all ranges of price and quantity along this curve. Measured over the price range $8 to $9, for example, the elasticity of demand is 5.66. Measured over the range $2 to $3, it is 0.33. (The full calculations are shown in the exhibit.)

**Exhibit 20.6**

**A demand curve with constant elasticity**

It is possible for a demand curve to have constant elasticity throughout its length. The calculations in the exhibit show that this curve has an elasticity of 1.0 wherever it is measured. This particular demand curve is a rectangular hyperbola with the formula $P \times Q = 100$.

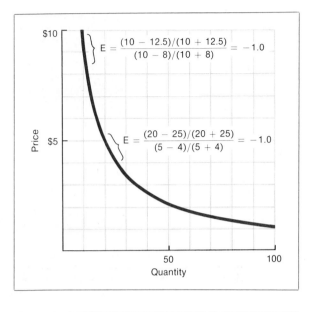

$$E = \frac{(10 - 12.5)/(10 + 12.5)}{(10 - 8)/(10 + 8)} = -1.0$$

$$E = \frac{(20 - 25)/(20 + 25)}{(5 - 4)/(5 + 4)} = -1.0$$

This illustrates the general principle that elasticity declines as one moves down along a straight-line demand curve. It is easy to see why: with a straight-line demand curve, a $1 reduction in price always produces the same absolute increase in quantity demanded. At the upper end of the demand curve, though, a $1 change in price is a small percentage change, while the absolute change in quantity, as a percentage of the small quantity already demanded, is large. At the lower end of the curve, the situation is reversed. A $1 change is now a large percentage of the price, while the constant absolute increase in quantity has now become smaller in percentage terms. Because it is percentages, not absolute amounts, that count in elasticity calculations, the demand curve is less elastic near the bottom than near the top. Because elasticity changes along a straight-line demand curve, it makes sense to apply the formula only to small changes.

Note the relationship between the elasticity of demand and total revenue, as shown by Exhibit 20.5b. In the elastic range of the demand curve, total revenue increases as price decreases. Total revenue reaches a peak at the point of unit elasticity and declines again in the range of inelastic demand.

**A Constant Elasticity Demand Curve** If the demand curve is not a straight line, the above results need not always apply. There is an important special case in which the demand curve has just the curvature needed to keep elasticity constant throughout its length. Such a curve is shown in Exhibit 20.6. As the calculations in the exhibit indicate, elasticity is exactly 1.0 everywhere on this curve. It is possible to construct demand curves with constant elasticities of any desired value. Such curves are often used in statistical studies of demand elasticity, as the following case study illustrates.

## Case 20.2
## Measuring Elasticity of Demand in the Cotton Market

The market for cotton has tended to be relatively unstable in the postwar period. Price changes from one year to the next have been very great. It is thought that one of the reasons for this instability is a very inelastic demand for cotton. With an inelastic demand, the price must fall a long way for producers to dispose of a relatively small surplus, and a considerable rise in price can occur when there is a shortage. Kenneth Lewis, an economist at Boston University, thought it would be useful for those concerned with the cotton market to know just how inelastic demand was.

Lewis began by assembling data on the price of cotton and the quantity of cotton purchased in sixteen industrialized countries during the period 1949 to 1964. To simplify his calculations, he followed a standard econometric practice and assumed that the cotton demand curve would have the shape needed to give constant elasticity throughout the normal range of prices. Next he had to deal with the problem of "other things being equal." A demand curve tells how the demand for cotton responds to the price for cotton when nothing else changes, but in the wide range of countries and years represented in Lewis's data, "other things" could hardly be expected to stand still. To deal with this problem, he used a statistical technique known as multiple regression analysis. This allowed an approximate correction for changes that had occurred over time in population, per capita consumer income, and the prices of other closely related products — particularly wool and synthetic fibers.

Lewis's statistical results confirmed that the demand for cotton was very inelastic — only 0.095, as nearly as he could estimate. This meant that more than a 10 percent change in price from one year to the next would be required to change the quantity demanded by 1 percent. Lewis suggested two reasons for the low elasticity of demand. One was that cotton is a raw material that often accounts for only a small portion of the value of a final product. For example, a 10 percent change in the price of cotton would have far less than a 10 percent effect on the price of a cotton shirt if the cost of manufacturing, labor, transportation, retailing, services, and the like remained unchanged. Second, the products made from cotton were necessities rather than luxuries, for the most part, and hence they too could be expected to have low elasticities of demand.

Source: Based on Kenneth Lewis, "Multi-Market Demand Functions in the Presence of Supply Constraints: International Demand for Cotton and Wool." *Southern Economic Journal* 38 (October 1971), pp. 200-208.

It is important to recognize the limitations of statistical estimates of demand elasticity. To say that the elasticity of demand for cotton is 0.095 is not to measure any inherent quality of the good itself. Neither is the measured elasticity really a constant of consumer behavior. The actual measurement is just a capsulized fragment of economic history. It tells us that at certain times and places in the past, a 1 percent change in price appears to have been associated with approximately a 0.095 percent change in quantity demanded.

Despite their limitations, however, statistical estimates of elasticity can be of considerable practical use. Economic decision makers in business and government must take past experience into account when planning for the future even though they know that market conditions in the future will not be exactly like those in the past.

### Determinants of Elasticity of Demand

Why is the price elasticity of demand high for some goods and low for others? One thing helping to determine the elasticity of demand for a good is the availability of substitutes or complements. If a good has close sub-stitutes, demand for that good tends to be elastic, because when its price rises, people can switch to something similar. For example, the demand for olive oil is more elastic than it would be if other salad oils were not available as substitutes. Similarly, the demand for cars is less elastic than it would be if good public transport were available everywhere, because cars and public transportation are reasonably close substitutes for each other. On the other hand, if something is a minor complement to an important good, its demand tends to be inelastic. For example, the demand for motor oil tends to be inelastic, because it is a complement to a more important good — gasoline. The price of gasoline is much more likely to influence the amount of driving a person does than is the price of motor oil.

Elasticity is also influenced by the portion of a person's budget spent on a good. Matches, for example, are no longer really a necessity, and good substitutes exist. Nonetheless, the demand for matches is thought to be very inelastic, just because people spend so little on them that they hardly notice a price change. In contrast, the demand for things like housing and transportation is not perfectly inelastic, even though they are necessities. Since they occupy a large part of people's budgets, changes in prices just cannot be ignored.

Finally, elasticity of demand is influenced by the time perspective being considered. Demand is often less elastic in the short run than in the long run. Consider the demand for home heating fuel, for example. In the short run, people find it hard to cut back the quantity they use when the price goes up. They are accustomed to living at a certain temperature, dressing a certain way, and so on. Given time, though, they may find ways to economize. They can put better insulation in their homes, get in the habit of dressing more warmly, or even move to a warmer climate.

## Other Elasticities

The concept of elasticity has, up to this point, been applied only to the price elasticity of demand for a good; but there are many other common applications of the concept. All of them are based on the idea of the ratio of the percentage change in one variable to the percentage change in another. Two of the most commonly used types of elasticity, in addition to the price elasticity of demand, are price elasticity of supply and income elasticity of demand.

**Price Elasticity of Supply** The definition of the **price elasticity of supply** for a good closely resembles that of the price elasticity of demand: it is the percentage change in the quantity of the good supplied divided by the percentage change in the price of the good. The formula for price elasticity of supply is exactly the same as that for price elasticity of demand. Because price and quantity change in the same direction along a positively sloped supply curve, the formula gives a positive value for the elasticity of supply. Exhibit 20.7 applies the elasticity formula to two supply curves, one having constant elasticity and the other having variable elasticity.

**Price elasticity of supply (elasticity of supply)** The ratio of the percentage change in the quantity of a good supplied to the percentage change in its price.

**Income Elasticity of Demand** As shown earlier in this chapter, changes in consumer income can cause changes in the demand for a good. Such changes are represented by shifts in the demand curve. The concept of

**Exhibit 20.7**
**Calculating price elasticities of supply**
This exhibit gives four examples of how supply elasticities are calculated — two for each of the two supply curves shown. The supply curve $S_1$, which is a straight line passing through the origin, has a constant elasticity of 1.0. The supply curve $S_2$, which is curved, is elastic for low quantities of output and inelastic for larger quantities. For example, in the range from twenty to thirty units of output, the elasticity of $S_2$ is 3.4, and in the range from eighty to ninety units of output, the elasticity is 0.41.

$$E = \frac{(50 - 40)/(50 + 40)}{(10 - 8)/(10 + 8)} = 1.0$$

$$E = \frac{(90 - 80)/(90 + 80)}{(8 - 6)/(8 + 6)} = 0.41$$

$$E = \frac{(30 - 20)/(30 + 20)}{(6 - 4)/(6 + 4)} = 1.0$$

$$E = \frac{(30 - 20)/(30 + 20)}{(2.25 - 2.0)/(2.25 + 2.0)} = 3.4$$

**Income elasticity of demand** The ratio of the percentage change in the demand for a good to the percentage change in the per capita income of buyers.

elasticity, in the form of the income elasticity of demand, can be applied to measure the size and direction of such changes. The **income elasticity of demand** for a good is defined as the ratio of the percentage change in demand for the good to the percentage change in income. In measuring the income elasticity of demand for a good, the price of the good is assumed not to change. Income is usually measured in per capita terms. Using $Q_1$ and $Q_2$ to represent quantities before and after the income change any $y_1$ and $y_2$ to represent per capita income before and after the change, the formula for income elasticity of demand can be written as follows:

$$\text{Income elasticity of demand} = \frac{(Q_1 - Q_2)/(Q_1 + Q_2)}{(y_1 - y_2)/(y_1 + y_2)} = \frac{\text{Percentage change in quantity}}{\text{Percentage change in income}}$$

Income elasticity of demand is positive for a normal good and negative for an inferior good. Suppose, for example, that a study of meat buying habits showed that for each 10 percent increase in income, the typical Canadian household tended to consume 12 percent more steak, 5 percent more chicken, and 2 percent less hamburger. One would conclude from these numbers that the income elasticity of demand was 1.2 for steak, 0.5

for chicken, and $-0.2$ for hamburger. Steak and chicken would thus be classified as normal goods and hamburger as an inferior good.

## CONCLUSIONS

This chapter has set the stage for asking a great many questions. First, what really lies behind the supply and demand curves? The text has given general commonsense explanations of why these curves have the shapes they do, but now it must show in more detail how they can be explained in terms of individual people's attempts to deal with the problems of scarcity and choice. This explanation will occupy several chapters.

Next, do the principles of supply and demand apply to all markets or to only certain types of markets? This chapter limited its examples to markets like those for wheat and strawberries, where there are many buyers and sellers and all of them are relatively small. But we need to know also how to apply the principles to markets that may be dominated by only one or a few large sellers.

Finally, how can the principles of supply and demand be applied to help in further understanding the role of government in the economy? In many markets, government regulations have important influences on the prices and quantities of goods that consumers can buy and producers can sell.

In answering all these questions, future chapters will continue to build on the basics reviewed in this chapter.

## SUMMARY

1. According to the law of demand, the quantity of a product demanded increases as its price decreases. It is also widely the case that sellers of a good are willing to increase the quantity supplied only if offered the inducement of a higher price. When these conditions hold, there is a market equilibrium price at the intersection of a good's supply and demand curves. That intersection represents the only price at which no one has an incentive to change the price asked or offered.

2. Economists use the term *elasticity* to refer to the responsiveness of quantity demanded to a change in price. For some goods, a 1 percent change in price produces more than a 1 percent change in quantity demanded, so that revenue increases as price decreases. Such goods are said to have elastic demand. Similarly, goods are said to have an elastic supply if a 1 percent change in price produces more than a 1 percent change in the quantity supplied. At the extreme, where supply or demand curves are horizontal, supply or demand is said to be perfectly elastic. For other goods, a 1 percent change in price will cause less than a 1 percent change in quantity demanded, so that revenue decreases as price decreases. Such goods are said to have inelastic demand. Similarly, goods are said to have an inelastic supply if a 1 percent change in price produces less than a 1 percent change in the quantity supplied. Perfectly inelastic demand or supply means a vertical supply or demand curve.

3. The formula for calculating the elasticity of supply or demand between two points on a supply or demand curve is:

$$\text{Elasticity} = \frac{(Q_1 - Q_2)/(Q_1 + Q_2)}{(P_1 - P_2)/(P_1 + P_2)}$$

In applying this formula to demand, it is conventional to drop the minus sign from the result and consider elasticity to be a positive number.

4. Changes in per capita income can cause shifts in demand curves. The ratio of the percentage change in quantity to the percentage change in per capita income is known as the income elasticity of demand. Income elasticity of demand is positive for a normal good and negative for an inferior good.

## DISCUSSION QUESTIONS

1. How much of each of the following goods or services do you buy now in comparison with the quantity you bought a year ago?
   a. Clothing       c. Gasoline
   b. Movie tickets    d. Beer

   If the quantity you buy has changed for any of these goods, do you think the change is best described as a movement along your demand curve, a shift in your demand curve, or a combination of the two? Explain.

2. How do firms and consumers recognize market disequilibrium in the real world? What are the specific tangible signs of a surplus or a shortage?

3. If you were the president of a union bargaining for a new contract and asking for higher wages, would you prefer that the demand for your firm's product were relatively elastic or relatively inelastic? Explain.

4. Suppose that Middle Eastern governments cut off imports of petroleum products into Canada and that the Canadian government imposed a price ceiling. Do you think the lines that might form at gas stations would be longer if the demand for gasoline were relatively elastic or if it were relatively inelastic?

5. Suppose that the supply of tobacco were relatively elastic and the demand relatively inelastic. Under these conditions, who do you think would protest an increase in the cigarette tax more strongly — consumers or producers? What if the elasticities were reversed?

6. The town manager of River City calls you in as a consultant to explain something puzzling. Last year, the city doubled its fares on its downtown buses. For a few months, the bus line reported a strong increase in revenues, but then the revenues began falling off and ended up lower than they had been to begin with. Does what you have learned about elasticity of demand and the determinants of that demand help you explain what happened?

7. Do you think it makes sense as a general principle to say that the demand for a broadly defined good such as cars, clothing, or meat will be less elastic than the demand for a corresponding narrowly defined good such as Fords, Levis, or pork chops? Explain.

8. Why would the slope of a demand curve not be just as good a measure as elasticity for the responsiveness of demand to price changes? Can you formulate a simple generalization relating the slope of a demand curve to the way in which total revenue changes when price changes?

9. Economists define the *cross elasticity of demand* between good A and good B as the ratio of the percentage change in the quantity of good A to the percentage change in the price of good B. Suppose that the price of olive oil was $5/L. Suppose also that a grocer found that customers bought 100L of olive oil a month when the price of safflower oil was $3/L and 150L of olive oil per month when the price of safflower oil was $4/L. What is the cross elasticity of demand between olive oil and safflower oil? Are the two kinds of salad oil complements or substitutes for each other?

# THE LOGIC OF CONSUMER CHOICE

## WHAT YOU WILL LEARN IN THIS CHAPTER

*According to the law of demand, people tend to buy more of a good when its price goes down. This chapter discusses some of the principles of consumer choice that lie behind the law of demand. It explains how consumers, facing the necessity of choosing among alternatives and having limited budgets, balance the relative satisfactions they get from various goods against the prices they must pay for those goods.*

## FOR REVIEW

*Here are some important terms and concepts that will be put to use in this chapter. If you do not understand them, review them before proceeding.*
- *Law of demand (Chapter 20)*
- *Normal and inferior goods (Chapter 20)*
- *Substitutes and complements (Chapter 20)*

People are used to the idea that when the price of a good goes down, the quantity of that good demanded by consumers tends to go up. The law of demand is easy to accept, because common sense and everyday experience show that it is the way things are. Still, knowing that a thing is so does not keep people from asking why it is so. In Newton's day, everyone knew that when apples fell from trees, they fell down and not up; but Newton asked why, and this led him to some valuable new insights about the laws of gravitation. In the same way, economists have often asked why people buy more of a good when its price falls. Trying to answer that question leads to some useful insights.

## CONSUMPTION AND UTILITY

The most basic question one can ask about the law of demand is why people demand goods and services at all. The answer seems to be that people want material goods and services because they get pleasure and satisfaction from them. A loaf of bread to eat, a warm bed to sleep in, or a book to read—each serves needs or desires in one way or another. Economists have their own term for this sort of thing. They say that the use or consumption of material goods gives people **utility**.

**Utility** The economist's term for the pleasure, satisfaction, and need fulfillment that people get from the consumption of material goods and services.

## Utility and Psychological Needs

To a psychologist, just saying that people want things because they get utility from them would sound very shallow. Some psychologists, at least, would want to go into detail about the nature and sources of human wants. Followers of Abraham Maslow, for example, find it useful to think in terms of five basic kinds of needs: (1) physiological needs; (2) safety and security needs; (3) affection and belonging needs; (4) the need for self-esteem and the esteem of others; and (5) the need for "self-actualization" or self-fulfillment.[1] For each person, the order of importance of the five needs is different.

This simple list of needs raises some important questions for psychologists. Is there a hierarchy among needs? Why is any given need more important to some people than to others? What factors in people's upbringing affect the needs they seek to satisfy in later life? Questions like these, however, get very little attention from economists. Smith may buy a tennis racket to satisfy a physiological need for exercise. Jones may buy one in order to gratify a need to belong by joining a tennis club. Baker may buy one in order to gain the esteem of others by playing in tournaments. What is true of tennis rackets is true of other goods and services too. People with very different psychological needs all have one thing in common. They get utility of one sort or another from material goods. Most economists feel that they do not really need to know any more psychology than that.

## Utility and Demand

Economists may not be interested in the origins of human wants, but they are interested in the intensity of those wants. The reason is that the intensity of people's wants for some goods relative to the intensity of their wants for others determines the quantity of those goods they will demand in the marketplace. Whether a person wants a new car intensely enough to pass up the opportunity to spend the same funds on a three-week Caribbean cruise is clearly an economic as well as a psychological question. It is a question about the demand for automobiles.

**Marginal utility** The amount of added utility obtained from a one-unit increase in consumption of a good.

**Principle of diminishing marginal utility** The principle that the greater the rate of consumption of some good, the smaller the increase in utility from a unit increase in the rate of consumption.

**Diminishing Marginal Utility** Economists made a major step forward in their understanding of the relationship between utility and economic behavior when, in the late nineteenth century, they first clearly formulated the principle of diminishing marginal utility. The **marginal utility** of a good to a consumer means the amount of added utility obtained from the consumption of one additional unit of the good in question. The **principle of diminishing marginal utility** says that the greater the quantity of any good consumed, the less the marginal utility from a unit increase in consumption.

For a simple but vivid example of the principle of diminishing marginal utility in action, imagine yourself in a blackberry patch eating berries by the handful. As you eat more and more berries, you get more and more satisfaction; but at the same time, the satisfaction from each additional

---

[1] See Abraham Maslow, *Motivation and Personality*, 2d ed. (New York: Harper & Row, 1970).

handful diminishes. If you eat enough, you may even get to a point where more berries give you no additional utility at all. Then you stop eating berries, at least until the next day.

Utility, to be sure, is a very subjective concept. No one has yet invented a "utility meter" that can be hooked up to a person's skull to read utility like blood pressure. But suppose, to indulge in a bit of science fiction, that there is such a utility meter. If you allow yourself to be hooked up to the meter during your spree in the blackberry patch, the results can be recorded in numerical or graphical form, as in Exhibit 21.1. The table and the graphs in this exhibit use the "util" as an imaginary unit for measuring utility. Both the table and the graphs show that as the quantity of berries consumed per day increases, total utility increases — but at a decreasing rate. Marginal utility — that is, the added utility obtained from each additional handful of berries — falls as the rate of consumption increases. For example, the third handful of berries increases utility by two units, from 5.5 to 7.5, whereas the fourth handful gives only 1.5 units more.

---

**Exhibit 21.1**
**Diminishing marginal utility**

As the rate at which a person consumes some good increases, the utility derived from one additional unit decreases. The table and figures here show that as the rate of consumption of berries increases, total utility increases — but at a decreasing rate. In Part b, a smooth curve is drawn through the stair-step total utility line, which is based on the table. Part c shows a marginal utility curve. The height of this curve at each point is equal to the slope of the smooth curve in Part b.

**(a)**

| Quantity of Berries (Handfuls per Day) | Total Utility (Utils) | | Marginal Utility (Utils per Handful) |
|---|---|---|---|
| 1 | 3.0 | | |
| 2 | 5.5 | | 2.5 |
| 3 | 7.5 | | 2.0 |
| 4 | 9.0 | | 1.5 |
| 5 | 10.0 | | 1.0 |
| 6 | 10.5 | | 0.5 |

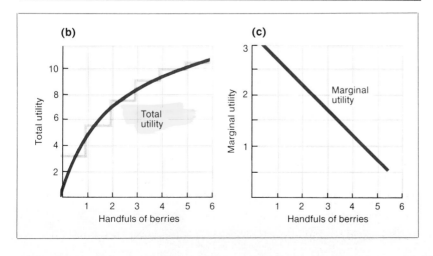

**The Consumer as Economizer**  For better or for worse, the world is not all one big blackberry patch where people can eat as much as they want without making choices. To put the principle of diminishing marginal utility to work in understanding consumer demand, one must look at a world more like the one that really exists. In particular, this is a world in which:

1. There are many different desirable goods.
2. Consumers must pay known prices for the goods they want.
3. Consumers have limited budgets.
4. Consumers try to get the greatest satisfaction they can from their limited budgets.

In such a world, consumers are faced with a classic problem in **pure economizing**: to maximize an objective (their own satisfaction) subject to known constraints (the prices of the goods and their budgets) by choosing among alternative activities (the consumption of various kinds of goods). In such a world, consumers have to make choices, and each choice involves an opportunity cost. If people spend more on one good, they have less to spend on something else. What can be said in a general way about how consumers economize their scarce resources?

**Pure economizing** The aspect of economic decision making that consists of choosing a pattern of activities from among a given set of alternative activities that will best serve a well-defined objective, subject to known constraints.

**Solving the Consumer Problem**  Begin with the consumer you know best—yourself. Suppose you are deciding how to divide your monthly spending between, say, food and clothing. If you spend an extra dollar a month on food, you get a certain added utility from doing so. At the same time, though, you must bear an opportunity cost equal to the utility you could instead have obtained by spending the dollar on clothing. Whether or not you actually think consciously in such terms, then, your choice will depend on which utility is greater—the extra dollar's worth of food or the extra dollar's worth of clothing.

Which is greater depends in turn on how much of each good you consume. If, relatively speaking, you have a lot of clothing and not much food, the marginal utility of clothing will tend to be low and that of food to be high. By shifting a dollar from clothing to food, you can give up a small utility and gain a large one, which will increase your total utility.

If, instead, you have relatively much food and little clothing, the marginal utilities may be reversed. You will gain a lot of utility from spending an extra dollar on clothing and only a little from spending an extra dollar on food. Again, you can gain in total utility by shifting your pattern of expenditure without spending any more over all.

**Consumer Equilibrium**  It is clear, then, that if the marginal utility of a dollar's worth of clothing is different from that of a dollar's worth of food, you have an incentive to change your pattern of consumption. The only condition in which you will not have an incentive to change your pattern of spending on food and clothing will be if the marginal utility per dollar's worth of the two goods is exactly the same.

Generalizing from this example, it can be said that consumers tend to shift their expenditures from one kind of good to another as long as they can increase their total utilities by doing so. When consumer expenditures are distributed among the various available goods in such a way that, for each consumer, the marginal utility of a dollar's worth of each good consumed is equal to the marginal utility of a dollar's worth of each other good consumed, no further increase in utility is possible within the given budget constraint. A state of **consumer equilibrium** is then said to prevail.

**An Alternative Statement** There is another, equivalent way to state the conditions for consumer equilibrium. Suppose that a person is consuming just the right quantities of, say, chicken and beef to make the marginal utility of a dollar's worth of chicken equal to the marginal utility of a dollar's worth of beef. It must be true, then, that the marginal utility of a kilogram of chicken divided by the price of chicken per kilogram is equal to the marginal utility per kilogram of beef divided by the price of beef per kilogram. In equation form, this comes out as:

**Consumer equilibrium** A state of affairs in which consumers cannot increase the total utility they obtain from a given budget by shifting expenditure from one good to another. (In consumer equilibrium, the marginal utility of a dollar's worth of one good must be equal to the marginal utility of a dollar's worth of any other good.)

$$\frac{\text{Marginal utility of chicken per kilogram}}{\text{Price of chicken per kilogram}} = \frac{\text{Marginal utility of beef per kilogram}}{\text{Price of beef per kilogram}}$$

Suppose, for example, that chicken costs $1/kg and beef costs $3. If the equation just given holds, then an extra kilogram of beef will give the consumer three times as much utility as an added kilogram of chicken.

---

The English economist William Stanley Jevons is generally credited with the first systematic exposition of the theory of marginal utility and with its first application to the problem of consumer equilibrium. Jevons was trained in mathematics and chemistry. With this background, it is not surprising that when his interest turned to economics, he would try to strengthen that science by restating its theories in mathematical form. It was the mathematical reworking of economics that led him to the theory of marginal utility.

Although Jevons wrote many books and papers, he is best remembered for his *Theory of Political Economy*, published in 1871. There he set forth the principle of diminishing marginal utility using this illustration:

Let us imagine the whole quantity of food which a person consumes on an average during twenty-four hours to be divided into ten equal parts. If his food be reduced by the last part, he will suffer but little; if a second tenth part be deficient, he will feel the want distinctly; the subtraction of the third part will be decidedly injurious; with every subsequent subtraction of a tenth part his sufferings will be more and more serious until at length he will be upon the verge of starvation. Now, if we call each of the tenth parts *an increment*, the meaning of these facts is, that each increment of food is less necessary, or possesses less utility, than the previous one.

Jevons was the first to put the new theory in print, but he shares credit for the "marginal revolution" in economics with at least three others who were working independently along the same lines at the same time. The Austrian Karl Menger published his version of marginal utility theory in 1871 also. Three years later, the Swiss economist Leon Walras, who did not know of either Jevons's or Menger's work, came out with still another version. Finally, Alfred Marshall worked out the basics of marginal analysis about the same time, although his own major work was not published until 1890.

Jevons had a strong interest in applied economics as well as in pure theory. He wrote on Australian gold mining, on the problem of Great Britain's coal reserves, on monetary questions, and on issues of social reform. As a consultant to the British government, he successfully recommended the abolition of the import duty on corn. In 1880, he resigned his teaching position at the University of London to devote full time to research. Sadly for the science of economics, however, this prolific writer died in a boating accident just two years later, at the age of forty-seven.

**William Stanley Jevons (1835-1882)**

This means, as in the earlier statement of the conditions for consumer equilibrium, that the marginal utility of a dollar's worth (one kilogram) of chicken is equal to the marginal utility of a dollar's worth (one-third of a kilogram) of beef.

The equation can be extended to a world with any number of goods and services. $MU_A$, $MU_B$, and so on stand for the marginal utilities of goods A, B, and so on. Likewise, $P_A$, $P_B$, and so on stand for the prices of the various goods. The general expression for consumer equilibrium then becomes:

$$\frac{MU_A}{P_A} = \frac{MU_B}{P_B} = \frac{MU_C}{P_C} = \frac{MU_D}{P_D} = \cdots$$

**From Consumer Equilibrium to the Law of Demand** The concepts of consumer equilibrium and diminishing marginal utility can be combined to give an explanation of the law of demand that is intuitively appealing, if not altogether precise. The explanation goes like this: suppose you have adjusted your pattern of consumption until you have reached an equilibrium in which, among other things:

$$\frac{MU \text{ of chicken}}{\$1} = \frac{MU \text{ of beef}}{\$3}$$

As long as this equality holds, it will not be to your benefit to increase your consumption of beef; to do so would, according to the principle of diminishing marginal utility, quickly push down the marginal utility of beef. The marginal utility per dollar's worth of beef would drop below the marginal utility per dollar's worth of chicken, and you would be better off to switch back toward more chicken.

But what if the price of beef were to drop, say to \$2.50/kg, upsetting the equality given above? To make the two ratios equal again, given the new price of beef, either the marginal utility of chicken would have to rise or the marginal utility of beef would have to fall. According to the principle of diminishing marginal utility, one way to get the marginal utility of beef to fall is to consume more beef, and one way to get the marginal utility of chicken to rise is to consume less chicken. Because chicken and beef are substitutes to most people, probably you would do a little of both—that is, cut back a little on chicken and consume a little more beef. In doing so, you would be acting exactly as the law of demand predicts: a fall in the price of beef would have induced you to buy more beef.

## SUBSTITUTION AND INCOME EFFECTS AND THE LAW OF DEMAND

The argument just given links the principle of diminishing marginal utility to the law of demand in an intuitively appealing way, but it leaves a few too many loose ends dangling to suit all economists. Is there a way to rationalize the law of demand without relying directly on the slippery, unmeasurable concept of utility? There is. The alternative approach relies on a breakdown of the effects of a change in price into two separate components, known as the substitution and income effect.

## The Substitution Effect

Go back in the earlier example to the point where you had adjusted your purchases to an equilibrium, given a price of beef of $3/kg and a price of chicken of $1/kg. As before, suppose that the price of beef dropped to $2.50/kg. With beef relatively cheaper than before, you would tend to substitute beef for chicken in your diet. You might substitute beef for other things too; with the price of a steak dinner cheaper, you might substitute an evening in a restaurant now and then for an evening at the movies. This effect of the change in the price of beef is known as the substitution effect. In general terms, the **substitution effect** of the change in the price of a good is that part of the change in the quantity demanded attributable to the tendency of consumers to substitute relatively cheap goods for relatively expensive ones.

**Substitution effect** The part of the increase in quantity demanded of a good whose price has fallen that is attributable to the tendency of consumers to substitute relatively cheap goods for relatively expensive ones.

## The Income Effect

The substitution effect is not, however, the only reason that a drop in the price of beef would be likely to increase your consumption of beef. Suppose that with the price of beef at $3/kg, you bought ten kilograms per month. The decline in the price to $2.50/kg would be welcome to you not only because it would allow you to substitute beef for chicken in your diet, but for another reason as well: it would increase the purchasing power of your monthly budget. With beef at $2.50/kg, you could buy the same quantities of all goods, including beef, and now have $5 left over at the end of the month to spend as you pleased. In short, a fall in the price of any good, other things being equal, produces an increase in real income.[2]

With your increased real income, you would tend to buy more of all normal goods and less of any inferior goods. For most people, beef is a normal good. Some of your new-found $5 in real income, then, would presumably go to the purchase of more beef. This effect of the change in the price of beef on the quantity of beef demanded is known as the income effect. In general terms, the **income effect** of a change in the price of a good is that part of the change in the quantity of the good demanded attributable to the change in real income resulting from the change in price.

**Income effect** The part of the change in quantity demanded of a good whose price has fallen that is attributable to the change in real income resulting from the price change.

## The Law of Demand for Normal and Inferior Goods

The concepts of the substitution and income effects of a price change are very helpful in understanding the law of demand itself and in understanding why the law of demand might, under rare circumstances, permit exceptions. Consider separately the cases of normal and inferior goods.

For a normal good, the law of demand holds absolutely, because the substitution and income effects work together to produce an increase in quantity demanded when the price of a good falls. The example given above

---

[2]Readers who have completed a course in macroeconomics will already be familiar with the concept of real income. For the benefit of those who have not taken such a course, real income means income adjusted for changes in prices to reflect actual purchasing power. The same number of dollars represents more real income when prices fall and less real income when prices rise.

is a case in point. When the price of beef dropped, you bought more beef partly because you substituted beef for chicken and for other goods and services that were now relatively more expensive than before. In addition, you bought more beef still because you spend part of your increased real income on beef—a normal good. Taking the two effects in combination, there is no doubt that a decline in the price of beef would increase the quantity of beef you demanded.

In the case of an inferior good, things are not quite so simple. Suppose that instead of considering a drop in the price of beef in general, you considered the effect of a drop in the price of hamburger only—with the price of all other cuts of beef held constant. Suppose further that you considered hamburger an inferior good—one that you would tend to phase out of your diet as your real income rose. A drop in the price of hamburger, as before, would tend to make you substitute hamburger for other foods that had become relatively more expensive. By itself, this would increase the quantity demanded. However, a drop in the price of hamburger would also produce a slight increase in your real income; and that, considered by itself, would tend to make you buy less hamburger. For an inferior good, then, the substitution and income effects operate in the opposite direction. The law of demand holds for an inferior good only if the size of the substitution effect is larger than that of the income effect.

### Are There Really Exceptions to the Law of Demand?

No one has ever come up with a fully convincing real-world case of an exception to the law of demand. It is reasonably certain that there are genuine examples of inferior goods. An earlier chapter cited intercity bus travel and shoe repair services as two likely examples. But as far as anyone knows, in all important cases, the substitution effect outweighs the income effect even for inferior goods, so that demand curves slope downward.

It is possible, however, to construct hypothetical examples of exceptions to the law of demand that, although perhaps farfetched, are logically possible. Consider the following hypothetical case: a family living in Manitoba spends each January in Florida. One year the price of home heating fuel goes up sharply. The family turns its thermostat down a little; but even so, the heating bills go up so much that it cannot afford to go to Florida that year. Staying home in January means that the house must be kept heated during that month. The extra fuel burned during January is more than what the family has been able to save with a lower thermostat setting in the other months. Thus the total quantity of fuel burned in the season increases as a direct result of the increase in the price of fuel.

This curious case can be analyzed in terms of the income and substitution effects as follows: when the price of fuel goes up, the substitution effect works normally. The family turns its thermostat down, substituting warm clothes for heating fuel as a source of winter comfort. The weekly demand for heating fuel, however, is inelastic; even though the quantity burned per week to heat the house is slightly reduced, total expenditures on it rise, cutting sharply into the real income that the family has to spend on other goods. Now comes the "gimmick" that makes the case work.

when Andrea and Ralph Smith left their jobs at a large corporation (where he had worked as a manager and she as an engineer) to set up a small firm of their own. Initial capital for the new firm was provided by $200,000 in personal savings that the Smiths had accumulated while working for their corporate employer.

During its first year, 1980, Smith Tool Company earned total revenues of $500,000. Total explicit costs, consisting of purchased materials and wages and salaries paid to persons other than the owners, came to $350,000, which left an accounting profit of $150,000.

The explicit costs of the new firm, however, did not represent all of the opportunity costs incurred by the firm during its first year of operation. Both Andrea and Ralph Smith gave up high-paying jobs to start the firm. Their combined former salary of $80,000 is listed in Exhibit 22.1 as an implicit cost of production because it represents the income they had to expect to derive from the firm in order to be attracted away from their former jobs.[1] Also listed as an implicit cost in Exhibit 22.1 is $20,000 of forgone interest income. This item is discussed in the next section.

After both implicit and explicit costs are subtracted from the firm's income, the firm is left with a pure economic profit of $50,000. This sum is profit, not cost, because it represents what the Smiths earned from their new company over and above the $100,000 assumed to be necessary to attract their labor and capital away from the best alternative use. It is their reward for acting as entrepreneurs — that is, for recognizing and entering a potentially profitable niche in the machine tool market that no other entrepreneur had yet exploited.

## Profit and Return to Capital

For some purposes, it is useful to calculate a firm's earnings in relation to the capital invested in the firm. In order to attract funds for investment, a firm must be able to provide prospective investors with the expectation of earning at least as much income as they would expect to earn from the best alternative use of their funds. Stated in terms of percent per year, this amount can be called the **normal rate of return to capital**, or **normal profit**. The normal rate of return represents the opportunity cost of capital to the firm. In the case of the Smith Tool Company, the normal rate of return to capital was assumed to be 10 percent per year. The Smiths could thus have earned $20,000 per year by putting their $200,000 of savings at the disposal of other firms in which they did not participate in an entrepreneurial capacity — for example, by using their savings to buy stocks and bonds of other companies.

**Normal rate of return to capital (normal profit)** The opportunity cost of capital to a firm — that is, the rate of return necessary to attract funds for investment from their best alternative uses.

As things worked out, the success of the Smith Tool Company permitted Andrea and Ralph Smith to earn much more than they would have if they had put their savings at the disposal of other firms. To be precise, they earned not only the $20,000 listed in Exhibit 22.1 as the opportunity cost of capital but also $50,000 in pure economic profit. The opportunity cost of

---

[1] The $80,000 combined former salary is really only an approximation of what would have been required to attract the Smiths away from their former jobs. Perhaps, because starting a new firm is a risky venture, the true opportunity cost — including lost peace of mind — would be more. Or perhaps, because the Smiths place some value on being their own boss, the true opportunity cost would be less.

**Total rate of return to capital** The opportunity cost of capital plus pure economic profit, expressed as a percentage of the capital invested in a firm.

capital plus pure economic profit, expressed as a percentage of capital invested in the firm, can be called the **total rate of return to capital** for the firm. In the case of the Smith Tool Company, the total rate of return to capital for 1980 was 35 percent:

$$\frac{\$20,000 + \$50,000}{\$200,000} = 0.35$$

From these definitions, it follows that a firm earning a total rate of return to capital greater than the normal rate of return is earning a positive pure economic profit (above normal profits); a firm earning a total rate of return less than the normal rate of return is earning a negative pure economic profit (that is, a pure economic loss); and a firm earning a total rate of return just equal to the normal rate of return is earning zero pure economic profit.

## PRODUCTION AND COSTS IN THE SHORT RUN

Now that the economic meaning of cost is clear, the next step is to build a theory of cost. The main purpose of such a theory is to explain how costs vary as the quantity of output produced by a firm varies. The exposition of the theory of cost will be divided into two parts corresponding to two time perspectives—the short run and the long run. The distinction between these two perspectives requires just a bit more preliminary explanation before the theory of cost itself is presented.

### The Long Run and the Short Run

A firm uses many kinds of inputs to produce its output. By varying the quantities of inputs it uses, the firm can vary the quantity of output produced. The quantities of some things a firm uses can often be adjusted very quickly, whereas others are not so easy to adjust. The inputs that cannot easily be varied as the level of output changes define the size of plant the firm must work with. The physical size of structures, the production capacity of major items of machinery, and specialized or not easily replaceable employees are among the inputs determining the size of a firm's plant. These inputs are known as **fixed inputs**. They can be distinguished from **variable inputs**—inputs that can be varied quickly and easily to adjust the quantity of output produced within a plant of a given size. Raw materials, energy, and hourly labor are among the major variable inputs for most firms.

**Fixed inputs** Inputs to the production process that cannot easily be increased or decreased in a short period of time (the quantity of fixed inputs employed by a firm defines the size of the firm's plant).

**Variable inputs** Inputs to the production process that can quickly and easily be varied to increase or decrease output within a plant of a given size.

The distinction between fixed and variable inputs in turn forms the basis for the distinction between the short run and the long run in cost theory. The **short run** is a time perspective too short to change the size of a firm's plant, so that variations in output can come only from changes in the quantities of variable inputs used. The **long run**, in contrast, is a time horizon long enough to permit changes in the quantities of fixed inputs and the size of the firm's plant.

**Short run** A time perspective within which output can be adjusted only by changing the quantities of variable inputs within a plant of fixed size.

**Long run** A time perspective long enough to permit changes in the quantities of all inputs, both fixed and variable.

### Production in the Short Run and Diminishing Returns

**Production with One Variable Input** With these preliminaries out of the way, the discussion of short-run cost theory can begin with a simple story

about the relationship between inputs and outputs in the short run for the Smith Tool Company. Imagine, for the sake of discussion, that the company has only one input that is variable in the short run—namely, labor—and that it produces only one product—say, a small, portable drill press. Beginning from a zero level of output, imagine that the rate of production of this tool is to be gradually increased, varying the quantity of labor while keeping the size of the plant fixed.

Initially, the firm might hire just one worker. This worker would have to walk from machine to machine, doing every step in the production process alone. The worker would lose time moving from machine to machine and would not become skilled at any particular task. This would not be very efficient, so costs would be relatively high in relation to output.

As more workers were taken on, output would increase rapidly. In fact, because workers could become more productive by specializing in particular tasks, it is very likely that the quantity of output produced per added unit of variable input would increase initially.

However, the rate of output per added unit of variable input could not continue to rise indefinitely. Eventually, a point would be reached beyond which the useful possibilities for specialization and division of labor within the plant would be exhausted. More workers might still increase output, of course. Each worker standing at a machine could be given a helper to pass along materials and carry away finished parts. Still more helpers could be added to pick up metal shavings for recycling or wave fans to keep the machine operators more comfortable and productive. Musicians could be hired to play string quartets to keep up morale in the stockroom. But obviously, long before that point was reached, each additional unit of variable input would be adding less and less to output. The fixed quantity of inputs other than labor would become increasingly inadequate to support the growing labor force. Eventually, additional workers would contribute nothing at all.

**A Numerical Example**  The preceding story, although somewhat fanciful, is put more precisely in the numerical example of Exhibit 22.2. This exhibit, like the story on which it is based, assumes that labor is the firm's only variable input. Columns 1 and 2 show the quantity of output, measured in units (drill presses) per day, and the quantity of the variable input, measured in labor hours per day. Output reaches one unit per day only after labor input reaches 38 hours per day. Seventy-two labor hours per day suffice to raise output to two units per day; 102 labor hours are enough to produce three units per day, and so on. By the time labor input rises to 880 hours per day, output has risen to twenty-four units per day.

Columns 3 and 4 of Exhibit 22.2 illustrate the relationship between inputs and outputs in marginal terms. Column 3 shows the number of added labor hours required to produce each added unit of output. Column 4 shows the number of units of output added by each added unit of labor. The entry in Column 4 is thus the reciprocal of the entry in Column 3. For example, to increase output from four units to five units requires that labor input be increased from 130 hours per day to 155 hours per day, an increase of 25 labor hours. In the range between four and five units of output, then, each added labor hour contributes 1/25th of a unit (0.04 units) of output.

| Quantity of Output (units per day) (1) | Quantity of Labor (labor hours per day) (2) | Added Labor Hours per Added Unit of Output (3) | Added Units of Output per Added Labor Hour (marginal physical product of labor) (4) |
|---|---|---|---|
| 1 | 38.0 | | |
| 2 | 72.0 | 34.0 | 0.029 |
| 3 | 102.5 | 30.5 | 0.032 |
| 4 | 130.0 | 27.5 | 0.036 |
| 5 | 155.0 | 25.0 | 0.040 |
| 6 | 178.0 | 23.0 | 0.043 |
| 7 | 199.5 | 21.5 | 0.047 |
| 8 | 220.0 | 20.5 | 0.049 |
| 9 | 240.0 | 20.0 | 0.050 |
| 10 | 260.5 | 20.5 | 0.049 |
| 11 | 282.0 | 21.5 | 0.047 |
| 12 | 305.0 | 23.0 | 0.043 |
| 13 | 330.0 | 25.0 | 0.040 |
| 14 | 357.5 | 27.5 | 0.036 |
| 15 | 388.0 | 30.5 | 0.032 |
| 16 | 422.0 | 34.0 | 0.029 |
| 17 | 460.0 | 38.0 | 0.026 |
| 18 | 502.5 | 42.5 | 0.024 |
| 19 | 550.0 | 47.5 | 0.021 |
| 20 | 603.0 | 53.0 | 0.019 |
| 21 | 662.0 | 59.0 | 0.017 |
| 22 | 727.5 | 65.5 | 0.015 |
| 23 | 800.0 | 72.5 | 0.014 |
| 24 | 880.0 | 80.0 | 0.013 |

**Exhibit 22.2**

**Short-run inputs and outputs for the Smith Tool Company**

This exhibit shows hypothetical input and output data for the Smith Tool Company. One variable input (labor) and one output (drill presses) are assumed. As the quantity of the variable input is increased — the quantities of fixed inputs remaining constant — output increases. Column 4 shows the additional output produced by each added labor hour for each one-unit range of output up to twenty-four units; this is called the marginal physical product of labor. Note that the marginal physical product of labor first rises but after nine units of output begins to fall again.

**Marginal physical product (of an input)** The quantity of output, expressed in physical units, produced by each added unit of the input.

For present purposes, the entries in Column 4 are of particular interest. The quantity of output added per unit of added labor is called the **marginal physical product of labor**. Exhibit 22.3a, based on Columns 1 and 2 of Exhibit 22.2, shows how the total physical product of labor (that is, the total quantity of output) varies as the total quantity of labor varies. Exhibit 22.3b, based on Columns 2 and 4 of Exhibit 22.2, shows how the marginal physical product of labor varies as the quantity of labor used varies. Both graphs are based on the same assumption as the table in Exhibit 22.2 — namely, that labor is the only variable input; the size of the plant and the quantities of all other inputs are assumed to remain fixed.

**The Law of Diminishing Returns** Notice that in Exhibit 22.3b, as the quantity of labor input varies, the marginal physical product of labor at first rises but then falls. This increase and then decrease in marginal product gives the total physical product curve its characteristic S-shape. The curves shown in Exhibit 22.3 illustrate a principle known as the **law of diminishing returns**, which says that as the quantity of one variable input used in a production process is increased, with the quantities of all other inputs remaining fixed, a point will eventually be reached beyond which the quantity of output added per unit of added variable input (that is, the marginal physical product of the variable input) will begin to decrease.

**Law of diminishing returns** The law stating that as the quantity of one variable input used in a production process is increased (with the quantities of all other inputs remaining fixed), a point will eventually be reached beyond which the quantity of output added per unit of added variable input (that is, the marginal physical product of the variable input) begins to decrease.

The law of diminishing returns is quite general. It applies to all known production processes and to all variable inputs. In the example above, the law was illustrated by the case of a manufacturing firm, with labor as the

## Exhibit 22.3
### Total and marginal physical product curves for the Smith Tool Company

The curves in this exhibit are drawn from the data given in Exhibit 22.2. Part a shows the total quantity of output produced by various quantities of the variable input labor, given the size of the firm's plant as defined by the quantities of fixed inputs. It is labeled the total physical product curve. Part b shows how much extra output is produced by each additional unit of labor. It is labeled the marginal physical product curve. Note that after labor input reaches approximately 230 hours per day, the marginal physical product of labor begins to decline. The downward-sloping section of the marginal physical product curve illustrates the law of diminishing returns.

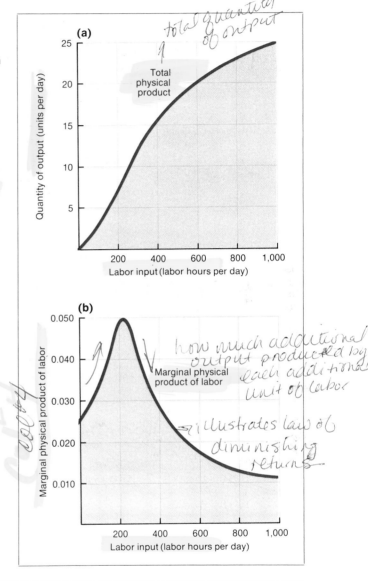

variable input. It could have been illustrated equally well by an example from farming, with, say, fertilizer as the variable input: as the quantity of fertilizer used per hectare of land increases, all other inputs remaining fixed, the number of cubic decimetres of output per hectare increases; but beyond some point, the quantity of output per added unit of fertilizer begins to decrease. Or an example from the energy industry could have been used: as the number of tonnes of coal burned per week in a power plant of a given size increases, the output of electricity increases; but beyond some point, the capacity of the plant is approached, and the added output of electricity per added tonne of coal per week decreases. In every case, the limited quantity of fixed input is unable, after a certain point, to adapt to increasing quantities of the variable input without a decline in marginal physical product of the variable input.

## Diminishing Returns and Short-Run Costs

It is a short step from the law of diminishing returns to an analysis of the short-run relationship between output and costs. To explore this relationship, return to the example of the Smith Tool Company. Assume that the company is able to hire production workers at a constant wage of $10 per hour. If, beyond a point, each added hour of labor adds less to output than the previous one, and each added labor hour costs the same as the previous one, it follows that beyond the point where diminishing returns begin, variable costs per unit of output must rise.

**Marginal Costs and Total Costs** The relationship between the law of diminishing returns and the behavior of short-run variable costs is illustrated numerically in Exhibit 22.4 and graphically in Exhibit 22.5. Exhibit 22.4 is based directly on Exhibit 22.2, assuming a labor cost of $10 per hour. Column 3 shows the total variable cost, at $10 per labor hour, of producing any given level of output. Column 4 shows the amount of added cost incurred to produce each added unit of output. This cost increase is known as the short-run **marginal cost** of production at that level of output. Note that the entries in Column 4 are equal to the differences between successive entries in Column 3.

**Marginal cost** The increase in cost required to increase output of some good or service by one unit.

Exhibit 22.5 is derived directly from the numbers given in Exhibit 22.4. A comparison of Exhibits 22.3 and 22.5 shows that the marginal cost and total cost curves are, roughly, the mirror images of the marginal product and total product curves. In particular, over the range of diminishing returns, marginal product falls and marginal cost rises. Correspondingly,

| Quantity of Output (units per day) (1) | Quantity of Labor Input (labor hours per day) (2) | Total Variable Cost ($10 per labor hour) (3) | Marginal Cost (4) |
|---|---|---|---|
| 1 | 38.0 | $ 380 | |
| 2 | 72.0 | 720 | $340 |
| 3 | 102.5 | 1,025 | 305 |
| 4 | 130.0 | 1,300 | 275 |
| 5 | 155.0 | 1,550 | 250 |
| 6 | 178.0 | 1,780 | 230 |
| 7 | 199.5 | 1,995 | 215 |
| 8 | 220.0 | 2,200 | 205 |
| 9 | 240.0 | 2,400 | 200 |
| 10 | 260.5 | 2,605 | 205 |
| 11 | 282.0 | 2,820 | 215 |
| 12 | 305.0 | 3,050 | 230 |
| 13 | 330.0 | 3,300 | 250 |
| 14 | 357.5 | 3,575 | 275 |
| 15 | 388.0 | 3,880 | 305 |
| 16 | 422.0 | 4,220 | 340 |
| 17 | 460.0 | 4,600 | 380 |
| 18 | 502.5 | 5,025 | 425 |
| 19 | 550.0 | 5,500 | 475 |
| 20 | 603.0 | 6,030 | 530 |
| 21 | 662.0 | 6,620 | 590 |
| 22 | 727.5 | 7,275 | 655 |
| 23 | 800.0 | 8,000 | 725 |
| 24 | 880.0 | 8,800 | 800 |

**Exhibit 22.4**

Total variable cost and marginal cost for the Smith Tool Company

The data given in this exhibit are based on those given in Exhibit 22.2; they assume a labor cost of $10 per hour. Column 3 gives the total variable cost (assuming labor to be the only variable input) of producing a given quantity of output per day. Column 4 shows the marginal cost at each level of output — that is, the added cost of increasing the level of output by one unit.

the slope of the total product curve becomes flatter as one moves to the right in the range of diminishing returns, while the slope of the total cost curve becomes steeper.

## A Family of Short-Run Cost Curves

The marginal cost and total variable cost curves shown in Exhibit 22.5 are only two of a whole family of short-run cost curves that can be constructed for the Smith Tool Company. The complete family is shown in numerical form in Exhibit 22.6c and graphically in Exhibits 22.6a and 22.6b.

Total variable cost, from Exhibit 22.4, appears in Column 2 of Exhibit 22.6c. Not all costs are variable in the short run. Fixed cost, which represents the costs of maintaining the plant within which the variable input labor is put to work, is assumed to amount to $2,000 per day in the case shown. Adding fixed cost (Column 3) to variable cost gives short-run total cost, shown in Column 4. The three total cost curves—total variable, total fixed, and total cost—are shown graphically in Exhibit 22.6a. Because

---

**Exhibit 22.5**
**Total variable and marginal cost curves for the Smith Tool Company**

The total variable and marginal cost curves shown in this exhibit are plotted from data given in Exhibit 22.4. Because marginal cost measures the amount by which total cost increases each time output is increased by one unit, the height of the marginal cost curve at each quantity of output is equal to the slope of the total variable cost curve at that output. Notice in particular that just at the point of minimal marginal cost, the total variable cost curve stops getting flatter and begins to get steeper.

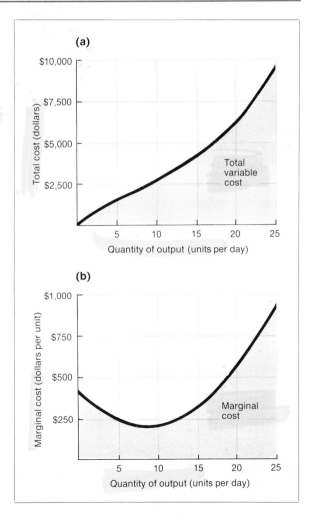

fixed cost by definition does not vary as output varies, the total fixed cost curve is a horizontal line at a distance equal to $2,000 above the horizontal axis. Adding fixed cost to variable cost gives total cost, so the total cost curve parallels the total variable cost curve at a level exactly $2,000 higher. The next entry in Exhibit 22.6c is again a familiar one — marginal cost. The marginal cost data given here are the same as those in Exhibit 22.4. They again appear on lines between the total cost entries to emphasize that marginal cost shows how total cost changes as the level of output changes. The marginal cost curve drawn in Exhibit 22.6b is the same as the one appearing in Exhibit 22.5.

The last three columns in Exhibit 22.6c are all average cost concepts: average variable cost, average fixed cost, and average total cost. Average variable cost is equal to total variable cost divided by the quantity of

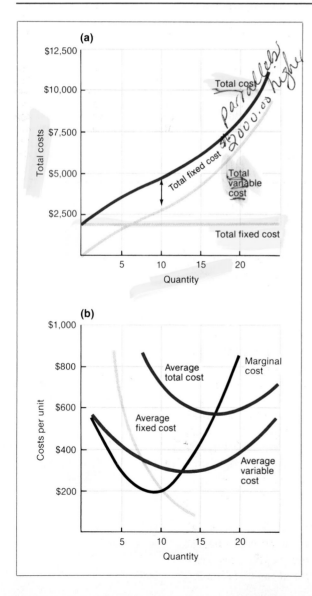

**Exhibit 22.6**
**A family of short-run cost curves**
A whole family of short-run cost curves can be derived from the cost data shown in Part c of this exhibit. Three kinds of total cost curves are shown in Part a, while average and marginal cost curves are shown in Part b. Note that the marginal cost curve intersects the average total cost and average variable cost curves at their lowest points.

*[handwritten annotations: "# of labor hours", "summation of Tv + TF = Tc", "increase in cost required to increase output by unit"]*

(c)

| Quantity of Output (units) (1) | Total Variable Cost (2) | Total Fixed Cost (3) | Total Cost (4) | | Marginal Cost (dollars per unit) (5) | Average Variable Cost (dollars per unit) (6) | Average Fixed Cost (dollars per unit) (7) | Average Total Cost (dollars per unit) (8) |
|---|---|---|---|---|---|---|---|---|
| 0 | $    0 | $2,000 | $ 2,000 | | | | | |
| 1 | 380 | 2,000 | 2,380 | | $380 | $380 | $2,000 | $2,380 |
| 2 | 720 | 2,000 | 2,720 | | 340 | 360 | 1,000 | 1,360 |
| 3 | 1,025 | 2,000 | 3,025 | | 305 | 342 | 667 | 1,009 |
| 4 | 1,300 | 2,000 | 3,300 | | 275 | 325 | 500 | 825 |
| 5 | 1,550 | 2,000 | 3,550 | | 250 | 310 | 400 | 710 |
| 6 | 1,780 | 2,000 | 3,780 | | 230 | 296 | 333 | 629 |
| 7 | 1,995 | 2,000 | 3,995 | | 215 | 285 | 286 | 571 |
| 8 | 2,200 | 2,000 | 4,200 | | 205 | 275 | 250 | 525 |
| 9 | 2,400 | 2,000 | 4,400 | | 200 | 266 | 222 | 488 |
| 10 | 2,605 | 2,000 | 4,605 | | 205 | 260 | 200 | 460 |
| 11 | 2,820 | 2,000 | 4,820 | | 215 | 256 | 181 | 437 |
| 12 | 3,050 | 2,000 | 5,050 | | 230 | 254 | 169 | 421 |
| 13 | 3,300 | 2,000 | 5,300 | | 250 | 254 | 154 | 408 |
| 14 | 3,575 | 2,000 | 5,575 | | 275 | 255 | 143 | 398 |
| 15 | 3,880 | 2,000 | 5,880 | | 305 | 259 | 133 | 392 |
| 16 | 4,220 | 2,000 | 6,220 | | 340 | 264 | 125 | 389 |
| 17 | 4,600 | 2,000 | 6,600 | | 380 | 271 | 118 | 389 |
| 18 | 5,025 | 2,000 | 7,025 | | 425 | 279 | 111 | 390 |
| 19 | 5,500 | 2,000 | 7,500 | | 475 | 289 | 105 | 394 |
| 20 | 6,030 | 2,000 | 8,030 | | 530 | 302 | 100 | 402 |
| 21 | 6,620 | 2,000 | 8,620 | | 590 | 315 | 95 | 410 |
| 22 | 7,275 | 2,000 | 9,275 | | 655 | 331 | 91 | 422 |
| 23 | 8,000 | 2,000 | 10,000 | | 725 | 348 | 87 | 435 |
| 24 | 8,800 | 2,000 | 10,800 | | 800 | 367 | 80 | 450 |

output; average fixed cost is equal to total fixed cost divided by output; and average total cost is equal to total cost divided by output. The three average cost curves are also drawn in Exhibit 22.6b.

## Some Geometric Relationships

A careful examination of Exhibits 22.6a and 22.6b reveals some important geometric relationships among the various average, marginal, and total cost curves represented there. First compare the marginal cost curve with the total variable cost curve drawn directly above it. The bottom of the U-shaped marginal cost curve occurs at exactly the same level of output where the slope of the reverse S-shaped total variable cost curve stops getting flatter and starts getting steeper. This occurs because the slope of the total variable cost curve is the *rate* at which the total variable cost curve is rising, just as marginal cost measures the *rate* at which total variable cost is rising. In graphical terms, then, the *height* of the marginal cost curve is always equal to the *slope* of the total cost curve.

A second feature of the cost curves drawn in Exhibit 22.6 deserves special comment. The marginal cost curve intersects both the average variable cost and average total cost curves exactly at their lowest points. This is not just coincidence. It is a consequence of a relationship that can be called the

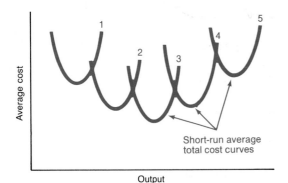

**Exhibit 22.7**
**Alternative short-run average total cost curves**
The position of the short-run average total cost curve for a firm depends on the size of the plant it constructs. In the long run, the firm has a choice of operating with any size plant it chooses. Each plant size can be represented by a different U-shaped short-run average total cost curve. Five such curves are shown in this exhibit. A new firm might begin with a plant corresponding to a curve such as the first one shown here. Then, as demand for its product expanded, it might move to those farther to the right.

**Marginal average rule** The rule that marginal cost must be equal to average cost when average cost is at its minimum.

**marginal average rule**. This rule can be explained as follows: beginning at any given point, ask what will be the cost of producing one more unit. The answer is given by marginal cost. Then ask whether this cost is more or less than the average cost of all units produced up to that point. If the added cost of the next unit produced is less than the average cost of previous units, then producing it will have the effect of pulling down the average. If the next unit costs more, its production will pull up the average. It follows that whenever marginal cost is below average variable cost, the average variable cost curve must be falling (that is, negatively sloped); and whenever marginal cost is above average variable cost, the average variable cost curve must be rising (that is, positively sloped). This in turn implies that the marginal cost curve cuts the average variable cost curve at its lowest point. All this is equally true of the relationship between marginal cost and average total cost.

## LONG-RUN COSTS AND ECONOMIES OF SCALE

### Short-Run and Long-Run Average Costs

Shifting perspective from the short run to the long run now, take another look at the costs of production for the Smith Tool Company. Remember the crucial distinction between the long run and the short run: in the long run, there are no fixed inputs. Not only can quantities of labor, raw materials, energy, and the like be varied, but, given time, the size of the firm's plant

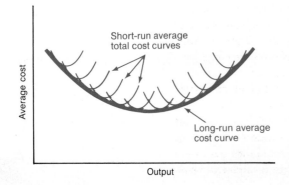

**Exhibit 22.8**
**Derivation of a long-run average cost curve**
A firm can build a plant of any size, and each possible plant size implies a different short-run total cost curve. Here are drawn a large number of possible short-run total cost curves, but even these curves are only a sample of all possible curves. As the firm expands, in the long run, it moves from one curve to another, always choosing the size of plant that minimizes the average total cost for the output the firm plans to produce at any particular time. The path along which a firm will expand — the firm's long-run average cost curve — is thus the "envelope" of all the possible short-run average total cost curves.

can be changed by building new structures, buying new capital equipment, and adding other fixed inputs as necessary.

It is sometimes said that firms operate in the short run and plan in the long run. This slogan reflects economists' distinction between variable and fixed costs: in the short run, one varies output within a plant of fixed size; and in the long run, one plans (and executes) expansions or contractions of the plant itself. Thinking of the long run as the firm's planning perspective and the short run as the firm's operating perspective makes it easier to understand the relationship between short-run and long-run average costs.

**Planning for Expansion**  Put yourself in the position of an entrepreneur just setting out to establish a small firm such as the Smith Tool Company. You think it will be wise to start with just a small plant, but you want to do some long-range planning too. After consulting with production engineers and other specialists, you sketch some average cost curves for various possible sizes of plant. Five such curves are drawn in Exhibit 22.7. The first one shows short-run average costs for the range of output that is feasible with a very small plant, the second one corresponds to a slightly larger plant, and so on. As you build up the market for your product, you hope to be able to expand your plant and move from one of these curves to the next.

Of course, the five short-run cost curves in the exhibit represent only a sample of plant sizes. Intermediate positions are also possible. The size of plant you actually choose to build will depend, in the long run, on the quantity of output you expect to produce. For any given level of output, you will choose the size of plant that will permit that output to be produced at the lowest possible average total cost.

**The Long-Run Average Cost Curve**  As your firm gradually expands, then, you can envision moving along a *long-run average cost curve* of the kind shown in Exhibit 22.8. This curve is the "envelope" of all possible short-run average cost curves. The size of plant chosen in the long run for each output will be the one that produces a short-run average total cost curve just tangent to the long-run average total cost curve at that point.

### Economies of Scale

Economists have developed some special terminology to describe what happens to long-run average costs as output increases. In any range of output where long-run average cost *decreases* as output increases, the firm for which the cost curves are drawn is said to experience **economies of scale**. In any range of output where long-run average cost *increases*, the firm is said to experience **diseconomies of scale**. Finally, if there is any range of output for which long-run average cost does not change as output changes, the firm is said to experience **constant returns to scale** in that range.

The long-run average cost curve in Exhibit 22.8 is smoothly U-shaped, but that is not the only possible shape for such a curve. In fact, statistical studies suggest that L-shaped long-run average cost curves are the rule, at least in many manufacturing industries. Such a curve appears in Exhibit 22.9, which shows an initial range of economies of scale followed by a range of approximately constant returns to scale. The curve could turn out to be a flat-bottomed U if it were followed out far enough (as the broken extension

**Economies of scale**
A phenomenon said to occur whenever long-run average cost decreases as output increases.

**Diseconomies of scale**
A phenomenon said to occur whenever long-run average cost increases as output increases.

**Constant returns to scale**
A phenomenon said to occur when there are neither economics nor diseconomies of scale.

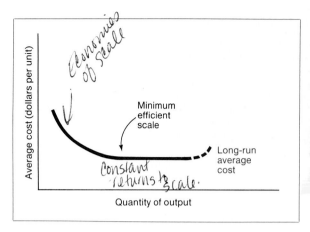

**Exhibit 22.9**

**An L-shaped average cost curve showing minimum efficient scale**

Statistical studies of long-run average cost suggest that long-run average cost curves are often L-shaped, as shown here. The point at which economies of scale are exhausted and the curve begins to flatten out is called the minimum efficient scale for the firm. Probably, if a firm continued to expand without limit, long-run average costs would eventually begin to rise. However, in many industries, there are no firms operating at a large enough scale to make the range of decreasing returns to scale visible to statistical observation. The upward-sloping portion of the curve is thus shown here as a broken line.

---

of the curve in Exhibit 22.7 indicates). In any single industry, however, there may be no firms large enough to show diseconomies of scale. If there are none, that range of the curve remains invisible to statistical observation.

Statistical studies of long-run average cost often concentrate on measuring the level of output where economies of scale are exhausted and constant returns to scale begin. This level is called the **minimum efficient scale** for the firm. As shown in Exhibit 22.9, it corresponds to the point where the L-shaped long-run average cost curve stops falling and begins to level out. If the cost curve does not have a sharp kink at this point — and there is no reason to think it must have — the minimum efficient scale can be identified only approximately. This is not a major problem, however, since statistical studies of cost must deal in approximations in any event.

Where do economies of scale come from? Why is it ever true that a large firm can produce at a lower unit cost than a smaller firm? Economists who have investigated these questions have found that there is no single source of economies of scale for all industries. Rather, there are a number of different sources, some of which are important in certain industries and others in other industries.

**Minimum efficient scale**
The level of output at which economies of scale are exhausted.

**Economies of Scale at the Plant Level** When most people think of economies of scale, what probably comes to mind first is an automobile assembly plant or a large steel mill. Costs per unit tend to decrease with the rate of output per plant per day in such industries as automobiles and steel for a number of reasons. One is that a metal-forming machine or steel furnace capable of producing twice as much as another usually costs less than twice as much to build. Another is that larger plants can take advantage of more specialized division of labor. The automobile assembly line, on which each worker performs a single operation on each car as it moves by, is the classical example of this effect. Economies of scale associated with the rate of output per plant per day can be referred to as *plant-level* economies of scale. The following case study describes one attempt to measure plant-level economies of scale for a sample of sixteen industries.

## Case 22.1
## Measuring Plant-Level Economies of Scale

In 1967, two University of Toronto economists, H.C. Eastman and S. Stykolt, published the results of an ambitious study of economies of scale in sixteen major Canadian industries. These industries accounted for about 22 percent of value added by manufacturing industries in Canada. The study was based on a series of interviews with engineers and industrialists carried out in the years 1955 to 1960. The respondents were asked questions relating to the level of technology in the industry at that time. Information was obtained on the smallest size of a new plant at which costs of production were minimized (that is, the point at which the L-shaped long-run average cost curve for a typical plant in each industry stopped falling and began to level out).

Exhibit 22.10 gives some of the major findings of this study. The first column of the table shows the study's estimates of how many plants each industry would contain if each plant were the minimum efficient size. The second column shows how many plants actually existed in the industries in the years indicated. In twelve of the sixteen industries, the actual number of plants exceeded the number that the market would contain if each plant were the minimum efficient size. In other words, in most industries plant size was smaller than the minimum size required by efficiency. The implication of this for the efficiency of Canadian industry is revealed in Column 3. In eight of the sixteen industries, half of the output or less was produced by plants operating at efficient size.

It appears from this study that a large number of plants in Canada are of sub-optimal size. This contrasts with similar studies in the United States, in which most plants appear to be near or slightly larger than optimal size. The result is that, in Canada, costs of production in manufacturing usually exceed the lowest level technically achievable. The authors of the study conjecture that the relatively small market in Canada makes firms reluctant to enlarge capacity because increased output would tend to depress prices. Limiting output enables Canadian firms to keep their prices high. These high prices can be maintained in the marketplace because the prices of competing goods from foreign countries are made artificially high by tariffs. Indeed, the study revealed that Canadian firms took the price of foreign goods entering the Canadian market as the level to which they could raise their own.

**Other Sources of Economies of Scale** Not all economies of scale are associated with increases in the rate of output of a single plant. Sometimes, for example, they have their origin in the total quantity of a product or model produced rather than in the rate at which it is produced. With a long production run, costs associated with product design, equipment set-up, and specialized training can be spread over a large number of units. A comparison of General Motors with Volkswagen can serve to illustrate the difference between economies of scale associated with the rate of production and those associated with the volume of production. General Motors achieves important economies of scale through a high rate of production but changes models frequently. Volkswagen, by comparison, produces fewer cars per year but keeps each model in production longer. Its famous Beetle, for example, was produced with minor variations for more than four decades.

In addition to the rate and volume of production at a single plant, attention must be given to economies of multi-plant operation. The McDonald's hamburger chain provides a good example. The minimum efficient scale for a single plant (a single restaurant) is obviously very small in the fast-food industry. Nonetheless, McDonald's apparently realizes

**Exhibit 22.10**
**Minimum efficient scale for sixteen industries**
This table presents the results of the study described in Case 22.1 The first column shows the number of plants that the existing Canadian market could contain if each plant were the smallest efficient size (that is assuming that each plant was operating at the point where the average cost curve stops falling and begins to level out). The second column shows the actual number of plants in each industry. The third column shows the percent of industry output produced by plants actually operating at the most efficient level.

| Industry | Year of Study | 1. Number of Plants of Smallest Efficient Size the Existing Canadian Market Could Contain | 2. Actual Number of Plants | 3. Percent of Output Produced by Plants at Most Efficient Size |
|---|---|---|---|---|
| Fruit canning | (1958) | 4 | 13 | 0 |
| Vegetable canning | (1958) | 24 | 43 | 50 |
| Cement | (1957) | 17.8 | 18 | 80 |
| Containerboard | (1960) | 4.7 | 10 | 57 |
| Shipping containers | (1958) | 28 | 37 | 72 |
| Synthetic solid detergents | (1959) | 7 | 3 | 100 |
| Synthetic liquid detergents | (1959) | 49 | ? | 75 |
| Refrigerators | (1960) | 0.6 | 10 | 0 |
| Electric ranges | (1960) | 0.9 | 23 | 0 |
| Wringer washing machines | (1960) | 8 | 14 | 58 |
| Newsprint | (1958) | 36 | 39 | 80 |
| Beef packing | (1959) | 42 | 47 | 68 |
| Pork Packing | (1959) | 16 | 45 | 9 |
| Petroleum refining | (1956) | 7 | 40 | 0 |
| Primary steel | (1955) | 4 | 4 | 0 |
| Rubber tire | (1959) | 7 | 9 | 20 |

Source: H.C. Eastman and S. Stykolt, *The Tariff and Competition in Canada* (Toronto: Macmillan 1967).

important economies by operating many restaurants as an integrated system. Some of the economies are production economies: individual food items and ingredients can be produced in efficient centralized kitchens, personnel can be trained at the famous "Hamburger University," and so on. A multi-plant firm such as McDonald's also realizes significant economies of scale with such functions as finance, advertising, and marketing.

## CONCLUSIONS

This chapter has only scratched the surface of the theory of cost. Advanced books on the subject go into a wealth of extensions, additional details, mathematical formulations, and special cases. Nonetheless, the limited treatment given here will serve quite well as a basis for the analysis of individual firms and industries in the following chapters.

Chapter 23 will show how short-run and long-run cost curves can be used to derive supply curves for an industry in which there are a large number of competing firms. Chapter 24 will then use cost curves to analyze business behavior in markets where a single firm has a monopoly. Chapter 25 will turn to the case of markets dominated not by a single firm but by a relatively small number of firms. At that point, the discussion will return to the theme of economies of scale, which are an important factor in determining the number of firms that exist in the market for a given product. Chapters 27 and 28 will develop a variety of applications of cost theory to important questions of public policy.

## SUMMARY

1. A firm's costs of production include all the sacrifices it must make in order to carry on production. Some of these sacrifices take the form of explicit payments to outsiders and are called explicit costs. Others are opportunity costs of using resources owned by the firm itself and are called implicit costs.

2. Economists use the term *profit* in a special sense: *pure economic profit* means the difference between a firm's revenues and its total costs, including both implicit and explicit costs. In everyday language, the term *profit* is instead often used to mean the difference between total revenue and explicit costs; economists refer to this difference as *accounting profit*.

3. The short run is a time period so short that not all of a firm's inputs can be varied in response to changes in output. According to the law of diminishing returns, in the short run, there must be some point beyond which the marginal physical product of a variable input diminishes. Short-run average and marginal cost curves for the typical firm are U-shaped. The marginal cost curve cuts the average variable cost and average total cost curves at their lowest points.

4. In the long run, a firm can adjust the quantities of all inputs in response to changes in output. A firm will choose the size of plant that will allow the expected long-run output to be produced at the minimum possible average cost. A long-run average cost curve can be constructed as the envelope of a set of short-run average total cost curves, one for each possible size of plant.

5. A firm is said to experience economies of scale over any range of output where its long-run average cost curve slopes downward. Over any range of output where the long-run average cost curve slopes upward, the firm experiences diseconomies of scale. If there are flat spots on the long-run average cost curve, the firm is said to experience constant returns to scale there.

## DISCUSSION QUESTIONS

1. Consider the costs of owning and operating an automobile. Which of the costs are implicit, and which are explicit? Are there any economy-wide opportunity costs of operating an automobile that do not show up at all in your tally of private costs?

2. Now divide the costs of owning and operating an automobile into fixed costs and variable costs. Suppose you were deciding whether to drive to a neighboring college to a football game or to take the bus instead. Would you take both fixed and variable costs into account? Suppose you were deciding whether to buy a house in a neighborhood where you could walk to work or a house located where you would have to buy a second car to drive to work every day. Would you then take both fixed and variable costs of the car into account?

3. What are the economies of scale and diseconomies of scale involved in running a university? Give specific examples.

4. Do you see any parallel between the law of diminishing returns and the principle of diminishing marginal utility? Do you think that both could be lumped together in a "law of diminishing marginal everything"? Try stating such a general law.

5. Take a piece of graph paper and draw, freehand, a typical reverse S short-run total cost curve. Then, as accurately as you can, construct the corresponding average total cost, average variable cost, average fixed cost, and marginal cost curves. When you have mastered these curves, try something harder. Draw some non-typical short-run total cost curves—curves with, say, funny kinks or bends or perhaps bumps like those on a roller coaster. They will not make much economic sense, but trying to draw the average and marginal cost curves for them will be an excellent test of whether you can really understand a graph like the one in Exhibit 22.6. If you cannot do this exercise successfully, you may need to review the Appendix to Chapter 1.

6. Turn to Exhibit 22.8. Copy this diagram onto a sheet of graph paper, drawing the long-run average cost curve and just one of the short-run average total cost curves. Use the curves you have drawn to construct the corresponding long-run and short-run cost curves. The total cost curves you get should both be reverse S-shaped and should be tangent to one another at the same level of output at which the average cost curves are tangent.

7. Suppose you had investigated the relationship between quantities of coal burned per week in a power plant of a given size and the output of electricity per week at that plant and had found the following: for tiny quantities of coal, not enough even to heat up the boiler, no electricity could be produced. After a critical minimum of coal was burned, the added electricity per added tonne of coal burned was constant over a considerable range. Then, abruptly, a capacity limit was reached beyond which putting more coal in would produce no added electricity at all. Sketch the marginal and total physical product of coal curves for the plant. Do they conform to the law of diminishing returns?

8. It has been said that if it were not for the law of diminishing returns, all the food that the world needs could be grown in a flowerpot. Discuss. (Hint: think of land as the only fixed factor and fertilizer as the only variable factor. How much food could be grown in the flowerpot if the marginal physical product of fertilizer were constant regardless of the quantity of fertilizer applied per unit of land?)

# SUPPLY UNDER PERFECT COMPETITION

---

## WHAT YOU WILL LEARN IN THIS CHAPTER

*The theory of cost developed in Chapter 22 provides a foundation for a theory of the supply curve. That theory will be developed in this chapter, using the concept of a perfectly competitive market. The chapter will first explain how a typical firm adjusts its quantity supplied to short-run changes in market prices. Next, it will show how a short-run supply curve for the market as a whole can be built up from the supply curves of separate firms. Then it will develop the relationship between short-run and long-run adjustments for both the firm and the market. Finally, it will briefly discuss what is perfect about perfect competition.*

## FOR REVIEW

*Here are some important terms and concepts that will be put to use in this chapter. If you do not understand them, review them before proceeding.*
- *Supply and demand (Chapter 20)*
- *Elasticity of supply (Chapter 20)*
- *Pure economizing (Chapter 21)*
- *Theory of cost (Chapter 22)*

---

The last two chapters have examined the nature of the firm and the cost structure of a typical firm. The discussion has supplied the background needed to develop a theory of what lies behind the supply curves so frequently drawn in earlier chapters. This chapter will begin with the simplest case — one in which the firm's supply decision is limited solely to determining how much to produce. Chapter 24 will extend the analysis to markets in which firms must also decide what price to put on their products as well as how much to produce.

## THE STRUCTURE OF PERFECT COMPETITION

The nature of the decisions a firm must make depends in large part on the structure of the market in which it operates. **Market structure** in this sense means such characteristics as the number of firms that operate in each industry, the extent to which the products of different firms are varied, and the ease or difficulty firms have in getting into and out of the market.

There are many possible market structures. This chapter will be occupied with one known as perfect competition. As a market structure, **perfect competition** has four defining characteristics:

**Market structure** Important characteristics of a market, including the number of firms that operate in it, the extent to which the products of different firms are diverse or homogeneous, and the ease of entry into and exit from the market.

**Perfect competition** A market structure characterized by a large number of relatively small firms, a homogeneous product, good distribution of information among all market participants, and freedom of entry and exit.

1. There are many sellers and buyers, each of which sells or buys only a small fraction of all that is bought and sold in the market.
2. The product traded in the market is entirely homogeneous; that is, the product sold by one firm is just like that sold by any other.
3. All participants in the market, buyers and sellers alike, are well-informed about prices, sources of supply, and so on.
4. Entry into and exit from the market are very easy.

### The Perfectly Competitive Firm as Price Taker

**Price taker** A firm that sells its outputs at fixed prices that are determined entirely by forces outside its own control.

These four characteristics of perfect competition, taken together, ensure that all firms in the market will be **price takers**—firms that sell their outputs at fixed prices determined entirely by forces outside their own control. If a firm makes, say, steel nails, and steel nails sell for $1.50/kg, that is that. The firm makes all its decisions and all its plans as if nothing it can do will change the $1.50 price tag.

It is easy to understand why firms operating in a perfectly competitive market are price takers. Because each producer contributes only a small fraction of the total output, its individual supply decisions will have no significant effect on the total quantity supplied in the market—and thus no significant effect on the market price as determined by supply and demand. Because the product is homogeneous, buyers are just as happy to buy from one firm as another. Thus a firm that raised its price even a fraction above what its competitors were charging would quickly lose all its customers. And because all buyers and sellers are well-informed, no one would, out of ignorance, be willing to pay or be able to get a price higher than the prevailing one.[1]

Under perfect competition, then, the decisions facing individual firms are very simple. The firm does not have to decide at what price to sell because price is completely beyond its control. It does not have to worry about product design or marketing decisions because, by definition, the product is the same for all firms and never changes. The only decision the firm needs to make is about quantity—how much to produce.

### Perfect Competition: The Ideal and the Reality

Perfect competition, as defined here, is an abstraction or ideal. Economists study it because it is a theoretically interesting benchmark, useful in judging the performance of real-world industries. No industry exactly fits all the conditions of perfect competition. Agriculture is often considered to be a very competitive industry, because there are thousands of independent producers of very standardized products. However, as Chapter 27 will show, farmers have reduced the competitive element through the creation of marketing boards. Before going on, it is important to take note of a paradox associated with perfect competition. The paradox is that perfect

---

[1] The fourth feature of perfect competition—easy entry and exit—is not strictly necessary, in the short run, to make firms price takers. But, as will be explained later in the chapter, it has considerable importance for how competitive markets work in the long run.

competition, as defined, is in many respects the exact opposite of competition as many people think of it in everyday business life.

When we think of business competition, we ordinarily think of rivalry and struggle. We think of Ford and General Motors battling for shares of the market. We think of advertising people talking up one product and putting down another. We think of Kodak working in secrecy to build an instant camera as good as Polaroid's.

Perfect competition, though, is none of these things. In a perfectly competitive market, there is no reason to battle for market shares because there is plenty of room for each small firm to sell as much as it wants at the going price. There is no advertising in such a market, because buyers are already well-informed, and goods are perfectly homogeneous — not only in fact but in the eyes of their consumers as well. There is no need for secrecy about techniques or innovations, because all technological knowledge is widespread and there are no innovations. The market environment is still competitive in the sense that any firms that fail to make their cost and supply decisions as accurately as their rivals may be forced out of the market. Firms are not sheltered from that kind of competition by any special privileges. Nonetheless, many more colorful or personalized aspects of competition are absent. Much more will be said about the relationship of "perfect" competition to real-world competition in the next few chapters.

## SHORT-RUN SUPPLY UNDER PERFECT COMPETITION
### Short-Run Profit Maximization for a Typical Firm

Now that the concept of perfect competition has been introduced, it is time to turn to the main subject of the chapter — what lies behind the supply curve in a perfectly competitive market. The investigation will begin at the level of the individual firm, using the Smith Tool Company as a typical example. The discussion will assume throughout that this firm and all others in the market make their production decisions with the object of earning maximum economic profits for the firms' owners, given prevailing prices of inputs and outputs and the production technology available. If prevailing market conditions make it impossible to earn positive economic profits, the firms will try to minimize losses.

A simple numerical example will show how a perfectly competitive firm adjusts the quantity of output it supplies to maximize profits. Exhibit 23.1a shows short-run cost data for Smith Tool Company (as first given in Chapter 22). It also shows the revenue earned by Smith Tool from the sale of each quantity of output, assuming a constant price of $500 per unit. The price per unit does not vary as output per day varies because it is assumed, for the sake of discussion, that the drill press produced by Smith Tool is essentially the same as that produced by a large number of other companies in this perfectly competitive market. The company is thus a price taker.

Subtracting total cost in Column 3 from total revenue in Column 2 gives the total profit the firm earns at each level of output. At a production level between eight and nine units a day, the firm reaches a breakeven point, where there are neither losses nor profits. The maximum profit is reached at nineteen units per day, where $2,000 profit per day is earned. Nineteen units per day is thus the quantity the firm will choose to supply at the price of $500 per unit, assuming that it wants to earn the maximum profit.

This profit maximizing quantity of output is also identified graphically in Exhibit 23.1b. In that diagram, the firm's total profit is indicated by the vertical distance between the total revenue and total cost curves. As shown, that distance is greatest at nineteen units of output.

**Exhibit 23.1**

**Short-run profit maximization under perfect competition—Smith Tool Company**

This exhibit shows the profit maximizing quantity of output chosen by a perfectly competitive firm—Smith Tool Company. The output can be found by comparing total cost and total revenue in Columns 2 and 3 of Part a. This approach is shown graphically in Part b, where total profit appears as the gap between the total revenue and total cost curves. Alternatively, the profit maximizing output can be found by comparing marginal cost and marginal revenue in Columns 5 and 6 of Part a. Profit increases up to the point where marginal cost begins to exceed marginal revenue and declines thereafter. Part c of the exhibit gives a graphical representation of the marginal approach. Whatever approach is used, the breakeven point with zero profits and losses occurs between 8 and 9 units per day; the profit maximizing output is seen to be nineteen units per day, and the maximum profit per day is seen to be $2,000.

(b)

(c)

(a)

| Quantity of Output (1) | Total Revenue (2) | Total Cost (3) | Total Profit (2)–(3) (4) | Marginal Cost (5) | Marginal Revenue (6) |
|---|---|---|---|---|---|
| 1 | $ 500 | $ 2,380 | $ –1,880 | | $500 |
| 2 | 1,000 | 2,720 | –1,720 | 340 | 500 |
| 3 | 1,500 | 3,025 | –1,525 | 305 | 500 |
| 4 | 2,000 | 3,300 | –1,300 | 275 | 500 |
| 5 | 2,500 | 3,550 | –1,000 | 250 | 500 |
| 6 | 3,000 | 3,780 | –780 | 230 | 500 |
| 7 | 3,500 | 3,995 | –495 | 215 | 500 |
| 8 | 4,000 | 4,200 | –200 | 205 | 500 |
| 9 | 4,500 | 4,400 | 100 | 200 | 500 |
| 10 | 5,000 | 4,605 | 395 | 205 | 500 |
| 11 | 5,500 | 4,820 | 680 | 215 | 500 |
| 12 | 6,000 | 5,050 | 950 | 230 | 500 |
| 13 | 6,500 | 5,300 | 1,200 | 250 | 500 |
| 14 | 7,000 | 5,575 | 1,425 | 275 | 500 |
| 15 | 7,500 | 5,880 | 1,620 | 305 | 500 |
| 16 | 8,000 | 6,220 | 1,780 | 340 | 500 |
| 17 | 8,500 | 6,600 | 1,900 | 380 | 500 |
| 18 | 9,000 | 7,025 | 1,975 | 425 | 500 |
| 19 | 9,500 | 7,500 | 2,000 | 475 | 500 |
| 20 | 10,000 | 8,030 | 1,970 | 530 | 500 |
| 21 | 10,500 | 8,620 | 1,880 | 590 | 500 |
| 22 | 11,000 | 9,275 | 1,725 | 655 | 500 |
| 23 | 11,500 | 10,000 | 1,500 | 725 | 500 |
| 24 | 12,000 | 10,800 | 1,200 | 800 | 500 |

**A Marginal Approach** As an alternative to comparing total cost and total revenue, a marginal approach can be used to determine the profit maximizing level of output for the competitive firm. Turn first to Columns 5 and 6 of Exhibit 23.1a. Column 5 gives data on marginal cost. As in Chapter 22, these data are printed on lines between the entries in the first four columns to indicate that marginal cost is the change in cost as output moves from one level to another. Column 6 presents a new concept — marginal revenue. **Marginal revenue** is the amount by which total revenue increases when output increases one unit. For a firm that is a price taker, as this one is, marginal revenue is equal to the price of the product. Each extra unit of output sold by the Smith Tool Company thus adds $500 to total revenue.

As Exhibit 23.1 is constructed, every unit increase in output adds to both total cost and total revenue. If the increase in revenue exceeds the increase in cost (that is, if marginal revenue is greater than marginal cost), increasing output by one unit increases total profit. If the increase in cost exceeds the increase in revenue (that is, if marginal cost is greater than marginal revenue), increasing output by one unit reduces profit. It follows that in order to maximize profit, a competitive firm should expand output so long as marginal revenue exceeds marginal cost. It should stop as soon as marginal cost begins to exceed marginal revenue. A comparison of Columns 5 and 6 of Exhibit 23.1 shows that for Smith Tool Company, this means producing nineteen units of output per day — the same number arrived at through a comparison of total cost and total revenue.

The marginal approach to short-run profit maximization is represented graphically in Exhibit 23.1c. Up to nineteen units of output, the marginal cost curve lies below the marginal revenue curve, so that each added unit of output increases profit. Beyond nineteen units, the marginal cost curve is above the marginal revenue curve, so that each added unit of output reduces profit. Note that the point of profit maximization, where the marginal cost and marginal revenue curves intersect, corresponds exactly to the point in Part b where the spread between total revenue and total cost is greatest.

**Minimizing Short-Run Losses** In the example just given, Smith Tool Company was able to make a comfortable profit at the prevailing market price of $500 per unit. But market conditions need not always be so favorable. Suppose, for example, the market price were to drop to $300. The firm, being a price taker, could do nothing about the price and would simply have to adjust its quantity of output as best it could to meet the new situation. The necessary adjustments can be determined from the table and diagrams of Exhibit 23.2. The table shows that there is no level of output at which the firm can earn a profit. *Unable to earn a profit, the firm must turn its attention to minimizing losses*. With a price of $300 per unit, the minimum loss occurs at fourteen units of output. As in the previous case, this is the level of output beyond which marginal cost begins to exceed the price of the product.

The two diagrams in Exhibit 23.2 give additional insight into the loss minimizing supply decision under the given market conditions. Exhibit 23.2b shows clearly why the firm cannot earn a profit: the total cost curve is everywhere higher than the total revenue curve. Nonetheless, total

**Marginal revenue** The amount by which total revenue increases as the result of a one-unit increase in quantity.

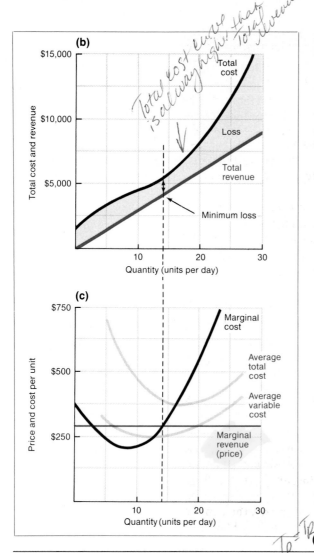

*(b)* handwritten: Total cost curve is always higher than Total Revenue

**Exhibit 23.2**
**Short-run loss minimization under perfect competition — Smith Tool Company**
If the product price is too low for the firm to earn a profit, the firm must turn its attention to minimizing losses. The same techniques illustrated in Exhibit 23.1 can be used to find the loss minimizing level of output, which is fourteen units of output for a price of $300 per unit, as shown here. Part c of this exhibit shows that the marginal revenue curve intersects the marginal cost curve at a point higher than average variable cost but lower than the average total cost. Each unit of output sold earns more than its share of average variable cost but not enough to pay its share of average total cost (including its share of average fixed cost).

| Quantity of Output (1) | Total Revenue (2) | Total Cost (3) | Total Profit or Loss (4) | Average Total Cost (5) | Average Variable Cost (6) | Marginal Cost (7) | Marginal Revenue (8) |
|---|---|---|---|---|---|---|---|
| 0 | $    0 | $2,000 | −$2,000 | – | – | | $300 |
| | | | | | | $380 | |
| 1 | 300 | 2,380 | −2,080 | $2,380 | $380 | | 300 |
| | | | | | | 340 | |
| 2 | 600 | 2,720 | −2,120 | 1,360 | 360 | | 300 |
| | | | | | | 305 | |
| 3 | 900 | 3,025 | −2,125 | 1,009 | 342 | | 300 |
| | | | | | | 275 | |
| 4 | 1,200 | 3,300 | −2,100 | 825 | 325 | | 300 |
| | | | | | | 250 | |
| 5 | 1,500 | 3,550 | −2,050 | 710 | 310 | | 300 |
| | | | | | | 230 | |
| 6 | 1,800 | 3,780 | −1,980 | 629 | 296 | | 300 |
| | | | | | | 215 | |
| 7 | 2,100 | 3,995 | −1,895 | 571 | 285 | | 300 |
| | | | | | | 205 | |
| 8 | 2,400 | 4,200 | −1,800 | 525 | 275 | | 300 |
| | | | | | | 200 | |
| 9 | 2,700 | 4,400 | −1,700 | 488 | 266 | | 300 |
| | | | | | | 205 | |
| 10 | 3,000 | 4,605 | −1,605 | 460 | 260 | | 300 |
| | | | | | | 215 | |
| 11 | 3,300 | 4,820 | −1,520 | 437 | 256 | | 300 |
| | | | | | | 230 | |
| 12 | 3,600 | 5,050 | −1,450 | 421 | 254 | | 300 |
| | | | | | | 250 | |
| 13 | 3,900 | 5,300 | −1,400 | 408 | 254 | | 300 |
| | | | | | | 275 | |
| 14 | 4,200 | 5,575 | −1,375 | 398 | 255 | | 300 |
| | | | | | | 305 | |
| 15 | 4,500 | 5,880 | −1,380 | 392 | 259 | | 300 |
| | | | | | | 340 | |
| 16 | 4,800 | 6,220 | −1,420 | 389 | 264 | | 300 |
| | | | | | | 380 | |
| 17 | 5,100 | 6,600 | −1,500 | 389 | 271 | | 300 |

handwritten notes: "Tp = TR − Tc", "marginal cost begins to exceed the price", "minimum losses" revenues come closest to meeting total costs at fourteen units of output.

Exhibit 23.2c is perhaps the most helpful of all for understanding why it is worthwhile for the firm to produce fourteen units of output even though it loses money by doing so. In addition to the marginal cost and marginal revenue curves, it shows average variable cost and average total cost curves. Notice that the point where marginal cost is equal to price lies between the two average cost curves. The vertical distance between the average variable cost and average total cost curves is equal to average fixed costs. Thus, at fourteen units of output, the price of $300 is more than enough to cover each unit's share of variable costs but not quite enough to cover each unit's share of fixed costs.

Without referring to technical terminology, it is easy to see that the firm's loss minimizing decision corresponds to simple common sense. Assume that the only variable input for Smith Tool Company is labor, and substitute the term *payroll* for the term *variable cost*. Similarly, assume that the firm's only fixed input is its factory building, and substitute *mortgage payment* for *fixed cost*. Clearly, with a price of $300, the firm is better off producing fourteen units of output than no units of output, because each unit more than pays for its share of the payroll and makes at least some contribution toward paying the mortgage.

*Shutting Down to Minimize Short-Run Losses* What would happen if the price dropped even lower? Would it always be worthwhile for the firm to keep grinding out drill presses even though it was losing money? The answer, as shown in Exhibit 23.3, is no.

Exhibit 23.3 is based on an assumed price of $225 per unit. The table in Part a shows that there is no way for the firm to make a profit with the price so low. Any supply decision will produce a loss. But this time, the loss can be minimized at a zero level of output. The best thing for the firm to do in the short run is to shut down. If things get better and the price rises again, the firm can restart production. If things never do get better, then, in the long run, the firm will have to wind up its affairs and go out of business altogether.

Notice that in this case it can be misleading to look only at the marginal revenue and marginal cost columns of the table. After seven units of output, marginal cost drops below the price of $225 and stays below until an output of eleven units is reached. *If* the firm were to stay in production, eleven units of output would give it a lower loss than any slightly greater or smaller level of output. But in this case the firm takes a still smaller loss by not producing at all.

As in the previous examples, the graphs tell the same story as the table. Exhibit 23.3b shows once again that the total revenue curve never reaches the total cost curve. It comes fairly close at eleven units of output but not as close as it comes at zero output.

Exhibit 23.3c shows that marginal cost and price are equal at eleven units of output. However, even at eleven units, the price does not cover average variable cost. Losses are minimized by shutting down. Once again, it may help to put the problem in payroll and mortgage terms. If the firm produced eleven drill presses per day and could sell them for only $225 apiece, it would not earn enough even to meet its payroll. Better to send the workers

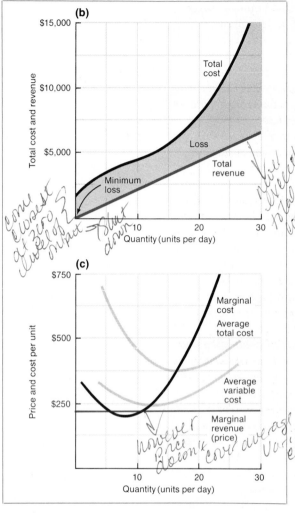

**Exhibit 23.3**
**Shutting down Smith Tool Company to minimize short-run losses**

Sometimes the price of a firm's output may drop so low that the firm must shut down altogether to minimize short-run losses. That possibility is illustrated here at the price of $225 per unit. Notice that eleven units of output yield a smaller loss ($2,345 per day) than any slightly greater or smaller output. However, the loss can be reduced to just $2,000 per day if the firm shuts down. Notice also that in Part c of the exhibit, the marginal cost curve intersects the marginal revenue curve at a point below minimum average variable cost. That is the signal to shut down.

**(a)**

| Quantity of Output (1) | Total Revenue (2) | Total Cost (3) | Total Profit or Loss (4) | Average Total Cost (5) | Average Variable Cost (6) | Marginal Cost (7) | Marginal Revenue (8) |
|---|---|---|---|---|---|---|---|
| 0 | $ 0 | $2,000 | −$2,000 | − | − | | |
| 1 | 225 | 2,380 | −2,155 | $2,380 | $380 | $380 | $225 |
| 2 | 450 | 2,720 | −2,270 | 1,360 | 360 | 340 | 225 |
| 3 | 675 | 3,025 | −2,350 | 1,009 | 342 | 305 | 225 |
| 4 | 900 | 3,300 | −2,400 | 825 | 325 | 275 | 225 |
| 5 | 1,125 | 3,550 | −2,425 | 710 | 310 | 250 | 225 |
| 6 | 1,350 | 3,780 | −2,430 | 629 | 296 | 230 | 225 |
| 7 | 1,575 | 3,995 | −2,420 | 571 | 285 | 215 | 225 |
| 8 | 1,800 | 4,200 | −2,400 | 525 | 275 | 205 | 225 |
| 9 | 2,025 | 4,400 | −2,375 | 488 | 266 | 200 | 225 |
| 10 | 2,250 | 4,605 | −2,355 | 460 | 260 | 205 | 225 |
| 11 | 2,475 | 4,820 | −2,345 | 437 | 256 | 215 | 225 |
| 12 | 2,700 | 5,050 | −2,350 | 421 | 254 | 230 | 225 |
| 13 | 2,925 | 5,300 | −2,375 | 408 | 254 | 250 | 225 |
| 14 | 3,150 | 5,575 | −2,425 | 398 | 255 | 275 | 225 |
| 15 | 3,375 | 5,880 | −2,505 | 392 | 259 | 305 | 225 |
| 16 | 3,600 | 6,220 | −2,620 | 389 | 264 | 340 | 225 |
| 17 | 3,825 | 6,600 | −2,775 | 389 | 271 | 380 | 225 |

home, suffer a loss equal to the mortgage payment, and hope for things to get better.

## The Firm's Short-Run Supply Curve

The preceding examples supply everything needed to construct a short-run supply curve for the profit maximizing firm in a perfectly competitive market. Exhibit 23.4 shows how this curve is constructed.

Work through this exhibit beginning with a price of $500. As before, Smith Tool Company would choose to produce nineteen units of output at this price. Point $E_1$ of the firm's short-run marginal cost curve must therefore be a point on the firm's supply curve.

Suppose now that the market price of the firm's product begins to fall as a result of forces beyond its control. As it does, the point where price equals marginal cost moves down along the firm's marginal cost curve. Soon Point $E_2$ is reached — the point where marginal cost and average total cost are equal. This occurs at an output of approximately seventeen units and a price of approximately $385. At this price, the best the firm can do is break even. Either a greater or a smaller output would result in a loss.

If the price falls still lower, the firm's problem becomes one of minimizing loss rather than maximizing profit. At a price of $300, for example, the firm minimizes losses by producing fourteen units, at Point $E_3$. In the range of prices lying between minimum average total cost and minimum average variable cost, the supply curve continues to follow the marginal cost curve.

Below a price of about $254, a change occurs. As before, when price is lower than the lowest point on the average variable cost curve, the firm minimizes losses by shutting down, rather than continuing to produce up

**Exhibit 23.4**

**Derivation of the short-run supply curve for Smith Tool Company**

This diagram traces Smith Tool Company's short-run supply curve. When the price is $500, the firm will produce at Point $E_1$. As the price falls, the firm moves down along its short-run marginal cost curve, as shown by Points $E_2$ and $E_3$. The firm will continue to produce where price equals marginal cost, until marginal cost falls below average variable cost. At that price, the firm will do just as well to shut down — that is, to produce at Point $E_4$.

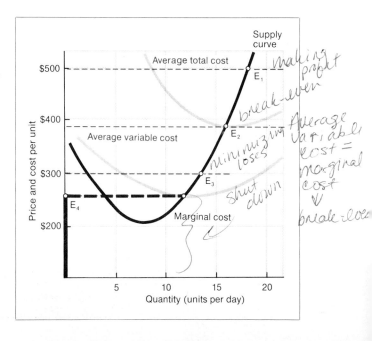

to the point where marginal cost begins to exceed price. For a price of $254, then, Point $E_4$ on the vertical axis is the preferred point of operation. This point must then be a point on the firm's short-run supply curve. As the diagram shows, for this and all lower prices, the supply curve coincides with the vertical axis.

All that has been learned so far about the firm's short-run supply decision can now be stated in the form of an important generalization: *the short-run supply curve for a profit maximizing firm operating in a perfectly competitive market coincides with the upward-sloping part of the marginal cost curve lying above its intersection with the average variable cost curve.*

### The Short-Run Industry Supply Curve

The supply curve for a whole industry can now be constructed on the basis of the supply curves of the individual firms. As a first approximation, an industry supply curve can be obtained by the horizontal addition of individual firms' supply curves, as shown in Exhibit 23.5. It is necessary to make one qualification, though. The assumption has been that any individual firm can expand output without any change in input prices; but if all firms in an industry expand simultaneously, input prices will rise unless the supply curve of the input is perfectly elastic. If input prices rise as industry output expands, the short-run industry supply curve will be somewhat steeper than the sum of the individual supply curves.

## LONG-RUN EQUILIBRIUM UNDER PERFECT COMPETITION

### Entry and Exit

For the individual firm, the long run is distinguished from the short run by the fact that all, not just some, inputs can be varied. In the long run, firms can go out of business entirely. (Sometimes firms go peaceably, with the owners selling off the assets and banking what is left. Other times they go with a crash, leaving their creditors to collect perhaps only pennies on the dollar for the mortgages, bonds, and other debts they hold.) Also in the long run, new firms can come into a market, building new plants and buying new equipment, which then become their short-run fixed inputs. As firms enter and exit, whole industries expand and contract.

One of the defining characteristics of perfect competition is that there must be no barriers to this free flow of firms into and out of the industry. This characteristic played no direct role in the discussion of a firm's short-run supply decision, but free entry and exit are crucial to explaining how a competitive market works in the long run.

### Equilibrium

Equilibrium, as explained here in many different contexts, is a state of affairs in which economic decision makers have no incentive to change their current patterns of behavior. In a perfectly competitive industry, short-run equilibrium means that each firm must have no incentive either

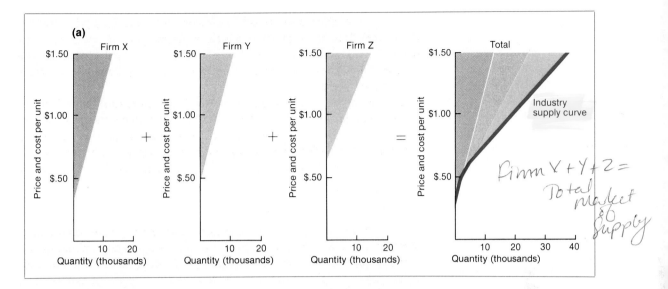

**(b)**

| | Quantity Supplied | | | |
|---|---|---|---|---|
| Price | Firm X | Firm Y | Firm Z | Total |
| $ .40 | 1,500 | | | 1,500 |
| $ .80 | 5,500 | 3,000 | 3,333 | 11,833 |
| $1.20 | 9,500 | 7,000 | 10,000 | 26,500 |
| $1.50 | 12,500 | 10,000 | 15,000 | 37,500 |

**Exhibit 23.5**

**Approximate derivation of short-run industry supply curve**

An approximation to the short-run industry supply curve can be obtained by horizontal summation of individual firms' supply curves. Here the method of summation is shown for an industry with just three firms. If the prices of inputs vary as industry output varies, it will be necessary to make an adjustment in the industry supply curve.

to increase or to decrease its quantity of output. That requires the firm to adjust its output to the point where marginal cost is equal to the price of the product. (Keep in mind that a perfectly competitive firm is a price taker, so price and marginal revenue are always equal.) In the long run, equilibrium in a perfectly competitive industry requires two other things as well. One is that each firm have no incentive to change the size of plant it uses to produce its current output, and the other is that firms have no incentive either to enter or to leave the industry.

Exhibit 23.6 shows graphically how all these requirements are satisfied simultaneously in long-run equilibrium for a perfectly competitive firm. First, marginal cost is equal to price at the equilibrium quantity of output. This equality ensures that there is no incentive in the short run either to increase or to decrease output.

Second, the firm is operating with a plant of just the size necessary to make short-run average total cost equal to the minimum possible long-run average cost at the equilibrium quantity of output. No change in the quantity of fixed inputs employed can reduce average cost, so the firm has no long-run incentive to change its plant size.[2]

---

[2] The reader may wish to review Exhibits 22.7 and 22.8, which show the relationship between short-run and long-run average cost curves for various plant sizes.

Third, average total cost (both long-run and short-run) is equal to price at the equilibrium quantity of output. As always, average total cost includes an allowance for a normal rate of return on capital—no more, no less. Thus, when average total cost is equal to price, there is no incentive for firms either to enter the industry (to seek pure economic profit in excess of the normal rate of return on capital) or to leave the industry (in order to avoid pure economic loss—that is, a rate of return on capital less than the normal rate).

The long-run equilibrium conditions shown graphically in Exhibit 23.6 can also be expressed in the form of the following equation:

$$\text{Price} = \frac{\text{Marginal}}{\text{cost}} = \frac{\text{Short-run}}{\text{average}} = \frac{\text{Long-run}}{\text{average}}$$
$$\text{total cost} \quad \text{cost}$$

If any part of this equation does not hold, there will be an incentive for firms to change the quantity of output they are producing within their current plants, to change the size of the plants they are using to produce their current output, or to enter or leave the industry. That is, unless all parts of the equation hold, the market cannot be in long-run equilibrium.

### Industry Adjustment to Falling Demand

A particular position of long-run equilibrium, such as the one shown in Exhibit 23.6, can continue undisturbed only so long as outside conditions remain unchanged. Exhibit 23.7, for example, shows how a perfectly competitive industry reacts to a long-run decrease in the demand for its product.

The exhibit consists of two parts. Part a shows a set of cost curves, much

**Exhibit 23.6**
**The typical perfectly competitive firm in long-run equilibrium**

Long-run equilibrium in a perfectly competitive industry requires that the typical firm (1) have no short-run incentive to change the quantity of output currently produced, (2) have no long-run incentive to change the size of plant used to produce its current output, and (3) have no long-run incentive to enter or leave the industry. This requires that price, short-run marginal cost, short-run average total cost, and long-run average cost all have the same value in equilibrium, as shown.

like those shown in Exhibit 23.6, for a typical individual firm in the industry. Part b is a simple supply and demand diagram representing the market in which the typical firm sells its output. The curves drawn there are short-run industry supply curves built up from the short-run supply curves of all the individual firms in the market (see Exhibit 23.5). The demand curves are short-run market demand curves of the usual kind.

Suppose that, initially, short-run supply curve $S_1$ and short-run demand curve $D_1$ applied. That would produce a market equilibrium price of $5. The individual firm would take this price as given and adjust its output accordingly, producing twenty-five units of output, as shown. At this price and output, it would be just breaking even. Remember, though, that breaking even in the economic sense means earning enough to cover all costs including the implicit cost of a normal rate of return on the owner's invested capital.

Suppose now that something happens — say, a change in consumer tastes or incomes — that shifts the demand curve to the new position, $D_2$. The short-run result of this demand shift will be a drop in the market price to $4 per unit. The individual firm, being a price taker, will consider this decline in price as something beyond its control and will adjust to it as best it can. As shown in Part a of the exhibit, this means cutting back output a little to minimize loss but not shutting down completely. The movement of each individual firm back down along its marginal cost curve is what produces the movement of the market as a whole down and to the left along short-run supply curve $S_1$.

*MC = marginal revenue.*

---

### Exhibit 23.7
**Long-run adjustment to a decline in demand**

In this exhibit, Part a represents a single typical firm and Part b the entire industry. Initially, both the firm and the industry are in long-run equilibrium at a price of $5. Then something happens to shift the demand curve leftward from $D_1$ to $D_2$. In the short run, the price falls to $4, at the intersection of $D_2$ and $S_1$. The firm's short-run reaction is to retreat down along its marginal cost curve. Eventually, some firms (not the one shown) get tired of taking losses and exit from the industry. Their exit causes the supply curve to shift toward $S_2$ and the market price to recover. The typical firm returns to breakeven operation. The market has traced out part of its long-run supply curve, as shown by the large arrow.

But the situation that the market is now in cannot prevail in the long run. The reason is that the typical firm and its fellows are operating at a loss. They are not giving their owners the normal rate of return they need to make an investment in this industry worthwhile. If the demand curve does not show any hope of shifting back to the right, some owners will become discouraged and will pull their capital out of the industry. Perhaps their firms will actually go bankrupt, or perhaps they will sell off their plant and equipment and get out while the going is good. Perhaps they will keep their firms intact but set to work to produce other goods for other, more profitable, markets. The particular form of exit does not much matter.

There is no real way to tell which firms will be the first to go; but for convenience, assume that the typical firm shown in the exhibit is not one of the first. Look what happens to it now as some of the others leave. As some firms withdraw, the market loses their contribution to the total supply. The market supply curve, now added together from fewer individual supply curves, shifts to the left toward $S_2$. As it does so, the market price begins to rise up along demand curve $D_2$. When the price gets all the way back up to $5, the firms still left in the industry will no longer be losing money. The exodus from the industry will stop, and the market will have reached a new long-run equilibrium. In the new equilibrium, price, marginal cost, short-run average total cost, and long-run average cost will once again be equal.

The entire sequence of events has traced out a portion of this industry's *long-run* supply curve, as shown by the arrow. A long-run supply curve for an industry shows the path along which equilibrium price and quantity move in response to persistent changes in demand, given time for individual firms to adjust the sizes of their plants, if necessary, and given time for entry and exit to occur. The long-run supply curve shown in Exhibit 23.7 is perfectly elastic, at least in the region shown. In the long run, the leftward shift of the demand curve causes no change in price, only a decrease in the quantity supplied.

### Industry Adjustment to Rising Demand

Freedom of entry plays the same role in the long-run adjustment of a perfectly competitive market to rising demand as freedom of exit plays in the adjustment to falling demand. This is illustrated in Exhibit 23.8.

The starting position in this exhibit is exactly the same as in Exhibit 23.7. Short-run supply curve $S_1$ and demand curve $D_1$ give an equilibrium price of $5. The individual firm just breaks even producing twenty-five units of output at this price. Now follow what happens as the demand curve shifts, this time to position $D_2$, to the right of $D_1$.

The short-run result of the shift in the demand curve is an increase in the market price to $6. The typical firm adjusts to this new price by moving up along its marginal cost curve to a somewhat higher level of output. As all firms do this, the market moves up and to the right along short-run supply curve $S_1$.

But again, this short-run adjustment does not result in a state of affairs that can last in the long run. For now, all the firms are making profits in

**Exhibit 23.8**

**Long-run adjustment to an increase in demand**

In this exhibit, both the firm and the industry are again initially in equilibrium at a price of $5. Then something happens to shift the demand curve rightward to $D_2$. In the short run, the price rises to $6, at the intersection of $D_2$ and $S_1$. The firm's short-run reaction is to move up along its marginal cost curve, earning better than normal profits. These high profits eventually attract new firms into the industry. As new firms enter, the supply curve shifts toward $S_2$. Profits for the typical firm return to normal, and entry activity ceases. Again, the market has traced out part of its long-run supply curve, as shown by the large arrow.

excess of the minimum needed to attract capital to the industry. Entrepreneurs elsewhere in the economy will soon spot this healthy, expanding market as a prime investment opportunity. Some of them may start brand new firms to produce for this market. Others may shift plants and equipment previously used to produce something else to making goods for this industry. It does not matter whether the entry is by brand new firms or by firms already existing in other industries that devote part of their capital to this particular market for the first time. In either case, new entry will cause the supply curve to shift to the right, toward $S_2$.

As the supply curve shifts, the price falls. It does not fall far enough to drive the new entrants back out again, but it does fall enough to drive everyone's profits back to the normal level. Entry will stop, and the market will be in a new long-run equilibrium at the intersection of $S_2$ and $D_2$.

Once again, a portion of the long-run supply curve for the industry has been traced out, as shown by the large arrow. And once again, this long-run supply curve is horizontal in the region investigated. A rightward shift in the demand curve has, in the long run, produced an increase in quantity supplied but no increase in price.

## Other Long-Run Supply Curves

In the examples just given, the industry long-run supply curve was a horizontal straight line, at least in the region examined. That is not the only possible shape such a supply curve can take, however. Exhibit 23.9 shows some other possibilities—upward-sloping, downward-sloping, and U-shaped.

Which shape the long-run industry supply curve takes depends primarily on what happens to the industry's input prices in the long run as output expands. If the long-run supply curve for all inputs is perfectly elastic, the price of those inputs will not change as the quantity of them demanded by the industry increases. Or perhaps the industry will use such a small part of the total supply of each unspecialized input that whatever change in input price does occur will be negligibly small. Industry output can thus expand without affecting the underlying costs of the individual firms. Thus the long-run supply curve of the industry using the outputs will be perfectly horizontal (that is, perfectly elastic) too. This is the case in Exhibits 23.7 and 23.8. Exhibit 23.9a shows a succession of short-run supply and demand curves lying along such a horizontal long-run supply curve. Each pair of short-run curves represents one stage in the industry's long-run expansion.

Suppose, though, that the industry uses some specialized input, the supply of which cannot easily be increased. Perhaps some special skilled labor is needed, and more workers can be induced to acquire the skill only by bidding up the wage rate. The rising price of this important input will cause an upward shift in the cost curves of all the firms in the industry as

**Exhibit 23.9**

**Possible long-run supply curves for a competitive industry**
The shape of an industry's long-run supply curve depends largely on what happens to the prices of the industry's inputs as demand and output expand in the long run. If input prices do not change significantly, the long-run supply curve willl be horizontal, as in Part a of this exhibit. If input prices rise, the long-run supply curve will slope upward, as in Part b. Falling input prices will produce a downward sloping long-run industry supply curve, as in Part c. Finally, mixed cases, where the long-run supply curve first falls and then rises are possible, as in Part d.

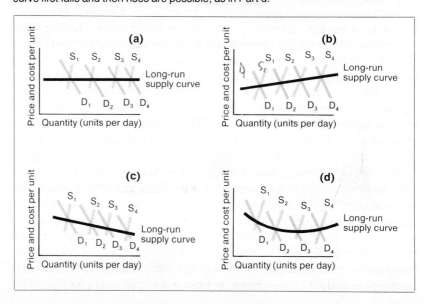

new firms enter the industry and output expands. In this case, the industry long-run supply curve will slope upward, as in Exhibit 23.9b.

It is also possible that the price of some important input can decrease as output of the industry expands. For example, as sales of electronic equipment expand, the firms making the components that go into that equipment may be able to adopt cheaper methods of production. If this occurs, the cost curves for all firms will drift downward as new firms enter the industry. The long-run supply curve will then be downward-sloping, as in Exhibit 23.9c.

Finally, it is possible that a combination of forces can be at work. In the industry shown in Exhibit 23.9d, long-run supply is at first influenced by the falling price of one specialized input; but beyond a point, some other specialized input becomes a bottleneck that causes the long-run supply curve to bend upward. Many variants are possible. Only actual observation of particular industries can determine which possibility applies.

## WHAT IS PERFECT ABOUT PERFECT COMPETITION?

The discussion of perfect competition is now very nearly complete. We have a fairly good picture of how perfectly competitive markets work. But there is one remaining question that deserves more attention than it has yet been given: what is so perfect about perfect competition?

As suggested early in the chapter, the answer is not that such a market is the perfect place to observe all forms of business rivalry. Far from it. Many familiar forms of rivalry are completely absent from perfectly competitive markets. Under perfect competition, business managers go blandly about their pure economizing without caring a whit what any particular other firm in the industry does. After all, those other firms cannot, by definition, be big enough to have any individual impact on market prices. They cannot, by definition, be getting ready to introduce a new, distinctive version of the industry's product. And they cannot, by definition, have any secrets. So it is not in any of these senses that perfectly competitive markets are perfect.

They are instead perfect in another sense. Think, for a moment, about just what a market really is. Very simply, it is a mechanism for getting buyers and sellers together to carry out mutually beneficial transactions. It would seem to make sense, then, to say that *a perfect market is one in which all potential mutually beneficial transactions are in fact carried out — a market in which none is missed*. That is exactly the sense in which perfectly competitive markets are perfect.

To see why, look at Exhibit 23.10. This is a quite ordinary supply and demand diagram (long-run variety) just like many shown before. But now look at it in a slightly different way.

Start with the demand curve. Usually, one thinks of a demand curve as showing the quantity that consumers are willing and able to buy at any given market price. But the demand curve can also be thought of as showing the maximum amount consumers are willing to pay for a marginal unit of the good, given the quantity already available. This particular demand curve, for example, has a height of $12 at 100 units of output. That means someone is willing to pay barely $12 for the marginal 100th unit and someone is willing to pay almost, but not quite, that much for the 101st.

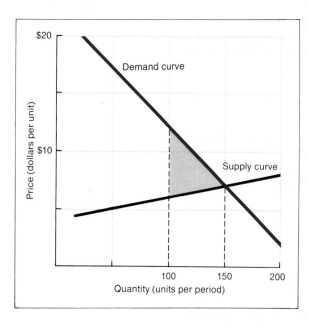

**Exhibit 23.10**
**Why perfectly competitive markets are perfect**
Think of the demand curve in this diagram as showing how much consumers would be willing to pay for additional units of output and the supply curve as showing how much producers would have to be offered to supply them. If production were limited to a rate of 100 units per period, mutually beneficial opportunities for exchange would be passed up. Consumers would be willing to pay nearly $12 for the 101st unit, while producers would have to be given barely more than $6 to produce it. Not all such worthwhile trades would take place until output were raised to 150 units. The shaded area provides a rough measure of the opportunities for mutual benefit that would be wasted if production were limited to 100 units. But a competitive market would carry output all the way to 150 units.

The supply curve can be interpreted in much the same way. Usually, one thinks of it as showing how much producers are willing to supply at a given price. But it also shows the minimum amount necessary to induce producers to supply the marginal unit. The supply curve in this exhibit, for example, has a height of $6 at an output of 100 units. That means someone is barely willing to supply the 100th unit for $6 and that no one will supply a 101st unit unless offered just a little bit more.

Now, suppose that for some reason, producers in fact are supplying goods to this market at a rate of only 100 units per period. At that level of output, the demand curve is above the supply curve. Some consumer out there is willing to pay nearly $12 for the 101st unit. And some producer is willing to supply it for anything just over $6. If production stops at 100 units, then, buyers and sellers will be passing up an opportunity for a mutually beneficial transaction. The market will not be perfect.

The same will be true, to a slightly lesser degree, if output stops at 101, 110, or 149 units. Even the production and sale of the 150th unit represents a mutually beneficial exchange, although only barely so. It can be said, then, that the whole shaded area in the diagram gives a measure of the accumulated potential for mutual benefit that will be wasted if production stops short at 100 units.

Now we can see the sense in which perfectly competitive markets, when they are in equilibrium, are perfect. In such markets, production is carried out up to, but not beyond, the point where the long-run supply and demand curves intersect. All possible mutually beneficial transactions between consumers and producers are thus carried out. And, as shown in the previous section, each firm in long-run perfectly competitive equilibrium produces at the minimum possible average total cost. That means no further gains are possible on the production side, at least within the limits of current technology. With no improvements possible through changes in either the quantity of output traded or the way that output is produced, the market does as well as it can in satisfying the needs of consumers. In that sense, it is a perfect market.

## CONCLUSIONS

It would be tempting to draw broad generalizations from the preceding section. Would not an economy in which all markets displayed all the structural characteristics of perfect competition be a perfect one in every economic respect? There is a sense in which this proposition is true, but its truth is hedged with a number of qualifications.

One very important qualification is that technology does not cooperate. Economies of scale make it altogether impractical in many industries to scatter production among a large number of very small firms.

A second qualification is the refusal of consumers to be indifferent between the products of different firms. Consumers demand variety, not homogeneity, from the firms they patronize. To enforce homogeneity in the name of perfect competition would be to pass up many mutually beneficial opportunities for firms to cater to the differing individual tastes of consumers.

A third qualification is inherent in the whole concept of perfect competition. General propositions about the efficiency of perfect competition place little weight on the entrepreneurial element in business life. The theories set forth in this chapter say little about how efficiently resources are allocated in a world where change occurs, where knowledge is not perfectly distributed, and where markets are not always in equilibrium. Do markets with large numbers of small firms guarantee efficient entrepreneurial decision making in a world of change and uncertainty? Are such markets most productive of new and better ways to satisfy human wants? The theory of perfect competition says nothing one way or the other in answer to these questions. Later chapters will return to them.

When all is said and done, perfect competition is one of the great abstractions of economics. As such, it produces many valuable insights. It makes it possible to think more clearly about what lies behind the law of supply and demand. It makes it easier to understand the element of pure economizing in business decision making—an important part of the real world of business but not all of it. It provides some insights into economic efficiency that, if not overgeneralized, can be of real use in comparing alternative economic policies. And, finally, for some kinds of markets, it is not so very far from the mark in a descriptive sense.

## SUMMARY

1. A firm is a price taker if it can do nothing to affect the prices of the outputs it sells. The characteristics of perfect competition are sufficient to make firms behave as price takers. Firms are too small to influence output prices by varying their own quantities supplied. The fact that consumers are indifferent between the products of different individual

firms makes it impossible for those firms to raise their prices above the prevailing level without losing all their customers. The "other things being equal" assumption applies in a particularly strong way to the price taking, perfectly competitive firm, which makes all its managerial calculations as if whatever it did would not affect in any way what others did.

2. Perfect competition, as the technical name of a particular market structure, must be carefully distinguished from real-world business competition. Many common types of business rivalry among entrepreneurs are absent in perfect competition.

3. For the typical firm with U-shaped short-run cost curves, the short-run supply curve is that upward-sloping portion of the short-run marginal cost curve that lies above the average variable cost curve. If price falls below average variable cost in the short run, the firm minimizes its losses by temporarily shutting down. The short-run industry supply curve is approximated by the summation of the supply curves of individual firms. An adjustment must be made, though, for any change in input prices that may occur when all firms in the industry expand or contract simultaneously.

4. In long-run equilibrium, product price, short-run marginal cost, long-run average cost, and short-run average total cost must all be equal for the competitive firm. If price rises above long-run average cost, new firms will be attracted to the industry, driving the price back down. If price is below long-run average cost, some firms will leave the industry, allowing the price to rise again. In the long run, variations in industry output take place primarily through the entry or exit of firms rather than through changes in the quantity produced by each individual firm.

5. Competitive markets are perfect in the sense that when they are in equilibrium, they leave no unrealized opportunities for mutually beneficial transactions between producers and consumers. One must, however, be cautious about generalizing from the perfection of particular markets, in this sense, to broad propositions about the economy as a whole.

## DISCUSSION QUESTIONS

1. Instead of saying that a perfectly competitive firm is a price taker, it is sometimes said that such a firm faces a perfectly elastic demand curve. Why are these two ways of putting the matter equivalent?

2. The concept of being a price taker can apply to consumers as well as producers. A price taking consumer is one who cannot influence the price paid for a product by changing the quantity purchased. For which of the goods and services that you buy are you a price taker? Are there any goods or services you buy for which you are not a price taker?

3. If the government imposes a price ceiling on some product, does that make the firms that sell the product price takers, regardless of whether their industry fits the market structure of perfect competition? Explain.

4. Make a list of half a dozen products that you purchase frequently. Do you buy any of these things from firms that are perfect competitors? If the firms you buy from are not perfect competitors, do they compete, in some other sense, with rivals for your business?

5. Explain the role that the free entry and exit assumption plays in determining the nature of long-run equilibrium in a competitive industry.

6. Here is a definition of efficiency that economists often use: an economy is said to be operating efficiently if and only if there is no possible change that will make at least one person better off and no person worse off. Can you show that perfectly competitive markets are efficient in this sense?

# THE THEORY OF MONOPOLY

## WHAT YOU WILL LEARN IN THIS CHAPTER

*This chapter is devoted to the analysis of pure monopoly, a market structure in which the entire quantity sold is supplied by a single firm. It will show that under pure monopoly a firm can potentially earn pure economic profits, even in long-run equilibrium. At the same time, it will show that pure monopoly is a less efficient market structure than perfect competition. In addition to the theory of pure monopoly, the chapter will discuss the closely related problems of price discrimination and cartels.*

## FOR REVIEW

*Here are some important terms and concepts that will be put to use in this chapter. If you do not understand them, review them before proceeding.*
- *Price elasticity of demand (Chapter 20)*
- *Pure economizing (Chapter 21)*
- *Pure economic profit (Chapter 22)*
- *Normal rate of return on capital (Chapter 22)*
- *Perfect competition (Chapter 23)*
- *Marginal revenue (Chapter 23)*

Perfect competition, with its very large number of very small firms, is one polar extreme of market structure. The other extreme is **pure monopoly** — the name given to a market structure in which one firm supplies 100 percent of industry sales.

As the sole supplier to its market, the pure monopolist is assumed not only to have no current competitors but also to be protected against the potential competition of new entrants into the market. Various kinds of barriers to entry can protect a pure monopolist from potential competition. In some cases, the barriers are technological, as when the nature of the product makes it inefficient for more than one firm to serve a market. Local utilities—such as the electric power, gas, water, and telephone companies—are the classic examples, in that it is likely to be wasteful for competing firms to provide duplicate lines or mains to any one neighborhood. Monopolies protected by technological barriers to entry are called **natural monopolies**. In monopolies of this type, both average and marginal costs will continue to decline over the range of demand. Monopolies based on the ownership of a unique natural resource can also be considered natural monopolies.

**Pure monopoly** A market structure in which one firm accounts for 100 percent of industry sales.

**Natural monopoly** An industry in which total costs are minimized by having just one producer serve the entire market.

**Franchised monopoly**
A monopoly protected from competition by a government grant of monopoly privilege, such as an exclusive license, permit, or patent.

Other monopolies are created or perpetuated by government grants of monopoly privilege that make it illegal for new firms to enter even when it is technologically feasible for them to do so. Monopolies protected by law against the entry of new competitors are called **franchised monopolies**. The Canadian post office is the classic example of a franchised monopoly. The law permits private carriers to compete with Canada Post in the transportation of parcels, but competition in first class mail has been prohibited. Monopolies based on patented inventions or processes can also be considered franchised monopolies.

The barriers to entry protecting natural and franchised monopolies from competition have their origin in technological or legal factors not directly created by the monopolistic firm itself. In addition, it may sometimes be possible for a firm or a group of firms acting in concert to erect other, artificial barriers to the entry of new competitors. This possibility will be discussed in Chapter 25, which examines certain market structures that are intermediate between perfect competition and pure monopoly.

Having defined pure monopoly, the chapter will turn now to an analysis of how a pure monopolist decides what quantity to supply to the market it dominates. As in the case of perfect competition, it will look first at the short run and then at the long run.

## PROFIT MAXIMIZATION FOR THE PURE MONOPOLIST

### The Monopolist Is Not a Price Taker

The short-run profit maximization decision for a pure monopolist, like that for a perfectly competitive firm, is a problem in pure economizing. With market demand conditions, the technology of the production process, and the prices of inputs given, the problem is to determine the quantity of output to supply in order to earn the maximum profit or minimum loss.

The supply decision for the pure monopolist, however, does differ from that of the perfectly competitive firm in one major respect: the pure monopolist is not a price taker. The perfectly competitive firm is assumed to be so small in relationship to its market that its individual supply decision has no noticeable impact on the market price. Not so for a monopolist. The pure monopolist, as the sole supplier to the market, must take into account the fact that the market demand curve has a negative slope. As the monopolist increases output, it must reduce the price at which it offers its product for sale in keeping with the law of demand.

**Output and Revenue** Consider Exhibit 24.1a, for example. Columns 1 and 2 give market demand for a typical pure monopolist. Exhibit 24.1b presents the same demand graphically. This demand curve provides the relationship between the quantity of output that the monopolist chooses to supply and the price at which that quantity can be sold. The greater the output, the lower the maximum price the monopolist can charge without leaving an excess supply unclaimed by any buyer.

The information contained in the demand curve can be used to determine what happens to the firm's revenue as its output changes. For any output, total revenue is equal to price times quantity. Column 3 of Part a

**Exhibit 24.1**

Demand, total revenue, and marginal revenue for a pure monopolist

This exhibit shows the relationships among demand, total revenue, and marginal revenue for a typical monopolist. Total revenue is found by multiplying price times quantity at each point on the demand curve. Marginal revenue is the increase in total revenue resulting from a one-unit increase in output. Part b of this exhibit shows the demand curve and marginal revenue curve in graphical form. Note that for a straight-line demand curve, the marginal revenue curve lies halfway between the demand curve and the vertical axis and that it cuts the horizontal axis at the point where price elasticity of demand is equal to zero. This point corresponds to the point of maximum total revenue, as shown in Part c.

**(a)**

| Quantity (1) | Price (2) | Total Revenue (3) | Marginal Revenue (4) |
|---|---|---|---|
| 1 | $10.00 | $10.00 | |
| | | | $9.40 |
| 2 | 9.70 | 19.40 | |
| | | | 8.80 |
| 3 | 9.40 | 28.20 | |
| | | | 8.20 |
| 4 | 9.10 | 36.40 | |
| | | | 7.60 |
| 5 | 8.80 | 44.00 | |
| | | | 7.00 |
| 6 | 8.50 | 51.00 | |
| | | | 6.40 |
| 7 | 8.20 | 57.40 | |
| | | | 5.80 |
| 8 | 7.90 | 63.20 | |
| | | | 5.20 |
| 9 | 7.60 | 68.40 | |
| | | | 4.60 |
| 10 | 7.30 | 73.00 | |
| | | | 4.00 |
| 11 | 7.00 | 77.00 | |
| | | | 3.40 |
| 12 | 6.70 | 80.40 | |
| | | | 2.80 |
| 13 | 6.40 | 83.20 | |
| | | | 2.20 |
| 14 | 6.10 | 85.40 | |
| | | | 1.60 |
| 15 | 5.80 | 87.00 | |
| | | | 1.00 |
| 16 | 5.50 | 88.00 | |
| | | | .40 |
| 17 | 5.20 | 88.40 | |
| | | | −.20 |
| 18 | 4.90 | 88.20 | |
| | | | −.80 |
| 19 | 4.60 | 87.40 | |
| | | | −1.40 |
| 20 | 4.30 | 86.00 | |
| | | | −2.00 |
| 21 | 4.00 | 84.00 | |
| | | | −2.60 |
| 22 | 3.70 | 81.40 | |
| | | | −3.20 |
| 23 | 3.40 | 78.20 | |
| | | | −3.80 |
| 24 | 3.10 | 74.40 | |
| | | | −4.40 |
| 25 | 2.80 | 70.00 | |
| | | | −5.00 |
| 26 | 2.50 | 65.00 | |
| | | | −5.60 |
| 27 | 2.20 | 59.40 | |
| | | | −6.20 |
| 28 | 1.90 | 53.20 | |
| | | | −6.80 |
| 29 | 1.60 | 46.40 | |
| | | | −7.40 |
| 30 | 1.30 | 39.00 | |
| | | | −8.00 |
| 31 | 1.00 | 31.00 | |
| | | | −8.60 |
| 32 | .70 | 22.40 | |
| | | | −9.20 |
| 33 | .40 | 13.20 | |
| | | | −9.80 |
| 34 | .10 | 3.40 | |

and the graph in Part c of the exhibit show that as output increases, total revenue first rises, then reaches a maximum at about seventeen units of output, and then falls. Notice the similarity between this exhibit, and

Exhibit 20.6, which appeared as part of the discussion of price elasticity of demand. There it was demonstrated that when demand is *elastic*, a decrease in price causes total revenue to increase. (The reason is that in percentage terms, the quantity sold increases by more than the price decreases, so the product of the two increases.) In contrast, when demand is *inelastic*, revenue falls when the price goes down. (That is because, with inelastic demand, the percentage increase in quantity is less than the percentage decrease in price.) With a straight-line demand curve like that of Exhibit 24.1b, the upper half is elastic and the lower half inelastic. That accounts for the shape of the "revenue hill" in Part c of this exhibit.

**Marginal Revenue**  The relationship between output and revenue for the pure monopolist can also be viewed in marginal terms. Chapter 23 defined *marginal revenue* as the change in total revenue resulting from a one-unit increase in a firm's output. Column 4 of Exhibit 24.1a gives data on marginal revenue for the firm in this example. Notice that the figures in this column are simply the differences between successive entries in Column 3. Part b of the exhibit shows a graph of marginal revenue, along with the demand curve that is the average revenue curve. Notice that the marginal revenue curve is above the horizontal axis when total revenue is increasing (elastic demand) and below the axis when total revenue is decreasing (inelastic demand). It intersects the horizontal axis just at the point of maximum total revenue.[1]

### Profit Maximization

The relationship between output and revenue for the pure monopolist forms the basis for an analysis of short-run profit maximization. Profit maximization for a pure monopolist can be demonstrated by means of a numerical example similar to that used for the case of perfect competition.

Exhibit 24.2 incorporates the demand and revenue data for a typical pure monopolist from Exhibit 24.1 and gives total and marginal cost data for the same firm. One way to determine the profit maximizing quantity of output for the firm is to compare total cost and total revenue, as given in Part a of the exhibit. Subtracting total cost in Column 6 from total revenue in Column 2 gives total profit in Column 7. A glance down Column 7 shows the profit maximizing level of output to be thirteen units. The total-revenue, total-cost approach to profit maximization is shown graphically in Exhibit 24.2b. Total profit appears in that exhibit as the vertical gap between the total cost and total revenue curves; it reaches a maximum at thirteen units of output, where the two curves are the maximum distance apart.

Note that maximizing profit is not the same thing as maximizing revenue. Between thirteen and seventeen units of output, total revenue continues to rise; but total cost rises even faster, so profit declines.

---

[1]Here is an easy rule that will help in sketching the marginal revenue curve corresponding to any downward sloping straight-line demand curve; *the marginal revenue curve for a straight-line demand curve always cuts the horizontal distance from the demand curve to the vertical axis exactly in half.* This rule does not work for curved demand curves, but the examples in this book will be kept simple.

**Exhibit 24.2**

**Profit maximization for a pure monopolist**

This exhibit demonstrates that a pure monopolist maximizes profits by producing that quantity of output for which marginal cost is equal to marginal revenue. Notice that maximizing profit is not the same as maximizing revenue. As this example is constructed, the profit maximizing output is thirteen units. In the range from thirteen to seventeen units of output, total revenue continues to increase. But because total cost increases even faster in this range, profits decline. Notice also that the profit maximizing price for the monopolist is determined by the height of the demand curve (not the marginal cost or marginal revenue curve) at the profit maximizing quantity of output.

**(a)**

| Output (1) | Price (2) | Total Revenue (3) | Marginal Revenue (4) | Marginal Cost (5) | Total Cost (6) | Total Profit (7) |
|---|---|---|---|---|---|---|
| 1 | $10.00 | $10.00 | | | $23.80 | −$13.80 |
| 2 | 9.70 | 19.40 | $9.40 | $3.40 | 27.20 | −7.80 |
| 3 | 9.40 | 28.20 | 8.80 | 3.05 | 30.25 | −2.05 |
| 4 | 9.10 | 36.40 | 8.20 | 2.75 | 33.00 | 3.40 |
| 5 | 8.80 | 44.00 | 7.60 | 2.50 | 35.50 | 8.50 |
| 6 | 8.50 | 51.00 | 7.00 | 2.30 | 37.80 | 13.20 |
| 7 | 8.20 | 57.40 | 6.40 | 2.15 | 39.95 | 17.45 |
| 8 | 7.90 | 63.20 | 5.80 | 2.05 | 42.00 | 21.20 |
| 9 | 7.60 | 68.40 | 5.20 | 2.00 | 44.00 | 24.40 |
| 10 | 7.30 | 73.00 | 4.60 | 2.05 | 46.05 | 26.95 |
| 11 | 7.00 | 77.00 | 4.00 | 2.15 | 48.20 | 28.80 |
| 12 | 6.70 | 80.40 | 3.40 | 2.30 | 50.50 | 29.90 |
| 13 | 6.40 | 83.20 | 2.80 | 2.50 | 53.00 | 30.20 |
| 14 | 6.10 | 85.40 | 2.20 | 2.75 | 55.75 | 29.65 |
| 15 | 5.80 | 87.00 | 1.60 | 3.05 | 58.80 | 28.20 |
| 16 | 5.50 | 88.00 | 1.00 | 3.40 | 62.20 | 25.80 |
| 17 | 5.20 | 88.40 | .40 | 3.80 | 66.00 | 22.40 |

**The Marginal Approach**  Alternatively, the profit maximizing level of output for the pure monopolist can be found by comparing marginal cost and marginal revenue, as shown in Columns 4 and 5 of Exhibit 24.2a. Marginal revenue is the amount by which total revenue increases as the result of a one-unit increase in output, and marginal cost is the amount by which total cost increases. It follows that so long as marginal revenue exceeds marginal cost, adding one more unit of output will add more to total revenue than to total cost and will hence add to total profit. Beyond thirteen units of output, marginal revenue falls below marginal cost, so further expansion of output reduces total profit.

Exhibit 24.2c makes the comparision between marginal revenue and marginal cost graphically. The profit maximizing quantity is found where the marginal cost and marginal revenue curves intersect. It corresponds to the point of maximum profit, shown in Exhibit 24.2b as the point where the gap between the total revenue and total cost curves is greatest.

The intersection of the marginal cost and marginal revenue curves in Exhibit 24.2c gives the profit maximizing quantity of output for the pure monopolist; the corresponding profit maximizing price is given by the height of the demand curve for this quantity. For the pure monopolist, this price is always above marginal cost. Marginal cost at thirteen units of output for the firm in the example is $2.50 per unit, but according to the demand curve, consumers would be willing to buy thirteen units of output for as much as $6.40. The price of $6.40 is thus what the monopolist will charge for the thirteen units of output in order to earn the maximum profit.

## Profit Maximization or Loss Minimization?

Just as for a perfectly competitive firm, profit maximization for a monopolist can sometimes mean loss minimization, at least in the short run. Whether there are actual profits to be made or only losses to be minimized depends on the position of the demand curve relative to the monopolist's average cost curves.

One possibility is illustrated in Exhibit 24.3. Here, demand is high enough relative to average cost for the monopolist to make a pure economic profit, above and beyond the normal rate of return on capital that is built into the definition of average total cost. As in Exhibit 24.2, the profit maximizing quantity, at the intersection of the marginal cost and marginal revenue curves, is roughly thirteen units of output. The demand curve indicates that the profit maximizing price for that quantity of output is approximately $6.40 per unit.

At thirteen units of output, average total cost is only $4 per unit. That means the monopolist earns a pure economic profit of $2.40 per unit above and beyond all costs, including the implicit cost of a normal rate of return on invested capital. At thirteen units of output, total profit is $31.20. This is shown graphically in Exhibit 24.3 as the shaded rectangle. The base of the rectangle is equal to the quantity of output (thirteen units). Its height is equal to the difference between the price of $6.40 per unit and the average total cost of $4 per unit—that is, to the $2.40 average profit the firm earns.

Under less favorable demand conditions, however, the same firm may be able to do no better than to minimize losses. This possibility is illustrated

## Exhibit 24.3

### A pure monopolist earning positive profits

The profit actually earned by a pure monopolist depends on the relationship of price to average total cost. In this example, the monopolist's demand curve is high enough to enable a pure economic profit to be earned. Total profit is shown in the diagram as the shaded rectangle with a height equal to the difference between price and average total cost and a width equal to the profit maximizing quantity of output.

*[handwritten annotations: "average profit earned 6.4 - 4.0 = 2.4", "output", "profit max.", "covers total costs"]*

## Exhibit 24.4

### Short-run loss minimization for a pure monopolist

Sometimes demand may not be sufficient to permit a pure monopolist to earn a pure economic profit. As this exhibit is drawn, for example, the demand curve lies below the average total cost curve at all points. The best the monopolist can do, in the short run, is to minimize losses by producing at the point where marginal cost equals marginal revenue. If the demand curve were to shift downward even farther, so that the firm could not obtain a price covering average variable cost, the short-run loss minimizing strategy would be to shut down.

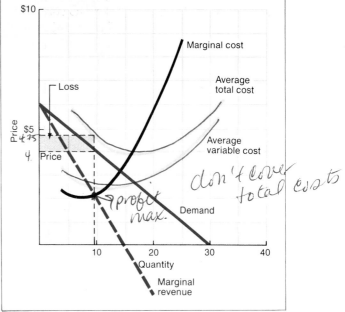

*[handwritten annotations: "4.75", "4", "profit max.", "don't cover total costs"]*

in Exhibit 24.4. The demand curve in the diagram lies below the average cost curve at all points. This can happen, for example, during a severe recession, when consumer incomes are abnormally low. Following the usual rule, the profit maximizing quantity of output is found to be about ten units, as Exhibit 24.4 is drawn. According to the demand curve, that much output can be sold for $4 per unit, but average total cost at ten units of output is $4.75. At a price of $4 per unit, the monopolist will lose $.75 on each unit sold. This total loss is shown in the exhibit by the shaded rectangle.

Although the monopolist suffers a loss at ten units of output, no other choice of output will yield a smaller loss. As Exhibit 24.4 is drawn, $4 per unit is more than enough to cover average variable costs. The monopolist, like the perfectly competitive firm, is better off staying in production in the short run, even at a loss, so long as the price at which the output can be sold is greater than the average variable cost. If the demand curve shifts so far to the left that it falls below the average variable cost curve at all points, the pure monopolist, like the perfectly competive firm, will minimize short-run losses by shutting down. In the long run, if demand conditions do not improve, the firm will go out of business.

### Long-Run Profit Maximization under Pure Monopoly

One of the most important conclusions reached in Chapter 23 was that, in the long run, pure economic profits are impossible under perfect competition. The reason is that if an increase in demand for the product raises the market price above average total cost, new firms will be attracted into the industry. As the new firms enter, the total quantity supplied to the market increases, driving the market price back to the level of average total cost.

Under pure monopoly, in contrast, pure economic profits can continue indefinitely if demand conditions are favorable. The reason is that a monopolist is assumed to be protected against competition by barriers to entry. Even if short-run demand conditions permit a higher than normal rate of return on capital, as in Exhibit 24.3, no other firm can enter the market. If nothing happens to disturb the favorable position of its cost and demand curves, a pure monopolist can earn pure economic profits above and beyond the normal rate of return even in the long run.

### Indirect Competition and Long-Run Profits

Although protection from direct competition makes it possible in some cases for pure monopolists to earn pure economic profits in the long run, there are other cases in which long-run profits are eroded by indirect competition. In one limiting case, a monopolist faced with indirect competition might find itself in the position pictured in Exhibit 24.5. In that exhibit, the demand curve just touched the average total cost curve at the quantity of output for which marginal revenue equals marginal cost, so that the best the firm can do is break even. It earns sufficient revenue to cover all its costs, including a normal rate of return on capital, but nothing more.

Two kinds of indirect competition in particular might push a monopolist toward this long-run breakeven position. One is competition in the process of establishing a monopoly in the first place. A firm may have to bid competitively for a key patent or for access to key natural resources in order to establish its monopoly. Perhaps it will have to hire expensive lawyers and consultants to convince a government agency that it, and not some other firm, should get a key license or permit. If entrepreneurs compete vigorously to establish a monopoly, it may very well turn out that the

**Exhibit 24.5**

**The breakeven position for a pure monopolist**

Being a pure monopolist in a market may make it possible to earn a pure economic profit in the long run, but it does not guarantee that positive profits will be earned. This exhibit shows a monopoly that is only breaking even (that is, earning only a normal rate of return on invested capital). Among other possibilities, this could be the result of high costs of obtaining or defending the firm's monopoly position or of erosion of demand through in-direct competition from substitute products.

winner never does better than break even. Its initial efforts, although successful, may cost so much that it ends up in the position shown in Exhibit 24.5.

Competition from substitute products can also force a monopolist to the breakeven position. A firm with a monopoly of steel production, for example, may find that, over time, clever entrepreneurs in the aluminum or plastics industries are stealing away more and more of its customers. The competition of substitutes may gradually erode demand for the monopolist's own product until, in the limiting case, the demand curve falls all the way to tangency with the average cost curve.

The likelihood of actually reaching the limiting position of zero profits depends on the closeness of the substitutes offered by the other firms. For example, a firm whose monopoly consists in owning the only Italian restaurant in town will clearly feel more competitive pressure than will a firm owning the only restaurant of any kind. In fact, when a firm's "monopoly" is so narrowly based that many competing firms offer products that are very close substitutes, economists no longer classify the firm as a pure monopolist. Instead, they call a market structure in which a large number of firms offer products that are relatively close substitutes for one another **monopolistic competition**. Chapters 25 and 26 will have more to say about monopolistic competition and about other forms of competition lying between pure monopoly and perfect competition.

**Monopolistic competition** A market structure in which a large number of firms offer products that are relatively close substitutes for one another.

## MONOPOLY, CONSUMER WELFARE, AND PRICE DISCRIMINATION

### Pure Monopoly as an Imperfect Market Structure

Chapter 23 showed that production is carried out in a perfectly competitive market up to the point where price is equal to marginal cost. This, it was

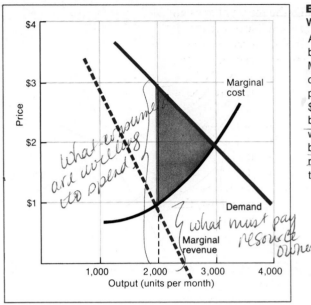

**Exhibit 24.6**
**Why monopoly markets are imperfect**

A perfect market is one in which all potential mutually beneficial exchanges are carried out and none is missed. Monopoly markets are not perfect in this sense. In the case illustrated here, a pure monopolist will maximize profits at a quantity of 2,000 units per month and a price of $3 per unit. But at that price and quantity, there is a gap between the demand curve and the marginal cost curve, which indicates that, in principle, further production can be carried out to the mutual benefit of consumers and resource owners. The shaded triangular area indicates the value of potential benefits forgone.

argued, makes perfect competition a "perfect" market form in the sense that all potential mutually beneficial transactions are carried out. Beyond the point of competitive equilibrium, consumer welfare cannot be further improved without imposing an actual loss on producers.

Under pure monopoly, in contrast, production stops short of the quantity necessary to bring market price down to the level of marginal cost. Consider Exhibit 24.6, for example. There, the monopolist maximizes profit by producing 2,000 units of output per month and selling each unit for $3. At a rate of output of 2,000 units per month, marginal cost is only $1 per unit. There is a $2 gap between marginal cost and the market price. This gap represents a market imperfection; it indicates that some potential mutually beneficial transactions are not being carried out.

One way to understand the nature of this market imperfection is to think of the monopolist as a middleman standing between the consumer and resource owners. The height of the demand curve at 2,000 units of output in Exhibit 24.6 represents what consumers are willing to pay for the 2,000th unit of output. The height of the marginal cost curve at this point represents what the firm has to pay resource owners for the various inputs necessary to produce the 2,000th unit. Clearly, production of the 2,000th unit is worthwhile; consumers value it at $3, and resource owners value the resources used up in producing it at only $1.

Reasoning in the same way, it would also be worthwhile to produce a 2,001st unit of output. Consumers would value the 2,001st unit at only slightly less than $3, and resource owners would be willing to release the necessary inputs for only a little more than $1. If it were feasible for consumers to negotiate directly with resource owners for production of the 2,001st unit, it would presumably be produced at a mutually agreeable price, such as $2. In this case, however, consumers do not deal with resource owners directly. They deal instead through the monopolist as an intermediary, and it is not worthwhile for the monopolist to produce a 2,001st unit of output. Even though the 2,001st unit could be sold at a price higher than its marginal cost, the marginal revenue earned by the monopolist from the transaction would be less than marginal cost. And it is not profitable for the monopolist to increase output beyond the point where marginal revenue falls below marginal cost.

What is true of the 2,001st unit is also true of the 2,002nd, the 2,003rd, and all units up to and including the 3,000th. Each of these units could be produced and sold at a price higher than marginal cost — that is, at a price high enough to fully compensate resource owners and low enough still to be agreeable to consumers. But as long as consumers deal with resource owners only at arm's length, through the agency of the monopolist, this potential mutual benefit, represented in Exhibit 24.6 by the shaded triangle, will not be realized. It is in this sense that pure monopoly is an imperfect market structure.

## Price Discrimination

This is a good place to emphasize an assumption that has been only implicit in the discussion to this point — the assumption that the pure monopolist sells all units of output at a uniform price. Such a pricing policy is forced on the monopolist whenever the nature of the product makes resale among buyers possible. For example, it is highly unlikely that your campus bookstore (a monopoly on many campuses) could get away with selling economics texts at list price to third year students and at a 25 percent discount to everyone else. If it tried to do so, it would not be long before some enterprising first year student went into buying books for resale to seniors at some split-the-difference price. The bookstore's list-price sales would soon fall to zero.

Some firms, however, do not sell their product to all customers at the same price. Such sellers are said to practice **price discrimination**. Two things are required if price discrimination is to be possible. First, resale of the product among consumers must be impossible, or at least inconvenient. And second, the seller must be able to classify potential customers into groups with highly inelastic demand, who can be charged high prices, and groups with more elastic demand, who will be driven away unless offered low prices. The following case study illustrates price discrimination in action.

**Price discrimination** The practice of charging more than one price for different units of a single product, when the price differences are not justified by differences in the cost of serving different customers.

### Case 24.1
### Price Discrimination in Private Schools

Private schools in Canada very commonly practice price discrimination in selling their main product — education. Usually, it works this way. First, the business office sets tuition at some ambitiously high level. Then, the admissions office gives its stamp of approval to a certain number of qualified applicants. After this is done, the financial aid office gets busy working out a price discrimination strategy. The strategy consists of offering selective price rebates, called scholarships, to those students who it thinks will not be willing or able to attend if charged full tuition.

A private school is in an ideal position to practice price discrimination. For one thing, the product is completely nontransferable. If you are admitted to both Upper Canada College in Toronto and Lower Canada College in Montreal, you can't sell your Upper Canada College admission to someone who didn't get into either place! Furthermore, the school collects a great deal of information that allows it to classify students according to willingness and ability to pay.

If the price discrimination strategy is successful, everyone involved may benefit. Students who would not have been able to attend a private school at all without financial aid probably benefit most. Students who pay full tuition find their school experience enriched by the diversity of a student population with a wider variety of backgrounds and abilities than could have been attracted without a scholarship program. Meanwhile, the school itself benefits by keeping its classrooms full with the help of scholarship students and its budget balanced with tuition and fees collected from those without scholarships.

## Pros and Cons of Price Discrimination

Price discrimination is widely perceived as unfair, especially by those who pay a high price while others pay less. Attempts have been made to outlaw price discrimination in some markets. However, as the preceding case study suggests, price discrimination should not be condemned without considering the alternatives.

The key question to ask in evaluating any price discrimination scheme is whether it moves the market closer to or farther from the ideal state in which all potential mutually beneficial trades are carried out. When price discrimination allows buying by those who are willing to pay a price at least equal to marginal cost but not as high as what a nondiscriminatory monopolist would charge, it may very well be beneficial. For example, price discrimination makes it possible for some students to attend schools they otherwise could not afford. It allows parents to take their young children to the movies. And it makes it possible for standby passengers, who could not afford the full fares business travelers pay, to fill airplane seats that would otherwise go empty. These forms of price discrimination almost certainly represent improvements in market performance compared with what would realistically be possible under uniform pricing.

On the other hand, price discrimination can sometimes be carried too far. In particular, it is important that the lowest price charged not fall below marginal cost. If that were to happen, another kind of market imperfection would be introduced: output would be too large, rather than too small, in comparison with a perfectly competitive market. Too many, rather than too few, resources would be attracted to the industry in question. For example, public utility commissions in some areas encourage electric utilities to discriminate against industrial users and in favor of residential users even to the point that some power for residential use is sold below long-run marginal cost. Many economists believe that this has encouraged wasteful use of electricity by homeowners and has thus made it necessary for utilities to overexpand their generating capacity.

Later chapters will discuss a number of additional examples of price discrimination. Case by case evaluations will show that some are good and others bad.

## CARTELS

### Pure Monopolies and Cartels

To the extent that it is motivated by profit maximization, every firm would like to be a monopolist. But most firms have no realistic chance of becoming pure monopolists. In most markets, firms face competitors that are far too numerous and far too vigorous ever to be bought up or driven away. Furthermore, in most markets, decreasing returns to scale would make it highly inefficient to concentrate all production in a single firm.

For would-be monopolists in such markets, there is a tempting alternative to the pure, single-firm monopoly. That alternative is a **cartel** — an agreement among a number of independent firms to stop competing and, instead, to coordinate their supply decisions so all of them will earn a monopoly profit.

### How Cartels Work

A simple example will show just how cartels work. Imagine an industry composed of one hundred identical small firms. For simplicity, assume that the marginal cost of production for all firms in the industry is a constant $1 per unit, regardless of the quantity produced. Because marginal cost is the same for all units of output, the marginal cost curve also serves as the long-run average cost curve and the long-run supply curve for the industry. This perfectly elastic long-run supply curve is shown, together with a hypothetical demand curve for the industry, in Exhibit 24.7.

The equilibrium price and quantity of output of the industry depend on how the market is organized. Suppose initially that all firms behave as perfect competitors. Under the theory set forth in Chapter 23, this situation will result in an equilibrium in which the market price is $1 per unit (equal to long-run average cost and long-run marginal cost) and in which

**Cartel** An agreement among a number of independent suppliers of a product to coordinate their supply decisions so all of them will earn monopoly profits.

**Exhibit 24.7**

**The effects of a cartel**
This exhibit represents an industry composed of one hundred identical firms, each producing at constant long-run average and marginal cost. If the firms behave as perfect competitors, the industry will be in equilibrium where the demand curve and marginal cost curve intersect. If the firms form a cartel, however, they can jointly earn profits by restricting output to the point where marginal cost is equal to marginal revenue and by raising the product price from $1 to $2.

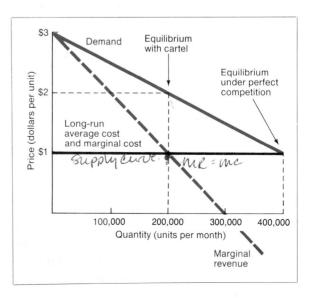

400,000 units of output are produced each month. In this equilibrium, each firm earns a normal rate of return on its capital and earns no pure economic profit.

Suppose now that one day the heads of the hundred firms get together to form a cartel. It is their hope that by replacing competition with cooperation, they can advance their mutual interests. They elect one of their number as cartel manager. The manager is instructed to work out a production and marketing plan that will maximize total profits for the industry and to share these profits fairly among the members.

The profit maximizing problem faced by the cartel manager is exactly the same as that faced by a pure monopolist. Industry profits are maximized at the output where marginal revenue for the industry equals marginal cost. That output is 200,000 units per month for this example. By restricting output to that quantity, the price can be raised to $2 per unit, and $200,000 per month of pure economic profit will be generated. To share this profit among all cartel members, each firm will be given an output quota of 2,000 units a month, half as much as it had been producing as a competitor. By this arrangement, the member firms will reap the benefits of pure monopoly despite their small size and large numbers.

### The Stability Problem for Cartels

For its members, a successful cartel is a wonderful thing. Each firm is able to share in the profits of a monopoly while maintaining its organizational independence. But for buyers of the product, a cartel is clearly no blessing. In this example, buyers end up spending the same amount of money on the product as under competition but getting only half the quantity.

Fortunately for consumers, relatively few markets are organized as cartels. Partly, this is because most cartels are illegal under Canadian law. (More on this subject in Chapter 27.) Even more importantly, though, cartels suffer from two big built-in problems that prevent most potential cartels from being formed at all and keep others from surviving for long if they are formed.

**Control over Entry** The first problem that cartels suffer from is control over entry. As long as competition in an industry keeps price down to the level of long-run average cost, membership in the industry tends to be stable. As soon as a cartel raises price above this level, however, the industry becomes a magnet for new entrants. The entry of new firms does not increase the total quantity that the cartel can sell at the profit maximizing price. It increases only the number of members among which profits have to be shared. Unless there is a way for a cartel to control entry into its market, it cannot effectively serve the interests of its members.

**Enforcement of Output Quotas** The second, even more serious, built-in problem of cartels is the enforcement of output quotas. In every cartel, each individual member always has an incentive to cheat on its quota by producing extra, unauthorized output. Take the cartel in Exhibit 24.7. The quota for each of the one hundred members is 2,000 units per month, just half of what each firm would produce under competitive conditions. What would happen if any single firm cheated on its quota by stepping up output to the precartel level while the others continued to play by the rules?

The answer is simple. An extra 2,000 units per month by one firm would have a negligible effect on the market price, because it would represent only a 1 percent increase in industry output. By producing 4,000 units a month, the cheater would double its monthly profit—as long as others did not cheat too.

What if the others did cheat? What if all the other ninety-nine firms stepped up output to 4,000 units while only one firm stuck to its quota? With industry output at 398,000 units, the price would be forced down virtually all the way to the competitive level of $1. The firm that played fair would gain nothing for its honesty.

Because cartels are potentially so profitable, cartel organizers sometimes undertake elaborate measures to suppress cheating and enhance stability. In the case of illegal cartels, these efforts go on behind locked doors, and outside observers rarely have a chance to learn the details. The following case study shows that such cartels suffer chronically from the stability problems identified here.

## Case 24.2
### Instability in an Actual Cartel

Mining is by no means a risk-free business. A single mine can cost hundreds of millions to develop, and interest on that money alone may mean high fixed payments for five or ten years. In the meantime, strikes, government intervention, and price fluctuations can chop out large chunks of revenue.

So mining companies seek out any way they can to reduce uncertainty. Their most common tactic is to form producers' cartels to prop up prices and regulate production. Recently, though, the cartel solution hasn't been working.

Cartels were originally organized by the great international mining finance houses such as Rio Tinto-Zinc, Le Nickel, Anglo American Corporation, and Charter Consolidated. Acting more as banks than operating companies, these firms would take participation in one another's projects, organize transportation and marketing, work out deals with governments, and set production and price levels.

As one mining finance man says, "The old cartels worked because the guys on top were willing to cut production ruthlessly when the market turned down. If a mining company attempted to produce more than its quota, it could find itself in trouble with its bankers and customers." All this was possible because governments didn't have the leverage to force companies to keep up payrolls and exports at unprofitable price levels.

The system also tended to work to the disadvantage of the new, small producer. As the head of the British copper cartel once said, "A high copper price is the cheapest form of exploration." Boom periods would suck in new, risk-taking prospectors and developers. The new guys would build new properties, and then find themselves overextended when the price dropped. Then the mining finance houses would come in and pick up the pieces. Their close ties to the banks made it possible for them to find the cash even as the doors were being closed on the entrepreneurs.

That system hasn't been working for a while. The mining finance houses are still around, to be sure. In Canada, for example, Britain's Rio Tinto-Zinc controls Rio Algom, the country's biggest uranium producer, and South Africa's Anglo American controls Hudson Bay Mining and Smelting Company. Increasingly, though, governments, rather than companies, are setting production and price policy, and they're not doing an especially good job.

In copper, for example, the old producers' cartel has been replaced by an organization called CIPEC, a sort of copper exporters' version of OPEC. Its members are Third World countries like Zaire, Zambia, Peru, and Chile. They have enormous burdens of debt, and they'll ship out copper at almost any price to meet the interest payments. This means that, unlike the old private cartel, they've been unable to cut production and prop up the price.

The breakdown of the international system has had serious effects on Canadian copper producers. They had their own cozy arrangement, the "North American Producer Price," which smoothed out fluctuations in the copper market. Now, in the face of attacks from the U.S. Justice Department and their industrial customers, most of the copper companies are being forced to go to something approaching a free market system. There are more competitive price cuts and fewer "orderly marketing arrangements" — the old euphemism for market-rigging deals.

Source: *Saturday Night*, Oct. 1978, pp. 80–81.

### Is OPEC an Exception?

But what about OPEC, the Organization of Petroleum Exporting Countries? Isn't OPEC a self-proclaimed cartel, which in less than a decade has engineered a twentyfold increase in the price of its product, bringing the rest of the world virtually to its knees? The following case study examines whether OPEC is indeed the rare example of a successful cartel or whether it is something else.

### Case 24.3
### OPEC: Is It a Cartel?

OPEC has often been called the world's most successful cartel. Its members call it a cartel. The OPEC oil ministers meet periodically to talk about raising prices. For many years they then went home and did what they said they would do — raised prices. The rise in oil prices from less than $2 a barrel in the 1960s to as much as $40 a barrel by 1980 left Western economists scrambling for an explanation of how it all happened.

*The Conventional Wisdom* Following the first price jump, in 1973, most discussions of OPEC took it for granted that the organization was in fact a cartel. Some said that this cartel would soon collapse because of the pressure of new entry and internal discord, but prices kept going up. Soon a conventional wisdom emerged to explain how OPEC overcame the forces that doomed ordinary cartels.

The conventional wisdom on OPEC-as-cartel rested on three propositions. First, OPEC was said to face no entry problem because it produced over half the oil of the noncommunist world and because large, new, non-OPEC reserves just weren't to be found. Second, OPEC was supposed to be able to avoid internal dissension because of the unifying force of Arab politics, catalyzed by the 1973 war with Israel. Third, it was said that even if some small producers broke rank and cheated on the cartel, Saudi Arabia alone, with more than a third of OPEC output capacity, would be able to absorb production cuts and hold aloft a price umbrella for the rest.

*The Revisionist View* By 1981 events had undermined this conventional wisdom. Mexico and the North Sea countries had emerged as major non-OPEC entrants, and the OPEC share of world production was falling. The political unity of OPEC was torn by the Iraq-Iran war, by Libyan radicalism, and by the strain between religious traditionalists and modernists throughout the Middle East. And Saudi Arabia's supposed price umbrella was inexplicably being held upside down. That country was pushing output to artificially high levels in an attempt to force other

OPEC members to lower their prices instead of cutting output to force the others to raise their prices.

To revisionist critics the decisive evidence against OPEC-as-cartel was the fact that the organization had no system of output quotas. Its members had attempted to establish quotas soon after OPEC was founded, in 1960, but these efforts failed because members couldn't agree on a formula. Venezuela, historically the largest oil producer, wanted a formula based on historical output. Saudi Arabia, with the biggest reserves, wanted a formula based on reserves. And Iran, with its large population, wanted a population-based formula. By the time prices finally took off, efforts to establish output quotas had long been abandoned. The revisionists claimed that OPEC could no more be a cartel without output controls than a bird could be a duck without webbed feet.

*What Really Happened?* If OPEC was not really a cartel, though, why did oil prices rise as they did in the 1970s? The revisionist theory would not be complete without an alternate explanation of the price explosion. This explanation, now gaining more and more adherents, rests on property rights and on supply and demand.

The key event that sparked the price rise of the 1970s, in the revisionist view, was the nationalization of property rights to Middle East oil, which had previously been held by the international oil companies. In the 1950s and 1960s, lacking secure ownership of reserves, the majors had every incentive to go for a quick profit while they could, even though the world price was less than $2 a barrel. Following 1973, the oil-producing countries themselves took over output and pricing decisions. To them, each barrel of cheap oil produced today carried an opportunity cost of a barrel less to sell in the future, when rising world demand would drive the price higher. Thus, in raising oil prices after 1973, each producing country was following the self-interest of a long-term profit maximizer. Its collective interest as a member of a cartel played a secondary role in the pricing decision, if any at all.

Additionally, in the revisionist view, supply and demand conditions created by U.S. energy policy favored a price run-up in the 1970s. In the 1950s and early 1960s, a U.S. policy of import restrictions had kept domestic prices and output artificially high. That had depressed world oil prices below the level they would have reached in a competitive international market. After 1973, U.S. policy was completely reversed. A price ceiling was imposed, and it kept domestic prices and output artificially low and demand for imports artificially high. U.S. oil imports ballooned, supporting the price-raising efforts of the oil-exporting countries.

The debate between the cartel theorists and the revisionists is not yet over. As long as world prices and demand were both rising steadily, either theory fitted the facts, at least in part. The test will come if world oil demand continues to fall, as it did in 1980 and 1981. Then it may become clear whether OPEC as a would-be cartel has any real capability of taking collective action to control price and output.

## CONCLUSIONS

It would be tempting to conclude this chapter with some sweeping comparisons of monopoly and competition. Competition is perfect; monopoly is flawed. So three cheers for competition, and down with monopoly! But not so fast. The implications that can legitimately be drawn from a comparison of the two market structures are more limited than they initially appear. And a lot more groundwork must be laid before even those limited conclusions can be drawn.

For one thing, remember that all of the analysis of perfect competition and pure monopoly has taken place on the level of pure economizing. We should be reluctant to draw any conclusions about the relative merits of alternative market structures until we know something about how they affect entrepreneurial decision making as well. That is a topic to be taken up in Chapters 25 and 26.

Second, even within the realm of pure economizing, we have seen only how to compare two *different* markets—one competitive and the other monopolistic. That is not at all the same thing as making an evaluation of how a single market would perform under two alternative forms of organization. In practice, it is rarely, if ever, possible to change the structure of a market without making other changes in it as well. In particular, any change in market structure that involves increasing or decreasing the number of firms among which production is divided is very likely to affect costs and product characteristics as well. If competition reduces costs and improves product characteristics, its degree of superiority over monopoly may be very much greater than the little triangle in Exhibit 24.6 indicates. On the other hand, if excessive fragmentation of production has adverse effects on cost or product quality, those effects may more than outweigh competitive benefits of the type looked at so far.

Finally, it would simply be premature to make any comparisons between perfect competition and pure monopoly until we have examined many other market structures that are neither one nor the other. That job will occupy most of the next five chapters.

## SUMMARY

1. Pure monopoly is a market structure in which one firm accounts for 100 percent of market supply. A firm operating as a pure monopolist is potentially much more profitable than one operating as a perfect competitor. Any short-run profits earned by a competitive firm will soon be eaten away by new entrants. But under pure monopoly, a price high enough to allow short-run profits need not immediately be driven down by competitors because, by definition, there are no competitors in that particular market.

2. The monopolist is not a price taker. Because the firm can expand sales only by lowering the price at which the product is sold, marginal revenue is always less than price. With a straight-line demand curve, the marginal revenue curve always lies exactly halfway between the demand curve and the vertical axis.

3. Once the demand curve, marginal revenue curve, and cost curves are given, profit maximization for the monopolist can be treated as a problem in pure economizing. To find the profit maximizing quantity, locate the point where marginal cost and marginal revenue curves intersect. Then, to find the profit maximizing price, go vertically up from that point to the demand curve.

4. Whether the profit maximizing supply decision actually yields a profit over and above the normal rate of return on invested capital or merely minimizes losses depends on the location of the demand curve relative to the average cost curves. If the demand curve is above the average total cost curve at the point where marginal cost and marginal revenue are equal, the firm will earn a positive profit. If the demand and average total cost curves are tangent at that point, the firm will break even. If the

demand curve passes below the average total cost curve but above the average variable cost curve, the firm will minimize losses in the short run by producing where marginal cost equals marginal revenue. If the demand curve is everywhere below average variable cost, the firm will minimize losses by shutting down.

5. A perfect market is one in which all potential mutually beneficial transactions are carried out. Pure monopoly is not perfect in this sense. At the profit maximizing quantity of output, there is a gap between the demand curve and the marginal cost curve; this indicates that further production will be beneficial to both consumers and resource owners. Sometimes these additional gains from trade, wasted under pure monopoly, can be realized if the monopolist engages in price discrimination. Price discrimination may result in some buyers paying even higher prices than under pure monopoly, but it also may permit buying by some who would be shut out of the market altogether under nondiscriminating monopoly.

6. A cartel is an agreement among a number of independent suppliers in a market to stop competing and, instead, to coordinate their activities in order to earn a monopoly profit. The profit maximizing rule for a cartel is the same as that for a pure monopolist: produce where industry marginal cost equals industry marginal revenue. Cartels are less common than they might otherwise be partly because they are often illegal and partly because they are often unstable. They are unstable because each firm has an incentive to cheat on the cartel's price and output decisions in order to earn more than its agreed-upon share of the cartel's total profits.

## DISCUSSION QUESTIONS

1. One sometimes hears it said that a firm with a monopoly in its particular market will charge "the highest price it can get" for its product. What is the fallacy in this statement?

2. The common form of price discrimination involves charging different prices to different customers when the price difference is not justified by differences in the cost of serving those customers. Can you think of any examples where the different prices a firm changes *are* justified by differences in the cost of service? Alternatively, can you think of any instances in which a firm charges the same price for all units it sells, even though the cost of serving various customers is not the same? Should this too be considered price discrimination? Explain.

3. Some postal services have traditionally maintained a special low rate for shipments of books. Can you think of any likely economic reasons for this particular instance of price discrimination? Do you think the policy is a desirable one? Explain.

4. In what respect do you think labor unions resemble cartels? In what respects do they differ from cartels? Do you think labor unions ever suffer from the instability problems that plague product market cartels?

5. What is the best example you know of a pure monopoly? What protects this monopoly from the entry of direct competitors? How significant is the indirect competition by substitute products that this monopoly faces?

# OLIGOPOLY: COMPETITION AMONG THE FEW

## WHAT YOU WILL LEARN IN THIS CHAPTER

*Most markets have neither a single firm, as required for pure monopoly, nor the many firms required for perfect competition. Markets in which there are only a few firms, at least some of which have a large share of industry sales, are called oligopolies. This chapter will explain how to measure the degree of concentration in an oligopolistic industry and what determines the degree of concentration. It will examine several attempts to construct formal theories of oligopoly and explain why none of these attempts has been entirely successful. It will also examine evidence regarding the relationship between profits and market concentration. Throughout the chapter, a major question will be how well oligopolistic markets perform.*

## FOR REVIEW

*Here are some important terms and concepts that will be put to use in this chapter. If you do not understand them, review them before proceeding.*
- *Economies of scale (Chapter 22)*
- *Minimum efficient scale (Chapter 22)*
- *Perfect competition (Chapter 23)*
- *Pure monopoly and cartels (Chapter 24)*

As pointed out before, the term *competition* has two distinct meanings in economics. Used in "perfect competition," it refers to market structure. A market is said to be perfectly competitive if it has large numbers of small firms, a homogeneous product, well-informed buyers and sellers, and easy entry and exit. In contrast, when used as the verb "to compete," competition refers to business rivalry. In this sense, it is a matter of conduct rather than market structure. Two firms are said to compete if they treat each other as rivals in their independent efforts to do the best they can in the market-place.

Up to this point, the emphasis has been almost entirely on the structural side of things. Rivalry has played little role in the theories that have been introduced. There is no rivalry in perfectly competitive markets because each firm sees each other firm as too small to have much influence on market conditions. Rivalry is absent from pure monopoly because there is only one firm in the market. And, in a cartel, rivalry disappears as the result of an explicit decision to replace competition with coordination.

In the vast majority of markets, however, rivalry plays too big a role to be pushed into the background. Most markets have more than a single firm but fewer than the large number required for perfect competition. Most such markets also lack explicit agreements among competing firms to refrain from business rivalry. Such markets are known as **oligopolies**.

**Oligopoly** A market structure in which there are two or more firms, at least one of which has a large share of total sales.

Under oligopoly, it matters very much to each firm what its rivals do. This is true even for the simplest kind of oligopoly, in which all firms produce a homogeneous product, because each firm is so large that a change in the quantity it supplies can significantly affect the market price. It is even more true in more complex forms of oligopoly, where the products of rival firms are not exactly alike. There, each firm must be prepared to react to moves that its rivals make in terms of style changes, product innovations, and promotional techniques as well as to changes in price and quantity of output and in many other areas.

The need to focus on the interaction of many firms rather than on the behavior of each firm in isolation makes it difficult to formulate a completely satisfactory theory of oligopoly. Rather than presenting a single, unified theory, then, this chapter will look at a number of fragmentary theories all tied together by one central question: *is perfect competition necessary for satisfactory market performance, or is competition among a few large rival firms good enough?* Some economists have argued that even without explicitly agreeing to do so, oligopolists can coordinate their actions to restrict output and raise prices almost as effectively as do members of formal cartels. Others reject this idea and argue instead that competition among the few works very efficiently to serve consumer needs. Still others hedge their bets by saying that some oligopolies seem to perform better than others for reasons that are not completely understood. Although the controversy cannot be settled here, at least a map of the territory can be provided.

## MARKET CONCENTRATION AND ITS DETERMINANTS

The main purpose of this chapter is to develop some insight into the performance of oligopolistic markets, but two preliminary questions need to be asked. First, how many markets are really dominated by just a few firms (and how many is "a few")? And second, what determines the number of firms in a market and the size of their market shares? Knowing the answers to these questions will make it easier to understand both how markets work and what government policy is toward monopoly and oligopoly.

## Measuring Market Concentration

**Concentration ratios** provide a rough-and-ready measure of the extent to which markets are dominated by a few firms. The most common of these ratios are the four-firm concentration ratio (which measures the percentage of sales attributed to the top four firms in a given market) and the eight-firm concentration ratio (which measures the share of the top eight firms).

**Concentration ratio** The percentage of all sales contributed by the four or eight largest firms in a market.

**Exhibit 25.1**

**Four-firm and eight-firm concentration for selected industries, 1980**

Concentration ratios measure the percentage of industry output contributed by the largest firms. This representative selection of thirty-three Canadian industries shows a wide range of concentration ratios. The figures given here do not take into account foreign competition or the fact that some industries produce mainly for local markets. (Dark = four-firm concentration; dark plus light = eight-firm concentration.)

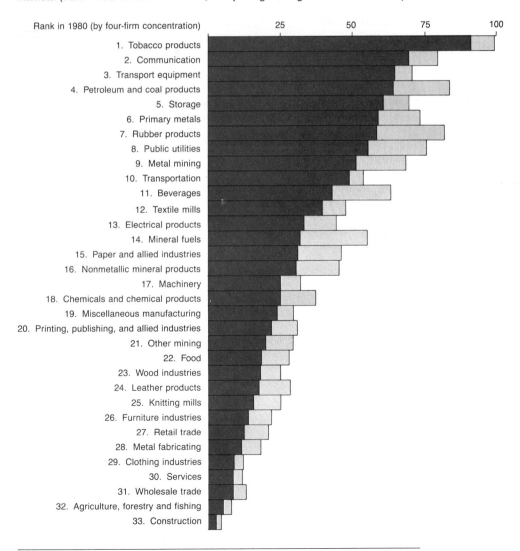

Rank in 1980 (by four-firm concentration)

1. Tobacco products
2. Communication
3. Transport equipment
4. Petroleum and coal products
5. Storage
6. Primary metals
7. Rubber products
8. Public utilities
9. Metal mining
10. Transportation
11. Beverages
12. Textile mills
13. Electrical products
14. Mineral fuels
15. Paper and allied industries
16. Nonmetallic mineral products
17. Machinery
18. Chemicals and chemical products
19. Miscellaneous manufacturing
20. Printing, publishing, and allied industries
21. Other mining
22. Food
23. Wood industries
24. Leather products
25. Knitting mills
26. Furniture industries
27. Retail trade
28. Metal fabricating
29. Clothing industries
30. Services
31. Wholesale trade
32. Agriculture, forestry and fishing
33. Construction

Source: Statistics Canada, *Annual Report of the Minister of Industry, Trade and Commerce under the Corporations and Labour Unions Returns Act* (Part 1: Corporations), 1980, p. 48.

Exhibit 25.1 gives concentration ratios for a representative selection of Canadian industries. At the top of the figure are industries that are classic oligopolies; they consist of a handful of firms that control virtually the entire market. For other industries, shown in the middle of the chart, the top four firms account for less than half of industry sales, although these firms are clearly large enough not to fit the strict requirements of perfect competition. Only in the case of services, such as hairdressing and shoe repair shops and in such industries as agriculture and construction, does it appear safe to say that there are "many" firms, each one of which is "small" relative to the size of the market. All in all, close to one-half of Canadian manufacturing output comes from markets in which the top four firms control half the markets or more. Canadian industry is considerably more concentrated than American industry.[1]

### Has Market Concentration Increased?

An interesting question, difficult to answer, is whether industry has become more or less concentrated in Canada. Case Study 25.1 describes recent attempts to answer that question. It is based on a more detailed survey of industries than that contained in Exhibit 25.1, so that concentration ratios in industry subsectors, like breweries (beverages) and automobile manufacture (transport equipment), are also provided.

### Case 25.1
### Trends in Industrial Concentration

There are pockets of sharply increasing corporate concentration in manufacturing industries but on the whole, competition has been on the increase since 1970 at least, Statistics Canada figures released this week suggest.

There was a "slight but noticeable downward trend" in industrial concentration in manufacturing industries between 1970 and 1980, says Statistics Canada official Ken Young.

The Statistics Canada figures on concentration levels measure the total market share held by the four top enterprises in each industry. The greater the market share, the greater the concentration and in general the less the competition.

Commenting on figures released this week, Young, an official with the agency's manufacturing and primary industries division, says the downward trend in concentration levels has been visible since 1970 when the agency began monitoring the country's 169 manufacturing industries on a regular basis.

The levels of concentration increased in 67 manufacturing industries between 1978 and 1980, declined in ninety-nine and remained unchanged in three.

The average level of concentration fell slightly to 49.8 percent in 1980 from 50.1 percent in 1978 and 50.6 percent in 1970.

The figures, published every second year, appear to contradict a report by the Consumer and Corporate Affairs Department released in 1981 which warned that unless competition laws are strengthened, "the trend towards higher industry concentration levels will remain unchallenged."

The 1981 Consumer and Corporate Affairs report is one of several used to

---

[1] A Canadian study showed that, in Canada, industries in which four or fewer firms produced 50 percent or more of total output accounted for 45 percent of all industries; in the United States such highly concentrated industries account for about 28 percent of industries. See B. Bock, "Is Concentration Rising?" *The Conference Board Record*, Vol. 13, No. 9, 1976, pp. 46–50.

support the latest of six government attempts to strengthen federal competition laws.

The latest attempt has failed to go beyond the discussion-paper stage and may fall victim to business opposition and the severe recession.

However, the author of the report, R.S. Khemani of the bureau of competition policy, noted that among other things, his study covered a much longer period—1948 to 1972—than covered by the Statistics Canada figures, and that the index used by Statistics Canada is only one of two used to measure industry concentration.

But Young says the other index, which measures the degree of concentration of all enterprises in an industry and not just the four largest, also suggests the level of competition increased marginally between 1970 and 1980.

He adds, however, that the levels in that index fluctuated in the intervening years and no trend is clearly visible.

The latest Statistics Canada figures also show industries where competition appears to be decreasing.

The publishing and printing industry, for example, continued to buck the trend with the top four enterprises holding 57.1 percent of the market share in 1980, up from 47.7 percent in 1978 and only 28.7 percent in 1965.

The sharp rise in concentration in that industry, specifically in newspapers, is a concern to Ottawa and some in the industry, and was the subject of a royal commission which recommended action be taken to reduce such concentration.

Young noted that mergers and take-overs have been responsible in many of the industries where there have been significant increases in corporate concentration.

However, the 1981 wave of corporate take-overs and the 1982 record onslaught of business bankruptcies are not included in the figures and could result in significant changes in the degree of concentration.

Young noted that levels of corporate concentration occur in lengthy cycles and that the last sharp increase was during the Depression.

Among the forty largest industries, the greatest concentration remained among breweries where the top four companies controlled 99 percent of the market, up from 98.9 in 1978 and 94 percent in 1970.

Other major industries where the four largest firms had a relatively high proportion of the market included: Automakers, where the big four held 93.7 percent of the market, virtually unchanged over the previous decade; electrical wire and cable manufacturers, with 80.2 percent of the market, down from 83 percent; and iron and steel mills, with 77.9 percent concentration, up from 76.2 percent since 1970.

While concentration levels are a measure of competition, they do not show the shifts in market share among the top four competitors or give any indication of the intensity of competition among them.

---

Source: Eric Beauchesne, "Competition Level on Increase," *Winnipeg Free Press*, June 15, 1983, p. 62.

## THE DETERMINANTS OF MARKET CONCENTRATION

Exhibit 25.1 gave a rough indication of the extent of industrial concentration. The next important question is: why are some industries more concentrated than others? The phenomenon of economies of scale provides a logical place to start answering this question.

### Economies of Scale

Chapter 22 introduced the concept of economies of scale. A firm is said to experience economies of scale if its long-run average costs decline as its scale of output increases. Shapes of long-run average cost curves vary from one industry to another, but statistical studies have indicated that many industries fit the pattern of an L-shaped long-run average cost curve. Such a cost curve shows economies of scale initially, followed by a range of constant returns to scale.

The point at which the average total cost curve stops falling and begins to flatten out is known as the minimum efficient scale for the firm — an important determinant of market concentration. The study of economies of scale by Eastman and Stykolt, discussed in Chapter 22, indicated that many industries in Canada appear to have *too many* plants. In contrast to American firms, which often build plants that appear to be larger than required by economies of scale, Canadian firms often build plants that are smaller than would be necessary to realize efficiencies of scale. Where this is the case, the concentration ratio might be said to be too low rather than too high. In view of the relatively small Canadian market and the existence of economies of scale, much of Canadian industry may be unavoidably oligopolistic in structure.

As was conjectured in Chapter 22, the reason Canadian firms build plants too small for economies of scale may be that they are reluctant to expand capacity because, given a relatively small market, substantial increases in capacity might require considerable reductions in price. Price reductions would threaten the profit margins of the firms in the industry.

It should also be noted that production costs of individual plants are not the only criteria used by firms in deciding the most efficient scale of operation. A recent study on the Canadian food processing industry observes that "plants which are too small to minimize production costs are often optimal in the sense of minimizing overall costs of production, assembly, and distribution."[2] Small tomato-canning plants in Ontario, for instance, can survive because they can locate close to raw materials and can specialize. These factors lead the multi-plant firms that we have in the meat packing, fish processing, and dairy processing industries to assume the higher production costs associated with small operations while retaining the advantages of size in bargaining, raising capital, advertising, and spreading overhead. Given such multi-plant economies, more industries may be operating at or close to their minimum efficient scale than otherwise appears to be the case.

Despite this, it is unlikely that economies of scale entirely determine the market concentration ratios presented in Exhibit 26.1. Many Canadian economists are convinced that, in a large number of industries, there are more plants now in operation than are warranted by considerations of efficiency, while simultaneously there are fewer firms than desirable. In other words, a relatively small number of firms — often operating numerous production or distribution units of less-than-efficient size — have

---

[2] John Morris, "The Competitive Characteristics of the Canadian Food Processing Industry," in *Competition and Public Policy on Competition in the Canadian Food Industry, Proceedings of Agricultural and Food Marketing Forum,* ed. R. M. A. Loyns and R. L. Louks, Department of Agricultural Economics and Farm Management, University of Manitoba, Occasional Series No. 7, May 1977.

come to dominate many industries.[3] Determinants other than efficiency must account for the maintenance of such market structures and for the absence of new rivals challenging existing firms. It is thus worth considering other possible determinants.

## Barriers to Entry Not Related to Economies of Scale

One reason why an industry may be more or less concentrated than economies of scale alone would indicate is that there may be barriers to entry of new firms. Even if profits in the industry are unusually high, prospective entrepreneurs may for some reason be unable to duplicate the performance of existing firms. As demand for the product expands, then, growth can come only through the expansion of existing firms, even after all economies of scale have been exhausted, or even if existing firms merely duplicate undersized production units.

**Legal Barriers** As in the case of pure monopoly, barriers to entry into oligopolistic industries are sometimes created on purpose by federal, provincial, or municipal government policy. In such industries, policy stops short of creating a pure franchised monopoly but still limits the number of competitors to fewer than would exist under free entry. For example, entry into many segments of the broadcasting industry was for years tightly controlled by the Canadian Radio-Television Commission (CRTC). Despite some recent reforms, these legal barriers to entry have still not been entirely dismantled. At the provincial level, entry into many professions and trades—law, medicine, plumbing, hairdressing, and dozens of others—is limited by licensing boards. Entry into rental housing or retailing in many communities is limited by local zoning regulations. The list of such legal barriers to entry goes on and on.

**Ownership of Resources** A second kind of barrier to entry is ownership of some nonreproducible resource. For example, entry into the ski resort industry is limited by the availability of suitable mountains. Entry into extractive industries is, in at least some cases, limited by ownership of the best available natural resources by existing firms. In other markets, the nonreproducible resources in question are human. Entry into the movie industry might be difficult, for example, if the top-quality stars were all under contract to existing firms. Whatever the reason, ownership of a nonreproducible resource gives existing firms an advantage over new entrants and thus constitutes a barrier to entry not directly related to economies of scale.

**Market Power** A third barrier to entry is market power. Market power is not the same thing as market performance, though in cases where economies of scale exist, it may depend at least partly on efficient performance.

**Market power** The strength that a firm possesses—because of exclusive control of resources, prior build-up of profits, or networks of influence and command—that gives it an advantage over its rivals.

---

[3] A recent study of the Canadian food retailing industry concludes that consumers are probably being harmed by the dominance of only four corporate chains in that industry (Dominion, Steinberg's, Canada Safeway, and Weston-Loblaw), which have simultaneously created overcapacity in the industry. (See Bruce Mallen, "Competition in Canadian Food Retailing," in *Competition and Public Policy on Competition in the Canadian Food Industry*.)

By **market power**, economists mean the strength that a firm may possess for reasons such as prior build-up of profits, or networks of influence and command—strength that gives it advantages over potential rivals.

The following hypothetical example illustrates one aspect of market power. A young engineer in Montreal develops a new method of manufacturing cement that, he claims, can reduce the cost of producing a certain type of cement by one-third. He arranges the financing, builds the plant, installs his new machines, and hires the necessary employees. Assume that his calculations are correct. On the day he opens his plant he announces a price for his cement that is one-third lower than the price charged by the large, single, long-established cement firm in the area. This larger firm cannot produce cement at that price, but, relying on its accumulation of past profits and its network of cement plants across the country, it cuts its price in the Montreal area by one-half. The new firm will now be driven out of business, not because it is unable to achieve efficient operation—it is *more* efficient than its rival—but because it doesn't have the market power of its older rival. The established firm does not have to lose much money, because it can retain higher prices in its other markets, nor does it have to lose money for long, because it can raise the price again as soon as the challenger declares bankruptcy. Incidentally, the practice of the hypothetical established firm in this case would be a violation of Canadian law. It is an example of "predatory pricing," meaning the temporary, localized use of below-cost prices to drive a rival out of business. However, such practices are difficult to prosecute, and the fines levied may be a small price to pay for the elimination of a competitor.

Firms may increase their market power by appointing bank presidents or other persons with specialized knowledge and influence to their boards of directors. Such appointments may give them advantages when it comes to examining new markets or arranging their financing. Several Canadian sociologists have documented the existence of a "corporate elite" in Canada: a social and economic network of about 1,000 business leaders who occupy most of the important directorships in the country.[4] One doesn't have to suffer from paranoia to assume that the social and economic connections thus established may provide benefits to the participants that place them at an economic advantage over those who operate outside the network.

Firms may also attempt to expand their power and control through formal mergers. Mergers can take many forms. A firm can merge *vertically* with a supplier or purchaser of its products, or *horizontally* with a competitor. It can engage in a *conglomerate* merger with firms producing completely different types of product and services. Horizontal mergers may result in economies of scale, and conglomerate mergers may give the firms more stability by reducing the danger of having all eggs in one basket. As Case Study 25.1 indicated, increases in corporate concentration occur in cycles, and the last one took place in the Depression of the 1930s at a time of great instability. The early 1980s may have been a period of further

[4]The classic study of this phenomenon remains John Porter, *The Vertical Mosaic* (Toronto: University of Toronto Press, 1965). See also Wallace Clement, *The Canadian Corporate Elite, An Analysis of Economic Power* (Toronto: McClelland and Stewart, 1975), and Peter Newman, *The Canadian Establishment* (Toronto: McClelland and Stewart, 1977), Vol. I.

**Exhibit 25.2**
The Thomson Empire

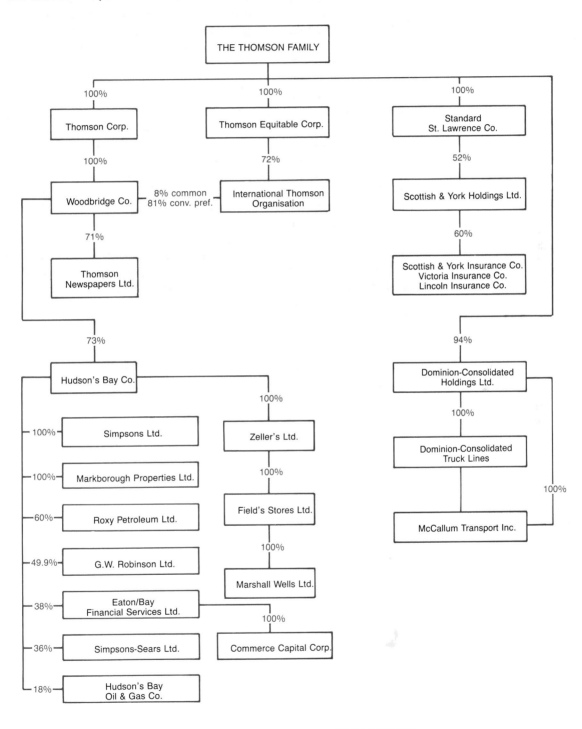

Source: *The Financial Post 500*, June 1981, p. 30.

concentrations through mergers, though full data are not yet available. Almost always, however, one objective of mergers is increased market power, and, from the point of view of potential competitors, the result may be increased barriers to entry. The largest conglomerate in Canada is Canadian Pacific Investment, which employs more than 100,000 people directly or through its many subsidiaries.

Some businesspeople are able to "pyrameid" their investments from one company to another, in order to establish effective control over a huge industrial empire without formal mergers. This is illustrated in Exhibit 25.2, which shows how the Thomson family, building on assets accumulated in Canada and England by the late Lord Thomson, gained substantial control of numerous firms, including the Hudson's Bay Co., Simpsons and Zeller's, and a chain of newspapers that includes *The Globe and Mail* of Toronto. It was the newspaper acquisitions of the Thomsons, combined with the acquisitions of Southam Press, which prompted the royal commission referred to in Case Study 25.1.

**Patents and Copyrights**  Patents and copyrights, another important class of barriers to entry, operate under oligopoly as well as under pure monopoly. A patent or copyright can be treated as a restrictive government regulation.

**Joan V. Robinson
(1903 –      )**

Joan Robinson is best known as a pioneer in the study of the behavior of firms in less than perfectly competitive markets. When she was a young assistant lecturer at Cambridge University, she decided to stand the accepted procedures of economics on their head. "It is customary," she wrote, "in setting out the principles of economic theory, to open with the analysis of a perfectly competitive world, and to treat monopoly as a special case. . . . This process can with advantage be reversed. . . . It is more proper to set out the analysis of monopoly, treating perfect competition as a special case." These words and the analysis to support them appeared in her *Economics of Imperfect Competition* in 1933. The book established her reputation immediately and remains one of the basic pioneering contributions to this branch of economics. (As often happens in economics, a similar theory was developed independently and published in the same year — by E. H. Chamberlin.)

Microeconomics was not Robinson's only interest, however. She was a pioneer of macroeconomic thinking. Even as her work on imperfect competition came out, she was involved in the debate that preceded the publication of Keynes's *General Theory*. In fact, in much of her later macro work, she is critical of the very kind of "partial" analysis on which her theory of imperfect competition rests.

Robinson has always been intensely interested in policy questions. In all her policy writings, she is a vehement critic of the market. In 1945, she wrote in *Private Enterprise and Public Control*:

The system of private property in its modern developments leads to great evils. Its inequality is not only an outrage on social justice, but also on common sense. It leads to large scale waste through unemployment, while the development of monopoly creates artificial scarcities and the dominance of the interests of property over the interests of human beings twists the whole system into a form for which it is impossible to find any reasonable justification.

Her opposition to the market and her interest in broad normative questions also led her to write *An Essay on Marxian Economics* (1956), *Economic Philosophy* (1962), and *Freedom and Necessity* (1970). Now long past retirement age, Robinson continues an active life as debater, social critic, and economic heretic.

Alternatively, ownership of a patent or copyright can be treated just like ownership of any other nonreproducible resource. Whichever point of view is adopted, patents and copyrights clearly can make entry difficult and thus can contribute to market concentration.

As the term is used here, a *barrier to entry* is something that prevents new entrants from duplicating the performance of existing firms in terms of cost or quality of product. It does not mean that every effort or expense that a firm must undertake to enter a market should be considered such a barrier. To start a new firm, a prospective entrepreneur must be willing to bear risks, must find investors to put up capital, must recruit a labor force, must attract customers, and so on. All these things are hard work — often hard enough to discourage less enterprising individuals from making the effort. Nonetheless, the need for hard work is not itself a barrier to entry in the economic sense. It is when entrepreneurs are not freely able to go out and buy the various building blocks of their new firms in the same market where existing firms buy their inputs, that barriers to entry become a determinant of market structure.

## COORDINATION AND INTERDEPENDENCE UNDER OLIGOPOLY

After this explanation of why some industries become concentrated, the chapter can turn to the behavior of firms in concentrated markets. In particular, it will examine the interdependence of firms in an oligopolistic market and the conditions under which the firms may be able to coordinate their price and output decisions to their mutual advantage.

### Oligopolistic Interdependence

When there are only a few firms in a market, it matters very much to each firm what its rivals do. Economists call the situation **oligopolistic interdependence**. This interdependence makes it very difficult to develop a theory of pure economizing in highly concentrated markets. A simple example will explain the problem.

Imagine a market in which there are only two firms — Alpha Company and Zed Enterprises. Their product costs $1 per unit to make. If both firms set their price at $5 per unit, each will sell 100 units per month at a profit of $4 per unit, for a total monthly profit of $400. If both firms set their price at $4 per unit, each will sell 120 units at a profit of $3 per unit for a total profit of $360. Which price will the firms actually set? Clearly, $5 is the price that will maximize their joint profits; but under oligopoly, this price may not represent a stable equilibrium.

Exhibit 25.3 shows why. It presents the alternative pricing strategies available *as they appear to Alpha Company*. In addition to the two possibilities already mentioned, Alpha must consider two more. One new possibility is to cut its price to $4 while Zed holds at $5. That will allow Alpha to steal away a lot of Zed's customers and to sell 150 units, for a profit of $450. The other new possibility is for Alpha to hold its price at $5 while Zed cuts to $4. Then Zed will steal a lot of Alpha's customers and leave Alpha selling only 60 units, for a total profit of $240.

**Oligopolistic interdependence** The necessity, in an oligopolistic market, for each firm to pay close attention to the behavior and likely reactions of its rivals when planning its own market strategy.

So what will happen? We just don't know! The theories that have helped explain many other market structures do not work for this simple oligopoly problem. We know how the firms can maximize joint profits if they coordinate their efforts. We know how to maximize Alpha's profits if we know what Zed is going to do. We know how to maximize Zed's profits if we know what Alpha is going to do. But none of that is enough. Something is still missing. The missing link needed to solve the problem of oligopolistic interdependence is some assumption about *how Alpha thinks Zed will react* to each possible move that Alpha might make.

All formal theories of oligopoly include some assumption about oligopolistic interdependence—about how each firm will react to its rival's market behavior. Although none of these can be upheld as the single correct theory, several are interesting enough to be worth describing briefly.

One very important possibility is that the rival firms in an oligopolistic market will recognize that they are all in the same boat and will tacitly coordinate their activities. Do unto others as you would have them do unto you will be the golden rule in such a market. Each firm will choose the price and output strategy that, if chosen by all the others, will maximize joint profits. In terms of the example in Exhibit 25.3, each firm will choose a price of $5. In the more general case, the golden rule will lead to a market equilibrium under oligopoly that will be the same as for a pure monopoly or a perfect cartel.

At the opposite extreme from the assumption of tacit coordination is the assumption that each firm will expect its rivals to do the worst thing possible. In the example, Alpha's managers will ask themselves what is the best they can do if Zed does the worst—that is, cuts its price. The answer is that Alpha must cut its price too. If Zed follows the same reasoning, both firms will end up charging $4.

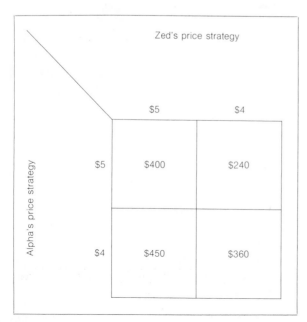

**Exhibit 25.3**
**Profits for Alpha Company under different pricing strategies**

This exhibit shows the profits that Alpha Company would earn under different pricing strategies for Alpha and its rival, Zed Enterprises. If both firms price at $5, each earns $400. If both cut their price to $4, they continue to split the market; and each earns $360. If Alpha cuts its price while Zed does not, Alpha steals many of Zed's customers and earns $450. If Zed cuts its price while Alpha's remains at $5, Zed steals many of Alpha's customers, leaving Alpha with only $240 in profit.

A more general variation of this theory is based on the assumption that each firm will expect its rivals to match its price decreases but not its increases. Under this assumption, a firm will be reluctant to lower its price because it knows that will only touch off a mutually destructive price war. At the same time, the firm will be reluctant to raise its price because its rivals will keep their prices down and steal customers. This theory has the curious property of saying that, under oligopoly, prices are not likely to change — without saying why prices are at one particular level rather than another in the first place. Nonetheless, it is claimed that some oligopolists actually do have exactly these expectations about their rivals' pricing strategies.

## The Kinked Demand Curve Theory

Another type of oligopolistic interdependence is illustrated in the so-called kinked demand curve theory, independently and simultaneously proposed by the British economists R.L. Hall and C.J. Hitch and the American economist Paul M. Sweezy in 1939. The kinked demand curve theory begins from a simple assumption about how oligopolists will react to price changes made by their rivals.

Specifically, each firm is supposed to assume that if it cuts its price, its rivals will match the cuts, but if it raises its price, no other firms will follow. Exhibit 25.4 shows how the market looks to an oligopolist who makes these two assumptions. Let P be the price ($1.70 in this case) that happens to prevail in the market at the moment, at 150 units of output. If the firm in question cuts its price below P, other firms will also lower their prices. Sales in the industry as a whole will then expand. The firm in question will keep approximately its same share of the market and will move down the lower slope of the demand curve, to the right of A. In contrast, if the firm raises its price, the others will not follow the move.

**Kinked demand curve** The demand curve possibly facing an oligopolistic business firm when it tries to depart from an established price. If it lowers prices, rivals will do the same and the curve will be inelastic. If it raises prices, rivals may not follow, and the curve will be elastic.

**Exhibit 25.4**
**The kinked demand curve theory of oligopoly**
An oligopolist will have a kinked demand curve (DAD) if its rivals will follow any price reduction it makes but not any price rise. There is a sharp step in the marginal revenue curve corresponding to the kink in the demand curve at A. Here, the marginal cost curve crosses the marginal revenue curve just at the step. That makes the equilibrium of 150 units and price P very stable.

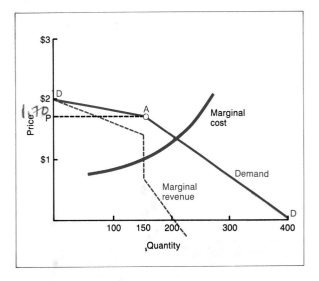

Instead of keeping its share of the market, our firm will lose customers to its rivals. As a result, the part of the firm's demand curve lying above established price P, to the left of A, is much more elastic than the part lying below.

Now bring marginal cost and marginal revenue into the picture. Give the firm a short-run marginal cost curve with the usual upward slope. The marginal revenue curve has a step in it that corresponds to the kink in the demand curve at A. To the left of the step, marginal revenue is very high, indicating that revenue will be lost rapidly if the firm moves up the very elastic part of the demand curve. To the right of the step, marginal revenue is much lower, indicating that little extra revenue can be obtained by moving down the less elastic part of the demand curve. As drawn, the marginal cost curve cuts the marginal revenue curve right at the step. The prevailing price is an equilibrium price for the firm, because it will be unprofitable to move in either one direction or the other.

The kinked demand curve equilibrium for an oligopolist is a particularly stable kind of equilibrium. Unlike a pure monopolist, the kinked demand curve oligopolist will not change price or output in response to small- or medium-sized changes in cost. The level of marginal cost shown in Exhibit 25.4 can move up or down by as much as 30 cents in either direction, and the firm will not change its price or output. The marginal cost curve will still cross the marginal revenue curve at the step. Only if cost changes by more than 30 cents per unit will the firm break with the prevailing industry price.

The kinked demand curve theory is simple and elegant, but it has a serious limitation. Although it cleverly explains why an oligopolist might be reluctant to change its price once the price was established, it fails to explain how the price comes to be established at any particular level in the first place.

## Oligopoly and Shared Monopoly

Although the simple theories of monopoly and perfect competition do not exactly fit the complex world of oligopolistic interdependence, they do provide a framework within which the search for a theory of oligopoly can be conducted. Such a framework is given by Exhibit 25.5, an adaptation of Exhibit 24.7, which was used to demonstrate the effects of a cartel. Now, however, we will assume that competition laws or other considerations eliminate the option of a formal cartel.

We will also assume that the industry we are examining is dominated by a few large firms, with perhaps some small-fry on the fringe. Profits are jointly maximized for these firms by a price of $2 and an output of 200,000 units per month, which corresponds to a point directly above the intersection of the marginal cost and marginal revenue curves. At this point the firms can be said to enjoy a **shared monopoly**. Such a monopoly is, in effect, a cartel without formal agreement or formal enforcement mechanisms.

**Shared monopoly** A situation in which the firms in an oligopolistic industry tacitly coordinate their activities in such a way as to earn maximum monopoly profits for the industry as a whole.

The opposite extreme is that of *cutthroat competition*—price competition so persistent and thoroughgoing that all pure economic profit is eliminated. This extreme is indicated in Exhibit 25.5 by the intersection

**Exhibit 25.5**
**Range of possible prices and quantities for an oligopoly**
The cost and demand curves given here represent a hypothetical oligopolistic industry. If the firms behave cooperatively, they can, at one extreme, jointly maximize profits and achieve a *shared monopoly*. At the other extreme they can compete so vigorously that all pure economic profit is eliminated and the price is driven down to the level of cost. This possibility is labeled "cutthroat competition." In practice, cooperation becomes more risky as the industry moves up along the demand curve toward the shared monopoly position. The likely outcome is a price somewhere between the $1 and $2 limits shown in the exhibit.

*likely price between this range*

of the demand and marginal cost curves. Cutthroat competition among oligopolists could, at the limit, duplicate the price-output performance of perfect competition. In the long run, no lower price could be sustained without driving firms and resources out of the industry altogether.

The range of price-quantity combinations that an oligopoly can achieve, then, includes the extremes of shared monopoly and cutthroat competition and the segment of the demand curve lying between the two. Where on this continuum will any given oligopolistic industry actually end up? The answer clearly depends on the balance struck between the risks and benefits of the tacit cooperation necessary to achieve, or approach, shared monopoly. The risks are of three kinds. First, there is a risk that the rivals with whom one tacitly seeks to cooperate will not be cooperative in return. Second, there is a risk that even if a firm does achieve tacit cooperation with its present rivals, the fruits of the effort will have to be shared with new entrants attracted by the resulting profits. And third, there is a legal risk if cooperation is pursued too openly. (More will be said about government competition policies in Chapter 27). The benefits of shared monopoly are clear enough to keep cutthroat competition at bay in some oligopolies at least some of the time, but the risks increase proportionately as rival firms edge their way up and to the left along the demand curve. As a result, it seems likely that most oligopolies operate somewhere between the two extremes shown in Exhibit 25.5

## Case 25.2
## Oligopoly Pricing: Meters and Automobiles

The following news items illustrate how closely oligopoly firms attempt to work with others in setting prices. In Winnipeg two producers of hydro house meters, Westinghouse and Sangamo, submitted the same price on the meters when responding to a tender from Winnipeg Hydro. A representative of Sangamo Co. Ltd. admitted openly that "all firms in the industry attempt to match prices," and Hydro's chief engineer observed that tenders in the last three years had resulted in identical price bids. One of the spokesmen for Westinghouse makes an interesting complaint about what would happen if the firms behaved as if they were independent of each other: "You would see prices juggling all over the place if one company's prices went up and another didn't." There was no price choice, so the city finally chose Westinghouse because it was situated in the city and paid taxes.

Winnipeg's works and operations committee had some difficulty finding an advantage in either of two identical bids submitted by two different firms on a Winnipeg Hydro tender for house meters.

After an hour-long debate, the committee awarded its $246,855 contract for kilowatt-hour meters and base adapters to Westinghouse Canada Ltd., on the grounds that the firm paid property taxes while its competitor did not.

Ted Glass of Westinghouse told committee members the industry has seen the pricing practice for 20 years.

"We are not about to change it," said Glass when asked if the firm would give the city a cost reduction.

"You would see prices juggling all over the place if one company's prices went up and another didn't," said the company representative.

The meters manufactured and distributed by both Canadian companies are almost identical in quality and performance, admitted Glass.

Glass appealed to the committee to accept his firm's bid to help it recover from a four-month strike by United Electrical Workers at its Hamilton plant this year.

Delivery of the meters will be delayed until four weeks after receipt of the order because of stock shortages, said Glass.

R.J. Brown of Sangamo Co. Ltd., which also submitted an identical price of $31.30 a meter, said all firms in the industry attempt to match prices.

Chief engineer, K.H. Hallson, said the city had received identical bids during all of the last three years and had awarded its annual contract to a different firm each time.[5]

The pricing of automobiles in Canada is quite similar. As the second news article indicates, General Motors, which is not only the biggest automobile company but also the biggest company (in sales) overall in Canada, acts as a price leader for the other automobile companies. This creates at least a semblance of price competition. Each fall General Motors announces its price increases on new models. The other automobile manufacturers then follow suit, perhaps over a period of a few weeks. Their increases may not be exactly the same as General Motors', but after a few adjustments back and forth the companies adopt virtually the same increases.

Despite a slight downturn on the sales charts, the Big Four auto makers in Canada will increase prices later this month, The Post has learned.

Paced by an average increase of 5.5 percent by General Motors of Canada Ltd., the North American makers should have new prices on their product lines by February 1.

The GM increase, which averages $255 per car, went into effect this week, but it will take at least a week before the other manufacturers can restructure their prices in line with GM, the traditional price leader. The auto firms always wait for the company's final lists before publishing their own price changes.[6]

---

[5]Source: "Identical Bid Wins City Contract," *Winnipeg Free Press*, November 15, 1978, p. 10.
[6]Source: Douglas Mepham, "Auto Makers to Follow GM Price Rise," *The Financial Post*, January 15, 1977, p. 1.

## Objections to Formal Theories

Unfortunately, all the assumptions about oligopolistic interdependence just described suffer from a common failing: they make business managers sound terribly naive.

Consider first the assumption of tacit coordination. The best evidence available is that rival firms are not likely to be able to achieve true joint profit maximization through tacit coordination alone. Cartels are explicit agreements among rivals to coordinate price and output strategies. Often cartel agreements are written up in a great detail, with elaborate enforcement and penalty clauses. Yet cartels are notoriously unstable. For each one that works, many fall apart before they get off the ground. And if explicit coordination is so difficult to achieve, how can tacit cooperation have any hope of working very well for very long?

On the other hand, it has been argued that it is just as naive for business-people always to assume that their rivals will do the very worst, when such behavior can clearly be mutually harmful. People have devised ingenious games in which, under controlled conditions, with carefully measured rewards and penalties, experimental subjects play the roles of rival managers. The results of some of these games have shown that after an initial period of all-out competition, opponents gradually learn to play cooperatively, even if they never meet or communicate directly.

## Informal Theories of Oligopoly

Many economists have simply given up the hope of developing a workable formal theory of oligopoly. Instead, they have resorted to various informal theories and rules of thumb that may be of some use in judging the performance of oligopolistic markets. These theories can be presented simply as a list of circumstances under which tacit coordination among oligopolists is likely to be more or less successful.

**Number and Size of Firms**  There is little doubt that the number and size of firms in a market make a lot of difference. Tacit coordination in a market with only two or three big firms of roughly equal size is surely more plausible than, say, coordination in a market with an eight-firm concentration ratio of 40 percent. A major reason is that the larger the number of firms, the more likely it is that any one firm can cut prices under the table without its rivals' knowledge.

The relative size of the various firms in the market is probably also important. Many observers have suggested that tacit coordination of prices is easier in an industry where there is one clearly dominant firm. That firm may then be able to act as a price leader. Under the strongest form of **price leadership**, firms are no longer uncertain about how their rivals will react to price changes. The leader can be confident that the others will follow it both up and down. The others can be certain that if they follow the leader, others will too; but if they initiate price increases (or decreases) of their own, others will not follow. Ideally, this arrangement can lead to joint monopoly profits for the industry.

However, tacit coordination cannot always be inferred solely from the timing of price changes. In any industry, someone has to be the first to

**Price leadership** A situation in an oligopolistic market where increases or decreases in price by one dominant firm, known as the price leader, are matched by all or most other firms in the market.

change prices if underlying market conditions change. Even if one particular firm is usually the first to make a move, its role may be no more than that of a barometer telling others that the pressure of demand or cost has made a change necessary.

**Nature of the Product** The nature of the product is also believed to affect the ease or difficulty of achieving tacit coordination. A homogeneous product with a smooth flow of orders tends to make coordination easier. A variable product with lumpy or irregular orders tends to make it more difficult. With a nonhomogeneous product, there are simply too many things to coordinate. It is not enough that all firms tacitly agree to sell at the same price. They also have to agree on a schedule of allowances above and below the basic price for changes in quality, accelerated or delayed delivery, size of the customer's order, and so on. Under these conditions, an agreement to raise the price above the competitive level, even if it can be sustained, will probably not lead to higher profits. It will more likely lead instead to an outbreak of competition in terms of quality, scheduling, volume discounts, and so on. These things will add to the cost of doing business until excess profits disappear. The next two chapters will return to this theme of nonprice competition several times.

**Information** Tacit coordination under oligopoly, if possible at all, is probable only in a market where firms have fairly good information about what their rivals are doing. Clearly, there can be no tacit understanding that all firms will charge the same price or follow a price leader if prices are kept secret. So there is little doubt that secrecy is an enemy of coordination under oligopoly.

There is a subtle danger in trying to reverse this formula, however. If secrecy is the enemy of coordination, does that make secrecy the friend of competition? From there it is only a short step to the proposition that bad information is the friend of good market performance. But this last statement is clearly nonsense. The primary function of the market system, after all, is to facilitate the flow of information among potential buyers and sellers. Perfect markets require perfect information, not perfect secrecy.

**Growth and Innovation** The rates of growth and innovation in a market are a final factor likely to affect the ease or difficulty of tacit coordination among rival oligopolists. In a market where product characteristics, production technologies, and the personalities of individual buyers and sellers do not change from year to year, an agreement among firms, whether tacit or explicit, need never be reworked once it is established. In a market where things change rapidly, any agreement that is reached will soon be rendered obsolete by changing circumstances or disrupted when newly entering buyers or sellers have to be accommodated. Given the uncertainties of establishing tacit agreements and the illegality of establishing explicit agreements, one would expect rival firms to be able to coordinate their activities less successfully the more rapid the pace of growth and change.

## MEASURING MARKET PERFORMANCE UNDER OLIGOPOLY

Neither the formal nor the informal theories of oligopoly just discussed give conclusive answers to the question asked at the outset of this chapter—namely, whether rivalry among a few firms in a concentrated market is sufficient to secure good market performance. Good market performance, in this context, means performance resembling that of a perfectly competitive market, with prices equal or close to marginal cost and all major opportunities for mutually competitive transactions among consumers, firms, and resource owners carried out. Poor performance means performance resembling that of a monopoly or cartel, in which efforts of firms to secure higher profits result in equilibrium prices higher than marginal cost and unrealized opportunities for potentially mutually beneficial trades between consumers and resource owners.

With pure theory unable to answer questions about market performance, it is natural for economists to try to answer the questions by the statistical examination of empirical data. Because it is usually difficult to measure directly whether a gap exists between a firm's output prices and its marginal costs, the most common approach taken is an indirect one. If firms in concentrated industries can be shown, on the average, to earn higher than normal rates of return on capital, it is reasoned, the inference that they are behaving more like monopolists than like perfect competitors can be drawn. If, on the other hand, firms in concentrated industries appear to earn rates of return no higher, on the average, than firms in relatively unconcentrated industries, it can be inferred that oligopolies perform about as well as more competitively structured industries.

### Early Empirical Studies

The first person to try this approach in a systematic way was University of California professor Joe Bain. In 1951, he published the results of a study of forty-two selected industries for the years 1936–1940. These results are shown in Exhibit 25.6. According to Bain's interpretation of the data,

---

**Exhibit 25.6**

**The relationship of market concentration to profits**

This table shows the relationship between market concentration and profits, according to a pioneering study published in 1951. The table appears to indicate that firms in industries with concentration ratios over 70 earn higher profits, on the average, than firms in less concentrated industries. The validity of the relationship shown by the figures has been the subject of lively debate ever since.

Average of Industry Average Profit Rates, by Concentration Groups, Forty-two Selected Industries, 1936–1940

| Eight-Firm Concentration Ratio | Average Profit Rate | Number of Industries |
|---|---|---|
| 90–100 | 12.7 | 8 |
| 80–89 | 9.8 | 11 |
| 70–79 | 16.3 | 3 |
| 60–69 | 5.8 | 5 |
| 50–59 | 5.8 | 4 |
| 40–49 | 8.6 | 2 |
| 30–39 | 6.3 | 5 |
| 20–29 | 10.4 | 2 |
| 10–19 | 17.0 | 1 |
| 0–9 | 9.1 | 1 |

Source: Joe S. Bain, "Relation of Profit-Rate to Industry Concentration," *Quarterly Journal of Economics* 65 (August 1951), p. 293. Copyright © 1951 by the President and Fellows of Harvard College; all rights reserved. Reprinted by permission.

industries with concentration ratios over 70 earned higher profits than less concentrated industries. The relationship between profits and concentration was not perfect and not overwhelmingly strong, but it did exist.

During the 1950s and 1960s, many of Bain's students and followers repeated his studies for other industries and other years. Most of them got the same results — a weak but persistent relationship between profits and concentration. It became part of the conventional wisdom of economics that the more highly concentrated an industry, the more likely its performance would resemble that of a cartel or monopoly. This would be true even if there were no conspiracy among rivals to raise prices and divide markets.

### More Recent Results

As faith in this proposition grew, economists tried harder and harder to verify it, using the more powerful statistical techniques and better data that became available year by year. Curiously, the harder they tried, the more elusive the relationship became. Some studies showed that if adjustments were made for the absolute size of firms in different markets, the relationship between concentration and profits tended to disappear. Other studies showed that if adjustments were made for differences in advertising expenditures, the relationship would disappear. Still other studies seemed to show that results like Bain's held only in years of depression and recession and disappeared with prosperity.

What is more, even as the relationship between concentration and profits was becoming less certain, economists were also becoming less certain about how such a relationship should be interpreted even if it were confirmed. New reasons were discovered why firms in more concentrated industries might appear to earn higher profits than firms in less concentrated industries. These reasons had nothing to do with monopoly pricing or tacit collusion. For example, a concentrated industry that was growing rapidly might need to earn high profits to attract the new capital it needed. Or the high profits of the largest firms in each concentrated industry might simply reflect the firms' superior efficiency relative to smaller firms in the same industry. Finally, the higher profits that some concentrated industries appeared to earn might not be profits at all in the economic sense. They might reflect only the fact that the categories used by accountants to classify business transactions are different from those used by economic theorists.

It is still too early to tell which team of econometricians will have the last word in the debate over concentration and profits or which team of theorists will have the last word on what the relationship means, if there really is one. For the moment, however, it appears that the empirical approach is not much more successful than the theoretical approach in solving the riddle of oligopoly behavior.

## CONCLUSIONS

This chapter began with the question of whether rivalry among the few is enough to guarantee satisfactory market performance. After reviewing the apparent determinants of market concentration, the informal theories of oligopoly behavior, and the empirical evidence on the relationship between concentration and profits, the answer is maybe yes, maybe no—it all depends.

Perhaps, though, economists are looking in the wrong place for an answer. The search for a theory of oligopoly is a search for a theory that is analogous to the theories of perfect competition and monopoly but lying somewhere in between. The theories of monopoly and competition, however, are theories of pure economizing. They deal with only a part of business reality—the search for maximum profits under *given* conditions of demand, technology, and resource availability. Perhaps economists would do better in their efforts to understand competition among the few if they broadened their focus to take into account more of the entrepreneurial elements in business decision making.

There have already been some hints that this is where they should look. The subjects of advertising competition and nonprice competition have come up more than once. These forms of competition involve entrepreneurial decision making. The question of barriers to entry has been raised. Entry of a new firm into an industry is an entrepreneurial decision. And such entrepreneurial variables as product homogeneity, growth, and innovation play major roles in determining how firms behave in concentrated markets. Without further delay, then, a new chapter will look into some of these things.

## SUMMARY

1. Markets that have more than one firm but fewer than many firms are called *oligopolies*. Any study of oligopoly must pay close attention to the phenomenon of business rivalry. The conduct of oligopolistic firms is very much influenced by what each firm expects its rivals to do in the competitive struggle for sales and profits.

2. The four-firm (or eight-firm) concentration ratio for a market is the percentage of industry output contributed by the top four (or eight) firms in the market. Close to one-half of all manufacturing output in Canada comes from markets with a four-firm concentration ratio of 50 or more.

3. Economies of scale are one major determinant of market concentration. Plant level economies alone, however, are not enough to explain observed concentration ratios. Economies of multi-plant operation must also be taken into account. Even when multi-plant scale economies are accounted for, some market concentration remains to be explained by barriers to entry having to do with such factors as legal support, ownership of resources and market power.

4. Many attempts have been made to construct a formal theory of oligopoly. Such a theory would resemble the theories of perfect competition and pure monopoly but would lie somewhere between the two. However, the formal theory of oligopoly to date has not been conspicuously successful. The reason is that it is very difficult to know how firms will react to the price and output decisions of their rivals. The kinked demand curve theory is one example of an attempt to formalize the analysis of oligopoly behavior.

5. Even in the absence of a formal theory of oligopoly, an attempt can be made to list factors that are likely to facilitate or hamper tacit coordination among rival firms. Among the most important factors are the number and size of firms in the market, the nature of the product, the availability of information about rival firms, and the rates of growth and innovation in the market.

6. Partly because oligopoly theory does not give clear answers about market performance in concentrated industries, economists have made many efforts to see whether firms in such industries are more profitable than those in less concentrated industries. If they were, that might indicate that oligopolists were able to achieve tacit coordination of their price and output decisions. Initial results reported during the 1950s appeared to indicate that concentrated industries were more profitable. More recent studies, however, have called these early results into question.

## DISCUSSION QUESTIONS

1. What is the difference between rivalry and competition? What does it mean to say that rivalry is a matter of conduct, while competition is a matter of structure?

2. The data on market concentration in Exhibit 25.1 relate only to major sectors of the economy. How highly concentrated do you think the following subsectors of the economy are: Oil? Banks? Funeral parlors? What factors do you think probably account for concentration or lack of concentration in each of these subsectors?

3. Evaluate the following statement: barriers to entry are lower in the restaurant industry than in the airline industry, because a restaurant requires only a few workers and a few thousand dollars in capital, while even a small airline requires hundreds of workers and millions of dollars in capital.

4. Would you consider the market for university education to be an oligopoly? What factors do you think determine the structure of the university "industry"? How important are economies of scale? Barriers to entry?

5. Oligopoly has sometimes been called a game, because each player's behavior depends on thinking ahead to outguess the strategies and reactions of rivals. How does oligopoly resemble such games as chess? Bridge? Tennis? War? Would it surprise you to learn that the formal theory of games is not much more practical help in understanding actual games than formal theories of oligopoly are in understanding actual oligopoly behavior? Explain.

# ADVERTISING AND MONOPOLISTIC COMPETITION

CHAPTER

TWENTY
S  I  X

---

## WHAT YOU WILL LEARN IN THIS CHAPTER

*This chapter introduces a number of topics in competition and market performance. First, it reviews an ongoing controversy concerning the conditions under which advertising can act as a barrier to entry into a market or industry. In connection with the discussion of advertising and nonprice competition, it introduces a formal theory of monopolistic competition. Finally, it distinguishes between static and dynamic efficiency and explains why both kinds of efficiency must be considered when evaluating the effects of market structure on market performance.*

## FOR REVIEW

*Here are some important terms and concepts that will be put to use in this chapter. If you do not understand them, review them before proceeding.*
- *Positive and normative economics (Chapter 1)*
- *Pure economizing (Chapter 21)*
- *Theory of consumer choice (Chapter 21)*
- *Pure monopoly and monopolistic competition (Chapter 24)*

---

There are still large pieces missing from the picture of competition assembled in the last four chapters. For one thing, up to this point the emphasis has been mainly on price and output decisions. Advertising, product innovation, and other forms of nonprice competition have remained in the background. In addition, the focus has been more on pure economizing than on entrepreneurial aspects of business conduct. This chapter will try to fill in some of the gaps and broaden the understanding of the process of competition.

It will begin with a discussion of advertising—first its effects on consumers and then its possible role as a barrier to entry into markets or industries. From there, it will move to a discussion of monopolistic competition—the market structure under which there are numerous firms and no barriers to entry but under which nonprice competition is very important. Finally, it will discuss the relationships among market structure, innovation, and competition for entrepreneurs.

## ADVERTISING AND THE CONSUMER

### The Consumer as Economizer and Entrepreneur

Chapter 21 presented the outlines of a long established economic theory of consumer choice. This theory sees consumer choice as a classic problem in pure economizing. Consumers are presented with certain givens—namely, their tastes, the size of their budgets, the characteristics of available goods, and the prices of those goods. Using these givens, consumers must calculate the mix of purchases that will give them the greatest satisfaction. They do this by equalizing the marginal utility per dollar's worth of goods for all goods.

In certain important respects, this theory of consumer choice resembles the theories of perfect competition and monopoly developed in Chapters 23 and 24. All are theories of pure economizing, which is to say that all are concerned with situations in which the decision maker confronts objectives, alternative activities, and constraints as givens—clearly known and not subject to manipulation. In addition, all these theories are concerned with decision-making situations in which price and quantity are the primary variables.

In reality, though, consumer choice is a matter of more than just pure economizing. Consumers are not fully aware of prices and product characteristics. They are not givens; they are constantly changing. Consumer decision making is not costless or instantaneous. Instead, it requires significant time and effort. The practical consequence is that consumers, just as much as business managers, must constantly be making entrepreneurial decisions. They have to be alert to new information, and they have to be willing to explore innovative ways of satisfying their wants.

Recognizing the entrepreneurial element in consumer decision making is the key to understanding how advertising works. It is not possible to understand why businesses spend money on advertising until it is understood why advertising affects the way consumers spend their money.

### Overcoming Consumer Ignorance

Any explanation of how advertising works must begin with the simple fact that because information is costly to acquire, consumers are always ignorant to some degree. They may have some idea how much eggs cost, but they do not automatically know whether this week eggs are cheaper at Dominion or at Loblaws. They know beds are bought in furniture stores, but they are not able to reel off a list of all the furniture stores in town—at least not if the town is very big. They know what a car is, but they do not always know which ones have front-wheel drive or which have side-window defrosters. Every firm can feel certain that there are consumers who would buy its product if they knew about it. By telling consumers of the price and characteristics of products and the places where they can be bought, advertisements attract enough customers to pay for the resources spent to produce the ads.

### Inducing Changes in Demand

Other kinds of advertising are aimed not at informing consumers about prices and products but at changing their tastes. If consumer tastes are changeable, firms can make profits by changing them. Making consumers like a firm's product more can increase the demand for the product and in some cases can make the demand more inelastic. Sales or prices or both can then be increased, which will raise profits. To understand advertising, then, it is useful to know something about the mechanisms by which consumer tastes are produced and modified.

**Changing Tastes** For one thing, people's tastes and preferences do not originate spontaneously. Instead, they are strongly influenced by the tastes and preferences of others. Some people are innovators and take up new styles or products of their own accord, but more people are imitators and change their buying patterns only after they see others change. The interaction of innovators and imitators in the consumer community keeps tastes and styles in flux. Through advertising, firms can hope to control the direction and pace of change. Controlled and predictable change is more profitable and less risky than random change. It can be worth the advertising resources invested to produce it.

**Changing Perceptions** Changing tastes is not the whole story, though. Market researchers have found that advertising changes not only tastes but also perceptions. It can influence not only which product people will like but how well they will like a given, unchanged product. The following case study provides an interesting illustration.

### Case 26.1
### Advertising and the Perceived Taste of Turkey Meat

In 1965, James C. Makens of Michigan Technological University conducted an experiment to determine the effect of a well-known brand name on consumers' preferences for turkey meat. In Part 1 of the experiment, 150 subjects from Detroit were presented with two plates, each containing a slice of turkey meat. Although the two slices were actually from the same turkey, they were labeled differently. One bore a brand name heavily advertised and well known in Detroit, and the other bore an unfamiliar brand name. Of the 150 subjects, only 10 percent indicated that they thought the two samples tasted alike; 56 percent expressed a definite preference for the known brand, and 34 percent preferred the unknown brand. Makens concluded that in the presence of brand name clues, the subjects tended to perceive identical portions of turkey as being different, and they tended to prefer the more familiar name.

In Part 2 of the experiment, sixty-one consumers were presented with two plates. One plate contained a slice of tender turkey meat and the other a slice of tough turkey meat. This time, no brand names were used. The tender sample was marked with one symbol and the tough sample with another. Forty-nine subjects said they preferred the tender meat, four said they preferred the tough meat, and eight said they could not tell the difference. The conclusion was that, in the absence of brand name clues, consumers generally can perceive an actual difference in quality.

In the final part of the experiment, the sixty-one subjects who had tasted the samples marked with symbols were asked to indicate which brand they thought each sample belonged to — after they had said which they preferred. Thirty-four subjects said that the turkey they preferred must have been the known brand; eighteen identified the preferred turkey as probably the unknown brand; and one did not express an opinion. The conclusion was that consumers tended to think it likely that the high quality product was the one with which they were familiar.

Makens summarized his results in these terms: "Brand preference for one well-known turkey brand was strong enough to influence the perceived taste for turkey meat among the subjects....[Also] the consumers expect a well-known brand to be of superior quality to an unknown brand" (p. 263).

Similar results have been reported elsewhere. These experiments leave us a long way from the idea that taste and preferences are a given of the consumer choice process.

Source Based on James C. Makens, "Effect of Brand Preferences upon Consumers' Perceived Taste of Turkey Meat," *Journal of Applied Psychology* 49 (November 4, 1965), p. 261-263. Used by permission.

**Brand Loyalty** In the idealized world of economic theory, the decisions consumers make are neither costly nor time-consuming. In the real world, this is not so. The shortcuts consumers take to simplify the decisions they have to make sometimes create openings for advertisers. An example is the phenomenon of brand loyalty.

A brand loyal consumer keeps decision costs down by choosing the same brand again and again. Where does brand loyalty come from? It can perhaps be explained to some degree on the basis of innate differences in tastes among consumers. (Some people may just be born with a liking for Molson Golden and others with a liking for Labatt 50.) The following case study, though, shows that there is more to brand loyalty.

### Case 26.2
### An Experimental Study of Brand Loyalty

In 1968, J. Douglass McConnell of the Stanford Research Institute reported the results of an experimental study of brand loyalty. The product chosen for the experiment was beer. It was chosen because people buy beer frequently and because McConnell judged that the nature of the product would help motivate subjects to stay with the experiment over the two-month period required. A random sample of sixty beer drinkers was drawn from Stanford University students living in married student housing. The subjects were told that the experiment was part of a marketing test of three types of beer produced by a local brewer.

Once a week, the subjects were presented, in their homes, with an opportunity to choose one bottle from among three bottles labeled "M," "L," and "P." They were told that Brand M was a high-priced beer, Brand L a medium-priced beer, and Brand P a bargain-priced beer. The subjects did not actually have to pay for their beer; but to make the price difference seem realistic, the medium-priced beer, had a $.02 "refund" taped to the bottle, and the low-priced beer had a $.05 "refund." The subjects could keep the refunds.

In point of fact, the three brands of beer were identical. They were all drawn from the same production run at the brewery, and they differed only in terms of the labels added by the experimenter. This, however, did not prevent the development of fierce brand loyalties by many of the subjects. One measure of brand loyalty that McConnell used was the occurrence of four consecutive choices of the same label. Although at first the subjects experimented with different brands, by the end of twenty-four trials, fifty-seven of the sixty had developed brand loyalty, as measured by the four-choice criterion. Of these fifty-seven, twenty-six chose Brand M, twelve Brand L, and nineteen Brand P.

Another measure of brand loyalty is the probability of making a switch in brands from one trial to the next. The lower the probability of switching, the more loyal. Exhibit 26.1 shows how the probability of switching decreased rapidly over the first twelve trials of the experiment.

Because the beer was actually all the same, these results could not be explained by any "given" differences in tastes. The results instead suggest that, by convincing themselves that one brand was better than another, the subjects avoided the painful task of having to make up their minds from scratch at each trial.

**Exhibit 26.1**

**Effects of repeated tasting on brand loyalty**

In the experiment, subjects were given a choice of three bottles of beer on each trial. The bottles had different labels, but their contents were the same. At first, consumers experimented, switching from brand to brand to find one they liked. Soon, though, the frequency of switching fell to a low level as brand loyalty developed.

Source J. Douglass McConnell, "The Development of Brand Loyalty: An Experimental Study." *Journal of Marketing Research 5* (February 1968), Table 3. Reprinted from *Journal of Marketing Research* published by the American Marketing Association.

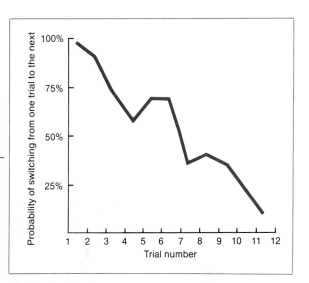

Given the nature of the choice the subjects were offered, it is remarkable how firmly set in their opinions some of them became. One woman reported, "M is a good strong malty beer, but I like L because it is lighter. Mmm!!! P would poison me —make me ill." A man who developed an enthusiasm for P once deviated to experiment with a bottle of M and reported, "Worst I've ever had; you couldn't give it away."

Source: Based on J. Douglass McConnell, "The Development of Brand Loyalty: An Experimental Study," *Journal of Marketing Research* 5 (February 1968), pp. 13-19. Used by permission.

## Normative Implications

So far, the chapter has discussed advertising and the consumer purely from the point of view of positive economics. It can, for example, be experimentally verified that external clues, such as exposure to advertising or differences in price, change consumer perceptions of unchanged products. This kind of positive analysis of the effects of advertising is all that is really needed in order to understand the role of advertising in the competitive process. In practice, though, advertising is an emotionally charged subject that invites normative as well as positive analysis. Before moving on to a discussion of advertising and market structure, then, the chapter will look at some of the normative issues that advertising raises.

**The Case against Advertising**  It is not hard for opponents of advertising to get an audience. Anyone who has ever been interrupted in the middle of a favorite Bogart film on late-night television is an automatic convert. But the case against advertising rests on much more than just the complaint that it is intrusive, annoying, ugly, and distracting. Following are some of the most common normative objections to advertising that economists make.

Heading the list of arguments against advertising is the complaint that it violates consumer sovereignty. Producers, it is said, do not adjust their output to consumer preferences. Instead, they use advertising to force consumers to buy whatever it is that they feel like producing. Harvard professor John Kenneth Galbraith has been one of the most vocal proponents of this view. In his book, *The Affluent Society*, he put the matter this way:

Were it so that a man arising each morning was assailed by demons which instilled in him a passion sometimes for silk shirts, sometimes for kitchen ware, sometimes for chamber pots, and sometimes for orange squash, there would be every reason to applaud the effort to find the goods, however odd, that quenched this flame....

Consumer wants can have bizarre, frivolous, or even immoral origins, and an admirable case can still be made for a society which seeks to satisfy them. But the case cannot stand if it is the process of satisfying wants that creates the wants. For then the individual who urges the importance of production to satisfy those wants is precisely in the position of the onlooker who applauds the efforts of the squirrel to keep abreast of the wheel that is propelled by his own effort.[1]

Advertising is identified as the chief method by which the people who satisfy the wants (that is, the economy's business firms) also create those wants. According to Galbraith, a distinction must be made between wants that are innate within the consumer and those that producers create through advertising. Consumer sovereignty means guiding production purely in accordance with innate wants. Advertising and all other means of want creation are a violation of that sovereignty.

Twenty years after the appearance of Galbraith's book, the ideas he expressed remain popular. Now they often take the form of the doctrine of consumer alienation, to use a term favored by Marxist-oriented economists. The doctrine is based on the idea that people have two sets of preferences. One set reflects their "true" wants and needs; the other reflects the "false" wants and needs created by advertising and other evils of modern capitalism. In this view, consumer sovereignty is a mockery unless preceded by consumer liberation from false needs and desires.

**John Kenneth Galbraith
(1908– )**

John Kenneth Galbraith, a native Canadian who has been teaching economics at Harvard University in Boston for many years, enjoys a unique distinction among economists today: his books regularly hit the best-seller list and stay there for long periods. Galbraith represents the opposite extreme from economists who, like Paul Samuelson, write primarily to gain the applause of other economists. On the contrary, his major books — *The Affluent Society* (1958) and *The New Industrial State* (1967) — are all-out attacks on conventional economics, written to be read by the widest possible nonprofessional audience.

Galbraith lumps everything he dislikes about modern economics under the heading of "the conventional wisdom." By this phrase, he means all the ideas that he claims are widely believed not because they are true but simply because they are often repeated. He saves his sharpest barbs for two particular elements of the conventional wisdom: consumer sovereignty and the law of supply and demand.

Consumers are not sovereign, Galbraith says, because their tastes and preferences are heavily manipulated by advertising. The ability of business to manipulate consumers knocks the "demand" leg out from under supply and demand theory. The "supply" leg is then knocked out with a second deftly aimed kick. The supply curve is valid only in an economy where firms aim to maximize profits. In the U.S. economy, says Galbraith, firms do not do this. How, then, can supply and demand determine price? The kinds of goods that consumers are persuaded to buy and the prices at which these goods are sold are determined by the whims of the "technostructure," Galbraith's name for the managerial-professional-academic elite who run the country.

[1] John Kenneth Galbraith, *The Affluent Society* (Boston: Houghton Mifflin, 1958), pp. 153-154.

Galbraith is many things other than an economist. He is a political activist, always promoting liberal and ultraliberal causes. He served as chairman of the Americans for Democratic Action, and he played a key role in securing the Democratic presidential nomination for George McGovern. He is also a diplomat and served as John Kennedy's ambassador to India. (At six feet eight inches, he towered almost comically over his local diplomatic counterparts there.) He once even turned his hand to writing a novel, *The Triumph*.

Few economists take the complete Galbraithian system seriously, but many admit that he is a useful critic. Economics, like other social science disciplines, is in fact always in danger of becoming excessively abstract and formalistic. Economists who talk only to other economists, and then only in mathematical language, do indeed often end up saying things that are just plain silly. Galbraith is determined that they not get away with it.

**Another Point of View** By no means do all economists accept the position that advertising is a violation of consumer sovereignty or an attempt to exploit some shameful, perverse side of human nature. Those who adopt a less hostile attitude toward advertising usually begin by making the point that there are no such things as natural, given, or innate consumer preferences, at least not if one means by this preferences for specific kinds of goods and services. People may well be born with basic needs for food, security, affection, self-esteem, and the rest; but there is an infinite variety of particular goods that can satisfy these needs. If the advertisers of one generation persuade people that their need to keep their feet dry is best satisfied with pointy-toed boots and those of the next that square-toed boots do the job better, so what? One should not be silly enough to think that, left to their own devices, people's "true" tastes in boot-toes would magically emerge, making everyone better off.

Perhaps, some go so far as to say, the idea of true and false preferences itself poses a potential threat to consumer sovereignty. Perhaps the so-called true preferences are just the preferences of a cultural elite who do not like the lowbrow life-styles of their neighbors. Because the members of this elite prefer Beaujolais to Baby Duck, or "tastefully" styled European cars to "tasteless" North American cars, they think that everyone else ought to share their preferences. It is a short step from a policy of forbidding the advertising of Baby Duck and Buicks to a policy of forbidding their production in the name of giving the people what they really want. And then what becomes of consumer sovereignty?

## ADVERTISING AND MARKET PERFORMANCE UNDER OLIGOPOLY AND MONOPOLISTIC COMPETITION

Having learned something about the normative economics of advertising, it is time to return to positive economics. For the economists' case against advertising does not consist entirely in the claim that it violates consumer sovereignty. There is also a group of issues concerning the effects of advertising on market performance under oligopoly and monopolistic competition. As we will see, these issues too are highly controversial.

### Is Advertising a Barrier to Entry?

Perhaps the most controversial issue of all is that of advertising as a barrier to entry. If advertising does represent such a barrier, then it may contribute to high levels of market concentration. And as shown in the last chapter, market concentration in turn may lead to poor market performance.

*Advertising as a Barrier*  The mechanism by which advertising acts as a barrier to entry is said to be the creation of brand loyalties. Consumers who might otherwise treat all cola drinks as close substitutes are divided into opposing camps, some fiercely loyal to Pepsi, others to Coca-Cola. Each firm can then raise its price with little fear that doing so will cause its customers to go elsewhere. And each firm will have to worry less that the resulting high profits will attract new entrants, because the new firms will not only have to spend money to build plants and hire workers but will also have to mount fabulously expensive advertising campaigns.

In 1967 this view of the effects of advertising received a substantial boost from economists W.S. Comanor and T.A. Wilson, who looked at the statistical relationship between advertising expenditures and profits in forty-one industries and reached the following conclusion:

> It is evident that . . . advertising is a highly profitable activity. Industries with high advertising outlays earn, on the average, at a profit rate which exceeds that of other industries by nearly four percentage points. This differential represents a 50 percent increase in profit rates. It is likely, moreover, that much of this profit rate differential is accounted for by the entry barriers created by advertising expenditures and by the resulting achievement of market power.[2]

*An Alternative View of Advertising and Entry*  Neither the theory of advertising as a barrier to entry nor the results of the Comanor and Wilson study have been accepted by everyone, however. Other economists, notably Yale Brozen of the University of Chicago business school, see the relationship between advertising and competition in a rather different light.[3]

According to Brozen, the theory that advertising is a barrier to entry stands reality on its head: advertising is not an impediment to competition; it is a means of competition. Existing firms have no advantage over new firms in buying advertising; ad agencies stand ready to sell their services to anyone willing to pay their fees. In fact, advertising is even more important for new firms than for existing firms. In Brozen's view, firms aim their advertising not so much at building loyalty in their own customers as at getting their rivals' customers to try something different. The real way to create a barrier to entry and protect established oligopolies, he says, would be to outlaw advertising. Then it would be far harder for a new firm to break into a market.

What about the Comanor and Wilson study, though? Brozen treats the apparent relationship between profits and advertising as an example of the fallacy of confusing accounting categories with categories of economic theory. Encouraged by certain features of the tax laws, accountants

---

[2] W. S. Comanor and T. A. Wilson, "Advertising, Market Structure, and Performance," *Review of Economics and Statistics* 49 (November 1967), p. 437.

[3] For a representative exposition of Brozen's views, see Yale Brozen, "Entry Barriers: Advertising and Product Differentiation," in *Industrial Concentration: The New Learning*, ed. Harvey J. Goldschmid, H. Michael Mann, and J. Fred Weston (Boston: Little, Brown, 1974), pp. 115-137. For a Canadian defense of advertising in somewhat similar terms see O. J. Firestone, *The Economic Implications of Advertising* (Toronto: Methuen, 1967).

treat advertising as a current expense, like wages or purchases of materials. In fact, Brozen contends, advertising is an investment having long-term effects. A brand image takes years to develop, and once developed, it is a valuable, long-lasting asset for the company that created it. If an adjustment is made to treat advertising as an investment, companies that advertise intensively no longer appear to be more profitable than the average.

## Advertising and Monopolistic Competition

Up to this point, the discussion of advertising and market performance has centered on markets that are oligopolistic in structure. Critics of advertising have charged that in such markets, advertising acts as a barrier to entry, that it contributes to market concentration, and that it is associated with excessively high rates of profit. Now attention will be given to the claim that even in markets where none of these things is true, advertising may have adverse effects on market performance. This effort will require a closer look at a type of market structure that has been mentioned before only in passing: monopolistic competition.

According to the definition given in Chapter 24, a monopolistically competitive market is one in which there are a large number of small firms, a differentiated product, and no significant barriers to entry. Examples can be found in such industries as restaurants, gasoline retailing, and personal services.

**Equilibrium for the Firm under Monopolistic Competition** The theory of monopolistic competition, like its definition, is a blend of monopolistic and competitive elements. The theory can be understood with the help of Exhibit 26.2, which shows short-run and long-run equilibrium positions for a typical firm under monopolistic competition.

The demand curve for a monopolistically competitive firm, like that for a pure monopolist, slopes downward, although it is likely to be more elastic than that of a monopolist. Each firm's product is a little different from the products of its competitors. Each firm can therefore raise its price at least a little without losing all its customers, because some customers attach more importance than others to the special style or location or whatever that the firm offers. Given this downward-sloping demand curve, the short-run profit maximizing position shown is analytically the same as that for a pure monopolist. The quantity of output is determined by the intersection of the marginal cost and marginal revenue curves, and the price charged is determined by the height of the demand curve at that point.

But this short-run equilibrium cannot also be a long-run equilibrium under monopolistic competition. The reason is freedom of entry. In the short-run position shown in Exhibit 26.2a, the firm is earning profits in excess of the normal rate of return on investment. (This is shown by the fact that price exceeds average total cost.) High profits attract new competitors. As new competitors come in, the demand curves of firms that are already there will shift downward, because the new entrants will sell products that are reasonably good substitutes for those of the original firms. If the original firms try to resist the shift in demand by improving their products or marketing them more aggressively, those efforts will raise their average total costs. The downward shift in the demand curve of the original firms and/or the upward shift in their cost curves will continue until there are no more profits to attract new entrants. The result is the long-run equilibrium position shown in Exhibit 26.2b.

**Market Performance**  In this long-run equilibrium position, it is claimed, markets perform poorly. For one thing, as under pure monopoly, each firm produces too little of its product. The gap between price and marginal cost indicates an unrealized potential for further mutually beneficial transactions. In addition, the monopolistically competitive firms do not operate at the minimum points on their long-run average cost curves. If there were fewer firms, each producing a greater quantity of output, the same quantity of products could be provided to consumers at a lower total cost. The hallmarks of monopolistic competition, then, are said to be too many gas stations, supermarkets, and restaurants, each operating at only a fraction of capacity and each charging inefficiently high prices, yet each earning no more than the minimum return needed to stay in business.

And what does advertising have to do with all this? Advertising is said to make the effects of monopolistic competition worse than they otherwise would be. The reason is that advertising exaggerates the differences among the products of various firms and thus makes each firm's demand curve less elastic than it would otherwise be. The performance gap between monopolistic competition and perfect competition is thus made even wider.

---

**Exhibit 26.2**

**Short-run and long-run equilibrium under monopolistic competition**

Under monopolistic competition, each firm has a downward-sloping demand curve, but there are no barriers to entry. In the short run, a firm producing at the point where marginal cost is equal to marginal revenue can earn profits in excess of the normal rate of return, as shown in Part a of the diagram. In the long run, however, new competitors are attracted. This diverts part of the demand from firms originally in the market, and the original firms may fight to retain their market shares, using promotional techniques that add to total costs. Entry will continue until a long-run equilibrium in which profits are eliminated is reached, as shown in Part b.

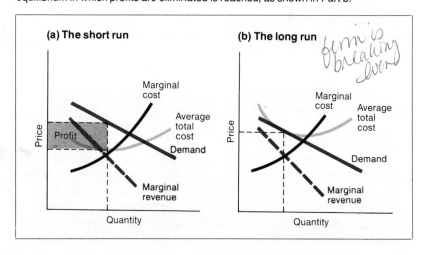

### Are Perfect Competition and Monopolistic Competition Different?

The analysis of market performance under monopolistic competition just given has not been accepted by all economists. Many scholarly articles have been written on the subject, and many elaborate mathematical variations on the theory have been suggested. Setting aside differences in detail, most of the attempts to defend monopolistic competition come down to the simple idea that monopolistic competition and perfect competition are not really significantly different.

One argument is that the illusion of a difference comes from a mistaken idea about the nature of the product being sold. Take restaurants, for example. The restaurants in any town sell meals that are highly differentiated according to location, national cuisine, atmosphere, service, and many other characteristics. But perhaps meals are not really the relevant product. Instead, think of all restaurants as selling a homogeneous good called dining pleasure. The differences among restaurants should be thought of not as differences in product but rather as differences in the technology used to produce dining pleasure and differences in the size of the package of dining pleasure being sold. By analogy, different farmers grow potatoes in assorted sizes and use a variety of farming methods, but the potato market is still considered to be close to perfectly competitive. The dining pleasure market, according to this line of reasoning, is no different from the potato market.

A variation of this defense of monopolistic competition acknowledges differences among products but points out that product diversity is valuable in and of itself. Suppose it were true, as the theory of monopolistic competition suggests, that prices would be a little lower if there were fewer barbershops, each not quite so conveniently located, or fewer supermarkets, each a little more crowded, or fewer flavors of ice cream. Would a move in that direction benefit consumers? Not necessarily, if consumers are willing to pay something for variety. Imagine that there were some way to split the market for, say, ice cream into two markets — one for the good called ice cream and the other for the good called variety. If that were possible, then each good could have its own separate price, and each market could be perfectly competitive. But such a split is simply impossible. In the real world, a single market for both goods, having the structure described as monopolistic competition, is as close as one can come to the ideal.

### Evidence on Advertising and Market Performance

As in so many cases where economic theorists disagree, attempts have been made to use empirical methods to settle the controversy about advertising and market performance under monopolistic competition. The studies on advertising and profits are not really relevant here, because firms would not be expected to earn profits under either perfect or monopolistic competition. Instead, evidence bearing more directly on the effect of advertising on market structure is needed. Is the natural state of the world one in which consumers tend to view all sources of supply as just alike and to move freely among them in response to small changes in price? Or is the natural state one in which inertia and ignorance on the part of consumers cause them to cling to familiar sources of supply, giving each firm a local monopoly vis-à-vis its own customers? And advertising—does it set up unnatural barriers between firms, thereby adding to their monopoly power, or does it break down natural barriers, thereby destroying monopoly power? A number of kinds of evidence might help answer these questions.

One kind of evidence comes from studies of consumer behavior, such as the two case studies earlier in this chapter. But these studies by themselves do not entirely settle the issue. Case 26.1, for example, showed that advertising affected the perceived taste of turkey meat that was actually all from the same turkey. This indicates that advertising can increase brand loyalty. On the other hand, Case 26.2 showed that in the case of beer, people not subjected to advertising also perceived great differences among actually identical goods and were very reluctant to switch from one "brand" to another. This indicates that brand loyalty can arise even in the absence of advertising.

Another kind of evidence comes from studies of how advertising is actually used by firms. For example, it has been shown that new products are advertised more intensively than old products. This may indicate that makers of old products tend to depend on consumer inertia and that advertising is a way of breaking down that inertia. It has also been shown that consumers in markets where advertising is heavy are less loyal to one brand than are consumers in markets where advertising is light. This too might indicate that advertising helps overcome consumer reluctance to try substitute products.[4]

## MARKET DYNAMICS AND COMPETITION AMONG ENTREPRENEURS

### Static Efficiency versus Dynamic Efficiency

**Static efficiency** The ability of an economy to get the greatest consumer satisfaction from given resources and technology.

**Dynamic efficiency** The ability of an economy to increase consumer satisfaction through growth and innovation.

Up to this point, the discussion of market structure and economic performance has focused almost entirely on the problem of **static efficiency**—the ability of an economy to get the greatest output of consumer satisfaction from given resources and technology. Static efficiency is a measure of how close an economy operates to its production possibility frontier. But market structure may also have an important impact on the economy's **dynamic efficiency**—its success in achieving growth in the rate of output per unit of resources. Dynamic efficiency is thus a measure of the rate at which the production possibility frontier of an economy shifts outward over time.

Of the two kinds of efficiency, dynamic efficiency is by far the most important in the long run. During the 1960s, Canada's real gross national product grew at an average rate of about 3.7 percent per year. One of the most important factors contributing to this growth was the improvement of knowledge—that is, innovation and technological change. Improvement in knowledge accounted for about a third of all economic growth, or

---

[4] The article by Brozen, cited in footnote 3, contains references to and discussions of these and several similar studies.

1.2 percent per year. The remaining economic growth is attributable to capital accumulation, population growth, increased education, and other factors. The contribution of innovation and technological change is very large compared to the estimate of the loss in static efficiency caused by monopolistic and oligopolistic market imperfections. The largest estimate of the static efficiency loss ever seriously put forward is about 2.5 percent of gross national product. Innovation and technological change add more than that to GNP each two years.

## The Schumpeter Hypothesis

If every policy promoting static efficiency also contributed to dynamic efficiency, the distinction between the two would not be important in a chapter dealing with market structure and economic performance. Unfortunately, however, it is not certain that things work out that way. In fact, there is a widely shared hypothesis according to which some sources of dynamic efficiency are to be found in just those concentrated markets that are suspected to be sources of static inefficiency. This will be referred to as the Schumpeter hypothesis, after economist Joseph Schumpeter, who first brought it to widespread attention.

According to Schumpeter, the source of innovation and growth is competition—but not the kind of competition found in those markets classified as perfectly competitive. Instead, he wrote:

Joseph Schumpeter was born in Trietsch, Moravia, then a part of Austria. He studied law at the University of Vienna, also attending the seminars of the leading economists of the Austrian school of the day. In 1906, he received a doctor of laws degree and briefly practiced law before turning to teaching as a career. He taught at several European universities, taking time out in 1919-1920 to serve as the Austrian minister of finance. In 1932, he emigrated to the United States. There, he accepted a post at Harvard University, which he held until his death in 1950. In 1948, he was honored with the presidency of the American Economic Association.

Schumpeter's writings are characterized by a broad scope rare in twentieth century economics. In his writings on economic development, business cycles, the history of economics, and economic systems, he attempted to portray the whole of the economic process. He had little use for the kind of economics that reduces everything to problems of managerial calculations and then reduces those problems to an arid set of mathematical equations. To him, the crucial figure in economic life was the entrepreneur, not the clerk or manager. What is more, he saw the entrepreneur as operating in an environment shaped as much by history, politics, and religion as by simple forces of supply and demand.

Although his *History of Economic Analysis* is probably Schumpeter's greatest scholarly achievement, it is *Capitalism, Socialism, and Democracy* that holds the most interest for the general student of economics. The book is, among other things, Schumpeter's reply to Karl Marx. The opening chapters of the book contain one of the most lucid and perceptive analyses of Marx's system ever written. Schumpeter went on to explain why he believed that capitalism would inevitably come to an end and be replaced by socialism. Unlike Marx, however, Schumpeter believed that capitalism would be killed not by its failures but by its successes. In the process of explaining this paradoxical proposition, he offered an analysis of the role of the entrepreneur in the market economy and explained why, in the twentieth century, the entrepreneur has come to face an increasingly hostile intellectual environment. A minor but significant role in the downfall of capitalism, Schumpeter believed, would be played by the economic profession's myopic focus on the fairyland of perfect competition and its blindness to the nature and importance of entrepreneurship.

**Joseph Alois Schumpeter (1883–1950)**

The competition that counts is the competition from the new commodity, the new technology, the new source of supply, the new type of organization (the largest scale unit of control, for instance) — competition which commands a decisive cost or quality advantage and which strikes not at the margins of the profits and the outputs of the existing firms, but at their foundations and their very lives. This kind of competition is as much more effective than the other as a bombardment is in comparison with forcing a door, and so much more important that it becomes a matter of comparative indifference whether competition in the ordinary sense functions more or less promptly; the powerful lever that in the long run expands output and brings down prices is in any case made of other stuff.[5]

"In this respect," he added in another place, "perfect competition is not only impossible but inferior, and has no title to being set up as a model of ideal efficiency."[6]

Just how is it that market concentration can actually promote, rather than retard, the kind of competition on which dynamic efficiency depends? There appear to be two mechanisms at work.

First, monopoly power is often the goal of competition among entrepreneurs and the chief incentive to engage in such competition. The first firm to seize on new knowledge and put it to use is able to make profits in excess of the normal rate of return precisely because its new discovery establishes a temporary monopoly that it can exploit until its competitors successfully imitate or outflank it. If each new product had to be introduced at a price that just covered costs, or if each cost-reducing innovation had to be followed immediately by a matching reduction in price, there would be little reason to introduce such innovations at all. If the first firm to adjust to changing circumstances were not able to increase the gap between its costs and its revenues by doing so, there would be no incentive to be first. Competition among entrepreneurs is competition for monopoly power of at least a temporary kind. In this sense, monopoly is not the opposite of competition but a normal result of it.

Second, monopoly power, once achieved, acts as a spur to competition. This is not only true in the now familiar sense that an industry where monopoly profits are being made tends to attract new entrants. It also applies to competition among different industries and product groups for the consumer's dollar. The OPEC countries' exploitation of their oil monopoly has subjected oil to greatly intensified competition from other sources of energy. The rate of innovation in methods of energy production and the rate of introduction of known energy-conserving technology have been greatly speeded up. Even if the oil cartel were now to be broken up, world energy markets would not return to their former equilibrium pattern. In this sense, monopoly is not the opposite of competition but a spur to it.

### Can the Schumpeter Hypothesis Be Tested?

The Schumpeter hypothesis poses a sweeping challenge to economic theory and policy. Not surprisingly, many attempts have been made to

---

[5] Joseph Schumpeter, *Capitalism, Socialism, and Democracy* (New York: Harper & Bros, 1942), pp. 84-85.
[6] Ibid, p. 106.

verify or refute it by examining the available data on economic growth, market concentration, and innovative activity. The results to date, however, are somewhat inconclusive.[7]

The major difficulty with testing the Schumpeter hypothesis lies in measuring innovative activity. Schumpeter had a fairly broad concept of innovation in mind. Inventing new products or processes, developing practical applications of new inventions, working out new forms of business organization, discovering new ways of financing investment, and creating new methods of marketing and distribution were, to Schumpeter, all equally important sources of dynamic efficiency. But clearly, most of these sources can be measured only indirectly, and some not at all. As a result, attempts to test the Schumpeter hypothesis have had to make do with rather crude approximations to the central concepts involved.

Looking at all the studies in perspective, it appears that firms of all sizes in markets of all levels of concentration are, under favorable circumstances, able to contribute positively to the dynamic efficiency of the economy. This implies that neither a policy of indiscriminately breaking up large firms into smaller ones nor a policy of indiscriminately welding small firms into larger ones can be counted on to speed the pace of innovation. The ability of the largest corporations to mass huge research and development teams on a difficult technical problem is important, but so is the flash of insight that may come to a lone inventor. In short, for all we know, the present mix of large and small firms may be just about right from the point of view of dynamic efficiency.

## CONCLUSIONS

Much of this chapter and the preceding one have been devoted to describing unresolved issues of market structure and performance, but they have been unable to offer firm conclusions. In preparation for the next chapter, which discusses public policy toward competition and market structure, it will be useful to summarize what has been covered up to this point in terms of two major areas of controversy.

The first area concerns the extent to which perfect competition, or something reasonably close to it, can be regarded as the natural state of the economy. If a substantial degree of concentration is necessary in most markets in order to take advantage of economies of scale, perfect competition appears to be an exceptional market structure, unattainable in most cases. On the other hand, if most market concentration can be explained on the basis of artificial barriers to entry, such as government franchises or the advertising and marketing strategies of firms dominating the market, public policies aimed at reducing such barriers may realistically be expected to be effective. Somewhat similarly, in the case of unconcentrated but monopolistically competitive industries, one can ask whether the existing degree of product differentiation is natural or contrived.

The second area of controversy concerns the question of whether perfect competition, or something closely approximating it, is a necessary or even

---

[7] For a survey of the most important efforts, see Jesse W. Markham, "Concentration, Stimulus or Retardant to Innovation," in *Industrial Concentration*, ed. Goldschmid, Mann, and Weston, pp. 247-272.

a sufficient condition for good market performance. If, in concentrated markets, tacit or explicit cooperation among firms is the exception and vigorous rivalry is the rule, perfect competition may not be necessary. And if, at least in some markets, economic concentration and large-scale operations are necessary to ensure dynamic efficiency, perfect competition may not be even a sufficient condition for good market performance.

Disagreements over these analytical issues, as will be shown in the next chapter, underlie many of today's public policy debates.

## SUMMARY

1. Some economists think that advertising may act as a barrier to new competition in concentrated industries. Their argument is twofold: (1) that advertising creates strong brand loyalties, thereby making the demand for each firm's product less elastic; and (2) that the necessity of mounting an advertising campaign adds to the start-up costs of a new firm. Other economists disagree; they see advertising as a means of competing rather than a barrier to competition. They argue that advertising is a way of attacking established brand loyalties and facilitating the entry of new firms.

2. A monopolistically competitive market is one in which there are large numbers of small firms, no significant barriers to entry, and a strongly differentiated product. Each firm in such a market faces a downward-sloping demand curve and maximizes profits at the point where marginal cost and marginal revenue are equal. If firms earn profits in the short run, then new firms will enter the market until those profits are eliminated. In long-run equilibrium under monopolistic competition, price must be equal to average total cost.

3. Economists disagree about market performance under monopolistic competition. Some argue that, in equilibrium, there will be too many firms in the market, each producing too little output. Others think that there is really little or no difference between monopolistic competition and perfect competition.

4. An economy's static efficiency is its ability to get the most out of given resources and technology; its dynamic efficiency is its ability to grow through innovation and technical change. According to the Schumpeter hypothesis, large firms in concentrated industries are the economy's major source of dynamic efficiency.

## DISCUSSION QUESTIONS

1. Discuss the controversy over advertising as a barrier to entry in terms of the following statement: a barrier to entry is something that prevents new entrants from duplicating the performance of existing firms in terms of cost or quality. Nonetheless, the need for hard work is not in itself a barrier to entry in the economic sense. When entrepreneurs are freely able to go out and buy the various building blocks of their new firms in the same markets where existing firms buy their inputs, barriers to entry are not a determinant of market structure.

    Do you think it is important that the market for advertising services is itself highly competitive?

2. In downtown Moscow, there are far fewer restaurants than in comparable Canadian cities. These restaurants are, on the average, much larger and much more

crowded than their Canadian counterparts. The quality of food served is high, although service leaves something to be desired by Canadian standards. Do these facts suggest to you that the central planners who control Moscow's restaurants have designed their system to perform better than the restaurant market in most Canadian cities? Using what you have learned about monopolistic competition, make a serious attempt to argue both sides of this question.

3. A landmark American study found that eyeglasses were cheaper in states where advertising was freely permitted than in states where it was restricted. Where advertising was completely banned, glasses cost an average of $37.48 per pair; where there were no restrictions, the average was $17.98.[8] Explain these results in terms of what you have learned in this chapter.

4. Evaluate the following argument in terms of what you have learned in this chapter: the apparent association between dynamic innovation and large firm size is an artificial result of the patent system, which allows firms to grow fat on the monopoly profits of their inventions. Without patents, new inventions could be equally shared among a large number of small firms, and there would be just as much dynamic efficiency without the need to suffer the present degree of market concentration.

## SUGGESTIONS FOR FURTHER READING

Department of Consumer and Corporate Affairs. *A Study on Consumer-Misleading and Unfair Trade Practices*. Ottawa: Information Canada, 1976.
*A critical examination of problems in Canada created by questionable forms of advertising.*

Firestone, O.J. *The Economic Implications of Advertising*. Toronto: Methuen, 1967.
*A quite deliberate but well-reasoned Canadian defense of advertising.*

Galbraith, John Kenneth. *The Affluent Society*. Boston: Houghton Mifflin, 1958.
*Contains Galbraith's well-known attack on advertising as a violation of consumer sovereignty.*

Goldschmid, Harvey J.; Mann, H. Michael; and Weston, J. Fred. *Industrial Concentration: The New Learning*. Boston: Little, Brown, 1974.
*Chapter 3 is a debate between Yale Brozen and H. Michael Mann on the topic of advertising as an impediment to competition. In Chapter 5, Jesse W. Markham discusses market concentration and innovation, citing several attempts to bring empirical evidence to bear on the Schumpeter hypothesis.*

Hayek, Friedrich A. von. "The Non Sequitur of the Dependence Effect." *Southern Economic Journal* 27 (April 1961).
*A reply to Galbraith's views on advertising and consumer sovereignty.*

Schumpeter, Joseph. *Capitalism, Socialism, and Democracy*. New York: Harper & Bros., 1942.
*Part 2 of this book contains Schumpeter's famous discussion of the relationship between market concentration and dynamic efficiency.*

---

[8] Lee Benham, "The Effect of Advertising on the Price of Eyeglasses," *Journal of Law and Economics* 15 (October 1972), pp. 337-352.

# MARKET FAILURE AND GOVERNMENT REGULATION

## WHAT YOU WILL LEARN IN THIS CHAPTER

*Chapters 20 to 23 showed that perfectly competitive markets satisfy consumer wants in the most efficient way. Unfortunately, as Chapters 24 to 26 demonstrated, many of the markets in which goods and services are produced and sold are not highly competitive. In monopolistic or "imperfectly competitive" markets, the market "fails" in its basic function of putting resources to their best use. This chapter examines how government in Canada has attempted to correct this type of market failure through legislation designed to curb business practices that lessen competition.*

*But markets sometimes fail to put resources to their best use for reasons other than the breakdown of competition. In some markets, such as agriculture, resources may be misallocated because of unique market uncertainties and "destructive competition." Such problems, and their attempted cures, are also described and evaluated here. Further, in some markets, as was noted in Chapter 24, "natural monopolies" appear to exist that require controls to curb potential abuses. The nature of such controls, and some of their accompanying problems, are examined briefly in this chapter. In addition, attention is given to the failure of markets to take account of external effects, both good and bad, of some market transactions.*

## FOR REVIEW

*Here are some important terms and concepts that will be put to use in this chapter. If you do not understand them, review them before proceeding.*
- *The functions of markets (Chapter 2)*
- *The role of prices in markets (Chapter 3)*
- *The benefits of perfect competition (Chapter 23)*
- *Natural monopoly (Chapter 24)*
- *Problems of monopoly and imperfect competition (Chapters 24 to 26)*

## A BRIEF REVIEW OF MARKET FAILURE AND GOVERNMENT INTERVENTION

We have completed the examination of various market structures in earlier chapters, and it is time now to review briefly what markets were intended to do, as well as why and how they sometimes fail. It was noted in Chapter 2 that one of the basic functions of an economy is to put resources to their best use. For this purpose, the economy must impart useful and accurate information, so that both producers and consumers know what their best choices are, and it must provide incentives to achieve the best results. In addition, it should distribute income according to some standard of fairness. That same chapter illustrated how the *market system*, despite imperfections (which were only briefly mentioned), does a reasonably good job of providing information and incentives and distributing income. Chapter 3 extended the analysis by showing how the *price system*, operating through the "laws" of supply and demand, creates an equilibrium between producer supply and consumer demand. A flexible price system is able to restore equilibrium when temporary imbalances exist. The example of rent controls was used, however, to show that some market prices may not be considered "fair" by large segments of the population. Attempts to impose a "fairer," more rigid price system seem to be accepted by voters, but they are not without problems of their own. Intervention by government in the market may require further interventions to "correct" the problems that the original intervention creates.

Chapter 4 showed how business organizations use principles of managerial coordination for efficient internal organization and the market system for efficient external operations. However, evidence of worker alienation was noted, accompanied by trends toward increased worker control. Chapter 4 also described the growth of government involvement in the Canadian economy. Governments have assumed extremely important roles for purposes of nation building, the provision of public goods, redistribution of income, stabilization of prices, employment and regional disparities, the regulation of private business, and the administration of justice. All these activities, to a greater or lesser extent, reflect a judgment that the market system by itself is not capable of meeting some basic needs of the population. The detailed attention given to fiscal and monetary policy by government underscore that impression.

In Chapters 20 to 23, however, we returned to the theme of how markets, when they are operating perfectly, guarantee that all mutually beneficial transactions in a society will be carried out. In perfect competition, each firm will produce at its lowest average cost, so no further gains are possible on the production side. Price will be equal to marginal cost, so marginal benefits will equal marginal cost. This potentially good result, however, is thwarted by the existence of monopoly or imperfect competition in some markets, as discussed in Chapters 24 to 26. In many cases, such imperfect market conditions seem to develop in defiance of economic necessity and society's good, while in others (in so-called "natural monopolies") the development appears to be inevitable. In either case, the failure of markets to achieve perfect competition provides additional reasons for governments to intervene in the economy. It is not surprising, therefore, that the scope of government regulation and control in modern markets has increased tremendously in the last few decades.

### The Scope of Government Regulations

The scope of government regulation in Canada affecting economic activity is illustrated in Exhibit 27.1. It would be impossible to provide details

**Exhibit 27.1**
## The scope of regulation in Canada

A wide range of federal, provincial, and municipal regulations has been developed in Canada to determine rates, entry and exit conditions, quality of output, health and safety, accuracy of information, and environmental effects in dozens of industries in Canada. Almost 30 percent of the Gross Domestic Product is affected by direct regulations.

- **Communications**

  Broadcasting
    Radio (AM, FM)
    Television
  Telecommunications
    Telephone
    Telegraph
    Satellite
    Cable TV

- **Consumer Protection/Information**

  Disclosure (product content label-
  ling, terms of sale, etc.)
  False and misleading advertising
  Sales techniques (merchandising)
  Packaging and labelling
  Prohibited transactions, e.g.,
  pyramid sales, referral sales
  Weights and measures

- **Cultural/Recreational**

  Residency requirements
  Language (bilingualism)
  Canadian content in broadcasting
  Horse racing
  Gambling (lotteries)
  Sports
  Film, theatre, literature, music
  e.g. Canadian content

- **Energy**

  Nuclear
  Natural gas
  Petroleum
  Hydro-electric
  Coal

- **Environmental Management**

  (a) Pollution control
      air
      water
      solid waste disposal
  (b) Resource development
      minerals
      forestry
      water
  (c) Wildlife protection
      hunting
      fishing
      parks/reserves
      endangered species

  (d) Land use
      planning/zoning
      development approval
      sub-division
      strata-title
  (e) Weather modification

- **Financial Markets and Institutions**

  Banks
  Non-banks
    Trust companies
    Management companies
    Finance companies
    Credit unions/
      Caisses populaires
  Pension plans
  Securities/commodities
    transactions
  Insurance

- **Food Production and Distribution**

  (a) Agricultural products
      marketing
      pricing
      grading
      storage
      distribution
      entry
      supply
  (b) Fisheries (marine, freshwater)
      price
      entry
      quotas
      gear

- **Framework**

  Competition policy
  Anti-dumping laws
  Foreign Investment Review Act
  Bankruptcy laws
  Corporation laws
  Intellectual and industrial
      property
      copyright
      industrial design
      patents
      trade marks
  Election laws
      contributors
      spending
      reporting

- **Health and Safety**

  (a) Occupational health and safety

  (b) Products — use
      explosives
      firearms
      chemicals
  (c) Product-characteristics
      purity
      wholesomeness
      efficacy
      accident risk
  (d) Building codes
  (e) Health services
      nursing homes
      private hospitals
      emergency services
  (f) Animal health
  (g) Plant health

- **Human Rights**

  Anti-discrimination legislation
  in respect to hiring, sale of goods
  or services etc.
  Protection of privacy, personal
  information reporting

- **Labour**

  Collective bargaining
  Minimum wage laws
  Hours of work, terms of employment

- **Liquor**

  Characteristics, e.g. alcoholic
  content
  Distribution and sale

- **Professions/Occupational Licensure**

  Certification/licensure
  Registration
  Apprenticeship

- **Transportation**

  Airlines (domestic, international)
  Marine (domestic, international)
  Railways
  Inter-city buses
  Taxis
  Pipelines
  Trucking (inter and intra-provincial)
  Urban public transit
  Postal express

- **Other**

  Rent control
  Metrication
  General wage and price controls

Source: Economic Council of Canada, *Responsible Regulation, An Interim Report*, 1979, p. 11.

**Direct regulation**
Government regulation of one or more of price, rate of return, output, entry, or exit, usually in a specific industry.

**Indirect or social regulation** Government regulation of the attributes of a product, information, methods of production, sale, and employment.

here on the nature and impact of such regulations on each one of the sectors listed. A distinction can be made, however, between *direct regulation*, involving government control over price and supply in a specific industry, and **indirect** or **social regulation**, which is aimed at controlling the attributes of a product or service and providing better information, working conditions, and protection for workers and consumers. Social regulation usually cuts across many industries, providing such things as health and safety standards, quality standards, and laws against air and water pollution. A recent Canadian study indicated that about 29 percent of the gross domestic product in Canada is subject to some form of direct regulation. An even larger proportion comes under some form of indirect legislation.[1] Very similar results were found for the United States, where, however, public ownership is much less extensive than it is in Canada.

In this chapter we will examine a few of the more important examples of both types of regulation. Laws designed to encourage greater competition fall into the indirect, social regulation category, as do laws dealing with the environment. On the other hand, regulations controlling rates in specific "natural monopolies," and establishing prices and production quotas for such diverse industries as agriculture and broadcasting are clearly direct regulations, affecting demand and supply in those industries. Both types of regulations are described and evaluated here. In following chapters, the special problems of the energy sector and the foreign control of some Canadian markets will be examined in greater detail.

## The Anticombines Laws

**Anticombines laws** A set of laws, including the acts of 1889 and 1923 and subsequent amendments, that seek to control market structure and the competitive behavior of firms.

Legislative attempts to curb monopoly in Canada—**anticombines laws**—go back to the Anticombines Act of 1889, which made it a misdemeanor "to conspire, combine, agree or arrange unlawfully, to unduly limit the transportation, production, or storage facilities for any trade commodity, to restrain the trade of such a commodity, or to unduly prevent or lessen competition in the production, sale, or price of any commodity."

In 1892 this act became a part of the Criminal Code, and an offense under the act became indictable. Subsequently, in 1910 and 1923, 1951 and 1960, further Combines Acts were enacted and revised, providing investigative and administrative support for prosecutions carried out under the Criminal Code.

When one compares these anticombines acts of Canada with the Sherman Antitrust Act and other antitrust laws in the United States, it becomes clear that the Canadian approach to monopoly is much less aggressive than the American.

A Canadian expert on anticombines legislation has noted: "Perhaps the most striking aspect of the history of the legislation dealing with restraints on competition in Canada is the mixed character of the economic beliefs and policies it discloses. For example, the early debates in the House of Commons on the Combines Investigation Act—and the more recent

---

[1] Fred Thompson and W. T. Stanbury, "The Scope and Coverage of Regulation in Canada and the United States: Implications for the Demand for Reform," Ottawa, Economic Council of Canada, cited in the Economic Council of Canada *Report on Responsible Regulation: An Interim Report*, 1979, p. 13.

debates for that matter—display no broad support for a general policy of competition."[2]

Canadian economic development, as we noted in Chapter 4, was promoted by the creation of virtual monopolies, such as the Hudson Bay Company and the Canadian Pacific Railway. There was considerable resentment toward abusive practices of these corporations, but there was simultaneously a widespread belief that large companies were necessary to develop the chief resources of the country. There was, therefore, no strong commitment to what Skeoch calls "a general rule of competition."

This helps to explain several important features of our anticombines policy. First, no attempt has been made to break up monopolies, as was done with Standard Oil of New Jersey in the United States in 1911. In Canada, the law has been primarily concerned with the prevention of such individual abuses as price fixing and price discrimination. Second, large sectors of the economy—banking and real estate, for instance—have until recently been exempt from prosecution. Third, the limited financial resources allotted by the government to anticombines investigation have never permitted more than a token approach to the problem.

Until 1967, anticombines investigation and prosecutions were carried out through a special branch of the Department of Justice. Since 1967, the Department of Consumer and Corporate Affairs has assumed responsibility for combines, mergers, monopolies, and other forms of restraint of trade. A new Competition Bill, before Parliament since 1977, would place strict limits on mergers and monopolies and would allow for their adjudication and even dissolution by a special civil tribunal. Strong lobbying by business groups has delayed the passage of this bill.

Over the years, the federal government has used its anticombines legislation to deal with two types of offenses: those that were considered to be illegal *per se*, and those that could be declared illegal only if it was shown that they had been detrimental to the public.

The pursuit of *per se* offenses has led to numerous successful prosecutions. Such offenses include *price fixing* (where firms agree to sell their similar products at a set price), *price discrimination* (charging different customers different prices for no justifiable economic reason), and *exclusive dealing and tied selling* (product supplied on condition that the purchaser buy only from the one supplier and buy other products as well). Interestingly, *resale price maintenance*, wherein manufacturers or wholesalers try to force a certain price on the retailer, is illegal in Canada (there can be only a "suggested price"), while in many American states it is protected by law. Canadian law seems to favor the consumer, while the United States is more concerned about protecting small businesses.

The prosecution of offenses involving mergers and monopolies has been uncommon. Before World War II, there was only one prosecution for a merger offense, the Western Fruits and Vegetables case, and it resulted in an acquittal. In 1959, charges were brought against Canadian Breweries and the Western Sugar Company, but both of these cases ended in acquittal. The Electric Reduction Company of Canada Limited pleaded guilty to a merger

---

[2] L.A. Skeoch, *Restrictive Trade Practices in Canada* (Toronto: McClelland and Stewart, 1966), p. 3. Much of this section is based on this book.

charge in 1970. K.C. Irving Limited, a Maritimes conglomerate, was convicted of merger charges in 1974, but the decision was reversed by the Supreme Court of Canada on grounds that detriment had not been proven. In Canada, therefore, there has never been a conviction after a full trial that was not reversed on appeal. As we have noted, new and tougher legislation has been stymied by strong business groups, calling into question the ability of a modern, industrial democracy to curb the power of important economic interests.

In addition to the protests of those who might be adversely affected by a more vigorous anticombines policy, there are arguments advanced by others against a basic change in policy.

Almost all economists would agree that, under given conditions of cost, competitive markets perform more efficiently than markets in which competition is restricted. But a major problem with anticombines policy, according to many critics, is that the law fails to recognize that cost conditions are not always given. Mergers, for example, may result in economies of scale. In condemning such mergers, the courts may prevent business from cutting costs, and the consumer may end up paying higher, rather than lower, prices as a result of anticombines or antitrust enforcement.

### The Royal Commission on Corporate Concentration

The idea that mergers may benefit consumers has been articulated by the Royal Commission on Corporate Concentration, which was established by Parliament in 1975. In its 1978 report, the Commission argued that the anticombines laws did not need any basic strengthening, because concentration had not been increasing in the past decade or more and there is nothing wrong with concentration in itself. Indeed, the report maintained that many industries would fare better in the international market if firms were able to become larger and utilize economies of scale. This, the report argued, should be allowed to happen "through internal growth and through mergers and acquisitions, even if this expansion resulted in higher concentration levels."[3]

In its recommendations, the Royal Commission advocated a form of *workable competition*, rather than the perfect competition idealized by economists, as a suitable model for the Canadian economy. It noted several important conditions for such workable competition.[4]

First, small and medium-sized firms must not be unfairly prevented from operating and expanding and must not face artificial barriers to entering new industries.

Second, there should be selective reductions in the tariff and nontariff barriers that protect most Canadian manufacturing industries. Such reductions, which would put more pressure on firms to achieve international standards of efficiency, should be accompanied by government sanction of specialization agreements under which competitors in a market would be

---

[3] *Report of the Royal Commission on Corporate Concentration*, 1978, p. 214.
[4] Ibid., p. 215 ff.

allowed to allocate production among themselves to achieve longer production runs and greater economies.

Third, there must be disclosure of accounting and profit information so that conglomerate firms are unable to hide areas of high profitability behind a protective shield of consolidated reporting.

Fourth, competition policy must be strong and vigorously enforced, particularly in the areas of restrictive trade practices and attempts to build or maintain barriers to entry.

Finally, another possible condition necessary for workable competition is that the proportion of the Canadian economy constrained by government regulation or ownership should be reviewed and possibly reduced.

While economists are aware of the difference between their model of perfect competition and the real world of imperfect competition, and while most are probably in favor of recognizing and protecting some form of workable competition, there is wide disagreement over the methods that should be pursued in achieving even this limited goal. The Royal Commission report has been severely criticized for downplaying the dangers of increased concentration and for not supporting more wholeheartedly the attempts made by the federal government in the 1970s to strengthen anticombines legislation. It is clear that government policy has been quite ineffective in lowering barriers to entry and in preventing mergers and other forms of business concentration.

## DIRECT GOVERNMENT REGULATION OF NATURAL MONOPOLIES

Up to now we have discussed examples of indirect government regulation, involving anticombines policy. If government is not willing to accept the outcome that the operation of the market produces in some industry, it does not need to limit itself to changing the market structure of that industry. One alternative is to leave the structure of the market untouched, but to subject producers to direct regulation. The discussion of such direct regulation can begin with a fairly simple case, that of utility regulation. Here, regulation presents itself as a direct alternative to anticombines policy. For various technical reasons, public utilities tend to be natural monopolies. A natural monopoly, as we noted in Chapter 24, is an industry in which total costs are minimized by having just one producer serve the entire market. Consider electricity, telephone service, water, or gas, to take the most common examples. It is easy for one utility to hook up extra customers in a neighborhood once it has run its basic lines, but wastefully expensive for separate companies to run duplicate sets of lines down each street. The problem is how to keep that one firm from restricting output and raising its price as a profit-maximizing pure monopolist would do.

A graphical example will help make the problem clear. Consider Exhibit 27.2. The firm represented there has roughly constant marginal costs and an L-shaped long-run average cost curve. The demand curve intersects the long-run average cost curve at a quantity $Q_1$, not far above the minimum economic scale of production. If this output were divided between even as

**Exhibit 27.2**
**Cost and revenue curves for a natural monopoly**
Because of the L-shaped average cost curve, one firm could supply the market with the quantity $Q_1$ more cheaply than could two firms, each producing half that much. A single unregulated firm, however, would behave as a monopolist, producing only $Q_2$ and selling at the price $P_2$. By imposing the price ceiling $P_1$, the firm is forced to act as a price taker and produces the desired quantity $Q_1$.

many as two firms, each producing half the quantity $Q_1$, cost per unit would be substantially higher.

If a single firm operates in the market, it will tend to behave as a pure monopolist. Instead of producing $Q_1$, it will produce $Q_2$, which corresponds to the intersection between the firm's marginal revenue and marginal cost curves. The price corresponding to this output is $P_2$, far in excess of marginal cost. This would be a smaller output and higher price than efficient resource allocation requires.

### Rate Regulation

In this analysis, then, competition by two or more firms is wasteful, and monopoly pricing by a single firm is wasteful too. A standard solution is to allow just one firm to operate either under private ownership or as a crown corporation, and to impose rate regulation on it. Instead of permitting the firm to charge the price $P_2$, the regulatory commission limits the price to no more than $P_1$, the price where the demand curve intersects the long-run average cost curve. The firm is forced to be a price taker, in effect, and chooses the quantity $Q_1$. Actually, maximum efficiency would require a price equal to *marginal* cost, and an output a little greater than $Q_1$. The problem is that the firm would then suffer a loss and eventually go bankrupt unless it were paid a subsidy. Most economists would agree that the price $P_1$, which avoids the necessity of paying a subsidy, is close enough to the ideal for practical policy purposes.

### Practical Problems

The argument for rate regulation of public utilities is based on the theories presented in Chapters 24 and 25. It is worth recalling the assumption on which those theories were based. For one thing, the theories assume that all participants in the market (including the regulators) possess accurate knowledge of cost and demand conditions. Second, they assume that when rate regulation is imposed on the monopoly, it will treat the rates as determined by forces beyond its own control, and will consequently behave as a price taker. Finally, they assume that underlying cost and demand conditions are stable and not subject to change.

In the real world, none of these conditions is wholly fulfilled. As a result, it is not quite so easy to make rate regulation work as Exhibit 27.2 suggests.

A major problem is that the regulators do not really know the shapes and positions of the firm's demand and cost curves. Not knowing these, they cannot directly identify the price and quantity where the demand and average cost curves intersect. They must use an indirect approach to finding the correct price instead, reasoning as follows: with the cost and demand curves shown in Exhibit 27.2, if the price were set above average cost, the firm would earn a higher rate of return than the average for other firms in the economy. If the price were set too low, the firm would earn a lower than average return. Therefore, if a price can be found that will allow the firm to earn just an average rate of return, that will be the price to charge.

Armed with this reasoning, the rate-setting process proceeds in five steps. First, the regulators measure the value of the firm's capital, which for our hypothetical firm is, say, $1,200,000. This is called the firm's *rate base*. Second, they measure the average rate of return for the economy, which, let us say, turns out to be 10 percent per year. (In practice, neither of these first two steps is quite as easy as it sounds, but we can afford to give the regulators the benefit of the doubt.) Third, they multiply the rate base by the permitted rate of return to figure out a total profit target for the firm. Step 4 is to ask the firm to propose a price or schedule of prices that it thinks will allow it to earn the target profit. Finally, as time goes by, the regulators monitor the firm's profits, cutting the price if profits rise too high and allowing the price to rise if profits fall below the target.

In an unchanging world where business decision makers behaved as price-taking managerial calculators, this approach might work fairly well. In a changing world, where business decision makers are entrepreneurs as well as calculators, rate regulation is less successful.

## Cost Control

For one thing, the procedures of rate regulation tend to weaken the firm's incentive for cost reduction. The regulated firm is not really a price taker. Its managers know that if they let costs rise, they will be able to complain about low profits to the regulatory commission, which will be bound to grant a rate increase big enough to restore the target rate of return. As an extreme case, imagine a regulated utility that spends $1 million on an investment project that adds absolutely nothing at all to output. The next time it goes before the regulatory commission, it can point to a million-dollar increase in its rate base, and legitimately ask for a corresponding increase in the profits it will be permitted to earn. Of course, because the new investment does not produce any new output, the only place the added profit can come from is a price rise. Not good for efficiency, but from the firm's point of view, profits from rate-base expansion are just as good as any other kind of profits.

Canadian governments regulate many industries in the manner described in Exhibit 27.2. Railways, electricity, gas, and telephone utilities (both private and government-owned), banks, pipelines, trucking companies, airlines, taxicabs, broadcasting companies, securities and insurance firms, are all subject to regulatory boards that concern themselves with their operation.[5] In some cases, for example railways and telephone companies, there is close scrutiny of prices, profits, and levels of service. In others, like insurance, banking, and securities, the regulatory authorities are interested mainly in financial integrity and do not control prices and profits. In broadcasting, the chief concern seems to be with service. In the transportation industry, the government has allowed more self-regulation by the Canadian Transport Commission, but recently it has tried to increase direct government control because it has felt that the public interest has not been well served by such policies as railway relocation. At the same time, de-regulation is occurring in the airline industry, where private airlines have not been permitted to compete on even terms with Air Canada.

## REGULATION IN AGRICULTURE

Another industry in which direct government regulation has become very important is agriculture. Many agricultural markets come close to fitting the four structural requirements of perfect competition: large numbers of small firms, homogeneous products, good information flows, and easy entry and exit. In Canada, there are some 300,000 farms altogether, about 90 percent of which are sole proprietorships—traditional family farms.

Most agricultural markets are characterized by a high degree of product homogeneity. Only rarely do consumers know or care about which particular farm produced the products they buy. The flow of information in agricultural markets is accomplished through highly organized commodity exchanges for major crops. The last structural requirement for perfect competition, easy entry and exit, is also well satisfied in agriculture.

As explained in Chapter 23, perfectly competitive markets have some important virtues. Whenever consumers are willing to pay more for a good than its marginal cost, a competitive market will bring forth the additional supply. If existing firms cannot handle the demand, new firms will enter. Similarly, if consumers are unwilling to buy all that is produced at a price at least equal to marginal cost, competition will accomplish the required reduction in supply. If a long-run reduction in supply is needed, some firms will withdraw from the market. In every case, the necessary adjustments occur in response to changes in the market price of the good, as determined by supply and demand. No central planner is needed to give orders; Adam Smith's "invisible hand" is at work.

---

[5]For a good brief discussion, on which this part of the chapter is based, see the *Report of the Royal Commission on Corporate Concentration*, Chapter 17, 1978.

Left alone, agricultural markets really do work in something quite close to this ideal fashion. But for farmers the ideal is a mixed blessing. In the short run, competition means unpredictable prices and unstable incomes as supply and demand curves shift with the weather and with patterns of world trade. In the long run, competition has driven more and more farmers from the land as new technology has increased crop yields per worker. Some economists use the term **destructive competition** to refer to industries like agriculture. In the absence of controls or some form of planned coordination, intensive competition accompanied by market uncertainty may lead to persistent excess capacity and unstable prices and income. So not despite but because of the perfectly competitive structure of agricultural markets, there is a farm problem.

The farm problem, it must be added, is a problem for *farmers*. From the consumer's point of view, and even more so from the detached point of view of the economist, fluctuating prices and declining farm population may not be problems at all; they may be merely the healthy functioning of competitive markets. Nonetheless, the farmer's point of view has traditionally dominated the Canadian government's farm policy. That being the case, it is worth examining more closely the cause of the problem, in order to evaluate the policies designed to cure it.

**Destructive competition**
This may occur in an industry with large fixed costs, relatively free entry, and long and recurrent periods of excess capacity. Marginal cost may be below average cost but at the same time equals price, leading to losses over long periods of time.

## Instability and Price Inelastic Demand

In a competitive market, the response of price and revenue to changes in the quantity supplied depends on the price elasticity of demand. This response is illustrated by Exhibit 27.3. Market A in the exhibit is characterized by relatively low price elasticity of demand and Market B by relatively high elasticity.

In both markets, the time horizon is the **very short run** — a time so short that producers cannot make any adjustments in inputs or outputs in response to a change in price. This is the case in the market for a perishable agricultural good after the crop has been harvested and before the farmers have a chance to respond to prices by adjusting their supply decision for the next year.

**Very short run** A time horizon so short that producers are unable to make any changes in input or output quantities in response to changing prices.

Suppose now that in the first year, 100,000 units of each crop are harvested. When the quantity of output is brought to market, an equilibrium price of $2 is established for both goods. The next year, because of improved weather, increased planting, or some other reason, output in both markets increases to 125,000 units. This is represented in the exhibit by a shift in the short-run supply curve from $S_1$ to $S_2$. What happens to price and revenue?

In Market A, where demand is inelastic, a large decrease in price is necessary to bring about the required increase in quantity demanded. As the price falls from $2 to $1, total revenue earned from the sale of the crop declines from $200,000 to $125,000. In Market B, however, a relatively small decline in price, from $2 to $1.80, is sufficient to increase the quantity demanded to 125,000 units. Because the price declines by a smaller percentage than the quantity of output increases in this market, revenue rises from $200,000 to $225,000.

Studies of actual agricultural markets indicate that they are more like

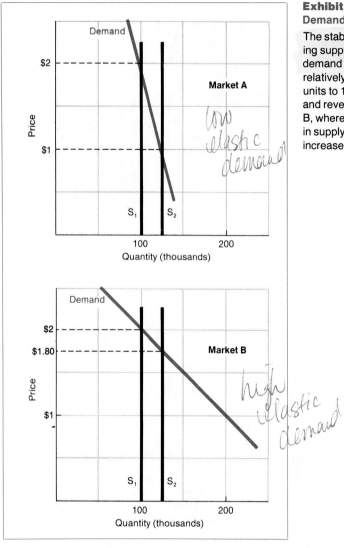

### Exhibit 27.3
**Demand elasticity and price instability**

The stability of prices and revenues in the face of changing supply conditions depends on the price elasticity of demand for the product. In Market A, where demand is relatively inelastic, an increase in supply from 100,000 units to 125,000 units brings the price down from $2 to $1 and revenue down from $200,000 to $125,000. In Market B, where demand is relatively elastic, the same increase in supply causes the price to drop to $1.80 and revenue to increase from $200,000 to $225,000.

Market A than Market B. For most farm products, the elasticity is less than one.

### The Historical Instability of Prices

Because demand for farm products is price inelastic, changing supply and demand conditions result in disproportionately large year-to-year price changes. The instability of agricultural prices is evident from Exhibit 27.4, which shows fluctuations in farm prices of Canadian agricultural products from 1961 to 1981. During that twenty-one year period, there were eight years in which agricultural prices actually declined. On the other hand, in 1973, when there appeared to be a worldwide shortage of agricultural commodities, accentuated by crop failures in the Soviet Union, the price of agricultural products in Canada rose by 49.3 percent. This was followed

**Exhibit 27.4**
Fluctuations in farm prices of
agricultural products, 1961–1981

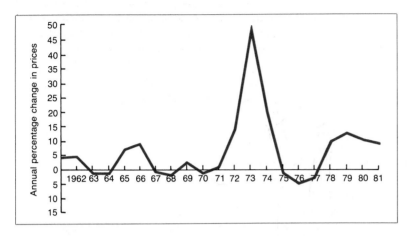

Source: Department of Finance, *Economic Review*, April 1979, p. 181, and April 1982, p. 174.

by a further 20.6 percent increase in 1974. This trend was abruptly reversed in 1975, when agricultural prices fell by 1.0 percent.

This price record tells the story of one aspect of the farm problem: short-term instability. There is a second aspect of the farm problem as well: long-term adjustment to rising productivity and slowly growing demand.

Canadian farmers, like farmers in most western countries, have increased output at an extraordinary rate. In 1946, one farm worker in Canada produced enough agricultural output for the consumption of fifteen people. By the 1970s, the worker produced enough for the consumption of fifty people. However, this increase in productivity has not been matched by increased demand. The demand for farm products is not only price inelastic, but *income* inelastic as well. As per capita income grows, the quantity of agricultural output demanded increases, but less than in proportion to the increase in income.

The result of slowly growing demand and rapidly growing farm productivity has been a steady decline in the farm population and a relatively poor income record for farmers. Currently about 4 percent of our population lives on farms. In 1929, one-third of the population lived on farms. In the past fifty years, the farm population has shrunk by about 2 million people.

The competitive market knows just one way to bring about the exit of resources from an industry in which they are no longer needed: reduce the amount those resources are paid. Not surprisingly, then, per capita farm income has fared more poorly than the income of many other groups in our society.

For most postwar years, per capita farm income has been considerably below that of the population as a whole. In the 1970s, the sharp increase in agricultural prices of 1973 and 1974 raised per capita agricultural incomes above the national average, but those years have been exceptions to the general rule.

Because of declining agricultural population and slowly growing income, the farm income share of net national income has declined from about 4 percent in 1962 to just over 2 percent in 1981. This is illustrated in Exhibit 27.5. The heavy line indicates how the share has fluctuated, demonstrating the instability of farm income, while the fine straight line indicates the long-run trend.

Because of such price and income instability, caused by unique demand and supply conditions, farmers have made numerous appeals to government for various types of assistance. These appeals have not gone unheeded. Policy makers in Ottawa and in the provincial capitals have heard the farmers' complaints and agreed that something should be done. Piece by piece, over the past half-century, a farm policy has been assembled that places a number of ingenious restrictions on competition. As a result, Canadian agriculture not only supplies textbook writers with some good illustrations of perfect competition in action, but also gives them a chance to develop applications of the theory of monopoly.

**Exhibit 27.5**
**Shares of net national income at factor cost**

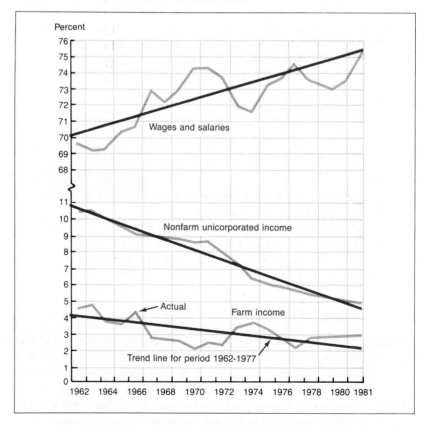

Source: Statistics Canada, *National Income and Expenditure Accounts*, Quarterly Catalogue 13-001, and Department of Finance, *Economic Review*, April 1982, p. 15.

## FARM POLICY

### Competition versus Coordination

Farmers could solve many of their own problems if only they could coordinate their activities instead of competing with each other. The theory developed in Chapter 24 suggests that one way to do this would be to form a comprehensive system of agricultural cartels. The cartel for each crop could limit the quantity supplied to the market and hold prices up. It could also carry one year's surplus over for sale at a higher price in a year when the crop was not so abundant. If there were more farmers than required to produce the profit maximizing output, the cartel could assign each member a fair share of the limited production while planning orderly withdrawal of unneeded resources.

But organizing such a system of agricultural cartels on a private, voluntary basis would be a completely hopeless undertaking. As Chapter 24 showed, cartels have built-in stability problems of their own. To be successful, a cartel must be able to restrict the entry of nonmembers into the industry, and it must be able to enforce its rules among its own members. Because the number of farms is so large and the barriers to entry are so low, these problems would quickly prove fatal for any privately organized agricultural cartel.

Unable to overcome their problems through voluntary coordination, then, it is not surprising that farmers have turned to the government for help.

The federal and provincial governments in Canada have helped to coordinate and support the activities of farmers in many different ways. Some assistance policies go back a long way, like the granting of agricultural land to new settlers in the late nineteenth century, and the use of subsidized railway rates — known as the Crow's Nest Pass Agreement — to encourage the export of grain and flour. However, with the creation of the Canadian Wheat Board in 1935, and the passing of the Agricultural Prices Support Act in 1944, Canadian governments began to develop institutions and procedures to support farm prices and incomes in the form of direct rather than indirect regulations.

There are, essentially, three ways that government supported agencies can directly help farmers to control prices and to cope with supply:

1. They can establish a minimum price and agree to buy all or a certain amount of the output at that price.
2. They can restrict output and guarantee a price for that output.
3. They can subsidize the price paid by the consumer.

### Price Supports

**Price supports** are the most venerable of all instruments of farm policy. Exhibit 27.6 shows how they work, taking the market for wheat as an example. As the figure is drawn, the competitive equilibrium price is $2 per dm³, and the equilibrium quantity of output is 2 billion dm³ per year. The supply curve is not completely inelastic because a longer period of time extending into another growing season is contemplated.

Suppose now that in order to raise farm incomes, the government

**Price support** A program under which the government guarantees a certain minimum price to farmers by undertaking to buy any surplus that cannot be sold to private buyers at the support price.

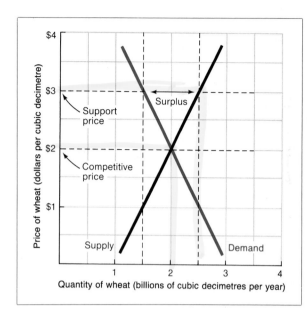

Price of wheat (dollars per cubic decimetre)

Quantity of wheat (billions of cubic decimetres per year)

**Exhibit 27.6**
**The effects of direct price supports**
To carry out its price support policy, the government agrees to pay $3/dm³ for all wheat that cannot be sold at that price in the open market. Because the support price is above the equilibrium price for a competitive market, this policy will reduce the quantity of wheat demanded and increase the quantity of wheat supplied. The resulting surplus will be purchased by the government and put into storage or otherwise disposed of.

declares a support price of $3 per dm³. At this price, farmers will produce 2.5 billion dm³ of wheat, but consumers will buy only 1.5 billion. The government will maintain the price at the support level by buying the 1 billion dm³ of surplus wheat at the support price and putting it in storage.[6]

But what is to be done with the surplus wheat? During the 1960s, the quantities of wheat stored by the government became a national problem. Luckily, most of the vast accumulation (or at least the part of it that had not spoiled) was cleared out during the 1973 world food crisis. Because of the surplus problem, the government has experimented with two other instruments of farm policy that potentially avoid the problem.

### Land-use Controls

**Land-use controls** Policies designed to raise agricultural prices by limiting the amount of land on which certain crops can be grown.

**Land-use controls** are one of the instruments intended to avoid the problem of surpluses. Exhibit 27.7 shows how they work. The demand curve, D, and supply curve $S_1$ in this exhibit are the same as in exhibit 27.6. The objective of government policy is also the same: raise the price of wheat from its equilibrium level of $2/dm³ to the desired level of $3/dm³.

The method of pushing the price up is different this time, however. Instead of offering to buy any wheat that goes unsold at the price of $3/dm³, the government attempts to restrict the quantity of wheat produced in order to drive the price up to the desired level. It does this by requiring each farmer to take some land out of wheat production.

---

[6]Through the Canadian Wheat Board the government allocates a wheat delivery quota to each farmer, and the wheat is sold by the board either at home or abroad. The farmer is paid an initial price (for example, $3/dm³), which is in effect the support price. If demand on the world market enables the price to rise higher than $3, farmers receive additional payments.

**Exhibit 27.7**
**The effects of land-use controls**
This exhibit shows how the government can raise the price of what to the desired level of $3/dm³ through the use of land-use controls. Land-use controls raise the cost of producing wheat, shifting the supply curve from $S_1$ to $S_2$. The effect is to push up the price of wheat without creating a surplus. However, more resources must be used to produce each cubic decimetre of wheat than would have been the case without land-use controls.

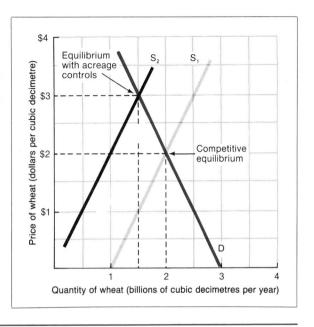

The effect of the artificial restriction of land for wheat is to raise the marginal cost of producing wheat. Ordinarily, farmers who want to grow more wheat will minimize their cost of production by adding a little more land, a little more labor, and a little more capital (machinery and fertilizer) in certain cost minimizing proportions. Now those same farmers face a new constraint: they can use more labor and capital but not more land. It is still possible to grow more wheat if the price is high enough to justify the added cost, so the new supply curve, $S_2$, still has an upward slope. But the increased marginal cost resulting from the constraint on farming practices pushes the supply curve to a higher level. If wheat production is restricted by just the right amount, as it is in Exhibit 27.7, the same price ($3/dm³) will be reached as was reached through direct price supports in the previous example.

## Subsidy Prices

Neither price supports nor land-use controls offer much to consumers but the prospect of spending more and getting less. With policy makers becoming more sensitive to consumer complaints, a third instrument of farm policy, **subsidy prices**, has received increased attention.

Exhibit 27.8 shows how such prices work. It begins with the same supply and demand curves as before and the same goal of getting the revenue received by farmers up to $3/dm³. Now, however, the government does not try to control either the quantity of wheat produced or the actual market price. Instead, it sets a target price of $3/dm³ and promises farmers a "deficiency payment" equal to the difference between the target price and the market price for each cubic decimetre produced. Knowing they will receive $3/dm³ regardless of how low the market price falls, farmers follow their supply curve up to an output of 2.5 billion cubic decimetres. When this quantity of wheat is thrown on the market, the price falls to $1/dm³.

**Subsidy price** A price guaranteed to farmers by the government; if the market price falls below the subsidy price, the government pays the farmers the difference.

Consumers gets lots of cheap wheat, and the government pays most of the bill.

## Alternative Policies Compared

Which of these three policy instruments—price supports, land-use controls, or subsidy prices—is the best? The answer turns out to depend on whose viewpoint is taken—the farmer's, the consumer's, the taxpayer's, the economist's, or the government policy maker's.

From the farmer's point of view, direct price supports and subsidy prices tie for best, and land-use controls are clearly inferior. As the examples here have been constructed, both price supports and subsidy prices raise total farm revenues from $4 billion to $7.5 billion, without any adverse impact on productivity. Land-use controls, in contrast, raise revenues to only $4.5 billion and simultaneously raise costs per unit. Valuable labor and capital was wasted cultivating some land too intensively, while other land lies altogether idle.

From the consumer's point of view, subsidy prices are by far the best, with price supports and land-use controls equally bad. Subsidy prices give consumers more wheat at a lower price per unit, while the other two instruments give them less wheat at greater cost.

From the taxpayer's point of view, land-use controls are the cheapest, involving only administrative costs. Both price supports and subsidy prices involve large payments directly to farmers. Which of the two is more expensive for taxpayers depends on the exact shape and position of the supply and demand curves.

It is not quite so easy to say which of the three policies looks best from the economist's point of view. The answer may again depend on the exact shape and position of the supply and demand curves. However, most economists would agree that, other things being equal, the cost required to

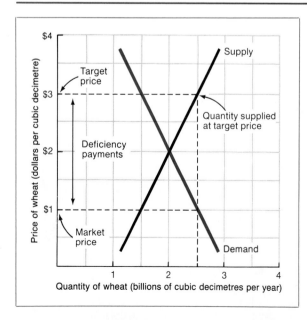

**Exhibit 27.8**
**The effects of subsidy prices**
Subsidy prices are a third way of raising the price of wheat to the desired level of $3/dm³. The government announces a subsidy price of $3/dm³ but does not actually offer to buy any wheat at this price. Farmers responding to the subsidy price increase the quantity they supply from 2 to 2.5 billion cubic decimetres. The increased quantity drives the market price down to $1/dm³. The government then makes a "deficiency payment" to farmers equal to the difference between the market price and the subsidy price.

secure a benefit of a given size should be minimized, regardless of who gets the benefit.

All three of the policy instruments discussed in this chapter involve some administrative costs. In the fiscal year 1978–1979, direct federal expenditures on agriculture amounted to close to $1.4 billion. All three also distort resource allocation in that they result in the wrong amount of wheat being produced. Under subsidy prices and price support, too much wheat is grown; and under land-use controls, too little is grown. Nonetheless, price supports and land-use controls involve certain additional costs that subsidy prices do not have. In the case of price supports, the cost is that of keeping wheat in storage to shore up the market price, instead of letting people eat it. In the case of land-use controls, the cost is the extra labor and capital required to grow each cubic decimetre of wheat when the use of land is artificially restricted. Without the alternative of a freely competitive market in wheat, many economists would therefore choose subsidy prices as the best of the three alternatives.

Case 27.1 illustrates the difficulty that government policy makers face when trying to enforce quota systems. Farmers, of course, see such quotas as a direct threat to their income. Further, the distorting effect of government-set prices should be noted. Because the set price for wheat was scheduled to fall by less than the set price for other grains such as barley, farmers were interpreting this to mean that more wheat should be grown, while policy makers were hoping that the production of *all* grain would decline.

## Case 27.1
## Farmer's Reactions to Grain Quotas

Grain farmer Peter Wiens of Midale, Sask., like thousands of other Prairies farmers, says he simply can't afford to go along with federal government recommendations to reduce grain planting this spring. [1983].

The proposal came from Senator Hazen Argue, minister responsible for the Canadian Wheat Board, and it was delivered hard on the heels of American programs that will idle one-third of U.S. grain acreage. The fiery Argue told Prairie producers last week they should cooperate with American efforts to reduce world grain stocks and bolster prices by seeding 3.5 million fewer acres of wheat and barley—a 9 percent cut.

"It is important, I think, in a world context that we have co-operation among the exporting nations," said the minister, known as Blazin' Hazen.

But farmers appear far more concerned with their individual balance sheets than the global outlook. As Wiens puts it: "What's the alternative? We have to produce enough to stay in business another year."

It seems most of the Prairies' 145,000 grain producers aren't in the mood for substantial cutbacks. Statistics Canada said late last week that grain farmers plan to reduce barley seeding less than Argue wants, while increasing their wheat acreages 7 percent over last year's record.

The survey was taken before Argue's recommendation and a further announcement that initial prices paid to farmers for grain—and guaranteed by the federal government—will be cut at the start of the new crop year, Aug. 1. But because the payment for wheat will be reduced just 2.5 percent, less than that for other crops, grain analysts say Argue has effectively told farmers to grow more wheat and not less.

Source: Edward Greenspon, "Grain Farmers Head for Peck of Trouble," *The Financial Post*, April 16, 1983, p.1.

There are now more than 120 marketing boards in Canada, controlling more than one-quarter of total agricultural output. Governments support these boards by making it compulsory for all producers of a given commodity to adhere to the regulations of their marketing board. The most powerful boards are the fluid milk boards or commissions, which directly fix prices and establish marketing quotas for dairy farmers.[7] Poultry product marketing boards set marketing quotas and minimum sales prices.

These boards have helped to ensure for all farmers the same basic price for their product, as well as uniform and fair quality standards. They are all, however, "monopoly" adaptations to what would otherwise be an extremely competitive industry.

## MARKET FAILURE IN THE FORM OF EXTERNALITIES

The market problems examined so far in this chapter have all been related to the breakdown of perfectly competitive markets. That is, the problems would not exist if markets could be kept perfectly competitive and non-destructive. However, even when markets are competitive and performing their functions as efficiently as possible, they may not always be able to provide for the best allocation of some goods and services.

Such market failure occurs when goods have negative or positive spill-over effects. (Economists sometimes call these external effects or externalities.) **Externalities** are the incidental benefits (positive externalities) or costs (negative externalities) that accompany economic activities. They have their effects upon persons whom the market neither charges for benefits nor compensates for costs. Economic theory shows that the market, left to itself, will produce too many goods with negative externalities and too few goods with positive externalities.

As an example of negative externalities, consider the pollution that accompanies the production of pulp and paper. Such pollution may reduce the income of fishermen and of people dependent on the tourist industry.

**Externality** This refers to an incidental benefit or "cost" that accompanies an economic activity and affects persons whom the market does not compensate or charge for the cost or the benefit.

---

[7]This information is based on G.A. Hiscocks and T.A. Bennett, "Marketing Boards and Pricing in Canada," in *The Canadian Economy*, ed. Ruggeri, (Toronto: Gage, 1977); pp. 265–272.

---

**Exhibit 27.9**
**Private and social costs for a hypothetical pulp and paper mill**

| a)          Costs | Tonnes of Paper | | | |
|---|---|---|---|---|
|  | 2,000 | 3,000 | 4,000 | 5,000 |
| Total private costs ($) | 100,000 | 300,000 | 600,000 | 1,000,000 |
| Marginal private costs ($) | | 200 | 300 | 400 |

| b)          Costs | Tonnes of Paper | | | |
|---|---|---|---|---|
|  | 2,000 | 3,000 | 4,000 | 5,000 |
| Total private costs ($) | 100,000 | 300,000 | 600,000 | 1,000,000 |
| Total external costs ($) | 25,000 | 75,000 | 150,000 | 250,000 |
| Total social costs ($) | 125,000 | 375,000 | 750,000 | 1,250,000 |
| Marginal social costs ($) | | 250 | 375 | 500 |

The mill owner's cost of producing an extra tonne of paper may be called the *marginal private cost*. The extra cost to fishermen and tourist operators may be called the *marginal external cost*. The two costs combined are the *marginal social cost*.

## Marginal Social Cost: The Example of a Paper Mill

Assume the cost structure shown in Exhibit 27.9a for a private, competitive mill operator. Increasing output from 2,000 t to 3,000 t increases the cost of each tonne by $200. Increasing output from 4,000 t to 5,000 t has a marginal private cost of $400/t. Assume that the competitively determined market price is $300/t. Each firm, in other words, faces a horizontal demand curve at a price of $300, as depicted in Exhibit 27.10. This firm, on the basis of the calculation of its private costs, will produce 4,000 t of paper, because the cost of the four thousandth tonne is $300, or MC = MR, where MC refers to marginal private costs and MR refers to marginal revenue. This is shown by the crossing of the MPC and demand curves in Exhibit 27.10, at $E_1$.

The problem is that, at an output level of 4,000 t, the marginal social cost may be greater than $300. In other words, the marginal benefit to society of the four thousandth tonne of paper, as measured by the price that society is willing to pay per tonne ($300), may be exceeded by the marginal cost to society of producing that four thousandth tonne. This possibility is illustrated in Exhibit 27.9b, where the external costs of producing paper are included in the cost calculations.

Assume that a social analysis of this hypothetical paper mill has revealed social costs to be 25 percent greater than private costs. That is, if the costs of pollution are added to direct private costs, the total "social cost" of producing 2,000 t of paper is $125,000, not $100,000, and the social cost of producing 4,000 t is $750,000, not $600,000. This result is depicted

---

**Exhibit 27.10**
**Demand and marginal cost curves for a hypothetical pulp and paper mill**

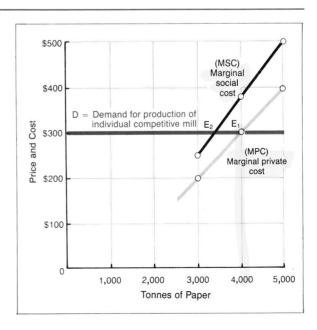

in Exhibit 27.10 by the marginal social cost (MSC) curve, representing costs that are 25 percent higher than the MPC curve. Note that if the producer were forced to consider the marginal social costs and not the marginal private costs, he would not produce 4,000 t of paper. At 4,000 t, marginal revenue is $300, but the marginal social cost is $375. In our example, marginal social costs at 4,000 t exceed by $75 the marginal social benefits as given by the demand curve. If forced to consider marginal social costs, the producer would reduce production to somewhere between 3,000 and 4,000 t where the MSC curve crosses his demand curve. The important conclusion that can be drawn from this is that when the producer considers only his private marginal costs, he will produce too much of a good with negative externalities. If he could be forced, somehow, to include external costs in his cost calculations, he would reduce output.

### Making Producers Responsive to Social Costs

Some way must be found to require such a producer to consider social costs, and not simply private costs, in determining his optimum level of output. In theory this could be done by having all private citizens who are harmed by the pollution take action against the producer, either by negotiating privately with him for compensation or by taking him to court. Actions of this type are not unknown, but the transactions costs of arranging for the numerous settlements that would likely be required could be enormous. It would likely be more efficient to have the government intervene on behalf of all those who are negatively affected.

The government could force the producer to compensate directly those who suffer from the pollution, or it might levy special taxes on the producer, the revenue of which would be used by the government to provide compensation to victims. The cost of such taxes would raise the marginal private cost of production so that it would approximate the marginal cost depicted in Exhibit 27.10. Alternatively, the government could force the producer to install equipment that would prevent the pollution from occurring. This too would increase the producer's private costs so that they approximate the true social costs of production.

### Positive Externalities

The external effects of production can be positive as well as negative. Take education as an example. The parents of children might, in a market system without government intervention, be the only purchasers of education for children. Yet many other people in society, including men and women without children, can be said to benefit from a school system set up to educate children. The market, however, cannot coerce them into paying for such benefits. In the absence of coercion, too little of the product "education" might be provided. This possibility is illustrated in Exhibit 27.11.

The marginal private cost curve indicates the additional costs that a private contractor might incur for each additional "pupil place" he would be willing to provide. The private contractor would build and organize a school in response to parents' demand for schooling. It might, for example, cost him $500,000 to build a school for 1,000 pupils, and $1,200,000 for a school to accommodate 2,000 pupils. The cost per pupil for the extra 1,000 pupils would be $700. This indicated at $E_1$ in Exhibit 27.11, as one point on the MPC curve. The additional cost per pupil of providing for another 1,000 pupils is shown along the MPC curve to be $800 (at 3,000 pupil places). If the contractor built a school for 4,000 pupils the additional cost per pupil would be $1,000.

The demand curve indicates that parents are willing to pay the contractor $700 for each child they wish to place in the school. The contractor is only one of many such contractors, so the demand curve that he faces is horizontal at $700. In the situation illustrated in Exhibit 27.11, the contractor would build a school for 2,000 pupils, where MPC = MR. (at $E_1$).

Assume now that the government decides that the schooling of each child provides a benefit of $100 to society at large. This means, in effect, that the marginal social cost of providing classroom space for a given number of pupils will be less than the marginal private cost. If, for example, the direct private cost of building a school for 1,000 pupils is $500,000, as was assumed above, the social cost is only $400,000 (a benefit of $100 being ascribed to each student). If the private cost of building a school for 2,000 pupils is again $1,200,000, the social cost would be $1,000,000. The additional per pupil cost of moving from the smaller to the larger school is only $600 in terms of social costs, not $700 as it was for private costs. This is illustrated in Exhibit 27.11 by the Marginal Social Cost curve (MSC)

**Exhibit 27.11**
**Private and social costs of providing a good or
service with positive externalities**
The social costs of providing an education for children
may be less than the private costs, after social benefits
have been added to private costs. In such a case, a private
market system might produce too little of the
good.

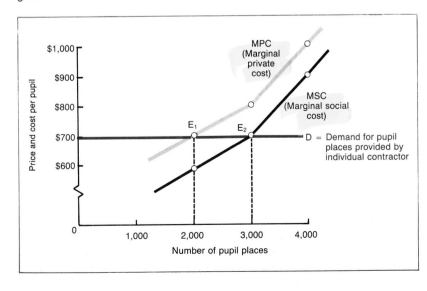

which lies below the MPC curve, increasing from $600 for an educational unit providing 2,000 pupil places to $700 for one providing 3,000 places.

If the contractor could be persuaded to produce where marginal social cost equals marginal revenue (at $E_2$), the best solution from society's point of view would be obtained. Now 3,000 pupil places would be provided instead of 2,000. This could be accomplished by having the government tax every citizen the equivalent of $100 for each pupil entering school and giving the contractor a subsidy per pupil of that amount. Such a subsidy would shift his marginal private cost down to the right, to lie along the marginal social cost curve. Alternatively, the government could give parents of school children a grant of $100 for each child enrolled in school, which would shift the demand curve up to $800. The new demand curve would cross the MPC curve at 3,000 pupil places, the same number as given at $E_2$.

In general, we can conclude that when external effects are negative the market will allocate too many resources to the production of that good. When the external effects are positive, not enough resources will be allocated by the market. In some extreme cases, where there are substantial, positive external effects but no practical way for the producer to charge most of the people who benefit, the market left to itself may allocate no resources to the production of such a good or service. For example, it would cost a private person an enormous amount to build an adequate military defense against a foreign power. Once the facility was built, there would be no incentive for the neighbors, who would also benefit from the defense system, to pay for the benefits. Without government provision of this service, and without taxes imposed on citizens to pay for it, society might be robbed of an adequate defense system. For citizens to possess such services the market system must, as a minimum, be supplemented by nonmarket institutions like government.

Case 27.2 illustrates this type of problem. Improvements to a major thoroughfare in a small town are delayed, partly because the benefits would be enjoyed by many people and, without government intervention, the costs would be borne by a few.

### Case 27.2
### An Example of Market Failure

Main Street property owners in Steinbach Monday overwhelmingly rejected a proposal to rebuild utilities, sidewalks, and boulevards along the thoroughfare at an estimated cost of well over $1 million.

The merchants told town council at a special meeting called to assess property owners' opinions on the proposal that the price of reconstruction is too steep during a period of economic recession.

Realtor George Penner added some property owners also believed the town's taxpayers at large should pay for a portion of Main Street improvements since he felt all residents benefitted from an attractive downtown appearance.

Source: "Merchants Say No to Main Street Proposal" *The Carillon*, Steinbach, Man. Vol. 38, No. 2 p.1.

### SUMMARY

1. Economic theory shows that competitive markets are remarkably efficient in satisfying consumer wants. However, many markets in

Canada are not very competitive, some suffer from destructive competitiveness, and in others with significant externalities, even perfect competition would not guarantee optimal results. Governments have tried to cope with such problems either through indirect social legislation, as in anticombines laws, or through direct control of prices, entry and exit conditions, and production quotas.

2. Anticombines policy is that area of public policy designed to control market structure and the competitive behavior of firms.

3. The foundations of anticombines policy in Canada go back to the first Anticombines Act of 1889, which preceded the Sherman Antitrust Act in the United States by one year. This act, together with amendments and subsequent court interpretations, places constraints on business behavior. The prohibition of price fixing has been the most important constraint on what firms can do. In addition, laws prohibiting certain kinds of *vertical restraints*—such as tied-sale contracts and resale price maintenance—and many forms of price discrimination have also been enforced with some success. However, attempts to limit the growth of companies through merger have largely failed.

4. Economists are far from united on what course anticombines policy should take in the future. Attempts by the federal government to establish a civil tribunal to adjudicate mergers and other forms of enterprise coordination have been stymied by strong opposition from the business community.

5. A natural monopoly is an industry in which total costs are minimized by having just one producer serve the entire market. The policy problem raised by natural monopoly is how to keep the single producer from exploiting its monopoly power to raise prices and restrict output. The traditional solution is to impose maximum price regulation in order to limit the firm's rate of return to a normal level. In practice, however, the effectiveness of such regulation may be rather limited.

6. Regulation, at least as currently practiced, is not highly regarded by most economists today. The economic case against regulation can be expressed in terms of two fundamental propositions. First, regulatory agencies and proceedings become dominated by efforts to redistribute income and wealth among participants in regulated markets, and this inevitably has a negative impact on economic efficiency. Second, even when regulators conscientiously try to make markets work more efficiently, they more often than not fail because regulation is not as effective as the market for making economic decisions and utilizing economic information.

7. Many agricultural markets fit the structural requirements of perfect competition very closely. They have large numbers of small firms, homogeneous products, good information systems, and free entry and exit. Farmers, however, regard perfect competition as a mixed blessing. The demand for most farm products is price inelastic; as a result, prices fluctuate sharply as the size of the crop varies from year to year. Demand is also income inelastic, with the result that the growth of demand for farm goods has not kept pace with the growth of farm productivity. This has led to depressed farm incomes.

8. One way for farmers to enhance their incomes and stabilize prices

would be to form cartels. However, it would be very difficult to form purely voluntary cartels in agriculture because of the large number of producers and the ease of entry. In some cases, government policy makes it possible for farmers to engage in cartel-like practices.

9. Price supports are an instrument of farm policy that can be used to stabilize prices and enhance farm incomes. The government announces a support price higher than the competitive equilibrium price. That induces farmers to move up along their supply curve, increasing total quantity supplied. To maintain the support price, the government must purchase the excess quantity supplied and keep it off the market. Price supports result in high prices to consumers and substantial storage costs for taxpayers.

10. Land-use controls are a policy sometimes used to raise farm prices without encouraging surplus production. They shift the supply curve upward, which means a higher equilibrium price and a lower equilibrium quantity than without controls. However, farmers respond to these controls by applying increased labor and capital to each piece of land, thereby raising the cost of production. These increased production costs offset the advantage that farmers get from the high prices.

11. Subsidy prices are a method of raising farm incomes without raising consumer prices. Under this policy, the government announces a subsidy price above the competitive equilibrium price but does not agree to buy surplus output. Farmers increase output, thereby driving down the market price. The government makes up the difference between the market price and the subsidy price with deficiency payments to farmers.

12. Canadian farm policies are subject to many criticisms. One objection is that the policies are very expensive for consumers. Another is that they pay too little attention to the goal of short-run stabilization and place too much emphasis on raising farm incomes. Still another is that they are ineffective in dealing with the problem of rural poverty, because most subsidies go to relatively prosperous farmers.

13. The production of some goods and services results in external benefits or "costs" for persons who can neither be charged nor compensated by the market.

14. Even a perfectly competitive market will not produce the optimal amount of such goods and services from the viewpoint of society. Without some mechanism for charging the producers of negative externalities, or for rewarding producers of positive externalities, too many goods and services with negative externalities will be produced, and two few with positive externalities.

15. The proper adjustments for such externalities may on occasion be made by private negotiations between the parties involved, but in many cases it is more efficient to have the government intervene to encourage production up to the point where marginal social costs equal marginal social benefits.

## DISCUSSION QUESTIONS

1. A young economist working for the Combines Branch in Ottawa was assigned to an investigation of a firm in Toronto accused of price fixing. When the young

investigator confronted the president of the firm and informed him that he would need to look at all of the firm's files, the president retorted: "The trouble with this country is government bureaucrats like you interfering in the operation of a free market economy. Why don't you leave us alone? Haven't you ever heard of Adam Smith?" How would you have responded to these remarks?

2. Compare and contrast anticombines laws and regulation as alternative policies toward monopoly. Why is sometimes one and sometimes another used?

3. In the case of a true natural monopoly, do you think it would be best to have regulated private monopoly, public ownership of the monopoly, or an unregulated private monopoly? How do considerations of efficiency enter into your choice? Considerations of fairness?

4. What aspects of the farm problem are problems from the farmer's point of view only, and what aspects are problems from the consumer's point of view as well? Is a low average level of farm prices a problem for consumers? For a given average level of farm prices, are unstable prices a problem for consumers? Explain.

5. Other things being equal, we would expect that a policy of land-use quotas but no output quotas would cause an increase in output per piece of land. (Explain why.) Would this policy also be expected to cause an increase in output per worker hour? Why or why not? If not, how could you explain the sharp rise in productivity per worker hour in agriculture that took place during the 1950s?

6. Many of the Great Lakes have become seriously polluted. Among the people damaged by this pollution are the owners of lakefront property. Do you think that these owners ought to be permitted to bring suit against any company polluting the lake on which their property is located? If such suits were permitted, do you think many would be brought? Should property owners who win their cases against polluters be able to obtain cease-and-desist orders stopping all further pollution, or should they simply be awarded monetary damages? Explain.

7. If a case is made for government intervention in the field of education, would it be sufficient to have the government impose taxes and redistribute the revenue to either parents or contractors, or is it necessary to have the government become involved in the provision of educational services? In Case 27.2, would it be necessary for the government actually to make the road improvement in order to have it done? What is the actual minimum function that governments must assume in such situations?

# THE ECONOMICS OF ENERGY

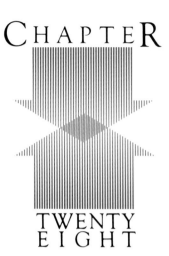

CHAPTER

TWENTY EIGHT

## WHAT YOU WILL LEARN IN THIS CHAPTER

*This chapter covers selected topics in the economics of energy. It begins by introducing a theory of the allocation of nonrenewable resources over time. It discusses both competitive markets and markets dominated by cartels. It then examines recent Canadian oil and natural gas policies in the light of this allocation theory, paying special attention to the effects of price controls and subsidies. The remainder of the chapter is devoted to the principal energy alternatives to oil and natural gas, coal, electricity, nuclear power, and solar power.*

## FOR REVIEW

*Here are some important terms and concepts that will be put to use in this chapter. If you do not understand them, review them before proceeding.*

- *Staple products (Chapter 1)*
- *Positive and normative economics (Chapter 1)*
- *The BNA Act (Chapter 4)*
- *Elasticity of supply and demand (Chapter 20)*
- *Monopoly and cartels (Chapter 24)*
- *Price discrimination (Chapter 24)*

This chapter will examine in detail an important industry sector—*natural resources*—for which a special branch of economic study has been developed. As was noted in Chapter 1, natural or primary resources have always played an important role in Canadian economic development. Beginning with the fish and fur industries, the resources of farming, forestry, mining, and energy production were developed in succession to form an important base for the whole economy. Even today, as Exhibit 28.1 illustrates, primary resources play a significant role in Canada's crucial export market.

Our main concern in this chapter is with nonrenewable natural resources, such as oil, gas and certain minerals, whose exploitation leads ultimately to its depletion and exhaustion. An important rationale for government intervention in such resource sectors, therefore, becomes one of conservation.[1]

---

[1]This observation, and some of the following analysis, is based on Nancy D. Olewiler, *The Regulation of Natural Resources in Canada: Theory and Practice*, Technical Report No. 4 (Ottawa: Economic Council of Canada, 1981).

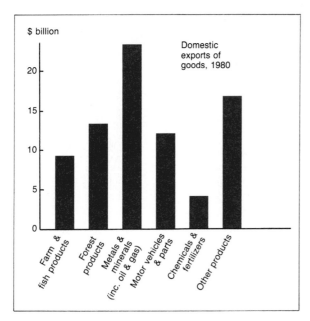

$ billion

Domestic exports of goods, 1980

Farm & fish products · Forest products · Metals & minerals (inc. oil & gas) · Motor vehicles & parts · Chemicals & fertilizers · Other products

**Exhibit 28.1**
**Canada's Exports, 1980**
Export numbers highlight Canada's dependency on resources. Consider, for instance, that basic products from the land, forest, ground and sea accounted for almost 60 percent of our foreign sales in 1980. By contrast, the U.S. resource tally in exports was in the order of one-third.

Our huge trading surplus in 1980 of about $25 billion in raw and semi-processed goods more than offset a deficit of $17 billion in fully manufactured goods, such as machinery and consumer products.

The resulting $8-billion surplus on trade in goods in 1980 stands out as a high point among most industrial nations. But every silver lining has a cloud and ours is an immense international deficit on services (interest, dividends, travel, shipping and the like), largely because of the payments we must make each year on the vast inflows of capital in years past.

Source: *The Financial Post* Sept. 5, 1981, p. 523.

We will focus particularly on those natural resources that make up the energy sector of the economy. The availability of energy is something that used to be taken for granted. Today, however, energy, more than any other commodity, symbolizes the problem of scarcity. Such diverse topics as inflation, unemployment, regional tensions, and international diplomacy cannot be discussed without bringing energy into consideration. As the Economic Council of Canada noted recently, "Although economists are often accused of not being able to agree on anything, there is virtual unanimity in the profession right now that the future of the Canadian economy over the next decade will depend on energy."[2] It seems appropriate, then, to devote a chapter to the economics of energy and energy policy, beginning with nonrenewable energy resources and moving on to possible alternatives.

## THE ECONOMICS OF OIL AND NATURAL GAS

As Exhibit 28.2 shows, the nonrenewable fossil fuels—oil and natural gas —are the most important current sources of energy in Canada. Together they made up 65 percent of our energy supplies in 1975. Though this proportion will decline in the next few decades, it is still predicted to be as high as 50 percent in the year 2000. Electricity is also a significant source of energy; about one-third of it is generated from nonrenewable sources such as coal and uranium, the other two-thirds from renewable hydro-electric power.

The economics of oil and gas, as well as part of the economics of

[2]Economic Council of Canada, *au courant*, Vol. 2, No. 2 (1980), p. 10.

electricity, is concerned mainly with allocation over time. When is it best to use the limited stocks available? We will begin to answer this question with an examination of the fairly well-developed branch of economics dealing with nonrenewable resources, sometimes called the **theory of the mine**.

**Theory of the mine** The branch of economics concerned with the allocation over time of nonrenewable natural resources.

**Exhibit 28.2**

**Changing patterns of energy supply in Canada**

Oil and natural gas together will remain the most important energy source in Canada into the twenty-first century. However, electricity will grow in significance as our nonrenewable sources of energy are used up. New sources of renewable energy such as solar energy, may also assume considerable importance by the year 2020.

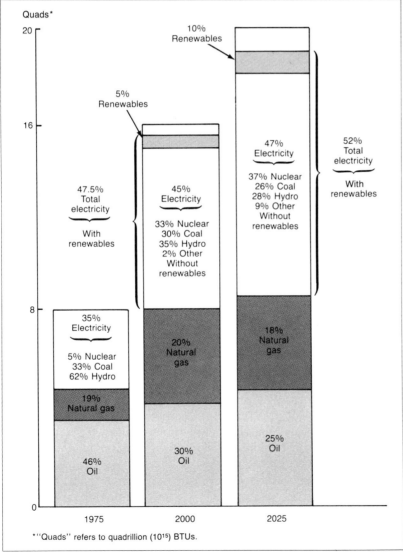

Quads*

| | 1975 | 2000 | 2025 |

10% Renewables

5% Renewables

47.5% Total electricity With renewables

45% Electricity
33% Nuclear
30% Coal
35% Hydro
2% Other
Without renewables

47% Electricity
37% Nuclear
26% Coal
28% Hydro
9% Other
Without renewables

52% Total electricity With renewables

35% Electricity
5% Nuclear
33% Coal
62% Hydro

19% Natural gas

46% Oil

20% Natural gas

30% Oil

18% Natural gas

25% Oil

*"Quads" refers to quadrillion ($10^{15}$) BTUs.

Source: *Business Life*, December 1979, p. 15.

## Introduction to the Theory of Nonrenewable Resources (Theory of the Mine)

The most vital economic decision, according to this theory, is when to extract and use the limited stock of resources that a mine contains. This decision involves a strict trade-off between the present and the future: what is used today cannot be used tomorrow, and what is conserved cannot be used today. Both immediate use and delayed use have advantages. Immediate use permits gratification of consumer demand without delay or permits use of the resource for investment purposes, thereby increasing tomorrow's supply of productive capital. Delayed use is advantageous because, to the extent that any of the resource is consumed today, what remains will be scarcer and hence more valuable in the future.

*The Case of Competitive Markets* The way resource owners handle the trade-off between present and future use depends, among other things, on the structure of the markets in which they operate. As often is true, the case of perfectly competitive markets provides a useful benchmark. Consider, for the sake of illustration, the market for natural gas, assuming for the present that the market is perfectly competitive, that the quantity of natural gas available for extraction is known, and that the cost of extracting it is zero.

Under these idealized conditions the only decision left to gas well owners is whether to extract their gas and sell it now or to conserve all or part of it for the future. If the owners are motivated primarily by financial considerations, they can be expected to make the choice that will maximize their total wealth. Keeping the gas in the ground means holding that wealth in the form of a reserve of energy that can be expected to increase in value in the future. Extracting the gas and selling it today allows the conversion of the wealth to other forms—for example, corporate stocks or government bonds—that can be expected to earn their owners a normal rate of return on the invested capital.

It follows that the decision of when to sell the gas depends on a comparison of the market rate of return available outside the gas industry with the rate at which the price of gas is expected to increase in the future. Suppose, for example, that the market rate of return on alternative investments is 10 percent per year, that the price of gas today is $3 per thousand litres and that this price is expected to rise at the rate of 5 percent per year. Selling 1 million litres of gas at today's prices and investing the proceeds at 10 percent will give a gas well owner a sum of $3,300 at the end of a year. Alternatively, leaving the same 1 million litres of gas in the ground and selling it at $3.15 per thousand litres next year will yield a sum of $3,150. Under these assumed conditions, then, it will be most profitable to sell the gas today.

However, there is a limit to how much gas will be sold currently, because today's sales of gas tend to change the conditions initially assumed to prevail. For one thing, greater supplies of gas brought to market today will tend to depress the price below the assumed level of $3 per thousand litres. In addition, more sales today will reduce the stocks available for the future, thereby reducing future supplies and increasing the future price. As

**Exhibit 28.3**
**Market allocation over time of a nonrenewable resource**
The market price of a nonrenewable resource tends to rise over time. Supply and
demand conditions limit the rate of depletion, so the price will not rise at a rate
faster than the rate of interest. As the price rises, the rate of use falls, other things
being equal.

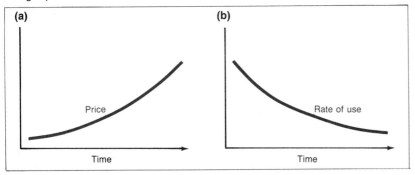

the price today falls and the expected future price rises, the expected percentage increase of next year's price over this year's price also rises. As
soon as the expected rate of price increase becomes equal to the rate of
return available on alternative investments, it will no longer be profitable
to sell today. Any owners who have not yet sold will conserve their supplies for the future, because it will pay them to do so.

In short, when a resource exists in known, fixed quantity and the cost of
extraction is low, a competitive market will allocate that resource over
time, as shown in Exhibit 28.3. The price will rise over time at a rate equal
to the market rate of interest. Other things being equal, the rate of use will
fall as the price rises.[3]

*Some Qualifications* The preceding argument puts a ceiling on the rate at
which the price of a scarce resource will increase and the rate at which it
will be used up. However, there are circumstances in which the rate of the
price increase is less rapid than the interest rate because the rate of
depletion is slower than implied. In particular, this will be the case if the
resource is costly to extract or if high prices stimulate a search for new
reserves or for substitutes.

If, for example, the current price of a resource is equal to the current
marginal cost of extracting it, the quantity supplied will be limited by the
quantity demanded at the current price rather than by the expected effect
of current use on future prices. The quantity demanded may very well not
be high enough to deplete the resource fast enough to push its future price
up at a rate equal to the interest rate. Alternatively, if there are reserves of a
resource that cannot be profitably extracted today but that can be used if
the price rises a little, the presence of those reserves will limit the rate of
price increase, because it will increase expected future supply.

---

[3]If economic growth or population growth causes demand for the resource to increase as time goes by,
this pattern may be somewhat modified. The rate of price increase will still not exceed the interest rate,
but the rate of use can, for a time, increase before it begins to taper off.

In practice, the usable reserves of many important resources do appear to increase quite elastically as demand and prices rise. This is partly because higher prices make it worthwhile to spend more money on exploration and partly because they make it worthwhile to exploit known low-grade reserves. Therefore, the assumption of absolutely fixed quantities of known reserves is a very restrictive one. In Canada, for example, natural gas reserves were increasing in the early 1980s, while reserves of crude oil were declining. The latter trend could, of course, be reversed with new discoveries.

*Effects of a Cartel* Up to this point, it has been assumed that the markets in which nonrenewable resources are bought and sold are perfectly competitive. With the rise of OPEC during the 1970s, however, economists have become increasingly interested in the situation where a nonrenewable resource is controlled by a cartel rather than supplied competitively.

Chapter 24 showed that under given conditions of demand and cost, a cartel tends to supply a smaller quantity at a higher price than does a competitively organized market. By reducing the quantity supplied and raising the price, the cartel benefits its members by increasing profit per unit sold. Profit is maximized at the point where marginal cost and marginal revenue are equal. Exhibit 28.4 makes the comparison between the output chosen by a cartel and that resulting from competition under the simplifying assumption of constant marginal cost.

Because they sell a smaller quantity at a higher price, cartels are more conservational than competitive markets. If, for example, a cartel were suddenly formed in a resource market that had been perfectly competitive,

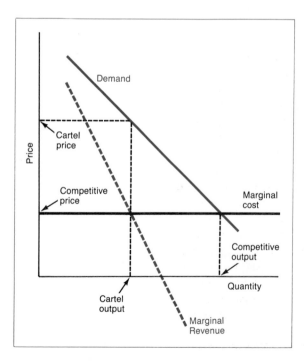

**Exhibit 28.4**
**Comparison of a competitive market and a cartel**
For the same conditions of cost and demand, producers in a competitive market will tend to supply more each period than will the same producers organized as a cartel. The competitive market produces a quantity that makes marginal cost equal to price; the cartel maximizes profits at the quantity that makes marginal cost equal to marginal revenue.

its first act would be to cut back production. Only in that way could the market price be raised. As a by-product of this profit-maximizing action, more of the resource would be left in the second and each subsequent year than would have been the case under competition.

What is more, an additional factor may tend to make natural resource cartels even more conservational than the preceding argument implies. That factor is the possibility that the cartels will try to practice intertemporal price discrimination. According to the theory of price discrimination, cartels will cut back production most sharply in markets with the most inelastic demand, because they can profit most by raising the price in such markets. Thus, if a cartel expects future demand for its product to be more elastic than present demand, it will discriminate against present buyers by raising the price very high initially. The high price will further slow the present rate of consumption. In the case of an oil cartel, it seems reasonable to believe that present demand is in fact less elastic than demand will be in the future, because the technology of substitute energy sources is constantly improving.

### Is the Market Rate of Use Optimal?

The theory of the mine shows that the market contains a built-in conservation mechanism. In effect, it transforms predictions of future scarcity into actions for present conservation, as profit-maximizing resource owners opt to sell at higher future prices rather than low present prices.

But an important question remains: might it not be wise to be more conservational still? That is, should current resource owners do future generations a favor by leaving them an even greater endowment of nonrenewable resources than that which the market forces dictate? The question of obligations toward future generations raises profound normative issues. Previous generations toiled in mines, fields, and factories, enduring great hardships to accumulate the stock of capital on which present wealth depends. Many people today believe that they themselves should do no less for their own descendants. Fortunately, it is not necessary to resolve all the great ethical questions of income distribution among the generations in order to answer the narrower question of how rapidly nonrenewable resources should be used up. The reason is that the conservation of nonrenewable resources is a question not of how much wealth should be left for future generations but of what form that wealth should be left in.

Basically, there are two tangible forms in which to leave wealth to future generations. One form is capital. It can be produced in as much quantity as people want, provided they are willing to abstain from the present consumption of income and to invest the resulting saving. The other form is natural resources. They cannot be created, but they can be conserved. Even after the decision of how much total wealth to leave to the next generation is made, there is still a need to decide how much of that wealth to leave in each of the two forms. At that point, it is surely ethically acceptable for people to think of themselves and to adjust the mix in such a way that their own sacrifices are minimized.

Once the matter is put this way, it is easy to determine, at least in principle, the optimum degree of conservation of nonrenewable resources. A dollar's worth of nonrenewable resources should be extracted today and invested in durable capital goods if and only if the future value of the resulting capital is greater than the future value of the natural resources if they are left in the ground. The future value of the capital can be determined by compounding the current rate of saving at the prevailing rate of interest. The rule just given can thus be restated as the instruction to extract resources in the present unless the value of those resources in the future, as measured by their market price, will be likely to rise at a rate more rapid than the interest rate. As previously shown, a competitive market economy operates in such a way as to ensure that this rule will not be violated. If monopolitistic tendencies make markets more conservational than the rule implies, people must bear a greater than necessary burden in the present for any given endowment that they choose to pass along to the future; but the error will be one of leaving too many, not too few, natural resources.

## The Canadian Oil and Gas Industry: Three Key Players

So far, we have assumed that the prices of oil and gas are determined in either a competitive market or a market dominated by an unrestricted cartel. Actual oil and gas policy in Canada has not corresponded to either of these assumptions for some time, however. Instead, both energy sources have been subject to price controls and other government measures.

*The Private Sector*  The determination of price and output in the oil and natural gas industry is the result of constant interaction between several key "players" in the industry. First, there are the large private oil companies, such as Imperial Oil, Texaco, and Shell, who explore, refine, and distribute the product. These private firms are mostly foreign owned— as the next chapter will discuss in more detail—and they are vertically integrated. This means that they control the various stages of production from exploration through to retail selling. The natural gas industry is not as concentrated. In addition to the large oil companies, which are also involved in the exploration and development of natural gas, there are three large companies that handle the transmission of natural gas, and a number of distribution companies whose rates are regulated by provincial governments, as we saw in Chapter 27. The privately owned companies are subject to numerous government restrictions and regulations, but they are powerful enough to influence at least some of the policies affecting them. When, for example, new price controls, taxes, and royalty payments were imposed on them in 1974, they moved some of their oil rigs to the United States and threatened to stall the development of the industry. After using such tactics, they were successful in obtaining tax and royalty concessions.

*Provincial Governments*  Provincial governments form a second set of important players in the oil and natural gas industry, particularly the government of Alberta. Alberta accounts for more than 85 percent of Canada's oil production and between 80 and 85 percent of its natural gas output (British

Columbia and Saskatchewan account for almost all the rest). Under the British North America Act, natural resources fall under the jurisdiction of the provinces. In most cases, this has meant that the provinces have claimed ownership rights to mineral resources on lands that are otherwise privately owned. In Alberta, for example, 80 percent of all oil resources are owned by the province and leased to private companies for development (the other 20 percent comes from "freehold land," that is, property on which private interests hold the mineral rights). In practice, private companies obtain rights to develop the oil that the government owns. Then, as Case 28.1 indicates, the oil is sold to a central marketing board, the Alberta Petroleum Marketing Commission, at a price established by the provincial government. Private refiners, owned by the developers, then buy the oil for refining and sell it for export or to their domestic dealers.

## Case 28.1
## How pricing works

The decision by the Alberta government to unilaterally raise the price of oil gives new currency to terms such as "domestic price," "oil-import subsidy" and "world price." Here's a primer compiled by The Post's staff on what the politicians and oil-company executives are talking about.

*Now that Alberta has established a new oil price of $16.75 a barrel, does that mean all oil sold in Canada is going at that price?*

No, in fact, very little does. What Alberta has done is set a base price for a particular grade of crude oil. The actual prices paid to producers will vary according to sulphur content, weight (whether it flows freely or not) and distance from the central gathering point at Edmonton.

Here's how it works. The Alberta Petroleum Marketing Commission (APMC) is offering $16.75 a barrel on the sweet (low-sulphur) crude measured at 42 degrees API (the standard set by the American Petroleum Institute) gravity. For every 10% of additional sulphur content, subtract 2¢ a barrel. On each degree of gravity variance, include a 3¢ price change. The more sulphur and the heavier the oil the lower the price to the producer.

APMC pays for the crude at the wellhead and then sells it to refiners at Edmonton. The buyers, of which there are 23, must qualify for inclusion in APMC's approved buyers' list before they may "nominate" for APMC's oil.

*What do we pay for imported oil?*

Canadian refiners pay what everyone else in the world pays. At the moment, the "target" price for OPEC oil is about US$32 per barrel. But, again, there is little oil available at that exact price. For instance, Mexican and Venezuelan crude costs much more. Other oil, such as that from Saudi Arabia, is somewhat less. According to officials at the federal Energy Department—who gather such data for the purpose of establishing a rate for subsidizing imports—the mixture of sources and types of oil being bought by Canadian buyers meant the average price for foreign oil delivered to Montreal in July was US$32.25, including transportation charges.

*How is the compensation level set?*

It's simple enough. Ottawa's Petroleum Compensation Board merely subtracts the average domestic price, including transportation charges to Montreal, from the average foreign price and pays the difference. The foreign price is calculated on the basis of a three-month moving average of oil source and type. The result can mean losses on some transactions if they involve higher-priced purchases or gains on others involving lower prices.

For July, Ottawa used a domestic price of C$15.42. That, with the foreign average pegged at US$32.25, left a subsidy of about C$21.35 a barrel. Canadian importers apply to Ottawa for a subsidy cheque covering each shipment of foreign oil.

*How much is the subsidy costing the taxpayer?*

Canada imports about 450,000 barrels of oil daily. So, in July, the subsidy was costing the federal treasury about $9.6 million a day. This month, with higher domestic prices, the tab will ease to about $8.7 million per day.

*But don't we also export oil?*

Canada exports significant quantities of both crude and oil products. Some of the exports are in the form of exchanges with the U.S. to cover regional needs. The 450,000-barrels-a-day estimate of imports ignores such trades. But, in addition, Canada sells a steadily declining quantity of heavy crudes to the northern U.S. refineries. In 1979, that flow amounted to about 57.5 million barrels, on which Ottawa collected an export tax worth about $576 million.

Canadian producers pumped more than 508 million barrels of oil in 1979. About 105 million barrels, including crude equivalents and exchanges, were exported. And we imported 222 million barrels, also including crude equivalents and exchanges.

*So that's why the nation remains energy-deficient?*

Actually, we enjoy a substantial *energy* surplus. We are simply *oil* deficient. The prebuild section of the Alaska Highway natural gas pipeline will mean greatly increased gas exports, but in 1979 alone, Western producers exported about one trillion cubic feet of gas, worth $2.9 billion. In addition, Canada exported coal worth $732 million and electricity worth $729 million.

Source: Excerpted from *The Financial Post*, August 9, 1982, p. 4.

Revenues for the provincial governments come from the sale of rights, from production royalties (which are really a form of direct tax), and from the provincial corporation income tax. These revenues have grown tremendously in the past decade, particularly in Alberta. In 1977, the Alberta government obtained more than $2 billion in royalties on oil and natural gas. In the four years from 1974 to 1977, royalty revenues exceeded $6 billion, or more than three times the amount collected in all previous years.

*The Federal Government* The third important player in this industry is the federal government. Its constitutional jurisdiction covers the interprovincial and foreign sale of oil and natural gas. Since most oil and natural gas is sold outside the producing provinces, the federal government has significant control over the ultimate price and sales conditions of these products. Further, the federal government derives revenue from the federal corporation income tax, from excise taxes on gasoline, and, more recently, from an oil export charge. In the fiscal year 1976–1977, these combined revenues exceeded $2 billion.

In addition, Ottawa has become heavily involved in oil exploration and development. In 1976 it created Petro-Canada, a 100 percent-owned crown corporation, for oil and gas production. Through a series of acquisitions of companies like Philips Petroleum and Pacific Petroleum, Petro-Canada has become the sixth-largest producer of oil in Canada, and the second-largest producer of natural gas. The federal government has also become a major participant in new oil exploration through substantial investments in companies like Panarctic Oils Ltd., Syncrude Oil, and a number of other companies.

## Conflict Over Energy Policies

With its control over export prices and federal taxes, and its aggressive move into oil and natural gas exploration and production, it was inevitable that the federal government would come into serious conflict with the major producing provinces, particularly Alberta. Overlapping jurisdictional problems became especially acute in the early 1970s, when the whole energy field was subject to new demand forces. Crude oil prices began to rise rapidly in 1971, as many countries perceived that there was a basic commodity shortage in the world. Prices accelerated in 1973 as a result of the Arab–Israeli war, which affected one of the major oil producing regions of the world, and the cartel-pricing policies of OPEC.

The major players in the Canadian oil and natural gas industry were faced with new profit opportunities as well as new problems. Each player of course, wanted to get a substantial piece of the rapidly expanding energy revenue pie. The private companies felt that they were entitled to increased profits because they were the risk takers in the industry. The provinces, as landlords of the natural resources, thought that they were entitled to increased rents on their property. The federal government, hard-pressed to balance its annual budgets, saw an opportunity to increase its revenues. It was also acutely aware of the impact that rising energy prices would have on the regional distribution of income and industry in the country. The sharp increase in energy revenues signified a substantial shift in Canada's development pattern. The shift was both a sectoral one —from manufacturing to natural resources—and a regional one, from Quebec and Ontario to Alberta and, to a lesser extent, British Columbia and Saskatchewan.[4]

For the sake of national economic efficiency, which involves the use of factors of production in their most profitable, productive way, it was desirable to shift resources such as labor and capital to the West. But not everyone can or will move to take advantage of new opportunities elsewhere. The relative increase in energy prices, combined with an inelastic demand for oil and natural gas, meant that incomes in the West would likely rise much more rapidly than in the East, both for companies and for individuals. The federal government felt compelled to even out some of the potential new disparities. But how? Federal taxes would appropriate a part of the increased energy revenues, but they could not touch the part of the revenues going to the province. To add to the federal dilemma, under the equalization programs described in Chapter 4, federal equalization payments to the have-not provinces were linked to the energy resources of the better-off provinces, but federal revenues were not. As energy prices rose sharply in 1973, Ottawa took steps to counteract some of their regional impact by freezing energy prices and by placing an export tax on shipments to the United States, equal to the difference between regulated Canadian prices and rising world prices. The federal government also placed limits on exports of oil and natural gas. Revenue from the export tax was used to subsidize imports of foreign oil to Eastern Canada

[4]This change is examined in Kenneth H. Norrie, "Energy, Canadian Federalism, and the West," *Research Paper No. 82-8*, University of Alberta. Some of the following analysis is based on this research paper.

from countries like Venezuela and Mexico. This policy of a uniform Canadian oil price, subject only to differences in transportation costs, was a major plank in the federal government's new efforts to dampen the effect of rising energy prices on oil-using provinces.

Not surprisingly, the federal government's freezing of prices, and its imposition of an export tax (meaning that producing provinces like Alberta could not take advantage of higher world prices), was met with considerable resistance by the oil and natural gas producing regions. The situation was exacerbated by the federal government's removal of previous tax concessions for the industry. The result was a series of vigorous confrontations and negotiations between private producers and government, and particularly between the provincial and federal governments. These discussions finally led to a compromise agreement, whereby taxes and other revenues from oil and natural gas would be apportioned so that the private producers and the producing provinces would each get 45 percent of the increased revenues and the federal government would get 10 percent. This agreement brought relative peace to the industry for several years. Domestic oil prices were permitted to increase, reaching 85 percent of the world level by 1978.

However, when world oil prices jumped sharply in 1979 and again in 1980, new conflicts developed. The federal government resisted pressures from the producing provinces to increase oil prices in line with world prices. In 1980 it introduced a new budget and simultaneously instituted a new **National Energy Program (NEP)**. Under this new program, oil and natural gas prices from existing wells would rise very slowly and remain considerably below world prices, but new oil and natural gas would obtain a higher price, around the world price level. At the same time, new federal excise taxes were imposed and a Canadianization levy was instituted to enable the federal government to purchase some of the foreign-owned oil companies with its revenues. The overall aim of NEP was to increase the federal share of oil revenues from 10 to 24 percent (primarily at the expense of private producers) and to give it more control over the energy sector through increased government participation and through more Canadianization of the industry. Canadian-owned firms were given preferential treatment in the granting of exploration subsidies.

**The National Energy Program (NEP)** The NEP was instituted in the fall of 1980 to slow the increase in the price of oil and natural gas, to provide the federal government with a greater share of revenues, and to further Canadianize the industry.

The previous system of levying export taxes and providing consumer subsidies to maintain a uniform price across the country was retained, but prices would now rise much more slowly than under the previous arrangements and more revenue would go to the federal coffers. It seemed to the Western producing provinces that through these new, unilateral initiatives, the federal government was usurping their constitutional rights. NEP led to a series of confrontations between the producing provinces and Ottawa. Alberta reduced oil deliveries to Eastern Canada and the federal government retaliated by raising excise taxes in order to pay for the increased imports that the partial provincial embargo necessitated. The development of the new oil sands project in Alberta was deliberately put on hold.

This damaging conflict finally produced a new agreement in September, 1981. The basic elements in this agreement were a faster increase in oil prices than permitted under NEP, with domestic prices allowed to rise to a maximum of 75 percent of world prices by 1986 (known as the 75 percent cap), and some additional federal taxes which, it was expected, would increase the federal share of oil and natural gas revenues to around 32 percent. Once again, a period of relative tranquility was achieved.

However, this last agreement proved to be vulnerable to the reversal in oil prices that occurred in 1982 to 1983. Partly because of the recession that was then taking place in most Western industrial nations, partly because of a successful shift on the part of these countries to substitutes for oil, and perhaps also because of growing instability within the OPEC cartel, world oil prices began to move down from their level of almost $35 per barrel to $30 or less. In the meantime, Canadian oil prices were scheduled under the latest agreement to rise in graduated steps. If they were allowed to continue to do so, they would soon exceed the 75 percent "cap" that had been placed on them. New agreements between the federal and provincial governments appeared to be necessary to resolve this problem. During these years too, as Case 28.1 showed, Canada moved from being a net exporter to a net importer of oil, causing the federal government to experience a sizable increase in its budget deficit, partly in order to pay the subsidy on the increased imports. Again the federal government looked to the energy sector as a possible source of increased revenues to solve its budget problems. For these reasons and others, the energy sector remained a source both of considerable promise and of sizable problems for the Canadian economy.

## An Economic Assessment of Canada's Oil and Natural Gas Policies

What can be said about the energy policies that have been followed in the oil and natural gas fields? First, much of the policy has been politically motivated. That is, all the principal players have sought to use energy

**Exhibit 28.5**
**Supply and demand for crude oil in Canada**
The graph illustrates the supply and demand for crude oil in Canada, with a world price of $P_F$ and an export tax/import subsidy of $P_F P_D$ per unit, which lowers the domestic price to $P_D$. A subsidy of ADEF is paid when the domestic price is kept at $P_D$. The government would save this amount if it allowed the price of oil to rise to the world level at $P_F$. At the same time, producer benefits would increase by the area $P_D FBP_F$ and consumer surplus would decrease by $P_D ECP_F$. The net benefit to society of the higher price would be represented by the shaded triangles ABF and CDE.

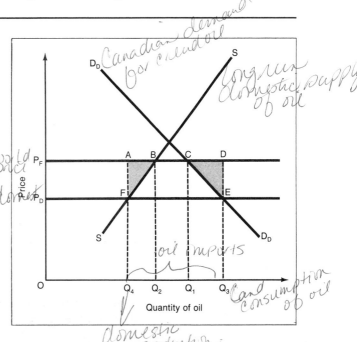

revenues to improve their budget positions, by tapping the increase in those revenues and by increasing their share of the revenues. Also, the federal government has followed national political objectives in supporting a one-Canadian-price policy and the increased Canadianization of the energy sector. Second, an attempt has been made to equalize the economic benefits and burdens of increased energy revenues for Canadians in different parts of the country. This has been done in the name of a fairer distribution of income.

An economic assessment of these policies must also examine their "efficiency" implications. Has the policy of keeping the Canadian price of oil below the world level, through a program of export taxes and consumer subsidies, permitted the most efficient utilization of oil and natural gas resources? An answer to this question can be formulated by using Exhibit 28.5.[5]

In this exhibit, the curve $D_D$ refers to Canadian domestic demand for crude oil, and S to the long-run domestic supply of oil. $P_F$ refers to the foreign demand for Canadian oil at world prices. It is assumed that Canada could export as much oil as it liked without affecting the current world price. The domestic price for Canadian oil is set at $P_D$, which is below the world price. A per-unit export tax equal to $P_F - P_D$ is imposed, equal to the difference between the world price and the domestic price. The effective price for Canadian purchasers of oil therefore is $P_D$, since it is assumed further that the tax is used to finance a subsidy so that even for foreign oil, Canadian purchasers pay only $P_D$. At the price $P_D$, total Canadian consumption of oil will be $Q_3$. Domestic production will be the lower amount, $Q_4$, and the difference, $Q_3 - Q_4$, represents net oil imports. The government is required to make subsidy payments of ADEF.

Assume now that the government decided to drop its export tax/subsidy policy and allowed the domestic price to rise to the world price, $P_F$. At $P_F$, domestic demand for oil would be $Q_1$, and domestic supply would be $Q_2$. There would be a domestic shortage of $Q_1 - Q_2$, but the amount imported would decline from $Q_3 - Q_4$ to $Q_1 - Q_2$. The government would no longer pay a subsidy, so it would save the amount represented by the rectangle ADEF. Along with this saving, a few other changes must be noted. In addition to the saving of the government, Canadian producers of oil would gain by the amount $P_DFBP_F$. Previously, their total revenue was $P_DFQ_4O$. Now, after the price increase, total revenue would be $P_FBQ_2O$. Therefore, total revenue increases by the area $P_DFQ_4Q_2BP_F$. However, of this amount, $FQ_4Q_2B$ represents increased costs, so that the net gain in profits to oil producers is $P_DFBP_F$.

On the negative side, Canadian purchasers of oil now pay higher prices and use less oil than before (consumption falls from $Q_3$ to $Q_1$ and price rises from $P_D$ to $P_F$). How does one measure their welfare loss? Consumers lose the amount $P_DECP_F$. This is known in economics as a loss in **consumer surplus**. This surplus refers to the difference between what consumers actually spend and what they would be willing to spend on a certain quantity of a good. This concept is illustrated in Exhibit 28.6.

**Consumer surplus** This is the difference between what consumers actually spend on a product and what they would be willing to spend for the same quantity.

---

[5]Exhibit 28.5 is adapted from an article by W.R. Thirsk and R.A. Wright, "The Impact of the Crude Oil Subsidy on Economic Efficiency in Canada," *Canadian Public Policy*, 3 (Summer, 1977), pp. 355-364.

**Exhibit 28.6**

**Consumer and producer surplus**

Consumer and producer surplus are illustrated in the diagram below. At $P_1$, consumers will demand $Q_1$. Their total expenditure will be $P_1EQ_1O$. However, if the sellers of the good had been able to charge consumers what they were actually willing to pay for each unit of the good, consumers would actually have spent the amount $AEQ_1O$. The area $AEP_1$ represents the amount that consumers were willing to pay but didn't pay—that is, *consumer surplus*. For the producer of the good, $P_1EQ_1O$ represents the total revenue received, and $BEQ_1O$ represent the amount paid out in costs to factors of production. The difference $(P_1EB)$ represents the net profit or *producer surplus*.

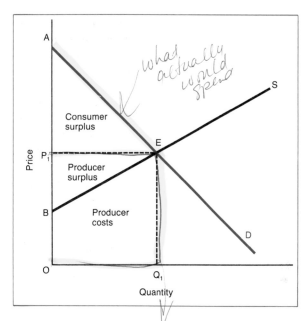

In this Exhibit, $P_1EQ_1O$ represents the amount that consumers actually spend on the quantity $Q_1$, while the area $AEQ_1O$ represents the amount that consumers would be willing to spend if they were required by the seller to pay the highest price they were willing to pay for each unit of the good. The difference between what they pay and what they would be willing to pay is $AEP_1$, the consumer surplus.

Now, referring back to Exhibit 28.5, as the price rises from $P_D$ to $P_F$ and the quantity consumed falls from $Q_3$ to $Q_1$, the consumer surplus falls by the amount $P_DECP_F$. Note that this loss in consumer surplus exceeds the increase in producer net profits (the increase in profits was $P_DFBP_F$) by the amount BCEF. However, the government (and the taxpayers) have gained an amount ADEF, which is greater than BCEF by the amount of the shaded triangles ABF and CDE. The general conclusion, therefore, is that society would realize a net gain from allowing the domestic price of oil to rise to the world price. The loss experienced by consumers would be more than offset by the gains experienced by producers and taxpayers combined.

The basic problem here is that, at the lower subsidized price, $P_D$, consumers were buying too much of the product, and producers were supplying too little. Economic inefficiency results when the domestic price is kept artificially below the world price, because the world price provides a measurement of the social benefit to Canada of its oil resources. However, in deciding how much to produce, Canadian oil producers are guided not by the world price, which is the true measure of the social benefit of oil, but by the artificially lower domestic price. Resources will then be shifted to other industries that provide lower benefits than the benefits that could be realized in the oil industry. In this respect, then, the energy policy pursued by the federal government has been misguided.

## THE ECONOMICS OF ALTERNATIVE ENERGY SOURCES

The analysis up to this point has been concerned with two nonrenewable energy sources, oil and natural gas. Before dealing briefly with a major renewable alternative—hydro-electricity—other nonrenewable energy sources such as coal and conventional nuclear power will be examined. Although they are nonrenewable, they present rather different economic problems from those relating to oil and natural gas, in that the availability of known fuel reserves is not the main barrier to their wider use.

### Coal

Like oil and natural gas, coal is a fossil fuel, but unlike them, its use as an energy source, at least for Western Canada, is limited on the demand side rather than the supply side. Canada's coal resources are growing; in the early 1980s we shifted from being net importers of the product to net exporters. However, mining capacity already in place is not being fully utilized. Most of the coal supplies are found in the provinces of British Columbia and Alberta. Their greater development depends on sales to Japan and Korea, and to Ontario, which currently meets a large part of its coal needs from the United States.

Besides the difficulty of getting Canada's coal resources to the right markets, the major factor limiting the use of coal is the cost of burning it in an environmentally acceptable way. Even in the wilderness areas where some of our coal is found, environmental problems are becoming worrisome. This raises two sets of economic issues—those concerned with setting the environmental standards for use of coal, and those concerned with meeting the standards.

*Setting the Standards* The major pollutant in coal is sulphur, which, when burned, produces sulphur dioxide. In urban areas, air pollution from unrestricted burning of coal is a major public health hazard. In agricultural and forest areas, sulphur dioxide pollution causes acid rain, which damages vegetation. And in wilderness areas, such as those of northern British Columbia, burning coal is a threat to visibility and hence to the attractiveness of outdoor recreation areas.

Chapter 27 discussed a number of alternative strategies for regulating air pollution, and little need be added to that discussion here. Suffice it to say that the regulation of emissions from coal combustion has until now emphasized a "command-and-control" approach, which is often criticized for its inefficiency. Certain minimum standards are set and firms are fined for exceeding them. Meanwhile environmental damage continues.

*Meeting the Standards* Work is under way on a number of technologies for the clean burning of coal. Presently, most coal is burned directly to fire boilers generating electricity, with the pollutants scrubbed out of the stack gases before they are released into the air. The major alternatives focus on preliminary conversion of coal into a clean synthetic fuel that can be burned without elaborate pollution control devices at the point of use. One technique, known as solvent refining, produces a liquid substitute for oil. Another technique bakes the coal and blasts it with air to produce a clean, flammable mixture of carbon monoxide and hydrogen, known as producer gas. This gas was widely manufactured in local gasworks around the turn of the century, but it was displaced by natural gas when long-distance pipelines were built. Although producer gas is unlikely to be reintroduced in the residential market (it has a much lower energy value per litre than natural gas), many industrial users are now finding it profitable to build on-site producer gas plants to meet their own needs.

### Nuclear Energy versus Coal: The Basics

Everyone's darling in the 1960s and already a contributor to Canadian energy supplies, nuclear energy now faces an uncertain future. Not all the objections to this form of energy are economic. However, the economic problems of nuclear energy are in a sense the most threatening ones, because they are producing disenchantment among its traditional friends as well as among its foes. Because nuclear energy is used almost exclusively to produce electricity, its major competitor is coal. It is appropriate, then, to cast the discussion of the economics of nuclear power in the form of a comparison with coal.

The basic economics of nuclear power versus coal is simple to state: nuclear power plants are more expensive to build but cheaper to operate. According to one set of estimates, as of 1978 a new nuclear power plant would cost $913 per kilowatt of capacity, compared with $639 per kilowatt for coal. Once built, however, the coal plant would gulp a hundred-car trainload of fuel every two days, while the nuclear plant would consume less than half a carload of fuel per year. At 1978 prices for coal and uranium, this would make the fuel cost of nuclear power just half the fuel cost for coal.

Whether the trade-off of higher construction costs for lower fuel costs is worthwhile depends on the cost of capital and the percent of capacity at which the plant is operated. Safety problems requiring more frequent shutdowns have seriously reduced the percentage of capacity at which nuclear plants have been able to operate. And although environmental regulations have increased the cost of coal-fired plants too, they have had even more of an impact on nuclear plants in that they have increased the gap in construction costs.

*Waste Disposal and Dismantling* One of the great unsolved problems of nuclear power is how to dispose of the radioactive wastes it produces. These wastes are extraordinarily toxic and must be kept isolated for thousands of years. No one really knows how the job can best be done, although there are a number of promising alternatives under exploration. Even if it is technically possible to dispose of nuclear wastes safely, however —something that some nuclear critics are willing to concede—there is no realistic way of knowing what the cost will be.

A similar problem concerns the dismantling of the reactors themselves at the end of their useful life of forty years or so. Estimates of the dismantling cost range anywhere from 5 to 25 percent of the original construction costs. Again, no one really knows, because no big nuclear power plant has ever been dismantled. Whatever the costs, however, they are not being fully charged against nuclear power now being generated. The economic advantage of nuclear power over coal is thereby exaggerated.

*Hazards of Coal*  Nuclear power, to be sure, is not unique in posing health and safety hazards. Pro-nuclear writers often point out that coal too has major health and safety problems. The hazards to which coal miners are exposed far exceed those confronted by workers in the nuclear industry, and air pollution is a very real public health hazard in contrast to the largely speculative hazards of low-level radiation or core meltdowns. Some calculations indicate that unrestricted burning of coal might be as much as a thousand times more hazardous than widespread use of nuclear power.

There can be no doubt that a balanced economic comparison of nuclear power versus coal must take into account the full health and safety costs of both alternatives. More research needs to be done, however, before this aspect of the debate can be said to favor nuclear power conclusively. For one thing, the health and safety costs of coal mining are not hidden; they are costs that the coal industry is already bearing in its wage bills, retirement benefits, workers' compensation premiums, and so on. As for the public health hazards of air pollution as compared with those of nuclear disasters, the question is not so much which is greater at present as which can be controlled at least cost through well-designed regulation.

## Renewable Energy Sources

*Electricity*  In view of the conservation problems associated with non-renewable energy sources, renewable sources such as hydro-electricity and solar energy might be expected, with their distinct advantages, to predominate in our society. Unfortunately, these energy sources are restricted by the availability of good streams close to population centres and by climatic conditions.

Hydro-electricity is much more important to Canada than it is to the United States. Measured in terms of "oil equivalence," hydro-power constitutes about 25 percent of total energy production in Canada, while in the United States its share is less than 5 percent.

As it becomes necessary to locate hydro-electric sites farther and farther away from major use centres, the capital cost of producing electricity rises very sharply. Currently, hydro-electricity is cheaper than oil, but more expensive than natural gas, as an industrial energy source in most centres.

In all provinces except Alberta, electricity, whether hydro or thermal (the latter produced through the use of coal), is generated and distributed by provincial utilities that form some of the largest corporations in the country. There is, therefore, much less dispute over the allocation of rents. There is relatively little export of hydro-electricity, so jurisdictional disputes are not significant. It is only geography that continues to limit the use of this important renewable energy source.

*Solar Energy*  The use of the sun, while strictly speaking not a "renewable" resource, provides such a long-run form of energy that it makes sense to treat it as renewable. At the moment, by far the most promising application of solar energy is passive solar heating for homes and commercial buildings. Passive solar systems are simple, unlike hi-tech active systems that require elaborate collectors, plumbing, and heat exchangers. Any building with a south-facing window is, to a degree, a passive solar building. The key to effective passive solar design is simply to maximize this window area while providing good insulation and a heat-storage mass such as a masonry wall or floor. During the early 1980s, when high mortgage rates drove the home construction industry to depression levels, passive solar construction remained one of the few healthy parts of the housing market.

For the future, many potentially attractive technologies exist for both large-scale and small-scale use of the sun. Wind power, photo-voltaic power, and large-scale solar steam plants are in the design or pilot plant stage. All, however, are still at least one technological generation away from being economically competitive with conventional fuels.

## CONCLUSIONS

The energy sector illustrates very succinctly some of the major themes developed in this chapter: government regulation, corporate concentration, and consumer ignorance. Perhaps the safest thing to say about the economics of energy is that it is a rapidly changing field. The prospects for oil and natural gas depend very much on supply and demand reactions to increasing world prices over the next five to ten years. Nuclear power appears at this time to have serious drawbacks preventing wider use, but existing plants contribute an indispensable part of Canada's electric power. Our coal is abundant, but its use is being limited by distance from good markets and the search for cost-efficient ways to overcome its environmental problems. Hydro-electric power is a major renewable energy source for some areas of the country. Solar power is growing in importance, but is unlikely to contribute more than 5 percent of Canadian energy needs in this century. Energy economics promises to be an exciting and changing field for years to come.

## SUMMARY

1. According to the theory of the mine, in a competitive market a nonrenewable resource will be depleted no faster than the rate that will cause its price to rise in step with the prevailing interest rate. Any faster rate of depletion would be self-correcting, because wealth-maximizing resource owners would begin to withhold present supplies from the market in order to sell them at higher prices later. When the market for such a resource is dominated by a cartel, the rate of depletion tends to be less than in a competitive market.

2. Price policies for oil and natural gas in Canada have partially insulated domestic markets from the effects of rising world prices. The result has been a lower rate of domestic consumption and a higher rate of imports than would have prevailed otherwise.

3. The major energy alternatives to oil and natural gas are electricity, coal, nuclear power, and solar energy. All these alternatives require greater capital expenditure per unit of energy output than oil and gas, especially if some of them are to meet health, safety, and environmental safeguards.

## DISCUSSION QUESTIONS

1. Imagine that you are snowed in for the winter in a small cabin in the mountains. Your food supply consists of a sack of potatoes. There are more than enough potatoes to survive on but less than enough to eat all you want every day. How will you allocate the potatoes over the winter? Will you eat an equal amount every day? More per day at first and then gradually taper off? Fewer at first and more toward the end? What does the theory of the mine have to say about this kind of situation?
2. The removal of the subsidy on oil prices might lead to a large increase in the price of oil in the immediate future but to a decline in the long run. Use supply and demand diagrams to explain this.
3. If solar energy came into increasing use, how do you think this would affect the elasticity of demand for oil and coal?
4. Discuss some pros and cons of letting oil prices rise to the world price level.

# FOREIGN OWNERSHIP AND CONTROL OF CANADIAN BUSINESS

## WHAT YOU WILL LEARN IN THIS CHAPTER

*When considering the economic behavior and performance of business enterprises in Canada—as we have done in the last few chapters—it is necessary to examine not only the domestic market structure in which they operate but also the degree to which they are controlled from abroad. For this reason the effect of foreign ownership on the nature of the Canadian firm is examined in this chapter. The issue of foreign control of Canadian business is part of a larger issue involving Canada's heavy dependence on other economies. The latter topic will be discussed briefly, but the main purpose of this chapter is to examine the extent to which Canadian firms are owned and controlled by foreigners, the effect this may have on those firms, the possible costs and benefits to Canadians, and the policies that are being used—or might be used—to reduce foreign ownership. A later chapter (Chapter 31) examines briefly the extent to which labor markets in Canada are subject to foreign controls and some possible consequences of such control.*

## FOR REVIEW

*Here are some important terms and concepts that will be put to use in this chapter. If you do not understand them, review them before proceeding.*

- *Staple production and foreign dependence (Chapter 1)*
- *The organization of business (Chapter 4)*
- *Balance of international payments (Chapter 15)*
- *The foreign sector and the multiplier (Chapter 16)*
- *The economics of energy (Chapter 28)*

One of the most hotly debated topics in Canada in recent years has been the dependence of the Canadian economy on that of other countries, particularly that of the United States. Canada is dependent on other economies in many different ways and has been throughout its history. First, Canada depends on foreign demand for more than one-quarter of its total output. This pattern began, as we saw in Chapter 1, with the early stress on staple or primary production for export markets. As late as 1960, over 90 percent of Canadian exports consisted of natural resources in crude or processed form. In the 1960s, finished products as a proportion of total exports increased from 8 percent to 38 percent, but in the 1970s and early 1980s the composition of exports showed no further significant change. The Canadian economy, then, continues to rely heavily on the export of primary products to other countries.

Second, Canada depends to a considerable extent on the importation of consumer durables and capital machinery. Its trade balance on end products is generally in deficit, and it reached a record deficit of more than $20 billion in 1981. It balances this by exporting more raw materials than it imports.

Third, Canada depends on foreign funds to finance the expansion of its output. This too has a long history. In the last half of the nineteenth century, foreigners provided much of the funding for the building of roads, canals, and railways, and for the development of mining and manufacturing. Most of this capital came from Great Britain. After World War I, the United States began to invest heavily in Canada. This investment often resulted in the establishment of new firms or the purchase of existing firms by "parent" companies in the United States. It is this development of numerous "subsidiary" firms in Canada (subsidiary to foreign parents) that has come to typify the way Canada is in general subservient to foreign interests.

## THE EXTENT OF FOREIGN INVESTMENT IN CANADIAN BUSINESS

Canada has actively encouraged foreign investment by erecting tariff barriers to trade, which have discouraged foreign firms from selling goods to Canada and encouraged them instead to establish subsidiaries in this country, and by selling bonds and shares abroad to finance large public and private undertakings. There seems to have been a pervasive feeling through much of our history that Canadian development desperately required the infusion of foreign funds. In the 1960s, when the United States tried to discourage its citizens from investing in other countries, Canada frantically — and successfully, as it turned out — sought exemption from such restrictions. Part of the concern was that inflows of foreign capital were necessary to finance the perennial current account deficit, but part was also the result of the long-standing conviction that Canada continually needs new infusions of foreign capital for the expansion of its industry.

One result of such favorable attitudes to foreign investment is that Canada has become, next to the United States (which has large short-term claims against it because its currency is virtually the world's currency), the world's largest net international debtor. The official value of our indebtedness is now over $55 billion, or about $2,400 for every person in the nation.[1] This net indebtedness is increasing at about $4 to $5 billion annually, and it has recently cost more than $8 billion annually just to service the debt, through interest and dividend payments and retained earnings. About 75 percent of total foreign assets are owned by Americans.

---

[1] Bruce W. Wilkinson, "Long-Term Capital Inflows and Balance of Payments Policy," *The Walter L. Gordon Lecture Series, 1978–79*, Vol. 3, p. 30.

## Portfolio Investment and Direct Investment

Not all foreign financing guarantees control of Canadian industry by foreigners. An important distinction must be made between portfolio investment and direct investment.

**Portfolio investment** includes minority holdings of corporate shares, which may or may not have voting power, and bond holdings, which do not carry voting rights. Most British investment in the pre-World War I period was of this kind, with Canadian bonds being sold in the London bond market. Such investment is more in the nature of a loan. For example, Canadian utilities like Quebec and Ontario Hydro do much of their current financing by selling bonds in the New York market. Such sales do not give Americans any control over those utilities because the bonds carry no voting rights.

**Portfolio investment**
Purchase of securities that involves no control of the company selling the securities.

**Direct investment** refers to holdings of securities with voting rights that are substantial enough to give the holder of those shares control over the business. It includes the establishment of subsidiaries by foreign companies that are financed through the earnings of the home company. Control is assumed when the investors own 50 percent or more of the securities or assets with voting rights. In contrast to Great Britain, American investors chose to put a large part of their financing into direct investments. Between 1945 and 1967, long-term investment by the United States in Canada increased from $5 billion to $28 billion, with direct investment rising from $2 billion to $17 billion. About half of the increase in direct investment was used to give Americans control of Canadian natural resources.

**Direct investment** Purchase of securities with voting rights substantial enough to give the investors control of the company invested in.

Direct investment by foreigners in Canada is generally carried out by corporations that have come to be called **multinationals**. These are companies that carry on business on a world-wide scale, and organize their world operations from a central headquarters. There are many foreign multinational firms operating in Canada, including such giants as General Motors, the Ford Motor Company, and Exxon Corporation. Canada also has its own multinational firms, such as Canadian Pacific Enterprises and Seagrams, which have large operations in other countries.

**Multinationals** Corporations that have enterprises in a number of countries.

## Foreign Ownership of Canadian Industry

Our main concern here is with direct foreign investment in Canada. A greater proportion of Canada's industry is foreign owned than that of any other industrialized country. As Exhibit 29.1 shows, about 68 percent of assets in the petroleum and natural gas industry, and between 50 and 60 percent of all assets in Canadian mining and manufacturing in 1976 were held by corporations in which foreigners had a controlling interest (that is, foreigners held more than 50 percent of the voting shares), and the proportion for all industry was 31 percent. Foreign-controlled companies accounted for 46 percent of all industry profits.

**Exhibit 29.1**
Percentage of assets in Canadian corporations that
are foreign-controlled (excluding finance), 1976

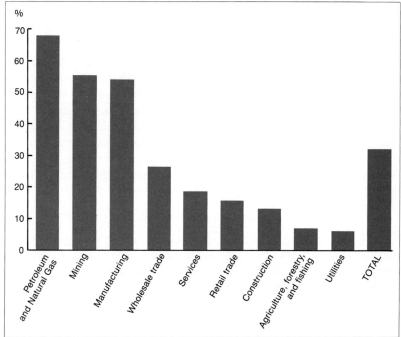

Source: *The Financial Post*, May 12, 1979, p. 8, and Statistics Canada, *Canada's International Investment Position, 1977.*

Utilities have only about 4 percent foreign ownership, because most are owned by provincial governments. Financial businesses, including banks, also have a low ratio of foreign ownership (about 10 percent) because of special legislation prohibiting substantial foreign investment. Current revisions to the Bank Act have opened the door to more foreign banks, however, in order to increase competition in that field.

More detail on individual firms in Canada is given in a recent survey of Canada's largest industrial companies. Exhibit 29.2 indicates that six of the ten largest Canadian industrial companies are owned by nonresidents. Only two have foreign ownership of less than 25 percent.

Of the 500 largest "Canadian" companies surveyed in that same report, 199 are owned 50 percent or more by nonresidents, and 141 companies are owned 100 percent by foreigners. Companies that are completely foreign owned include Chrysler, General Motors, F.W. Woolworth, Alberta and Southern Gas Co., and IBM Canada, all among the fifty largest companies in Canada.

In addition to ownership, economists are interested in the actual control of Canadian companies by nonresidents. Ownership may not always be a good indicator of control. Some subsidiaries wholly owned by foreigners will be much less tightly controlled than others by the parent company, while many companies in Canada that are technically owned by Canadians

**Exhibit 29.2**
**Foreign ownership in Canada's ten largest industrial corporations**

| Ranked by Sales (1982)[1] | Company | Major Shareholders | Foreign Ownership |
|---|---|---|---|
| | | | (Percentage) |
| 1 | Canadian Pacific Ltd. | Wide distribution | 25 |
| 2 | General Motors of Canada Ltd. | General Motors Corp. Detroit | 100 |
| 3 | Imperial Oil Ltd. | Exxon Corp. N.Y. | 74 |
| 4 | Bell Canada | Wide distribution | 4 |
| 5 | George Weston Ltd. | Weston family | 1 |
| 6 | Ford Motor Co. of Canada | Ford Motor Co. Dearborn, Mich. | 92 |
| 7 | Alcan Aluminum Ltd. | Wide distribution | 49 |
| 8 | Shell Canada Ltd. | Shell, Netherlands Britain | 79 |
| 9 | Texaco Canada Inc. | Texaco Inc. | 90 |
| 10 | Gulf Canada Ltd. | Gulf Oil Corp. | 75 |

[1]The Canadian Wheat Board, listed No. 9 in sales, is excluded here because it is not an industrial corporation.
Source: *The Financial Post 500: The 1983 Ranking of Canada's 500 Largest Companies.* (June, 1983), p. 69.

are influenced substantially by foreign interests. For instance, movie houses in Canada owned by Canadians show movies in accordance with agreements made with foreign movie producers. Fast-food businesses in Canada are, in many cases, franchised from U.S. companies, and the nature of the product and service are determined almost entirely by the American firms.[2]

There is no doubt, however, that foreign ownership of Canadian firms will affect the behavior of those firms. Why else would foreign firms want to own and control Canadian resources? Some academic economists have disputed this, but as others have pointed out, "The argument that foreign ownership does not matter is clearly false. If certain Canadian resources are worth more to a foreign firm than they are to a Canadian firm [which must be the reason why a foreign firm rather than a Canadian firm has come to own them], some change in the allocation of the Canadian resources must take place if they are under the control of an international firm. If the acquisition of Canadian resources by a foreign firm had no effect at all on the employment of those resources, their value to the foreign firm and a Canadian firm would have to be equal. The reason the foreign firm succeeds in bidding Canadian resources away from Canadian firms is that it expects to be able to make changes in the allocation of those resources that will be to its advantage."[3]

Whether the changes made to the Canadian economy by foreign ownership of its resources are good or bad for that economy is another and much more difficult question. It is necessary, therefore, to examine the possible costs and benefits, to Canadians, of the extensive foreign investment in this country.

[2] This point is made by Jack Carr, Frank Mathewson, and John C. McManus in *Cents and Nonsense: The Economics of Canadian Policy Issues* (Toronto: Holt, Rinehart and Winston, 1972), p. 90.

[3] Carr, Mathewson, and McManus, *Cents and Nonsense*, p. 92.

## THE BENEFITS AND COSTS OF FOREIGN OWNERSHIP OF CANADIAN BUSINESS

Economists have tried in various ways to determine the benefits that Canadians derive from the foreign ownership of Canadian business, and to compare such benefits with the apparent costs.

Before examining some of the approaches used to measure these things and the results obtained, it is important to note one point that is beyond dispute and that is central to the whole debate. Regardless of what foreign control may or may not do to Canadians, it clearly compromises their sovereignty. Sovereignty has been defined as "the capacity to develop and exercise choice."[4] One leading Canadian economist has posed this issue in the following way: "To those who want to be shown how the political interests of domestic and foreign controlled firms differ, I would say: 'Suppose the right to vote in Canadian elections were confined to the inhabitants of, let us say, Cleveland, Ohio. Would that be all right? Would that not be an infringement of Canadian independence in and of itself? Would it be necessary to show that the resulting Canadian government was worse than one elected by residents of Canada?'"[5]

To use an even more prosaic analogy, it may not be too facetious to suggest that Canada is in many ways like a young couple who prize their high standard of living and their apparent ability to stand on their own feet, but have in fact achieved at least some of their success through borrowings from their parents. Could they have done as well on their own? It is difficult, if not impossible, to tell. Will the parents interfere? They will not necessarily interfere overtly, or very often, but it would certainly be an illusion for the young couple to think that they are truly independent or, when it comes to a difference of opinion as to how they should spend their money, that pressure will not be brought to bear on their decision. In addition, their dependence on "outside" financing may create a spirit of caution and dependence that will retard their future financial development.

Empirical studies of the Canadian economy have anticipated these possibilities and others. On the positive side, a number of economists have drawn attention to the superior technology and management skills that foreign capital often brings with it. It is argued that if investment were restricted to the portfolio type, foreign firms would not be as likely to risk the application of some of their best techniques in other countries. The late Harry G. Johnson in particular argued that American-owned corporations have made possible the low-cost diffusion of technology and ideas in Canada, and have undoubtedly contributed to the growth of the Canadian economy.[6] One study reported that in the years 1950–1956 net foreign investment (both portfolio and direct) contributed from 8 to 20 percent of

[4] John J. Shepherd, "An Economic Strategy for Canada: Our Political Economy Regained," *The Walter L. Gordon Lecture Series, 1978 –79*, Vol. 3, p. 10.

[5] Gideon Rosenbluth, "Canadian Policy on Foreign Ownership and Control of Business," in *The Canadian Economy: Problems and Policies*, ed. G.C. Ruggeri (Toronto: Gage, 1977), p. 346.

[6] H.G. Johnson, "Economic Benefits," in *Nationalism and the Multinational Enterprise*, ed. H.R. Hahlo, Graham Smith, and Richard W. Wright (Leiden, The Netherlands: Sijthoff, 1973).

the growth in per capita real income in Canada.[7] Another study indicated that if only Canadian capital had been used, the gross domestic product in Canada would be 16.5 percent lower.[8]

Studies of this kind are based on assumptions that are themselves very difficult to verify, but they represent a serious effort to measure the possible benefits derived from foreign investment and ownership.

On the negative side, economists and other social scientists have stressed, in addition to the general loss of sovereignty already noted, the possibility that Canadian subsidiaries of foreign multinationals may be induced to do things that are in the interest of the parent company rather than in the interest of the subsidiary or the Canadian economy.

First, the influx of managerial talent that often accompanies a foreign takeover and may contribute to increased efficiency in the firm that has been taken over, may simultaneously cause a long-run dependence on expertise and services lodged in the parent company. This represents a loss of business to Canadian firms that might otherwise supply such a company with architectural, legal, and advertising services. The tendency to limit the development of services and skills in the foreign-owned subsidiary, because they are concentrated in the parent company, is known as **truncation**. It has been estimated that the migration of services to the United States will result in a projected $1.5 billion deficit in our balance of payments by 1985.[9]

Related to this is the concentration of research and development (R & D) activities in the parent company, at the possible expense of such activities being undertaken in the Canadian subsidiary. Early studies of this subject indicated that foreign-owned firms were as committed to research and development as Canadian-owned firms, but recently developed data show that, in several sectors of the economy, Canadian-owned companies perform more R & D per dollar of sales than do foreign-owned companies.[10]

The impact of foreign ownership on exports and imports has also been examined. It has been conjectured that subsidiaries of foreign companies would be constrained from exporting, because their exports might compete with exports of the same commodity produced by the parent company, while at the same time they would import more than similar domestically owned companies because of their reliance on services and capital equipment from the parent company. (Though in the absence of the foreign subsidiary, Canadian imports of goods produced by that subsidiary might increase.) In view of Canada's chronic deficit on current account, this possibility has been viewed with great concern. The detailed studies of A.E.

(legal, advertising, architectural)

**Truncation** Limits placed on the development of skills and services in and by a Canadian subsidiary because they are concentrated in the parent company.

[7] Rudolph G. Penner, "The Benefits of Foreign Investment in Canada, 1950 –1956," *Canadian Journal of Economics and Political Science*, May 1966, pp. 172 –83. Cited by A.E. Safarian, "Issues Raised by Foreign Direct Investment in Canada," in *Issues in Canadian Economics*, ed. L.H. Officer and L.B. Smith (Toronto: McGraw-Hill Ryerson, 1974), p. 82. The estimate deducts Canadian investment abroad; the contribution of gross inflows alone would be greater.

[8] Philip A. Neher, "Capital Movement, Foreign Ownership and Dependence on Foreign Investment in Canada and British Columbia," and John Helliwell and Jillian Broadbent, "How Much Does Foreign Capital Matter?" both in *B.C. Studies*, Department of Economics, University of British Columbia, Spring 1972, 13, pp. 31 –42. Cited by Safarian, "Issues," p. 82.

[9] John J. Shepherd, "An Economic Strategy for Canada: Our Political Economy Regained," *The Walter L. Gordon Lecture Series*, 1978 –79, Vol. 3, p. 17.

[10] John J. Shepherd, "Economic Strategy," p. 23.

Safarian, a Toronto economist, indicate that foreign-owned firms seem to export as freely as their Canadian-owned counterparts. At the same time they also import more.[11] The net impact on the balance of payments of the export and import behavior of foreign-owned firms does not appear to be as serious as some have thought. At the same time, it should not be forgotten that the capital flows that are part and parcel of foreign investment have a profound impact on the balance of payments. Insofar as they represent the creation of new foreign debt for Canada, which must be paid back in the form of interest and dividends, they increase the already serious deficit in Canada's current account—a deficit that we have traditionally tried to cover by even larger inflows of capital and larger current account deficits. Simultaneously, the inflow of capital, under a system of flexible exchange rates, increases the value of the Canadian dollar and reduces the cost of imports. However, this beneficial result must be balanced against the fact that our exports are simultaneously made more expensive. The net effect of such capital flows in this respect is hard to gauge.

General, tentative conclusions of this kind should not obscure the fact that, in many individual cases, Canadians have come to feel that they have good reason to want more control of their economy.

In 1971, Robert L. Perry, a reporter for *The Financial Post*, made a detailed examination of the foreign control of Canadian industry in Galt, Ontario. His award-winning study was called *Galt, U.S.A.* He discovered that many American-owned firms in Galt were tightly controlled by their American headquarters and were making decisions that, in the opinion of Canadian personnel of these firms, were not in the best interests of Canada. As one of the Canadian managers of a subsidiary noted, "I was being manipulated and controlled by Americans—by people outside the day-to-day work environment." This manager thought it was in the interest of the company to purchase a steel mill owned by Bethlehem Steel just across the border from Ontario, but the American parent firm vetoed the idea because "the American market belonged to the parent."[12]

Eight years later, in 1979, Perry returned to that same community to bring his research up to date. He found now that many American firms were selling their branch plants because they had discovered what their Canadian-based managers had been trying to tell them: that many of the subsidiaries had been performing badly under absentee ownership and control. It is too early to tell whether the movement of some American firms out of the Galt area (since renamed Cambridge) represents a nation-wide trend that will reduce the American presence in Canadian industry.

Another experience linked to foreign ownership is described in Case 29.1. American firms like Westinghouse may decide at any time that it would pay them to consolidate their multinational operations at the expense of individual plants somewhere in their operation.

---

[11] A.E. Safarian, *Foreign Ownership of Canadian Industry* (Toronto: McGraw-Hill, 1966).

[12] Robert L. Perry, *Galt, U.S.A.*, rev. ed. (Toronto: The Financial Post, 1979). Excerpt reprinted in *The Financial Post*, Sept. 1, 1979, p. 15.

## Case 29.1
## Who Decides for Westinghouse Canada Ltd.?

Early in 1979, Westinghouse of Canada Ltd., with headquarters in Hamilton, Ontario, announced plans to "decentralize" its Hamilton operations. The 700 workers in the Hamilton plant were naturally concerned. What did "decentralization" mean? Would they lose their jobs? Would they be dispersed to other parts of Canada? Would the operation be moved to the United States, where the parent company seemed to make the decisions? The Ontario government and the labor unions demanded clarification. As the following news item indicates, it was Westinghouse of Canada's dependence on its U.S. parent that created much of the concern, illustrating a problem created for the Canadian economy by foreign ownership. As *The Financial Post* reported:

The gut issue in the controversy swirling about the possible decentralization of Westinghouse Canada Ltd.'s switchgear and control division is who exactly is calling the shots? Executives in Hamilton, Ont., or chiefs back in Pittsburgh, Pa., home-base of Westinghouse Electric Corp.?

The other key question is why is the move necessary when even company officials admit the division, which produces devices to distribute and measure electrical power, is the second most profitable at Westinghouse?

Leaders of the United Electrical Radio & Machine Workers Union of America say Pittsburgh has snapped its fingers.

"They just want to get the heck out of Canada, and away from the union," says John Ball of Local 504.

The union claims the switchgear plant is viable for future growth and that the division will become a "warehousing and service operation" if decentralized.

With the support of provincial opposition parties and Hamilton city council, the union is pressing the Ontario government to introduce legislation that would guarantee the jobs of 700 Hamilton workers and force Westinghouse to accept its "social responsibility" to the community.

Late last week, Westinghouse management finally issued a point-by-point reply to the charges.

C. F. MacNeil, vice-president, told *The Post* the decision to move to a multi-location operation "with internal strategies to match" will be Canadian. "There is a 1% chance the division will leave Canada, but that is not part of our study," he says.

Source: *The Financial Post*, March 31, 1979, p. 5.

Another major problem associated with foreign-owned firms is **extraterritoriality**: the intrusion of foreign law and policy into Canada. The United States, in particular, has always insisted that subsidiaries of American corporations operating in Canada are subject to American laws. This has had a number of important, and highly publicized, repercussions for Canadian subsidiaries of American firms. For example, under the U.S. Trading with the Enemy Act, trade by American-owned corporations with countries like Cuba, China, Vietnam, and North Korea has at times been expressly prohibited. Several sales of goods to Cuba by Canadian subsidiaries were stopped by the U.S. government in the 1970s, though after a vigorous appeal by the Canadian government one of them eventually went through. As Case 29.2 indicates, actions of this type have been repeated recently, posing serious problems for Canadian trade.

**Extraterritoriality** The application of foreign laws to Canadian companies.

The problems just cited do not amount to indisputable evidence that foreign-owned corporations have done serious and irreparable damage to the Canadian economy. In fact, on balance it would be extremely difficult to prove whether or not the costs have outweighed the benefits. However, as was observed at the beginning of this section, there is no question that the extensive foreign ownership of Canadian firms represents a substantial diminution of Canadian sovereignty.

### Case 29.2
### Extraterritoriality in the Energy Industry

U.S. trade sanctions against the Soviet Union have all but scuttled Canadian hopes to improve industrial exports to Russia in the energy sector.

Two major Canadian projects have already been undermined, and Canadian trade officials believe several smaller export activities may also be threatened. Given the strong U.S. technology and ownership content of the Canadian energy industry, there are few corners the broad U.S. trade sanctions do not touch.

Whatever damage this may do to Canadian exports and job opportunities in future, the most immediate threat is to already damaged Canada–U.S. relations.

Ottawa and many in Canadian industry are incensed by the extraterritorial extension of the U.S. trade sanctions. Diplomatic notes and ministerial face-to-face protests have already been launched.

And there is fresh fear within industry that the U.S. sanction is ready-made ammunition for Canadian nationalists who want to strengthen, not weaken, the National Energy Program and foreign investment ownership restrictions.

''The change in U.S. policy won't win friends for the U.S. either in Western Europe or here in Canada,'' says Sam Hughes, president of the Canadian Chamber of Commerce. ''It will only increase the clamor among nationalists to limit or control American foreign investment.''

The scope of the most recent U.S. sanctions has shocked all of Washington's major industrial allies and brought forth almost totally negative reactions.

Although Canada was never a direct target of the sanctions, Canadian diplomats fear this country could be the hardest hit over time.

The initial sanctions were aimed at U.S. companies supplying goods for the new Siberian pipeline which will send Soviet gas to Western Europe. The sanctions were imposed in retaliation for Polish and Soviet restrictions of human rights.

In the past, Canada has been in the forefront in opposing U.S. efforts to extend its jurisdiction over U.S. companies and their subsidiaries abroad. This time, however, the charge was led by France and West Germany, two of several European countries with extensive interests in the Siberian pipeline project.

Canada was inadvertently dragged into the latest crisis when President Ronald Reagan, over the protests of several members of his cabinet, decided to extend the sanctions to cover U.S. involvement in all Soviet oil-and-gas-sector projects. The ban, to the dismay of Canadian diplomats, extended not only to U.S. companies and their subsidiaries abroad, but to U.S. technology licenses to Canadian and other foreign companies abroad.

''We thought we were making some progress getting the Americans to soften their extraterritorial stance in the case of Cuban sanctions,'' one Canadian diplomat told The Post. ''But Reagan has just reversed course totally and extended the principle further than any recent president.''

Canadian officials say the definition of U.S. jurisdiction appears so broadly defined that it may cover many foreign companies with as little as 25 percent of U.S. ownership.

Source: Hyman Solomon, ''Reagan's 'No' on Soviet Pipeline Reverberates Here,'' *The Financial Post*, July 17, 1982. p. 1.

## POLICIES TO CURB THE FOREIGN OWNERSHIP OF CANADIAN BUSINESS

Though Canada has generally welcomed the inflow of foreign capital to support the development of its industry, in the last decade or so a large number of Canadians, including governments at both the provincial and federal levels, have become concerned about the extent of foreign ownership. A number of policies have been undertaken by governments to reduce the size of new capital inflows and to repatriate some of the assets already owned by nonresidents. A federal government study in 1972 described three types of policies that have emerged.[13]

First, legislation has been passed limiting direct foreign investment in sectors of the economy deemed crucial to Canada's cultural and financial development. In the field of broadcasting, no broadcasting system in Canada is permitted to have more than 20 percent nonresident participation. In the field of publishing, attempts have been made, through tax laws and government subsidies, to discourage Canadian advertising in foreign magazines and to establish Canadian publishing houses in a field largely dominated by American companies. In banking, the Bank Act revision of 1967 limits to 25 percent the proportion of shares that can be transferred to nonresidents. The actual participation of foreigners in this important field is considerably smaller than that. Similar legislation applies to insurance companies.

A second strategy has been to provide guidelines for the behavior of American (and other foreign) firms in Canada. In 1975, the federal minister of Industry, Trade and Commerce issued a document entitled *The New Principles of International Business Conduct*, advising foreign corporations on matters such as interference in the operation of Canadian subsidiaries and the need for more research and technological development in Canada. It is doubtful, however, that such public relations efforts have had much impact on the performance of foreign-owned corporations.

An important exception to this may be the Foreign Investment Review Agency (FIRA), which was established in 1973 by the federal Parliament to monitor prospective foreign takeovers, and to encourage more Canadian participation at the management level and more use of Canadian resources and skills by foreign corporations permitted to enter the Canadian market. The review agency has denied few applications and is generally felt to have exercised little real control over the entry of new foreign firms.

A third type of policy consists of encouraging increased Canadian ownership of business firms. Many measures have been adopted to accomplish this. For example, corporations that are partly Canadian owned pay lower dividend taxes than those that are wholly foreign owned; pension funds, which are an extremely important source of capital funding, are required to pay a special tax if they do not keep at least 90 percent of their assets in Canada.

The most serious effort of this kind has occurred since October 1980 in the petroleum industry. Under the National Energy Program (NEP) announced at that time, the federal government responded to growing oil prices and revenues by attempting to gain more control over the industry and by increasing the "Canadianization" of the industry. The main concern was that more of the growing oil revenue should accrue to Canadians (including, of course, Canadian governments). The stated objective of the

---

[13] *Foreign Direct Investment in Canada*, a report prepared under the direction of the Hon. Herb Gray (Ottawa: Information Canada, 1972).

NEP was to increase Canadian ownership of the petroleum industry from about 30 percent to at least 50 percent by 1990. The strategies designed to achieve this objective included a Petroleum Incentives Program (PIP), which provided higher exploration rebates to companies with 75 percent Canadian ownership, and requirements that only firms with 50 percent Canadian ownership could participate in offshore oil and oil sands developments. In addition, billions of dollars were allocated to the purchase of foreign firms like Petrofina.

By the spring of 1982 it was reported by the Minister of Energy, Mines and Resources that as a direct result of this program the percentage of revenues generated by Canadian-owned companies had increased from 28 to 35 percent of industry revenues. As Case 29.3 illustrates, the program was beginning to affect the ownership of companies in significant ways.

### Case 29.3
### Inter-City Gas and the National Energy Program

Inter-City Gas Ltd. of Winnipeg is studying various ways to increase the company's Canadian ownership percentage in order to benefit from further exploration incentives under the federal National Energy Program.

President Robert G. Graham told the annual meeting last week the problem of core Canadian ownership is "the paramount corporate question facing us now."

When the new incentives for drilling on Crown lands under the NEP were announced in October, the Winnipeg-based energy company was more than half owned by American investors. Since then, the percentage of Canadian ownership has increased to the present level of about 61 percent to 62 percent.

Graham says the shift has occurred largely by itself, without management interference, although the company has stopped actively promoting the shares in the U.S. But, he says, if the Canadian core ownership does not increase to the corporate goal of 65 percent, "we may well have to take some initiative to raise our core rating."

"To take advantage of the various goodies offered under the NEP, we want to be 65 percent Canadian-owned by the end of the year," he said.

Graham says management is examining several alternatives, including issuing a new block of shares for sale to Canadians only, or spinning off the exploration interests in a separate Canadian company.

When the NEP was announced, Inter-City was one of the few Canadian energy companies which did not condemn it outright. The reason is that, while the company's exploration division suffered immediate penalties from increased taxes, several other company divisions stood to gain a great deal from federal incentives to convert from oil to other fuels and from increased gas distribution.

Source: Susan Hoeschen, "ICG Wants to be More Canadian," *The Financial Post*, June 6, 1981, p. W4.

Despite all of these efforts, Canada remains an economy peculiarly dependent on other economies, particularly that of the United States. It is clear that Canadian business firms are profoundly affected by foreign ownership, though the actual costs and benefits of such ownership are extremely difficult to assess.

## SUMMARY

1. Canada's economy has, throughout its history, been dependent on the economies of other countries. Canada depends heavily on its exports of

primary goods and on its imports of finished products. Further, Canada has always encouraged foreign investment for industrial expansion. This has led to the development of numerous "subsidiary" firms, operating in Canada but responsible to parent companies in other countries.

2. Even without much documented evidence that foreign multinational firms interfere frequently in decisions made by their Canadian subsidiaries, the very fact that such Canadian enterprises have been purchased by foreigners is reason enough to believe that their performance is different from the way it would have been under Canadian control.

3. Whether the difference mentioned works for or against Canada is a matter for legitimate dispute. Recent evidence seems to indicate that, in terms of its balance of payments position, research and development, and in the development of highly skilled Canadian managers, the costs may exceed the benefits.

4. A number of approaches have been developed by governments to restrain foreign investment, to make foreign investors conform to Canadian needs and practices, and to encourage a partial repatriation of foreign-owned assets by Canadians. The National Energy Program represents the most radical attempt to regain Canadian control over a major industry.

## DISCUSSION QUESTIONS

1. Does it appear to you, from what has been said in this chapter and on the basis of your previous reading, that the problem of Canada's dependence on other countries is primarily a political, social, or economic one? Explain.

2. Why do you think multinational corporations want to own the firms in which they invest? Why don't they just use contractual agreements, franchises, etc., to purchase the resources that they want from Canada?

3. Suggest ways, other than those being followed today, by which Canada might "buy back" the companies now owned by foreigners. Try to obtain data from the sources listed in this chapter on how expensive this might be. Do you think Canadians are willing to pay a considerable price for an increase in their economic autonomy?

# FACTOR
# MARKETS
# AND INCOME
# DISTRIBUTION

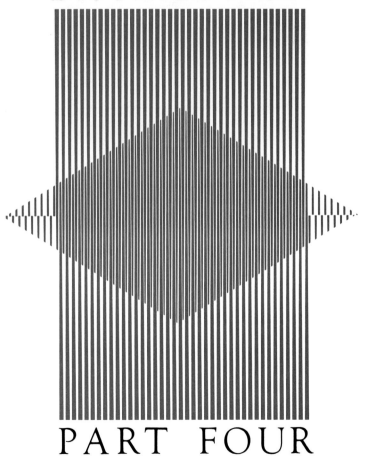

# PART FOUR

# FACTOR MARKETS AND MARGINAL PRODUCTIVITY THEORY

## WHAT YOU WILL LEARN IN THIS CHAPTER

*This chapter is the first of three that discuss the operation of factor markets—the markets in which labor, capital, and natural resources are bought and sold. These markets are much like the product markets studied earlier, with one major exception: in factor markets, households are the sellers and firms the buyers. Accordingly, a theory of factor supply can be developed as an outgrowth of the theory of consumer choice, and a theory of factor demand can be developed as an outgrowth of the theory of the firm. The factor market theory discussed in this chapter covers both perfectly competitive and less than perfectly competitive cases.*

## FOR REVIEW

*Here are some important terms and concepts that will be put to use in this chapter. If you do not understand them, review them before proceeding.*
- *Factors of production (Chapter 1)*
- *Marginal utility and consumer equilibrium (Chapter 21)*
- *Income and substitution effect (Chapter 21)*
- *Marginal physical product (Chapter 22)*
- *Pure economic profit (Chapter 22)*
- *Law of diminishing returns (Chapter 22)*
- *Normal rate of return (Chapter 22)*

One very important set of markets in the economy has been referred to so far only indirectly: **factor markets**—the markets in which labor, capital, and natural resources are bought and sold. (In Chapter 1 entrepreneurship—the innovative, risk-taking function—was identified as a possible fourth factor of production. It is discussed later in this chapter in relation to profit income.) Factor markets perform two major functions in a market economy. They help determine how goods and services are produced and for whom they are produced. This chapter and the next three chapters will look at both functions.

Factor markets are important in determining how goods and services are produced because most goods and services can be produced in more than

**Factor markets** The markets in which the factors of production—labor, natural resources, and capital — are bought and sold.

one way. Wheat, for example, can be grown by extensive cultivation of large areas of land with a lot of machinery and little labor or by intensive cultivation of small areas with little machinery and much labor. The choice of production methods depends on the relative prices of the various factors. As those prices change, production methods can change too. Factors that are relatively cheap are used intensively, while those that are relatively expensive are used sparingly.

At the same time, factor markets help determine for whom output is produced, because most people earn their incomes by selling whatever factors of production they own. The greatest number sell their labor services. Many also sell or rent land or capital that they own. Because markets determine factor prices, they also determine how much of the total product will go to the owners of labor services, capital, and natural resources.

**Functional distribution of income** The distribution of income according to factor ownership—that is, the distribution among workers, natural resource owners, and owners of capital.

The distribution of income among factor owners is called the **functional distribution of income**. Functional distribution partly explains for whom output is produced, but it is not the whole story. The **personal distribution of income** — which specific people receive the income — depends both on the functional distribution of income and on the way ownership of factors is distributed among people. This chapter and the next will be largely concerned with the functional distribution of income. First, the outlines of marginal productivity theory will be presented and applied to the factor markets for natural resources and capital. Chapter 31 will apply this theory to labor markets and use it to help explain the nature and functions of labor unions.

**Personal distribution of income** The distribution of income among individuals, taking into account both the functional distribution of income and the distribution of factor ownership among persons.

Finally, Chapter 32 will take up the subject of the personal distribution of income and, in particular, the problem of poverty. It will show how the operation of factor markets helps determine the incidence of poverty and will discuss various government policies aimed at reducing or eliminating poverty.

## THE DEMAND FOR FACTORS OF PRODUCTION

### The Firm in Factor Markets

In many ways, factor markets are much like the product markets already studied. The theories of supply and demand and the tools of marginal analysis apply to factor markets just as to product markets. But factor markets do differ from product markets in one major respect. In factor markets, it is firms that are the buyers and households that are the sellers, rather than the other way around. A theory of the demand for factors of production must be based on the same considerations of price, revenue, and profit that determine the supply of products. A theory of factor supply must be an extension of the theory of consumer choice.

In taking the first steps toward a theory of factor demand the assumption, as earlier, will be that firms aim to maximize profits. Each profit maximizing firm must take three things into account when it makes its hiring decisions. The first is the quantity of output produced by a unit of the factor in question, the second is the revenue derived from the sale of the output that will be produced, and the third is the cost of obtaining the factor.

## Marginal Physical Product

Chapter 22 defined the *marginal physical product* of a factor as the increase in output resulting from a one unit increase in the input of that factor when the quantity of all other factors used remains unchanged. For example, if employing one additional worker hour of labor in a light bulb factory yields an added output of five light bulbs, when no other inputs to the production process are increased, the marginal physical productivity of labor in that factory is five bulbs per hour. To take another example, if giving a farmer one more hectare of land makes it possible for the farmer to produce twenty more cubic decimetres of wheat per year—without any increase in the amount of work performed, the amount of machinery used, or anything else—the marginal physical product of land on that farm is twenty cubic decimetres per hectare. Finally, if having one extra dollar of capital allows a taxi company to carry one extra passenger one extra kilometre each year, that puts the marginal physical product of capital for the company at one passenger kilometre per dollar's worth of capital.

**Exhibit 30.1**

**Total and marginal physical product of a factor of production**

As the quantity of one factor increases with the quantity of other factors remaining unchanged, total physical product increases, but at a decreasing rate. Marginal physical product, as Part c of this exhibit and Column 3 of the table in Part a show, decreases as the quantity of the factor employed increases. This decrease in marginal physical product is a direct consequence of the law of diminishing returns.

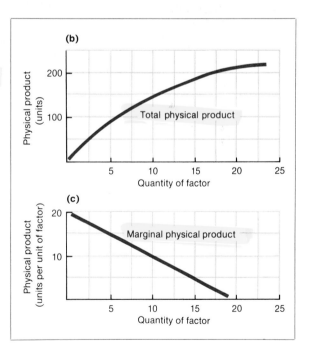

**(a)**

| Quantity of Factor (1) | Total Physical Product (2) | Marginal Physical Product (3) |
|---|---|---|
| 0 | 0 | |
| | | 20 |
| 1 | 20 | |
| | | 19 |
| 2 | 39 | |
| | | 18 |
| 3 | 57 | |
| | | 17 |
| 4 | 74 | |
| | | 16 |
| 5 | 90 | |
| | | 15 |
| 6 | 105 | |
| | | 14 |
| 7 | 119 | |
| | | 13 |
| 8 | 132 | |
| | | 12 |
| 9 | 144 | |
| | | 11 |
| 10 | 155 | |
| | | 10 |
| 11 | 165 | |
| | | 9 |
| 12 | 174 | |
| | | 8 |
| 13 | 182 | |
| | | 7 |
| 14 | 189 | |
| | | 6 |
| 15 | 195 | |
| | | 5 |
| 16 | 200 | |
| | | 4 |
| 17 | 204 | |
| | | 3 |
| 18 | 207 | |
| | | 2 |
| 19 | 209 | |
| | | 1 |
| 20 | 210 | |

**Law of Diminishing Returns** As Chapter 22 showed, the marginal physical product of a factor varies as the quantity of the factor used varies, other things being equal. In particular, as the quantity of a single variable factor increases, with the quantities of all other factor inputs remaining fixed, a point will be reached beyond which the marginal physical product of the variable factor will decline. This principle is known as the *law of diminishing returns*.

Exhibit 30.1 shows total and marginal physical product curves for a firm subject to the law of diminishing returns throughout the range of zero to twenty units of factor input. (At this point, it does not matter whether the factor in question is labor, capital, or natural resources; the principle is the same for all.) As the quantity of this one factor is increased, with the quantities of all other factors used held constant, output increases — but at a diminishing rate. The first unit of the factor yields a marginal physical product of twenty units of output, the second a marginal physical product of nineteen units of output, and so on. After the twentieth unit of output, as the example is constructed, marginal physical product drops to zero. This implies that some absolute capacity ceiling has been reached, so that adding more of the variable factor cannot produce more output unless the quantities of some of the fixed factors are also increased. For example, if the variable factor in question is labor, it may be that adding more than twenty workers will do nothing to increase output unless, say, the quantity of machinery available for use by the workers is also increased. Note that beyond twenty units of output, where the marginal physical product of the variable factor drops to zero, the total physical product curve becomes horizontal.

## Marginal Revenue Product

To determine what quantity of each factor of production it should hire to maximize profit, a firm must take into account the revenue that will be earned from the sale of the product of an added unit of factor input as well as the size of the marginal physical product. Here, a new term will be useful. The change in revenue resulting from the sale of the product produced by one additional unit of factor input is called the **marginal revenue product** of that factor.

**Marginal revenue product (of a factor)** The change in revenue resulting from the sale of the product produced by one additional unit of factor input.

**Marginal Revenue Product for a Competitive Firm** What happens to the marginal revenue product of a factor as the quantity of that factor is varied depends on what happens to both the marginal physical product of the factor and the marginal revenue earned by selling the product. The simplest case to consider is that of a perfectly competitive firm. Because such a firm is a price taker, as shown in Chapter 23, the quantity of output it produces has no effect on the price at which its output is sold. Marginal revenue for the competitive firm is thus equal to the price of the firm's output, which is constant for all quantities of output. To calculate marginal revenue product of a factor for such a firm, then, the marginal physical product of the factor is multiplied by the price of the output.

Exhibit 30.2 gives an example of how marginal revenue product is calculated for a perfectly competitive firm. The marginal physical product

**Exhibit 30.2**

**Marginal revenue product for a typical price taking firm**

For a price taking firm, the marginal revenue product of a factor is equal to the factor's marginal physical product times the price of the product. This table is constructed on the assumption that the product price is $1 per unit and that marginal physical product is the same as in Exhibit 30.1.

| Quantity of Factor (1) | Total Physical Product (2) | Marginal Physical Product (3) | Revenue per Unit (Price) (4) | Marginal Revenue Product (5) |
|---|---|---|---|---|
| 0 | 0 | | | |
| | | 20 | $1 | $20 |
| 1 | 20 | | | |
| | | 19 | 1 | 19 |
| 2 | 39 | | | |
| | | 18 | 1 | 18 |
| 3 | 57 | | | |
| | | 17 | 1 | 17 |
| 4 | 74 | | | |
| | | 16 | 1 | 16 |
| 5 | 90 | | | |
| | | 15 | 1 | 15 |
| 6 | 105 | | | |
| | | 14 | 1 | 14 |
| 7 | 119 | | | |
| | | 13 | 1 | 13 |
| 8 | 132 | | | |
| | | 12 | 1 | 12 |
| 9 | 144 | | | |
| | | 11 | 1 | 11 |
| 10 | 155 | | | |
| | | 10 | 1 | 10 |
| 11 | 165 | | | |
| | | 9 | 1 | 9 |
| 12 | 174 | | | |
| | | 8 | 1 | 8 |
| 13 | 182 | | | |
| | | 7 | 1 | 7 |
| 14 | 189 | | | |
| | | 6 | 1 | 6 |
| 15 | 198 | | | |
| | | 5 | 1 | 5 |
| 16 | 200 | | | |
| | | 4 | 1 | 4 |
| 17 | 204 | | | |
| | | 3 | 1 | 3 |
| 18 | 207 | | | |
| | | 2 | 1 | 2 |
| 19 | 209 | | | |
| | | 1 | 1 | 1 |
| 20 | 210 | | | |

schedule is the same as that given in Exhibit 30.1, and a constant price of $1 per unit of output is assumed.

**Marginal Revenue Product for a Monopolist**  If the firm in question is not perfectly competitive, the price at which it sells its output will tend to vary as the quantity of output varies. Suppose, for example, that the firm is a pure monopolist. As Chapter 24 demonstrated, a pure monopolist must decrease the price at which its product is sold each time it wants to increase the quantity sold, in accordance with the downward-sloping demand curve for its product. Because the price per unit decreases as output increases, marginal revenue per unit of output is always less than price per unit for a monopolist.

To calculate the increase in revenue resulting from a one unit increase in factor input for a monopolist, then, requires taking changes in both marginal physical product and marginal revenue into account. Exhibit 30.3 illustrates how this is done. The exhibit is constructed using the same total physical product schedule as Exhibits 30.1 and 30.2; but this time, the firm is assumed to be a monopolist. Column 3 gives the firm's demand curve, showing that the price at which output can be sold drops from $1.40 per unit at 20 units of output to $.45 at 210 units of output. Multiplying price times total physical product gives the total revenue corresponding to each quantity of factor input, shown in Column 4.

The differences between successive entries in the total revenue column give the marginal revenue product data, shown in Column 5. For example, as the quantity of factor input increases from 4 units to 5 units, the total output increases from 74 units to 90 units, while the price falls from $1.13 per unit to $1.05. As Column 4 shows, total revenue increases from $83.62

when 4 units of factor input are used to $94.50 when 5 units of factor input are used. This gives a marginal revenue product of $10.88 in the range from 4 to 5 units of factor input.

As the price continues to fall, marginal revenue eventually becomes negative. Beyond that point, additional units of factor input, even though they increase total physical product, reduce total revenue. The turning point comes at 10 units of factor input, as Exhibit 30.3 is constructed. Beyond that point, marginal revenue product is negative, even though marginal physical product remains positive.

At every level of factor input, the marginal revenue product of the factor is equal to the marginal physical product times the marginal revenue per unit of output. This relationship is shown in Columns 5 through 7 of Exhibit 30.3. Note that the marginal revenue figures in Column 7 are expressed in terms of dollars per unit of output, whereas the marginal revenue product figures in Column 5 are expressed in terms of dollars per unit of factor input.

**Exhibit 30.3**

**Marginal revenue product for a monopolistic firm**

This exhibit shows how marginal revenue product varies as the quantity of factor input varies for a firm that is a pure monopolist. As Column 3 shows, price falls as outputs increase, in accordance with the demand for the firm's product. Total revenue begins to decline after ten units of output, as marginal revenue per unit of output becomes negative, even though marginal physical product remains positive. Marginal revenue product can be calculated either as the difference between successive entries in the total revenue column or as the product of marginal physical product and marginal revenue per unit of output.

| Quantity of Factor (1) | Total Physical Product (2) | Price of Output (3) | Total Revenue (4) | Marginal Revenue Product (5) | Marginal Physical Product (6) | Marginal Revenue per Unit of Output (7) |
|---|---|---|---|---|---|---|
| 0 | 0 | — | 0 | | | |
| 1 | 20 | $1.40 | $28.00 | $28.00 | 20 | $1.40 |
| 2 | 39 | 1.31 | 51.09 | 23.09 | 19 | 1.21 |
| 3 | 57 | 1.22 | 69.54 | 18.45 | 18 | 1.02 |
| 4 | 74 | 1.13 | 83.62 | 14.08 | 17 | .84 |
| 5 | 90 | 1.05 | 94.50 | 10.88 | 16 | .68 |
| 6 | 105 | .98 | 102.38 | 7.88 | 15 | .52 |
| 7 | 119 | .91 | 107.70 | 5.32 | 14 | .38 |
| 8 | 132 | .84 | 110.88 | 3.18 | 13 | .24 |
| 9 | 144 | .78 | 112.32 | 1.44 | 12 | .12 |
| 10 | 155 | .73 | 112.38 | .06 | 11 | .01 |
| 11 | 165 | .68 | 111.38 | −1.00 | 10 | −.10 |
| 12 | 174 | .63 | 109.62 | −1.76 | 9 | −.20 |
| 13 | 182 | .59 | 107.38 | −2.24 | 8 | −.28 |
| 14 | 189 | .56 | 104.90 | −2.48 | 7 | −.35 |
| 15 | 195 | .53 | 102.38 | −2.52 | 6 | −.42 |
| 16 | 200 | .50 | 100.00 | −2.38 | 5 | −.47 |
| 17 | 204 | .48 | 97.92 | −2.08 | 4 | −.52 |
| 18 | 207 | .47 | 96.26 | −1.66 | 3 | −.55 |
| 19 | 209 | .46 | 95.10 | −1.16 | 2 | −.58 |
| 20 | 210 | .45 | 94.50 | −.60 | 1 | −.60 |

Figures in Columns 3, 4, 5, and 7 are rounded to the nearest cent.

## Marginal Factor Cost

The third consideration a firm must take into account to determine the profit maximizing quantity of a factor is the cost of obtaining each additional unit of that factor—the factor's **marginal factor cost**.

To keep things simple for the moment, consider only the case where a firm is a price taker in the market where it buys its factors of production. This will happen if the firm is only one among a large number of firms competing to hire that particular factor and if the quantity of the factor it uses is only a small fraction of the total used by all firms. For a firm that buys as a price taker, marginal factor cost is simply equal to the market price of the factor. If, for example, the market wage rate for typists is $7 per hour, then the marginal factor cost for this particular type of labor is $7 per hour for any firm that is a price taker in the market for typists.

**Marginal factor cost** The amount by which a firm's total factor cost must increase in order for it to obtain an additional unit of that factor.

## Profit Maximization

Profit maximization requires that a firm hire just enough of each factor of production to equalize marginal revenue product and marginal factor cost. If marginal revenue product exceeds marginal factor cost, hiring one more unit of the factor will add more to the revenue than to the cost and hence will increase profit. If marginal factor cost exceeds marginal revenue product, reducing input of the factor by one unit will reduce cost by more than revenue and hence will also increase profit. Only when marginal revenue product and marginal factor cost are equal will it be impossible for any change in factor input to raise profit. This rule applies both to a firm that is a perfect competitor in its output market and to a monopolist.

Exhibit 30.4 illustrates this profit maximization rule. The exhibit, which contains both a table and a corresponding diagram, is constructed on the assumption that the firm is a perfect competitor in the output market and that it sells its product at $1 per unit, as in Exhibit 30.2. The firm is also assumed to be a price taker in the factor market, buying inputs of the factor at $5 per unit. Notice that profit rises as more of the factor is hired—up to the fifteenth unit of input. The firm just breaks even on the hiring of the sixteenth unit of input, and profit declines thereafter. It is between the fifteenth and sixteenth units of factor input that marginal revenue product becomes exactly equal to marginal factor cost.

## Factor Demand Curves

It follows from this analysis of profit maximization that a firm's marginal revenue product curve for a factor is also the firm's demand curve for that factor. A demand curve must indicate the quantity demanded at each price, and it has just been shown that the quantity of the factor demanded will be whatever quantity makes the factor's price (more precisely, its marginal factor cost) equal to marginal revenue product.

Individual firm demand curves for a factor of production can be added together to get a market demand curve for that factor. Such a market demand is said to be a *derived* demand curve, because the demand for a factor of production does not arise from the usefulness of the factor services themselves. Instead it is derived indirectly from the usefulness of the products the factor can produce. The market demand for farmland is derived from the market demand for food, the market demand for printers from the market demand for books, and so on.

## Changes in Factor Demand

The demand for factors, like the demand for products, changes in response to changes in economic conditions. Consider Exhibit 30.5. Suppose that the demand curve $D_0$ is the market demand curve for some factor of production. A change in the market price of that factor will cause the quantity of the factor demanded to change. This is represented by a movement along the demand curve. (See the arrow drawn parallel to $D_0$.) Changes in economic conditions other than a change in the factor's price

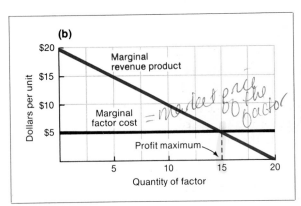

(b)

**Exhibit 30.4**
**Profit maximization for a price taking firm**
Profit maximization requires that a firm hire just enough of each factor of production to equalize marginal revenue product and marginal factor cost. Here it is assumed that the firm is a price taker, as in Exhibit 30.2. The point of profit maximization falls between fifteen and sixteen units of the factor.

(a)

| Quantity of Factor (1) | Marginal Revenue Product (2) | Marginal Factor Cost (3) | Total Factor Cost (4) | Fixed Costs (5) | Total Revenue (6) | Total Profit (7) |
|---|---|---|---|---|---|---|
| 1 | | | $5 | $100 | $ 20 | −$85 |
| | $19 | $5 | | | | |
| 2 | | | 10 | 100 | 39 | −71 |
| | 18 | 5 | | | | |
| 3 | | | 15 | 100 | 57 | −58 |
| | 17 | 5 | | | | |
| 4 | | | 20 | 100 | 74 | −46 |
| | 16 | 5 | | | | |
| 5 | | | 25 | 100 | 90 | −35 |
| | 15 | 5 | | | | |
| 6 | | | 30 | 100 | 105 | −25 |
| | 14 | 5 | | | | |
| 7 | | | 35 | 100 | 119 | −16 |
| | 13 | 5 | | | | |
| 8 | | | 40 | 100 | 132 | −8 |
| | 12 | 5 | | | | |
| 9 | | | 45 | 100 | 144 | −1 |
| | 11 | 5 | | | | |
| 10 | | | 50 | 100 | 155 | 5 |
| | 10 | 5 | | | | |
| 11 | | | 55 | 100 | 165 | 10 |
| | 9 | 5 | | | | |
| 12 | | | 60 | 100 | 174 | 14 |
| | 8 | 5 | | | | |
| 13 | | | 65 | 100 | 182 | 17 |
| | 7 | 5 | | | | |
| 14 | | | 70 | 100 | 189 | 19 |
| | 6 | 5 | | | | |
| 15 | | | 75 | 100 | 195 | 20 |
| | 5 | 5 | | | | |
| 16 | | | 80 | 100 | 200 | 20 |
| | 4 | 5 | | | | |
| 17 | | | 85 | 100 | 204 | 19 |
| | 3 | 5 | | | | |
| 18 | | | 90 | 100 | 207 | 17 |
| | 2 | 5 | | | | |
| 19 | | | 95 | 100 | 209 | 14 |
| | 1 | 5 | | | | |
| 20 | | | 100 | 100 | 210 | 10 |

can cause a change in demand for a factor—for example, a shift in the demand curve from $D_0$ to $D_1$ or $D_2$.

Three kinds of changes in particular are capable of causing shifts in the demand curve for a factor of production. First, an increase in demand for the product that the factor produces will shift the factor demand curve to the right. Similarly, a decrease in demand for the product will cause the factor demand curve to shift to the left. Second, a change in the price of another factor of production used in combination with the given factor can also cause the demand for the given factor to shift. An increase in the price of a factor that is a substitute for the given factor will cause the demand curve for the given factor to shift to the right, while an increase in the price of a factor that is a complement to the given factor will cause the demand curve of that factor to shift to the left. Third, any change in technology that increases the marginal physical productivity of a factor will cause its demand curve to shift to the right, other things being equal, while a decrease in the marginal physical product of the factor will shift the curve to the left.

## SUPPLY AND DEMAND IN THE LABOR MARKET

Up to this point, marginal productivity and factor demand have been discussed in general terms. It is time now to turn to the specifics of markets for particular factors. This section begins the analysis of such markets by looking at the supply and demand for labor, land, and capital. It concludes with a discussion of a unique and controversial form of income called profit. The discussion on labor will be limited at first to the case where individual workers compete with one another for jobs. The next chapter will take up the case of organized labor markets, where workers join together into unions to bargain with employers rather than competing with one another for jobs on an individual basis.

---

**Exhibit 30.5**
**Movements along a factor demand curve and shifts in the curve**

Changes in the price of a factor, other things being equal, will produce movements along a given factor demand curve, as shown by the arrow. Other kinds of changes can shift the factor demand curve. An increase in demand for the product produced by the factor might shift the curve from $D_0$ to $D_1$. An increase in the price of another factor that is a complement to the given factor might shift the curve from $D_0$ to $D_2$.

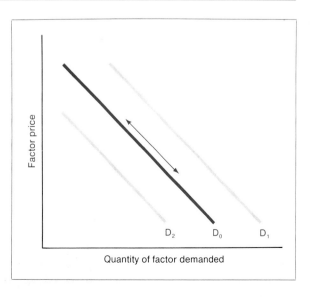

## The Labor Supply Curve

The general analysis of a factor demand given in the previous section can be applied to the labor market without special modification. A labor supply curve is now needed to go with the labor demand curve. A look at the labor supply decision for an individual worker will begin the analysis.

**Labor Supply for the Individual** As individuals, people's decisions regarding how much labor to supply to the market are part of the general problem of consumer choice and can be analyzed in terms of the theory developed in Chapter 21. The best way to approach the problem is to think in terms of a trade-off between two alternative sources of utility — leisure and the consumption of purchased goods and services. Leisure is valued for relaxation, recreation, and the accomplishment of assorted household tasks. Time spent at leisure is time taken away from work, however, and thus is time taken away from earning income that can be used to buy goods and services. Within the limits of a twenty-four-hour day, people balance the relative advantages of work and leisure to achieve a consumer equilibrium in which, ideally, the marginal utility per hour of leisure exactly equals the marginal utility of the goods that can be bought with an hour's earnings.

The hourly wage rate can be thought of as the price — or, more precisely, as the opportunity cost — of leisure to the worker, in that it represents the dollar equivalent of the goods and services that must be sacrificed in order to enjoy an added hour of leisure. As the wage rate increases, it affects work versus leisure decisions in two ways. First, there is a substitution effect; the increased wage rate provides an incentive to work more, because each hour of work now produces more income to be spent on goods and services. In effect, purchased goods and services are substituted for leisure. Second, however, the increase in the wage rate has an income effect that tends to reduce hours worked. The higher wage rate, assuming that the prices of goods and services in general remain unchanged, increases workers' real incomes. With higher real incomes, they tend to consume more of all goods that are normal goods and less of those that are inferior goods. Leisure is a normal good. Other things being equal, people generally seek more leisure, in the form of shorter working hours and longer vacations, as their incomes rise. Taken by itself, then, the income effect of a wage increase is the reduction of the quantity of labor supplied by workers.

It can be seen, therefore, that the net effect of an increase in the wage rate on the quantity of labor supplied by an individual worker depends on the relative strength of the substitution and income effects. It is generally believed that for very low wage rates, the substitution effect predominates, so that the quantity of labor supplied increases as the wage increases. As the wage rises, however, the income effect becomes stronger. People tend to treat leisure as a luxury good; after they have assured themselves of a reasonable material standard of living, they begin to consider "spending" any further wage increases on increased time off from work. The labor supply curve for an individual to whom this generalization applies has a backward-bending shape, like the one shown in Exhibit 30.6. Over the positively sloped low wage section, the substitution effect of wage changes predominates, and over the negatively sloped high wage section, the income effect predominates.

## Exhibit 30.6
### An individual's labor supply curve

On the one hand, a higher wage tends to increase the amount of work an individual is willing to do, because the extra money compensates for time taken away from leisure activities. On the other hand, a higher wage allows a person to take more time off work and still enjoy a high standard of living. Taken together, the two effects tend to give the individual labor supply curve the backward-bending shape shown here.

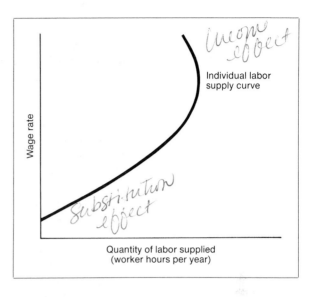

**Market Labor Supply Curves** Even though the labor supply curves for all individual workers may bend backwards, at least over some range of wages, the supply curve for any particular type of labor as a whole is likely to be positively sloped throughout. Consider, for example, the supply of electrical engineers, the supply of typists in Montreal, or the supply of farm laborers in Saskatchewan. Each individual engineer or typist or laborer might, beyond some point, respond to an increased wage by cutting back on hours worked; but for the market as a whole, this tendency would be more than offset by new workers drawn into that particular labor market from other occupations or areas. Thus, other things being equal, if the wage rate for electrical engineers rose, more engineering students would take up that specialty; if the wage rate for typists in Montreal rose, more people would become typists than, say, filing clerks; and if the wage for farm laborers in

## Exhibit 30.7
### Hypothetical supply curve for typists

Although each individual typist may have a backward-bending supply curve, the supply curve for typists in any particular local market will have the usual upward-sloping shape. As the wage rises, people will be drawn into this occupation from other kinds of work or other localities.

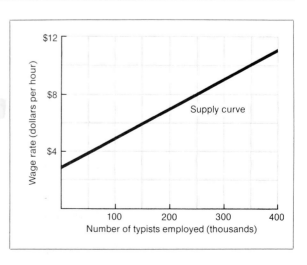

Saskatchewan rose, workers would be drawn in from Alberta, Manitoba, and Ontario. As a result, for any discussion of the market for a particular category of labor at a particular time and place, it is reasonable to draw the labor supply curve with the usual positive slope, as in Exhibit 30.7, regardless of the shape of the individual labor supply curves underlying it.

## Competitive Equilibrium

Determining the wage rate in a labor market that is fully competitive on both sides is a straightforward exercise in supply and demand analysis. Exhibit 30.8, for example, shows a supply and demand curve representing the labor market for typists in Montreal. It assumes that a large number of typists compete with one another for jobs and that a large number of employers compete with one another for typists, so that both are price takers. The demand curve for typists is the employers' combined marginal revenue curve. The supply curve is the same as that in Exhibit 30.7.

Equilibrium in this market requires a wage rate of $7 per hour, with 200,000 typists employed. If the wage rate were lower, there would be a shortage of typists. Some firms, unable to fill all their job openings, would offer premium wages to workers from other jobs or other regions. The wage rate would be driven up to the equilibrium level. If, on the other hand, the wage rate were above $7 per hour, there would be a surplus of typists. Many people would be looking for typing jobs and not finding them. After sufficient fruitless search, some would become willing to accept work at lower than expected wages, thus pushing the wage rate down toward equilibrium. Others would drift into other occupations or regions.

In a labor market such as this one, where both employers and employees are price takers, the equilibrium wage rate is equal to the marginal revenue product of labor. In the special case where all employers are price takers (perfect competitors) in the market where they sell their output as well as in the market where they purchase inputs, the equilibrium wage rate is

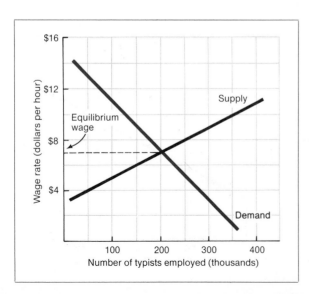

**Exhibit 30.8**
**Determination of the equilibrium wage in a competitive labor market**
When both employers and workers are price takers in the labor market, the point of equilibrium is found where the supply and demand curves intersect. Here the equilibrium wage rate is $7 per hour, and the equilibrium quantity of labor is 200,000 typists employed.

equal to the marginal physical product of labor times the price per unit of output.

## Monopsony

Not every factor market has a large number of buyers competing with one another. The extreme situation where there is only one buyer in a market is called **monopsony**.

There is an important difference between the case of competition and the case of monopsony. For a monopsonist, marginal factor cost is not equal to the price of the factor. Exhibit 30.9 shows why. The table and graph in this exhibit represent the supply side of the market for typists in a small town where there is just one big employer — an insurance company — which employs all or almost all the town's typists.

The supply schedule of typists shows that no one will work as a typist if the wage rate is $3 per hour or less. Above that wage, each extra two cents per hour will attract one more worker. Suppose that the monopsonistic employer has hired 150 typists, paying them $6 per hour. The total labor cost for a labor force of this size is $900 per hour. What will happen to the firm's total labor cost if it expands its labor force by one additional worker?

According to the supply curve, to hire 151 typists requires a wage of $6.02 per hour. That wage must be paid not just to the 151st worker but to all workers. The total cost of a labor force of 151 typists, then, is $6.02 times 151, or $909.02. The addition of one more worker has raised the total labor cost from $900 to $909.02, a marginal factor cost of $9.02. Similar results can be obtained by choosing other starting points from the table. *In every case, the marginal factor cost for the monopsonist is greater than the factor price (the wage rate).*

Exhibit 30.9b shows a marginal factors cost curve based on the marginal

**Monopsony** A market in which there is only one buyer; from the Greek words *mono* ("single") and *opsonia* ("buying").

---

**Exhibit 30.9**

**Marginal factor cost under monopsony**

Under monopsony, marginal factor cost exceeds factor price. Consider an increase in quantity from 150 to 151 units of labor in this exhibit. The wage rate must be raised from $6 to $6.02 not just for the 151st employee but for all the previous 150 as well. Marginal labor cost in this range is thus $9.02 per hour, not $6.02 per hour.

**(a)**

| Quantity of Labor Supplied (1) | Wage Rate (2) | Total Factor Cost (3) | Marginal Factor Cost (4) |
|---|---|---|---|
| 1 | $3.02 | $  3.02 | |
| 2 | 3.04 | 6.08 | $ 3.06 |
| 3 | 3.06 | 9.18 | 3.10 |
| | | | |
| 150 | 6.00 | 900.00 | |
| 151 | 6.02 | 909.02 | 9.02 |
| 152 | 6.04 | 918.08 | 9.06 |
| | | | |
| 200 | 7.00 | 1,400.00 | |
| 201 | 7.02 | 1,411.02 | 11.02 |
| 202 | 7.04 | 1,422.08 | 11.06 |

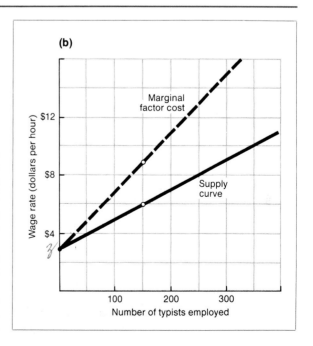

factor cost column of the table in Part a. This curve lies above the supply curve at every point. The relationship between the supply curve and the marginal cost curve for a monopsonist, as shown in this figure, is analogous to the relationship between the demand and marginal revenue curves for a monopolist.

### Monopsony Equilibrium

Given the monopsonist's marginal factor cost curve—derived from the factor's market supply curve—determining the equilibrium level of employment for the firm is a matter of routine. Exhibit 30.10 shows the monopsonistic employer's marginal revenue product curve along with the labor supply and marginal factor cost curves from Exhibit 30.9. Following the general rule that profit is maximized where marginal factor cost is equal to marginal revenue product, it can be seen that the monopsonist will hire 150 typists at a wage rate of $6 per hour.

Note that when a labor market is in monopsony equilibrium, the wage rate is lower than the marginal revenue product of labor. In the example shown, the equilibrium wage rate is $6 per hour, although the marginal revenue product is $9 per hour. Despite the gap between the wage rate and the marginal revenue product, this increase in the quantity of labor hired will not increase revenue by enough to offset higher labor costs. The reason is that the cost of hiring another worker is not just the $6.02 per hour that must be paid to the 151st worker but that sum plus the extra two cents per hour by which the wages of all 150 previously hired workers must be raised. The complete marginal factor cost for the 151st worker is thus $6.02 + $3.00, or $9.02 per hour.

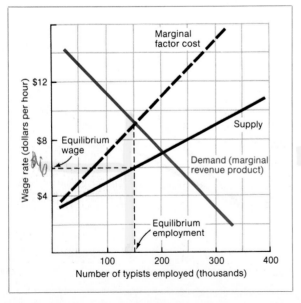

**Exhibit 30.10**
**Wage determination under monopsony**

Here are a monopsonist's marginal revenue product of labor curve, labor supply curve, and marginal factor cost curve. The quantity of labor required to maximize profits is found where the marginal revenue product curve and the marginal factor cost curves intersect. Note that the equilibrium wage rate is *not* shown by the intersection of the marginal factor cost and marginal revenue product curves. Instead, the rate is equal to the height of the supply curve directly below that intersection.

## RENT, INTEREST, AND PROFITS

Wages and salaries are a big part of the income distribution picture in the Canadian economy. Recently, they have accounted for some three-quarters of all net national income. They are not the whole picture, however.

The remaining quarter of personal income (excluding transfer payments) is composed of rent, interest, and profits. These sources of income, although relatively small, deserve the same careful analysis given to wages and salaries. Rent, interest, and profits play a key role in the resource allocation process. They also play an important role in determining the overall personal distribution of income, since they are distributed some-what less equally than labor income.

### Rent

**Economic Rent**  **Pure economic rent** is the income earned by a factor of production that is in completely inelastic supply. The classic example of such a factor is land, which in this context means the natural productive powers of the earth and the locational advantages of particular sites. It does not include artificial improvements; nor does it include such matters as destruction of the soil through erosion or creation of new land through reclamation.

Exhibit 30.11 shows how rent is determined by supply and demand in a competitive market. It considers a particular category of land — Saskatche-wan wheatland. The supply curve for Saskatchewan wheatland is a vertical line, because the quantity of land supplied does not vary as the rent that it earns varies. The demand curve is the marginal revenue product curve for that land as seen by Saskatchewan wheat farmers. The marginal product of land falls as more land is used in combination with fixed quantities of labor and capital because of diminishing returns. The demand curve thus slopes downward to the right.

> **Pure economic rent** The income earned by any factor of production that is in perfectly inelastic supply.

**Exhibit 30.11**
**Determination of rent by supply and demand**
Pure economic rent is earned only by a factor that has a perfectly inelastic supply curve. This figure shows hypo-thetical supply and demand curves for Saskatchewan wheatland. No account is taken of any possibilities for creating or destroying such land, so the supply curve is vertical. The demand curve, as for other factors, is based on the land's marginal revenue product.

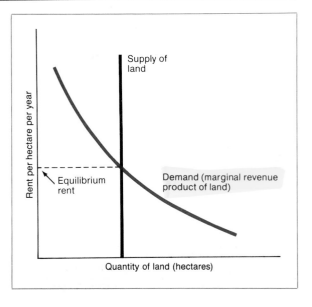

The rent the land earns is determined by the intersection of the supply curve, representing the scarcity of land, and the demand curve, representing its productivity. If the rent is higher than the equilibrium shown, not all land will be put to use. The rent will then fall as landowners compete with one another to find tenants. If the rent is lower than the equilibrium rate, farmers will be unable to find all the land they want. They will bid against one another for the limited available supply and drive rents up.

**Capitalization of Rents** The price of land is called rent; but much land, of course, is used by the person who owns it and is therefore not rented by a tenant from a landlord. That use does not change the way supply and demand determine the value of land. It does mean, though, that it is sometimes useful to speak of the price of land in terms of a lump-sum sales price rather than as a rent per month or year.

There is a simple relationship between the value of a piece of land expressed as a rent and the price at which that piece can be sold in the market. The market price of a piece of land is said to be the **capitalized value of its rent** — that is, the sum that would earn an annual return equal to the annual rent if it were invested at the market rate of interest.

> **Capitalized value of a rent**
> The amount equal to the value of the sum of money that would earn a periodic interest return equal to the rent if invested at the current market rate of interest.

Consider, for example, a piece of land with an expected real rental value of $1,000 per year in perpetuity. If the expected real rate of interest were 5 percent per year, a buyer would be willing to pay $20,000 for title to the land. If the expected real rate of interest were 2 percent per year, the price of the land would rise to $50,000, and so on. In general, the price of a parcel of land having a perpetual expected real annual rental value of R dollars per year, capitalized at the real rate of interest r is given by the formula $R/r$.

**Other Rents** The term *rent* can refer to the market return earned by any factor of production that is unique or that is in perfectly inelastic supply. Consider the very high incomes of people with unique talents, such as singers, actors, and some executives. These incomes are more plausibly thought of as rents earned on talents rather than as wages earned for work done. Artificially created legal privileges can be said to earn rents, too. For instance, part of the earnings of a Winnipeg taxicab can be counted as rent earned from the license that gives it the legal privilege to operate, so long as the supply of licenses is strictly limited by city authorities.

The hallmark of pure economic rent is inelasticity of supply. Pure economic rent should not be confused with what is loosely called the rental income earned by manufactured assets that are not in perfectly inelastic supply. Consider rental income of an apartment house owner, for example. It may in part be pure economic rent earned by some uniquely convenient site on which the building is located. In addition, though, the owner's income includes implicit wages for any custodial work done in the building, implicit interest on the money invested to build it, and so on.

What is pure economic rent and what is not depends in part on the time framework within which the income is considered. In the short run—say a period too short for new buildings to be constructed—a case could be made for considering the income earned from buildings as a pure economic rent. In the long run, however, when additional buildings can be supplied at a price, such rental income is clearly not a pure economic rent.

## INTEREST AND CAPITAL

**Two Aspects of Interest** The theory of capital and interest is in many ways the most complicated part of factor market theory, and care must be taken to understand the relationship between two different aspects of interest. The term *interest* is used to express both the price paid by borrowers to lenders for the use of loanable funds and the market return earned by capital as a factor of production. A person who loans $1,000 to another in return for a payment of $100 per year (plus eventual repayment of the principal) is said to earn 10 percent interest per year on the money. At the same time, a person who buys a machine for $1,000 and earns $100 a year by employing the productive services of that machine is said to earn 10 percent interest on capital.

**Consumption Loans** The discussion of interest and capital will begin by looking at how credit markets work in a simplified economy where households are the only suppliers of credit — that is, of loanable funds. Savers are households that earn incomes now but consume less than they earn in order to put something aside for expected future needs. Not all households in the economy are savers, however; some want to consume more than their current incomes permit. The latter may be households that want to tide themselves over a temporary decrease in income, or they may be households with steady incomes that just do not want to wait to buy a car or take a vacation. These and other households that borrow for any number of reasons are one source of demand for loanable funds. The loans they take out are called consumption loans.

**The Productivity of Capital** Nothing has yet been said about production or capital. Opportunities to use capital as a factor of production are a second source of demand for loanable funds, in addition to the demand for pure consumption loans. To understand the demand for loans of this kind, it is necessary to understand why capital is productive.

Using capital means using a roundabout method of production rather than a direct method. Consider, as an example, a person whose business is making bricks. There are two ways to make bricks. The direct way is to form them by hand out of raw clay scooped up from the ground and to bake them over an open fire. Suppose that by using this method, a worker can make 100 bricks per month. The alternative way of making bricks is a roundabout one. The brickmaker first spends a month forming bricks by hand and putting them together to make a kiln. When the kiln is completed, its hotter fire and lower fuel consumption make it possible to produce 110 bricks per month from then on. The roundabout method using capital (the kiln) lengthens the period between the time work starts and the time finished bricks begin to appear. In return, it increases the eventual rate of output. That is the sense in which capital is productive.

The brickmaker's experience is repeated in a more elaborate way whenever a firm makes a capital investment. Producing automobiles on an assembly line is a roundabout method of production compared to producing them one by one with hand tools. Constructing a building in which to hold economics classes is a roundabout method of education compared with holding classes in the woods under a tree. In every case, time is taken to construct aids to production in order to produce more effectively later on.

**Investment Loans** The brickmaker in the example invested directly by actually building the needed capital equipment. In a market economy, firms need not build their own capital equipment. Anyone who sees an opportunity for increasing output by using a more capital intensive (that is, a more roundabout) production process can borrow money and buy capital. The productivity of capital thus creates a source of demand for loanable funds in addition to the demand for consumption loans. Loans for increasing productivity can be called investment loans.

Exhibit 30.12 shows how the rate of interest is determined when the demand for investment loans is added to the demand for consumption loans. The demand curve for loans is downward sloping because consumers experience diminishing satisfaction from extra consumption and will borrow more, in order to finance increased consumption, only if they can do so at lower rates of interest. Because of the diminishing marginal productivity of capital, businesses will be inclined to borrow more money for building more capital equipment only if they can do so at lower interest rates. The supply of loanable funds slopes upward to the right because those who provide the funds sacrifice current consumption. The more they sacrifice, the more painful it becomes, the greater will be the interest they demand in compensation. The equilibrium interest rate is simply the price that those who supply the funds exact for their sacrifice, and a reflection of the increased benefits anticipated by those who borrow the funds. In other words, at the equilibrium interest rate, S = D.

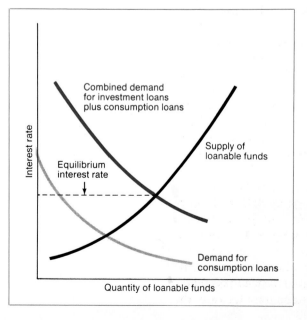

**Exhibit 30.12**
**Determination of the interest rate with both consumption and investment loans**

The demand for investment loans must be added to the demand for consumption loans to get the combined demand curve for loanable funds.

## PROFIT AND ENTREPRENEURSHIP

The term *pure economic profit* was introduced in Chapter 22 to refer to the income, if any, remaining to owners of a firm after they deduct all implicit and explicit costs of production. Explicit costs include factor payments to workers, resource owners, and suppliers of capital, together with the cost of semifinished inputs, if any, purchased from other firms. Implicit costs include a normal rate of return on capital supplied by owners of the firm plus the opportunity costs of using natural resources or labor supplied by owners of the firm or owned by the firm itself. What is left over is pure economic profit.

This definition of profit leaves unanswered two very important questions that have not yet been raised explicitly. Why does a firm ever earn any pure economic profit at all? Why is the entire value of the product of all firms not divided up among the owners of the labor, natural resources, and capital used in the production process? These are subtle questions that have occupied the minds of many great economists, who have not yet come up with answers that everyone agrees with. Still, it will be worthwhile to look at some of the kinds of answers that have been suggested.

### Theories of Profit

**Risk and Profit** According to one theory, profits are a reward that the owners of business receive for bearing risk. Every business venture is subject to the risk of failure. That is the nature of economic life in a world where the future is not known with certainty. People who merely hire out their factor services largely escape risk. A new business is usually expected to offer workers contractual guarantees that the payroll will be met even if the firm loses money. It is also expected to offer security against default to banks or bondholders who provide capital. The owner or owners of the firm (stockholders if the firm is organized in the corporate form) bear most of the risk of loss if the firm fails. In return, they get the privilege of keeping the profits if revenues turn out to be more than enough to pay off the obligations to hired factors. Why is it, though, that the profits earned by successful risk takers are not exactly offset by the losses of the unsuccessful? The answer has to do with people's attitudes toward risk.

It is possible that some people are indifferent to risk. A person who is indifferent to risk will be indifferent between the opportunity to earn $10,000 a year with absolute certainty and the opportunity to try for $20,000, subject to a fifty-fifty chance of failing and earning nothing. People who are indifferent to risk may launch new businesses even when the expected profit if the business succeeds is exactly offset by the expected loss if the business fails.

In practice, though, most people dislike risk. If they know they can earn a secure $10,000 a year, they will not launch a business with a fifty-fifty chance of failure unless that business, if successful, will pay more than $20,000. Because most people dislike risk, somewhat fewer business ventures are launched than would be otherwise. That makes opportunities a little more favorable, on the average, for those who are willing to bear some risk. When successes and failures are averaged out over the whole economy, profits more than offset losses. The excess of profits over losses is the reward earned by the people who bear business risks. Factor owners are willing to accept less than the whole value of the product of the firm to the extent that they are shielded from these risks.

**Arbitrage** The activity of earning a profit by buying a good for a low price in one market and reselling it for a higher price in another market.

**Profits as Arbitrage** A second theory equates profits with the return to the activity of **arbitrage** — buying a good at a low price in one market and selling it at a higher price in another. Examples of pure arbitrage can be found in markets for agricultural commodities, precious metals, foreign currencies, and other markets where completely standardized goods are traded at different points in the world. Consider, for example, the gold markets in London and Hong Kong. Economic policies, daily news developments, and other events may initially affect supply and demand in these two gold markets differently.

A political crisis in the British government, for example, might prompt an increase in demand in the London market, sending the price of gold there up relative to the price in Hong Kong. Before the prices got far apart, however, alert arbitrageurs in Hong Kong would start buying gold at the low Hong Kong price for resale at the higher London price. This activity would raise demand in Hong Kong and increase supply in London until the price in the two markets was equalized. (In practice, because of various transactions costs, the prices would be only approximately equalized on any given day.) In the process of acting as a crucial link in the international transmission of information through the price system, the arbitrageurs would turn a handy profit.

Arbitrage cannot always be seen in a form so pure as the international gold market. However, New York University economist Israel Kirzner has pointed out in an influential book that there is an element of arbitrage in every profit-making transaction.[1] Consider the entrepreneur-owner-manager of, say, a small shoe factory. This person buys inputs in one set of markets at the lowest prices possible and, after combining the inputs to form finished shoes, sells the product in other markets at the highest prices possible. In a hypothetical world where all markets were in perfectly competitive long-run equilibrium, it would no more be possible to make a profit by buying labor and leather and selling shoes than it would be by buying gold in Hong Kong and selling it in London. In such a world, the price of the leather and labor would be bid up to just equal the price of the finished shoes. In the real world, though, the alert entrepreneur can find arbitrage opportunities in a great variety of markets and can earn profits accordingly.

**Profits and Innovation** A third theory associates the profit and the activity of innovation. This theory has achieved considerable popularity through the writings of Joseph Schumpeter.[2] In subtle contrast to the entrepreneur as arbitrageur, taking advantage of spontaneously occurring opportunities to buy low and sell high, the entrepreneur as innovator creates new profit opportunities by devising a new product, a new production process, or a

---

[1]Israel Kirzner, *Competition and Entrepreneurship* (Chicago: University of Chicago Press, 1974).
[2]See, for example, Joseph Schumpeter, *Capitalism, Socialism, and Democracy* (New York: Harper & Bros., 1942).

new marketing strategy. If successful, the entrepreneur achieves a position of temporary monopoly that permits pure economic profits to be earned until rival firms catch on or leap ahead with innovations of their own.

## Further Comments on the Nature of Profit

**Entrepreneurship as a Factor of Production** It is probably pointless to argue which of the three theories of profit just discussed is the correct one. The economic activity called entrepreneurship is best thought of as an inseparable blend of risk taking, alertness to opportunities for arbitrage, and innovation.

Because entrepreneurs, like workers, resource owners, and suppliers of capital, earn a reward for their contribution to production, entrepreneurship is sometimes spoken of as a fourth factor of production. In some ways, it is indeed a little like the three factors of production—labor, natural resources, and capital. First, entrepreneurship, like the others, is scarce. Not everyone possesses the ability to organize business undertakings and recognize new economic opportunities. Second, entrepreneurs do earn an income in the form of the profit that remains after all the costs of their firms have been covered. Third, as is true for labor, natural resources, and capital, production cannot take place without entrepreneurship.

There is a limit, however, to how far the parallel between entrepreneurship and other factors can be pushed. The chief problem is that entrepreneurship is an intangible, not subject to measurement. There is no quantitative unit of entrepreneurship and hence no way to determine a price per unit. Applying supply and demand analysis to this fourth factor of production just does not work.

**Monopoly Profits** Up to this point, no distinction has been made between the profits earned in the short run by a competitive firm (before those profits are eroded by the competition of new entrants) and the profits earned by a monopolist (which under proper conditions of demand can persist indefinitely). Some writers have suggested that monopoly profits are a separate category of income that cannot be explained either as a reward to labor, capital, or natural resources or in terms of the entrepreneurial activities of risk bearing, arbitrage, and innovation. On close inspection, however, it turns out that most, if not all, of monopoly profit can be explained without introducing a special new category of income.

Consider, for example, the case of a monopoly based on a patented invention. When explicit costs are subtracted from revenue for such a firm, more than enough will be left over to provide a normal rate of return on capital. The firm might be said to earn a pure economic profit, but it would more accurately be said to earn an implicit rent as owner of the patent. It could, after all, sell or lease the patent rights to some other firm, in which case the patent owner would earn an explicit rent and the firm using the patent would earn only a normal return on capital after paying to acquire the patent. The opportunity cost to a monopolist of not renting the patent to another firm should thus be counted as an implicit cost, not as part of pure economic profit. The same applies to firms having a monopoly based on any other unique advantage that is in perfectly inelastic supply, such as a government franchise, a uniquely suitable location, or a unique natural resource.

If a monopolistic firm does not possess any unique advantage, its monopoly cannot be more than temporary. Sooner or later, other entrepreneurs will enter into competition with the firm and begin the process of reducing its pure economic profits to zero. Temporary monopoly profits of this type are not a separate category of income; they are simply the return earned by the monopolistic entrepreneur who was alert enough to get into the market before any competitors did so.

In Exhibit 30.13 are listed the sales, assets, earnings, and rates of return on capital investment for a select number of large and well-known corporations in Canada in 1982. These data help us to see how profit rates are calculated and how they vary from one corporation to another.

Column 2 shows the value of sales, and Column 3 lists the estimated value of all assets owned by each company. Column 4 indicates the net income earned by each corporation. Net income is close to the businessperson's definition of profit. It is the value of sales recorded in Column 2, *minus* operating expenditures (but not minus extraordinary expenditures).

To determine the profit *rate*, we should calculate net income as a percentage of the funds or assets that investors have committed to a particular corporation. But how does one determine the amount committed? Column 3 provides one such measurement—the estimated market value of the company's assets. This value will usually be considerably higher than the amount actually invested in the company by shareholders. Many assets will have been purchased over the years out of the company's retained earnings. However, if Column 3 accurately measures the current value of the company's assets, and if these assets could be pulled out of the company at any time by the shareholders and sold for that value, then Column 3 represents the amount that shareholders actually have tied up in the corporation. Under such circumstances, shareholders should compare profit calculated as a percent of asset value with the best alternative return they might enjoy if they sold their assets and invested them elsewhere. For example, Column 5 tells us that, for the Bell Telephone Company, net income was only 4.6 percent of asset value in 1982. If Bell Telephone could actually sell its assets for $13.4 billion, it should clearly do so. It could

---

**Exhibit 30.13**

Sales, assets, earnings, and rates of return for selected Canadian corporations, 1982

| Company (1) | Sales or Operating Revenue $000's (2) | Assets $000's (3) | Net Income $000's (4) | Net Income as Percent of Assets (5) | Net Income as Percent of Shareholders' Equity[a] (6) | Net Income as Percent of Sales (7) |
|---|---|---|---|---|---|---|
| Canadian Pacific Ltd. | 12,289,487 | 17,273,034 | 188,924 | 1.1 | 4.8 | 1.5 |
| Imperial Oil Ltd. | 8,618,000 | 7,486,000 | 267,000 | 3.6 | 6.5 | 3.1 |
| Bell Canada Inc. | 8,411,300 | 13,421,800 | 622,200 | 4.6 | 13.8 | 7.4 |
| Canada Safeway Ltd. | 3,300,252 | 1,009,927 | 68,539 | 6.8 | 12.0 | 2.1 |
| IBM Canada Ltd. | 2,204,000 | 1,153,000 | 172,000 | 14.9 | 26.5 | 7.8 |

[a]After taxes.
Source: *The Financial Post 500*, June 1983.

direct the $13.4 billion that it received from the sale of its assets into bonds earning about 10 percent, which would give it net earnings of about $1.3 billion instead of only $622 million.

However, it is extremely unlikely that the sales value of the assets would be anywhere near $13.4 billion. Used equipment will seldom bring to its owners the value that accountants attribute to it, even though the value of such assets is depreciated. Still, the ratio of net earnings to assets does give the owners (shareholders) of a corporation some idea of how well the company is using its resources.

Another more common way of measuring the profit rate is to calculate net income as a percentage of the amount that shareholders have actually invested in the company (shareholder's equity). We don't have these figures, but *The Financial Post* used them to calculate such a profit rate in Column 6. That column informs us that the last three corporations listed earned a higher rate of profit on investment in 1982 than the going interest rate of about 10 percent. Shareholders of Canadian Pacific and Imperial Oil earned considerably less on their actual investment than they could have earned in many alternate forms of investment. This result is not surprising in view of the fact that 1982 was marked by a serious recession.

Sometimes corporations will calculate their profit as a percentage of sales. Supermarkets often do this because, in their case, sales are unusually large in relation to their investment, so that the profit/sales ratio will be much lower than the profit/investment ratio. By focusing on sales, supermarkets can try to counteract consumer criticism that they are earning high profits. They may also have good internal reasons for keeping track of profits in relation to sales, but for purposes of comparing their profit rates with other corporations, the profit/investment ratio is much more meaningful.

## CONCLUSIONS

The introduction to this chapter mentioned that factor markets determine not only how productive inputs are allocated among competing uses but also how total output is divided among individual factor owners. Consider the case in which several factors of production are used by a firm and factor markets are competitive. Profit maximization then requires that each factor be used up to the point where its marginal revenue product is equal to its price.

This suggests that each unit of each factor receives a reward that is equal to the contribution it makes to the firm's revenue. The idea that factors are rewarded according to their marginal productivity is known as the **marginal productivity theory of distribution**. The theory applies only to cases in which all factors are purchased in competitive input markets.

In an economy where all markets are perfectly competitive—not only input markets but output markets as well—the marginal productivity theory applies in an even stronger form. It has been shown that when output markets as well as factor markets are competitive, marginal revenue product is equal to output price times marginal physical product. In such an economy, the reward that each unit of each factor receives is exactly equal

**Marginal productivity theory of distribution**
A theory of the functional distribution of income according to which each factor receives a payment equal to its marginal revenue product.

to the value of its marginal physical product. If an extra hour's labor in a T-shirt factory produces two extra T-shirts, and each T-shirt sells for $5, the wage rate must be $10 per hour—no more, no less.

This principle of distribution, in which every factor receives a reward equal to the value of its marginal product, appeals to many people as the most just one possible. The reward of every worker is exactly equal to the contribution of that worker to the productive process. If a worker or factor owner were to decide to withhold a unit of productive services from the market, that person would suffer a loss of earnings exactly equal to the value of production that would be lost to the economy as a whole.

Not everyone favors distribution according to marginal productivity, however. Some people do not believe it leads to the best personal distribution of income. There are two main lines of criticism. Some critics argue that it is fine for factors to earn their marginal products but that a just personal distribution of income also requires that the ownership of factors be justly distributed among people. Others argue that productivity is completely irrelevant as a basis for distribution. Instead, distribution should be carried out on the principle of "to each according to needs." These issues lie somewhat beyond the scope of this chapter, but the chapters on poverty and on capitalism versus socialism will return to them.

## SUMMARY

1. In factor markets, firms are the buyers, and households are the sellers. The theory of demand for a factor of production is thus an extension of the theory of the firm. A profit maximizing firm must take three things into account when it makes a hiring decision for any factor: (a) the quantity of output produced by a unit of the factor in question (marginal physical product), (b) the revenue derived from the sale of the output that will be produced by the extra unit of the factor (marginal revenue product), and (c) the cost of obtaining an extra unit of the factor (marginal factor cost).

2. A profit maximizing firm will hire just enough of each factor of production to equalize marginal revenue product and marginal factor cost. In the special case where a firm is a price taker both in the market where it buys its inputs and in the market where it sells its outputs, profit maximization requires that each factor's price be equal to its marginal physical product times the product price. So long as the firm is a price taker in the factor market, its demand for a factor of production is that factor's marginal revenue product curve.

3. The theory of labor supply for an individual household is an extension of the theory of consumer choice. Given the alternatives of work and leisure, each consumer works just enough that the marginal utility per hour of leisure exactly equals the marginal utility of the goods that can be bought with an hour's wage. The labor supply curve for a single individual tends to have a backward-bending shape. The market labor supply curve for a particular occupation or locality, however, ordinarily has the conventional upward-sloping shape.

4. In a market where both workers and employers are price takers, the equilibrium wage rate and equilibrium quantity of labor are found at the

intersection of the labor supply and labor demand curves. If the workers are price takers but their employer is a monopsonist, the equilibrium quantity of labor is found at the intersection of the marginal revenue product curve and the marginal factor cost curve, and the equilibrium wage rate is determined by the height of the supply curve directly below this intersection.

5. In a competitive market where there are several factors of production, profit maximization requires that each factor be used up to the point where its marginal product is equal to its price. Each factor thus receives a reward equal to its marginal revenue product. This distribution is thought by some to be the most just distribution of income possible.

6. Pure economic rent is the income earned by any factor of production that is in completely inelastic supply. Land is the classic example of a factor that earns a pure economic rent. Rent can be expressed in terms of either a periodic payment or a lump-sum price paid when a piece of land is transferred from one owner to another. The market price of a piece of land is the capitalized value of the rent it can earn. Rent can also be said to be earned by other factors that are in perfectly inelastic supply. The special talents of uniquely gifted persons earn rents, as do artificially created legal privileges.

7. The term *interest* expresses both the price paid by borrowers to lenders in credit markets and the income earned by capital as a factor of production. The interest rate is determined in credit markets. The supply of credit depends on the willingness of savers to lend. The demand for credit is composed of the demand for consumption loans plus the demand for investment loans. There is a demand for investment loans because capital-using, roundabout methods of production are more productive than direct methods.

8. There are several theories about the true nature of profits. One theory holds that profit is the reward that entrepreneurs earn for performing the function of bearing risks. Another sees profits as earned primarily through arbitrage. Still another emphasizes innovation. In practical terms, profit usually appears to arise from a mixture of these three sources.

## DISCUSSION QUESTIONS

1. What is meant by the statement that factor markets help determine for whom things are produced? Is it that workers consume exactly the things they produce? Do they ever do this? When they do not, what other markets also help determine for whom things are produced?

2. The text examined only factor markets in which the buyers are firms. Are households ever the buyers of factors of production? Are you the direct purchaser of a factor of production when you hire someone to type a term paper for you? When you get your hair cut? When you buy or rent a plot of land for a vegetable garden? What changes would have to be made in the theory of factor markets to take into account the case where both buyers and sellers are households?

3. Is a monopsonist necessarily a monopolist, and vice versa? Try to imagine a firm that is a monopolist in its product market but not a monopsonist in its factor markets. Then try to imagine a firm that is a monopsonist but not a monopolist.

4. Do you think there is any close connection between the value of what somebody produces and the amount that person earns? Consider these specific examples: an auto worker; a real estate salesperson; a rock star; your economics professor. Why does the connection between earnings and product seem closer in some cases than in others?

5. Suppose a friend said to you that it was just fine to let factor markets determine how things were produced, but the matter of for whom ought to be handled according to the principle of "to each according to need." Sketch a reply to this remark that begins: "But that won't work. If you don't let markets determine for whom, they won't be able to determine the how...."

6. The chapter has suggested that part of the income of persons with exceptional talents might best be considered pure economic rent earned on those talents. Suppose a certain opera singer makes $100,000 per year. How could you tell what part of that income is wages and what part is rent? Here are three possible tests for finding what part is rent: (a) ask how big a pay cut the singer would take before switching to a job where singing talent would be of no use; (b) measure the difference between this singer's income and the income of a singer with the same training but only average natural talent; (c) measure the difference between the singer's income in opera and the income he or she could earn in the next-best nonsinging job available. Which test is best? Do they all give about the same answer? Explain.

7. How would the burden of a tax on pure economic rent be divided between resource owners and consumers? What about a tax on the "rental" income of apartment house owners?

8. Suppose you decide to start a Christmas tree farm. You already own a suitable piece of land. You get seeds from pine cones picked in the woods. You plant the seeds with your bare hands, using no tools or equipment of any kind. Five years later, you harvest the trees, breaking them off with your hands rather than using any tools whatsoever. You sell the trees and earn a handsome income. How should that revenue be divided into wages, rent, interest, and profit? Did you use any capital? If so, what form did it take? (Hint: did you use a roundabout method of production?)

9. Suppose a contractor places an ad for laborers in the newspaper, offering to pay them $1/m$^2$ for removing rocks and dirt from a cellar hole. Four workers show up and start the job. Alice is a person of average build. She uses a simple shovel and bucket for the job and manages to earn $2 a day. Baker, a giant of a man, also uses a shovel and bucket but earns $5 a day. Charles brings a wheelbarrow with him and earns $6 a day even though he is no stronger than Alice. Donna uses a bucket and shovel and, like Alice, earns only $2 a day at first. Not satisfied with this, she takes a month off to go through an intensive course of physical conditioning. When she comes back, she can earn $5 a day. How should the income of each worker be categorized in terms of wages, rent, income, and profits?

CHAPTER

THIRTY
O N E

# LABOR UNIONS AND COLLECTIVE BARGAINING

---

## WHAT YOU WILL LEARN IN THIS CHAPTER

*This chapter completes the discussion of labor markets begun in the previous chapter. It explains how labor markets operate when workers organize into unions and bargain collectively with their employers. It begins with a brief history of the union movement in Canada. Next, it shows how to interpret the effects of unionization in terms of supply and demand curves. Finally, it reviews the history of public policy toward labor unions and discusses some contemporary issues in labor union economics.*

## FOR REVIEW

*Here are some important terms and concepts that will be put to use in this chapter. If you do not understand them, review them before proceeding.*
- *Cost-push inflation (Chapter 17)*
- *Incomes policy (Chapter 19)*
- *Anticombines Act (Chapter 27)*
- *Monopsony (Chapter 30)*

---

## THE NATURE OF UNIONS IN CANADA

In 1980, 3,092,852 Canadian workers belonged to labor unions—approximately one-third of all nonagricultural paid workers in the country. Of this total union membership, 1,554,082, or 50.2 percent, belonged to international unions based in the United States and affiliated there with the American Federation of Labor (AFL) and the Congress of Industrial Organizations (CIO). Some of these unions were also members of the Canadian Labour Congress (CLC), the Canadian federation of labor to which 73.2 percent of all union members in Canada belonged.

Canadian union membership, although substantial, is not large by European standards. In Austria and Sweden, more than two-thirds of all workers belong to unions. In England, Germany, and the Netherlands, more than one-third are members. Only France, among the major European countries, has a comparably low level of unionization, with just 29 percent of the labor force unionized.

In the United States, the largest unions are virtually all "blue collar" unions, representing manufacturing and transportation workers. In

**Exhibit 31.1**

**Membership of the ten largest Canadian unions, 1980**

Almost 40 percent of all union members belong to these ten largest unions. Of the ten, only the International Brotherhood of Teamsters, the Ontario Public Service Employees, and the Quebec Teaching Congress are independent.

| Name of Union | Affiliation | 1980 Membership |
|---|---|---|
| 1. Canadian Union of Public Employees | CLC | 271,652 |
| 2. United Steelworkers of America | AFL-CIO/CLC | 189,905 |
| 3. Public Service Alliance of Canada | CLC | 154,546 |
| 4. Food and Commercial Workers | AFL-CIO/CLC | 141,378 |
| 5. United Auto Workers | AFL-CIO/CLC | 121,829 |
| 6. International Brotherhood of Teamsters | Independent | 89,340 |
| 7. Quebec Teaching Congress | Independent | 86,615 |
| 8. Carpenters | AFL-CIO/CLC | 81,717 |
| 9. Ontario Public Service Employees | Independent | 73,377 |
| 10. Social Affairs Federation | CNTU-Quebec | 73,135 |

Source: Statistics Canada, *Annual Report of the Minister of Industry, Trade and Commerce under the Corporations and Labour Unions Returns Act* (Part II: *Labour Unions*), 1980, p. 34.

Canada, the practice is quite different. As Exhibit 31.1 shows, the single largest union is the Canadian Union of Public Employees (CUPE), representing mostly "white collar" government employees. Several other important unions (ranked third, seventh, ninth, and tenth), represent similar types of workers.

Exhibit 31.2 illustrates the relative strength of the union movement in various economic sectors and the significance in each sector of national and international unions. The public sector is the most highly unionized industry in Canada. However, it contributes only 16 percent of total union membership, while the larger manufacturing sector, though less unionized, contributes about 29 percent. It is significant that virtually all of the public administration workers belong to national unions. International unionism is strongest in such private industrial sectors as construction, mines and oil wells, and manufacturing.

In Europe, union membership is associated with political support for socialist political parties. In the United States, the popular image of unionists is somewhat the reverse. Union workers are often represented as being

**Exhibit 31.2**

**Percentage of workers unionized, by industry and by international and national unions, 1980**

| Industry Group | Percentage of Workers Unionized | Percentage in International Unions | Percentage in National Unions |
|---|---|---|---|
| Public Administration | 67.8 | 3.2 | 64.6 |
| Construction | 57.6 | 52.6 | 5.0 |
| Fishing and Trapping | 55.3 | 8.7 | 46.6 |
| Transportation | 53.2 | 25.2 | 28.0 |
| Manufacturing | 43.2 | 32.5 | 10.7 |
| Forestry | 38.6 | 29.5 | 9.1 |
| Mines and Oil Wells | 32.5 | 26.0 | 6.5 |
| Service Industries | 24.2 | 5.7 | 18.5 |
| Trade | 8.9 | 7.4 | 1.5 |
| Finance | 2.5 | 1.6 | 0.9 |

Source: Statistics Canada, *Annual Report of the Minister of Industry, Trade and Commerce under the Corporations and Labour Unions Returns Act* (Part II: *Labour Unions*), 1980, p. 61.

more conservative on political and social questions than the nonunion public. In fact, on a broad range of issues, including social programs, national defense, and foreign affairs, surveys in the United States have shown that the opinions of union members differ very little from the opinions of the rest of the public.

In Canada, the leadership of the Canadian Labour Congress and of some of the major unions is openly committed to the New Democratic Party, but rank-and-file union members have voting preferences similar to those of the rest of the public. A concerted effort by union leaders to rally their workers behind the NDP in the 1979 federal election had little success.

So much for generalities. These statistics and observations are enough to show that Canadian unions, although not as strong as in some other countries, are large enough to play quite a significant role in the economy. Let us now turn to a more detailed look at their origins and functions.

## THE HISTORY OF CANADIAN UNIONISM

The history, structure, and philosophy of Canadian unions have been shaped by the various forces that we have discussed earlier in this book: the extreme regional disparities of the country, the large-scale development of resources requiring considerable capital investment and resulting in concentration levels higher than those in the U.S., the extreme seasonal and cyclical fluctuations, and the close economic dependence on the United States. These factors have, in the words of one scholar, "all worked to produce a Canadian labor movement that could be described as decentralized, fragmented, relatively weak, and strongly influenced by American international unions."[1]

The development of local unions in Great Britain and the United States at the beginning of the nineteenth century found an echo in scattered industrial centers in Canada by the 1820s and 1830s. Small **craft unions**, which were unions of skilled workers all practicing the same craft, were formed in the shops of tailors, printers, and foundry operators in several places in Quebec, the Maritimes, and Ontario. These early attempts at unionization usually failed, because of sharp opposition from owners, generally hostile courts, and poor organization. In 1873, in Toronto, the first attempt was made to form a coordinating body, the Canadian Labour Union. It lasted only until 1877. A somewhat more successful effort was made by an American union, the Knights of Labor, which began to organize Canadian unions shortly after Confederation. It was founded as a secret society (the Noble Order of the Knights of Labor), but its growth began only after it abandoned secrecy in 1878. It reached a peak membership of about 12,000 in Canada in 1887.

Many local unions of skilled craftsmen were affiliated with the Knights of Labor, but the Knights' principles went far beyond the narrow bounds of craft unionism. They welcomed anyone who worked for a living, including

**Craft unions** Unions of skilled workers practicing a single craft.

---

[1]M. Saunderson, "Labour Relations in Canada," in *The Canadian Economy: Problems and Policies*, ed. G.C. Ruggeri (Toronto: Gage, 1977), pp. 274–275.

**Industrial unions** A union representing all workers in an enterprise, regardless of trade.

farmers and unskilled laborers. In this they resembled an **industrial union**, which is a union of all workers in an industry, including both skilled and unskilled workers and workers practicing various trades. Only such "undesirables" as bankers, liquor dealers, Pinkerton detectives, and lawyers were excluded by the Knights. Their program was not limited to narrow economic concerns. It stressed workers' education and producer co-operatives that would help counteract the "evil of wealth."

The Knights ran into conflict with other craft unions and declined rapidly after they were associated (without proof) with the killing of a policeman during Chicago's Haymarket Riot of 1886.

Despite the ultimate failure of the American-based Knights of Labor, many Canadian workers found it advantageous to turn to American unions for financial and organizational support in establishing unions in their craft. Naturally, most of these unions became affiliates of the American unions.

The United Brotherhood of Carpenters and Joiners in the United States had dozens of affiliates in Canada, from Nova Scotia to British Columbia, by 1890.

One of the first successful confederations of labor in Canada, the Trades and Labour Council of Canada (TLC) was founded in 1886, and affiliated itself with the rapidly growing American Federation of Labor (AFL). Thereafter, the philosophy of the AFL, as expressed by its founder Samuel Gompers, came to dominate much of the Canadian labor scene. No Canadian labor leader has so influenced the philosophy of unionism in Canada as this powerful American unionist. Gompers sought to avoid the mistakes that had led to the downfall of the Knights of Labor. The AFL owes its success largely to three features of its organization and philosophy that were prominent from its earliest years:

1. The AFL was based solidly on the principle of craft unionism. Its leaders thought that the dangers of economic depressions and employer opposition could be overcome only by relying on skilled workers who could not easily be replaced during strikes. The AFL itself was, in effect, an umbrella organization of national craft unions.

2. The AFL emphasized business unionism; that is, it devoted most of its energies to bread-and-butter issues of pay and working conditions. Unlike many European labor unions, it was content to work within the capitalist system. It did not seek the overthrow of private property or the establishment of socialism.

3. The AFL limited its political role to that of a lobbyist on labor's behalf. Again in contrast to European labor movements, it did not found a labor party. Gompers thought that excessive political involvement would lead to internal conflict within the labor movement and would weaken its ability to achieve concrete economic objectives.

The TLC, through its affiliation with the businesslike and highly successful AFL, was the guiding force for unionism in Canada for half a century after its founding.

Partly because of the strength of the international unions affiliated with the TLC and the AFL, several rival, autonomous confederations were established on a provincial basis, notably the B.C. Federation of Labour in 1911 and the Federation of Catholic Workers of Canada (Quebec) in 1921.

Samuel Gompers was born in a London tenement, the son of a skilled cigar maker. When he was thirteen, his family moved to the United States and settled on the East Side of New York. Gompers followed his father into the cigar trade.

Although his formal education ended at the age of ten, Gompers was very active in the workers' self-education movement of the time. In the cigar-making shops, jobs were organized on a piecework basis. Groups of workers would have one of their members read to them while they worked, "paying" the reader by making his cigars for him. Gompers became acquainted with the works of Marx, Engels, and other European socialists in this way. Often he was chosen as the reader.

The cigar makers' union to which Gompers belonged fell apart during the depression of 1873. Gompers rebuilt it as a model of the craft unions he was later to unite under the American Federation of Labor. Key features of this union were high membership dues, central control of funds, national officers with control over local unions, and union-organized accident and unemployment benefits for members.

Gompers became disillusioned with radical socialism. The main role of unions, in his view, was to watch after the economic interests of their members. He wrote:

Unions, pure and simple, are the natural organization of wage workers to secure their present material and practical improvement and to achieve their final emancipation. . . . The working people are in too great need of immediate improvements in their condition to allow them to forgo them in the endeavor to devote their entire energies to an end however beautiful to contemplate. . . . The way out of the wage system is through higher wages.

**Samuel Gompers
(1850–1924)**

During the 1890s, a socialist faction emerged within the AFL. It adopted a program calling for the collective ownership of all means of production and other radical measures. Gompers opposed the group, and in the 1895 election for the AFL presidency, he was defeated. He fought back, however, and succeeded in regaining the presidency the next year. He remained president until his death in 1924.

Gompers was an ardent patriot throughout his career. During World War I, he opposed pacifism and supported the war effort. In 1918, he said: "America is a symbol; it is an ideal; the hopes of the world can be expressed in the ideal—America."

---

Until the rise of strong, independent public workers' unions after World War II, these provincial federations formed the main bulwark against the complete dominance of the TLC.

The period 1914 to 1919 saw the development of a more radical form of unionism. Union membership increased sharply in this period, partly as a result of the increased union activity permitted by the federal government in all industries devoted to the war effort. The war itself brought Canadian union members in touch with more militant forms of industrial conflict in Europe, particularly the aims and methods of the 1917 Bolshevik Revolution. There is also evidence that rising prices immediately after the war, and a poor job market, led to a decline in real wages for many workers. The result of such new opportunities, ideas, and economic pressures was growing political action by labor in British Columbia, the formation of the One Big Union (OBU) by western radicals in 1918, and the most dramatic event in Canadian labor history, the Winnipeg General Strike of 1919. The police put down the strikers in Winnipeg, and several, including J.S. Woodsworth, later the founder of the CCF (the precursor of the NDP party), were put in jail. In 1920, however, eleven labor members were elected to the Manitoba Legislature, and J.S. Woodsworth became a member of Parliament for Central Winnipeg.

However, despite (and because of) the new radicalism and the political successes, the union movement showed few new advances in the interwar period. The Great Depression of the 1930s caused massive unemployment, accompanied by new labor–management conflict. In the Estevan coal miners strike of 1931, for example, three workers were killed. There were approximately 400,000 union members in Canada in 1920, and about the same number in 1940. As we shall see, social, legal, and legislative changes were required to give the union movement new momentum.

New union structures were also needed. The TLC and the AFL had turned their backs on the type of industrial unionization favored by the Knights of Labor. In the 1920s and 1930s, several unions in Canada and the United States promoted industrial unionism and laid the foundation for a major change in union strategy. In the United States, the fight was carried on by the Congress of Industrial Organizations (CIO) led by the Mine-workers leader, John L. Lewis. In Canada, the Canadian Brotherhood of Railway Employees (CBRE) led the way, creating first the All-Canadian Congress of Labour (ACCL) and assisting, in 1940, in the formation of the Canadian Congress of Labour (CCL). The CCL, in turn, affiliated with the CIO but never came under the latter's dominance (unlike the TLC, which was clearly subservient to the AFL).

After World War II, the AFL in the United States modified its stand on craft unionism and began to espouse industrial unionism. This helped to lead to a merger of the AFL and the CIO in 1955. A similar merger occurred in Canada in 1956, when most of the members of the TLC and the CCL created one confederation of labor, the Canadian Labour Congress (CLC). Most unions outside of Quebec are now affiliated with the CLC. In Quebec, the Confederation of National Trade Unions (CNTU) continues to represent most of the provincial trade unions.

As this brief historical survey has made clear, the Canadian labor union movement has been deeply influenced by ideas and organizations originating outside of Canada, particularly in the United States. Today, about half of all Canadian union members are affiliated with unions based in the United States. Although many of their unions are also affiliated with the Canadian Labour Congress, their main direction comes from their U.S. affiliates. As a recent Statistics Canada report observes: "In terms of industrial coverage, as well as membership and financial resources, international unions with headquarters in the United States remain the dominant force in the Canadian labour movement and constitute one of the major economic links between Canada and the United States."[2] Questions raised in Chapter 29 with regard to Canada's economic autonomy are therefore relevant for the labor sector as well as for the business sector. It should be pointed out, however, that the Canadian labor movement has become less tied to U.S. labor in the last few decades. Membership in the international unions grew by only 54 percent between 1962 and 1980, while membership in national unions grew by 222 percent. The result is that during this period the proportion of the unionized membership in international unions declined from 67 percent to 50 percent. This development is linked

---

[2]Statistics Canada, *Annual Report of the Minister of Industry, Trade and Commerce under the Corporations and Labour Unions Returns Act.* (Part II: *Labour Unions*), 1980, p. 60.

## Bilateral Monopoly

The example just given assumes that the monopsonistic employer will accept the union demand on a take-it-or-leave-it basis. Not all employers react this way. A strong employer may counter the union demand with the threat of a lockout or of some take-it-or-leave-it offer of its own. The kind of bargaining situation that develops when neither party to the labor contract acts competitively and neither passively accepts the demands of the other is called **bilateral monopoly**. The outcome of bargaining under bilateral monopoly is impossible to predict with the type of analysis used here. Economic theory can only specify a range of outcomes within which a settlement can take place. The actual outcome depends simply on the relative bargaining strength and skill of the two sides. The headline-making disputes in which "big labor" clashes with "big business" often fall into the category of bilateral monopoly. Bilateral monopoly is also characteristic of the increasingly important negotiations between large public sector unions and the governments they confront. Under the federal government's "6 and 5" wage-guideline program for 1983–84, arbitrarily low wage settlements were unilaterally imposed by several provincial governments.

> **Bilateral monopoly** A market in which both buyer and seller exercise monopoly power and neither passively accepts the demands of the other.

## Relative Wages

How successful unions are in raising the relative wages of their members depends primarily on three things: (1) whether the unions are strong enough to make a creditable strike threat; (2) how willing they are to sacrifice jobs in order to gain higher wages; and (3) what the demand conditions are in their sector of the labor market. No purely theoretical analysis can tell which unions will be able to win higher relative wages and which will not. This is an empirical question that has drawn the attention of many economists.

In the United States, a 1963 study by H.G. Lewis indicated that unions were able to raise the wages of their members above those of nonunion workers in the same industry, especially in the first few years of the union's existence. However, only rarely were unions able to raise union wages more than 25 percent above the nonunion level. The general difference seemed to be about 5 to 20 percent.[3] A Canadian study by G. Starr indicated that for production workers in Ontario, the increase in relative wages for union members ranged from 10 to 17 percent.[4]

One problem, of course, is that nonunion workers may have their wages and salaries set in accordance with those negotiated by union members in the same or a related firm or industry. In such cases, it may only be in times of economic slack, when employees are being laid off and management can afford to alienate some of its staff, that the strength of the union for its own members becomes apparent. This is illustrated in Case 31.1. According to this article, the rise of unemployment in 1982 prompted some firms to lower the wages and salaries of nonunion workers, while

---

[3]H.G. Lewis, *Unionism and Relative Wages in the U.S.* (Chicago: University of Chicago Press, 1963).
[4]G. Starr, *Union-Non Union Wages Differentials*, Ontario Minister of Labour, 1973.

**Case 31.1**
**Upward Pressure on Wage Levels**

Serious distortions in traditional wage relationships are beginning to appear as a direct result of federal and provincial restraint programs.

As more and more government workers start to swallow wage rollbacks, nearly three-quarters of their private-sector counterparts are holding firm to rich wage contracts negotiated during better times.

New private-sector wage contracts are beginning to reflect the severity of the recession, but there are relatively few private-sector pacts up for renewal—which means general wage levels in industry are moving down far more slowly than in government.

Since companies cannot reduce costs by reducing hourly wage rates within bargaining units, they must resort to layoffs. In the past year, nearly 500,000 jobs disappeared across the country—75 percent of these in mining, manufacturing, and construction. At the same time, governments laid off 21,000 workers.

The base wage rates of union members are becoming significantly higher than those enjoyed by nonunion employees who work in the same company.

Last year, for example, Hamilton, Ont.-based Stelco signed a three-year deal with its 12,500 hourly-rated workers (following a 125-day strike) that will see wages rise about 50 percent. But last July, the company announced its 6,000 nonunion, salaried workers would have to accept a wage freeze (though they still receive a form of cost-of-living adjustment).

One industrial relations specialist notes: "What better way to encourage unionization than discriminating against nonunion workers?"

But many companies have apparently concluded that the risk of further unionization—particularly when union coffers are fairly low—is smaller than the risk of losing corporate solvency.

Source: James Bagnall, "Upward Pressure on Wage Levels," *The Financial Post*, October 2, 1982, p. 9 (excerpted).

---

unions were able to protect their members against wage controls and wage reductions. They were not able, however, to protect their members against massive layoffs.

## Unions and Absolute Wages

It seems well established, then, that unions can affect relative wages. Are they also able to raise the average wages of all workers, as measured by the share of wages in national income? That is a quite separate question. This time, there is little theoretical basis for believing they can. Except in cases of true monopsony, which are likely to be temporary and purely localized, unions win their higher wages at the expense of fewer jobs. As the wage in unionized industries rises, the supply of labor to nonunionized sectors increases, keeping nonunion wages down.

National income statistics show labor's share of national income to be remarkably stable over time. Unadjusted figures show the proportion of wages in national income rising from about 60 percent in the 1920s to around 75 percent today, but this change reflects factors other than unionization. It is largely explained by the relative growth of sectors of the economy that employ much labor (especially government and services) and the decline of sectors using less labor in proportion to other inputs. When an adjustment is made for this, labor's share of national income appears to have increased by only about 2 percent over the past half-century. Since this period coincides with the period of fastest union growth, the impression left is that the impact of unionization on average wages has been small.

## PUBLIC POLICY TOWARD UNIONS

What should be the government's policy toward unions? This question has been a topic of impassioned political debate ever since unions began. Some have argued that all unions should be suppressed as illegal restraints on trade. Others have advocated government support for unions to promote industrial stability and high living standards for all. Still others have favored a laissez-faire policy, letting workers and management bargain without government interference. The debate has been clouded by disagreements about the true effect of unions on relative and absolute wages and on industrial efficiency. Without taking a position, the next section will survey the changing course of government policy over time, showing how first one and then another opinion has become dominant.

Unions had trouble with the courts from their earliest days. Under precedents from English common law, they were often treated as illegal conspiracies in restraint of trade. Businesses were able to get the support of the courts in most cases to have the unions declared illegal. Often they didn't bother resorting to courts. Workers who were caught participating in the formation of a union, or just listening sympathetically to a union organizer, were summarily fired. Such workers were often blacklisted, so that they had trouble getting a job anywhere else. Confrontations were often violent, both in Canada and the United States. Some employers used "yellow-dog" contracts, whereby workers signed an agreement not to engage in union activity. This then became a condition of employment.

In the United States, the Sherman Antitrust Act was used vigorously against unions as a form of restraint of trade, but in Canada the anticombines legislation was not used in a similar fashion. Canadian governments, both provincial and federal, created few laws either for or against unions, so that unions had neither the disadvantages of the Sherman Act nor the advantages of pro-union laws passed in the U.S. in the 1930s. The first supportive act was passed by Parliament in 1900. This set out a framework of conciliation to handle disputes between labor and management. This was followed by the Industrial Dispute Act of 1907, which included the acceptance of the right of workers to organize and bargain collectively, but did not require management to recognize a union.

It was only in 1939 that changes in the Criminal Code made it an offence for an employer to harass employees who were unionizing. During World War II, a special Order-in-Council laid the basic foundation for collective bargaining, by forcing management to bargain with an elected union "in good faith."

A unique Canadian decision in 1946, by Mr. Justice Ivan Rand of the Supreme Court of Canada, who had been appointed to arbitrate and settle a bitter strike at the Ford Motor Company, gave unions a new type of power and security. His ruling, which has come to be known as the *Rand Formula*, required both union and nonunion members at Ford to pay union dues. This has given strong support to the practice of compulsory union dues.

**Exhibit 31.6**
**Person-Days lost through industrial disputes, 1974–1980**

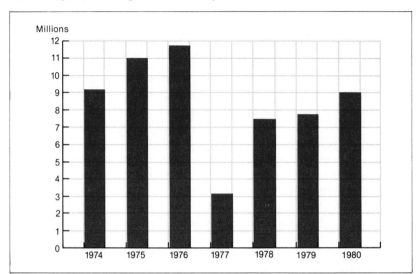

Since World War II, unions have enjoyed the right to organize, to bargain collectively with the employer, and to strike if a settlement cannot be reached. Both federal and provincial labor laws have been created to support these developments, though laws still differ from one province to another. Despite considerable legislative support, however, the Canadian experience in management–labor relations has been one of the most disappointing among western industrialized nations.

Union leaders in Canada generally frown on the cozy relationship that some American union leaders seem to have with their employers, which may have made the American unions less militant and which has also led to many glaring abuses of power and finances by American union leaders. At the same time, both union and management are skeptical of experiments in "industrial democracy" in such countries as Sweden and West Germany, where a greater spirit of cooperation has been developed between employers and employees by granting workers considerable rights in the management of companies.

Canadian labor and management seem to prefer the adversary system of bargaining, based on the assumption of class conflict. The result is continued industrial strife, millions of hours of work lost through strikes and lockouts, and the use of tactics that sometimes seem to fall just short of war. In 1980, almost 9 million person-days were lost through industrial disputes, or about 800 days per 1,000 workers. This compares with 5 lost days per 1,000 workers in West Germany and 6 lost days per thousand workers in Sweden.[5] Exhibit 31.6 shows that the number of person-days lost was even higher in the mid-1970s, but Canada still has one of the worst records in the west.

---

[5]International Labour Office, *1981 Year Book of Labour Statistics*, Geneva, 1982. Days lost per 1,000 workers in the U.K. were about 450, and in Japan, 16.

### Case 31.2
### Continuing Conflict between Labor and Management

The news article reproduced here from *The Financial Post* shows that Canada's deeply rooted management-labor conflicts are far from resolved. Perhaps no area of our economy is more in need of innovation and change.

Following hard on the heels of a remarkable growth in membership, union organization drives show signs of degenerating into brutal trench warfare with managements that shudder at the thought of union shops.

It's been that way for some time in Quebec, where celebrated battles such as that between the Canadian Tire outlet in Sherbrooke and the Retail Clerks International Union stayed on the boil for months in and out of court. And there've been some tough battles in British Columbia. But the fighting seems now to have spread to Ontario with a vengeance.

In two rulings this year, the Ontario Labor Relations Board (OLRB) — more noted for its restraint than anger — has come down hard on management. In one ruling, it said Toronto-based Norseman Plastics Ltd. conducted what "could only be described as a concerted campaign of terror aimed at employees who supported the union."

Then late last month, Dylex Ltd. was charged with criminal conspiracy to commit unfair labor practices. Dylex manufactures and distributes clothing through such well-known chains as Tip Top, Harry Rosen and Suzy Shier, among others.

The charges related to an unsuccessful attempt to organize the 175 employees in Dylex's central distribution centre in Toronto 2½ years ago. Included in the indictments were two Dylex executives—marketing director Lewis Pearsall and manager Gunter Leverenz — and private detective firm Centurion Investigation Ltd. (which has since had its license suspended) and its president, Daniel McGarry. The charges include the claim that Dylex hired two Centurion employees to pick a fight with the two leading union organizers on Dylex's payroll, giving the company reason to fire all four of them.

Dylex officials declined to comment when contacted by The Post.

Sam Fox, Canadian director of the Amalgamated Clothing & Textile Workers' Union (which was conducting the organizing campaign), claims there is a "whole new breed of labor experts advising management how to beat or break a union drive."

Fox says Dylex is just one of a series of companies that have started to dig in against the unions. S. S. Kresge Co. and Radio Shack, Barrie, are examples. But labor leaders say most are within the "ghetto industries" — small companies of less than 50 employees, labor intensive, such as metal fabrication or clothing, and employing immigrants. Generally they are less sophisticated in labor relations and belong to industries without a tradition of trade union organization.

Source: Peter Silverman, "Unions Facing Tough Battles in Ontario as Managements 'Dig In,'" *The Financial Post*, May 12, 1979, p. 36.

## SUMMARY

1. The first local craft unions in Canada were established in the early decades of the nineteenth century. In the 1870s and 1880s a confederation of labor was attempted by the U.S.-based Knights of Labor. The Knights were soon succeeded by the Trades and Labour Council of Canada (TLC), in affiliation with the AFL in the United States. The philosophy and practice of the latter was shaped by the strong leader Samuel Gompers. The TLC emphasized craft unionism and concentrated on the bread-and-butter issue of higher wages. There were some early successes in industrial unionism in some provinces and in some independent unions, but it became widespread only with the formation

of the Canadian Congress of Labour (CCL) in 1940, in affiliation with the CIO in the U.S. At first the TLC and CCL feuded bitterly, but in 1956, following the merger of the AFL and the CIO, the two organizations united and formed the Canadian Labour Congress (CLC). Today about two-thirds of all union members in Canada are in unions affiliated with the CLC. About half of Canadian union members are affiliated with unions in the U.S., a declining but still significant percentage.

2. The strike threat is a union's ultimate weapon in bargaining with employers for higher wages. A union wage demand backed up by a strike threat has the effect of bending the labor supply curve so that it becomes horizontal at the level of the wage demand. In a market where employers are price takers, a higher wage can usually be won only at the expense of jobs lost. Sometimes, featherbedding or other kinds of work sharing are used to spread available work among all union members. Within certain limits, a union can win higher wages from a monopsonistic employer and gain higher employment at the same time.

3. Empirical studies show that many unions actually do succeed in raising the relative wages of their members. Often, though, the relative wage advantage of union members is only a few percent. It is doubtful that unions have a significant effect on the average wages of all workers, as measured in terms of the share of wages in national income.

4. Public policy toward unions has gone through several phases. Until the 1930s courts were generally hostile toward unions. Beginning in 1900, but accelerating in the late 1930s and during World War II, legislation was passed giving unions the rights they now enjoy. The Rand Formula of 1946 has provided the foundation for compulsory payment of union dues, a source of new security for unions. Despite legislative progress, labor and management operate in a sometimes fierce adversary system, resulting in a comparatively high rate of days lost through industrial disputes.

## DISCUSSION QUESTIONS

1. Why do you think that unions are stronger in the public service and, for example, in manufacturing, than in service industries and in such sectors as banking and agriculture?

2. Why has socialism never been a strong political force in Canadian unionism, even though the labor movements of almost every other country are strongly socialist or communist?

3. Is the nonteaching staff of your college or university unionized? If so, what union or unions represent them? Is the teaching faculty unionized? If not, are there any active attempts underway to unionize the faculty? Describe.

4. Why do some unions encourage wasteful featherbedding rather than simple work sharing in the form of, say, shorter hours or longer vacations?

5. In what ways do labor unions resemble cartels? Do you think labor unions deserve more public policy support than cartels of producers? Explain.

6. Refer to Exhibit 31.5, which illustrates the effects of unionization in a monopsonistic labor market. Using the demand and supply curves of that exhibit, identify the maximum wage that a union might get while keeping employment at 220,000. Alternatively, what would be the maximum employment level if wages were held to $6.50 per hour by the union?

## SUGGESTIONS FOR FURTHER READING

Anderson, John C., and Gunderson, Morley (editors). *Union Management Relations in Canada.* Don Mills, Ontario: Addison-Wesley, 1982.

Craig, Alton W.J. *The System of Industrial Relations In Canada.* Toronto: Prentice-Hall, 1983.

Williams, Jack. *The Story of Unions in Canada.* Toronto: J.M. Dent, 1975.

*The book by Williams provides an excellent history of the Canadian labor movement. The others are more analytical and emphasize current policies concerning labor.*

# THE PROBLEM
# OF POVERTY

## CHAPTER

## THIRTY
## T W O

---

**WHAT YOU WILL LEARN IN THIS CHAPTER**

*Factor markets do not distribute income equally among Canadian families. Even in an economy that supplied families with an average income of $27,398 in 1980, some three to four million Canadians are officially classified as poor. Federal, provincial, and local governments have many ambitious antipoverty programs. These have somewhat reduced the inequality of income distribution over recent decades, but they have not eliminated the problem. Current programs are so expensive that there has been much discussion of streamlined transfer schemes such as the negative income tax. Not all economists think that transfers are the best answer to the poverty problem. Policies that aim to improve poor workers' chances in the job market also generate much current interest.*

## FOR REVIEW

*Here are some important terms and concepts that will be put to use in this chapter. If you do not understand them, review them before proceeding.*

- *Economic functions of government (Chapter 27)*
- *Functional distribution of income (Chapters 30 and 31)*

---

## THE DISTRIBUTION OF INCOME IN CANADA

The factor markets that we have been studying distribute income very unequally among Canadian families. Exhibit 32.1 gives an idea of who received how much in 1980. The table shows a median family income in 1980 of $25,244. Although this median was sufficient to provide a comfortable standard of living, it is worth noting that about 20 percent of all families received less than half of that. It is the lower end of the income distribution profile that will particularly concern us in this chapter.

| Income Bracket (by Families) | Percentage of Families in Each Bracket | Percentage of Families in Each Bracket and Below[1] |
|---|---|---|
| Under $5,000 | 2.8 | 2.8 |
| $5,000–$6,999 | 3.0 | 5.8 |
| 7,000– 9,999 | 7.0 | 12.8 |
| 10,000–11,999 | 4.6 | 17.4 |
| 12,000–13,999 | 3.8 | 21.2 |
| 14,000–15,999 | 4.6 | 25.8 |
| 16,000–17,999 | 5.2 | 31.0 |
| 18,000–19,999 | 5.2 | 36.2 |
| 20,000–24,999 | 13.2 | 49.4 |
| 25,000–29,999 | 13.4 | 63.2 |
| 30,000–34,999 | 11.1 | 74.3 |
| 35,000–39,999 | 8.6 | 82.9 |
| 40,000–44,999 | 5.5 | 88.4 |
| 45,000 and over | 11.7 | 100.0 |

Average income = $27,398 ( = total income divided by number of families)
Median Income = $25,244 (half of families have income less than this; half have more).

[1]Figures do not add up to exactly 100, because of rounding.
Source: Statistics Canada, *Income Distribution by Size in Canada*, 1980, p. 37.

**Exhibit 32.1**
**Personal distribution of income in Canada, 1980**
Income is not distributed equally among families in Canada. About 20 percent of them receive less than half the median income.

## Measuring Inequality by Quintile Shares

One way of measuring the inequality of income distribution is to divide people into equal groups and then order them from poorest to richest. If, for example, the population is divided into five equal groups, each group is called a *quintile.* Exhibit 32.2 gives the shares of different quintiles of Canadian families for selected years from 1965 to 1980. If income were distributed equally among these groupings, each quintile should receive 20 percent of total family income. This is clearly not the case.

The share of total family income received by the richest fifth of families in Canada is consistently more than seven times greater than the share received by the lowest fifth. What is perhaps most remarkable is the stability of the distribution pattern over time. There has been virtually no change in it since World War II. The lowest fifth has consistently received about 6 percent of family income, the second fifth about 13 percent, and the highest fifth between 38 and 39 percent.

**Exhibit 32.2**
**Income Shares of Canadian Families by Quintiles, 1965 to 1980**
In 1980, the poorest fifth of family groups in Canada received only 6 percent of family income, while the richest fifth received 38.6 percent. This unequal pattern of income distribution remained remarkably constant between 1965 and 1980.

| Year | Lowest 20% | Second Quintile | Third Quintile | Fourth Quintile | Top 20% | Total |
|---|---|---|---|---|---|---|
| 1965 | 6.2 | 13.1 | 18.0 | 23.6 | 39.0 | 100.0 |
| 1969 | 6.2 | 12.6 | 17.9 | 23.5 | 39.7 | 100.0 |
| 1973 | 6.1 | 12.9 | 18.1 | 23.9 | 38.9 | 100.0 |
| 1977 | 5.9 | 13.1 | 18.5 | 24.4 | 38.0 | 100.0 |
| 1980 | 6.0 | 12.8 | 18.3 | 24.1 | 38.6 | 100.0 |

Source: Statistics Canada, *Income Distributions by Size in Canada, 1980,* p. 85.

### The Lorenz Curve and the Gini Index of Inequality

In 1905, M.O. Lorenz demonstrated a method of illustrating income inequality that has been used extensively by economists ever since. In Exhibit 32.3, a **Lorenz Curve** is developed by plotting the cumulative percentage of family units along the horizontal axis and the cumulative percentage of income received by those families along the vertical axis. The data in Exhibit 32.2 can be used for this purpose. A is the point at which the poorest 20 percent of family units received 6.0 percent of family income, B is the point at which the poorest 40 percent received 18.8 percent of family income (6.0 + 12.8), and C is the point at which the poorest 60 percent of families received 37.1 percent of family income (6.0 + 12.8 + 18.3). D represents the cumulative income received by the fourth quintile of family groups. Connecting these points enables us to approximate a Lorenz curve for Canadian families. If income were broken down into many more income intervals a more accurate curve would be possible.

If every family quintile had the same share of family income (that is, 20 percent) the Lorenz curve would be the straight line, OE. The distance from the line OE of the actual Lorenz curve connecting points A, B, C, and D provides us with a measurement of the income inequality in the country. In 1912, Corrado Gini proposed that the extent of inequality in a society could be measured in this way, by determining the ratio of the area between the actual Lorenz curve for a society and the OE line (the area shaded in Exhibit 32.3) *and* the area of the entire triangle OPE. The greater the inequality, the larger the shaded area would be and the more it would approximate the entire area of the OPE triangle. Therefore the ratio, known as the **Gini coefficient**, would also be greater.

In summary, the lower the Gini ratio or coefficient, the greater the *equality* of income within a society, and the higher the ratio, the greater

**The Lorenz curve** This curve graphs the cumulative percentage of income units along the horizontal axis and the cumulative percentage of income received by those units along the vertical axis.

**The Gini co-efficient** This is a ratio of the area between the Lorenz curve and the line OE, and the area of the entire triangle OPE.

---

**Exhibit 32.3**

**The Lorenz curve and the Gini coefficient of inequality**

The Lorenz curve for Canada for 1980 is derived from the data in Exhibit 32.2. The percentage of income units, measured cumulatively, is plotted along the horizontal axis, and the percentage of income received by those family units, again measured cumulatively, is plotted along the vertical axis. Points A, B, C, D, and E are derived in this way. If each family quintile received 20 percent of family income, the Lorenz curve would be the line OE. The deviation of the actual Lorenz curve, OABCDE, from that line represents the degree of inequality between families. This is measured more exactly by the Gini coefficient, which calculates the ratio of the actual inequality (given by the shaded area) to the greatest possible inequality (which would be given by the whole triangle OPE).

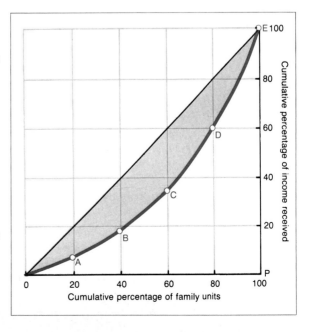

**Exhibit 32.4**
**Effects of government taxes and expenditures on income distribution in Canada, 1961–1969**

| Income Group (1) | Percent of Households in Group (2) | Percent of Broad Income by Group (3) 1961 | Percent of Adjusted Broad Income, 1961 (4) | Percent of Broad Income by Group, 1969 (5) | Percent of Adjusted Broad Income, 1969 (6) |
|---|---|---|---|---|---|
| 1. Poorest | 21.7 | 3.1 | 5.8 | 3.3 | 6.9 |
| 2. Lower-middle | 25.5 | 15.7 | 18.2 | 14.9 | 17.9 |
| 3. Middle | 25.5 | 27.5 | 27.6 | 25.8 | 25.7 |
| 4. Upper-middle | 22.2 | 33.6 | 31.6 | 35.7 | 32.0 |
| 5. Richest | 5.0 | 20.1 | 16.8 | 20.3 | 17.6 |
| Total | 100.0 | 100.0 | 100.0 | 100.0 | 100.0 |

Source: W. Irwin Gillespie, "On the Redistribution of Income in Canada," *Canadian Tax Journal*, No. 24, 1976, p. 432, 450.

the *inequality*. In the early 1970s, the Gini coefficient for families in Canada was calculated to be .348, while for the U.S. it was .369. Canada's coefficient of inequality was thus about halfway between that of the most unequal country among western industrial nations, France (.417) and that of the most equal, the Netherlands (.264).[1]

## Effects of Government Spending on Income Distribution

The previous exhibits, we should note, record only the distribution of before-tax money income, including government transfer payments. To get a more accurate picture of the relative welfare of upper and lower-income households, and of changes in the distribution of income over time, we must make certain adjustments. (A household consists of families *and/or* individuals living alone.) First, we have to correct for the different impact of taxes on households at different levels of income. Second, we should adjust for differences in the average size of household. Unfortunately, this is not done by Statistics Canada.

Exhibit 32.4 shows that, when some of these adjustments are made, the income distribution in Canada has become somewhat more equal over time.

The data in Exhibit 32.4 are based on a study in which income groups were selected, not on the basis of a constant level of income, but on the basis of constant percentages of households in each group. Thus, in both 1961 and 1969, the two years chosen for comparison, the poorest group consisted of the bottom 21.7 percent of all households, the next group consisted of the next 25.5 percent of households, and so on. Column 3 indicates the percentage of income that would have been received by each group in 1961 if governments at all levels had not intervened with both taxes and transfer payments (and with expenditures on such items as hospitals and schools, whose benefits for each group are also calculated). Column 4 illustrates the difference in these percentages after income has been adjusted by taking account of such government activity.

Comparing Columns 3 and 4, we see that in 1961 the three lowest income

---

[1]This information and some of the preceding analysis is derived from Lars Osberg, *Economic Inequality in Canada* (Toronto: Butterworth), 1981.

groups had income redistributed in their favor by government taxation and expenditure programs. In general, this occurs not because of the tax system—which tends on the whole to be only slightly progressive—but because of government expenditures that favor lower-income groups. In 1969, only the two lowest income groups had income redistributed in their favor by the combination of government taxes and expenditures. Based on the experience of those two years, it can be said that government activities redistribute income from higher to lower-income classes.

### Income Distribution over Time

What happens to income distribution over time? Comparing Columns 3 and 5, we see that the picture is extremely ambiguous. Without the presence of government, the percentage of income going to the poorest group would have increased slightly, from 3.1 to 3.3 percent. In fact, an even greater shift occurred for this group, because of government activity. The adjusted broad income share (Columns 4 and 6) increased from 5.8 percent to 6.9 percent. However, the lower-middle class fared quite differently. Both when government activity is considered, and when it is not, the share of this group declined between 1961 and 1969. The same holds true for the middle class. On the other hand, both the upper-middle and the richest classes enjoyed a greater share of income, adjusted and unadjusted, in 1969 than in 1961. It seems that the poorest and the richest classes benefitted in the interval at the expense of the middle-income groups. One can hardly say, therefore, that income was clearly distributed in favor of lower-income people in the decade of the 1960s. It appears that government programs do not bring about much change in income shares.

This rather dismal conclusion was challenged in 1979, however, by Professor Clarence Barber of the University of Manitoba. "A more careful look suggests that Gillespie's conclusion, widely shared among economists, has a major pitfall. The studies assume that the structure of households today is roughly the same as 20–25 years ago. In fact, there have been quite major changes. And when allowance has been made for these, it is no longer clear just what changes have occurred in our income distribution."[2]

Barber notes that in recent years many young people who previously would have been at home contributing to family income have established separate households. Since many of these young people are just starting out, their incomes will be relatively low. This will increase the number of low-income households in the data, but we would not be justified in saying that these young people are worse off than their counterparts a generation earlier. He notes other changes in family living that would have a similar effect. He concludes, therefore, that "the contention that the growth in government welfare spending... has had little effect on income distribution is a contention no one is justified in making."[3]

## A PROFILE OF POVERTY IN CANADA

If we are to discuss poverty as a policy problem, we must know how income

[2]Clarence Barber, *The Financial Post*, July 14, 1979, p. 8.
[3]Ibid.

distribution and poverty are related. We might say, in a sense, that income distribution is a matter of numbers, while poverty is a matter of people and values. Measuring income distribution is just a routine task of positive economics. Measuring poverty, however, requires a normative judgment. It requires us to say how far down the income scale a family can fall before they do not have enough or have less than they ought to have.

## Definitions of Poverty

There is no single definition of poverty that everyone accepts. Some want an absolute income figure, indicating the minimum income that a household would need to satisfy its basic wants. Others see poverty in relative terms. When income in general is rising the income of the poor may also rise, but if their relative position is unchanged their sense of being poor will remain. By a definition of this kind it is possible to have "poor" in Canada who are better off than the "rich" in some other countries, but they are poor in relation to the rest of society, with which they will inevitably compare their situation.

Statistics Canada and the Economic Council of Canada have tried to establish absolute poverty lines for different-sized families in different locations. These lines were originally calculated on the basis of studies in the 1960s that indicated Canadian families spent, on average, about half of their income on the basic essentials of food, clothing, and shelter. It was arbitrarily decided that a family which spent a considerably greater proportion of its income on such essentials — say 70 percent — could be considered poor. The "poverty line" was drawn at that point, and any household spending 70 percent or more on essentials was considered to be below it. Since then, with rising real incomes, the line has been lowered to those income levels that require the expenditure of 58.5 percent or more of income on food, shelter, and clothing.

Exhibit 32.5 indicates how much income different-sized households, in rural and urban areas, would require in 1980 to be able to spend no more than 58.5 percent of their income on essentials (or to be able to devote 41.5 percent of their income to non-essentials).

There is, of course, much room for debate about the validity of these figures. Some critics contend that the figures are too high because, for example, some households below the poverty line are seemingly able to afford cars and television sets. Others argue that the figures are too low,

---

**Exhibit 32.5**

**Poverty lines by household size and location, 1980**

| Persons Per Household | Poverty Line for Large Cities (500,000 plus) | Poverty Line for Rural Areas |
|---|---|---|
| 1 | $ 7,152 | $ 5,289 |
| 2 | 9,436 | 6,912 |
| 3 | 12,622 | 9,256 |
| 4 | 14,545 | 10,699 |
| 5 | 16,949 | 12,441 |
| 6 | 18,511 | 13,583 |
| 7 or more | 20,375 | 14,966 |

Source: Statistics Canada, *Income Distribution by Size in Canada, 1980*, p. 125.

**Exhibit 32.6**
**The geographical distribution of poverty in Canada, 1980**

The data presented in this table show the percentage of families who fell below the poverty line in different regions of the country in 1980.

| Region | Percentage of Families below Poverty Line |
|---|---|
| Atlantic Provinces | 16.4 |
| Quebec | 15.2 |
| Ontario | 10.2 |
| Prairie Provinces | 11.4 |
| British Columbia | 9.6 |

Source: Statistics Canada, *Income Distributions by Size in Canada, 1980,* p. 137.

because people do not live "by bread alone" and many families close to the poverty line are unable to share in the cultural and social amenities which their society offers. The debate will never be settled, but the figures at least give social planners something definite to work with. We shall use them in other parts of this chapter.

## Who Are the Poor?

As of 1980, more than three million Canadians, or about 15 percent of the population, were living below the official poverty line. The poor were not distributed evenly across the population, either demographically or geographically. A higher proportion of families in rural areas (13.9 percent) were poor than were families in cities (for example, 11.1 percent of families in cities with populations from 100,000 to 500,000). This was true despite the fact that for a family of two persons, for example, the poverty line in rural areas was only $6,912 while in cities with populations of 500,000 or more the line was drawn at $9,436. Poverty is unevenly distributed across the country. Exhibit 32.6 shows the percentage of families below the poverty line by region in 1980. British Columbia had the lowest proportion of families below the line (9.6 percent) and the Atlantic provinces had the highest (16.4 percent).

Still other data can shed light on why some persons or families fall below the poverty line. Exhibit 32.7 shows that 43.2 percent of households headed by a woman, usually widowed or divorced, live in poverty, as compared to only 8.8 percent of households in which the head is a male. Age is also important, as Exhibit 32.7 indicates. Both very young families (age of family head below twenty-five) and old families (age of family head sixty-five and over) have a very high poverty rate. The level of education of the head of the family is also very important. Only 4.5 percent of families in which the head has a university degree live in poverty, compared to 18.8 percent for those with 0–8 years of schooling.

About ten years ago, the Special Senate Committee on Poverty determined in the course of extensive hearings that the poor can be classified in three general categories:

1. About one-quarter of the poor are unable to work because of severe disability.
2. About one-half of the poor are working, but are not able to earn an adequate income.

**Exhibit 32.7**
**Incidence of poverty by selected characteristics, 1980**

| Characteristics | Incidence of Poverty (Percentage of families below poverty line) |
|---|---:|
| Sex of family head | |
| Male | 8.8 |
| Female | 43.2 |
| Age of Family Head | |
| 24 and under | 21.1 |
| 25–34 | 12.2 |
| 35–44 | 11.6 |
| 45–54 | 10.1 |
| 55–64 | 11.4 |
| 65 and over | 14.2 |
| By Education of Head | |
| 0–8 years | 18.8 |
| some high school – no post secondary | 12.2 |
| university degree | 4.5 |

Source: Statistics Canada, *Income Distribution by Size in Canada, 1980*, pp. 137 and 140.

3. The remaining quarter of the poor are seemingly able to work but can't or won't find employment.[4]

The first group can be helped through special assistance programs and personal charity. The second group, the working poor, poses many special problems. Its members are the victims of erratic employment patterns related to swings in the business cycle; low-productivity jobs and low pay, often associated with low levels of education; and low mobility. Some members of this group may also be the victims of discrimination.

The third group, made up of those who are not working but are potentially able to work, also poses acute problems. To what extent are they simply not motivated to work, either because of generous social assistance programs that reduce the penalty for not working, or because of the absence of inner drive and a sense of responsibility? To what extent are they unable to match their limited skills with the prevailing job market? We simply don't have many reliable answers to these questions. We noted in a previous chapter that unemployment insurance provisions have undoubtedly contributed to some of the unemployment in the country. Some feel that generous welfare programs do the same. However, a study of welfare in Manitoba observed: "Contrary to a popular view, the typical individual on welfare is not an able-bodied person with a large family who prefers living in idleness drawing his welfare cheque to taking a job and supporting himself. Indeed, insofar as the provincial welfare rolls are concerned, the employable category makes up only a small proportion of the total, usually five percent or less."[5]

---

[4]Special Senate Committee on Poverty, *Poverty in Canada*, 1971. See also T. Courchene, "Some Reflections on the Senate Hearings on Poverty," in *Economic Canada: Selected Readings*, eds. B.S. Keirstead, J.F. Earl, et al. (Toronto: Macmillan of Canada, 1974), pp. 205–206.

[5]Clarence L. Barber, *Welfare Policy in Manitoba*, A Report to the Planning and Priorities of Cabinet Secretariat, Province of Manitoba, December, 1972, p. 8.

## WHAT IS TO BE DONE ABOUT POVERTY?

This profile of poverty in Canada gives us an idea of the dimensions and diversity of the problem. Next we shall look at what is being done to alleviate poverty, and what else might be done but is not.

We have divided the poor into three main categories, and this suggests that three different types of approaches may be necessary to alleviate poverty in Canada.

For those who are clearly disabled or unable to participate in the work force because of age, a program of social assistance, involving transfer payments, is required. We noted in Chapter 4 that all three levels of government in Canada have instituted programs of this type. At least a dozen transfer programs are now in existence, coordinated through the Canada Assistance Plan (1966). Programs include the Old Age Security Pension, Blind Persons' Assistance, Veterans' Benefits, Family Allowances, and Workmen's Compensation. In addition there are social insurance schemes, in which the amount paid out is related to premiums paid by the recipient. These include the Canada (and Quebec) Pension plans and unemployment insurance. In 1982, almost 1.8 million Canadians depended on welfare assistance of one kind or another, with the federal government contributing more than $3 billion to the Canada Assistance Plan.

Such assistance programs are generous enough to prevent extreme hardship among most of the unemployed poor in the country, but it could be argued that, in a wealthy nation like Canada, assistance to the disabled and the aged could and should be sufficient to lift them above the poverty line entirely.

For the employable poor, other types of programs are required. Various types of manpower training programs and fiscal and monetary measures are currently utilized to create more and better jobs. These need to be supplemented by other measures. It would appear, for example, that more vigorous efforts are necessary to moderate excessive wage and income differentials by curbing the monopolistic power of large corporations, professional groups, and labor unions.

A comprehensive approach to poverty through changes to the income tax act, which would use "negative taxes" to provide assistance without discouraging work incentives, has also been advocated in Canada. This is related to what is known as a Guaranteed Annual Income policy (GAI) for Canada. In November 1970 the federal government published a White Paper, "Income Security for Canadians," calling for study of "an overall guaranteed income program for the whole population." The government agreed to cooperate with provincial governments in researching the feasability of such a program. The only provincial government to take up the offer was Manitoba, which launched a three-year research project in 1975 (see Case 32.1). In 1973 the federal government issued a "Working Paper on Social Security in Canada," which gave broad support to new initiatives in the area of social security including a negative income tax approach.

### The Negative Income Tax

Economists concerned about the disincentive effects of the present welter of poorly coordinated transfer programs have long advocated "cashing out"

**Negative income tax** A general name for transfer systems that emphasize cash benefits, beginning with a basic benefit available to households with zero earned income that is then subject to a benefit reduction rate of substantially less than 100 percent.

all in-kind transfers and rolling all transfer programs into a single negative income tax program. The basic idea behind a negative income tax is very simple. Under a positive income tax — the kind currently used — individuals pay the government an amount that varies according to how much they earn. A **negative income tax** puts the same principle to work in reverse. It makes the government pay individuals an amount that varies in proportion to their earnings.

Exhibit 32.8 shows how a negative income tax could be set up. The horizontal axis of the figure measures the income a household earns. The vertical axis measures what it actually receives after payments from or to the government. The 45 degree line represents the amount of disposable income households would have if there were no tax of any kind. The negative and positive income tax schedules show the disposable income of families with the negative income tax program in force.

As the exhibit is drawn, the benefit received by a family with no income at all is just equal to the average low income level, assumed to be $6,000, that is necessary if the scheme is to eliminate officially measured poverty entirely. Starting from zero earnings, benefits are reduced by $.50 for each $1 earned. When earned incomes reach a level equal to twice the low income level, a breakeven point where no taxes are paid and no benefits received is reached. Beyond that point, a positive income tax schedule of the familiar kind takes over.

The negative income tax has the great advantage of maintaining work incentives for all beneficiaries. The marginal tax rate for poor families is only 50 percent as the exhibit is drawn. This rate is presumably low enough to prevent widespread withdrawal of effort. Note, however, that the cost of the program is still much greater than the initial size of the aggregate income deficit. All but the very poorest families receive more than the minimum they need to reach the low income cutoff. What is more, many

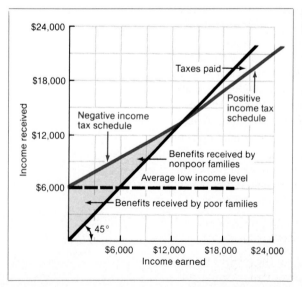

**Exhibit 32.8**

**Possible schedules for a negative income tax**

A negative income tax redistributes income without imposing extremely high marginal tax rates on either taxpayers or beneficiaries. In order to maintain low marginal tax rates, some benefits are given to nonpoor families, and some poor families are given more than they need to reach the low income level. The cost of a negative income tax scheme must therefore always be greater than the aggregate income deficit.

nonpoor families—those with earned incomes in the $6,000 to $12,000 range—also receive benefits.

Many practical questions about the cost and workability of a negative income tax cannot be answered by armchair economics. They can be answered only on the basis of actual experience with running such a program. Some significant experiments have now been carried out; two of them are described in the following case study.

### Case 32.1
### The New Jersey Graduated Work Incentive Experiment and the Basic Annual Income Experiment in Manitoba

From 1968 to 1972, a negative income tax experiment involving 1,300 low-income families was carried out in four eastern cities. The program was called the New Jersey Graduated Work Incentive Experiment. A variety of different benefit schedules were used with different groups of subjects. The level of guaranteed minimum income ranged from 50 to 100 percent of the poverty-level income, and the marginal tax rate for the beneficiaries varied from 30 to 70 percent. Only households headed by a male were included in the experimental group.

The central objective of the experiment was to investigate the effect of the negative income tax on work incentives and labor supply. Results of the experiment indicated strongly that the labor supply effects of such a program are small. Over all, it appeared that there might be a 5 to 10 percent reduction in the amount of work done by participants in the program. Somewhat surprisingly, no statistically measurable differences in labor supply response were observed within the range of 30 to 70 percent marginal tax rates. Some experimenters tentatively took this to indicate that marginal tax rates of at least 50 percent could be used without seriously eroding work incentives.

A detailed study of the labor supply response of beneficiaries revealed some further items of interest. In particular, it appeared that the 5–10 percent overall reduction in hours worked did not take the form of total withdrawal from the labor force of any significant number of workers. Rather, reductions came from fewer hours worked, fewer dual jobs and, in some cases, longer periods of job search between jobs. Reductions in labor supply appeared to be more pronounced for secondary than for primary workers. They were also more pronounced for whites than for blacks or Spanish-speaking workers.

A secondary purpose of the experiment was to test the administrative feasibility of a negative income tax. Results were encouraging in this respect also. Despite problems of interpreting some of the data, and lack of clearcut statistical results in some areas, it was felt that, as an experiment in experimentation, the New Jersey program had been a success. It has encouraged further investigation of the negative income tax as a practical policy alternative.

Manitoba decided to initiate further experimentation in 1975, under a three-year program called Mincome Manitoba, costing over $17 million. This was financed jointly by the federal government (75 percent) and the Manitoba government (25 percent).

Several areas in Manitoba were selected for the experiment, and participants were chosen on a random basis. In addition, the community of Dauphin was chosen for saturation experimentation. In total over a thousand families were involved. Participants were guaranteed a minimum level of income, to be paid in full if they had no other form of income. For each dollar of income earned through employment the assistance was reduced by 50 percent (up to a limit of $7,600 for a family of four, with the guaranteed income level set at $3,800). Unfortunately, when the experiment was concluded in 1978, further funding became uncertain.

Recently the federal government granted research support to a new research institute at the University of Manitoba to salvage as much useful information as possible from the accumulated data. No results have yet been published.

Source: Joseph A. Pechman and Michael Timpane (eds.), *Work Incentives and Income Guarantees. The New Jersey Negative Income Tax Experiment*, (Washington, D.C.: Brookings Institution, 1975).

## Political Problems

In addition to problems posed by the need for more practical information on cost and effects, the negative income tax scheme faces a number of political problems. One such problem is posed by the diversity of living standards in different parts of the country. The business of setting benefits would be greatly complicated by the need to reconcile regional interests. A further problem is how the negative income tax should relate to other programs. Many economists believe that it would make great sense to use a comprehensive negative income tax to replace all existing social insurance and public charity programs. Existing programs are not easy to eliminate, however. Each has its own army of lobbyists among beneficiaries, politicians, and public officials. Yet simply to tack a negative income tax onto the existing welter of programs would increase rather than diminish the total cost of all transfer programs. It would increase rather than diminish the complexity, overlaps, and conflicting incentives that characterize the current system. For the moment, it appears that political realities will keep the negative income tax in the textbooks, but interest in the scheme has become so widespread that it may not stay there forever.

## HELPING THE POOR: JOB MARKET STRATEGIES

Transfer strategies for helping the poor are based on the diagnosis that people are poor because they do not have enough money. The implied cure is to give them additional resources in cash or in kind. A different approach to the problem of poverty is based on the diagnosis that poverty results from a failure of factor markets to allocate human resources properly. By implication, putting wasted labor to work would make many poor households self-supporting.

The diagnosis that poverty is a matter of factor market failure must be broadly interpreted if it is to have any credibility at all. Research data suggest that very few of the poor are adults in households headed by unemployed, able-bodied males aged eighteen to sixty-five. A narrowly conceived jobs-for-the-poor approach that focused just on this group would not make much of a dent on the overall poverty picture. In a broader sense, though, much more poverty is attributable to job related sources. The number of elderly poor and working poor would be reduced if the market provided higher paying jobs. The number of families headed by women, where the highest proportion of poor children are concentrated, would be less if it were not for the destructive effect on family life of men's inability to get good jobs. In the long run, job market strategies for alleviating poverty could benefit all the poor.

## The Dual Labor Market Theory

Job market failure as a source of poverty is not just a matter of unemployment. According to one theory, the problem lies in the existence of a dual labor market. One sector of the labor market contains high wage jobs with profitable firms. These jobs not only pay more but are more likely to be unionized, to offer opportunities for advancement, and to be less affected by macroeconomic fluctuations. The secondary job market, in contrast, contains low paying jobs with marginal firms. These jobs are held by unorganized workers with unstable work patterns. They are largely dead-end jobs with few opportunities for advancement, and they are heavily hit by cyclical swings in unemployment.

According to proponents of the dual labor market theory, the two parts of the job market are kept separate by a complex of interacting factors. Discrimination, attitudes, motivation, and work habits determine which sector a worker is in. Once in the secondary sector, a worker develops attitudes and work habits that make discrimination more likely. The dual labor market theory has clear implications for antipoverty policy—namely, that such a policy must aim at breaking down the barriers between the two market sectors. The following section looks at some possible means of doing this.

**Education** Economists like to view education as an investment. By spending money and taking time away from current employment, people can improve their skills and productivity. Later, they can sell their services at higher wages in the labor market. One antipoverty strategy, then, is to make good quality education available to the poor and to the children of the poor, in the hope that this education will make them self-supporting.

There are actually two different ways in which education can have an impact on the problem of poverty. On the one hand, education benefits the particular individuals who are educated, thus taking people one by one out of poverty. On the other hand, improved education has a general impact on the equality of income distribution; by increasing the supply of highly educated workers, it lowers their relative wages. Both effects are slow, however, and far from foolproof.

Looking first at elementary education, one encounters the problem of an uncertain relationship between the quantity of educational inputs and the quality of educational outputs. Despite numerous studies, it is by no means clear that spending more on schools improves the performance of the pupils who go to them. To a considerable extent, the home and community environment may be more powerful than formal education in transmitting the crucial attitudes, motivations, and work habits that decide which sector of the labor market a person will end up in.

Increased spending on higher education appears to be an even less certain method for combating poverty. It is true that a college education gives upward mobility for many individuals from impoverished backgrounds. Those who succeed in college, however, are likely to be those with the attitudes and abilities that would bring them success in any event, even if they never had the chance to go to college. There is some evidence that in the early 1970s, salaries for college trained workers began to fall in response to an increased supply of college graduates. This may be having some effect on the inequality of income distribution. There are probably other, better ways to achieve the same effect, though. It would seem better to bring up the income of the poor rather than to push down the income of college graduates by encouraging their oversupply.

One thing remains to be said in favor of education as an antipoverty measure. Although the economic effects of subsidizing education may be difficult to measure, a good education is something that most disadvantaged parents want for their children. Improvements in education thus fill a perceived need. This may be important in itself.

## CONCLUSIONS

The economics of poverty is, in many ways, the most discouraging branch of economics to study. Economists, of course, have plenty of simple and elegant solutions. If we really want to eliminate poverty, what we need to do is abolish all existing programs and replace them with a single, streamlined negative income tax, or something like it. But our political system is not built to pursue a goal such as eliminating poverty in a straightforward, single-minded way. It is a system of give and take that responds to many opposing interests, and the current array of poverty programs is the natural outcome.

## SUMMARY

1. In 1980, some three to four million Canadians were officially classified as poor, according to poverty lines established by Statistics Canada. These lines are based on the amount of income required by different-sized families in different locations of the country to enable them to spend no more than 58.5 percent of their income on basic necessities. In classifying families as poor or nonpoor, only before-tax money incomes are taken into account. This practice leads to an overstatement of the difference between the two groups. If the effects of taxes and all benefits are taken into account, the distribution of income in Canada appears to have become somewhat more equal in recent decades.
2. The Lorenz curve and the Gini coefficient provide useful measurements of the extent of income inequality in a society. They also enable comparisons to be made between different countries, with respect to their income inequality.
3. The Canada Assistance Plan is the heart of government transfer efforts. Many benefits are paid to families on the basis of need. Social insurance benefits are paid with some relationship to premiums that have been contributed.
4. The negative income tax is a simplified transfer scheme often suggested as an alternative to current antipoverty efforts. A key feature of the negative income tax is a relatively low marginal tax rate for families at all income levels. Limited local experiments tentatively confirm the practicality of the negative income tax. The idea is not yet as popular in governments, however, as it is among economists.
5. Job market strategies for aiding the poor approach poverty as a problem of factor market failure. More is involved than just unemployment. One theory states that antipoverty efforts must aim at breaking down a dual labor market. Some think that the government should approach the problem from the supply side with education and job training programs. Others emphasize demand-side programs including antidiscrimination measures and public employment.

## DISCUSSION QUESTIONS

1. It is sometimes said that poverty is not the fault of individuals, but the fault of society. Do you agree? What do you think the statement means? Because "society" is itself composed of individuals, does it mean that certain nonpoor individuals are responsible for the poverty of poor individuals? If so, which individuals are responsible? Do you think that any of your own actions may be at fault in causing someone else to be poor?

2. According to the logic of the federal government's low-income standard, an officially poor family is likely not to be able to afford an adequate diet. Do you think it odd that so many poverty-level families, who cannot afford adequate nutrition, do seem able to afford cars, television sets, clothes dryers, and air conditioners? Is it natural and reasonable that a poor family should own such things? Would you favor legislation that attempted to force poor families to spend more on food and less on seemingly unnecessary appliances? Could the data on appliances indicate a defect in the official method of measuring poverty?

3. What are the relative merits of cash versus in-kind transfers? Review Chapter 21, paying particular attention to the concepts of marginal utility and consumer equilibrium. Suppose that program A gives a family a $1,000 cash benefit, and program B gives the family $1,000 worth of goods in kind, in proportions not selected by the family itself. Which program do you think would be likely to give the family greater utility? To make the question easier to answer, assume a simplified economy where there are only two goods, food and clothing. What if the two goods were food and whiskey?

4. Suppose that there were a universally effective negative income tax in force, so that measured poverty was entirely eliminated. Would you then be willing to see other social insurance programs, including social security (retirement), unemployment insurance, and medicare abolished? Why or why not?

5. According to data in this chapter, in which country is family income more evenly distributed, in Canada or the United States?

## SUGGESTIONS FOR FURTHER READING

Osberg, Lars. *Economic Inequality in Canada*. Toronto: Butterworth, 1981.
*A recent, thorough discussion of the apparent causes and characteristics of income inequality and poverty in Canada.*
Special Senate Committee on Poverty, *Report on Poverty in Canada*, 1971.
*An early, major, and thoughtful study of poverty in Canada.*

# THE
# WORLD
# ECONOMY

# PART FIVE

# CHAPTER

# THIRTY THREE

# THE ECONOMICS OF POPULATION AND DEVELOPMENT

**WHAT YOU WILL LEARN IN THIS CHAPTER**

*Most of the inhabitants of the planet earth are very poor, and the numbers of the poor are increasing more rapidly than those of the more well-to-do. This chapter discusses some of the economic problems faced by the inhabitants of the less developed countries. It begins with a lesson in basic population arithmetic. Then it compares population growth trends over time in the developed and less developed countries and shows why the population problem of the less developed world is in many respects more serious than that faced in earlier times by the now developed countries. Finally, the chapter turns from the population problem itself to the problem of producing sufficient food to feed the ever-growing third world population.*

**FOR REVIEW**

*Here is an important concept that will be put to use in this chapter. If you do not understand it, review it before proceeding.*

*• Sources of economic growth (Chapter 7)*

How will the ever-increasing numbers of people in the world find room to live? How are they going to be fed? These are among the most pressing worldwide problems to be faced in the closing years of the twentieth century.

The problems of food and population have largely been solved in the world's industrialized market economies. For that reason, this chapter will focus on the less developed countries, where two-thirds of the world's people already live. It begins with a brief discussion of the nature of the economic development process itself. Next, it turns to the topic of population. Finally, it reviews the status of world food production, on which the solution of the problems of development and population so heavily depend.

## THREE FACES OF ECONOMIC GROWTH

### Economic Development as Growth

The less developed countries that make up what is called the "third

**$3,001 to more than $7,000**

| | | |
|---|---|---|
| Australia | Gabon | Norway |
| Austria | Greenland | Oman |
| Bahamas Islands | Iceland | Qatar |
| Bahrain | Israel | San Marino |
| Belgium | Italy | Saudi Arabia |
| Bermuda | Japan | Spain |
| Brunei | Kuwait | Sweden |
| Canada | Libya | Switzerland |
| Czechoslovakia | Liechtenstein | United Arab Emirates |
| Denmark | Luxembourg | United Kingdom |
| East Germany | Monaco | United States |
| Faroe Islands | Nauru | USSR |
| Finland | Netherlands | West Germany |
| France | New Zealand | |

**$201 to $1,000**

| | |
|---|---|
| Albania | Dominica |
| Algeria | Dominican |
| Angola | Republic |
| Antigua | Djibouti |
| Belize | Ecuador |
| Benin | Egypt |
| Bolivia | El Salvador |
| Botswana | French Guiana |
| Cameroon | Gambia |
| Chile | Ghana |
| Colombia | Gibraltar |
| Congo | Gilbert Islands |
| Cook Islands | Grenada |
| Cuba | Guadeloupe |

**$1,001 to $3,000**

| | |
|---|---|
| Andorra | |
| Argentina | |
| Barbados | |
| Brazil | |
| Bulgaria | |
| Costa Rica | |
| Cyprus | |
| Falkland Islands | |
| Fiji | |
| French Polynesia | |
| Greece | |
| Hong Kong | |
| Hungary | Portugal |
| Iran | Puerto Rico |
| Iraq | Romania |
| Ireland | Singapore |
| Jamaica | South Africa |
| Malta | Surinam |
| Martinique | Taiwan |
| Mexico | Trinidad and |
| Netherlands Antilles | Tobago |
| New Caledonia | Turkey |
| Panama | Uruguay |
| Poland | Venezuela |
| | Yugoslavia |

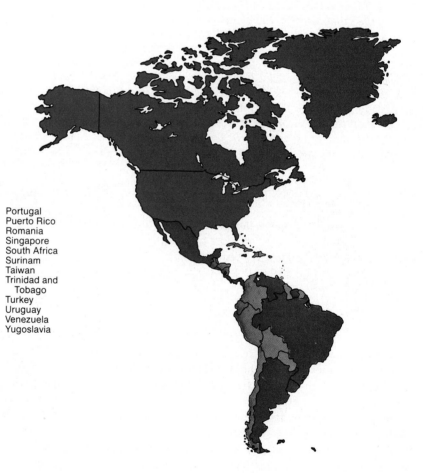

**Exhibit 33.1**

**Gross national product per capita, 1977 (in 1977 U.S. dollars)**

The countries of the world exhibit an enormous range in per capita incomes. There is no sharp dividing line between the developed and less developed countries. Here, four groups are distinguished. The most poverty stricken countries are those with incomes of less than $201 GNP per capita. Those with per capita incomes of less than $1,001 are also very poor, but many are experiencing promising self-sufficient

| Guatemala | Malaysia | People's Republic | South Yemen |
|-----------|----------|-------------------|-------------|
| Guyana | Mauritania | of China | Sri Lanka |
| Haiti | Mauritius | Peru | Sudan |
| Honduras | Mongolia | Philippines | Swaziland |
| Indonesia | Morocco | Rhodesia | Syria |
| Ivory Coast | Mozambique | St. Christopher- | Thailand |
| Jordan | Namibia | Nevis-Anguilla | Togo |
| Kenya | Nicaragua | St. Lucia | Tonga |
| Lebanon | Nigeria | St. Vincent | Tunisia |
| Lesotho | North Korea | Sao Tome/Principe | Uganda |
| Liberia | North Yemen | Senegal | Western Sahara |
| Macao | Papua-New | Seychelles | Western Samoa |
| Madagascar | Guinea | Sierra Leone | Zambia |
| Republic | Paraguay | South Korea | |

**Less than $201**

Afghanistan
Bangladesh
Bhutan
Burma
Burundi
Cambodia
Cape Verde Islands
Central African
 Empire
Chad
Equatorial Guinea
Ethiopia
Guinea-Bissau
India
Laos
Malawi
Mali
Nepal
Niger
Pakistan
Rwanda
Somalia
Tanzania
Upper Volta
Vietnam
Zaire

economic growth. Countries in the $1,001 to $3,000 range belong in the less developed category in some respects; but in other ways, they more closely resemble the countries with more than $3,000 per capita GNP. This last group includes the oil-rich countries of the Middle East as well as the industrialized countries of Europe and North America.

Source: Adapted from U.S. Central Intelligence Agency, National Foreign Assessment Center, *Handbook of Economic Statistics* (Washington, D.C., 1978), Figure 1, p. 1.

world"[1] differ from one another and from the developed countries in many ways, but they have one conspicuous thing in common—low per capita income. No magic number divides the rich countries from the poor; there is a continuous range of degrees of poverty, as shown in the map in Exhibit 33.1. At the very bottom of the range are the poorest of poor countries— those with per capita GNP of less than $200 per year. These countries are found in southern Asia, from Afghanistan to Vietnam, and in a band through central Africa reaching from Guinea on the west coast to Tanzania on the east. The map also distinguishes countries with per capita GNP in the range of $201 to $1,000, clearly in the less developed group but somewhat better off. A third group, in the $1,001 to $3,000 range —including much of Latin America as well as such countries as Portugal, Yugoslavia, and Taiwan—straddles the ill-defined border between developed and less developed status. Countries with still higher levels of per capita GNP include the truly developed countries as well as the somewhat anomalous oil-rich countries of the Middle East.

To draw these distinctions in terms of per capita incomes implies that economic development equals economic growth. That is the traditional view of the matter, and it is a view that still has much truth to it. Economic development implies changes in the *kinds* of goods that people produce and use (not just changes in their quantity), and it involves changes in the techniques of production, but it is hard to see how a better life for all can come without at least some growth. This is especially true for the least developed countries that have less than $200 of GNP per capita.

Much of development economics, then, focuses on ways to enable a country to grow. Growth-oriented development studies usually emphasize capital accumulation as the great key. Capital accumulation has accounted for only about 20 percent of economic growth in Canada in recent years, but it is more important for less developed countries, which have a great shortage of capital. Typically, saving and investment are only 5 to 7 percent of GNP, compared to over 15 percent in Canada and 35 percent in Japan and the Soviet-type economies. Without capital accumulation, it is difficult to put unemployed and underemployed people to work. Without capital it is equally difficult to improve the level of education or to take advantage of imported technology. Yet, although capital accumulation and growth are important, they are not the whole story of economic development.

## Development as Industrialization

The developed countries are not only richer than the less developed countries; they are also more highly industrialized. Developed countries typically have between a fifth and a quarter of their populations engaged in industry. In the less developed countries, the proportion is likely to be 10 percent or less. A second interpretation of economic development, then, is

---

[1]It has become a popular practice to divide the world into three groups: first, the advanced market economies, second, the advanced centrally planned economies, and third, the less developed countries, or "third world" countries.

that it means industrializing, just as the advanced countries have done in the past.

The view that development means industrialization, like the view that development means economic growth, has much truth to it. The less developed countries have large and growing urban populations. Only industrialization offers them much hope of employment. As incomes rise in a developing country, the demand for manufactured goods increases rapidly. It makes sense to meet many of these needs with domestic sources of supply. Many less developed countries have valuable raw materials that they now export for processing; these materials could be processed domestically instead. Still, despite all this, the importance of industrialization to development should not be exaggerated.

For one thing, an overemphasis on industrialization may cause resources to be wasted on ill-conceived showcase projects. Not every less developed country needs a steel mill and an automobile plant. Even small-scale industrial projects may be inappropriate if they mean building an exact replica of some plant originally designed for Manchester or Milwaukee, where labor or capital scarcities and other market conditions are completely different.

What is more, an overemphasis on industrialization can lead to the neglect of other development objectives. The third face of economic development shows why.

## Development as Depauperization

It is a widely shared opinion that a major goal of economic development should be a better life for the poorest of the poor — the people at the low end of the income distribution in the poorest countries. They are the true paupers — lacking adequate food, often lacking all access to medical care, and not infrequently lacking even the most primitive shelter.

Development economists once were confident that the benefits of growth and industrialization would automatically trickle down to the poorest of the poor. Unfortunately, this optimism may not be justified, as the research of Irma Adelman and C.T. Morris has shown.[2] Their work focuses on the range of development from sub-Saharan Africa to the poorest countries of South America — that is, from about $100 to $500 per capita income. In these countries, development tends to bring both relative and absolute impoverishment to the poorest 60 percent of the population. At very low levels of development, there appears to be no trickling down at all. The poor begin to benefit only after an intermediate level of development has been reached.

Adelman and Morris have concluded that the policies needed to benefit the poor are different from those needed to maximize growth rates. The ideas of development as growth or industrialization, they say, should be

---

[2]Irma Adelman and C.T. Morris, *Society, Politics, and Economic Development* (Baltimore: Johns Hopkins University Press, 1967).

**Depauperization** Economic development of a kind that benefits the poorest of the poor, providing them not only with the material necessities of life but also with access to education, status, security, self-expression, and power.

replaced with the idea of **depauperization**—the provision not only of the necessary material basis for life but also of access to education, security, self-expression, status, and power. Depauperization stresses the removal of social, political, and spiritual deprivation as much as physical deprivation. It has as much to do with equity as with growth.

## Two Strategies

The choice of development goals strongly influences the strategy that can best promote the development process. The Soviet Union represents one extreme. For early Soviet planners, development meant industrialization above all else. Through high rates of saving, they sacrificed consumption to achieve rapid growth. Through collectivization, they sacrificed the growth of agriculture to achieve the growth of industry. Eventually, the benefits of successful industrialization began to trickle down to the population at large. Initially, though, living standards declined, and the overall distribution of income shifted in favor of industrial workers and against peasants.

Even where industrialization as an end in itself is not made a higher priority than overall growth, the benefits of development may be spread unevenly. Many less developed countries suffer from what is called a **dual economy**. In such an economy, a modern, Westernized industrial sector provides high wages for better educated workers and a tax base to pay a middle class of civil servants. Meanwhile, a secondary, traditional sector remains largely untouched. Sometimes, the overall growth rate of GNP can be maximized by concentrating available development resources on the modern sector, at least in the short run. Often also foreign aid and the investments of multinational corporations are concentrated on the modern sector of dual economies.

**Dual economy** An economy that is sharply divided into a modern, westernized industrial sector capable of rapid growth and a traditional rural sector that remains stagnant.

There is a second kind of development strategy that contrasts with the industry-first approach. It emphasizes redistribution and mass education first and growth later. Redistribution in the context of less developed countries means, most importantly, the redistribution of land ownership. Education means mass education in literacy and general knowledge, rather than just specialized training for participation in the modern sector. If this strategy works, redistribution can provide the basis for rural development and education the basis for the growth of broadly based, labor-intensive industry. Adelman and Morris cite Israel, Japan, South Korea, Singapore, and Taiwan as countries that have successfully followed this strategy. China should probably be added to the list. In the last century, U.S. economic development followed this strategy much more than did economic development in Europe.

## POPULATION AND DEVELOPMENT

Whatever development strategy they choose, all less developed countries face certain common problems that they must somehow solve. None is more serious than the problem of population growth. As background for a discussion of population problems in the less developed countries, here is a review of some basic population arithmetic.

**Exhibit 33.2**
**Birthrates, death rates, and the rate of natural increase of the population for selected countries**

The rate of natural increase for a population is found by subtracting the current death rate per thousand from the current birthrate per thousand. If the rate of natural increase is greater than zero, it can also be expressed as the number of years that would be required for the population to double if that rate were to continue.

| Country | Crude Birthrate | Crude Death Rate | Rate of Natural Increase | Doubling Time of Population (years) |
|---|---|---|---|---|
| Honduras | 47 | 12 | 35 | 20 |
| Mexico | 41 | 7 | 34 | 20 |
| Algeria | 48 | 14 | 33 | 21 |
| Nigeria | 50 | 18 | 32 | 22 |
| Ghana | 48 | 17 | 31 | 22 |
| Pakistan | 44 | 14 | 30 | 23 |
| Somalia | 48 | 20 | 28 | 25 |
| Brazil | 36 | 8 | 28 | 25 |
| Haiti | 42 | 16 | 26 | 27 |
| Ethiopia | 50 | 25 | 25 | 28 |
| Afghanistan | 50 | 27 | 23 | 30 |
| Yemen | 48 | 25 | 23 | 30 |
| Thailand | 32 | 9 | 23 | 30 |
| Argentina | 22 | 9 | 13 | 53 |
| China | 20 | 8 | 12 | 58 |
| Japan | 15 | 6 | 9 | 77 |
| Canada | 16 | 7 | 9 | 77 |
| USSR | 18 | 10 | 8 | 87 |
| Czechoslovakia | 19 | 12 | 7 | 99 |
| United States | 15 | 9 | 6 | 116 |
| France | 14 | 10 | 4 | 173 |
| Italy | 13 | 10 | 4 | 173 |
| Sweden | 12 | 11 | 1 | 693 |
| United Kingdom | 12 | 12 | 0 | — |
| West Germany | 10 | 12 | −2 | — |

Source: Reprinted by permission from *1979 World Population Data Sheet* (Washington, D.C.: Population Reference Bureau, 1979). Data refer to 1976–77.

## Population Arithmetic

For a population to increase, it is obvious that more people must be born than die each year. (In this section and in what follows, immigration and emigration are ignored.) The number of people born into a population per thousand per year is the **crude birthrate** for that population. The number who die per thousand per year is the **crude death rate**. The difference between the two is the **rate of natural increase**.

Exhibit 33.2 shows crude birthrates, crude death rates, and rates of natural increase for a selection of countries, according to the latest available data. In interpreting data such as these, it sometimes helps to translate rates of natural increase into population doubling times. This is done in the last column of the table. The faster the rate of natural increase, the shorter the period of time required for the population to double in size.

**Growth Curves** A population that grew indefinitely at a constant rate of natural increase would double each time a fixed number of years elapsed. It would reach 2, 4, 8, 16, 32, 64 (and so on) times its original size, following

**Crude birthrate** The number of people born into a population per thousand per year.

**Crude death rate** The number of people in a population who die per thousand per year.

**Rate of natural increase** The current growth rate of a population calculated as the crude birthrate minus the crude death rate.

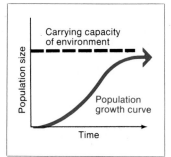

**Exhibit 33.3**
**Typical S-shaped curve of population growth**
A living population cannot grow indefinitely in a finite environment. Under laboratory conditions, populations of bacteria or fruit flies or other organisms tend to follow S-shaped growth curves such as the one shown here. In the long run, it seems inevitable that the growth curve of human population will also begin to decrease.

the same sort of growth path as that followed by the value of a sum of money invested at compound interest.

Normally, however, living populations are not able to grow exponentially without limit. Suppose that bacteria are allowed to multiply in a glass jar of nutrient, or a population of fruit flies is allowed to grow in a glass cage or room of fixed size, or a breeding pair of dogs is introduced on an island previously inhabited only by rabbits. Under such conditions, the growth of the population of bacteria, fruit flies, or dogs typically follows the kind of S-shaped growth curve shown in Exhibit 33.3. At first, the population will expand at the exponential rate. The biological characteristics of the species in question determine the population doubling time under optimal conditions. Sooner or later, though, the population will begin to fill up its jar or cage or island or whatever. Then, under more crowded conditions, the time needed to double the population will increase. Eventually, overcrowding will bring population growth to a halt.

Must the growth of human population also be subject to this S-curve pattern? In the long run, it surely must. Estimates of the maximum human population of earth vary widely, but no one doubts that there is some finite ceiling. (One admittedly fanciful estimate places the limit as high as 20 million times the present world population. This would require people to live 120 to the square meter in a two-thousand-story building covering the entire earth. Even that limit would take only 890 years to reach at the present growth rate of world population!)

In the short run, though, the growth of human population has not followed the simple S-curve pattern. In fact, over as long a period as any kind of population estimates can be made, the world rate of natural increase has been accelerating, not slowing down. World population has doubled in about the last forty-five years and would double again in the next thirty-five if the current growth rate were to continue. The last preceding doubling of population took about eighty years, from 1850 to 1930. The doubling before that took some two hundred years. It is hard to imagine that this trend will continue. There are now indications that the world is reaching the bend in the population growth curve and that world population growth, for the first time, is beginning to slow.[3]

---

[3]For example, Donald J. Bogue and Amy Ong Tsui, in "Zero World Population Growth," *Public Interest*, no. 55 (Spring 1979), pp. 99–113, go so far as to declare the once-feared population bomb a dud. Between 1968 and 1975, they report, fertility declined in 103 countries having a total population of 3.2 billion and increased or was unchanged in only 45 countries with a total population of 749 million.

## Population Equilibrium

There can be no doubt that in the long run the level of human population is headed for an equilibrium state in which births will just balance deaths. The really interesting question is: what will that equilibrium look like? Let's explore some possibilities.

First, imagine a market economy in which people earn money to buy the necessities of life only by selling factor services. The population begins to approach some fixed limit to population growth defined, for example, by the food supply. Income is distributed unequally in this society. As population nears the ceiling, the price of food rises relative to the wage rate. The lowest income groups find their standard of living reduced, and this eventually affects their birth and death rates. At some point, an excess of deaths over births will occur among the poorest classes. This will be accompanied by a balance between births and deaths for those living just at the margin of subsistence. An excess of births will be possible only among the well-to-do. When enough people have finally been pushed down to or below the margin of subsistence, population growth as a whole will cease. The result can be called a marginal subsistence equilibrium for population.

This equilibrium assumes great inequality. It implies affluence for a few against the backdrop of destitute masses whose members are continuously replenished by the excess children of the rich driven down into poverty. If the assumption of inequality is removed, the result is a second type of population equilibrium, which can be called the absolute subsistence equilibrium. Under this solution, as crowding begins to lower the living standards of a population, taxes and transfers are used to divide the burden equally among all. This equality permits population growth to go on longer; no one is starved or crowded to the point of being unable to reproduce until everyone reaches that point. The total number of people living in poverty in the absolute subsistence equilibrium is greater than in the marginal subsistence equilibrium.

---

Thomas Robert Malthus was born in England in 1766 and received what was, for his time, a radical upbringing. His father was an admirer of Rousseau and Condorcet, and one of his tutors was imprisoned for expressing the wish that the French revolutionaries would invade and liberate England. Malthus studied at Cambridge, took holy orders, and became a curate.

In 1793, a book appeared that had a great impact on the circles in which young Malthus moved. The book was *Enquiry Concerning Political Justice and Its Influence on Morals and Happiness* by the anarchist and socialist William Godwin. As a result of many lively debates over this book and subsequent essays by Godwin, Malthus decided to write down his own view that population growth constituted an insurmountable barrier to a society of absolute equality and abundance. This writing appeared as *An Essay on the Principle of Population* in 1798.

The heart of Malthus's argument was the doctrine that population tended to grow in geometric progression (2, 4, 8, 16, and so on) while the means of subsistence grew only in arithmetic progression (2, 4, 6, 8, and so on). As population increased, increasingly less fertile land would have to be brought into cultivation. Population would outstrip food production, and wages would be driven down to the subsistence level.

Famine, vice, misery, and war could be avoided only if people engaged in "moral restraint"—later marriages with fewer children per family. Schemes such as the Poor

**Thomas Robert Malthus (1766–1834)**

Laws or subsidized housing for the poor were worse than useless, according to Malthus. They simply encouraged population growth and led to an actual deterioration of conditions.

Malthus's views influenced Darwin in developing his survival of the fittest doctrine in the nineteenth century. More than anyone else, it was Malthus who was responsible for earning political economy the name of the "dismal science." Not everyone has interpreted the man in such a negative light, however. John Maynard Keynes placed Malthus firmly in "the English tradition of humane science. . . a tradition marked by a love of truth and a most noble lucidity, . . . and by an immense disinterestedness and public spirit."

Population projections like these were what once caused economics to be called the "dismal science." As long ago as 1798, Thomas Malthus forecast a marginal subsistence population equilibrium for humanity that would come about through the operation of the law of diminishing returns, as a growing population caught up with a fixed supply of agricultural land. According to Malthus's theory, only the landlords, who owned the means of producing precious food, would escape eventual poverty. Even the capitalists would eventually be ground down and their profits reduced to zero.

Malthus's prophecy has not come true for Great Britain, the United States, or other advanced industrial countries. These countries have instead achieved, or nearly achieved, a nonsubsistence population equilibrium with low birthrates, low death rates, and high living standards. The process by which this equilibrium has been achieved is a good illustration of how economic and demographic processes interact.

### The Demographic Transition

In a preindustrial society, birthrates and death rates are both very high, and the rate of natural increase of population is low. With industrialization and economic development, per capita incomes begin to rise. The first demographic effect of rising income is a reduction in the death rate brought about by better nutrition, better hygiene, and better medical care. With the birthrate remaining high, the drop in the death rate increases the rate of natural increase. Population enters a phase of very rapid growth.

If there are sufficient natural resources and enough investment in new capital, economic growth can outstrip population growth. Per capita income then rises. This has happened in all the major industrialized countries of the world. In these countries, rising per capita incomes have eventually caused the birthrate to fall. Population growth has then slowed, and population equilibrium has been approached.

**Demographic transition**
A population cycle that accompanies economic development, beginning with a fall in the death rate, continuing with a phase of rapid population growth, and concluding with a decline in the birthrate.

The whole cycle, from falling death rates to rapid population growth to falling birthrates and equilibrium, is called the **demographic transition**. Exhibit 33.4 provides a graphical view of the demographic transition. Part a represents the course of the crude birthrate and death rate over time. Part b shows what happens to the rate of natural increase as it first rises and then falls. Part c shows the familiar S-curve pattern of population growth that results from the demographic transition. The human population growth curve shown in Part c differs in an important respect from

**Exhibit 33.4**
**The demographic transition**
In a preindustrial society, both birthrates and death rates are high, so that population growth is slow. The first effect of economic development is a drop in the death rate. This brings on a period of rapid population growth. As economic development continues, the birthrate begins to fall. Population growth decelerates and eventually may fall to zero.

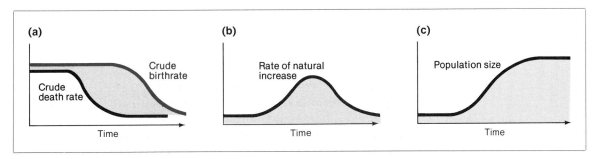

that of flies in a jar or dogs on an island; it levels off at an equilibrium population below the biologically maximum level set by subsistence requirements.

The crucial part of the demographic transition is the fall in birthrates produced by rapid economic development. Demographers do not completely understand the mechanisms that bring about this decline. In large part, it is probably caused by increasing urbanization. Traditionally, a large number of children is an economic asset to a farm family, because children can contribute to production from an early age. In the city, children tend to be an economic burden. There is no guarantee of remunerative jobs for them, and their food, clothing, and housing cannot be produced at home. More subtle changes in life-styles and attitudes toward family life, which occur as income rises, also seem to be involved in the demographic transition.

## Net Reproduction

To complete the demographic transition and approach an equilibrium population takes many decades. To understand why the transition takes so long, one needs to know more about population growth than crude birthrates and crude death rates alone can offer.

Crude birthrates and death rates can be misleading because they depend on both the underlying reproductive behavior of a population and its age structure. A more direct measure of reproductive behavior is the **net reproduction rate** for a population—the average number of daughters born to each female child in the population over her lifetime. If the net reproduction rate is equal to 1, then the population is, in the long run, just replacing itself. If it is greater than 1, then the population has a long-run tendency to grow. If it is less than 1, it has a long-run tendency to shrink.

In the short run, the rate of natural increase in a population may be positive even when the net reproduction rate is 1 or less. In particular, this

**Net reproduction rate** The inherent long-term growth rate of a population, measured as the average number of daughters born to each female child over her lifetime.

**Exhibit 33.5**
**The demographic transition and the economic growth**

Here, the effects of the demographic transition are shown in terms of economic growth and population growth. It is assumed that death rates begin to fall once per capita income reaches Level A, and that birthrates begin to fall once per capita income reaches Level B. During the transition, population growth speeds up and per capita income growth slows. Economic growth always stays above population growth, however.

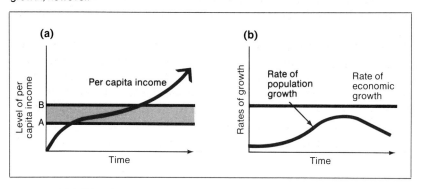

will happen when population growth has been slowing in the recent past. The present situation in Canada provides a case in point. The Canadian net reproduction rate is now less than 1, but it has fallen to that level only recently. The elderly people now in high mortality brackets are members of the relatively small generation born around the turn of the century. People in the high fertility range are members of the much larger generation who were born immediately after World War II. The disproportion in the size of the generations causes the crude death rate to be lower—and the crude birthrate to be higher—than will be the case in the long-run equilibrium. If there is no further change in reproductive behavior, and if the net reproduction rate remains slightly less than 1, it will take some forty to sixty years for the rate of natural increase to fall to 0. Only at that point will the demographic transition in this country be complete.

## The Population Trap

Birthrates, death rates, economic growth, and income levels are in very delicate balance during economic development. Countries that develop successfully undergo a process called the demographic transition. During that process, rising income levels first depress death rates, causing population growth rates to accelerate, and then depress birthrates, causing population growth to slow.

Exhibit 33.5 shows what happens to per capita income and population growth, assuming steady economic growth, during the demographic transition. In Part a, the vertical axis measures the level of per capita income. When income is below Level B, people are so poor that death rates are high, and when it is above A, people are prosperous enough that birthrates are low. (Of course, things are really more complicated than this. There are not really any sharp cutoff levels of income, but this simple assumption makes the point.) In Part b, the vertical axis measures growth rates of total GNP and population. Note that population growth never exceeds the growth of GNP. The curve of per capita income in Part a always moves upward, although it rises less rapidly in the zone between A and B while the demographic transition is under way.

Can today's less developed countries complete this process as the developed countries have done? It is to be hoped that they can, but it is by no means certain. There is a real danger that they will get caught in a **population trap**, which will abort their attempt to make it through the demographic transition.

Exhibit 33.6 shows schematically how a country can fall foul of the population trap. Suppose that such a country begins development normally, as did the country represented in Exhibit 33.5. This time, though, either population growth is more rapid or economic growth is slower. At Time T, population growth begins to exceed the growth of income, and per capita income starts to fall. Instead of completing the demographic transition, the country falls back into a subsistence equilibrium with birth and death rates both high and per capita income stagnant.

**Population trap** A situation in which the rate of population growth rises above the rate of economic growth, halting the growth of per capita income and aborting the demographic transition.

**Escaping the Population Trap** In the nineteenth century, when Western Europe and North America were industrializing, death rates fell only slowly—and only after living standards had already begun to improve. Population growth rates did not rise above 1 percent per year in most cases. Today, modern death control techniques have reached almost every corner of the globe, no matter how poor. Such controls include public health programs and better sanitation systems, all helping to reduce the death rate. That makes it more difficult for today's less developed countries to escape the population trap. During the nineteenth century, the Canadian economy experienced growth rates of GNP in the range of 3.5 to 4.5 percent per year. Growth rates in that range are no longer good enough for less developed countries, where population itself can grow as fast as 3.5 percent per year. Any growth rate for GNP slower than 6 to 7 percent per year

**Exhibit 33.6**
**The population trap**

If at some point during the demographic transition the rate of population growth exceeds the rate of economic growth, a country may be caught in a population trap. As this exhibit is drawn, the country enters the trap at Time T. At that point, per capita income begins to fall and the demographic transition is aborted.

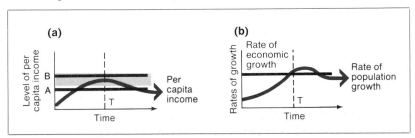

gives little hope for escaping the population trap just by outrunning it. Countries like South Korea or Taiwan may make it, but those like Haiti, Chad, or Dahomey, where per capita incomes are already falling, will not.

The only other way to escape the population trap is to bring down the birthrate while per capita incomes are still low. Although headway has been made in some countries, serious problems remain elsewhere, as the examples in the following three-part case study show.

### Case 33.1
### Three Experiments in Population Control

Saying that less developed countries need to bring population growth under control is one thing; accomplishing the feat is another. Here is a report on population programs in three of the largest countries of the third world. Each has made major efforts, but the results are not uniformly encouraging.

*Pakistan*. Few countries have a more serious population problem than Pakistan. Development planners were thus delighted when, in 1973, Pakistan was chosen as the laboratory for a massive experiment in the "inundation" approach to family planning. Using $58 million in U.S. aid as well as local resources, the plan was literally to flood the countryside with condoms and birth control pills at a price so low — 2.5 cents for a month's supply — that even the poorest people could afford them. The flood of birth control devices was to be followed by teams of "continuous motivators," who were to visit each household three or four times a year to give encouragement and instruction.

Today, the program appears to be a total failure. The birthrate has gone up, not down. Only 9 percent of fertile couples in the country have ever tried birth control, and only 6 percent practice it regularly. Why the failure? Poor administration is part of the reason, but the real flaw in the program was its assumption that families *wanted* to have fewer children. In rural Pakistan, each child, male and female, begins to contribute positively to the support of the family as early as the age of four by tending goats or chickens, running errands, or driving a bullock cart. And in this conservative Moslem society, children are a source of social prestige. The condoms were turned into children's playthings or melted down by contractors to make caulking material.

*India*. India, a neighbor of Pakistan, faces a population problem of much the same magnitude. Under the leadership of Prime Minister Indira Gandhi and her controversial son, Sanjay, however, India adopted a very different approach to birth control. To make certain that families stayed on the birth control track once they got on it, the government emphasized sterilization and insertion of IUDs as the main birth control techniques. An elaborate program of incentives and disincentives included transistor radios; the disincentives included disqualification for government housing for men not willing to accept sterilization after two children. When even this program proved unequal to the task of getting the birthrate down to a level of 25 per 1,000, the government turned to outright coercion. At a rate of a million a month, men were herded into sterilization clinics.

It soon became apparent, though, that the Gandhi policy had gone too far. After a period of nationwide political disruption, Gandhi was swept out of office by India's voters, who feared and detested the birth control program. Under the new government, birth control efforts collapsed, and the birthrate began to creep up again. It has already risen to 35 per 1,000 from its low of 33 in 1977 and is likely to reach 40 soon unless the government takes strong action — something that is now almost impossible politically. Gandhi has in the meantime returned to power with more moderate policies.

*Indonesia*. Meanwhile, on the Indonesian island of Bali, a population program is achieving heartening success. In the tiny village of Banjar Kangin, for example, 218 of the village's 243 fertile couples are practicing some form of birth control. At monthly town meetings, each man is asked what he has done about birth control that month — and then the next month's supply of condoms and pills is handed out.

Why the contrast? Several things appear to contribute to it. For one thing, the Hindus of Banjar Kangin have much more open and permissive attitudes toward sex than do the Moslem Pakistanis. (But even Moslem areas of Indonesia do better than Pakistan.) For another, the administrative structure of the village is much stronger. But perhaps most important of all is that the village economic structure is such that children are perceived as liabilities, not assets. Even with these successes, though, Indonesia's population is expected to soar from 132 million in 1978 to 215 million in 2000.

Source: The descriptions of the programs in Pakistan and Indonesia are based on Bill Peterson, "Battling the Birth Boom — Small Wins, Big Failures," *Washington Post*, May 19, 1978, p. A-1. India's story is based in part on Barry Kramer. "The Politics of Birth Control," *Wall Street Journal*, May 8, 1978, and in part on William Borders, "Birth Control Slows in India," *New York Times*, February 6, 1978, p. A-2.

## FOOD AND DEVELOPMENT[4]

### Hunger

The aspect of economic development that causes the greatest concern of all is the problem of hunger. Hunger comes in varying degrees. People are said to be undernourished if they suffer from a quantitative lack of calories. They are said to suffer from malnutrition if the food they do get contains insufficient protein and other nutrients, even if energy requirements are met. Undernourishment leads to actual starvation. In recent years it has been a major problem in the countries just south of the Sahara in Africa; in India, Bangladesh, and Sri Lanka in Asia; and in Bolivia, Haiti, and El Salvador in the Americas, to list only a few. Malnutrition is much more widespread and has long-run effects that are hardly less devastating. A protein insufficiency in the diets of young children and breast-feeding women is especially dangerous, because it retards brain development. People who survive a malnourished childhood are likely to suffer from lethargy and lack of productive ability in later life. These are hardly the traits required for the labor forces of poor countries struggling to achieve development.

Accurate statistics on world hunger are hard to come by. Definitions vary, and the governments of some of the worst-hit countries are reluctant to supply information. Some who have studied the problem believe that as many as two-thirds of the world's population may suffer from undernourishment or malnutrition in some form. The data in Exhibit 33.7 are based on much more conservative methods of estimation, but they still show an appallingly serious problem.

### Hunger and Population

The relationship between hunger and population is complex. It is natural to think of overpopulation causing hunger, with a Malthusian growth of numbers of people outstripping food production. Hunger can be a spur to population growth, too, however. Malnutrition leads to high infant mortality. High infant mortality in turn leads to the desire to have a large family, so that at least some children will survive. Perhaps the relationship between

[4]This section draws on many points in the useful survey *World of Hunger*, by Jonathan Power and Anne-Marie Holenstein (London: Temple Smith, 1976). Material used by permission.

**Exhibit 33.7**

**Estimated numbers of people with insufficient protein/energy supply, by regions, 1970**

According to the relatively conservative estimates reported in this table, some 388 million people had less than minimum standards of nutrition in 1970. Some observers think that nearly two-thirds of the world's population may suffer from malnutrition to some extent.

| Region | Population (billions) | Percentage below Lower Limit | Number below Lower Limit (millions) |
|---|---|---|---|
| Developed regions | 1.07 | 3 | 28 |
| Developing regions (excluding Asian centrally planned economies) | 1.75 | 20 | 360 |
| Latin America | 0.28 | 13 | 37 |
| Far East | 1.02 | 22 | 221 |
| Near East | 0.17 | 20 | 34 |
| Africa | 0.28 | 25 | 68 |
| World (excluding Asian centrally planned economies) | 2.83 | 14 | 388 |

Source: Jonathan Power and Anne-Marie Holenstein, *World of Hunger* (London: Temple Smith, 1976). Reprinted by permission.

malnutrition and desired family size is part of the reason why birthrates have fallen earliest in those countries that have distributed the benefits of development widely among their populations.

When the world food problem is presented as a race between production and growth of demand, the results are sobering. Information presented at the World Food Conference in 1974 placed seventy-one less developed countries in three groups according to food and population trends during the period 1953–1971. In twenty-four of these countries, the rate of increase in food production fell short of population growth. In an additional seventeen, the rate of increase of food production exceeded the rate of population growth but fell short of the growth rate of domestic demand. Because rising incomes permitted people to eat more, these countries had to increase food imports (or decrease food exports), thereby making things harder yet for the countries in the first group. In the thirty remaining countries, the growth rate of food output exceeded the growth rate of demand, but even some of these countries experienced regional problems because of maldistribution within their borders.[5]

What can be done about the world food problem? The remainder of this section will examine some possible approaches.

## Food Aid

Canada, the United States, and many other Western countries are giving direct aid, including food, medical supplies, and other necessary products and services, to the less developed countries. Food surpluses created by

[5]Preliminary Assessment of the World Food Situation, World Food Conference, 1974, UNIE/Conf. 65/ Prep./6. Data also presented as Table 7 in Power and Holenstein, *World of Hunger*, pp. 41–43.

government support programs have been used on occasion as part of the aid program. Canada gives its aid through the Canadian International Development Agency (CIDA). Such aid has recently averaged about $1 billion a year, or about 0.5 percent of Canada's GNP. This is far less than the 1 percent of more of GNP that Prime Minister Pearson set as a goal for Canada in the 1960s, but it is considerably higher, on a per capita basis, than some other countries, including the United States, are giving. Canada has concentrated much of its aid in the form of special development programs, assisted by more than 1,500 Canadians serving abroad. The United States has tended to focus much of its attention on food distribution. During the 1960s, the United States gave up to 84 percent of all world food aid. The less developed countries were able to rely on food aid for 30 to 45 percent of their food imports. However, such food-aid programs have been restricted by quotas on hectares under cultivation in Canadian and U.S. agriculture, which are designed to curb the growth of surplus output.

## Need for Rural Development

Throughout the world, less developed countries are urbanizing rapidly — far more rapidly than today's developed countries did at comparable stages of their own growth. The reasons for this urbanization are complex. Partly the modernity and the promise of a better life in the city attract people. Partly the problem is education systems that do not emphasize agricultural topics. Whatever the causes, cities are not able to meet the aspirations of all those who arrive in them. Urban unemployment rates are very high. Many people who are employed work in tertiary services — from shining shoes to hustling — that contribute little to economic development or to the development of the individuals. Huge shantytowns surrounding third world cities are the rule rather than the exception.

Current rates of urbanization far exceed the potential for industrial development in most poor countries. One study calculated that, just to keep urban unemployment from rising in a typical less developed country, industrial output would have to grow at 18 percent per year.[6] Even in Brazil, which has had outstanding success with industrialization and urban development, industrial growth has run at only 15 percent per year. To get rid of the 20 to 25 percent unemployment common in cities of less developed countries, industry would have to grow at something like 30 to 35 percent per year for a decade.

When urban unemployment and the food problem are considered together, it is not surprising that many development economists believe that the real hope for the less developed countries lies in the countryside. The hope is to hold people on the land and to make them productive there within a meaningful community structure. If the third world nations can do that, they may be able to feed themselves, distribute what little they

---

[6]David Turnham, *The Employment Problem in Less Developed Countries* (Paris: Organization for Economic Cooperation and Development, 1971), as cited by Power and Holenstein, *World of Hunger*, pp. 74–75.

have more equitably, meet the nonmaterial aspirations of their populations, and retain their independence. That, at least, is what the advocates of rural development say. They all recognize that there are problems, though.

**Technological Problems** Rural development does not mean just the introduction of new agricultural methods. It also means the growth of small-scale industry in villages and towns, which is necessary to meet local needs and provide employment for those whom even the most ambitious land reform program would leave landless. Is the technological basis for such development available?

In some respects, technological progress has been remarkable. The most talked-about development is the appearance of new, high-yield varieties of wheat and rice. Under laboratory conditions, these new varieties can triple food output per hectare. They provide the best hope for less developed countries to escape from the sheer shortage of land.

Unfortunately, high-yield wheat, rice, and other grains cannot just be stuck in the ground and expected to do their magic. The secret of their success lies in their ability to absorb huge quantities of fertilizer. If ordinary varieties of grain are overfertilized, they produce only luxuriant growth of stems and leaves or seedheads so heavy that they break the stalk of the plant. With high-yield varieties, extra fertilization produces growth where it is needed. Without such fertilization, the new varieties actually produce less than traditional crops. (In many cases, heavy use of pesticides and irrigation is needed as well.)

As the use of high-yield varieties has spread, less developed countries have become more dependent on imported fertilizers. They now produce barely half their own fertilizer needs. What is worse, fertilizer production depends critically on oil. This is particularly true of nitrogen fertilizers, which make up half the total used. These are made almost entirely from natural gas and petroleum products. The "green revolution" has been extremely hard hit by high oil prices, because outside the Middle East, few less developed countries have their own oil supplies. Once again, the adoption of practices from advanced countries that rely on the unique technology and resources of those countries has not always brought success.

Rural industrial development faces technological problems that are, if anything, greater than those faced by agricultural development. Western industrial research has developed technology designed to use cheap capital and save expensive labor. The opposite conditions prevail in rural areas of the third world. Too little research has gone into the development of simple but sophisticated labor-intensive ways of doing things.

**Institutional Problems** A number of institutional problems also threaten rural development. Chief among them are the problem of land reform and the problem of supplying credit to rural areas.

Advocates of rural development support land reform, which involves buying (or sometimes confiscating) the large holdings of absentee landlords and distributing the land in the smallest feasible parcels among those who actually till the soil. The effects of land reform, if it works, are threefold. First, a small landowner has a greater incentive than a tenant farmer to improve the land and introduce better production techniques. Second,

In October 1979, the Royal Swedish Academy awarded the Nobel Memorial Prize in Economic Science jointly to two men noted for their work in the economics of development. The two — Sir William Arthur Lewis, professor of economics at Princeton University, and Theodore Schultz, professor of economics at the University of Chicago — had never worked together directly. Their writings, however, shared a common theme: the importance of the agricultural sector in the development process, and the hazards of a development strategy overemphasizing industrialization.

Lewis was born on the island of St. Lucia in the British West Indies. He was educated in London and lectured at the University of London from 1938 to 1948. Before coming to Princeton in 1963, he served for several years as vice-chancellor of the University of the West Indies and was knighted by Queen Elizabeth for this work. The author of a number of books on development and development planning, he is best known for *The Theory of Economic Growth*, published in 1955. Lewis has served as an adviser to the governments of many developing nations, to the British government, and to the United Nations. It was this practical experience in particular that led him to recognize the central importance of agriculture in the economies of the less developed countries.

**William Arthur Lewis
(1915 – )**

Theodore Schultz grew up on a farm in South Dakota in a community of German settlers. In 1930, he received a Ph.D. from the University of Wisconsin; in that same year, he joined the faculty at Iowa State College. During the 1930s and 1940s, Schultz worked to make agricultural economics a branch of general economics that would benefit from advances in other parts of the discipline. The numerous New Deal farm programs of the period provided many opportunities for research, and he published a series of books on U.S. agricultural policy. At the same time, he developed an interest in the process of economic growth — in particular, the contribution of investment in human capital to growth and development. This line of research led eventually to the publication, in 1964, of his book *Transforming Traditional Agriculture*. In this book, he argued that traditional farmers were efficient in the use of whatever resources they had available and would quickly adopt new methods of production when given the chance to do so. The popularity among third-world farmers of the new, high-yield crop varieties stands as a case in point.

Both men continue to be active scholars and advocates of their common point of view. The Nobel award will no doubt act as a further spur to their work in the economics of agricultural development.

**Theodore W. Schultz
(1902 – )**

---

wide distribution of ownership means wide distribution of the product, with all the benefits this is believed to bring. Third, land reform can lead to more stable rural community structures, which help stop the rush to the city. They also help provide the dignity and sense of personal worth that are part of the process of depauperization.

Many countries have carried out thorough land reforms, but many others have not. Two problems hold back further land reform. One major problem is political. The land-owning classes often dominate the political structures of less developed countries and are reluctant to relinquish their hold. The second problem is economic. Under some circumstances, technological considerations may make it more productive to consolidate land holdings into bigger farms to realize economies of scale. To some extent, land reform can involve a trade-off between growth and depauperization.

The other major institutional weakness that holds back small-scale rural development is a weakness of credit markets. In many less developed countries, small farmers have no access to banks and other modern credit facilities. They must rely on local money lenders or merchants, who charge extremely high interest rates.

High-yield crops have made the credit problem more serious than ever. The green revolution can actually work against the small farmer. Higher yields drive land rents up and put downward pressure on output prices. The new varieties cannot be used without expensive fertilizers and pesticides, but buying these goods puts the small farmer more at the mercy of the money lender. Thus, if land reform is carried out without credit reform, it can in fact retard the introduction of new techniques.

## THE NEW INTERNATIONAL ECONOMIC ORDER

Many of the financial and other economic problems of the third world are blamed on the trade and pricing practices of the more industrialized nations. It has been argued that these more advanced economies have used their economic power to set prices on traded goods that favor them at the expense of the less developed economics, and that they used the latter as places to "dump" their manufactured goods, restricting the less developed countries to the provision of cheap raw materials. In response to these concerns, the U.N. General Assembly in 1974 passed a resolution calling for the establishment of a New International Economic Order. The more advanced world economies were asked to restructure their trade and financial relations with third world countries in such a way as to further the economic development of the latter. A vigorous North-South debate preceded and followed this declaration. In the past few years, however, several countries, including the United States, Canada, several European countries and Japan have begun to implement trading strategies designed to favor countries in the third world.

Unfortunately, this favorable development has taken place in the midst of a worsening world economic situation and rapidly rising energy prices. Some of the less developed countries therefore find themselves in a worse financial situation than ever before. This is discussed in Case 33.2. It is pointed out in this article that private commercial bankers in the industrialized West have actively promoted the growth of lucrative industries in some of the less developed countries, and now are alarmed at the inability of these countries to meet their obligations. At the same time, other less promising third world economies have relied heavily on aid from official sources like the International Monetary Fund and the World Bank. The author, a leading banker in Canada, calls for a cooperative approach by both private and official bankers that will sustain the economies to whom they have lent money—both for their own good and for the good of the developing countries.

**Case 33.2**
**The Third World's Debts**

Canadians are suffering, with the citizens of virtually every industrial country, from the cumulative effects on their economies of oil price increases, an extended bout of high interest rates and the most severe world-wide economic downturn in post-war history.

Nowhere is the pain more acute, however, than in the developing countries, particularly in the ones that have not had the good fortune of being self-sufficient in fuel, or better yet, fuel exporters. In the process of financing their massive trade deficits, the non-oil developing countries have built up a debt burden in excess of $500 billion, approximately $300 billion of which is owed to the commercial banks of the industrial world.

The immediate challenge is to keep funds flowing to the developing world. The countries in this group will remain for a long time in need of large sums of new capital. Without the injection of capital their further development would stagnate. Such stagnation would not remain limited to the developing world; it would also affect the industrialized countries.

Meeting that challenge will require a concerted effort by the public and private sectors of the international financial community. By the private sector, I mean the international commercial and investment bankers who regularly raise large amounts of funds — about $185 billion in 1981 — on world capital markets. By the public sector, I mean finance ministers, central bankers and international organizations such as the International Monetary Fund, the World Bank and the Bank for International Settlements. These institutions provide the channels for national governments to pool their resources and co-ordinate policies.

What is at stake? The industrial world could not hope to insulate itself from a sudden reduction in imports by developing countries. More than a quarter of its exports go South, as it were. These exports account for about four percent of the combined Gross National Products of the OECD countries. Thus, a downward spiral of reduced output in the industrial world would be precipitated, which would in turn depress exports from the developing world, and so on. World trade and world production would inevitably contract.

Source: William D. Mulholland, ''The Third World's Debts,'' *Policy Options*, March/April, 1983, p. 13.

## CONCLUSIONS

The tone of much of this chapter has been pessimistic. There is no doubt that the problems of the less developed countries will be very difficult to surmount and that some countries will fail. There is every doubt of the ability and the will of the industrialized countries to carry the burden of development. Nonetheless, there are places where things are going right rather than wrong. It is fitting to end this chapter with one of these success stories.

### Case 33.3
### Daniel Benor's Agricultural Revolution

In India, Turkey, Thailand, Nepal, Sri Lanka, and Indonesia, Daniel Benor is producing a remarkable agricultural revolution. His revolution, sponsored by the World Bank, is quite different from the highly technological green revolution that has been so widely publicized. And it works. Small farmers are doubling and tripling their crop yields wherever the system is tried.

Benor's program is deceptively simple. It is based on what he calls the "T&V" (training and visitation) system of passing information from top experts to farmers in the field. The key link in the system consists of a network of village level extension workers whose responsibility it is to pass carefully limited and digestible doses of information along to a limited group of farmers. The extension worker visits each assigned village on a regular schedule, each week to two weeks. The emphasis is on such labor-intensive basics as proper spacing, weeding, and the use of the most promising seeds.

Even more importantly, in some cases, the program guards against misuse of the green revolution technologies. Take insecticides, for example. In the Gujarat area of India, cotton is the principal crop. The hybrid variety most widely grown responds well to good fertilization and care, but it is vulnerable to insect pests. The farmers' instinctive reaction was to spray heavily with insecticides. They sprayed so heavily, in fact, that they not only increased costs but upset the entire regional ecology. The pest problem actually got worse, not better. Cotton also uses up nutrients in the soil.

Benor's solution to this problem was to put his T&V system to work teaching farmers when *not* to spray. He trained special "scouts," armed with magnifying glasses, to count the number of pests per plant. The fields would be sprayed only when a threshold — say twenty pests per plant — was reached. As soon as the number started to decline, spraying stopped. Using this simple approach, one agricultural cooperative of two hundred members increased its profits by a third in a single year. Elsewhere, the same principle is applied to prevent overfertilization.

Benor has become a hero to Asian farmers. Traditional development specialists were skeptical of his method at first, but it has now been so widely validated that they too are convinced of its effectiveness. Former World Bank President Robert S. McNamara, once a skeptic, became one of Benor's biggest boosters. Countries all over the world are now eager to try the T&V system in the hope that as agricultural yields rise, the race between population and food may one day be won by food.

Source: Based on Hobart Rowen, "Poorest of Poor's Crop Yield Soars," *Washington Post*, November 12, 1978, p. K–1. © 1978 The Washington Post. Used by permission.

## SUMMARY

1. Economic development is a complex phenomenon, a major part of which is sheer economic growth—increasing the size of GNP as a whole. Development also means industrialization. This involves the use of more advanced techniques and business organizations, not only in industry itself, but also in the development of agriculture, transportation, and other sectors of the economy. A third aspect of economic development is depauperization—not only growing but distributing the benefits of growth to the poorest classes. An industry-first growth strategy may hamper depauperization.

2. A population grows whenever its crude birthrate exceeds its crude death rate. In a finite environment, living populations cannot grow indefinitely. If the birthrate does not fall to the death rate, overcrowding will force the death rate up to the birthrate. Population growth in developed countries has undergone a process known as the demographic transition. In preindustrial society, both birth and death rates were high. As industrialization began, death rates fell and a period of rapid population growth began. Economic growth was even more rapid than population growth, however, so per capita incomes rose. This brought birthrates down and reduced the rate of population growth.

3. Virtually all less developed countries face serious population pressures. Modern death control techniques have been introduced to all corners of the globe, no matter how poor. Where birthrates are still high, population growth rates are more rapid than they ever were during the demographic transition in developed countries. If the growth rate of GNP does not keep up with the growth of population, a country may be caught in a population trap. In order to complete the demographic transition successfully, many countries will have to find a way of lowering birthrates while per capita incomes are still at a very low level.

4. Some observers believe that as many as two-thirds of the world's people suffer from undernourishment or malnutrition in some form. In many developing countries population growth is outstripping food production, thereby making the problem worse. In the past, food aid has been an important stopgap measure, but food aid alone is not the long-run solution. Rural development is needed if less developed countries are to be able to feed themselves. Technological advances, including high-yield grains, provide a potential basis for rural development. Economic and institutional problems remain, however. Some way must be found to provide the fertilizers, pesticides, and capital needed to make the best use of high-yield grains. Land reform and credit reform are also necessary parts of successful rural development.

## DISCUSSION QUESTIONS

1. In what ways are the problems faced by the less developed countries similar to the problems faced by Canada one hundred years ago? In what ways are they different? Will today's less developed countries follow a similar path to economic development, or is a different route more promising? Explain.
2. In early phases of industrialization, urbanization seems to be a major factor in bringing birthrates down. Today, birthrates are still falling in Canada, even though the degree of urbanization is no longer changing rapidly. What other factors do you think are at work causing the continued decline in birthrates?
3. Less developed countries are short of capital. Foreign firms are often willing to invest in such countries. Is foreign investment a good way for the countries to solve their capital shortage? What are the advantages and disadvantages to the countries of such foreign investment?
4. Less developed countries tend to have less equally distributed incomes than do developed countries. Why do you think this is so? Why does development sometimes increase inequality rather than reduce it?
5. Do you see any similarity between the dual economy of some less developed countries and the dual labor market that some economists believe exists in Canada?
6. People in Canada eat huge quantities of meat. Each kilogram of meat requires up to ten kilograms of grain to produce. It is sometimes said that the world food problem could be solved in part simply by people eating less meat. Suppose that this advice were taken to heart, and meat consumption in Canada were cut in half, with more bread eaten instead. Would the grain thus saved ever actually reach the hungry poor in the developing countries? If so, explain how shifts in market prices and changes in supply and demand conditions would operate to get it there. If not, explain why the market would fail to move the grain in the desired direction.
7. It is sometimes said that it is pointless to give money to developing countries to buy food, because this money will just end up lining the pockets of Saskatchewan farmers without doing the less developed countries themselves any good. Is this concern wholly justified, partly justified, or wholly unjustified? Why?

## SUGGESTIONS FOR FURTHER READING

Bogue, Donald J., and Ong Tsui, Amy. "Zero World Population Growth." *Public Interest*, no. 55 (Spring 1979), pp. 99–113.
*A report on recent declines in fertility in many countries that are disproving some of the more pessimistic population forecasts made only a few years ago. The authors suggest that the "population bomb" may turn out to be a dud.*

Ehrlich, Paul, and Ehrlich, Ann. *Population, Resources, and Environment*. 2d ed. San Francisco: W. H. Freeman, 1972.
*A good introduction to population arithmetic, the debate over optimal population size, and population control techniques.*

Johnson, D. Gale. *World Food Problems and Prospects*. Washington, D.C.: American Enterprise Institute, 1975.
*A survey of the world food outlook from the perspective of 1975.*

Meier, Gerald M., ed. *Leading Issues in Economic Development*. 3rd ed. New York: Oxford University Press, 1976.
*A good introduction to the field of development economics.*

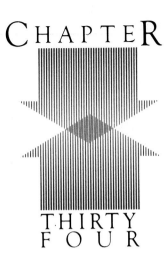

CHAPTER

THIRTY
FOUR

# CAPITALISM VERSUS SOCIALISM

---

**WHAT YOU WILL LEARN IN THIS CHAPTER**

*Beyond all the particular issues of economic policies lies the wider issue of capitalism versus socialism. This chapter begins by defining the two terms and distinguishing several particular varieties of each type of economic system. Next, it surveys major elements of the long-standing debate over the relative merits of capitalism and socialism, first from the point of view of efficiency and then from the point of view of equity.*

**FOR REVIEW**

*Here are some important terms and concepts that will be put to use in this chapter. If you do not understand them, review them before proceeding.*
- *Efficiency and perfect competition (Chapter 23)*
- *Functional distribution of income (Chapter 30)*

---

The term *economic system* refers to the whole pattern of economic institutions that determine the way resources are allocated in a society. In most branches of economics, systems and institutions are among the givens. For example, macroeconomics develops theories about how an increase in the money supply will affect prices and interest rates, assuming a given institutional structure of the banking system and credit markets. Sometimes it examines the effects of the change in one particular institution while assuming that others do not change. An example is the study of the effects of fixed versus flexible exchange rates on world trade. In the branch of economics called comparative economic systems, though, the scope of analysis is much broader. Institutions and whole systems of institutions become the variables rather than the givens of analysis.

Economic systems can be grouped into broad categories on the basis of certain common traits. One way to classify them is on the basis of property rights. Property can be owned privately by individuals or corporations, owned cooperatively by voluntary associations of individuals, or owned by the government. In practice, examples of each kind of ownership can be found in almost every economic system, but often one form or another predominates. In economies called capitalist, for example, there is widespread private ownership of nonlabor factors of production. In socialist economies, cooperative or government ownership prevails.

Economic systems can also be classified in terms of their organizational structure. We can refer to two general principles by which the division of labor in an economy can be coordinated. One is the managerial principle, which depends on centralized decision making; coordination is accomplished by means of orders passed from superiors to subordinates within a hierarchical organization. The other is the market principle, which depends on decentralized decision making and the use of the price system as a means of coordination. In capitalist economies, there is a tendency for managerial coordination to be confined to the internal business of individual firms. Relationships among firms are coordinated on a market basis. In socialist economies, there is usually an attempt to introduce managerial coordination on a larger scale, in the form of national economic planning.

This chapter will show how the two bases of classification can be used in various combinations to identify a variety of different subtypes of capitalist and socialist economies. It will also enter briefly into the general debate on the relative merits of the various systems, involving a more detailed look at one of the largest socialist economies—that of the Soviet Union.

## CAPITALISM

**Capitalism** Any economic system based on private ownership of all factors of production in which owners of capital act as entrepreneurs and coordinate their activity through use of the market.

Most of this book has described the operation of a capitalist economy. Therefore, the description of it here can be relatively brief. The discussion of capitalism begins with a formal definition. **Capitalism** is any economic system based on private ownership of all factors of production in which owners of capital act as entrepreneurs and coordinate their activity through use of the market. Under capitalism, the principle of managerial coordination is limited to the internal workings of firms. Capitalism is sometimes also referred to as a *free enterprise system* because production and consumption activities are carried out on the basis of free contracts and voluntary exchange. The rules of the game under which capitalism operates formally prohibit the use of force, violence, threats, and fraud in market transactions.

The term *capitalism* has been applied to so many economic systems that it is necessary to distinguish several different varieties. The following section will discuss two kinds of capitalism that differ from one another in terms of the economic role played by government. This role can range from nothing at all to very substantial.

### Classical Liberal Capitalism

**Classical liberal capitalism** A capitalist economic system in which government performs only the limited role of protecting property rights and settling private disputes.

Under the tenets of **classical liberal capitalism**, the government plays an important, but strictly limited, role in the economy. In the classical liberal conception, government is a referee that enforces the rules of the game. It has just two functions: (1) to maintain a police force, a system of courts, and, if necessary, a military establishment to protect property rights against criminal activity and foreign aggression; and (2) to provide a court system for the peaceable settlement of disputes that arise over the terms of private contracts. Marxist opponents of capitalism say that this means that the government simply acts as the "executive committee" of the capitalist class and settles all disputes in favor of the owners of capital. Classical liberals deny the executive committee doctrine. Their ideal is a government that is impartial—one that is as vigilant in protecting the personal and property rights of consumers and workers as in protecting those of capitalists.

Under classical liberal capitalism, the government has a monopoly on the legitimate use of force, but it uses its coercive powers only against those who violate the personal and property rights of others. The sole exception is that the government can force private citizens to pay whatever minimal taxes are needed to finance its defense and law enforcement agencies.

## Anarcho-capitalism

Some supporters of capitalism are even more strongly opposed to the use of force in economic affairs and even more strongly in favor of the free market than are the classical liberals. This combination of a radical attack on government (anarchism) with a defense of private property (capitalism) is called **anarcho-capitalism**, or, alternatively, **radical libertarianism.**

Radical libertarians believe that in an anarcho-capitalist society, profit-seeking private firms would take over all the legitimate functions now performed by government. Like classical liberals, they believe that private firms could deliver the mail, dispose of garbage, and collect tolls from motorists to pay for the construction and repair of highways. Unlike classical liberals, they believe that private arbitration firms could settle disputes between parties to business contracts, that private insurance companies could provide protection against criminal activity, and that the criminals themselves could be tracked down by private detectives (hired by the insurance companies) and locked up in privately run jails. A few hours spent with a radical libertarian tract such as Murray Rothbard's *For a New Liberty* have convinced many a skeptic that the principles of private enterprise are much more widely applicable than they ever imagined.[1]

> **Anarcho-capitalism (radical libertarianism)** A capitalist system under which no state exists and all goods and services — including defense, police, and court services — are supplied by private firms.

## SOCIALISM

At the other end of the spectrum from radical libertarianism is socialism. The doctrines and systems that have been called socialist are so diverse that any short definition is bound to offend at least some people who call themselves socialists. If these cautionary words are kept in mind, however, there is no reason not to at least try a definition. As the term is used here, **socialism** means any of a number of doctrines that include two tenets: (1) that some major share of nonlabor factors of production ought to be owned in common or by the state; and (2) that justice requires incomes to be distributed at least somewhat more equally than under classical liberal capitalism. No more will be said here about socialism in general; instead, the chapter will turn to a number of particular types of socialism.

> **Socialism** Any of a number of doctrines that include the following tenets: (1) that some major share of nonlabor factors of production ought to be owned in common or by the state, and (2) that justice requires incomes to be distributed at least somewhat more equally than under classical liberal capitalism.

---

[1]Murray N. Rothbard, *For a New Liberty* (New York: Macmillan, 1972).

## Centralized Socialism and the Soviet Economy

Perhaps the most widely discussed variety of socialism—and, to many, the only "pure" variety—is **centralized socialism**. In such a system, all capital and natural resources are government owned. The government sets up some kind of central planning board that coordinates all production according to managerial principles. The board issues plans that have binding force on all individual units where production is actually carried out. In a literal sense, the entire economy is one big firm.

In the most commonly described form of centralized socialism, planning is carried out in physical terms. The plans drawn up by the central planning board specify the number of tonnes of steel or number of metres of cloth or whatever to be made in each factory. The plans also specify the number of tonnes of coal or kilograms of yarn or whatever to be used up in producing the output. Labor is the only factor of production not directly owned by the state. Workers are free to choose their own jobs within the framework of the plans. (Forms of centralized socialism in which workers are assigned to specific jobs are by no means unknown, however.) Governments that have espoused centralized socialism have generally tried to bring agriculture as well as industry under the sway of central planning. The Soviet Union provides the best example of a modern industrialized nation that is based on the concept of centralized socialism.

## ORIGINS OF THE SOVIET ECONOMY

### Marxism-Leninism

The discussion of the Soviet economy begins with an explanation of its ideological origins as a system founded on the principles of Marxism-Leninism. The voluminous writings of Karl Marx are devoted largely to the evolution and structure of capitalism. Marx wanted to pave the way for revolution by demonstrating that capitalism was headed for a breakdown, but he did not attempt to draw a detailed blueprint for the coming socialist economy. There is little doubt, though, that he envisioned the socialist economy in highly centralized terms. Private ownership of nonlabor factors of production would be abolished, and planning would replace the market as the primary means of resource allocation.

Karl Marx, together with a close colleague, Friedrich Engels, was the great nineteenth century theoretician of communism. He provided the vision. It took a twentieth century Russian revolutionary, Lenin, to implement that vision. V.I. Lenin, the leader of the Russian Revolution, was, if anything, more of a centralist than Marx himself. The secret of Lenin's political success in Russia was the highly centralized, disciplined structure of the Bolshevik Communist Party he led. It was natural for him to apply the same methods of administration to the economy. In a book written just before he came to power, Lenin likened the task of running the economy to that of running the post office or any other bureaucratic administrative agency. The important thing would be a strong party leadership to define economic goals clearly and to provide the discipline and the will necessary to carry them out.

Karl Marx—German philosopher, international revolutionary, and patron saint of Soviet communism—was also a prominent member of the British classical school of economics. His study of economics began in earnest when he moved to London in 1849 at the age of thirty-one. As it was for his contemporary, John Stuart Mill, the study of economics for Marx was first and foremost the study of the works of David Ricardo. But whereas other economists of the classical school were for the most part sympathetic to the capitalist system, Marx took the tools of Ricardian economic analysis and turned them against the social system that had spawned them.

The keystone of classical economics was the labor theory of value—the doctrine that the values and relative prices of various goods are determined primarily by the number of labor hours that go into their production. For Ricardo, the labor theory had been just a description of how the economy worked; but Marx went on to argue that if labor is the source of all value, workers ought to receive the whole product of their labor. Instead, under capitalism, a large part of that product was siphoned off into the pockets of capitalists in the form of profits or "surplus value."

Marx did not limit himself to exposing the inner workings of the capitalist system and condemning it as unjust. In addition, he attempted in his massive work, *Capital*, to prove that capitalism was headed for an inevitable breakdown, to be followed by a socialist revolution. Marx worked all his life with international revolutionary groups to prepare the way for this coming revolution.

**Karl Marx (1818–1883)**

Despite his faith in the inevitability of the socialist revolution, Marx had practically nothing to say about the operation of a socialist economy. The few remarks he did make suggest, however, that the socialism he envisioned would be of a centralized variety in which the "planning principle" would replace the "anarchy of the market." The rest he left to be worked out by future socialists in the course of their practical experience.

## War Communism

Within months of the revolution of October 1917, the Bolsheviks were engaged in a civil war with their White Russian opponents. From the beginning of the civil war, the market economy was abandoned. Trade between the city and countryside was replaced with forced requisitioning of agricultural products. Virtually all industry was nationalized, including many small-scale businesses. Retail trade was also nationalized, although a substantial black market soon emerged. Industrial labor was put under semimilitary discipline, with workers sent to jobs wherever the need was most pressing. As a final blow to the market, a massive outpouring of paper currency from the new government sent inflation spiraling so high that money became uesless. Workers in essential positions were paid in food or other goods. Party ideologists proclaimed that socialism had come to the Russian economy.

Either the civil war or the government's radical policies taken one at a time would have produced economic chaos. In combination, they were a disaster. Militarily, the Bolsheviks scraped through against the odd assortment of White Russians and Western armies of intervention who opposed them. By 1921, however, with the war over, the economy was in sad shape. Agricultural production was down by one-third, and industrial workers had fled to the countryside in search of food. It was time for a change of direction.

## The NEP

With the threat of war removed, Lenin launched his New Economic Policy, in order to get production back on its feet. Trade and small industry went back to private hands. Buying replaced forced requisitioning in agriculture. The peasants once again found it worth their while to sow the fields they had let go fallow. Currency reform put the brakes on inflation, and the money economy reappeared. The "commanding heights," communist terminology for heavy industry, transportation, banking, and foreign trade — remained in government hands, while the rest of the economy followed its own course. Planning was reduced to the issuance of "control figures," which were not directives but merely forecasts intended to help guide investment decisions.

As an instrument for economic recovery, the NEP was a great success. By 1928, prewar production levels had been surpassed in both industry and agriculture. Lenin died in 1924, and Stalin was busy consolidating his power in the party. It was time to take the two steps forward that Lenin had promised.

## Collectivization and the Five-Year Plan

The two steps forward taken in 1928 were the Five-Year Plan for industry and the policy of collectivization in agriculture. These steps were designed to overcome two features of the NEP that Stalin saw as serious defects. First, as long as the NEP was in force, central authorities were altogether unable to control the direction of the market economy. Events went their own way while the nominal planners sat on the side and collected statistics after the fact. Second, the NEP provided no mechanism for transferring resources from agriculture to industry. The party needed such a transfer in order to pursue its industry-first development strategy. Higher taxes, lower agricultural prices, or forced requisitioning of grain would result only in a withdrawal of effort by the peasants, as during the civil war.

In industry, the Five-Year Plan was, for the first time, supposed to set the course of development in advance. Annual operational plans were to be drawn up in accordance with it. These plans were to include assignments of the necessary raw materials to producers on a nonmarket basis. Above all, the Five-Year Plan envisioned a massive program of capital investment.

Industrial growth was to be financed by obtaining more agricultural produce. Collectivization was the technique used to make sure that the needed grain moved from the country to the city. Between 1928 and 1932, some 15 million peasant households — about two-thirds of the rural population — were formed into 211,000 collective farms. On the collectives, land and livestock were owned in common, while agricultural machinery was supplied by independent machine-tractor stations. Land was worked in common too, and a complex system of payment to collective farmers was introduced. Party control over the peasantry was immeasurably strengthened. Party policy could be imposed on the collectives in a way that had never been possible while agriculture was in private hands.

Collectivization was at least a qualified success. The policy wreaked havoc with agricultural production. The number of livestock fell nearly by half as peasants slaughtered them rather than turn them over to the collectives. Grain output also fell sharply, both because of the general chaos accompanying collectivization and because the incentive structure of the collectives themselves discouraged effort. Despite the disruption of production, though, the flow of goods from the countryside to the city increased; and that, after all, had been a major objective of the policy.

The increased flow to the cities occurred partly because collectivization put the grain where party authorities could get their hands on the first share, before the remainder was distributed to the peasants, and partly because there were fewer livestock left to eat it in the countryside. There were fewer people in the countryside too. Several millions died in the initial turmoil of collectivization and the subsequent famine of 1932–1934.

## Emerging Outlines

Out of the disorder of the early 1930s emerged an economic system that displayed most of the major features of the Soviet economy today. Industry, trade, banking, transportation, and foreign commerce were all completely nationalized—with only the most trivial exceptions. Agriculture was almost entirely collectivized. At the top of the system sat Gosplan, the state planning agency. This agency and the ruling party guided the economy with a development strategy emphasizing centralization and planning in physical terms.

The next section of this chapter will look at some details of the structure and functioning of this system. Alternative socialist systems will also be described, followed by an evaluation of their performance.

## STRUCTURE OF THE SOCIALIST SYSTEMS TODAY
### Central Hierarchy in the Soviet Union

According to the official party handbook, *Fundamentals of Marxism-Leninism*, the Soviet economy functions as a single enterprise, directed by a single will. At the top of the economic hierarchy are the highest political organs of the Soviet government—the Supreme Soviet and its Council of Ministers. Under the Council of Ministers come a number of specialized agencies, including Gosplan, the Central Statistical Administration, and the State Bank. Also under the Council of Ministers are a long list of ministries with specific industrial responsibilities, such as coal, railroads, and ferrous metallurgy. Subordinate to these ministries are numerous regional agencies that act as intermediaries between the central government and the individual firms that stand at the bottom of the hierarchy.

Parallel to the government administrative structure is a Communist Party hierarchy, which also has important economic responsibilities. One of them is to observe, check, and report to the party leadership what is going on in firms and administrative agencies throughout the economy. A second responsibility is to control appointments to administrative and managerial posts at all levels. A third is to mobilize and exhort the labor force to greater efforts in service of the plan. In addition to these specific responsibilities, local party officials consult and participate in many kinds of managerial decision making at the enterprise level.

## Enterprise Status

Operation of the individual Soviet enterprise is governed by a so-called technical-industrial-financial plan. This plan, issued annually, is broken down into quarterly and monthly segments. Its most important part is the production plan, which specifies how much output is to be produced, what assortment of products is to be included in total output, and when output is to be delivered. Other parts of the plan specify the quantities of labor and material inputs allotted to individual firms. A financial section gives targets for costs, wage bills, profits, use of short-term credit, and so on. In all, the plan may contain two dozen or more specific physical and financial targets that a particular firm is to meet.

The plan has the binding force of law on enterprise management. In principle, criminal penalties can be imposed for failure to fulfill the plan, although administrative penalties such as demotion or transfer to less desirable jobs are more commonly used. Positive incentives are also provided. Very substantial bonuses are given to managers who successfully fulfill or overfulfill the various parts of their plans.

This centralized planning system continues to be the chief characteristic of the Soviet system, and a model to many followers of Marx around the world. Economies like East Germany and Czechoslovakia are closely modelled on it. Today, however, one often encounters people who think of themselves as Marxian socialists without being strict centralists on economic matters. Many Eastern European reformers and Western Marxist radicals are non-centralists.

## Lange's Market Socialism: An Alternative System

From the early days of this century, one aspect of centralized socialism has been consistently criticized by economists: the principle of planning in physical terms. Opponents of socialism have argued that it is beyond the capacity of central planners to specify the physical quantities of the millions of inputs required for thousands of firms. Even if workable sets of plans could be drawn up, planners could not guarantee that they had found the most efficient combination of inputs for production of the given outputs and the most efficient pattern of outputs to satisfy consumer demands.

During the 1930s, economist Oskar Lange issued a justly famous reply to these critics. In a series of articles entitled "On the Economic Theory of Socialism," Lange claimed that central planning in physical terms was neither the only nor the best way of running a socialist economy. Instead, he proposed a system — **market socialism** — in which the socialist managers of individual firms would mimic the behaviour of managers under perfectly competitive capitalism. A central planning board would exist, but its major function would no longer be to issue commands; instead, it would set prices for goods and factors of production. Managers would take these prices into account and would conduct the actual operation of their firms according to two rules:

**Market socialism** A socialist system in which details of resource allocation are made through market mechanisms rather than through central planning.

1. The quantity of output produced by each firm would be the quantity that would make the marginal cost of production equal to the assigned price of the product.
2. A combination of factor inputs would be chosen to produce each product; this would make the marginal physical product per dollar's worth

of each factor equal to the marginal physical product per dollar's worth of any other factor.

Managers would requisition whatever quantities of factors of production they needed to produce according to these rules. They would produce whatever quantities of outputs the rules required. In any particular period, the uncoordinated actions of individual firms might result in a surplus or shortage of some goods or factors. If this were to occur, the central planning board would correct any imbalances. It would raise the prices of any factors or goods of which there was a shortage, thereby discouraging their use. Similarly, it would lower the prices of any goods or factors of which there was a surplus, thereby encouraging greater use. In this way, production and use would be brought into equilibrium and the plans of individual firms coordinated.

Lange's system, of which this is only the barest sketch, immediately caught the imagination of his readers. It appeared to offer two major advantages over centralized socialism with physical planning. First, the burden of work on central planners would be lessened because they would be responsible only for prices. Individual managers would do their own planning of physical input and output requirements. Second, Lange's rules for managers closely resembled the rules of managerial calculation under perfect competition. That resemblance made it seem likely that inputs and outputs would be chosen more efficiently than under a regime of physical planning. (These points will be discussed in more detail later in the chapter.)

---

In his sixty-one years, Oskar Lange achieved not one but two distinguished careers as an economist. Born in Tomaszow, Poland, he went to the United States to study at the University of California and Stanford University. He remained in the United States to teach at the University of Michigan, Stanford University, and the University of Chicago. His famous article, "On the Economic Theory of Socialism," appeared in the *Review of Economic Studies* in 1937 and gave him an international reputation.

Lange's interests as an economist went beyond the question of the economics of socialism. He was a pioneer in econometrics and did important early work in macroeconomics as well. In 1944, he wrote *Price Flexibility and Full Employment*, in which he attempted to establish Keynes's employment theory as a special case within a general equilibrium theory.

By this time, Lange had acquired U.S. citizenship. In 1945, however, he renounced it to become the Polish ambassador to the United States. After serving as ambassador, he became Poland's delegate to the United Nations. Finally, in 1947, he returned to Poland to begin the second phase of his career as an economist. He held various positions in the Communist Party and government and in 1957 became the chairman of the Polish Economic Council.

As a leading economist in communist Poland, Lange turned to electronic computers and cybernetics to reconcile his earlier views on market socialism with Soviet-type central planning. He described the market as a cumbersome and slow-working servomechanism—the best available in the days before computers, but now obsolete. Without repudiating his earlier work, he characterized its proposed trial-and-error system as quaintly out of date. He continued to write on econometrics and economic cybernetics until his death in 1965.

Oskar Lange (1904–1965)

## Participatory Socialism: Another Alternative System

**Participatory socialism** A socialist system under which the means of production are owned collectively by the workers of individual firms, who participate democratically in the process of management and share the profits of their firms.

Under **participatory socialism**, the third socialist system to be looked at, the means of production belong neither to the state nor to private capitalists. Instead, they are owned in common by the workers who actually operate them. The workers of each firm participate democratically in management; hence the name. Relationships among firms and between firms and consumers are coordinated by markets, as in a capitalist economy.

Under participatory socialism, workers, not capital owners, are the entrepreneurs. If successful, they share in the profits. The functional distribution of income is determined by marginal productivity principles, much as under capitalism; but the principles that govern the personal distribution of income are quite different. The ownership of nonlabor factors of production is not highly concentrated, as it is under capitalism; instead, it is widely shared by all workers. As a result, workers receive in addition to their wages a bonus or "social dividend" that represents their share of the profits and of the product of resources owned in common. To the extent necessary, of course, this principle of distribution can be supplemented by social insurance to meet the needs of the elderly, the disabled, and the nonworkers.

**Participatory Socialism in Yugoslavia** Participatory socialism is not just a creature of abstract theory. An entire national economy, that of Yugoslavia, has operated under a system of worker management since the early 1950s. In the Yugoslav economy, a new firm can be created by central or local government, by an existing firm, or by a group of individuals. Once it comes into being, it takes on an independent life of its own, entering into market relationships with its customers and suppliers. The basic governing unit of a Yugoslav firm is the workers' council, in which all workers participate. The council directly reviews and approves basic long-run policy decisions, including the important decisions regarding distribution of the firm's income. The council also elects a smaller executive council and a director to handle the day-to-day business of the firm. Although Yugoslavia's communist government claims to find authority in Marx's writings for this brand of socialism, the system could hardly be in greater contrast to the centralized blueprint of official Soviet doctrine.

In many respects, participatory socialism has worked well in Yugoslavia. Although the country was very nearly the poorest one in Europe at the end of World War II, over the next two decades it enjoyed one of the fastest economic growth rates in Europe. Furthermore, Yugoslavs have enjoyed a far greater degree of political and personal freedom than their comrades in other Eastern European countries. This fact is by no means unrelated to the difference in economic systems. Yugoslavia has its share of economic problems, ranging from high inflation and regional disparities in income to complaints that workers spend too much time at factory meetings and not enough on the production line. Nonetheless, it is a system from which there is much to be learned in both the East and the West.

## European Social Democracy

The fourth kind of socialism to be looked at is European social democracy.

Social democratic parties have either held power or been a strong opposition party in most countries of Western Europe and Scandinavia since World War II. Although there are important differences among the parties of various countries, the main principles of social democracy can be illustrated with the example of the British Labour Party. The defining characteristics of British social democracy are an overriding concern for the poor and a belief in equality. By equality, in the words of a leading member of the Labour Party, "we mean more than a simple redistribution of income. We want a wider social equality embracing the distribution of property, the educational system, social class relationships, power and privilege in industry — indeed, all that is enshrined in the age-old socialist dream of classless society."[2] In pursuit of this goal of equality, the Labour Party, like its counterparts on the continent of Europe, instituted wide-ranging "welfare state" policies. These policies were supposed to guarantee to every citizen, as a matter of political right, minimum standards of health care, education, food, and housing. At the other end of the scale, high rates of taxation were imposed on people with inherited wealth (or even simply high earned incomes). Great Britain's Labour governments also made strong efforts to reduce selectivity in education in an attempt to eliminate an important source of class distinction.

On the matter of ownership of the means of production, the more moderate Labour Party leaders are not dogmatists. The same person just quoted writes that a "mixed economy is essential to social democracy. For while a substantial public sector is clearly needed to give us the necessary control over the economy, complete state collectivism is without question incompatible with liberty and democracy."[3] Great Britain's public sector is indeed substantial by Canadian standards. In its various periods in power, Labour governments extensively nationalized steel, coal, railroads, shipbuilding, aircraft, automobiles, and several other important industries, although still leaving a large part of the private sector. British nationalized industries are supposed to be run on competitive business principles and are supposed to turn a profit to help finance the government's welfare state policies. In practice, though, the managers of nationalized industry have complained of capricious political interference in their affairs. Many of the largest nationalized industries have operated at a loss and have required heavy subsidies from the taxpayers. The Conservative government elected in 1979 and again in 1983 returned some nationalized industry to private hands.

Although they lie to the "left" of the two major Canadian political groupings, the European social democrats represent the "right" within the broad spectrum of possible socialisms.

## SOCIALISM: PRO AND CON

Having made this catalog of capitalist and socialist economic systems, the chapter turns now to a brief survey of the ongoing debate over the relative merits of various systems. Socialist slogans have long proclaimed the

---

[2]Anthony Crosland, *Social Democracy in Europe*, Fabian Tract 438 (London: Fabian Society, 1975), p. 1.
[3]Ibid.

superiority of socialism over capitalism. Socialism, it has been said, replaces the "anarchy of the market" with the "planning principle." It also replaces "production for profit" with "production for use" and replaces capitalist exploitation of the working classes with a system in which the whole product goes to the real producers. Such slogans are impressive to hear but difficult to evaluate. What exactly is the planning principle? What is the difference between production for profit and production for use? And what is meant by "exploitation"? What standards can be used to shed some light on the merits of socialism?

## Static Efficiency

The first standard that can be used for comparing economic systems is static efficiency. In comparative economics, static efficiency is the efficiency of resource allocation under hypothetical conditions of universal equilibrium. In this system, resources, production technologies, and consumer tastes are known to everyone and are forever unchanging.

**Lange's Claims for the Static Efficiency of Socialism**     Under perfect competition, a capitalist economy can, in principle, operate with complete static efficiency. If claims are to be made for socialism on grounds of static efficiency, then, it must be shown that it can do at least as well as capitalism under the same ideal conditions. That is what Oskar Lange set out to prove. He accepted the idea that any kind of socialism relying on central planning in physical terms would score poorly in terms of static efficiency. In his own system, however, efficiency would be guaranteed. Managers would be instructed to make the proper adjustments in marginal costs and marginal products, while central planners would be instructed to adjust prices to market-clearing, equilibrium levels.

That was only a starting point. It was not enough for Lange to show that under ideal circumstances, his socialist system could function at least as efficiently as capitalism. He went on to argue that under the circumstances that actually prevailed in the real world, his system would do better. First, he claimed that his system solved the problem of monopoly. Under capitalism, in an industry with only one or a few firms, managers tend to equate marginal cost with marginal revenue rather than with price. That tendency violates static efficiency conditions. In Lange's system, in contrast, managers would be instructed to follow the same rule—marginal cost equals price—no matter how few firms there were in a market.

Furthermore, Lange pointed out that even competitive markets would not operate efficiently when pollution or other distorting factors caused private costs to deviate from opportunity costs. Under his system, central planners could automatically correct for such things. They would simply build the appropriate incentives or penalties into the prices they set.

**Counterclaims**     Lange's claims for the superior static efficiency of his system have brought forth three kinds of counterclaims. First, some critics have attacked the system directly in Lange's own terms. They have suggested, for example, that the trial-and-error pricing system that Lange's central planners were to use would be too time-consuming and might even be unstable. Also, they have pointed out that it is not clear how the trial-and-error method for finding market-clearing prices could be applied to goods that were custom-made, as much important industrial equipment is. Finally, they have argued that Lange's system would do poorly where considerations of time and risk played an important role in the pricing process.

A second, rather different, kind of criticism comes from advocates of liberal capitalism and moderate social democrats. They argue that a full transition to socialism is not necessary to achieve the desired gains in static efficiency. Instead, it would make more sense to keep a market economy and to introduce ad hoc corrections to deal with problems such as monopoly and pollution where necessary.

Finally, the most important of all the criticisms of Lange's system is a simple rejection of static efficiency as a standard of evaluation. Any gains in static efficiency from Lange's system, according to the critics, would be offset by disadvantages. This rejection raises the issues of dynamic efficiency and economic growth, to which the chapter now turns.

## Dynamic Efficiency and Economic Growth

Dynamic efficiency and economic growth are standards for evaluating economic systems that accept the world as it is, with changing technologies, resource availabilities, and consumer preferences. The two standards are closely related. Economic growth measures the overall rate of expansion of output of goods and services. Part of any increase in economic growth that occurs may be attributable to increased supplies of factors of production. More capital is accumulated through saving, more labor through population growth or more hours of work per capita, and more natural resources through mineral discoveries or territorial expansion. Dynamic efficiency refers to the growth rate that can be sustained with a given rate of expansion of factor supplies. High dynamic efficiency depends partly on the ability of a system to generate scientific and technical advances. It depends even more on the ability of its entrepreneurs to take advantage of opportunities as they emerge, quickly and effectively. The best way to test the dynamic efficiency of different systems is to compare the growth rate of two very different industrial powers; for example, the Soviet Union and the United States.

## PERFORMANCE OF THE SOVIET ECONOMY
### Growth Record

Soviet leaders, and indeed ordinary Soviet citizens, are extremely proud of one aspect of their economy's performance: its growth record. Within the lifetimes of millions, Russia has been transformed from an economic backwater into one of the world's leading industrial powers. In 1917, Russia had achieved only something like the level of economic development of today's Brazil. It had only a small industrial sector set against a backdrop of vast rural poverty. Today, Soviet living standards are comparable to those of, say, Italy. Soviet industrial capacity exceeds that of West Germany; and in certain particular fields, such as steel output and military technology, it equals or surpasses that of the United States.

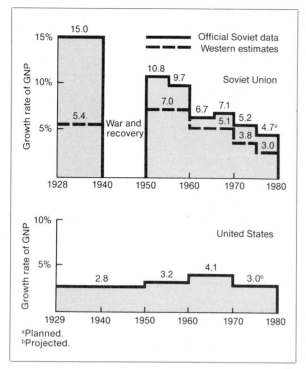

Sources: From Paul R. Gregory and Robert C. Stuart, *Soviet Economic Structure and Performance* (New York: Harper & Row, 1974), p. 378. (Soviet data recomputed from Abram Bergson.) Also from "Brezhnev's Russia," *Economist*, February 14, 1976, p. 63. All Soviet official data from published sources. Early Western estimates from Abram Bergson, *Real National Income of Soviet Russia since 1928* (Cambridge, Mass.: Harvard University Press, 1961), pp. 180, 210, 261. Most recent estimates from U.S. Joint Economic Committee, *Western Perceptions of Soviet Economic Trends* (Washington D.C.: Government Printing Office, 1978), pp. 3-4.

**Exhibit 34.1**
**Growth rates of GNP: The Soviet Union and the United States**

The Soviet Union has a very impressive record of economic growth. Western and Soviet estimates of this growth use different methods and arrive at different numbers; but even by Western measures, growth has consistently been more rapid in the Soviet Union than in the United States until quite recently. It should be noted, however, that the Soviet base was smaller in 1928, so percentage changes would naturally tend to be higher at first.

Exhibit 34.1 presents the Soviet growth record and compares it to growth in the United States. In the upper figure, representing economic growth in the Soviet Union, two sets of data are presented. The official Soviet statistics show an enormous surge of growth during the 1930s, interrupted by the devastation of World War II and continuing at very high, but gradually declining, rates thereafter. On the same chart, a Western estimate of Soviet growth also shows very respectable growth rates in the earlier periods, but by no means so spectacular a growth as the official Soviet figures show. In the 1970s, both Soviet and Western estimates indicate a slowdown.

**Explaining Differing Estimates** Why do Western and official Soviet estimates of early Soviet growth differ so much? The answer is largely a matter of the accounting conventions used. Real GNP statistics are always derived by using some index of prices to adjust nominal GNP data in a way that will make it possible to compare data for different years. It turns out to make a great deal of difference which base year is chosen for the index. Choice of an early base year gives rise to numbers that exaggerate the growth rate, especially for an economy that is undergoing rapid structural changes. Soviet statisticians like to use the earliest possible year. The 15 percent growth rates of the 1930s reflect the use of 1928 prices as a basis for calculations. Western practice makes use of a later base year. Soviet accounting practices differ from Western ones in other ways as well, including the way output of services is measured, the way introduction of new kinds of products is taken into account, and the way agricultural harvests are computed.

In many cases, it is not a matter of Soviet statistics being wrong and Western calculations of Soviet performance being right; it is merely a matter of arbitrary choices of accounting convention. What is important for comparative purposes is to express the growth performance of different countries by using conventions that are as nearly the same as possible. It is the Western estimates of Soviet growth that ought to be compared with the figures given for the United States in the lower part of Exhibit 34.1.

**Explaining the Slowdown** Soviet economic growth, according to Western estimates, slowed markedly during the 1970s and is unlikely to recover to earlier rates during the 1980s. Over the next decade, Soviet growth is judged unlikely to exceed 3.5 percent, with 2.5 percent a realistic possibility. Various explanations are offered for the slowdown. For one thing, the growth rate of the Soviet labor force is slowing, and population growth in the relatively little-industrialized Central Asian republics is exceeding that in the industrialized areas. The Soviet energy outlook also is not bright. The U.S. Central Intelligence Agency projects a decline in Soviet oil and natural gas production in the 1980s; the Soviet Union may be forced to stop oil exports to Eastern Europe and in the worst case may even become a net oil importer. This would drain scarce reserves of Western currency away from much-needed industrial imports. Finally, weather conditions for Soviet agriculture are not likely to be as favorable on the average during the 1980s as during the 1970s. Comparing these projections of Soviet economic growth with the estimated 3 percent growth rate of potential real GNP in the United States, one can see that the historic gap between Soviet and U.S. growth rates may be drawing to an end.

## Sources of Soviet Economic Growth

In the past, the major source of rapid economic growth in the Soviet Union was the ability of the centrally planned economy to mobilize vast new supplies of factor inputs. In the decades immediately before and after World War II, the number of labor hours employed in the Soviet economy increased at a rate of 2.2 percent per year, while they were increasing at only 0.5 percent per year in the United States. Even more impressive, the Soviet capital stock grew at a rate of 7.4 percent per year, compared with just 1 percent per year in the U.S. economy. These very rapid growth rates of factor supplies more than compensated for the inferior dynamic efficiency of centralized socialism. The type of growth experienced by the Soviet Union, based primarily on expansion of inputs, is often called **extensive growth**; the type of growth experienced in the United States, based on better utilization of inputs, is called **intensive growth**.

**Extensive growth** Growth based predominantly on the mobilization of increasing quantities of factor inputs.

**Intensive growth** Growth based predominantly on improvements in the quality of factor inputs and in the efficiency with which they are utilized.

Extensive growth is just as effective as intensive growth in adding to the economic power and prestige of a nation as a political unit, but it has certain disadvantages for individual citizens. Most important, a much larger share of GNP has been diverted from consumption into investment in the Soviet Union than in the United States. The figures for 1964 were 35 percent versus 17 percent. As a result, Soviet consumption per capita is only about a third that of the United States, even though GNP per capita is nearly half. It is also worth noting that Japan, the only noncommunist industrial nation to invest as high a fraction of GNP as the Soviet Union, has grown twice as fast in recent years. The Japanese experience shows what can be accomplished when rapid growth of inputs is combined with high dynamic efficiency rather than employed as a substitute for it.

### Soviet Agriculture

If rapid industrial growth is the Soviet Union's proudest accomplishment, agriculture is its most distressing failure. While Soviet industry grew at a rate of 6.5 percent per year in the first half of the 1970s, agriculture crept ahead at only 2 percent (both official figures). In 1961, then-Premier Nikita Khrushchev set a target of 274 million tonnes of grain for 1980. In 1975, with three-quarters of Khrushchev's allotted time span elapsed, output was a mere 127 million tonnes. That was an exceptionally bad year, to be sure, but even the official 1980 target had to be scaled down to 198 million tonnes.

The roots of Soviet agricultural problems date from the earliest days of collectivization. In the Stalin era, agriculture was a cow to be milked for the benefit of industrial development. Now that it has become a serious constraint on industrial development, it is proving difficult to reverse the effects of decades of neglect.

## CONCLUSIONS

It would be very misleading to think that socialism owes its widespread support solely to its purportedly superior economic performance. There are many socialists for whom the problems of production are secondary to the problems of economic justice. Economic justice, of course, means different things to different people, but here are at least some of the things it means to socialists.

First, socialists conceive of economic justice as equality. In their time-honored phrase, it means "from each according to ability, to each according to need." Some socialists are willing to accept the degree of inequality of labor income that would result from wage payments proportional to marginal productivity. Even these people, however, advocate supplementing wages with interest, rent, and profits earned by collectively owned non-labor factors.

Second, socialist economic justice is supposed to mean an end to exploitation. In this view, the profits, rents, and interest earned by nonworkers under capitalism do not reflect any real productive contribution of inanimate factors of production. They are instead unfairly deducted from the just earnings of labor. Socialists thus often oppose the nonwage earnings even of small-scale shopkeepers, land owners, and moneylenders, despite the fact that these earnings may not raise their recipients very high up the ladder of income distribution.

Finally, many socialists hold that economic justice requires not only that workers get a fair share of the product but also that they have some voice in the actual management of business affairs. Some socialists pay only lip service to this principle. They promote systems in which workers end up as remote from the functions of the central planning bureaucracies as they are from boardroom management under capitalism. Others—the participatory socialists—make this the first and foremost element of economic justice.

Whatever the specific content given to the concept of economic justice, any argument that a socialist economy is inefficient can, in the last resort, be met by the reply that one can afford to tolerate inefficiency in the name of equity.

Two kinds of counterclaims are advanced against the contention that socialism is necessary to achieve economic justice. One comes from left-wing liberal capitalists. These people are basically in sympathy with the egalitarian aims of socialism. They simply argue that the government of a capitalist country can, if it has the will to do so, use tax and transfer policies to distribute income however desired. As mentioned earlier, this variety of opinion merges imperceptibly at some point with the position taken by moderate European social democrats.

The less moderate view on capitalism, socialism, and economic justice is heard from radical libertarians. These people conceive of economic justice primarily in terms of what has been called market justice. What economic justice requires, they say, is a system in which all people are able to devote their own energies and abilities exclusively to the pursuit of their own chosen objectives, without coercive intervention by anyone. In this view, the first requirement is a free market in which workers, consumers, and resource owners can participate on a purely voluntary basis. In such a system, no person has a right to demand that another turn over property or produce without offering a fair exchange. Nationalization of the means of production and redistributive taxation are thus unjust per se; equality has nothing to do with the matter.

The Soviet Union is an industrialized nation based on the concept of centralized socialism. What sort of future does it face? Since the early 1960s, there has been a great amount of talk, both in the Soviet Union and in the West, about economic reform. To many, the declining Soviet growth rate indicates a necessity to switch from an extensive to an intensive growth strategy, and that cannot be done within current economic institutions. These institutions were designed to mobilize resources and to implement vast structural changes, not to use scarce resources as efficiently as possible.

Reform proposals have centered on three areas. First, there is a need to reform managerial incentives so that, in the Soviet phrase, the interests of management will coincide with the interests of the national economy. The most important part of reforming incentives must be to make profit replace the dozens of indicators of output, assortment, cost, and productivity. Second, there must be a radical price reform. Profit cannot be used as an indicator of economic performance unless industrial prices reflect opportunity costs. Third, there is a need for decentralizing some decision making and establishing direct links among firms, bypassing the cumbersome planning bureaucracy. The Soviet government has responded to these reform proposals by encouraging discussion, but it has done little else. Compared to the radical changes envisioned by some reformers, what has actually been accomplished is very little.

What the future will bring is a matter of speculation. The most hopeful sign is the great amount of reform and experimentation being carried out in Eastern Europe. Every country in Eastern Europe except Albania has introduced reforms that go far beyond anything tried in the Soviet Union. Each set of reforms is different from the others. Perhaps when a new, more daring leadership comes on the scene in the Soviet Union, it will find in one or another of these experiments a path worth following.

## SUMMARY

1. Any market economy in which all factors of production are privately owned and in which the owners of capital for the most part play the role of entrepreneurs can be called a capitalist economy. In both theory and practice, there is a broad range of kinds of capitalism. Classical liberals advocate limiting the role of government to the provision of police, defense, and court services. Anarcho-capitalists favor reducing the role of government all the way to zero, with even the minimal functions of the classical liberal state being performed by private firms.

2. Any system can be called socialist if at least substantial parts of nonlabor factors of production are collectively owned and if an attempt is made to distribute incomes more equally than under classical liberal capitalism. Socialist systems differ widely from one another in the role they assign to the market. Centralized socialism envisions an economy run as one big firm in which the market plays no role at all. Lange's socialist economy, participatory socialism, and European-style social democracy all depend heavily on the market as a mechanism of resource allocation but use redistribution policies to modify the personal distribution of income.

3. The origins of the Soviet economic system are found first in the Marxist-Leninist ideology and second in the practical experience of the first years of Soviet rule. After the 1917 revolution, an overambitious attempt to abolish the market economy all at once (war communism) was followed by a temporary restoration of the market (the new economic policy). The main features of what is now known as the Soviet-type economy—central planning in physical terms plus collectivization of agriculture—were established around 1928. They were designed to serve the government's objectives of complete political control of the economy and extensive, industry-first economic growth. The combination of planning plus collectivization was effective in achieving those objectives.

4. In its formal structure, the Soviet economy is a fully centralized hierarchy. Individual firms receive plans that specify inputs and outputs in physical terms, along with many other targets. These plans are legally binding on firms.

5. The static efficiency of an economy is its theoretical efficiency under idealized conditions in which resources, production technologies, and consumer tastes are completely known and unchanging. A capitalist economy could achieve complete static efficiency under perfect competition. Centralized socialism is widely thought to score poorly in

terms of static efficiency. Lange built the case for his own brand of socialism largely on consideration of static efficiency. He argued that under ideal conditions his system would operate as well as a capitalist market economy and that under real-world conditions it could achieve higher static efficiency.

6. Dynamic efficiency and economic growth are additional standards by which to judge the performance of an economic system. Centralized socialism claims a superior growth potential because of its ability to mobilize resources of capital and labor and focus them on the task of economic expansion.

7. Socialists claim that their systems provide greater economic justice than does capitalism. By economic justice, they mean distributive justice. Some liberal capitalists claim that the welfare state can achieve distributive justice without socialism. Other critics of socialism emphasize the standard of market justice and see capitalism as superior to socialism according to that standard.

8. The outstanding feature of Soviet economic performance has been rapid economic growth. The rate of growth, has, however, slowed in recent years. The need to switch from a strategy of extensive growth to one of intensive growth has focused attention on the inefficiency of the Soviet system. Soviet economic efficiency is hampered by inadequate managerial incentives and a price system that does not reflect opportunity costs. Many proposals have been put forward for reforming the system, but there has been little practical progress with reform in the Soviet Union. In the Soviet-type economies of Eastern Europe, however, a number of interesting and far-reaching reform experiments have been carried out.

## DISCUSSION QUESTIONS

1. Why is it that owners of capital so often perform the entrepreneurial function in an economy where factors of production are privately owned? Why should land owners not play this role? Why not workers? Why not people who own no resources at all but who hire everything they need on a contract basis? Can you think of exceptions to the rule that entrepreneurs are also owners of capital? Explain.

2. What position do you think an advocate of classical liberal capitalism would take on each of the following issues: Antitrust policy? Regulation? Poverty? Pollution? Protectionism? How would the classical liberal position on these issues differ from the anarcho-capitalist position—if at all?

3. Of all the kinds of economic systems discussed in this chapter, which kind would you expect Canadian "big businesses" to favor? Why? On what evidence do you base your answer?

4. Explain just what it means to say that under centralized socialism the whole economy is run as one big firm. In an anarcho-capitalist economy, which would entirely lack any government antitrust policy, do you think private businesses would grow and merge with one another to the point that the whole economy would become one big private firm? Explain.

5. There are no serious legal barriers to the emergence of participatory socialist firms in the Canadian economy. If the workers in a private firm pooled all their resources (perhaps making temporary sacrifices to increase their rate of saving), they could buy up the firm's stock share by share until they owned a controlling interest. They would then be in more or less the same position as the worker-owners of a Yugoslav firm. Why do workers so rarely do this in the Canadian

economy? Do you know of any example of worker-owned and operated firms in the Canadian economy? Explain.

6. In what ways do you think a centralized socialist economy of the Soviet type might be better equipped than a capitalist economy to deal with problems of population, resources, and pollution? In what ways is it less well equipped?

## SUGGESTIONS FOR FURTHER READING

Friedman, Milton. *Capitalism and Freedom*. Chicago: University of Chicago Press, 1972.
*A classic defense of classical liberal capitalism.*

Gregory, Paul R., and Stuart, Robert C. *Soviet Economic Structure and Performance*. New York: Harper & Row, 1974.
*A short textbook on the Soviet economy, covering all major aspects of history, structure, and performance.*

Lange, Oskar, and Taylor, Fred M. *On the Economic Theory of Socialism*. New York: McGraw-Hill, 1964.
*This volume conveniently reprints Lange's classical articles of the 1930s, together with a closely related essay by Taylor.*

# GLOSSARY

**Absolute advantage** (2) In trade theory, the ability of a region or country to produce a good at absolutely lower cost, measured in terms of factor inputs, than its trading partners.

**Accommodating monetary policy** (14) A policy under which the Bank of Canada expands the money supply in an attempt to keep interest rates from rising and provides the money to allow financial intermediaries to buy the bonds when the government sells bonds to cover a budget deficit.

**Accounting profit** (22) Total revenue minus explicit costs.

**Adaptive expectations hypothesis** (18) The hypothesis that people form their expectations of the future rate of inflation primarily on the basis of inflationary experience in the immediate past.

**Aggregate demand** (5, 8) The total planned expenditure for an economy, consisting of consumption, planned investment, government purchases, and net exports.

**Aggregate nominal demand schedule** (9) A graph showing the relationship between aggregate nominal demand (the nominal value of total planned expenditure) and nominal national income.

**Aggregate nominal supply schedule** (9) A graph showing the relationship between aggregate nominal supply (nominal national product) and nominal national income. The schedule has the form of a 45 degree line passing through the origin.

**Aggregate real demand curve** (17) A curve showing the amount of real output purchased at any given price level for a given aggregate nominal demand.

**Aggregate real supply curve** (17) A curve showing how much real output is produced at different price levels.

**Aggregate supply** (5) The total value of all goods and services supplied in the economy; identical to *national product*.

**Allocation of resources** (2) Determination of what will be produced, how it will be produced, who will produce it, and for whom it will be produced.

**Anarcho-capitalism (radical libertarianism)** (34) A capitalist system under which no state exists and all goods and services—including defense, police, and court services—are supplied by private firms.

**Anticombines laws** (27) A set of laws, including the acts of 1889 and 1923 and subsequent amendments, that seek to control market structure and the competitive behavior of firms.

**Arbitrage** (30) The activity of earning a profit by buying a good for a low price in one market and reselling it for a higher price in another market.

**Automatic stabilizers** (10) Changes in taxes, transfers, and government purchases that occur automatically as nominal GNP rises or falls.

**Autonomous consumption** (8) The level of consumption shown by a consumption schedule for a zero disposable income level.

**Autonomous imports (Ma)** (8) The amount of imports when disposable income is zero.

**Balance of payments** (15) A record of all economic transactions between Canada and other countries in a given year. The balance is in surplus when receipts in the current and capital account exceed total payments to foreigners. It is in deficit when such receipts are less than total payments.

**Balance of payments equilibrium** (16) A situation in which transactions in the capital account exactly match transactions in the current account, so that there is no loss or build-up of foreign currency reserves.

**Balanced budget multiplier effect** (10) The ability of an increase in government purchases, matched dollar for dollar by an increase in taxes, to raise the equilibrium level of nominal national income.

**Bank rate** (12) The interest rate paid by chartered banks to borrow reserve funds from the Bank of Canada. Acts as a signal as to desired changes in interest rates charged by chartered banks.

**Bilateral monopoly** (31) A market in which both buyer and seller exercise monopoly power and neither passively accepts the demands of the other.

**Bond** (13) A promise, given in recognition of a loan, to make a fixed annual or semiannual payment over a period of years plus a larger final payment equal to the sum initially borrowed.

**Budget line** (21) A line showing the various combinations of goods that can be purchased at given prices within a given budget.

**Capital** (1) As a factor of production, all manufactured productive resources such as tools, industrial equipment, structures, and artificial improvements to land.

**Capital account** (15) The account whose transactions include all international borrowing and lending and all international purchases and sales of assets for investment purposes.

**Capital inflow** (15) Purchases of domestic assets by foreigners and borrowing by domestic residents from foreigners.

**Capital outflow** (15) Purchases of foreign assets by domestic residents and borrowing by foreigners from domestic sources.

**Capitalism** (34) Any economic system based on private ownership of all factors of production in which owners of capital act as entrepreneurs and coordinate their activity through use of the market.

**Capitalized value of a rent** (30) The amount equal to the value of the sum of money that would earn a periodic interest return equal to the rent if invested at the current market rate of interest.

**Cartel** (24) An agreement among a number of independent suppliers of a product to coordinate their supply decisions so all of them will earn monopoly profits.

**Centralized socialism** (34) A socialist system under which all capital and natural resources are owned by the government, which plans all production as if the economy were one big firm.

**Circular flow of income and product** (5) The flow of goods from firms to households and factor services from households to firms, counterbalanced by the flow of expenditures from households to firms and factor payments from firms to households.

**Classical liberal capitalism** (34) A capitalist economic system in which government performs only the limited role of protecting property rights and settling private disputes.

**Common stock or shares** (4) A certificate of part ownership in a corporation that gives the owner a vote in the selection of management and the right to share in dividend payments, if any.

**Comparative advantage** (2) In trade theory, the ability of a region or country to produce a good at lower opportunity cost, measured in terms of other foregone goods, than its trading partners.

**Complements** (3) A pair of goods for which an increase in the price of one causes a decrease in the demand for the other, other things being equal.

**Concentration ratio** (25) The percentage of all sales contributed by the four or eight largest firms in a market.

**Constant returns to scale** (22) A phenomenon said to occur when there are neither economies nor diseconomies of scale.

**Consumer equilibrium** (21) A state of affairs in which consumers cannot increase the total utility they obtain from a given budget by shifting expenditure from one good to another. (In consumer equilibrium, the marginal utility of a dollar's worth of one good must be equal to the marginal utility of a dollar's worth of any other good.)

**Consumer price index (CPI)** (6) A price index based on a "representative market basket" of about 400 goods and services purchased by urban wage earners. This index is calculated using base year quantities.

**Consumer surplus** (28) This is the difference between what consumers actually spend on a product and what they would be willing to spend for the same quantity.

**Consumption schedule** (8) A graphical or numerical representation of how nominal consumption expenditure varies as nominal income varies, other things being equal.

**Contractual savings institutions** (11) Financial intermediaries such as insurance companies and pension funds, to which individuals and groups commit savings on a long-term contractual basis.

**Corporation** (4) A firm in which the ownership is divided into equal parts called shares, with each shareholder's liability limited to the amount of his or her investment in the firm.

**Cost-push inflation** (17) Inflation produced by an upward or leftward shift in the aggregate real supply curve relative to the aggregate real demand curve.

**Craft unions** (31) Unions of skilled workers practicing a single craft.

**Crowding out effect** (14) The tendency of expansionary fiscal policy to cause a drop in private planned investment expenditure as a result of a rise in the interest rate.

**Crude birthrate** (33) The number of people born into a population per thousand per year.

**Crude death rate** (33) The number of people in a population who die per thousand per year.

**Currency** (12) Coins and paper money.

**Current account** (15) The account whose transactions include imports and exports of goods and services plus international unilateral transfer payments.

**Deficit** (5) In referring to government budgets, and excess of government purchases over net taxes.

**Deflationary gap** (10) The difference between planned expenditures and national product at the target level of national income when aggregate supply exceeds aggregate demand at that level.

**Demand curve** (3) A graphical representation of the relationship between the price of a good and the quantity of it demanded.

**Demand deposits** (12) Deposits at chartered banks that permit the depositor to make payments to others by writing a cheque against the deposit. Demand deposits are what we commonly call chequing accounts.

**Demand equation** (3) This equation can be written as $Qd = a - bP$, where $Qd$ = quantity demanded, $a$ = quantity demanded when the price is zero, and $bP$ expresses the rate at which $Qd$ declines when the price rises.

**Demand-pull inflation** (17) Inflation caused by an expansion of aggregate nominal demand relative to the productive capacity of the economy.

**Demand schedule** (3) A table showing the quantity of a good demanded at various prices.

**Demographic transition** (33) A population cycle that accompanies economic development, beginning with a fall in the death rate, continuing with a phase of rapid population growth, and concluding with a decline in the birthrate.

**Depauperization** (33) Economic development of a kind that benefits the poorest of the poor, providing them not only with the material necessities of life but also with access to education, status, security, self-expression, and power.

**Depreciation and appreciation of the exchange rate** (16) The Canadian dollar is said to depreciate when its price falls in terms of foreign currency, and to appreciate when its price rises in terms of foreign currency.

**Destructive competition** (27) This may occur in an industry with large fixed costs, relatively free entry, and long and recurrent periods of excess capacity. Marginal cost may be below average cost, but at the same time equalling price, leading to losses over a long period of time.

**Direct investment** (29) Purchase of securities with voting rights substantial enough to give the investors control of the company invested in.

**Direct regulation** (27) Government regulation of one or more of price, rate of return, output, entry, or exit, usually in a specific industry.

**Discretionary fiscal policy** (10) Changes in the levels of taxes, transfers, or government purchases made for the specific purpose of economic stabilization.

**Diseconomies of scale** (22) A phenomenon said to occur whenever long-run average cost increases as output increases.

**Dissaving** (8) Negative saving—the difference between disposable income and consumption expenditure when consumption exceeds disposable income.

**Division of labor** (1) The division of the production process for a commodity into numerous specialized functions.

**Draw downs and redeposits** (12) Transfer of government deposits between the Bank of Canada and the chartered banks.

**Dual economy** (33) An economy that is sharply divided into a modern, westernized industrial sector capable of rapid growth and a traditional rural sector that remains stagnant.

**Dynamic efficiency** (26) The ability of an economy to increase consumer satisfaction through growth and innovation.

**Econometrician** (1) A specialist in the statistical analysis of economic data.

**Economic historian** (1) An economist who explains events after the fact (*ex post*) and is content to find the most plausible reason for an event.

**Economic ideology** (1) A set of judgments and beliefs concerning efficiency and fairness as goals of economic policy, together with a set of beliefs concerning matters of positive economics.

**Economies of scale** (22) A phenomenon said to occur whenever long-run average cost decreases as output increases.

**Efficiency** (1) The property of producing or acting with a minimum of expense, waste, and effort.

**Elastic demand** (20) The situation in which quantity changes by a larger percentage than price along the demand curve, so that total revenue increases as price decreases.

**Empirical** (1) A term referring to data or methods based on observation of actual past experience or on controlled experiments.

**Entrepreneurship** (1) A unique form of business activity that consists of inventing new ways of doing things, being alert to new opportunities, taking risks, overcoming constraints, and developing new products and organizations.

**Equation of exchange** (13) An equation showing the relationship between the money stock (M), the velocity of money (V), the price level (P), and the level of real income (Q), written $MV = PQ$.

**Excess quantity demanded** (3) The amount by which the quantity of a good demanded exceeds the quantity supplied when the price of the good is below the equilibrium level.

**Excess quantity supplied** (3) The amount by which the quantity of a good supplied exceeds the quantity demanded when the price of the good is above the equilibrium level.

**Excess reserves** (12) Reserves held by chartered banks in excess of required reserves.

**Expected rate of interest** (7) The nominal rate of interest minus the expected rate of inflation.

**Explicit costs** (22) Costs taking the form of explicit payments to nonowners of a firm.

**Extensive growth** (34) Growth based predominantly on the mobilization of increasing quantities of factor inputs.

**Externality** (27) This refers to an incidental benefit or "cost" that accompanies an economic activity and affects persons whom the market does not compensate or charge for the cost or the benefit.

**Extraterritoriality** (29) The application of foreign laws to Canadian companies.

**Factor markets** (30) The markets in which the factors of production—labor, natural resources, and capital—are bought and sold.

**Factor payments** (5) The payments with which firms purchase factors of production (natural resources, labor, and capital).

**Factors of production** (1, 5) The basic elements of natural resources, labor, and capital used in the production of all goods.

**Featherbedding** (31) The practice of negotiating purposefully inefficient work rules so that more workers will be needed to do a job.

**Final goods and services** (6) Goods and services sold directly for household consumption, business investment, or government purchase. Excludes intermediate goods sold for use as inputs in the production of other goods.

**Financial intermediary** (11) Any financial institution that performs the function of channeling funds from savers to investors.

**Fiscal policy** (10) The collective term for the policies that determine the levels of government purchases and net taxes.

**Fixed inputs** (22) Inputs to the production process that cannot easily be increased or decreased in a short period of time (the quantity of fixed inputs employed by a firm defines the size of the firm's plant).

**Fixed investment** (5) Purchases by firms of newly produced capital goods, such as production machinery, newly built structures, and office equipment.

**Flows** (5) Processes occurring continuously through time, measured in units per time period.

**Foreign exchange market** (16) The complex of institutions through which the currency of one country may be exchanged for that of another.

**Franchised monopoly** (24) A monopoly protected from competition by a government grant of monopoly privilege, such as an exclusive license, permit, or patent.

**Fraser Institute** (4) An independent economic and social research organization with headquarters in Vancouver. It is firmly committed to the study and preservation of a competitive market system.

**Full employment** (7) The greatest possible utilization of the labor force consistent with price stability and allowing for unavoidable unemployment of workers between jobs.

**Functional distribution of income** (30) The distribution of income according to factor ownership—that is, the distribution among workers, natural resource owners, and owners of capital.

**General equilibrium analysis** (14) An approach to the study of markets along the lines of: if Event X occurs, the effect on Market Y will be Z, provided that other markets also adjust fully to the event in question.

**The Gini coefficient** (32) This is a ratio of the area between the Lorenz curve and the line OE, and the area of the entire triangle OPE.

**GNE implicit price deflator (GNE deflator)** (6) A measure of the price level equal to the ratio of current nominal GNP to current real GNP times 100.

**Government purchases of goods and services (government purchases)** (4) Expenditures made by federal, provincial, and municipal governments to purchase goods from private firms and to hire the services of government employees.

**Gross national expenditure** (6) A measurement of aggregate economic activity arrived at by adding together the nominal expenditure of all economic units on newly produced final goods and services.

**Gross national product (GNP)** (6) The dollar value at current market prices of all final goods and services produced annually by the nation's economy.

**Homogeneous** (2) Having the property that every unit is just like every other unit.

**Implicit costs** (22) The opportunity costs to a firm of using resources owned by the firm itself or contributed by owners of the firm.

**Import quota** (15) A limitation on the quantity of a good that can be imported in a given time period.

**Import schedule** (8) A graphical or numerical representation of how nominal import purchases vary as nominal income varies, other things being equal. It is assumed here that: Imports (M) = Ma + $m$ DI, where Ma is autonomous imports, $m$ is the marginal propensity to import, and DI is disposable income.

**Income approach** (6) A method of estimating aggregate economic activity by adding together the incomes earned by all households.

**Income effect** (21) The part of the change in quantity demanded of a good whose price has fallen that is attributable to the change in real income resulting from the price change.

**Income elasticity of demand** (20) The ratio of the percentage change in the demand for a good to the percentage change in the per capita income of buyers.

**Incomes policy** (19) A policy that attempts to control wages, salaries, earnings, and prices directly in order to fight inflation.

**Indexing** (17) The practice of automatically adjusting wages, salaries, or other payments to compensate for changes in the price level.

**Indifference curve** (21) A graphical representation of an indifference set.

**Indifference map** (21) A representative selection of indifference curves for a single consumer and pair of goods.

**Indifference set** (21) A set of consumption alternatives each of which yields the same utility, so that no member of the set is preferred to any other.

**Indirect or social regulation** (27) Government regulation of the attributes of a product, information, methods of production, sale, and employment.

**Industrial democracy** (19) Arrangements whereby workers are able to participate more fully in economic decision making.

**Industrial unions** (31) A union representing all workers in an enterprise, regardless of trade.

**Inelastic demand** (20) The situation in which quantity changes by a smaller percentage than price along the demand curve, so that total revenue decreases as price decreases.

**Inferior good** (3) A good for which an increase in the income of buyers causes a leftward shift in the demand curve.

**Inflationary gap** (10) The difference between planned expenditures and national product at the target level of national income when aggregate demand exceeds aggregate supply at that level.

**Inflationary recession (or stagflation)** (17) An episode characterized by simultaneous high (or rising) inflation, low (or falling) real output, and high (or rising) unemployment.

**Injections** (5) The part of total expenditures that does not originate from domestic households—that is, investment, government purchases, and exports.

**Intensive growth** (34) Growth based predominantly on improvements in the quality of factor inputs and in the efficiency with which they are utilized.

**Inventory investment** (5) Changes in the stocks of finished products and raw materials that firms keep on hand. If stocks are increasing, inventory investment is positive; if they are decreasing, it is negative.

**Investment** (5) The sum of fixed investment and inventory investment.

**Keynesian cross** (9) A figure formed by the intersection of the aggregate nominal demand and aggregate nominal supply schedules.

**Kinked demand curve** (25) The demand curve facing an oligopolistic business firm when it tries to depart from an established price. If it lowers prices, rivals will do the same, and the curve will be inelastic. If it raises prices, rivals may not follow and the curve will be elastic.

**Labor** (1) As a factor of production, the contributions to production made by people working with their minds and their muscles.

**Labor force** (7) All members of the noninstitutionalized civilian population over the age of 15 who are either officially employed or looking for employment.

**Land-use controls** (27) Policies designed to raise agricultural prices by limiting the amount of land on which certain crops can be grown.

**Law of demand** (3) The law that the quantity of a good demanded by buyers in any market tends to increase as the price of the good decreases and to decrease as the price increases, other things being equal.

**Law of diminishing returns** (22) The law stating that as the quantity of one variable input used in a production process is increased (with the quantities of all other inputs remaining fixed), a point will eventually be reached beyond which the quantity of output added per unit (that is, the marginal physical product of the variable input) begins to decrease.

**Law of increasing costs** (2) As resources are shifted from one use to another, an additional unit of output of one good requires an increasing rate of sacrifice of other goods as greater and greater shifts occur.

**Leakages** (5) The part of national income not devoted to consumption (saving plus net taxes) plus domestic expenditures on foreign-made goods (imports).

**Liquid** (12) Description of an asset that can be used as a means of payment or easily converted to a means of payment without risk of gain or loss in nominal value.

**Long run** (22) A time perspective long enough to permit changes in the quantities of all inputs, both fixed and variable.

**The Lorenz Curve** (32) This curve graphs the cumulative percentage of income units along the horizontal axis and the cumulative percentage of income received by those units along the vertical axis.

**Lump sum taxes** (8) Taxes that do not vary as income varies.

$M_1$ (12) The money supply defined as currency plus demand deposits in chartered banks.

$M_2$ (12) The money supply defined as $M_1$ plus notice (savings and term) deposits at chartered banks.

**Macroeconomics** (1) The study of large-scale economic phenomena, especially inflation, unemployment, and economic growth.

**Managerial coordination** (4) Coordination of economic activity through directives from managers to subordinates.

**Marginal average rule** (22) The rule that marginal cost must be equal to average cost when average cost is at its minimum.

**Marginal cost** (22) The increase in cost required to increase output of some good or service by one unit.

**Marginal efficiency of investment** (8) The rate of return expected to be obtained on an additional dollar of planned investment.

**Marginal factor cost** (30) The amount by which a firm's total factor cost must increase in order for it to obtain an additional unit of that factor.

**Marginal physical product (of an input)** (22) The quantity of output, expressed in physical units, produced by each added unit of the input.

**Marginal productivity theory of distribution** (30) A theory of the functional distribution of income according to which each factor receives a payment equal to its marginal revenue product.

**Marginal propensity to consume** (8) The proportion of each added dollar of disposable income that goes to added consumption. Algebraically, it can be written:

$$MPC = b = \frac{\Delta C}{\Delta DI}$$

where MPC is the marginal propensity to consume, C is consumption, and DI is personal disposable income.

**Marginal propensity to import** (8) The proportion of each added dollar of disposable income (DI) that goes to added imports.

$$MPM = m = \frac{\Delta M}{\Delta DI}$$

In our model of the economy, where the only difference between disposable income and national income is a lump-sum tax, the marginal propensity to import out of disposable income will be the same as the marginal propensity to import out of national income. For purposes of analysis we will often express MPM in terms of national income, i.e.

$$MPM = \frac{\Delta M}{\Delta Y}, \text{ where}$$

Y = national income.

**Marginal propensity to save** (8) The proportion of each added dollar of disposable income that is not consumed. Algebraically, it can be written:

$$MPS = \frac{\Delta S}{\Delta DI},$$

where MPS is the marginal propensity to save, S is saving, and DI is personal disposable income.

**Marginal rate of substitution** (21) The rate at which one good can be substituted for another without gain or loss in satisfaction (equal to the slope of an indifference curve at any point).

**Marginal revenue** (23) The amount by which total revenue increases as the result of a one-unit increase in quantity.

**Marginal revenue product (of a factor)** (30) The change in revenue resulting from the sale of the product produced by one additional unit of factor input.

**Marginal utility** (21) The amount of added utility obtained from a one-unit increase in consumption of a good.

**Market coordination** (4) Coordination of economic activity using the price system to transmit information and provide incentives.

**Market equilibrium** (3) A condition in which the separately formulated plans of buyers and sellers of some good exactly mesh when tested in the marketplace, so that the quantity supplied is exactly equal to the quantity demanded at the prevailing price.

**Market power** (25) The strength that a firm possesses—because of exclusive control of resources, prior build-up of profits, or networks of influence and command—that gives it an advantage over its rivals.

**Market socialism** (34) A socialist system in which details of resource allocation are made through market mechanisms rather than through central planning.

**Market structure** (23) Important characteristics of a market, including the number of firms that operate in it, the extent to which the products of different firms are diverse or homogeneous, and the ease of entry into and exit from the market.

**Markets** (2) All the various arrangements people have for trading with one another.

**Microeconomics** (1) The study of the economic behavior of individual households and firms and the determination of the market prices of individual goods and services.

**Minimum efficient scale** (22) The level of output at which economies of scale are exhausted.

**Monetarists** (14) Economists who believe that movements in the money supply are the primary causes of ups and downs in business activity.

**Money** (12) Anything that serves as a unit of account, a medium of exchange, and a store of purchasing power.

**Money demand schedule** (13) A schedule showing the quantity of money that people desire to hold in their portfolios given various values for the nominal interest rate and the level of nominal income.

**Money multiplier** (12) The ratio of the quantity of money to the total reserves in a banking system. Various money multipliers can be defined, depending on the definition of money used. In the simplified banking system, the formula for the money multiplier is: Money multiplier =

$$\frac{1}{\text{Required reserve ratio}}$$

**Monopolistic competition** (24) A market structure in which a large number of firms offer products that are relatively close substitutes for one another.

**Monopoly power** (2) A seller's power to raise the price of a product without losing all, or nearly all, customers.

**Monopsony** (30) A market in which there is only one buyer; from the Greek words *mono* ("single") and *opsonia* ("buying").

**Moral suasion** (12) Direct attempts by the Bank of Canada to influence the practices of the chartered banks.

**Multinationals** (29) Corporations that have enterprises in a number of countries.

**Multiplier** (9) The ratio of an induced change in the equilibrium level of national income to an initial change in planned expenditure. For an economy in which imports play an important role, the value of the multiplier is given by the formula

$$\text{Multiplier} = \frac{1}{1 - (MPC - MPM)}$$
$$\text{or } \frac{1}{1 - MPC_D}.$$

MPC_D is the marginal propensity to consume domestic output.

$$MPC_D = \frac{\Delta C}{\Delta DI} - \frac{\Delta M}{\Delta DI}.$$

Note that MPC_D + MPM + MPS = Y, where Y = national income.

**Multiplier effect** (9) The ability of a $1 shift in the aggregate nominal demand schedule to induce a change of more than $1 in the equilibrium level of nominal national income.

**The National Energy Program (NEP)** (28) This policy was instituted in the fall of 1980 to slow the increase in the price of oil and natural gas, to provide the federal government with a greater share of revenues, and to further Canadianize the industry.

**National income** (5) The total of all incomes, including wages, rents, interest payments, and profits received by households.

**National product** (5) The total value of all goods and services supplied in the economy.

**Natural monopoly** (24) An industry in which total costs are minimized by having just one producer serve the entire market.

**Natural resources** (1) As a factor of production, land and mineral deposits.

**Near-banks** (11) Institutions that accept deposits on which cheques can be written but that are not chartered banks and not subject to direct Bank of Canada control.

**Near-money** (12) Assets that are less than perfectly liquid but still liquid enough to be reasonably good substitutes for money.

**Negative income tax** (32) A general name for transfer systems that emphasize cash benefits, beginning with a basic benefit available to households with zero earned income that is then subject to a benefit reduction rate of substantially less than 100 percent

**Net exports** (5) Total exports minus total imports.

**Net incidence of taxation** (4) The difference between the amount paid to government in taxes and the amount received from government, calculated as a percentage of income.

**Net national income** (6) Total income received by a nation's productive factors, including wages and salaries, interest and rent, corporate taxes before profits, and income of unincorporated enterprises. It is also equal to GNP – capital consumption allowances and indirect business taxes.

**Net reproduction rate** (33) The inherent long-term growth rate of a population, measured as the average number of daughters born to each female child over her lifetime.

**Net tax multiplier** (10) A multiplier showing how much equilibrium nominal national income will change in response to a change in net taxes. The formula for the net tax multiplier is

$$- \frac{(MPC - MPM)}{MPS + MPM} \quad \text{or} \quad \frac{-MPC_D}{1 - MPC_D}$$

**Net taxes** (5) Total tax revenues collected by government at all levels minus total transfer payment disbursed.

**Nominal price** (3) The price at which goods and services are actually sold, without adjustment for inflation.

**Nominal rate of interest** (7) The rate of interest measured in the ordinary way, without adjustment for inflation.

**Nominal values** (6) Measurements of economic values made in terms of actual market prices at which goods are sold.

**Normal good** (3) A good for which an increase in the income of buyers causes a rightward shift in the demand curve.

**Normal rate of return to capital (normal profit)** (22) The opportunity cost of capital to a firm—that is, the rate of return necessary to attract funds for investment from their best alternative uses.

**Normative economics** (1) The part of economics devoted to making value judgments about what economic policies or conditions are good or bad.

**Notice deposits** (12) Interest-paying accounts at chartered banks against which it is not ordinarily possible to write cheques.

**Official reserve account** (15) The account whose transactions include purchases and sales of reserves of foreign currency by central banks.

**Okun's law** (18) Each 1 percent increase (decrease) in unemployment results in a 3 percent decrease (increase) in real economic growth. Or, conversely, each 3 percent increase (decrease) in real economic growth results in a 1 percent decrease (increase) in unemployment.

**Oligopolistic interdependence** (25) The necessity, in an oligopolistic market, for each firm to pay close attention to the behavior and likely reactions of its rivals when planning its own market strategy.

**Oligopoly** (25) A market structure in which there are two or more firms, at least one of which has a large share of total sales.

**Open market operation** (12) A purchase of securities from the public or a sale of securities to the public made by the Bank of Canada for the purpose of altering the quantity of reserves available to chartered banks.

**Opportunity cost** (2) The cost of doing something as measured by the loss of the opportunity to do something else with the same amount of time or resources.

**Par** (16) The point at which one unit of a currency is traded for exactly one unit of another currency.

**Partial equilibrium analysis** (14) An approach to the study of markets along the lines of: if Event X occurs, the effect on Market Y will be Z, provided that the equilibrium of other markets is not disturbed.

**Participatory socialism** (34) A socialist system under which the means of production are owned collectively by the workers of individual firms, who participate democratically in the process of management and share the profits of their firms.

**Partnership** (4) A firm formed by two or more persons to carry on a business as co-owners. Each partner bears full legal liability for the debts of the firm.

**Perfect competition** (23) A market structure characterized by a large number of relatively small firms, a homogeneous product, good distribution of information among all market participants, and freedom of entry and exit.

**Perfectly elastic demand** (20) The situation in which the demand curve is a horizontal line.

**Perfectly inelastic demand** (20) The situation in which the demand curve is a vertical line.

**Personal disposable income (disposable income)** (6) Personal income minus personal taxes.

**Personal distribution of income** (30) The distribution of income among individuals, taking into account both the functional distribution of income and the distribution of factor ownership among persons.

**Personal income** (6) The total of all income, including transfer payments, actually received by households before payment of personal income taxes and other transfer payments to government.

**Phillips curve** (17) A curve showing the relationship between the rate of inflation and the level of unemployment. Inflation, usually placed on the vertical axis of such a figure, can be measured in terms of either the rate of change in wages or the rate of change in a price index.

**Planned investment schedule** (8) A downward-sloping schedule showing the relationship between planned investment and the interest rate, other things being equal.

**Population trap** (33) A situation in which the rate of population growth rises above the rate of economic growth, halting the growth of per capita income and aborting the demographic transition.

**Portfolio** (13) A short-hand term for a person's collection of assets.

**Portfolio investment** (29) Purchase of securities that involves no control of the company selling the securities.

**Positive economics** (1) The part of economics limited to making scientific predictions and purely descriptive statements.

**Potential output growth** (17) The average growth that can be expected each year as a result of changes in population, in labour force participation, and in labour productivity.

**Potential real GNP (potential real output)** (7) The level of real GNP that the economy could, in principle, produce if resources were fully employed.

**Preferred share** (4) A certificate of part ownership in a corporation that gives the owner voting rights and a fixed return paid out from profits before payments of dividends to common stock holders.

**Price discrimination** (24) The practice of charging more than one price for different units of a single product, when the price differences are not justified by differences in the cost of serving different customers.

**Price elasticity of demand (elasticity of demand)** (20) The ratio of the percentage change in the quantity of a good demanded to the percentage change in the price of the good.

**Price elasticity of supply (elasticity of supply)** (20) The ratio of the percentage change in the quantity of a good supplied to the percentage change in its price.

**Price leadership** (25) A situation in an oligopolistic market where increases or decreases in price by one dominant firm, known as the price leader, are matched by all or most other firms in the market.

**Price support** (27) A program under which the government guarantees a certain minimum price to farmers by undertaking to buy any surplus that cannot be sold to private buyers at the support price.

**Price taker** (23) A firm that sells its outputs at fixed prices that are determined entirely by forces outside its own control.

**Principle of diminishing marginal utility** (21) The principle that the greater the rate of consumption of some good, the smaller the increase in utility from a unit increase in the rate of consumption.

**Production possibility frontier** (2) A curve showing the possible combinations of goods that can be produced by an economy, given the quantity and quality of factors of production available.

**Progressive tax** (4) A tax that takes a larger percentage of income from people whose income is high.

**Proportional tax** (4) A tax that takes a constant percentage of income from people of all income levels.

**Protectionism** (15) Policies of shielding domestic industry from foreign competition.

**Public goods** (4) Goods or services having the properties that (1) they cannot be provided to one citizen without being supplied also to that person's neighbors, and (2) once they are provided for one citizen, the cost of providing them to others is zero.

**Purchasing power parity theory (of exchange rates)** (16) The theory holding that the price of a unit of Currency A in terms of Currency B will, in the long run, tend to be equal to the ratio of the price level in Country B to the price level in Country A.

**Pure economic profit** (22) The sum remaining after both explicit and implicit costs are subtracted from total revenue.

**Pure economic rent** (30) The income earned by any factor of production that is in perfectly inelastic supply.

**Pure economizing** (21) The aspect of economic decision making that consists of choosing a pattern of activities from among a given set of alternative activities that will best serve a well-defined objective, subject to known constraints.

**Pure monopoly** (24) A market structure in which one firm accounts for 100 percent of industry sales.

**Rate of natural increase** (33) The current growth rate of a population calculated as the crude birthrate minus the crude death rate.

**Real values** (6) Measurements of economic values that include adjustments for changes in prices between one year and another.

**Realized real rate of interest** (7) The nominal rate of interest minus the actual rate of inflation.

**Reflation** (18) An episode in which demand management policy becomes more expansionary while the expected rate of inflation is falling.

**Regressive tax** (4) A tax that takes a larger percentage of income from people whose income is low.

**Required reserve ratios** (11, 12) Legally required minimum quantities of reserves, expressed as ratios of reserves to various types of deposits; the fraction of each type of deposit that the Bank of Canada requires chartered banks to hold in the form of non-interest-bearing assets.

**Reservation wage** (18) The wage (adjusted for nonmonetary advantages and disadvantages of a job) below which a person will not accept a job offer.

**Reserves (of chartered banks)** (11) Money held by chartered banks as cash or non-interest-bearing deposits with the Bank of Canada.

**Residual error of estimate** (6) The difference between the initial measurements of GNP and GNE.

**Saving** (5) The part of household income not used to purchase goods and services or to pay taxes.

**Saving schedule** (8) A graphical or numerical representation of how nominal saving varies as nominal disposable income varies, other things being equal.

**Scientific prediction** (1) A conditional prediction having the form "if A, then B, other things being equal."

**Shared monopoly** (25) A situation in which the firms in an oligopolistic industry tacitly coordinate their activities in such a way as to earn maximum monopoly profits for the industry as a whole.

**Short run** (22) A time perspective within which output can be adjusted only by changing the quantities of variable inputs within a plant of fixed size.

**Shortage** (3) As used in economics, an excess quantity demanded.

**Socialism** (34) Any of a number of doctrines that include the following tenets: (1) that some major share of nonlabor factors of production ought to be owned in common or by the state, and (2) that justice requires incomes to be distributed at least somewhat more equally than under classical liberal capitalism.

**Sole proprietorship** (4) A firm owned and usually managed by a single person, who receives all profits of the firm and who personally bears all of the firm's liabilities.

**Special drawing rights (SDRs)** (15) Accounts that the larger trading nations hold with the International Monetary Fund to settle their international transactions with each other.

**Stabilization policy** (4) An effort by government to control the level of national income and the related conditions of inflation, unemployment, and the balance of payments.

**Staple product** (1) A commodity on which the economy of a settlement or region concentrates much of its labor and capital.

**Static efficiency** (26) The ability of an economy to get the greatest consumer satisfaction from given resources and technology.

**Stocks** (5) Accumulated quantities existing at a particular time, measured in terms of simple units.

**Subsidy price** (27) A price guaranteed to farmers by the government; if the market price falls below the subsidy price, the government pays the farmers the difference.

**Substitutes** (3) A pair of goods for which an increase in the price of one causes an increase in the demand for the other, other things being equal.

**Substitution effect** (21) The part of the increase in quantity demanded of a good whose price has fallen that is attributable to the tendency of consumers to substitute relatively cheap goods for relatively expensive ones.

**Supply curve** (3) A graphical representation of the relationship between the price of a good and the quantity of it supplied.

**Supply equation** (3) This equation expresses the idea that quantity supplied (Qs) is a function of price, or Qs = $a + b$P.

**Supply schedule** (3) A table showing the quantity of a good supplied at various prices.

**Surplus** (3, 5) As used in economics, an excess quantity supplied; in referring to government budgets, an excess of net taxes over government purchases.

**Target level of nominal national income (income target)** (10) The level of nominal national income judged by policy makers to be most nearly compatible with the goals of full employment, price stability, real economic growth, regional economic balance and balance of payments stability.

**Tariff** (15) A tax levied on imported goods.

**Tax incidence** (4) Measures the extent to which producers and consumers bear the burden of a tax.

**Theory of the mine** (28) The branch of economics concerned with the allocation over time of nonrenewable natural resources.

**Total rate of return to capital** (22) The opportunity cost of capital plus pure economic profit, expressed as a percentage of the capital invested in a firm.

**Transfer payments** (4) All payments made by government to individuals that are not made in return for goods or services currently supplied. Social security benefits, welfare payments, and unemployment compensation are major forms of transfer payments.

**Transitivity** (21) The situation where if A is preferred to B and B is preferred to C, then A must be preferred to C.

**Truncation** (29) Limits placed on the development of skills and services in and by a Canadian subsidiary because they are concentrated in the parent company.

**Unemployment rate** (7) Percentage of the labor force who are actively looking for employment but who are not employed.

**Unit elastic demand** (20) The situation in which price and quantity change by the same percentage along the demand curve, so that total revenue remains unchanged as price changes.

**Unit labor cost** (18) The wage payment per one unit of output.

**Utility** (21) The economist's term for the pleasure, satisfaction, and need fulfillment that people get from the consumption of material goods and services.

**Variable inputs** (22) Inputs to the production process that can quickly and easily be varied to increase or decrease output within a plant of a given size.

**Velocity** (13) The ratio of nominal national income to the money stock; a measure of the average number of times each dollar of the money stock is used each year for income-generating purposes.

**Very short run** (27) A time horizon so short that producers are unable to make any changes in input or output quantities in response to changing prices.

**Weighted average** (6) An average that gives appropriate weights to products in proportion to their relative importance in the total basket of goods purchased.

**The White Paper of 1945** (7) Committed the federal government to the maintenance of stable, full-employment economic growth.

# INDEX